Practical Programming in Tcl & Tk

Third Edition

Brent B. Welch

Prentice Hall PTR
Upper Saddle River, NJ 07458
www.phptr.com

Library of Congress Cataloging-in-Publication Data

Welch, Brent. B.
    Practical programming in Tcl and Tk / Brent B. Welch.-- 3rd ed.
    p. cm.
    ISBN 0-13-022028-0
    1. Tcl (Computer program language) 2. Tk toolkit. I. Title.

QA76.73.T44 W45 1999
005.13'3--dc21   99-047206

Editorial/Production Supervision: *Joan L. McNamara*
Acquisitions Editor: *Mark Taub*
Marketing Manager: *Kate Hargett*
Editorial Assistant: *Michael Fredette*
Cover Design Director: *Jerry Votta*
Cover Design: *Design Source*
Manufacturing Manager: *Alexis R. Heydt*

 © 2000, 1997 by Prentice Hall PTR
Prentice-Hall, Inc.
Upper Saddle River, New Jersey 07458

Prentice Hall books are widely used by corporations and government agencies for training, marketing, and resale. The publisher offers discounts on this book when ordered in bulk quantities. For more information, contact:
Corporate Sales Department, Prentice Hall PTR, One Lake Street, Upper Saddle River, NJ 07458
Phone: 800-382-3419; Fax: 201-236-7141; email: corpsales@prenhall.com

Printed in the United States of America
10 9 8 7 6 5

ISBN: 0-13-022028-0

Prentice-Hall International (UK) Limited, *London*
Prentice-Hall of Australia Pty. Limited, *Sydney*
Prentice-Hall Canada Inc., *Toronto*
Prentice-Hall Hispanoamericana, S.A., *Mexico*
Prentice-Hall of India Private Limited, *New Delhi*
Prentice-Hall of Japan, Inc., *Tokyo*
Prentice-Hall (Singapore) Pte. Ltd., *Singapore*
Editora Prentice-Hall do Brasil, Ltda., *Rio de Janeiro*

to

Jody,
Christopher, Daniel, and Michael

Contents

List of Examples

List of Tables

Preface

Tcl stands for *Tool Command Language*. Tcl is really two things: a scripting language, and an interpreter for that language that is designed to be easy to embed into your application. Tcl and its associated graphical user-interface toolkit, Tk, were designed and crafted by Professor John Ousterhout of the University of California, Berkeley. You can find these packages on the Internet (as explained on page lii) and use them freely in your application, even if it is commercial. The Tcl interpreter has been ported from UNIX to DOS, Windows, OS/2, NT, and Macintosh environments. The Tk toolkit has been ported from the X window system to Windows and Macintosh.

I first heard about Tcl in 1988 while I was Ousterhout's Ph.D. student at Berkeley. We were designing a network operating system, Sprite. While the students hacked on a new kernel, John wrote a new editor and terminal emulator. He used Tcl as the command language for both tools so that users could define menus and otherwise customize those programs. This was in the days of X10, and he had plans for an X toolkit based on Tcl that would help programs cooperate with each other by communicating with Tcl commands. To me, this cooperation among tools was the essence of Tcl.

This early vision imagined that applications would be large bodies of compiled code and a small amount of Tcl used for configuration and high-level commands. John's editor, *mx*, and the terminal emulator, *tx*, followed this model. While this model remains valid, it has also turned out to be possible to write entire applications in Tcl. This is because the Tcl/Tk shell, *wish*, provides access to other programs, the file system, network sockets, plus the ability to create a graphical user interface. For better or worse, it is now common to find applications that contain thousands of lines of Tcl script.

This book was written because, while I found it enjoyable and productive to use Tcl and Tk, there were times when I was frustrated. In addition, working at Xerox PARC, with many experts in languages and systems, I was compelled to understand both the strengths and weaknesses of Tcl and Tk. Although many of my colleagues adopted Tcl and Tk for their projects, they were also just as quick to point out its flaws. In response, I have built up a set of programming techniques that exploit the power of Tcl and Tk while avoiding troublesome areas. This book is meant as a practical guide to help you get the most out of Tcl and Tk and avoid some of the frustrations I experienced.

It has been about 10 years since I was introduced to Tcl, and about five years since the first edition of this book. During the last several years I have been working under John Ousterhout, first at Sun Microsystems and now at Scriptics Corporation. I have managed to remain mostly a Tcl programmer while others in our group have delved into the C implementation of Tcl itself. I've been building applications like HTML editors, e-mail user interfaces, Web servers, and the customer database we run our business on. This experience is reflected in this book. The bulk of the book is about Tcl scripting, and the aspects of C programming to create Tcl extensions is given a lighter treatment. I have been lucky to remain involved in the core Tcl development, and I hope I can pass along the insights I have gained by working with Tcl.

Why Tcl?

As a scripting language, Tcl is similar to other UNIX shell languages such as the Bourne Shell (sh), the C Shell (csh), the Korn Shell (ksh), and Perl. Shell programs let you execute other programs. They provide enough programmability (variables, control flow, and procedures) to let you build complex scripts that assemble existing programs into a new tool tailored for your needs. Shells are wonderful for automating routine chores.

It is the ability to easily add a Tcl interpreter to your application that sets it apart from other shells. Tcl fills the role of an extension language that is used to configure and customize applications. There is no need to invent a command language for your new application, or struggle to provide some sort of user-programmability for your tool. Instead, by adding a Tcl interpreter, you structure your application as a set of primitive operations that can be composed by a script to best suit the needs of your users. It also allows other programs to have programmatic control over your application, leading to suites of applications that work well together.

The Tcl C library has clean interfaces and is simple to use. The library implements the basic interpreter and a set of core scripting commands that implement variables, flow control, and procedures (see page 22). There is also a set of commands that access operating system services to run other programs, access the file system, and use network sockets. Tk adds commands to create graphical user interfaces. Tcl and Tk provide a "virtual machine" that is portable across UNIX, Windows, and Macintosh environments.

The Tcl virtual machine is extensible because your application can define new Tcl commands. These commands are associated with a C or C++ procedure that your application provides. The result is applications that are split into a set of primitives written in a compiled language and exported as Tcl commands. A Tcl script is used to compose the primitives into the overall application. The script layer has access to shell-like capability to run other programs, has access to the file system, and can call directly into the compiled part of the application through the Tcl commands you define. In addition, from the C programming level, you can call Tcl scripts, set and query Tcl variables, and even trace the execution of the Tcl interpreter.

There are many Tcl extensions freely available on the Internet. Most extensions include a C library that provides some new functionality, and a Tcl interface to the library. Examples include database access, telephone control, MIDI controller access, and *expect*, which adds Tcl commands to control interactive programs.

The most notable extension is Tk, a toolkit for graphical user interfaces. Tk defines Tcl commands that let you create and manipulate user interface widgets. The script-based approach to user interface programming has three benefits:

- Development is fast because of the rapid turnaround; there is no waiting for long compilations.
- The Tcl commands provide a higher-level interface than most standard C library user-interface toolkits. Simple user interfaces require just a handful of commands to define them. At the same time, it is possible to refine the user interface in order to get every detail just so. The fast turnaround aids the refinement process.
- The user interface can be factored out from the rest of your application. The developer can concentrate on the implementation of the application core and then fairly painlessly work up a user interface. The core set of Tk widgets is often sufficient for all your user interface needs. However, it is also possible to write custom Tk widgets in C, and again there are many contributed Tk widgets available on the network.

There are other choices for extension languages that include Visual Basic, Scheme, Elisp, Perl, Python, and Javascript. Your choice between them is partly a matter of taste. Tcl has simple constructs and looks somewhat like C. It is easy to add new Tcl primitives by writing C procedures. Tcl is very easy to learn, and I have heard many great stories of users completing impressive projects in a short amount of time (e.g., a few weeks), even though they never used Tcl before.

Java has exploded onto the computer scene since this book was first published. Java is a great systems programming language that in the long run could displace C and C++. This is fine for Tcl, which is designed to glue together building blocks written in any system programming language. Tcl was designed to work with C, but has been adapted to work with the Java Virtual Machine. Where I say "C or C++", you can now say "C, C++, or Java," but the details are a bit different with Java. This book does not describe the Tcl/Java interface, but you can find *TclBlend* on the CD-ROM. TclBlend loads the Java Virtual Machine into your Tcl application and lets you invoke Java methods. It also lets you implement Tcl commands in Java instead of C or C++.

Javascript is a language from Netscape that is designed to script interactions with Web pages. Javascript is important because Netscape is widely deployed. However, Tcl provides a more general purpose scripting solution that can be used in a wide variety of applications. The Tcl/Tk Web browser plugin provides a way to run Tcl in your browser. It turns out to be more of a Java alternative than a JavaScript alternative. The plugin lets you run Tcl applications inside your browser, while JavaScript gives you fine grain control over the browser and HTML display. The plugin is described in Chapter 20.

Tcl and Tk Versions

Tcl and Tk continue to evolve. See `http://www.beedub.com/book/` for updates and news about the latest Tcl releases. Tcl and Tk have had separate version numbers for historical reasons, but they are released in pairs that work together. The original edition of this book was based on Tcl 7.4 and Tk 4.0, and there were a few references to features in Tk 3.6. This third edition has been updated to reflect new features added through Tcl/Tk 8.2:

- Tcl 7.5 and Tk 4.1 had their final release in May 1996. These releases feature the port of Tk to the Windows and Macintosh environments. The Safe-Tcl security mechanism was introduced to support safe execution of network applets. There is also network socket support and a new Input/Output (I/O) subsystem to support high-performance event-driven I/O.
- Tcl 7.6 and Tk 4.2 had their final release in October 1996. These releases include improvements in Safe-Tcl, and improvements to the grid geometry manager introduced in Tk 4.1. Cross-platform support includes virtual events (e.g., <<Copy>> as opposed to <Control-c>), standard dialogs, and more file manipulation commands.
- Tcl 7.7 and Tk 4.3 were internal releases used for the development of the Tcl/Tk plug-in for the Netscape Navigator and Microsoft Internet Explorer Web browsers. Their development actually proceeded in parallel to Tcl 7.6 and Tk 4.2. The plug-in has been released for a wide variety of platforms, including Solaris/SPARC, Solaris/INTEL, SunOS, Linux, Digital UNIX, IRIX, HP/UX, Windows 95, Windows NT, and the Macintosh. The browser plug-in supports Tcl applets in Web pages and uses the sophisticated security mechanism of Safe-Tcl to provide safety.
- Tcl 8.0 features an on-the-fly compiler for Tcl that provides many-times faster Tcl scripts. Tcl 8.0 supports strings with embedded null characters. The compiler is transparent to Tcl scripts, but extension writers need to learn some new C APIs to take advantage of its potential. The release history of 8.0 spread out over a couple of years as John Ousterhout moved from Sun Microsystems to Scriptics Corporation. The widely used 8.0p2 release was made in the fall of 1997, but the final patch release, 8.0.5, was made in the spring of 1999.

- Tk changed its version to match Tcl at 8.0. Tk 8.0 includes a new platform-independent font mechanism, native menus and menu bars, and more native widgets for better native look and feel on Windows and Macintosh.
- Tcl/Tk 8.1 features full Unicode support, a new regular expression engine that provides all the features found in Perl 5, and thread safety so that you can embed Tcl into multithreaded applications. Tk does a heroic job of finding the correct font to display your Unicode characters, and it adds a message catalog facility so that you can write internationalized applications. The release history of Tcl/Tk 8.1 also straddled the Sun to Scriptics transition. The first alpha release was made in the fall of 1997, and the final patch release, 8.1.1, was made in May 1999.
- Tcl/Tk 8.2 is primarily a bug fix and stabilization release. There are a few minor additions to the Tcl C library APIs to support more extensions without requiring core patches. Tcl/Tk 8.2 went rapidly into final release in the summer of 1999.

Who Should Read This Book

This book is meant to be useful to the beginner in Tcl as well as the expert. For the beginner and expert alike, I recommend careful study of Chapter 1, *Tcl Fundamentals*. The programming model of Tcl is designed to be simple, but it is different from many programming languages. The model is based on string substitutions, and it is important that you understand it properly to avoid trouble in complex cases. The remainder of the book consists of examples that demonstrate how to use Tcl and Tk productively. For your reference, each chapter has tables that summarize the Tcl commands and Tk widgets they describe.

This book assumes that you have some programming experience, although you should be able to get by even if you are a complete novice. Knowledge of UNIX shell programming will help, but it is not required. Where aspects of window systems are relevant, I provide some background information. Chapter 2 describes the details of using Tcl and Tk on UNIX, Windows, and Macintosh.

How to Read This Book

This book is best used in a hands-on manner, trying the examples at the computer. The book tries to fill the gap between the terse Tcl and Tk manual pages, which are complete but lack context and examples, and existing Tcl programs that may or may not be documented or well written.

I recommend the on-line manual pages for the Tcl and Tk commands. They provide a detailed reference guide to each command. This book summarizes much of the information from the manual pages, but it does not provide the complete details, which can vary from release to release. HTML versions of the on-line manual pages can be found on the CD-ROM that comes with this book.

Other Tcl Books

This book was the second Tcl book after the original book by John Ousterhout, the creator of Tcl. Since then, the number of Tcl books has increased remarkably. The following are just some of the books currently available.

Tcl and the Tk Toolkit (Addison-Wesley, 1994) by John Ousterhout provides a broad overview of all aspects of Tcl and Tk, even though it covers only Tcl 7.3 and Tk 3.6. The book provides a more detailed treatment of C programming for Tcl extensions.

Exploring Expect (O'Reilly & Associates, Inc., 1995) by Don Libes is a great book about an extremely useful Tcl extension. *Expect* lets you automate the use of interactive programs like *ftp* and *telnet* that expect to interact with a user. By combining *expect* and Tk, you can create graphical user interfaces for old applications that you cannot modify directly.

Graphical Applications with Tcl & Tk (M&T Press, 1996) by Eric Johnson is oriented toward Windows users. The second edition is up-to-date with Tcl/Tk 8.0.

Tcl / Tk Tools (O'Reilly & Associates, Inc., 1997) by Mark Harrison describes many useful Tcl extensions. These include Oracle and Sybase interfaces, object-oriented language enhancements, additional Tk widgets, and much more. The chapters were contributed by the authors of the extensions, so they provide authoritative information on some excellent additions to the Tcl toolbox.

CGI Developers Resource, Web Programming with Tcl and Perl (Prentice Hall, 1997) by John Ivler presents Tcl-based solutions to programming Web sites.

Effective Tcl / Tk Programming (Addison Wesley, 1997) by Michael McLennan and Mark Harrison illustrate Tcl and Tk with examples and application design guidelines.

Interactive Web Applications with Tcl/Tk (AP Professional, 1998) by Michael Doyle and Hattie Schroeder describes Tcl programming in the context of the Web browser plugin.

Tcl / Tk for Programmers (IEEE Computer Society, 1998) by Adrian Zimmer describes Unix and Windows programming with Tcl/Tk. This book also includes solved exercises at the end of each chapter.

Tcl / Tk for Real Programmers (Academic Press, 1999) by Clif Flynt is another example-oriented book.

Tcl / Tk in a Nutshell (O'Reilly, 1999) by Paul Raines and Jeff Tranter is a handy reference guide. It covers several popular extensions including Expect, [incr Tcl], Tix, TclX, BLT, SybTcl, OraTcl, and TclODBC. There is a tiny pocket-reference guide for Tcl/Tk that may eliminate the need to thumb through my large book to find the syntax of a particular Tcl or Tk command.

Web Tcl Complete (McGraw Hill, 1999) by Steve Ball describes programming with the Tcl Web Server. It also covers Tcl/Java integration using *TclBlend*.

[incr Tcl] From The Ground Up (Osborn-McGraw Hill, 1999) by Chad Smith describes the [incr Tcl] object-oriented extension to Tcl.

On-line Examples

The book comes with a CD-ROM that has source code for all of the examples, plus a selection of Tcl freeware found on the Internet. The CD-ROM is created with the Linux *mkhybrid* program, so it is readable on UNIX, Windows, and Macintosh. There, you will find the versions of Tcl and Tk that were available as the book went to press. You can also retrieve the sources shown in the book from my personal Web site:

```
http://www.beedub.com/book/
```

Ftp Archives

The primary site for the Tcl and Tk distributions is given below as a Universal Resource Location (URL):

```
ftp://ftp.scriptics.com/pub/tcl
```

You can use FTP and log in to the host (e.g., `ftp.scriptics.com`) under the `anonymous` user name. Give your e-mail address as the password. The directory is in the URL after the host name (e.g., `/pub/tcl`). There are many sites that mirror this distribution. The mirror sites provide an archive site for contributed Tcl commands, Tk widgets, and applications. There is also a set of Frequently Asked Questions files. These are some of the sites that maintain Tcl archives:

```
ftp://ftp.neosoft.com/pub/tcl
ftp://ftp.syd.dit.csiro.au/pub/tk
ftp://ftp.ibp.fr/pub/tcl
ftp://src.doc.ic.ac.uk/packages/tcl/
ftp://ftp.luth.se/pub/unix/tcl/
ftp://sunsite.cnlab-switch.ch/mirror/tcl
ftp://ftp.sterling.com/programming/languages/tcl
ftp://ftp.sunet.se/pub/lang/tcl
ftp://ftp.cs.columbia.edu/archives/tcl
ftp://ftp.uni-paderborn.de/pub/unix/tcl
ftp://sunsite.unc.edu/pub/languages/tcl
ftp://ftp.funet.fi/pub/languages/tcl
```

You can use a World Wide Web browser like *Mosaic*, *Netscape*, *Internet Explorer*, or *Lynx* to access these sites. Enter the URL as specified above, and you are presented with a directory listing of that location. From there you can change directories and fetch files.

If you do not have direct FTP access, you can use an e-mail server for FTP. Send e-mail to `ftpmail@decwrl.dec.com` with the message `Help` to get directions. If you are on BITNET, send e-mail to `bitftp@pucc.princeton.edu`.

You can search for FTP sites that have Tcl by using the *Archie* service that indexes the contents of anonymous FTP servers. Information about using *Archie* can be obtained by sending mail to `archie@archie.sura.net` that contains the message `Help`.

World Wide Web

Start with these World Wide Web pages about Tcl:

```
http://www.scriptics.com/
http://www.sco.com/Technology/tcl/Tcl.html
http://www.purl.org/NET/Tcl-FAQ/
```

The home page for this book contains errata for all editions. This is the only URL I control personally, and I plan to keep it up-to-date indefinitely:

```
http://www.beedub.com/book/
```

The Prentice Hall Web site has information about the book, but you must use its search facility to find the exact location. Start at:

```
http://www.prenhall.com/
```

Newsgroups

The `comp.lang.tcl` newsgroup is very active. It provides a forum for questions and answers about Tcl. Announcements about Tcl extensions and applications are posted to the `comp.lang.tcl.announce` newsgroup.

Typographic Conventions

The more important examples are set apart with a title and horizontal rules, while others appear in-line. The examples use courier for Tcl and C code. When interesting results are returned by a Tcl command, those are presented below in *oblique courier*. The => is not part of the return value in the following example.

```
expr 5 + 8
=> 13
```

The courier font is also used when naming Tcl commands and C procedures within sentences.

The usage of a Tcl command is presented in the following example. The command name and constant keywords appear in courier. Variable values appear in *courier oblique*. Optional arguments are surrounded with question marks.

```
set varname ?value?
```

The name of a program is in italics:

xterm

Hot Tips

The icon in the margin marks a "hot tip" as judged by the reviewers of the book. The visual markers help you locate the more useful sections in the book. These are also listed in the index under Hot Tip.

Book Organization

The chapters of the book are divided into seven parts. The first part describes basic Tcl features. The first chapter describes the fundamental mechanisms that characterize the Tcl language. This is an important chapter that provides the basic grounding you will need to use Tcl effectively. Even if you have programmed in Tcl already, you should review Chapter 1. Chapter 2 goes over the details of using Tcl and Tk on UNIX, Windows, and Macintosh. Chapter 3 presents a sample application, a CGI script, that illustrates typical Tcl programming. The rest of Part I covers the basic Tcl commands in more detail, including string handling, data types, control flow, procedures, and scoping issues. Part I finishes with a description of the facilities for file I/O and running other programs.

Part II describes advanced Tcl programming. It starts with `eval`, which lets you generate Tcl programs on the fly. Regular expressions provide powerful string processing. If your data-processing application runs slowly, you can probably boost its performance significantly with the regular expression facilities. Namespaces partition the global scope of procedures and variables. Unicode and message catalogs support internationalized applications. Libraries and packages provide a way to organize your code for sharing among projects. The introspection facilities of Tcl tell you about the internal state of Tcl. Event driven I/O helps server applications manage several clients simultaneously. Network sockets are used to implement the HTTP protocol used to fetch pages on the World Wide Web. Safe-Tcl is used to provide a secure environment to execute applets downloaded over the network. *TclHttpd* is an extensible web server built in Tcl. You can build applications on top of this server, or embed it into your existing applications to give them a web interface.

Part III introduces Tk. It gives an overview of the toolkit facilities. A few complete examples are examined in detail to illustrate the features of Tk. Event bindings associate Tcl commands with events like keystrokes and button clicks. Part III ends with three chapters on the Tk geometry managers that provide powerful facilities for organizing your user interface.

Part IV describes the Tk widgets. These include buttons, menus, scrollbars, labels, text entries, multiline and multifont text areas, drawing canvases, listboxes, and scales. The Tk widgets are highly configurable and very programmable, but their default behaviors make them easy to use as well. The resource database that can configure widgets provides an easy way to control the overall look of your application.

Part V describes the rest of the Tk facilities. These include selections, keyboard focus, and standard dialogs. Fonts, colors, images, and other attributes that are common to the Tk widgets are described in detail. This part ends with a few larger Tk examples.

Part VI is an introduction to C programming and Tcl. The goal of this part is to get you started in the right direction when you need to extend Tcl with new commands written in C or integrate Tcl into custom applications.

Part VII provides a chapter for each of the Tcl/Tk releases covered by the book. These chapters provide details about what features were changed and added. They also provide a quick reference if you need to update a program or start to use a new version.

What's New in the Third Edition

The third edition is up-to-date with Tcl/Tk 8.2. The main new Tcl/Tk features are Internationalization, which is covered in Chapter 15, a new regular expression engine, which is described in Chapter 11, and thread-safety. There is a new chapter about compiling C extensions, and there is a more complete C extension example. The chapters on Eval and the Web browser plugin received a thorough update. I made a light sweep through the remainder of the book correcting errors and improving examples. Perhaps the best addition for the reader is an all-new index.

My favorite addition to the book is Chapter 18 that describes *TclHttpd*, a Web server built in Tcl. *TclHttpd* provides a number of nice ways to integrate a Web server with a Tcl application, replacing the standard CGI interface with something that is much more flexible and efficient. I have been using this server for the last year to build www.scriptics.com. This freely available server has been used to build several other products, plus it provides an easy way for you to bring up your own Web server.

First Edition Thanks

I would like to thank my managers and colleagues at Xerox PARC for their patience with me as I worked on this book. The tips and tricks in this book came partly from my own work as I helped lab members use Tcl, and partly from them as they taught me. Dave Nichols' probing questions forced me to understand the basic mechanisms of the Tcl interpreter. Dan Swinehart and Lawrence Butcher kept me sharp with their own critiques. Ron Frederick and Berry Kerchival adopted Tk for their graphical interfaces and amazed me with their rapid results. Becky Burwell, Rich Gold, Carl Hauser, John Maxwell, Ken Pier, Marvin Theimer, and Mohan Vishwanath made use of my early drafts, and their questions pointed out large holes in the text. Karin Petersen, Bill Schilit, and Terri Watson kept life interesting by using Tcl in very nonstandard ways. I especially thank my managers, Mark Weiser and Doug Terry, for their understanding and support.

I thank John Ousterhout for Tcl and Tk, which are wonderful systems built with excellent craftsmanship. John was kind enough to provide me with an advance version of Tk 4.0 so that I could learn about its new features well before its first beta release.

Thanks to the Tcl programmers out on the Net, from whom I learned many tricks. John LoVerso and Stephen Uhler are the hottest Tcl programmers I know.

Many thanks to the patient reviewers of early drafts: Pierre David, Clif Flynt, Simon Kenyon, Eugene Lee, Don Libes, Lee Moore, Joe Moss, Hador Shemtov, Frank Stajano, Charles Thayer, and Jim Thornton.

Many folks contributed suggestions by e-mail: Miguel Angel, Stephen Bensen, Jeff Blaine, Tom Charnock, Brian Cooper, Patrick D'Cruze, Benoit Desrosiers, Ted Dunning, Mark Eichin, Paul Friberg, Carl Gauthier, David Gerdes, Klaus Hackenberg, Torkle Hasle, Marti Hearst, Jean-Pierre Herbert, Jamie Honan, Norman Klein, Joe Konstan, Susan Larson, Håkan Liljegren, Lionel Mallet, Dejan Milojicic, Greg Minshall, Bernd Mohr, Will Morse, Heiko Nardmann, Gerd Neugebauer, TV Raman, Cary Renzema, Rob Riepel, Dan Schenk, Jean-Guy Schneider, Elizabeth Scholl, Karl Schwamb, Rony Shapiro, Peter Simanyi, Vince Skahan, Bill Stumbo, Glen Vanderburg, Larry Virden, Reed Wade, and Jim Wight. Unfortunately, I could not respond to every suggestion, even some that were excellent.

Thanks to the editors and staff at Prentice Hall. Mark Taub has been very helpful as I progressed through my first book. Lynn Schneider and Kerry Reardon were excellent copy and production editors, respectively.

Second Edition Thanks

I get to thank John Ousterhout again, this time for supporting me as I worked in the Tcl/Tk group at Sun Microsystems. The rest of the group deserve a lot of credit for turning Tcl and Tk into a dynamite cross-platform solution. Scott Stanton led the Tk port to the PC. Ray Johnson led the Tk port to the Macintosh. Jacob Levy implemented the event-driven I/O system, Safe-Tcl, and the browser plug-in. Brian Lewis built the Tcl compiler. Ken Corey worked on Java integration and helped with the *SpecTcl* user interface builder. Syd Polk generalized the menu system to work with native widgets on the Macintosh and Windows. Colin Stevens generalized the font mechanism and worked on internationalization for Tk.

Stephen Uhler deserves special thanks for inspiring many of the cool examples I use in this book. He was the lead on the *SpecTcl* user interface builder. He built the core HTML display library on which I based an editor. We worked closely together on the first versions of *TclHttpd*. He taught me how to write compact, efficient Tcl code and to use regular expression substitutions in amazing ways. I hope he has learned at least a little from me.

Thanks again to Mark Taub, Eileen Clark, and Martha Williams at Prentice Hall. George Williams helped me assemble the files for the CD-ROM.

Third Edition Thanks

John Ousterhout continues his wonderful role as Tcl benefactor, now as founder of Scriptics Corporation. I'd like to thank every one of the great folks that I work with at Scriptics, especially the pioneering crew of Sarah Daniels, Scott Stanton, Ray Johnson, Bryan Surles, Melissa Hirschl, Lee Bernhard, Suresh Sastry, Emil Scaffon, Pat P., Scott Redman, and Berry Kercheval. The rest of the gang deserves a big thanks for making Scriptics such an enjoyable place to work. Jerry Peek, who is a notable author himself, provided valuable advice and wonderfully detailed comments! Ken Jones told me about a great indexing tool.

I'd like to thank all the readers that drop me the encouraging note or probing question via e-mail. I am always interested in new and interesting uses of Tcl!

Thanks to the editors at Prentice Hall: Mark Taub, Joan McNamara, and Joan Eurell. Mark continues to encourage me to come out with new editions, and the Joans helped me complete this third edition on time.

Finally, I thank my wonderful wife Jody for her love, kindness, patience, wit, and understanding as I worked long hours. Happily, many of those hours were spent working from home. I now have three sons, Christopher, Daniel, and Michael, who get the credit for keeping me from degenerating into a complete nerd.

Contact the Author

I am always open to comments about this book. My e-mail address is welch@acm.org. It helps me sort through my mail if you put the word "book" or the title of the book into the e-mail subject line. Visit my Web site at:

        http://www.beedub.com/

for current news about the book and my other interests.

P A R T I

Tcl Basics

Part I introduces the basics of Tcl. Everyone should read Chapter 1, which describes the fundamental properties of the language. Tcl is really quite simple, so beginners can pick it up quickly. The experienced programmer should review Chapter 1 to eliminate any misconceptions that come from using other languages.

Chapter 2 is a short introduction to running Tcl and Tk on UNIX, Windows, and Macintosh systems. You may want to look at this chapter first so you can try out the examples as you read Chapter 1.

Chapter 3 presents a sample application, a CGI script, that implements a guestbook for a Web site. The example uses several facilities that are described in detail in later chapters. The goal is to provide a working example that illustrates the power of Tcl.

The rest of Part I covers basic programming with Tcl. Simple string processing is covered in Chapter 4. Tcl lists, which share the syntax rules of Tcl commands, are explained in Chapter 5. Control structure like loops and if statements are described in Chapter 6. Chapter 7 describes Tcl procedures, which are new commands that you write in Tcl. Chapter 8 discusses Tcl arrays. Arrays are the most flexible and useful data structure in Tcl. Chapter 9 describes file I/O and running other programs. These facilities let you build Tcl scripts that glue together other programs and process data in files.

After reading Part I you will know enough Tcl to read and understand other Tcl programs, and to write simple programs yourself.

Tcl Fundamentals

This chapter describes the basic syntax rules for the Tcl scripting language. It describes the basic mechanisms used by the Tcl interpreter: substitution and grouping. It touches lightly on the following Tcl commands: `puts`, `format`, `set`, `expr`, `string`, `while`, `incr`, and `proc`.

Tcl is a string-based command language. The language has only a few fundamental constructs and relatively little syntax, which makes it easy to learn. The Tcl syntax is meant to be simple. Tcl is designed to be a glue that assembles software building blocks into applications. A simpler glue makes the job easier. In addition, Tcl is interpreted when the application runs. The interpreter makes it easy to build and refine your application in an interactive manner. A great way to learn Tcl is to try out commands interactively. If you are not sure how to run Tcl on your system, see Chapter 2 for instructions for starting Tcl on UNIX, Windows, and Macintosh systems.

This chapter takes you through the basics of the Tcl language syntax. Even if you are an expert programmer, it is worth taking the time to read these few pages to make sure you understand the fundamentals of Tcl. The basic mechanisms are all related to strings and string substitutions, so it is fairly easy to visualize what is going on in the interpreter. The model is a little different from some other programming languages with which you may already be familiar, so it is worth making sure you understand the basic concepts.

Tcl Commands

Tcl stands for Tool Command Language. A command does something for you, like output a string, compute a math expression, or display a widget on the screen. Tcl casts everything into the mold of a command, even programming constructs like variable assignment and procedure definition. Tcl adds a tiny amount of syntax needed to properly invoke commands, and then it leaves all the hard work up to the command implementation.

The basic syntax for a Tcl command is:

```
command arg1 arg2 arg3 ...
```

The `command` is either the name of a built-in command or a Tcl procedure. White space (i.e., spaces or tabs) is used to separate the command name and its arguments, and a newline (i.e., the end of line character) or semicolon is used to terminate a command. Tcl does not interpret the arguments to the commands except to perform *grouping*, which allows multiple words in one argument, and *substitution*, which is used with programming variables and nested command calls. The behavior of the Tcl command processor can be summarized in three basic steps:

- Argument grouping.
- Value substitution of nested commands, variables, and backslash escapes.
- Command invocation. It is up to the command to interpret its arguments. This model is described in detail in this Chapter.

Hello, World!

Example 1–1 The "Hello, World!" example.

```
puts stdout {Hello, World!}
=> Hello, World!
```

In this example, the command is `puts`, which takes two arguments: an I/O stream identifier and a string. `puts` writes the string to the I/O stream along with a trailing newline character. There are two points to emphasize:

- Arguments are interpreted by the command. In the example, `stdout` is used to identify the standard output stream. The use of `stdout` as a name is a convention employed by `puts` and the other I/O commands. Also, `stderr` is used to identify the standard error output, and `stdin` is used to identify the standard input. Chapter 9 describes how to open other files for I/O.
- Curly braces are used to group words together into a single argument. The `puts` command receives `Hello, World!` as its second argument.

The braces are not part of the value.

The braces are syntax for the interpreter, and they get stripped off before the value is passed to the command. Braces group all characters, including newlines and nested braces, until a matching brace is found. Tcl also uses double quotes for grouping. Grouping arguments will be described in more detail later.

Variables

The set command is used to assign a value to a variable. It takes two arguments: The first is the name of the variable, and the second is the value. Variable names can be any length, and case *is* significant. In fact, you can use any character in a variable name.

It is not necessary to declare Tcl variables before you use them.

The interpreter will create the variable when it is first assigned a value. The value of a variable is obtained later with the dollar-sign syntax, illustrated in Example 1–2:

Example 1–2 Tcl variables.

```
set var 5
=> 5
set b $var
=> 5
```

The second set command assigns to variable b the value of variable var. The use of the dollar sign is our first example of substitution. You can imagine that the second set command gets rewritten by substituting the value of var for $var to obtain a new command.

```
set b 5
```

The actual implementation of substitution is more efficient, which is important when the value is large.

Command Substitution

The second form of substitution is *command substitution*. A nested command is delimited by square brackets, [ ]. The Tcl interpreter takes everything between the brackets and evaluates it as a command. It rewrites the outer command by replacing the square brackets and everything between them with the result of the nested command. This is similar to the use of backquotes in other shells, except that it has the additional advantage of supporting arbitrary nesting of commands.

Example 1–3 Command substitution.

```
set len [string length foobar]
=> 6
```

In Example 1–3, the nested command is:

```
string length foobar
```

This command returns the length of the string foobar. The string command is described in detail starting on page 45. The nested command runs first.

Then, command substitution causes the outer command to be rewritten as if it were:

```
set len 6
```

If there are several cases of command substitution within a single command, the interpreter processes them from left to right. As each right bracket is encountered, the command it delimits is evaluated. This results in a sensible ordering in which nested commands are evaluated first so that their result can be used in arguments to the outer command.

Math Expressions

The Tcl interpreter itself does not evaluate math expressions. Tcl just does grouping, substitutions and command invocations. The expr command is used to parse and evaluate math expressions.

Example 1–4 Simple arithmetic.

```
expr 7.2 / 4
=> 1.8
```

The math syntax supported by expr is the same as the C expression syntax. The expr command deals with integer, floating point, and boolean values. Logical operations return either 0 (false) or 1 (true). Integer values are promoted to floating point values as needed. Octal values are indicated by a leading zero (e.g., 033 is 27 decimal). Hexadecimal values are indicated by a leading 0x. Scientific notation for floating point numbers is supported. A summary of the operator precedence is given on page 20.

You can include variable references and nested commands in math expressions. The following example uses expr to add the value of x to the length of the string foobar. As a result of the innermost command substitution, the expr command sees 6 + 7, and len gets the value 13:

Example 1–5 Nested commands.

```
set x 7
set len [expr [string length foobar] + $x]
=> 13
```

The expression evaluator supports a number of built-in math functions. (For a complete listing, see page 21.) Example 1–6 computes the value of *pi*:

Example 1–6 Built-in math functions.

```
set pi [expr 2*asin(1.0)]
=> 3.1415926535897931
```

The implementation of `expr` is careful to preserve accurate numeric values and avoid conversions between numbers and strings. However, you can make `expr` operate more efficiently by grouping the entire expression in curly braces. The explanation has to do with the byte code compiler that Tcl uses internally, and its effects are explained in more detail on page 15. For now, you should be aware that these expressions are all valid and run a bit faster than the examples shown above:

Example 1–7 Grouping expressions with braces.

```
expr {7.2 / 4}
set len [expr {[string length foobar] + $x}]
set pi [expr {2*asin(1.0)}]
```

Backslash Substitution

The final type of substitution done by the Tcl interpreter is *backslash substitution*. This is used to quote characters that have special meaning to the interpreter. For example, you can specify a literal dollar sign, brace, or bracket by quoting it with a backslash. As a rule, however, if you find yourself using lots of backslashes, there is probably a simpler way to achieve the effect you are striving for. In particular, the `list` command described on page 61 will do quoting for you automatically. In Example 1–8 backslash is used to get a literal `$`:

Example 1–8 Quoting special characters with backslash.

```
set dollar \$foo
=> $foo
set x $dollar
=> $foo
```

Only a single round of interpretation is done.

The second `set` command in the example illustrates an important property of Tcl. The value of `dollar` does not affect the substitution performed in the assignment to `x`. In other words, the Tcl parser does not care about the value of a variable when it does the substitution. In the example, the value of `x` and `dollar` is the string `$foo`. In general, you do not have to worry about the value of variables until you use `eval`, which is described in Chapter 10.

You can also use backslash sequences to specify characters with their Unicode, hexadecimal, or octal value:

```
set escape \u001b
set escape \0x1b
set escape \033
```

The value of variable `escape` is the ASCII ESC character, which has character code `27`. The table on page 20 summarizes backslash substitutions.

A common use of backslashes is to continue long commands on multiple lines. This is necessary because a newline terminates a command. The backslash in the next example is required; otherwise the expr command gets terminated by the newline after the plus sign.

Example 1–9 Continuing long lines with backslashes.

```
set totalLength [expr [string length $one] + \
        [string length $two]]
```

There are two fine points to escaping newlines. First, if you are grouping an argument as described in the next section, then you do not need to escape newlines; the newlines are automatically part of the group and do not terminate the command. Second, a backslash as the last character in a line is converted into a space, and all the white space at the beginning of the next line is replaced by this substitution. In other words, the backslash-newline sequence also consumes all the leading white space on the next line.

Grouping with Braces and Double Quotes

Double quotes and curly braces are used to group words together into one argument. The difference between double quotes and curly braces is that quotes allow substitutions to occur in the group, while curly braces prevent substitutions. This rule applies to command, variable, and backslash substitutions.

Example 1–10 Grouping with double quotes vs. braces.

```
set s Hello
=> Hello
puts stdout "The length of $s is [string length $s]."
=> The length of Hello is 5.
puts stdout {The length of $s is [string length $s].}
=> The length of $s is [string length $s].
```

In the second command of Example 1–10, the Tcl interpreter does variable and command substitution on the second argument to puts. In the third command, substitutions are prevented, so the string is printed as is.

In practice, grouping with curly braces is used when substitutions on the argument must be delayed until a later time (or never done at all). Examples include loops, conditional statements, and procedure declarations. Double quotes are useful in simple cases like the puts command previously shown.

Another common use of quotes is with the format command. This is similar to the C printf function. The first argument to format is a format specifier that often includes special characters like newlines, tabs, and spaces. The easiest way to specify these characters is with backslash sequences (e.g., \n for newline and \t for tab). The backslashes must be substituted before the format command is called, so you need to use quotes to group the format specifier.

```
puts [format "Item: %s\t%5.3f" $name $value]
```

Here `format` is used to align a name and a value with a tab. The `%s` and `%5.3f` indicate how the remaining arguments to `format` are to be formatted. Note that the trailing `\n` usually found in a C `printf` call is not needed because `puts` provides one for us. For more information about the `format` command, see page 52.

Square Brackets Do Not Group

The square bracket syntax used for command substitution does not provide grouping. Instead, a nested command is considered part of the current group. In the command below, the double quotes group the last argument, and the nested command is just part of that group.

```
puts stdout "The length of $s is [string length $s]."
```

If an argument is made up of only a nested command, you do not need to group it with double-quotes because the Tcl parser treats the whole nested command as part of the group.

```
puts stdout [string length $s]
```

The following is a redundant use of double quotes:

```
puts stdout "[expr $x + $y]"
```

Grouping before Substitution

The Tcl parser makes a single pass through a command as it makes grouping decisions and performs string substitutions. Grouping decisions are made before substitutions are performed, which is an important property of Tcl. This means that the values being substituted do not affect grouping because the grouping decisions have already been made.

The following example demonstrates how nested command substitution affects grouping. A nested command is treated as an unbroken sequence of characters, regardless of its internal structure. It is included with the surrounding group of characters when collecting arguments for the main command.

Example 1–11 Embedded command and variable substitution.

```
set x 7; set y 9
puts stdout $x+$y=[expr $x + $y]
=> 7+9=16
```

In Example 1–11, the second argument to `puts` is:

```
$x+$y=[expr $x + $y]
```

The white space inside the nested command is ignored for the purposes of grouping the argument. By the time Tcl encounters the left bracket, it has already done some variable substitutions to obtain:

```
7+9=
```

When the left bracket is encountered, the interpreter calls itself recursively to evaluate the nested command. Again, the $x and $y are substituted before calling expr. Finally, the result of expr is substituted for everything from the left bracket to the right bracket. The puts command gets the following as its second argument:

```
7+9=16
```

Grouping before substitution.

The point of this example is that the grouping decision about puts's second argument is made before the command substitution is done. Even if the result of the nested command contained spaces or other special characters, they would be ignored for the purposes of grouping the arguments to the outer command. Grouping and variable substitution interact the same as grouping and command substitution. Spaces or special characters in variable values do not affect grouping decisions because these decisions are made before the variable values are substituted.

If you want the output to look nicer in the example, with spaces around the + and =, then you must use double quotes to explicitly group the argument to puts:

```
puts stdout "$x + $y = [expr $x + $y]"
```

The double quotes are used for grouping in this case to allow the variable and command substitution on the argument to puts.

Grouping Math Expressions with Braces

It turns out that expr does its own substitutions inside curly braces. This is explained in more detail on page 15. This means you can write commands like the one below and the substitutions on the variables in the expression still occur:

```
puts stdout "$x + $y = [expr {$x + $y}]"
```

More Substitution Examples

If you have several substitutions with no white space between them, you can avoid grouping with quotes. The following command sets concat to the value of variables a, b, and c all concatenated together:

```
set concat $a$b$c
```

Again, if you want to add spaces, you'll need to use quotes:

```
set concat "$a $b $c"
```

In general, you can place a bracketed command or variable reference anywhere. The following computes a command name:

```
[findCommand $x] arg arg
```

When you use Tk, you often use widget names as command names:

```
$text insert end "Hello, World!"
```

Procedures

Tcl uses the `proc` command to define procedures. Once defined, a Tcl procedure is used just like any of the other built-in Tcl commands. The basic syntax to define a procedure is:

```
proc name arglist body
```

The first argument is the name of the procedure being defined. The second argument is a list of parameters to the procedure. The third argument is a *command body* that is one or more Tcl commands.

The procedure name is case sensitive, and in fact it can contain any characters. Procedure names and variable names do not conflict with each other. As a convention, this book begins procedure names with uppercase letters and it begins variable names with lowercase letters. Good programming style is important as your Tcl scripts get larger. Tcl coding style is discussed in Chapter 12.

Example 1–12 Defining a procedure.

```
proc Diag {a b} {
    set c [expr sqrt($a * $a + $b * $b)]
    return $c
}
puts "The diagonal of a 3, 4 right triangle is [Diag 3 4]"
=> The diagonal of a 3, 4 right triangle is 5.0
```

The `Diag` procedure defined in the example computes the length of the diagonal side of a right triangle given the lengths of the other two sides. The `sqrt` function is one of many math functions supported by the `expr` command. The variable `c` is local to the procedure; it is defined only during execution of `Diag`. Variable scope is discussed further in Chapter 7. It is not really necessary to use the variable `c` in this example. The procedure can also be written as:

```
proc Diag {a b} {
    return [expr sqrt($a * $a + $b * $b)]
}
```

The `return` command is used to return the result of the procedure. The return `command` is optional in this example because the Tcl interpreter returns the value of the last command in the body as the value of the procedure. So, the procedure could be reduced to:

```
proc Diag {a b} {
    expr sqrt($a * $a + $b * $b)
}
```

Note the stylized use of curly braces in the example. The curly brace at the end of the first line starts the third argument to `proc`, which is the command body. In this case, the Tcl interpreter sees the opening left brace, causing it to ignore newline characters and scan the text until a matching right brace is found. *Double quotes have the same property.* They group characters, including newlines, until another double quote is found. The result of the grouping is that the third argument to `proc` is a sequence of commands. When they are evaluated later, the embedded newlines will terminate each command.

The other crucial effect of the curly braces around the procedure body is to delay any substitutions in the body until the time the procedure is called. For example, the variables a, b, and c are not defined until the procedure is called, so we do not want to do variable substitution at the time `Diag` is defined.

The `proc` command supports additional features such as having variable numbers of arguments and default values for arguments. These are described in detail in Chapter 7.

A Factorial Example

To reinforce what we have learned so far, below is a longer example that uses a `while` loop to compute the factorial function:

Example 1–13 A `while` loop to compute factorial.

```
proc Factorial {x} {
    set i 1; set product 1
    while {$i <= $x} {
        set product [expr $product * $i]
        incr i
    }
    return $product
}
Factorial 10
=> 3628800
```

The semicolon is used on the first line to remind you that it is a command terminator just like the newline character. The `while` loop is used to multiply all the numbers from one up to the value of x. The first argument to `while` is a boolean expression, and its second argument is a command body to execute. The `while` command and other control structures are described in Chapter 6.

The same math expression evaluator used by the `expr` command is used by `while` to evaluate the boolean expression. There is no need to explicitly use the `expr` command in the first argument to `while`, even if you have a much more complex expression.

The loop body and the procedure body are grouped with curly braces in the same way. The opening curly brace must be on the same line as `proc` and `while`. If you like to put opening curly braces on the line after a `while` or `if` statement, you must escape the newline with a backslash:

```
        while {$i < $x} \
        {
            set product ...
        }
```

Always group expressions and command bodies with curly braces.

Curly braces around the boolean expression are crucial because they delay variable substitution until the while command implementation tests the expression. The following example is an infinite loop:

```
set i 1; while $i<=10 {incr i}
```

The loop will run indefinitely.[*] The reason is that the Tcl interpreter will substitute for $i *before* while is called, so while gets a constant expression 1<=10 that will always be true. You can avoid these kinds of errors by adopting a consistent coding style that groups expressions with curly braces:

```
set i 1; while {$i<=10} {incr i}
```

The incr command is used to increment the value of the loop variable i. This is a handy command that saves us from the longer command:

```
set i [expr $i + 1]
```

The incr command can take an additional argument, a positive or negative integer by which to change the value of the variable. Using this form, it is possible to eliminate the loop variable i and just modify the parameter x. The loop body can be written like this:

```
while {$x > 1} {
    set product [expr $product * $x]
    incr x -1
}
```

Example 1–14 shows factorial again, this time using a recursive definition. A recursive function is one that calls itself to complete its work. Each recursive call decrements x by one, and when x is one, then the recursion stops.

Example 1–14 A recursive definition of factorial.

```
proc Factorial {x} {
    if {$x <= 1} {
        return 1
    } else {
        return [expr $x * [Factorial [expr $x - 1]]]
    }
}
```

More about Variables

The set command will return the value of a variable if it is only passed a single argument. It treats that argument as a variable name and returns the current value of the variable. The dollar-sign syntax used to get the value of a variable is really just an easy way to use the set command. Example 1–15 shows a trick you can play by putting the name of one variable into another variable:

---

[*] Ironically, Tcl 8.0 introduced a byte-code compiler, and the first releases of Tcl 8.0 had a bug in the compiler that caused this loop to terminate! This bug is fixed in the 8.0.5 patch release.

Example 1–15 Using `set` to return a variable value.

```
set var {the value of var}
=> the value of var
set name var
=> var
set name
=> var
set $name
=> the value of var
```

This is a somewhat tricky example. In the last command, $name gets substituted with var. Then, the set command returns the value of var, which is the value of var. Nested set commands provide another way to achieve a level of indirection. The last set command above can be written as follows:

```
set [set name]
=> the value of var
```

Using a variable to store the name of another variable may seem overly complex. However, there are some times when it is very useful. There is even a special command, upvar, that makes this sort of trick easier. The upvar command is described in detail in Chapter 7.

Funny Variable Names

The Tcl interpreter makes some assumptions about variable names that make it easy to embed variable references into other strings. By default, it assumes that variable names contain only letters, digits, and the underscore. The construct $foo.o represents a concatenation of the value of foo and the literal ".o".

If the variable reference is not delimited by punctuation or white space, then you can use curly braces to explicitly delimit the variable name (e.g., ${x}). You can also use this to reference variables with funny characters in their name, although you probably do not want variables named like that. If you find yourself using funny variable names, or computing the names of variables, then you may want to use the upvar command.

Example 1–16 Embedded variable references.

```
set foo filename
set object $foo.o
=> filename.o
set a AAA
set b abc${a}def
=> abcAAAdef
set .o yuk!
set x ${.o}y
=> yuk!y
```

The unset Command

You can delete a variable with the unset command:

```
unset varName varName2 ...
```

Any number of variable names can be passed to the unset command. However, unset will raise an error if a variable is not already defined.

Using info to Find Out about Variables

The existence of a variable can be tested with the info exists command. For example, because incr requires that a variable exist, you might have to test for the existence of the variable first.

Example 1–17 Using info to determine if a variable exists.

```
if {![info exists foobar]} {
    set foobar 0
} else {
    incr foobar
}
```

Example 7–6 on page 86 implements a new version of incr which handles this case.

More about Math Expressions

This section describes a few fine points about math in Tcl scripts. In Tcl 7.6 and earlier versions math is not that efficient because of conversions between strings and numbers. The expr command must convert its arguments from strings to numbers. It then does all its computations with double precision floating point values. The result is formatted into a string that has, by default, 12 significant digits. This number can be changed by setting the tcl_precision variable to the number of significant digits desired. Seventeen digits of precision are enough to ensure that no information is lost when converting back and forth between a string and an IEEE double precision number:

Example 1–18 Controlling precision with tcl_precision.

```
expr 1 / 3
=> 0
expr 1 / 3.0
=> 0.333333333333
set tcl_precision 17
=> 17
expr 1 / 3.0
# The trailing 1 is the IEEE rounding digit
=> 0.33333333333333331
```

In Tcl 8.0 and later versions, the overhead of conversions is eliminated in most cases by the built-in compiler. Even so, Tcl was not designed to support math-intensive applications. You may want to implement math-intensive code in a compiled language and register the function as a Tcl command as described in Chapter 44.

There is support for string comparisons by `expr`, so you can test string values in `if` statements. You must use quotes so that `expr` knows to do string comparisons:

```
if {$answer == "yes"} { ... }
```

However, the `string compare` and `string equal` commands described in Chapter 4 are more reliable because `expr` may do conversions on strings that look like numbers. The issues with string operations and `expr` are discussed on page 48.

Expressions can include variable and command substitutions and still be grouped with curly braces. This is because an argument to `expr` is subject to two rounds of substitution: one by the Tcl interpreter, and a second by `expr` itself. Ordinarily this is not a problem because math values do not contain the characters that are special to the Tcl interpreter. The second round of substitutions is needed to support commands like `while` and `if` that use the expression evaluator internally.

Grouping expressions can make them run more efficiently.

You should always group expressions in curly braces and let `expr` do command and variable substitutions. Otherwise, your values may suffer extra conversions from numbers to strings and back to numbers. Not only is this process slow, but the conversions can loose precision in certain circumstances. For example, suppose `x` is computed from a math function:

```
set x [expr {sqrt(2.0)}]
```

At this point the value of `x` is a double-precision floating point value, just as you would expect. If you do this:

```
set two [expr $x * $x]
```

then you may or may not get 2.0 as the result! This is because Tcl will substitute `$x` and `expr` will concatenate all its arguments into one string, and then parse the expression again. In contrast, if you do this:

```
set two [expr {$x * $x}]
```

then `expr` will do the substitutions, and it will be careful to preserve the floating point value of `x`. The expression will be more accurate and run more efficiently because no string conversions will be done. The story behind Tcl values is described in more detail in Chapter 44 on C programming and Tcl.

Comments

Tcl uses the pound character, #, for comments. Unlike in many other languages, the # must occur at the beginning of a command. A # that occurs elsewhere is not treated specially. An easy trick to append a comment to the end of a command is to precede the # with a semicolon to terminate the previous command:

```
# Here are some parameters
set rate 7.0      ;# The interest rate
set months 60     ;# The loan term
```

One subtle effect to watch for is that a backslash effectively continues a comment line onto the next line of the script. In addition, a semicolon inside a comment is not significant. Only a newline terminates comments:

```
# Here is the start of a Tcl comment \
and some more of it; still in the comment
```

The behavior of a backslash in comments is pretty obscure, but it can be exploited as shown in Example 2–3 on page 27.

A surprising property of Tcl comments is that curly braces inside comments are still counted for the purposes of finding matching brackets. I think the motivation for this mis-feature was to keep the original Tcl parser simpler. However, it means that the following will not work as expected to comment out an alternate version of an if expression:

```
# if {boolean expression1} {
if {boolean expression2} {
    some commands
}
```

The previous sequence results in an extra left curly brace, and probably a complaint about a missing close brace at the end of your script! A technique I use to comment out large chunks of code is to put the code inside an if block that will never execute:

```
if {0} {
unused code here
}
```

Substitution and Grouping Summary

The following rules summarize the fundamental mechanisms of grouping and substitution that are performed by the Tcl interpreter before it invokes a command:

- Command arguments are separated by white space, unless arguments are grouped with curly braces or double quotes as described below.
- Grouping with curly braces, { }, prevents substitutions. Braces nest. The interpreter includes all characters between the matching left and right brace in the group, including newlines, semicolons, and nested braces. The enclosing (i.e., outermost) braces are not included in the group's value.
- Grouping with double quotes, " ", allows substitutions. The interpreter groups everything until another double quote is found, including newlines and semicolons. The enclosing quotes are not included in the group of char-

acters. A double-quote character can be included in the group by quoting it
with a backslash, (e.g., `\"`).

- Grouping decisions are made before substitutions are performed, which
  means that the values of variables or command results do not affect grouping.
- A dollar sign, `$`, causes variable substitution. Variable names can be any
  length, and case is significant. If variable references are embedded into
  other strings, or if they include characters other than letters, digits, and the
  underscore, they can be distinguished with the `${varname}` syntax.
- Square brackets, `[ ]`, cause command substitution. Everything between the
  brackets is treated as a command, and everything including the brackets is
  replaced with the result of the command. Nesting is allowed.
- The backslash character, `\`, is used to quote special characters. You can
  think of this as another form of substitution in which the backslash and the
  next character or group of characters are replaced with a new character.
- Substitutions can occur anywhere unless prevented by curly brace grouping.
  Part of a group can be a constant string, and other parts of it can be the
  result of substitutions. Even the command name can be affected by substitutions.
- A single round of substitutions is performed before command invocation.
  The result of a substitution is not interpreted a second time. This rule is
  important if you have a variable value or a command result that contains
  special characters such as spaces, dollar signs, square brackets, or braces.
  Because only a single round of substitution is done, you do not have to
  worry about special characters in values causing extra substitutions.

Fine Points

- A common error is to forget a space between arguments when grouping with
  braces or quotes. This is because white space is used as the separator, while
  the braces or quotes only provide grouping. If you forget the space, you will
  get syntax errors about unexpected characters after the closing brace or
  quote. The following is an error because of the missing space between `}` and
  `{`:

  ```
  if {$x > 1}{puts "x = $x"}
  ```
- A double quote is only used for grouping when it comes after white space.
  This means you can include a double quote in the middle of a group without
  quoting it with a backslash. This requires that curly braces or white space
  delimit the group. I do not recommend using this obscure feature, but this
  is what it looks like:

  ```
  set silly a"b
  ```
- When double quotes are used for grouping, the special effect of curly braces
  is turned off. Substitutions occur everywhere inside a group formed with

double quotes. In the next command, the variables are still substituted:

```
set x xvalue
set y "foo {$x} bar"
=> foo {xvalue} bar
```

- When double quotes are used for grouping and a nested command is encountered, the nested command can use double quotes for grouping, too.

```
puts "results [format "%f %f" $x $y]"
```

- Spaces are *not* required around the square brackets used for command substitution. For the purposes of grouping, the interpreter considers everything between the square brackets as part of the current group. The following sets x to the concatenation of two command results because there is no space between] and [.

```
set x [cmd1][cmd2]
```

- Newlines and semicolons are ignored when grouping with braces or double quotes. They get included in the group of characters just like all the others. The following sets x to a string that contains newlines:

```
set x "This is line one.
This is line two.
This is line three."
```

- During command substitution, newlines and semicolons *are* significant as command terminators. If you have a long command that is nested in square brackets, put a backslash before the newline if you want to continue the command on another line. This was illustrated in Example 1–9 on page 8.

- A dollar sign followed by something other than a letter, digit, underscore, or left parenthesis is treated as a literal dollar sign. The following sets x to the single character $.

```
set x $
```

Reference

Backslash Sequences

Table 1–1 Backslash sequences.

\a	Bell. (0x7)
\b	Backspace. (0x8)
\f	Form feed. (0xc)
\n	Newline. (0xa)
\r	Carriage return. (0xd)
\t	Tab. (0x9)
\v	Vertical tab. (0xb)
\<newline>	Replace the newline and the leading white space on the next line with a space.
\\	Backslash. ('\')
\ooo	Octal specification of character code. 1, 2, or 3 digits.
\xhh	Hexadecimal specification of character code. 1 or 2 digits.
\uhhhh	Hexadecimal specification of a 16-bit Unicode character value. 4 hex digits.
\c	Replaced with literal c if c is not one of the cases listed above. In particular, \$, \", \{, \}, \], and \[are used to obtain these characters.

Arithmetic Operators

Table 1–2 Arithmetic operators from highest to lowest precedence.

- ~ !	Unary minus, bitwise NOT, logical NOT.
* / %	Multiply, divide, remainder.
+ -	Add, subtract.
<< >>	Left shift, right shift.
< > <= >=	Comparison: less, greater, less or equal, greater or equal.
== !=	Equal, not equal.
&	Bitwise AND.
^	Bitwise XOR.
|	Bitwise OR.
&&	Logical AND.
||	Logical OR.
$x?y:z$	If x then y else z.

Built-in Math Functions

Table 1–3 Built-in math functions.

`acos(x)`	Arccosine of x.
`asin(x)`	Arcsine of x.
`atan(x)`	Arctangent of x.
`atan2(y,x)`	Rectangular (x,y) to polar (r, th). `atan2` gives th.
`ceil(x)`	Least integral value greater than or equal to x.
`cos(x)`	Cosine of x.
`cosh(x)`	Hyperbolic cosine of x.
`exp(x)`	Exponential, e^x.
`floor(x)`	Greatest integral value less than or equal to x.
`fmod(x,y)`	Floating point remainder of x/y.
`hypot(x,y)`	Returns `sqrt(x*x + y*y)`. r part of polar coordinates.
`log(x)`	Natural log of x.
`log10(x)`	Log base 10 of x.
`pow(x,y)`	x to the y power, x^y.
`sin(x)`	Sine of x.
`sinh(x)`	Hyperbolic sine of x.
`sqrt(x)`	Square root of x.
`tan(x)`	Tangent of x.
`tanh(x)`	Hyperbolic tangent of x.
`abs(x)`	Absolute value of x.
`double(x)`	Promote x to floating point.
`int(x)`	Truncate x to an integer.
`round(x)`	Round x to an integer.
`rand()`	Return a random floating point value between 0.0 and 1.0.
`srand(x)`	Set the seed for the random number generator to the integer x.

Core Tcl Commands

The pages listed in Table 1–4 give the primary references for the command.

Table 1–4 Built-in Tcl commands.

Command	Pg.	Description
after	218	Schedule a Tcl command for later execution.
append	51	Append arguments to a variable's value. No spaces added.
array	91	Query array state and search through elements.
binary	54	Convert between strings and binary data.
break	77	Exit loop prematurely.
catch	77	Trap errors.
cd	115	Change working directory.
clock	173	Get the time and format date strings.
close	115	Close an open I/O stream.
concat	61	Concatenate arguments with spaces between. Splices lists.
console	28	Control the console used to enter commands interactively.
continue	77	Continue with next loop iteration.
error	79	Raise an error.
eof	109	Check for end of file.
eval	122	Concatenate arguments and evaluate them as a command.
exec	99	Fork and execute a UNIX program.
exit	116	Terminate the process.
expr	6	Evaluate a math expression.
fblocked	223	Poll an I/O channel to see if data is ready.
fconfigure	221	Set and query I/O channel properties.
fcopy	237	Copy from one I/O channel to another.
file	102	Query the file system.
fileevent	219	Register callback for event-driven I/O.
flush	109	Flush output from an I/O stream's internal buffers.
for	76	Loop construct similar to C `for` statement.
foreach	73	Loop construct over a list, or lists, of values.
format	52	Format a string similar to C `sprintf`.
gets	112	Read a line of input from an I/O stream.
glob	115	Expand a pattern to matching file names.
global	84	Declare global variables.

Table 1–4 Built-in Tcl commands. (Continued)

history	185	Use command-line history.
if	70	Test a condition. Allows else and elseif clauses.
incr	12	Increment a variable by an integer amount.
info	176	Query the state of the Tcl interpreter.
interp	274	Create additional Tcl interpreters.
join	65	Concatenate list elements with a given separator string.
lappend	61	Add elements to the end of a list.
lindex	63	Fetch an element of a list.
linsert	64	Insert elements into a list.
list	61	Create a list out of the arguments.
llength	63	Return the number of elements in a list.
load	607	Load shared libraries that define Tcl commands.
lrange	63	Return a range of list elements.
lreplace	64	Replace elements of a list.
lsearch	64	Search for an element of a list that matches a pattern.
lsort	65	Sort a list.
namespace	203	Create and manipulate namespaces.
open	110	Open a file or process pipeline for I/O.
package	165	Provide or require code packages.
pid	116	Return the process ID.
proc	81	Define a Tcl procedure.
puts	112	Output a string to an I/O stream.
pwd	115	Return the current working directory.
read	113	Read blocks of characters from an I/O stream.
regexp	148	Match regular expressions.
regsub	152	Substitute based on regular expressions.
rename	82	Change the name of a Tcl command.
return	80	Return a value from a procedure.
scan	54	Parse a string according to a format specification.
seek	114	Set the seek offset of an I/O stream.
set	5	Assign a value to a variable.

Table 1–4 Built-in Tcl commands. (Continued)

socket	226	Open a TCP/IP network connection.
source	26	Evaluate the Tcl commands in a file.
split	65	Chop a string up into list elements.
string	45	Operate on strings.
subst	132	Substitute embedded commands and variable references.
switch	71	Test several conditions.
tell	114	Return the current seek offset of an I/O stream.
time	191	Measure the execution time of a command.
trace	183	Monitor variable assignments.
unknown	167	Handle unknown commands.
unset	13	Delete variables.
uplevel	130	Execute a command in a different scope.
upvar	85	Reference a variable in a different scope.
variable	197	Declare namespace variables.
vwait	220	Wait for a variable to be modified.
while	73	Loop until a boolean expression is false.

Getting Started

This chapter explains how to run Tcl and Tk on different operating system platforms: UNIX, Windows, and Macintosh. Tcl commands discussed are: `source`, `console` **and** `info`.

*T*his chapter explains how to run Tcl scripts on different computer systems. While you can write Tcl scripts that are portable among UNIX, Windows, and Macintosh, the details about getting started are different for each system. If you are looking for a current version of Tcl/Tk, check the Internet sites listed in the Preface on page *lii*.

The main Tcl/Tk program is *wish. Wish* stands for windowing shell, and with it you can create graphical applications that run on all these platforms. The name of the program is a little different on each of the UNIX, Windows, and Macintosh systems. On UNIX it is just *wish*. On Windows you will find *wish.exe*, and on the Macintosh the application name is *Wish*. A version number may also be part of the name, such as *wish4.2, wish80.exe*, or *Wish 8.2*. The differences among versions are introduced on page *xlviii*, and described in more detail in Part VII of the book. This book will use *wish* to refer to all of these possibilities.

Tk adds Tcl commands that are used to create graphical user interfaces, and Tk is described in Part III. You can run Tcl without Tk if you do not need a graphical interface, such as with the CGI script discussed in Chapter 3. In this case the program is *tclsh, tclsh.exe* or *Tclsh*.

When you run *wish,* it displays an empty window and prompts for a Tcl command with a % prompt. You can enter Tcl commands interactively and experiment with the examples in this book. On Windows and Macintosh, a console window is used to prompt for Tcl commands. On UNIX, your terminal window is used. As described later, you can also set up standalone Tcl/Tk scripts that are self-contained applications.

The source Command

You can enter Tcl commands interactively at the % prompt. It is a good idea to try out the examples in this book as you read along. The highlighted examples from the book are on the CD-ROM in the `exsource` folder. You can edit these scripts in your favorite editor. Save your examples to a file and then execute them with the Tcl `source` command:

        source *filename*

The `source` command reads Tcl commands from a file and evaluates them just as if you had typed them interactively.

Chapter 3 develops a sample application. To get started, just open an editor on a file named `cgi1.tcl`. Each time you update this file you can save it, reload it into Tcl with the `source` command, and test it again. Development goes quickly because you do not wait for things to compile!

UNIX Tcl Scripts

On UNIX you can create a standalone Tcl or Tcl/Tk script much like an `sh` or `csh` script. The trick is in the first line of the file that contains your script. If the first line of a file begins with `#!pathname`, then UNIX uses `pathname` as the interpreter for the rest of the script. The "Hello, World!" program from Chapter 1 is repeated in Example 2–1 with the special starting line:

Example 2–1 A standalone Tcl script on UNIX.

```
#!/usr/local/bin/tclsh
puts stdout {Hello, World!}
```

Similarly, the Tk hello world program from Chapter 21 is shown in Example 2–2:

Example 2–2 A standalone Tk script on UNIX.

```
#!/usr/local/bin/wish
button .hello -text Hello -command {puts "Hello, World!"}
pack .hello -padx 10 -pady 10
```

The actual pathnames for *tclsh* and *wish* may be different on your system. If you type the pathname for the interpreter wrong, you receive a confusing "command not found" error. You can find out the complete pathname of the Tcl interpreter with the `info nameofexecutable` command. This is what appears on my system:

        info nameofexecutable
        => /home/welch/install/solaris/bin/tclsh8.2

Watch out for long pathnames.

On most UNIX systems, this special first line is limited to 32 characters, including the `#!`. If the pathname is too long, you may end up with `/bin/sh` trying to interpret your script, giving you syntax errors. You might try using a symbolic link from a short name to the true, long name of the interpreter. However, watch out for systems like Solaris in which the script interpreter cannot be a symbolic link. Fortunately, Solaris doesn't impose a 32-character limit on the pathname, so you can just use a long pathname.

The next example shows a trick that works around the pathname length limitation in all cases. The trick comes from a posting to `comp.lang.tcl` by Kevin Kenny. It takes advantage of a difference between comments in Tcl and the Bourne shell. Tcl comments are described on page 16. In the example, the Bourne shell command that runs the Tcl interpreter is hidden in a comment as far as Tcl is concerned, but it is visible to `/bin/sh`:

Example 2–3 Using `/bin/sh` to run a Tcl script.

```
#!/bin/sh
# The backslash makes the next line a comment in Tcl \
exec /some/very/long/path/to/wish "$0" ${1+"$@"}
#    ... Tcl script goes here ...
```

You do not even have to know the complete pathname of *tclsh* or *wish* to use this trick. You can just do the following:

```
#!/bin/sh
# Run wish from the users PATH \
exec wish -f "$0" ${1+"$@"}
```

The drawback of an incomplete pathname is that many sites have different versions of *wish* and *tclsh* that correspond to different versions of Tcl and Tk. In addition, some users may not have these programs in their PATH.

If you have Tk version 3.6 or earlier, its version of *wish* requires a `-f` argument to make it read the contents of a file. The `-f` switch is ignored in Tk 4.0 and higher versions. The `-f`, if required, is also counted in the 32-character limit on `#!` lines.

```
#!/usr/local/bin/wish -f
```

Windows 95 Start Menu

You can add your Tcl/Tk programs to the Windows start menu. The command is the complete name of the *wish.exe* program and the name of the script. The trick is that the name of *wish.exe* has a space in it in the default configuration, so you must use quotes. Your start command will look something like this:

```
"c:\Program Files\TCL82\wish.exe" "c:\My Files\script.tcl"
```

This starts `c:\My Files\script.tcl` as a standalone Tcl/Tk program.

The Macintosh and *ResEdit*

If you want to create a self-contained Tcl/Tk application on Macintosh, you must copy the *Wish* program and add a Macintosh resource named `tclshrc` that has the start-up Tcl code. The Tcl code can be a single `source` command that reads your script file. Here are step-by-step instructions to create the resource using *ResEdit*:

- First, make a copy of *Wish* and open the copy in *ResEdit*.
- Pull down the `Resource` menu and select `Create New Resource` operation to make a new `TEXT` resource.
- *ResEdit* opens a window and you can type in text. Type in a `source` command that names your script:

      source "Hard Disk:Tcl/Tk 8.1:Applications:MyScript.tcl"
- Set the name of the resource to be `tclshrc`. You do this through the `Get Resource Info` dialog under the `Resources` menu in *ResEdit*.

This sequence of commands is captured in an application called *Drag n Drop Tclets*, which comes with the Macintosh Tcl distribution. If you drag a Tcl script onto this icon, it will create a copy of *Wish* and create the `tclshrc` text resource that has a `source` command that will load that script.

If you have a Macintosh development environment, you can build a version of *Wish* that has additional resources built right in. You add the resources to the `applicationInit.r` file. If a resource contains Tcl code, you use it like this:

      source -rcrc *resource*

If you don't want to edit resources, you can just use the *Wish* `Source` menu to select a script to run.

The `console` Command

The Windows and Macintosh platforms have a built-in console that is used to enter Tcl commands interactively. You can control this console with the `console` command. The console is visible by default. Hide the console like this:

      console hide

Display the console like this:

      console show

The console is implemented by a second Tcl interpreter. You can evaluate Tcl commands in that interpreter with:

      console eval *command*

There is an alternate version of this console called *TkCon*. It is included on the CD-ROM, and you can find current versions on the Internet. *TkCon* was created by Jeff Hobbs and has lots of nice features. You can use *TkCon* on Unix systems, too.

Command-Line Arguments

If you run a script from the command line, for example from a UNIX shell, you can pass the script command-line arguments. You can also specify these arguments in the shortcut command in Windows. For example, under UNIX you can type this at a shell:

```
% myscript.tcl arg1 arg2 arg3
```

In Windows, you can have a shortcut that runs *wish* on your script and also passes additional arguments:

```
"c:\Program Files\TCL82\wish.exe" c:\your\script.tcl arg1
```

The Tcl shells pass the command-line arguments to the script as the value of the argv variable. The number of command-line arguments is given by the argc variable. The name of the program, or script, is not part of argv nor is it counted by argc. Instead, it is put into the argv0 variable. Table 2–2 lists all the predefined variables in the Tcl shells. argv is a list, so you can use the lindex command, which is described on page 59, to extract items from it:

```
set arg1 [lindex $argv 0]
```

The following script prints its arguments (foreach is described on page 73):

Example 2–4 The EchoArgs script.

```
# Tcl script to echo command line arguments
puts "Program: $argv0"
puts "Number of arguments: $argc"
set i 0
foreach arg $argv {
    puts "Arg $i: $arg"
    incr i
}
```

Command-Line Options to *Wish*

Some command-line options are interpreted by *wish*, and they do not appear in the argv variable. The general form of the *wish* command line is:

```
wish ?options? ?script? ?arg1 arg2?
```

If no script is specified, then *wish* just enters an interactive command loop. Table 2–1 lists the options that *wish* supports:

Table 2–1 Wish command line options.

-colormap new	Use a new private colormap. See page 538.
-display *display*	Use the specified X *display*. UNIX only.
-geometry *geometry*	The size and position of the window. See page 570.
-name *name*	Specify the Tk application name. See page 560.

Table 2–1 Wish command line options. (Continued)

`-sync`	Run X synchronously. UNIX only.
`-use id`	Use the window specified by `id` for the main window. See page 578.
`-visual visual`	Specify the visual for the main window. See page 538.
`--`	Terminate options to *wish*.

Predefined Variables

Table 2–2 Variables defined by *tclsh* and *wish*.

`argc`	The number of command-line arguments.
`argv`	A list of the command-line arguments.
`argv0`	The name of the script being executed. If being used interactively, `argv0` is the name of the shell program.
`embed_args`	The list of arguments in the `<EMBED>` tag. Tcl applets only. See page 296.
`env`	An array of the environment variables. See page 117.
`tcl_interactive`	True (one) if the *tclsh* is prompting for commands.
`tcl_library`	The script library directory.
`tcl_patchLevel`	Modified version number, e.g., 8.0b1.
`tcl_platform`	Array containing operating system information. See page 182.
`tcl_prompt1`	If defined, this is a command that outputs the prompt.
`tcl_prompt2`	If defined, this is a command that outputs the prompt if the current command is not yet complete.
`tcl_version`	Version number.
`auto_path`	The search path for script library directories. See page 162.
`auto_index`	A map from command name to a Tcl command that defines it.
`auto_noload`	If set, the library facility is disabled.
`auto_noexec`	If set, the auto execute facility is disabled.
`geometry`	(*wish* only). The value of the `-geometry` argument.

The Guestbook CGI Application

This chapter presents a simple Tcl program that computes a Web page. The chapter provides a brief background to HTML and the CGI interface to Web servers.

*T*his chapter presents a complete, but simple guestbook program that computes an HTML document, or Web page, based on the contents of a simple database. The basic idea is that a user with a Web browser visits a page that is computed by the program. The details of how the page gets from your program to the user with the Web browser vary from system to system. The Tcl Web Server described in Chapter 18 comes with this guestbook example already set up. You can also use these scripts on your own Web server, but you will need help from your Webmaster to set things up.

The chapter provides a very brief introduction to HTML and CGI programming. HTML is a way to specify text formatting, including hypertext links to other pages on the World Wide Web. CGI is a standard for communication between a Web server that delivers documents and a program that computes documents for the server. There are many books on these subjects alone. *CGI Developers Resource, Web Programming with Tcl and Perl* by John Ivler (Prentice Hall, 1997) is a good reference for details that are left unexplained here.

A guestbook is a place for visitors to sign their name and perhaps provide other information. We will build a guestbook that takes advantage of the World Wide Web. Our guests can leave their address as a Universal Resource Location (URL). The guestbook will be presented as a page that has hypertext links to all these URLs so that other guests can visit them. The program works by keeping a simple database of the guests, and it generates the guestbook page from the database.

The Tcl scripts described in this chapter use commands and techniques that are described in more detail in later chapters. The goal of the examples is to demonstrate the power of Tcl without explaining every detail. If the examples in this chapter raise questions, you can follow the references to examples in other chapters that do go into more depth.

A Quick Introduction to HTML

Web pages are written in a text markup language called HTML (HyperText Markup Language). The idea of HTML is that you annotate, or mark up, regular text with special tags that indicate structure and formatting. For example, the title of a Web page is defined like this:

```
<TITLE>My Home Page</TITLE>
```

The tags provide general formatting guidelines, but the browsers that display HTML pages have freedom in how they display things. This keeps the markup simple. The general syntax for HTML tags is:

```
<tag parameters>normal text</tag>
```

As shown here, the tags usually come in pairs. The open tag may have some parameters, and the close tag name begins with a slash. The case of a tag is not considered, so `<title>`, `<Title>`, and `<TITLE>` are all valid and mean the same thing. The corresponding close tag could be `</title>`, `</Title>`, `</TITLE>`, or even `</TiTlE>`.

The `<A>` tag defines hypertext links that reference other pages on the Web. The hypertext links connect pages into a Web so that you can move from page to page to page and find related information. It is the flexibility of the links that make the Web so interesting. The `<A>` tag takes an `HREF` parameter that defines the destination of the link. If you wanted to link to my home page, you would put this in your page:

```
<A HREF="http://www.beedub.com/">Brent Welch</A>
```

When this construct appears in a Web page, your browser typically displays "Brent Welch" in blue underlined text. When you click on that text, your browser switches to the page at the address "http://www.beedub.com/". There is a lot more to HTML, of course, but this should give you a basic idea of what is going on in the examples. The following list summarizes the HTML tags that will be used in the examples:

Table 3–1 HTML tags used in the examples.

HTML	Main tag that surrounds the whole document.
HEAD	Delimits head section of the HTML document.
TITLE	Defines the title of the page.
BODY	Delimits the body section. Lets you specify page colors.

Table 3–1 HTML tags used in the examples. (Continued)

H1 - H6	HTML defines 6 heading levels: H1, H2, H3, H4, H5, H6.
P	Start a new paragraph.
BR	One blank line.
B	Bold text.
I	Italic text.
A	Used for hypertext links.
IMG	Specify an image.
DL	Definition list.
DT	Term clause in a definition list.
DD	Definition clause in a definition list.
UL	An unordered list.
LI	A bulleted item within a list.
TABLE	Create a table.
TR	A table row.
TD	A cell within a table row.
FORM	Defines a data entry form.
INPUT	A one-line entry field, checkbox, radio button, or submit button.
TEXTAREA	A multiline text field.

CGI for Dynamic Pages

There are two classes of pages on the Web, static and dynamic. A static page is written and stored on a Web server, and the same thing is returned each time a user views the page. This is the easy way to think about Web pages. You have some information to share, so you compose a page and tinker with the HTML tags to get the information to look good. If you have a home page, it is probably in this class.

In contrast, a dynamic page is computed each time it is viewed. This is how pages that give up-to-the-minute stock prices work, for example. A dynamic page does not mean it includes animations; it just means that a program computes the page contents when a user visits the page. The advantage of this approach is that a user might see something different each time he or she visits the page. As we shall see, it is also easier to maintain information in a database of some sort and generate the HTML formatting for the data with a program.

A CGI (Common Gateway Interface) program is used to compute Web pages. The CGI standard defines how inputs are passed to the program as well as a way to identify different types of results, such as images, plain text, or HTML markup. A CGI program simply writes the contents of the document to its standard output, and the Web server takes care of delivering the document to the user's Web browser. The following is a very simple CGI script:

Example 3–1 A simple CGI script.

```
puts "Content-Type: text/html"
puts ""
puts "<TITLE>The Current Time</TITLE>"
puts "The time is <B>[clock format [clock seconds]]</B>"
```

The program computes a simple HTML page that has the current time. Each time a user visits the page they will see the current time on the server. The server that has the CGI program and the user viewing the page might be on different sides of the planet. The output of the program starts with a `Content-Type` line that tells your Web browser what kind of data comes next. This is followed by a blank line and then the contents of the page.

The `clock` command is used twice: once to get the current time in seconds, and a second time to format the time into a nice looking string. The `clock` command is described in detail on page 173. Fortunately, there is no conflict between the markup syntax used by HTML and the Tcl syntax for embedded commands, so we can mix the two in the argument to the `puts` command. Double quotes are used to group the argument to `puts` so that the `clock` commands will be executed. When run, the output of the program will look like this:

Example 3–2 Output of Example 3–1.

```
Content-Type: text/html

<TITLE>The Current Time</TITLE>
The time is <B>Wed Oct 16 11:23:43  1996</B>
```

This example is a bit sloppy in its use of HTML, but it should display properly in most Web browsers. Example 3–3 includes all the required tags for a proper HTML document.

The `guestbook.cgi` Script

The `guestbook.cgi` script computes a page that lists all the registered guests. The example is shown first, and then each part of it is discussed in more detail later. One thing to note right away is that the HTML tags are generated by procedures that hide the details of the HTML syntax. The first lines of the script use the UNIX trick to have *tclsh* interpret the script. This trick is described on page 26:

Example 3–3 The guestbook.cgi script.

```
#!/bin/sh
# guestbook.cgi
# Implement a simple guestbook page.
# The set of visitors is kept in a simple database.
# The newguest.cgi script will update the database.
# \
exec tclsh "$0" ${1+"$@"}

# The cgilib.tcl file has helper procedures
# The guestbook.data file has the database
# Both file are in the same directory as the script

set dir [file dirname [info script]]
source [file join $dir cgilib.tcl]
set datafile [file join $dir guestbook.data]

Cgi_Header "Brent's Guestbook" {BGCOLOR=white TEXT=black}
P
if {![file exists $datafile]} {
    puts "No registered guests, yet."
    P
    puts "Be the first [Link {registered guest!} newguest.html]"
} else {
    puts "The following folks have registered in my GuestBook."
    P
    puts [Link Register newguest.html]
    H2 Guests
    catch {source $datafile}
    foreach name [lsort [array names Guestbook]] {
        set item $Guestbook($name)
        set homepage [lindex $item 0]
        set markup [lindex $item 1]
        H3 [Link $name $homepage]
        puts $markup
    }
}
Cgi_End
```

Using a Script Library File

The script uses a number of Tcl procedures that make working with HTML and the CGI interface easier. These procedures are kept in the cgilib.tcl file, which is kept in the same directory as the main script. The script starts by sourcing the cgilib.tcl file so that these procedures are available. The following command determines the location of the cgilib.tcl file based on the location of the main script. The info script command returns the file name of the script. The file dirname and file join commands manipulate file names in a platform-independent way. They are described on page 102. I use this trick to avoid putting absolute file names into my scripts, which would have to be changed if the program moves later:

```
set dir [file dirname [info script]]
source [file join $dir cgilib.tcl]
```

Beginning the HTML Page

The following command generates the standard information that comes at the beginning of an HTML page:

```
Cgi_Header {Brent's GuestBook} {bgcolor=white text=black}
```

The `Cgi_Header` is shown in Example 3–4:

Example 3–4 The `Cgi_Header` procedure.

```
proc Cgi_Header {title {bodyparams {}}} {
    puts stdout \
"Content-Type: text/html

<HTML>
<HEAD>
<TITLE>$title</TITLE>
</HEAD>
<BODY $bodyparams>
<H1>$title</H1>"
}
```

The `Cgi_Header` procedure takes as arguments the title for the page and some optional parameters for the HTML `<Body>` tag. The guestbook.cgi script specifies black text on a white background to avoid the standard gray background of most browsers. The procedure definition uses the syntax for an optional parameter, so you do not have to pass `bodyparams` to `Cgi_Header`. Default values for procedure parameters are described on page 81.

The `Cgi_Header` procedure just contains a single `puts` command that generates the standard boilerplate that appears at the beginning of the output. Note that several lines are grouped together with double quotes. Double quotes are used so that the variable references mixed into the HTML are substituted properly.

The output begins with the CGI content-type information, a blank line, and then the HTML. The HTML is divided into a head and a body part. The `<TITLE>` tag goes in the head section of an HTML document. Finally, browsers display the title in a different place than the rest of the page, so I always want to repeat the title as a level-one heading (i.e., `H1`) in the body of the page.

Simple Tags and Hypertext Links

The next thing the program does is to see whether there are any registered guests or not. The `file` command, which is described in detail on page 102, is used to see whether there is any data:

```
if {![file exists $datafile]} {
```

If the database file does not exist, a different page is displayed to encourage a registration. The page includes a hypertext link to a registration page. The newguest.html page will be described in more detail later:

```
puts "No registered guests, yet."
P
puts "Be the first [Link {registered guest!} newguest.html]"
```

The P command generates the HTML for a paragraph break. This trivial procedure saves us a few keystrokes:

```
proc P {} {
    puts <P>
}
```

The Link command formats and returns the HTML for a hypertext link. Instead of printing the HTML directly, it is returned, so you can include it in-line with other text you are printing:

Example 3–5 The Link command formats a hypertext link.

```
proc Link {text url} {
    return "<A HREF=\"$url\">$text</A>"
}
```

The output of the program would be as below if there were no data:

Example 3–6 Initial output of guestbook.cgi.

```
Content-Type: text/html

<HTML>
<HEAD>
<TITLE>Brent's Guestbook</TITLE>
</HEAD>
<BODY BGCOLOR=white TEXT=black>
<H1>Brent's Guestbook</H1>
<P>
No registered guests.
<P>
Be the first <A HREF="newguest.html">registered guest!</A>
</BODY>
</HTML>
```

If the database file exists, then the real work begins. We first generate a link to the registration page, and a level-two header to separate that from the guest list:

```
puts [Link Register newguest.html]
H2 Guests
```

The H2 procedure handles the detail of including the matching close tag:

```
proc H2 {string} {
    puts "<H2>$string</H2>"
}
```

Using a Tcl Array for the Database

The datafile contains Tcl commands that define an array that holds the guestbook data. If this file is kept in the same directory as the guestbook.cgi script, then you can compute its name:

```
set dir [file dirname [info script]]
set datafile [file join $dir guestbook.data]
```

By using Tcl commands to represent the data, we can load the data with the source command. The catch command is used to protect the script from a bad data file, which will show up as an error from the source command. Catching errors is described in detail on page 79:

```
catch {source $datafile}
```

The Guestbook variable is the array defined in guestbook.data. Array variables are the topic of Chapter 8. Each element of the array is defined with a Tcl command that looks like this:

```
set Guestbook(key) {url markup}
```

The person's name is the array index, or key. The value of the array element is a Tcl list with two elements: their URL and some additional HTML markup that they can include in the guestbook. Tcl lists are the topic of Chapter 5. The following example shows what the command looks like with real data:

```
set {Guestbook(Brent Welch)} {
    http://www.beedub.com/
    {<img src=http://www.beedub.com/welch.gif>}
}
```

The spaces in the name result in additional braces to group the whole variable name and each list element. This syntax is explained on page 90. Do not worry about it now. We will see on page 42 that all the braces in the previous statement are generated automatically. The main point is that the person's name is the key, and the value is a list with two elements.

The array names command returns all the indices, or keys, in the array, and the lsort command sorts these alphabetically. The foreach command loops over the sorted list, setting the loop variable x to each key in turn:

```
foreach name [lsort [array names Guestbook]] {
```

Given the key, we get the value like this:

```
set item $Guestbook($name)
```

The two list elements are extracted with lindex, which is described on page 63.

```
set homepage [lindex $item 0]
```

```
set markup [lindex $item 1]
```

We generate the HTML for the guestbook entry as a level-three header that contains a hypertext link to the guest's home page. We follow the link with any HTML markup text that the guest has supplied to embellish his or her entry. The H3 procedure is similar to the H2 procedure already shown, except it generates <H3> tags:

```
H3 [Link $name $homepage]
puts $markup
```

Sample Output

The last thing the script does is call Cgi_End to output the proper closing tags. Example 3–7 shows the output of the guestbook.cgi script:

Example 3–7 Output of guestbook.cgi.

```
Content-Type: text/html

<HTML>
<HEAD>
<TITLE>Brent's Guestbook</TITLE>
</HEAD>
<BODY BGCOLOR=white TEXT=black>
<H1>Brent's Guestbook</H1>
<P>
The following folks have registered in my guestbook.
<P>
<A HREF="newguest.html">Register</A>
<H2>Guests</H2>
<H3><A HREF="http://www.beedub.com/">Brent Welch</A></H3>
<IMG SRC="http://www.beedub.com/welch.gif">
</BODY>
</HTML>
```

Defining Forms and Processing Form Data

The guestbook.cgi script only generates output. The other half of CGI deals with input from the user. Input is more complex for two reasons. First, we have to define another HTML page that has a form for the user to fill out. Second, the data from the form is organized and encoded in a standard form that must be decoded by the script. Example 3–8 on page 40 defines a very simple form, and the procedure that decodes the form data is shown in Example 11–6 on page 155.

The guestbook page contains a link to newguest.html. This page contains a form that lets a user register his or her name, home page URL, and some additional HTML markup. The form has a submit button. When a user clicks that button in their browser, the information from the form is passed to the newguest.cgi script. This script updates the database and computes another page for the user that acknowledges the user's contribution.

The newguest.html Form

An HTML form contains tags that define data entry fields, buttons, checkboxes, and other elements that let the user specify values. For example, a one-line entry field that is used to enter the home page URL is defined like this:

```
<INPUT TYPE=text NAME=url>
```

The INPUT tag is used to define several kinds of input elements, and its type parameter indicates what kind. In this case, TYPE=text creates a one-line text entry field. The submit button is defined with an INPUT tag that has TYPE=submit, and the VALUE parameter becomes the text that appears on the button:

```
<INPUT TYPE=submit NAME=submit VALUE=Register>
```

A general type-in window is defined with the TEXTAREA tag. This creates a multiline, scrolling text field that is useful for specifying lots of information, such as a free-form comment. In our case we will let guests type in HTML that will appear with their guestbook entry. The text between the open and close TEXTAREA tags is inserted into the type-in window when the page is first displayed.

```
<TEXTAREA NAME=markup ROWS=10 COLS=50>Hello.</TEXTAREA>
```

A common parameter to the form tags is NAME=*something*. This name identifies the data that will come back from the form. The tags also have parameters that affect their display, such as the label on the submit button and the size of the text area. Those details are not important for our example. The complete form is shown in Example 3–8:

Example 3–8 The newguest.html form.

```
<!Doctype HTML PUBLIC "-//IETF//DTD HTML 2.0//EN">
<HTML>
<HEAD>
<TITLE>Register in my Guestbook</TITLE>
<!-- Author: bwelch -->
<META HTTP-Equiv=Editor Content="SunLabs WebTk 1.0beta 10/
11/96">
</HEAD>
<BODY>

<FORM ACTION="newguest.cgi" METHOD="POST">

<H1>Register in my Guestbook</H1>
<UL>
<LI>Name <INPUT TYPE="text" NAME="name" SIZE="40">
<LI>URL  <INPUT TYPE="text" NAME="url" SIZE="40">
<P>
If you don't have a home page, you can use an email URL like
"mailto:welch@acm.org"
<LI>Additional HTML to include after your link:
<BR>

<TEXTAREA NAME="html" COLS="60" ROWS="15">
</TEXTAREA>
<LI><INPUT TYPE="submit" NAME="new" VALUE="Add me to your
```

```
guestbook">
<LI><INPUT TYPE="submit" NAME="update" VALUE="Update my
guestbook entry">
</UL>
</FORM>

</BODY>
</HTML>
```

The newguest.cgi Script

When the user clicks the Submit button in their browser, the data from the form is passed to the program identified by the Action parameter of the form tag. That program takes the data, does something useful with it, and then returns a new page for the browser to display. In our case the FORM tag names newguest.cgi as the program to handle the data:

```
<FORM ACTION=newguest.cgi METHOD=POST>
```

The CGI specification defines how the data from the form is passed to the program. The data is encoded and organized so that the program can figure out the values the user specified for each form element. The encoding is handled rather nicely with some regular expression tricks that are done in Cgi_Parse. Cgi_Parse saves the form data, and Cgi_Value gets a form value in the script. These procedures are described in Example 11–6 on page 155. Example 3–9 starts out by calling Cgi_Parse:

Example 3–9 The newguest.cgi script.

```
#!/bin/sh
# \
exec tclsh "$0" ${1+"$@"}
# source cgilib.tcl from the same directory as newguest.cgi

set dir [file dirname [info script]]
source [file join $dir cgilib.tcl]
set datafile [file join $dir guestbook.data]

Cgi_Parse

# Open the datafile in append mode

if [catch {open $datafile a} out] {
    Cgi_Header "Guestbook Registration Error" \
        {BGCOLOR=black TEXT=red}
    P
    puts "Cannot open the data file"
    P
    puts $out;# the error message
    exit 0
}
```

```
# Append a Tcl set command that defines the guest's entry

puts $out ""
puts $out [list set Guestbook([Cgi_Value name]) \
    [list [Cgi_Value url] [Cgi_Value html]]]
close $out

# Return a page to the browser

Cgi_Header "Guestbook Registration Confirmed" \
    {BGCOLOR=white TEXT=black}

puts "
<DL>
<DT>Name
<DD>[Cgi_Value name]
<DT>URL
<DD>[Link [Cgi_Value url] [Cgi_Value url]]
</DL>
[Cgi_Value html]
"

Cgi_End
```

The main idea of the newguest.cgi script is that it saves the data to a file as a Tcl command that defines an element of the Guestbook array. This lets the guestbook.cgi script simply load the data by using the Tcl source command. This trick of storing data as a Tcl script saves us from the chore of defining a new file format and writing code to parse it. Instead, we can rely on the well-tuned Tcl implementation to do the hard work for us efficiently.

The script opens the datafile in append mode so that it can add a new record to the end. Opening files is described in detail on page 110. The script uses a catch command to guard against errors. If an error occurs, a page explaining the error is returned to the user. Working with files is one of the most common sources of errors (permission denied, disk full, file-not-found, and so on), so I always open the file inside a catch statement:

```
if [catch {open $datafile a} out] {
    # an error occurred
} else {
    # open was ok
}
```

In this command, the variable out gets the result of the open command, which is either a file descriptor or an error message. This style of using catch is described in detail in Example 6–14 on page 77.

The script writes the data as a Tcl set command. The list command is used to format the data properly:

```
puts $out [list set Guestbook([Cgi_Value name]) \
    [list [Cgi_Value url] [Cgi_Value html]]]
```

There are two lists. First the `url` and `html` values are formatted into one list. This list will be the value of the array element. Then, the whole Tcl command is formed as a list. In simplified form, the command is generated from this:

```
list set variable value
```

Using the `list` command ensures that the result will always be a valid Tcl command that sets the variable to the given value. The `list` command is described in more detail on page 61.

The cgi.tcl Package

The `cgilib.tcl` file included with this book just barely scratches the surface of things you might like to do in a CGI script. Don Libes has created a comprehensive package for CGI scripts known as `cgi.tcl`. You can find it on the Web at

```
http://expect.nist.gov/cgi.tcl/
```

One of Don's goals in `cgi.tcl` was to eliminate the need to directly write any HTML markup at all. Instead, he has defined a whole suite of Tcl commands similar to the P and H2 procedures shown in this chapter that automatically emit the matching close tags. He also has support procedures to deal with browser cookies, page redirects, and other CGI features.

Next Steps

There are a number of details that can be added to this example. A user may want to update their entry, for example. They could do that now, but they would have to retype everything. They might also like a chance to check the results of their registration and make changes before committing them. This requires another page that displays their guest entry as it would appear on a page, and also has the fields that let them update the data.

The details of how a CGI script is hooked up with a Web server vary from server to server. You should ask your local Webmaster for help if you want to try this out on your local Web site. The Tcl Web Server comes with this guestbook example already set up, plus it has a number of other very interesting ways to generate pages. My own taste in Web page generation has shifted from CGI to a template-based approach supported by the Tcl Web Server. This is the topic of Chapter 18.

The next few chapters describe basic Tcl commands and data structures. We return to the CGI example in Chapter 11 on regular expressions.

4

String Processing in Tcl

This chapter describes string manipulation and simple pattern matching. Tcl commands described are: `string`, `append`, `format`, `scan`, and `binary`. The `string` command is a collection of several useful string manipulation operations.

Strings are the basic data item in Tcl, so it should not be surprising that there are a large number of commands to manipulate strings. A closely related topic is pattern matching, in which string comparisons are made more powerful by matching a string against a pattern. This chapter describes a simple pattern matching mechanism that is similar to that used in many other shell languages. Chapter 11 describes a more complex and powerful regular expression pattern matching mechanism.

The `string` Command

The `string` command is really a collection of operations you can perform on strings. The following example calculates the length of the value of a variable.

```
set name "Brent Welch"
string length $name
=> 11
```

The first argument to `string` determines the operation. You can ask `string` for valid operations by giving it a bad one:

```
string junk
=> bad option "junk": should be bytelength, compare,
equal, first, index, is, last, length, map, match, range,
repeat, replace, tolower, totitle, toupper, trim, trim-
left, trimright, wordend, or wordstart
```

This trick of feeding a Tcl command bad arguments to find out its usage is common across many commands. Table 4–1 summarizes the `string` command.

Table 4–1 The `string` command.

`string bytelength str`	Returns the number of bytes used to store a string, which may be different from the character length returned by `string length` because of UTF-8 encoding. See page 210 of Chapter 15 about Unicode and UTF-8.
`string compare ?-nocase? ?-length len? str1 str2`	Compares strings lexicographically. Use `-nocase` for case insensitve comparison. Use `-length` to limit the comparison to the first *len* characters. Returns 0 if equal, -1 if *str1* sorts before *str2*, else 1.
`string equal ?-nocase? str1 str2`	Compares strings and returns 1 if they are the same. Use `-nocase` for case insensitve comparison.
`string first str1 str2`	Returns the index in *str2* of the first occurrence of *str1*, or -1 if *str1* is not found.
`string index string index`	Returns the character at the specified *index*. An index counts from zero. Use end for the last character.
`string is class ?-strict? ?-failindex varname? string`	Returns 1 if *string* belongs to *class*. If `-strict`, then empty strings never match, otherwise they always match. If `-failindex` is specified, then *varname* is assigned the index of the character in *string* that prevented it from being a member of *class*. See Table 4–3 on page 50 for character class names.
`string last str1 str2`	Returns the index in *str2* of the last occurrence of *str1*, or -1 if *str1* is not found.
`string length string`	Returns the number of characters in *string*.
`string map ?-nocase? charMap string`	Returns a new string created by mapping characters in *string* according to the input, output list in *charMap*. See page 51.
`string match pattern str`	Returns 1 if *str* matches the *pattern*, else 0. Glob-style matching is used. See page 48.
`string range str i j`	Returns the range of characters in *str* from *i* to *j*.
`string repeat str count`	Returns *str* repeated *count* times.
`string replace str first last ?newstr?`	Returns a new string created by replacing characters *first* through *last* with *newstr*, or nothing.
`string tolower string ?first? ?last?`	Returns *string* in lower case. *first* and *last* determine the range of *string* on which to operate.
`string totitle string ?first? ?last?`	Capitalizes *string* by replacing its first character with the Unicode title case, or upper case, and the rest with lower case. *first* and *last* determine the range of *string* on which to operate.

Table 4–1 The string command. (Continued)

string toupper *string* ?*first*? ?*last*?	Returns *string* in upper case. *first* and *last* determine the range of *string* on which to operate.
string trim *string* ?*chars*?	Trims the characters in *chars* from both ends of *string*. *chars* defaults to whitespace.
string trimleft *string* ?*chars*?	Trims the characters in *chars* from the beginning of *string*. *chars* defaults to whitespace.
string trimright *string* ?*chars*?	Trims the characters in *chars* from the end of *string*. *chars* defaults to whitespace.
string wordend *str ix*	Returns the index in *str* of the character after the word containing the character at index *ix*.
string wordstart *str ix*	Returns the index in *str* of the first character in the word containing the character at index *ix*.

These are the string operations I use most:

- The equal operation, which is shown in Example 4–2 on page 48.
- String match. This pattern matching operation is described on page 48.
- The tolower, totitle, and toupper operations convert case.
- The trim, trimright, and trimleft operations are handy for cleaning up strings.

These new operations were added in Tcl 8.1 (actually, they first appeared in the 8.1.1 patch release):

- The equal operation, which is simpler than using string compare.
- The is operation that test for kinds of strings. String classes are listed in Table 4–3 on page 50.
- The map operation that translates characters (e.g., like the Unix *tr* command.)
- The repeat and replace operations.
- The totitle operation, which is handy for capitalizing words.

String Indices

Several of the string operations involve string indices that are positions within a string. Tcl counts characters in strings starting with zero. The special index end is used to specify the last character in a string:

```
string range abcd 2 end
=> cd
```

Tcl 8.1 added syntax for specifying an index relative to the end. Specify end-*N* to get the *N*th caracter before the end. For example, the following command returns a new string that drops the first and last characters from the original:

```
string range $string 1 end-1
```

There are several operations that pick apart strings: `first`, `last`, `wordstart`, `wordend`, `index`, and `range`. If you find yourself using combinations of these operations to pick apart data, it will be faster if you can do it with the regular expression pattern matcher described in Chapter 11.

Strings and Expressions

Strings can be compared with `expr`, `if`, and `while` using the comparison operators `==`, `!=`, `<` and `>`. However, there are a number of subtle issues that can cause problems. First, you must quote the string value so that the expression parser can identify it as a string type. Then, you must group the expression with curly braces to prevent the double quotes from being stripped off by the main interpreter:

> `if {$x == "foo"}` *command*

`expr` *is unreliable for string comparison.*

Ironically, despite the quotes, the expression evaluator first converts items to numbers if possible, and then converts them back if it detects a case of string comparison. The conversion back is always done as a decimal number. This can lead to unexpected conversions between strings that look like hexadecimal or octal numbers. The following boolean expression is true!

> `if {"0xa" == "10"} { puts stdout ack! }`
> `=> ack!`

A safe way to compare strings is to use the `string compare` and `equal` operations. These operations work faster because the unnecessary conversions are eliminated. Like the C library `strcmp` function, `string compare` returns 0 if the strings are equal, minus 1 if the first string is lexicographically less than the second, or 1 if the first string is greater than the second:

Example 4–1 Comparing strings with `string compare`.

```
if {[string compare $s1 $s2] == 0} {
    # strings are equal
}
```

The `string equal` command added in Tcl 8.1 makes this simpler:

Example 4–2 Comparing strings with `string equal`.

```
if {[string equal $s1 $s2]} {
    # strings are equal
}
```

String Matching

The `string match` command implements *glob*-style pattern matching that is modeled after the file name pattern matching done by various UNIX shells.

The heritage of the word "glob" is rooted in UNIX, and Tcl preserves this historical oddity in the `glob` command that does pattern matching on file names. The `glob` command is described on page 115. Table 4–2 shows the three constructs used in `string match` patterns:

Table 4–2 Matching characters used with `string match`.

`*`	Match any number of any characters.
`?`	Match exactly one character.
`[chars]`	Match any character in *chars*.

Any other characters in a pattern are taken as literals that must match the input exactly. The following example matches all strings that begin with `a`:

```
string match a* alpha
=> 1
```

To match all two-letter strings:

```
string match ?? XY
=> 1
```

To match all strings that begin with either `a` or `b`:

```
string match {[ab]*} cello
=> 0
```

Be careful! Square brackets are also special to the Tcl interpreter, so you will need to wrap the pattern up in curly braces to prevent it from being interpreted as a nested command. Another approach is to put the pattern into a variable:

```
set pat {[ab]*x}
string match $pat box
=> 1
```

You can specify a range of characters with the syntax `[x-y]`. For example, `[a-z]` represents the set of all lower-case letters, and `[0-9]` represents all the digits. You can include more than one range in a set. Any letter, digit, or the underscore is matched with:

```
string match {[a-zA-Z0-9_]} $char
```

The set matches only a single character. To match more complicated patterns, like one or more characters from a set, then you need to use regular expression matching, which is described on page 148.

If you need to include a literal `*`, `?`, or bracket in your pattern, preface it with a backslash:

```
string match {*\?} what?
=> 1
```

In this case the pattern is quoted with curly braces because the Tcl interpreter is also doing backslash substitutions. Without the braces, you would have

to use two backslashes. They are replaced with a single backslash by Tcl before
`string match` is called.

```
string match *\\? what?
```

Character Classes

The `string is` command tests a string to see whether it belongs to a particular *class*. This is useful for input validation. For example, to make sure something is a number, you do:

```
if {![string is integer $input]} {
        error "Invalid input. Please enter a number."
}
```

Classes are defined in terms of the Unicode character set, which means
they are more general than specifying character sets with ranges over the ASCII
encoding. For example, `alpha` includes many characters outside the range of `[A-
Za-z]` because of different characters in other alphabets. The classes are listed in
Table 4–3.

Table 4–3 Character class names.

`alnum`	Any alphabet or digit character.
`alpha`	Any alphabet character.
`ascii`	Any character with a 7-bit character code (i.e., less than 128.)
`boolean`	0, 1, `true`, `false` (in any case).
`control`	Character code less than 32, and not NULL.
`digit`	Any digit character.
`double`	A valid floating point number.
`false`	0 or `false` (in any case).
`graph`	Any printing characters, not including space characters.
`integer`	A valid integer.
`lower`	A string in all lower case.
`print`	A synonym for `alnum`.
`punct`	Any punctuation character.
`space`	Space, tab, newline, carriage return, vertical tab, backspace.
`true`	1 or `true` (in any case).
`upper`	A string all in upper case.
`wordchar`	Alphabet, digit, and the underscore.
`xdigit`	Valid hexadecimal digits.

Mapping Strings

The `string map` command translates a string based on a character map. The map is in the form of a input, output list. Whereever a string contains an input sequence, that is replaced with the corresponding output. For example:

```
string map "food" {f p d l}
=> pool
```

The inputs and outputs can be more than one character and do not have to be the same length:

```
string map "food" {f p d ll oo u}
=> pull
```

Example 4–3 is more practical. It uses `string map` to replace fancy quotes and hyphens produced by Microsoft Word into ASCII equivalents. It uses the `open`, `read`, and `close` file operations that are described in Chapter 9, and the `fconfigure` command described on page 223 to ensure that the file format is UNIX friendly.

Example 4–3 Mapping Microsoft World special characters to ASCII.

```
proc Dos2Unix {filename} {
    set input [open $filename]
    set output [open $filename.new]
    fconfigure $output -translation lf
    puts $output [string map {
        \223    "
        \224    "
        \222    '
        \226    -
    } [read $input]]
    close $input
    close $output
}
```

The append Command

The `append` command takes a variable name as its first argument and concatenates its remaining arguments onto the current value of the named variable. The variable is created if it does not already exist:

```
set foo z
append foo a b c
set foo
=> zabc
```

The append *command is efficient with large strings.*

The `append` command provides an efficient way to add items to the end of a string. It modifies a variable directly, so it can exploit the memory allocation scheme used internally by Tcl. Using the `append` command like this:

```
append x " some new stuff"
```
is always faster than this:
```
set x "$x some new stuff"
```

The `lappend` command described on page 61 has similar performance benefits when working with Tcl lists.

The `format` Command

The `format` command is similar to the C `printf` function. It formats a string according to a format specification:

```
format spec value1 value2 ...
```

The `spec` argument includes literals and keywords. The literals are placed in the result as is, while each keyword indicates how to format the corresponding argument. The keywords are introduced with a percent sign, `%`, followed by zero or more modifiers, and terminate with a conversion specifier. Example keywords include `%f` for floating point, `%d` for integer, and `%s` for string format. Use `%%` to obtain a single percent character. The most general keyword specification for each argument contains up to six parts:

- position specifier
- flags
- field width
- precision
- word length
- conversion character

These components are explained by a series of examples. The examples use double quotes around the `format` specification. This is because often the format contains white space, so grouping is required, as well as backslash substitutions like \t or \n, and the quotes allow substitution of these special characters. Table 4–4 lists the conversion characters:

Table 4–4 Format conversions.

d	Signed integer.
u	Unsigned integer.
i	Signed integer. The argument may be in hex (0x) or octal (0) format.
o	Unsigned octal.
x or X	Unsigned hexadecimal. 'x' gives lowercase results.
c	Map from an integer to the ASCII character it represents.
s	A string.
f	Floating point number in the format a.b.

Table 4–4 Format conversions. (Continued)

e or E	Floating point number in scientific notation, a.bE+-c.
g or G	Floating point number in either %f or %e format, whichever is shorter.

A position specifier is *i*$, which means take the value from argument *i* as opposed to the normally corresponding argument. The position counts from 1. If a position is specified for one format keyword, the position must be used for all of them. If you group the format specification with double quotes, you need to quote the $ with a backslash:

```
set lang 2
format "%${lang}\$s" one un uno
=> un
```

The position specifier is useful for picking a string from a set, such as this simple language-specific example. The message catalog facility described in Chapter 15 is a much more sophisticated way to solve this problem. The position is also useful if the same value is repeated in the formatted string.

The flags in a format are used to specify padding and justification. In the following examples, the # causes a leading 0x to be printed in the hexadecimal value. The zero in 08 causes the field to be padded with zeros. Table 4–5 summarizes the format flag characters.

```
format "%#x" 20
=> 0x14
format "%#08x" 10
=> 0x0000000a
```

Table 4–5 Format flags.

–	Left justify the field.
+	Always include a sign, either + or -.
space	Precede a number with a space, unless the number has a leading sign. Useful for packing numbers close together.
0	Pad with zeros.
#	Leading 0 for octal. Leading 0x for hex. Always include a decimal point in floating point. Do not remove trailing zeros (%g).

After the flags you can specify a minimum field width value. The value is padded to this width with spaces, or with zeros if the 0 flag is used:

```
format "%-20s %3d" Label 2
=> Label                  2
```

You can compute a field width and pass it to `format` as one of the arguments by using * as the field width specifier. In this case the next argument is used as the field width instead of the value, and the argument after that is the value that gets formatted.

```
set maxl 8
format "%-*s = %s" $maxl Key Value
=> Key      = Value
```

The precision comes next, and it is specified with a period and a number. For %f and %e it indicates how many digits come after the decimal point. For %g it indicates the total number of significant digits used. For %d and %x it indicates how many digits will be printed, padding with zeros if necessary.

```
format "%6.2f %6.2d" 1 1
=>    1.00     01
```

The storage length part comes last but it is rarely useful because Tcl maintains all floating point values in double-precision, and all integers as long words.

The scan Command

The scan command parses a string according to a format specification and assigns values to variables. It returns the number of successful conversions it made. The general form of the command is:

```
scan string format var ?var? ?var? ...
```

The format for scan is nearly the same as in the format command. There is no %u scan format. The %c scan format converts one character to its decimal value.

The scan format includes a set notation. Use square brackets to delimit a set of characters. The set matches one or more characters that are copied into the variable. A dash is used to specify a range. The following scans a field of all lowercase letters.

```
scan abcABC {%[a-z]} result
=> 1
set result
=> abc
```

If the first character in the set is a right square bracket, then it is considered part of the set. If the first character in the set is ^, then characters *not* in the set match. Again, put a right square bracket immediately after the ^ to include it in the set. Nothing special is required to include a left square bracket in the set. As in the previous example, you will want to protect the format with braces, or use backslashes, because square brackets are special to the Tcl parser.

The binary Command

Tcl 8.0 added support for binary strings. Previous versions of Tcl used null-terminated strings internally, which foils the manipulation of some types of data. Tcl now uses counted strings, so it can tolerate a null byte in a string value without truncating it.

This section describes the `binary` command that provides conversions between strings and packed binary data representations. The `binary format` command takes values and packs them according to a template. For example, this can be used to format a floating point vector in memory suitable for passing to Fortran. The resulting binary value is returned:

```
binary format template value ?value ...?
```

The `binary scan` command extracts values from a binary string according to a similar template. For example, this is useful for extracting data stored in binary format. It assigns values to a set of Tcl variables:

```
binary scan value template variable ?variable ...?
```

Format Templates

The template consists of type keys and counts. The types are summarized in Table 4–6. In the table, *count* is the optional count following the type letter.

Table 4–6 Binary conversion types.

a	A character string of length *count*. Padded with nulls in `binary format`.
A	A character string of length *count*. Padded with spaces in `binary format`. Trailing nulls and blanks are discarded in `binary scan`.
b	A binary string of length *count*. Low-to-high order.
B	A binary string of length *count*. High-to-low order.
h	A hexadecimal string of length *count*. Low-to-high order.
H	A hexadecimal string of length *count*. High-to-low order. (More commonly used than h.)
c	An 8-bit character code. The *count* is for repetition.
s	A 16-bit integer in little-endian byte order. The *count* is for repetition.
S	A 16-bit integer in big-endian byte order. The *count* is for repetition.
i	A 32-bit integer in little-endian byte order. The *count* is for repetition.
I	A 32-bit integer in big-endian byte order. The *count* is for repetition.
f	Single-precision floating point value in native format. *count* is for repetition.
d	Double-precision floating point value in native format. *count* is for repetition.
x	Pack *count* null bytes with `binary format`. Skip *count* bytes with `binary scan`.
X	Backup *count* bytes.
@	Skip to absolute position specified by *count*. If *count* is *, skip to the end.

The count is interpreted differently depending on the type. For types like integer (`i`) and double (`d`), the count is a repetition count (e.g., `i3` means three integers). For strings, the count is a length (e.g., `a3` means a three-character string). If no count is specified, it defaults to 1. If count is `*`, then `binary scan` uses all the remaining bytes in the value.

Several type keys can be specified in a template. Each key-count combination moves an imaginary cursor through the binary data. There are special type keys to move the cursor. The `x` key generates null bytes in `binary format`, and it skips over bytes in `binary scan`. The `@` key uses its *count* as an absolute byte offset to which to set the cursor. As a special case, `@*` skips to the end of the data. The X key backs up *count* bytes.

Numeric types have a particular byte order that determines how their value is laid out in memory. The type keys are lowercase for little-endian byte order (e.g., Intel) and uppercase for big-endian byte order (e.g., SPARC and Motorola). Different integer sizes are 16-bit (s or S), 32-bit (i or I), and possibly 64-bit (l or L) on those machines that support 64-bit integers. Note that the official byte order for data transmitted over a network is big-endian. Floating point values are always machine-specific, so it only makes sense to format and scan these values on the same machine.

There are three string types: character (a or A), binary (b or B), and hexadecimal (h or H). With these types the *count* is the length of the string. The a type pads its value to the specified length with null bytes in `binary format` and the A type pads its value with spaces. If the value is too long, it is truncated. In `binary scan`, the A type strips trailing blanks and nulls.

A binary string consists of zeros and ones. The b type specifies bits from low-to-high order, and the B type specifies bits from high-to-low order. A hexadecimal string specifies 4 bits (i.e., nybbles) with each character. The h type specifies nybbles from low-to-high order, and the H type specifies nybbles from high-to-low order. The B and H formats match the way you normally write out numbers.

Examples

When you experiment with `binary format` and `binary scan`, remember that Tcl treats things as strings by default. A "6", for example, is the character 6 with character code 54 or 0x36. The c type returns these character codes:

```
set input 6
binary scan $input "c" 6val
set 6val
=> 54
```

You can scan several character codes at a time:

```
binary scan abc "c3" list
=> 1
set list
=> 97 98 99
```

The previous example uses a single type key, so `binary scan` sets one corresponding Tcl variable. If you want each character code in a separate variable, use separate type keys:

```
binary scan abc "ccc" x y z
=> 3
set z
=> 99
```

Use the H format to get hexadecimal values:

```
binary scan 6 "H2" 6val
set 6val
=> 36
```

Use the a and A formats to extract fixed width fields. Here the * count is used to get all the rest of the string. Note that A trims trailing spaces:

```
binary scan "hello world " a3x2A* first second
puts "\"$first\" \"$second\""
=> "hel" " world"
```

Use the @ key to seek to a particular offset in a value. The following command gets the second double-precision number from a vector. Assume the vector is read from a binary data file:

```
binary scan $vector "@8d" double
```

With `binary format`, the a and A types create fixed width fields. A pads its field with spaces, if necessary. The value is truncated if the string is too long:

```
binary format "A9A3" hello world
=> hello     wor
```

An array of floating point values can be created with this command:

```
binary format "f*" 1.2 3.45 7.43 -45.67 1.03e4
```

Remember that floating point values are always in native format, so you have to read them on the same type of machine that they were created. With integer data you specify either big-endian or little-endian formats. The `tcl_platform` variable described on page 182 can tell you the byte order of the current platform.

Binary Data and File I/O

When working with binary data in files, you need to turn off the newline translations and character set encoding that Tcl performs automatically. These are described in more detail on pages 114 and 209. For example, if you are generating binary data, the following command puts your standard output in binary mode:

```
fconfigure stdout -translation binary -encoding binary
puts [binary format "B8" 11001010]
```

Related Chapters

- To learn more about manipulating data in Tcl, read about lists in Chapter 5 and arrays in Chapter 8.
- For more about pattern matching, read about regular expressions in Chapter 11.
- For more about file I/O, see Chapter 9.
- For information on Unicode and other Internationalization issues, see Chapter 15.

Tcl Lists

This chapter describes Tcl lists. Tcl commands described are: `list`, `lindex`, `llength`, `lrange`, `lappend`, `linsert`, `lreplace`, `lsearch`, `lsort`, `concat`, `join`, **and** `split`.

Lists in Tcl have the same structure as Tcl commands. All the rules you learned about grouping arguments in Chapter 1 apply to creating valid Tcl lists. However, when you work with Tcl lists, it is best to think of lists in terms of operations instead of syntax. Tcl commands provide operations to put values into a list, get elements from lists, count the elements of lists, replace elements of lists, and so on. The syntax can sometimes be confusing, especially when you have to group arguments to the list commands themselves.

Lists are used with commands such as `foreach` that take lists as arguments. In addition, lists are important when you are building up a command to be evaluated later. Delayed command evaluation with `eval` is described in Chapter 10, and similar issues with Tk callback commands are described in Chapter 27.

However, Tcl lists are not often the right way to build complicated data structures in scripts. You may find Tcl arrays more useful, and they are the topic of Chapter 8. List operations are also not right for handling unstructured data such as user input. Use regular expressions instead, which are described in Chapter 11.

Tcl Lists

A Tcl list is a sequence of values. When you write out a list, it has the same syntax as a Tcl command. A list has its elements separated by white space. Braces or quotes can be used to group words with white space into a single list element.

Because of the relationship between lists and commands, the list-related commands described in this chapter are used often when constructing Tcl commands.

Big lists were often slow before Tcl 8.0.

Unlike list data structures in other languages, Tcl lists are just strings with a special interpretation. The string representation must be parsed on each list access, so be careful when you use large lists. A list with a few elements will not slow down your code much. A list with hundreds or thousands of elements can be very slow. If you find yourself maintaining large lists that must be frequently accessed, consider changing your code to use arrays instead.

The performance of lists was improved by the Tcl compiler added in Tcl 8.0. The compiler stores lists in an internal format that requires constant time to access. Accessing the first element costs the same as accessing any other element in the list. Before Tcl 8.0, the cost of accessing an element was proportional to the number of elements before it in the list. The internal format also records the number of list elements, so getting the length of a list is cheap. Before Tcl 8.0, computing the length required reading the whole list.

Table 5–1 briefly describes the Tcl commands related to lists.

Table 5–1 List-related commands.

`list arg1 arg2 ...`	Creates a list out of all its arguments.
`lindex list i`	Returns the *i*th element from `list`.
`llength list`	Returns the number of elements in `list`.
`lrange list i j`	Returns the *i*th through *j*th elements from `list`.
`lappend listVar arg arg ...`	Appends elements to the value of `listVar`.
`linsert list index arg arg ...`	Inserts elements into `list` before the element at position `index`. Returns a new list.
`lreplace list i j arg arg ...`	Replaces elements *i* through *j* of `list` with the `args`. Returns a new list.
`lsearch ?mode? list value`	Returns the index of the element in `list` that matches the `value` according to the `mode`, which is `-exact`, `-glob`, or `-regexp`. `-glob` is the default. Returns -1 if not found.
`lsort ?switches? list`	Sorts elements of the list according to the switches: `-ascii`, `-integer`, `-real`, `-dictionary`, `-increasing`, `-decreasing`, `-index ix`, `-command command`. Returns a new list.
`concat list list ...`	Joins multiple lists together into one list.
`join list joinString`	Merges the elements of a list together by separating them with `joinString`.
`split string splitChars`	Splits a string up into list elements, using the characters in `splitChars` as boundaries between list elements.

Constructing Lists

Constructing a list can be tricky because you must maintain proper list syntax. In simple cases, you can do this by hand. In more complex cases, however, you should use Tcl commands that take care of quoting so that the syntax comes out right.

The list command

The list command constructs a list out of its arguments so that there is one list element for each argument. If any of the arguments contain special characters, the list command adds quoting to ensure that they are parsed as a single element of the resulting list. The automatic quoting is very useful, and the examples in this book use the list command frequently. The next example uses list to create a list with three values, two of which contain special characters.

Example 5–1 Constructing a list with the list command.

```
set x {1 2}
=> 1 2
set y foo
=> foo
set l1 [list $x "a b" $y]
=> {1 2} {a b} foo
set l2 "\{$x\} {a b} $y"
=> {1 2} {a b} foo
```

The list command does automatic quoting.

Compare the use of list with doing the quoting by hand in Example 5–1. The assignment of l2 requires carefully constructing the first list element by using quoted braces. The braces must be turned off so that $x can be substituted, but we need to group the result so that it remains a single list element. We also have to know in advance that $x contains a space, so quoting is required. We are taking a risk by not quoting $y because we know it doesn't contain spaces. If its value changes in the future, the structure of the list can change and even become invalid. In contrast, the list command takes care of all these details automatically.

When I first experimented with Tcl lists, I became confused by the treatment of curly braces. In the assignment to x, for example, the curly braces disappear. However, they come back again when $x is put into a bigger list. Also, the double quotes around a b get changed into curly braces. What's going on? Remember that there are two steps. In the first step, the Tcl parser groups arguments. In the grouping process, the braces and quotes are syntax that define groups. These syntax characters get stripped off. The braces and quotes are not part of the value. In the second step, the list command creates a valid Tcl list. This may require quoting to get the list elements into the right groups. The list command uses curly braces to group values back into list elements.

The lappend Command

The lappend command is used to append elements to the end of a list. The first argument to lappend is the name of a Tcl variable, and the rest of the arguments are added to the variable's value as new list elements. Like list, lappend preserves the structure of its arguments. It may add braces to group the values of its arguments so that they retain their identity as list elements when they are appended onto the string representation of the list.

Example 5–2 Using lappend to add elements to a list.

```
lappend new 1 2
=> 1 2
lappend new 3 "4 5"
=> 1 2 3 {4 5}
set new
=> 1 2 3 {4 5}
```

The lappend command is unique among the list-related commands because its first argument is the name of a list-valued variable, while all the other commands take list values as arguments. You can call lappend with the name of an undefined variable and the variable will be created.

The lappend command is implemented efficiently to take advantage of the way that Tcl stores lists internally. It is always more efficient to use lappend than to try and append elements by hand.

The concat Command

The concat command is useful for splicing lists together. It works by concatenating its arguments, separating them with spaces. This joins multiple lists into one list where the top-level list elements in each input list become top-level list elements in the resulting list:

Example 5–3 Using concat to splice lists together.

```
set x {4 5 6}
set y {2 3}
set z 1
concat $z $y $x
=> 1 2 3 4 5 6
```

Double quotes behave much like the concat command. In simple cases, double quotes behave exactly like concat. However, the concat command trims extra white space from the end of its arguments before joining them together with a single separating space character. Example 5–4 compares the use of list, concat, and double quotes:

Example 5–4 Double quotes compared to the concat and list commands.

```
set x {1 2}
=> 1 2
set y "$x 3"
=> 1 2 3
set y [concat $x 3]
=> 1 2 3
set s { 2 }
=>  2
set y "1 $s 3"
=> 1  2  3
set y [concat 1 $s 3]
=> 1 2 3
set z [list $x $s 3]
=> {1 2} { 2 } 3
```

The distinction between list and concat becomes important when Tcl commands are built dynamically. The basic rule is that list and lappend preserve list structure, while concat (or double quotes) eliminates one level of list structure. The distinction can be subtle because there are examples where list and concat return the same results. Unfortunately, this can lead to data-dependent bugs. Throughout the examples of this book, you will see the list command used to safely construct lists. This issue is discussed more in Chapter 10.

Getting List Elements: llength, lindex, and lrange

The llength command returns the number of elements in a list.

```
llength {a b {c d} "e f g" h}
=> 5
llength {}
=> 0
```

The lindex command returns a particular element of a list. It takes an index; list indices count from zero.

```
set x {1 2 3}
lindex $x 1
=> 2
```

You can use the keyword end to specify the last element of a list, or the syntax end-N to count back from the end of the list. The following commands are equivalent ways to get the element just before the last element in a list.

```
lindex $list [expr {[llength $list] - 2}]
lindex $list end-1
```

The lrange command returns a range of list elements. It takes a list and two indices as arguments. Again, end or end-N can be used as an index:

```
lrange {1 2 3 {4 5}} 2 end
=> 3 {4 5}
```

Modifying Lists: `linsert` and `lreplace`

The `linsert` command inserts elements into a list value at a specified index. If the index is zero or less, then the elements are added to the front. If the index is equal to or greater than the length of the list, then the elements are appended to the end. Otherwise, the elements are inserted before the element that is currently at the specified index.

`lreplace` replaces a range of list elements with new elements. If you don't specify any new elements, you effectively delete elements from a list.

Note: `linsert` and `lreplace` do not modify an existing list. Instead, they return a new list value. In the following example, the `lreplace` command does not change the value of x:

Example 5–5 Modifying lists with `linsert` and `lreplace`.

```
linsert {1 2} 0 new stuff
=> new stuff 1 2
set x [list a {b c} e d]
=> a {b c} e d
lreplace $x 1 2 B C
=> a B C d
lreplace $x 0 0
=> {b c} e d
```

Searching Lists: `lsearch`

`lsearch` returns the index of a value in the list, or -1 if it is not present. `lsearch` supports pattern matching in its search. Glob-style pattern matching is the default, and this can be disabled with the `-exact` flag. The semantics of glob pattern matching is described in Chapter 4. The `-regexp` option lets you specify the list value with a regular expression. Regular expressions are described in Chapter 11. In the following example, the glob pattern `l*` matches the value `list`.

```
lsearch {here is a list} l*
=> 3
```

Example 5–6 uses `lreplace` and `lsearch` to delete a list element by value. The value is found with `lsearch`. The value is removed with an `lreplace` that does not specify any replacement list elements:

Example 5–6 Deleting a list element by value.

```
proc ldelete { list value } {
    set ix [lsearch -exact $list $value]
    if {$ix >= 0} {
        return [lreplace $list $ix $ix]
    } else {
        return $list
    }
}
```

Sorting Lists: `lsort`

You can sort a list in a variety of ways with `lsort`. The list is not sorted in place. Instead, a new list value is returned. The basic types of sorts are specified with the `-ascii`, `-dictionary`, `-integer`, or `-real` options. The `-increasing` or `-decreasing` option indicate the sorting order. The default option set is `-ascii` `-increasing`. An ASCII sort uses character codes, and a dictionary sort folds together case and treats digits like numbers. For example:

```
lsort -ascii {a Z n2 n100}
=> Z a n100 n2
lsort -dictionary {a Z n2 n100}
=> a n2 n100 Z
```

You can provide your own sorting function for special-purpose sorting. For example, suppose you have a list of names, where each element is itself a list containing the person's first name, middle name (if any), and last name. The default sorts by everyone's first name. If you want to sort by their last name, you need to supply a sorting command.

Example 5–7 Sorting a list using a comparison function.

```
proc NameCompare {a b} {
    set alast [lindex $a end]
    set blast [lindex $b end]
    set res [string compare $alast $blast]
    if {$res != 0} {
        return $res
    } else {
        return [string compare $a $b]
    }
}
set list {{Brent B. Welch} {John Ousterhout} {Miles Davis}}
=> {Brent B. Welch} {John Ousterhout} {Miles Davis}
lsort -command NameCompare $list
=> {Miles Davis} {John Ousterhout} {Brent B. Welch}
```

The `NameCompare` procedure extracts the last element from each of its arguments and compares those. If they are equal, then it just compares the whole of each argument.

Tcl 8.0 added a `-index` option to `lsort` that can be used to sort lists on an index. Instead of using `NameCompare`, you could do this:

```
lsort -index end $list
```

The `split` Command

The `split` command takes a string and turns it into a list by breaking it at specified characters and ensuring that the result has the proper list syntax. The `split` command provides a robust way to turn input lines into proper Tcl lists:

```
set line {welch:*:28405:100:Brent Welch:/usr/welch:/bin/csh}
split $line :
=> welch * 28405 100 {Brent Welch} /usr/welch /bin/csh
lindex [split $line :] 4
=> Brent Welch
```

Do not use list operations on arbitrary data.

Even if your data has space-separated words, you should be careful when using list operators on arbitrary input data. Otherwise, stray double quotes or curly braces in the input can result in invalid list structure and errors in your script. Your code will work with simple test cases, but when invalid list syntax appears in the input, your script will raise an error. The next example shows what happens when input is not a valid list. The syntax error, an unmatched quote, occurs in the middle of the list. However, you cannot access any of the list because the `lindex` command tries to convert the value to a list before returning any part of it.

Example 5–8 Use `split` to turn input data into Tcl lists.

```
set line {this is "not a tcl list}
lindex $line 1
=> unmatched open quote in list
lindex [split $line] 2
=> "not
```

The default separator character for `split` is white space, which contains spaces, tabs, and newlines. If there are multiple separator characters in a row, these result in empty list elements; the separators are not collapsed. The following command splits on commas, periods, spaces, and tabs. The backslash–space sequence is used to include a space in the set of characters. You could also group the argument to `split` with double quotes:

```
set line "\tHello, world."
split $line \ ,.\t
=> {} Hello {} world {}
```

A trick that splits each character into a list element is to specify an empty string as the split character. This lets you get at individual characters with list operations:

```
split abc {}
=> a b c
```

However, if you write scripts that process data one character at a time, they may run slowly. Read Chapter 11 about regular expressions for hints on really efficient string processing.

The join Command

The join command is the inverse of split. It takes a list value and reformats it with specified characters separating the list elements. In doing so, it removes any curly braces from the string representation of the list that are used to group the top-level elements. For example:

```
join {1 {2 3} {4 5 6}} :
=> 1:2 3:4 5 6
```

If the treatment of braces is puzzling, remember that the first value is parsed into a list. The braces around element values disappear in the process. Example 5–9 shows a way to implement join in a Tcl procedure, which may help to understand the process:

Example 5–9 Implementing join in Tcl.

```
proc join {list sep} {
    set s {}   ;# s is the current separator
    set result {}
    foreach x $list {
        append result $s $x
        set s $sep
    }
    return $result
}
```

Related Chapters

- Arrays are the other main data structure in Tcl. They are described in Chapter 8.
- List operations are used when generating Tcl code dynamically. Chapter 10 describes these techniques when using the eval command.
- The foreach command loops over the values in a list. It is described on page 73 in Chapter 6.

Control Structure Commands

This chapter describes the Tcl commands that implement control structures: if, switch, foreach, while, for, break, continue, catch, error, and return.

*C*ontrol structure in Tcl is achieved with commands, just like everything else. There are looping commands: while, foreach, and for. There are conditional commands: if and switch. There is an error handling command: catch. Finally, there are some commands to fine-tune control structures: break, continue, return, and error.

A control structure command often has a command body that is executed later, either conditionally or in a loop. In this case, it is important to group the command body with curly braces to avoid substitutions at the time the control structure command is invoked. Group with braces, and let the control structure command trigger evaluation at the proper time. A control structure command returns the value of the last command it chose to execute.

Another pleasant property of curly braces is that they group things together while including newlines. The examples use braces in a way that is both readable and convenient for extending the control structure commands across multiple lines.

Commands like if, for, and while involve boolean expressions. They use the expr command internally, so there is no need for you to invoke expr explicitly to evaluate their boolean test expressions.

If Then Else

The if command is the basic conditional command. If an expression is true, then execute one command body; otherwise, execute another command body. The second command body (the else clause) is optional. The syntax of the command is:

        if *expression* ?then? *body1* ?else? ?*body2*?

The then and else keywords are optional. In practice, I omit then but use else as illustrated in the next example. I always use braces around the command bodies, even in the simplest cases:

Example 6–1 A conditional if then else command.

```
if {$x == 0} {
    puts stderr "Divide by zero!"
} else {
    set slope [expr $y/$x]
}
```

Curly brace positioning is important.

The style of this example takes advantage of the way the Tcl interpreter parses commands. Recall that newlines are command terminators, except when the interpreter is in the middle of a group defined by braces or double quotes. The stylized placement of the opening curly brace at the end of the first and third lines exploits this property to extend the if command over multiple lines.

The first argument to if is a boolean expression. As a matter of style this expression is grouped with curly braces. The expression evaluator performs variable and command substitution on the expression. Using curly braces ensures that these substitutions are performed at the proper time. It is possible to be lax in this regard, with constructs such as:

        if $x break continue

This is a sloppy, albeit legitimate, if command that will either break out of a loop or continue with the next iteration depending on the value of variable x. This style is fragile and error prone. Instead, always use braces around the command bodies to avoid trouble later when you modify the command. The following is much better (use then if it suits your taste):

```
if {$x} {
    break
} else {
    continue
}
```

When you are testing the result of a command, you can get away without using curly braces around the command, like this:

        if [*command*] *body1*

However, it turns out that you can execute the if statement more efficiently if you always group the expression with braces, like this:

        if {[*command*]} *body1*

You can create chained conditionals by using the `elseif` keyword. Again, note the careful placement of curly braces that create a single `if` command:

Example 6–2 Chained conditional with `elseif`.

```
if {$key < 0} {
    incr range 1
} elseif {$key == 0} {
    return $range
} else {
    incr range -1
}
```

Any number of conditionals can be chained in this manner. However, the `switch` command provides a more powerful way to test multiple conditions.

Switch

The `switch` command is used to branch to one of many command bodies depending on the value of an expression. The choice can be made on the basis of pattern matching as well as simple comparisons. Pattern matching is discussed in more detail in Chapter 4 and Chapter 11. The general form of the command is:

```
switch flags value pat1 body1 pat2 body2 ...
```

Any number of pattern-body pairs can be specified. If multiple patterns match, only the body of the first matching pattern is evaluated. You can also group all the pattern-body pairs into one argument:

```
switch flags value { pat1 body1 pat2 body2 ... }
```

The first form allows substitutions on the patterns but will require backslashes to continue the command onto multiple lines. This is shown in Example 6–4 on page 72. The second form groups all the patterns and bodies into one argument. This makes it easy to group the whole command without worrying about newlines, but it suppresses any substitutions on the patterns. This is shown in Example 6–3. In either case, you should always group the command bodies with curly braces so that substitution occurs only on the body with the pattern that matches the value.

There are four possible flags that determine how *value* is matched.

`-exact`	Matches the *value* exactly to one of the patterns. This is the default.
`-glob`	Uses glob-style pattern matching. See page 48.
`-regexp`	Uses regular expression pattern matching. See page 134.
`--`	No flag (or end of flags). Necessary when *value* can begin with -.

The `switch` command raises an error if any other flag is specified or if the *value* begins with -. In practice I always use the `--` flag before *value* so that I don't have to worry about that problem.

If the pattern associated with the last body is `default`, then this command body is executed if no other patterns match. The `default` keyword works only on the last pattern-body pair. If you use the `default` pattern on an earlier body, it will be treated as a pattern to match the literal string `default`:

Example 6–3 Using `switch` for an exact match.

```
switch -exact -- $value {
    foo { doFoo; incr count(foo) }
    bar { doBar; return $count(foo)}
    default { incr count(other) }
}
```

If you have variable references or backslash sequences in the patterns, then you cannot use braces around all the pattern-body pairs. You must use backslashes to escape the newlines in the command:

Example 6–4 Using `switch` with substitutions in the patterns.

```
switch -regexp -- $value \
    ^$key { body1 }\
    \t### { body2 }\
    {[0-9]*} { body3 }
```

In this example, the first and second patterns have substitutions performed to replace `$key` with its value and `\t` with a tab character. The third pattern is quoted with curly braces to prevent command substitution; square brackets are part of the regular expression syntax, too. (See page Chapter 11.)

If the body associated with a pattern is just a dash, -, then the `switch` command "falls through" to the body associated with the next pattern. You can tie together any number of patterns in this manner.

Example 6–5 A `switch` with "fall through" cases.

```
switch -glob -- $value {
    X* -
    Y* { takeXorYaction $value }
}
```

Comments in switch Commands

A comment can occur only where the Tcl parser expects a command to begin. This restricts the location of comments in a `switch` command. You must put them inside the command body associated with a pattern, as shown in Example 6–6. If you put a comment at the same level as the patterns, the `switch` command will try to interpret the comment as one or more pattern-body pairs.

Example 6–6 Comments in `switch` commands.

```
switch -- $value {
    # this comment confuses switch
    pattern { # this comment is ok }
}
```

While

The `while` command takes two arguments, a test and a command body:

```
while booleanExpr body
```

The `while` command repeatedly tests the boolean expression and then executes the body if the expression is true (nonzero). Because the test expression is evaluated again before each iteration of the loop, it is crucial to protect the expression from any substitutions before the `while` command is invoked. The following is an infinite loop (see also Example 1–13 on page 12):

```
set i 0 ; while $i<10 {incr i}
```

The following behaves as expected:

```
set i 0 ; while {$i<10} {incr i}
```

It is also possible to put nested commands in the boolean expression. The following example uses `gets` to read standard input. The `gets` command returns the number of characters read, returning -1 upon end of file. Each time through the loop, the variable `line` contains the next line in the file:

Example 6–7 A `while` loop to read standard input.

```
set numLines 0 ; set numChars 0
while {[gets stdin line] >= 0} {
    incr numLines
    incr numChars [string length $line]
}
```

Foreach

The `foreach` command loops over a command body assigning one or more loop variables to each of the values in one or more lists. Multiple loop variables were introduced in Tcl 7.5. The syntax for the simple case of a single variable and a single list is:

```
foreach loopVar valueList commandBody
```

The first argument is the name of a variable, and the command body is executed once for each element in the list with the loop variable taking on successive values in the list. The list can be entered explicitly, as in the next example:

Example 6–8 Looping with `foreach`.

```
set i 1
foreach value {1 3 5 7 11 13 17 19 23} {
    set i [expr $i*$value]
}
set i
=> 111546435
```

It is also common to use a list-valued variable or command result instead of a static list value. The next example loops through command-line arguments. The variable `argv` is set by the Tcl interpreter to be a list of the command-line arguments given when the interpreter was started:

Example 6–9 Parsing command-line arguments.

```
# argv is set by the Tcl shells
# possible flags are:
# -max integer
# -force
# -verbose
set state flag
set force 0
set verbose 0
set max 10
foreach arg $argv {
    switch -- $state {
        flag {
            switch -glob -- $arg {
                -f*     {set force 1}
                -v*     {set verbose 1}
                -max    {set state max}
                default {error "unknown flag $arg"}
            }
        }
        max {
            set max $arg
            set state flag
        }
    }
}
```

The loop uses the `state` variable to keep track of what is expected next, which in this example is either a flag or the integer value for `-max`. The `--` flag to `switch` is *required* in this example because the `switch` command complains about a bad flag if the pattern begins with a - character. The `-glob` option lets the user abbreviate the `-force` and `-verbose` options.

 If the list of values is to contain variable values or command results, then the `list` command should be used to form the list. Avoid double quotes because if any values or command results contain spaces or braces, the list structure will be reparsed, which can lead to errors or unexpected results.

Example 6–10 Using `list` with `foreach`.

```
foreach x [list $a $b [foo]] {
    puts stdout "x = $x"
}
```

The loop variable x will take on the value of a, the value of b, and the result of the `foo` command, regardless of any special characters or whitespace in those values.

Multiple Loop Variables

You can have more than one loop variable with `foreach`. Suppose you have two loop variables x and y. In the first iteration of the loop, x gets the first value from the value list and y gets the second value. In the second iteration, x gets the third value and y gets the fourth value. This continues until there are no more values. If there are not enough values to assign to all the loop variables, the extra variables get the empty string as their value.

Example 6–11 Multiple loop variables with `foreach`.

```
foreach {key value} {orange 55 blue 72 red 24 green} {
    puts "$key: $value"
}
orange: 55
blue: 72
red: 24
green:
```

If you have a command that returns a short list of values, then you can abuse the `foreach` command to assign the results of the commands to several variables all at once. For example, suppose the command `MinMax` returns two values as a list: the minimum and maximum values. Here is one way to get the values:

```
set result [MinMax $list]
set min [lindex $result 0]
set max [lindex $result 1]
```

The `foreach` command lets us do this much more compactly:

```
foreach {min max} [MinMax $list] {break}
```

The `break` in the body of the `foreach` loop guards against the case where the command returns more values than we expected. This trick is encapsulated into the `lassign` procedure in Example 10–4 on page 131.

Multiple Value Lists

The `foreach` command has the ability to loop over multiple value lists in parallel. In this case, each value list can also have one or more variables. The `foreach` command keeps iterating until all values are used from all value lists. If a value list runs out of values before the last iteration of the loop, its corresponding loop variables just get the empty string for their value.

Example 6–12 Multiple value lists with `foreach`.

```
foreach {k1 k2} {orange blue red green black} value {55 72 24} {
    puts "$k1 $k2: $value"
}
orange blue: 55
red green: 72
black : 24
```

For

The `for` command is similar to the C `for` statement. It takes four arguments:

> for *initial test final body*

The first argument is a command to initialize the loop. The second argument is a boolean expression that determines whether the loop body will execute. The third argument is a command to execute after the loop body:

Example 6–13 A `for` loop.

```
for {set i 0} {$i < 10} {incr i 3} {
    lappend aList $i
}
set aList
=> 0 3 6 9
```

You could use `for` to iterate over a list, but you should really use `foreach` instead. Code like the following is slow and cluttered:

```
for {set i 0} {$i < [llength $list]} {incr i} {
    set value [lindex $list $i]
}
```

This is the same as:

```
foreach value $list {
}
```

Break **and** Continue

You can control loop execution with the break and continue commands. The break command causes immediate exit from a loop, while the continue command causes the loop to continue with the next iteration. There is no goto command in Tcl.

Catch

Until now we have ignored the possibility of errors. In practice, however, a command will raise an error if it is called with the wrong number of arguments, or if it detects some error condition particular to its implementation. An uncaught error aborts execution of a script.[*] The catch command is used to trap such errors. It takes two arguments:

```
catch command ?resultVar?
```

The first argument to catch is a command body. The second argument is the name of a variable that will contain the result of the command, or an error message if the command raises an error. catch returns zero if there was no error caught, or a nonzero error code if it did catch an error.

You should use curly braces to group the command instead of double quotes because catch invokes the full Tcl interpreter on the command. If double quotes are used, an extra round of substitutions occurs before catch is even called. The simplest use of catch looks like the following:

```
catch { command }
```

A more careful catch phrase saves the result and prints an error message:

Example 6–14 A standard catch phrase.

```
if {[catch { command arg1 arg2 ... } result]} {
    puts stderr $result
} else {
    # command was ok, result contains the return value
}
```

A more general catch phrase is shown in the next example. Multiple commands are grouped into a command body. The errorInfo variable is set by the Tcl interpreter after an error to reflect the stack trace from the point of the error:

---

[*] More precisely, the Tcl script unwinds and the current Tcl_Eval procedure in the C runtime library returns TCL_ERROR. There are three cases. In interactive use, the Tcl shell prints the error message. In Tk, errors that arise during event handling trigger a call to bgerror, a Tcl procedure you can implement in your application. In your own C code, you should check the result of Tcl_Eval and take appropriate action in the case of an error.

Example 6–15 A longer `catch` phrase.

```
if {[catch {
    command1
    command2
    command3
} result]} {
    global errorInfo
    puts stderr $result
    puts stderr "*** Tcl TRACE ***"
    puts stderr $errorInfo
} else {
    # command body ok, result of last command is in result
}
```

These examples have not grouped the call to `catch` with curly braces. This is acceptable because `catch` always returns an integer, so the `if` command will parse correctly. However, if we had used `while` instead of `if`, then curly braces would be necessary to ensure that the `catch` phrase was evaluated repeatedly.

Catching More Than Errors

The `catch` command catches more than just errors. If the command body contains `return`, `break`, or `continue` commands, these terminate the command body and are reflected by `catch` as nonzero return codes. You need to be aware of this if you try to isolate troublesome code with a `catch` phrase. An innocent looking `return` command will cause the `catch` to signal an apparent error. The next example uses `switch` to find out exactly what `catch` returns. Nonerror cases are passed up to the surrounding code by invoking `return`, `break`, or `continue`:

Example 6–16 There are several possible return values from `catch`.

```
switch [catch {
    command1
    command2
    ...
} result] {
    0 {                     # Normal completion }
    1 {                     # Error case }
    2 { return $result    ;# return from procedure}
    3 { break             ;# break out of the loop}
    4 { continue          ;# continue loop}
    default {               # User-defined error codes }
}
```

Error

The error command raises an error condition that terminates a script unless it is trapped with the catch command. The command takes up to three arguments:

```
error message ?info? ?code?
```

The *message* becomes the error message stored in the result variable of the catch command.

If the *info* argument is provided, then the Tcl interpreter uses this to initialize the errorInfo global variable. That variable is used to collect a stack trace from the point of the error. If the *info* argument is not provided, then the error command itself is used to initialize the errorInfo trace.

Example 6–17 Raising an error.

```
proc foo {} {
    error bogus
}
foo
=> bogus
set errorInfo
=> bogus
    while executing
"error bogus"
    (procedure "foo" line 2)
    invoked from within
"foo"
```

In the previous example, the error command itself appears in the trace. One common use of the info argument is to preserve the errorInfo that is available after a catch. In the next example, the information from the original error is preserved:

Example 6–18 Preserving errorInfo when calling error.

```
if {[catch {foo} result]} {
    global errorInfo
    set savedInfo $errorInfo
    # Attempt to handle the error here, but cannot...
    error $result $savedInfo
}
```

The *code* argument specifies a concise, machine-readable description of the error. It is stored into the global errorCode variable. It defaults to NONE. Many of the file system commands return an errorCode that has three elements: POSIX, the error name (e.g., ENOENT), and the associated error message:

```
POSIX ENOENT {No such file or directory}
```

In addition, your application can define error codes of its own. Catch phrases can examine the code in the global errorCode variable and decide how to respond to the error.

Return

The return command is used to return from a procedure. It is needed if return is to occur before the end of the procedure body, or if a constant value needs to be returned. As a matter of style, I also use return at the end of a procedure, even though a procedure returns the value of the last command executed in the body.

Exceptional return conditions can be specified with some optional arguments to return. The complete syntax is:

```
return ?-code c? ?-errorinfo i? ?-errorcode ec? string
```

The -code option value is one of ok, error, return, break, continue, or an integer. ok is the default if -code is not specified.

The -code error option makes return behave much like the error command. The -errorcode option sets the global errorCode variable, and the -errorinfo option initializes the errorInfo global variable. When you use return -code error, there is no error command in the stack trace. Compare Example 6–17 with Example 6–19:

Example 6–19 Raising an error with return.

```
proc bar {} {
    return -code error bogus
}
catch {bar} result
=> 1
set result
=> bogus
set errorInfo
=> bogus
    while executing
"bar"
```

The return, break, and continue code options take effect in the caller of the procedure doing the exceptional return. If -code return is specified, then the calling procedure returns. If -code break is specified, then the calling procedure breaks out of a loop, and if -code continue is specified, then the calling procedure continues to the next iteration of the loop. These -code options to return enable the construction of new control structures entirely in Tcl. The following example implements the break command with a Tcl procedure:

```
proc break {} {
    return -code break
}
```

Procedures and Scope

Procedures encapsulate a set of commands, and they introduce a local scope
for variables. Commands described are: proc, global, and upvar.

Procedures parameterize a commonly
used sequence of commands. In addition, each procedure has a new local scope
for variables. The scope of a variable is the range of commands over which it is
defined. Originally, Tcl had one global scope for shared variables, local scopes
within procedures, and one global scope for procedures. Tcl 8.0 added
namespaces that provide new scopes for procedures and global variables. For
simple applications you can ignore namespaces and just use the global scope.
Namespaces are described in Chapter 14.

The proc Command

A Tcl procedure is defined with the proc command. It takes three arguments:

```
proc name params body
```

The first argument is the procedure name, which is added to the set of commands understood by the Tcl interpreter. The name is case sensitive and can contain any characters. Procedure names do not conflict with variable names. The
second argument is a list of parameter names. The last argument is the body of
the procedure.

Once defined, a Tcl procedure is used just like any other Tcl command.
When it is called, each argument is assigned to the corresponding parameter and
the body is evaluated. The result of the procedure is the result returned by the
last command in the body. The return command can be used to return a specific
value.

Procedures can have default parameters so that the caller can leave out some of the command arguments. A default parameter is specified with its name and default value, as shown in the next example:

Example 7–1 Default parameter values.

```
proc P2 {a {b 7} {c -2} } {
    expr $a / $b + $c
}
P2 6 3
=> 0
```

Here the procedure P2 can be called with one, two, or three arguments. If it is called with only one argument, then the parameters b and c take on the values specified in the proc command. If two arguments are provided, then only c gets the default value, and the arguments are assigned to a and b. At least one argument and no more than three arguments can be passed to P2.

A procedure can take a variable number of arguments by specifying the args keyword as the last parameter. When the procedure is called, the args parameter is a list that contains all the remaining values:

Example 7–2 Variable number of arguments.

```
proc ArgTest {a {b foo} args} {
    foreach param {a b args} {
        puts stdout "\t$param = [set $param]"
    }
}
set x one
set y {two things}
set z \[special\$
ArgTest $x
=> a = one
    b = foo
    args =
ArgTest $y $z
=> a = two things
    b = [special$
    args =
ArgTest $x $y $z
=> a = one
    b = two things
    args = {[special$}
ArgTest $z $y $z $x
=> a = [special$
    b = two things
    args = {[special$} one
```

The effect of the list structure in args is illustrated by the treatment of variable z in Example 7–2. The value of z has special characters in it. When $z is passed as the value of parameter `b`, its value comes through to the procedure unchanged. When `$z` is part of the optional parameters, quoting is automatically added to create a valid Tcl list as the value of `args`. Example 10–3 on page 127 illustrates a technique that uses `eval` to undo the effect of the added list structure.

Changing Command Names with `rename`

The `rename` command changes the name of a command. There are two main uses for `rename`. The first is to augment an existing procedure. Before you redefine it with `proc`, rename the existing command:

```
rename foo foo.orig
```

From within the new implementation of `foo` you can invoke the original command as `foo.orig`. Existing users of `foo` will transparently use the new version.

The other thing you can do with `rename` is completely hide a command by renaming it to the empty string. For example, you might not want users to execute UNIX programs, so you could disable `exec` with the following command:

```
rename exec {}
```

Scope

By default there is a single, global scope for procedure names. This means that you can use a procedure anywhere in your script. Variables defined outside any procedure are global variables. However, as described below, global variables are not automatically visible inside procedures. There is a different namespace for variables and procedures, so you could have a procedure and a global variable with the same name without conflict. You can use the namespace facility described in Chapter 7 to manage procedures and global variables.

Each procedure has a local scope for variables. That is, variables introduced in the procedure live only for the duration of the procedure call. After the procedure returns, those variables are undefined. Variables defined outside the procedure are not visible to a procedure unless the `upvar` or `global` scope commands are used. You can also use qualified names to name variables in a namespace scope. The `global` and `upvar` commands are described later in this chapter. Qualified names are described on page 198. If the same variable name exists in an outer scope, it is unaffected by the use of that variable name inside a procedure.

In Example 7–3, the variable `a` in the global scope is different from the parameter `a` to `P1`. Similarly, the global variable `b` is different from the variable `b` inside `P1`:

Example 7–3 Variable scope and Tcl procedures.

```
set a 5
set b -8
proc P1 {a} {
    set b 42
    if {$a < 0} {
        return $b
    } else {
        return $a
    }
}
P1 $b
=> 42
P1 [expr $a*2]
=> 10
```

The `global` Command

Global scope is the toplevel scope. This scope is outside of any procedure. Variables defined at the global scope must be made accessible to the commands inside a procedure by using the `global` command. The syntax for `global` is:

    global *varName1 varName2* ...

The `global` command goes inside a procedure.

The `global` command adds a global variable to the current scope. A common mistake is to have a single `global` command and expect that to apply to all procedures. However, a `global` command in the global scope has no effect. Instead, you must put a `global` command in all procedures that access the global variable. The variable can be undefined at the time the `global` command is used. When the variable is defined, it becomes visible in the global scope.

Example 7–4 shows a random number generator. Before we look at the example, let me point out that the best way to get random numbers in Tcl is to use the `rand()` math function:

    expr rand()

    => .137287362934

The point of the example is to show a state variable, the seed, that has to persist between calls to `random`, so it is kept in a global variable. The choice of `randomSeed` as the name of the global variable associates it with the random number generator. It is important to pick names of global variables carefully to avoid conflict with other parts of your program. For comparison, Example 14–1 on page 196 uses namespaces to hide the state variable:

Example 7–4 A random number generator.[*]

```
proc RandomInit { seed } {
    global randomSeed
    set randomSeed $seed
}
proc Random {} {
    global randomSeed
    set randomSeed [expr ($randomSeed*9301 + 49297) % 233280]
    return [expr $randomSeed/double(233280)]
}
proc RandomRange { range } {
    expr int([Random]*$range)
}
RandomInit [pid]
=> 5049
Random
=> 0.517686899863
Random
=> 0.217176783265
RandomRange 100
=> 17
```

Call by Name Using upvar

Use the upvar command when you need to pass the name of a variable, as opposed to its value, into a procedure. The upvar command associates a local variable with a variable in a scope up the Tcl call stack. The syntax of the upvar command is:

upvar *?level? varName localvar*

The *level* argument is optional, and it defaults to 1, which means one level up the Tcl call stack. You can specify some other number of frames to go up, or you can specify an absolute frame number with a #*number* syntax. Level #0 is the global scope, so the global foo command is equivalent to:

upvar #0 foo foo

The variable in the uplevel stack frame can be either a scalar variable, an array element, or an array name. In the first two cases, the local variable is treated like a scalar variable. In the case of an array name, then the local variable is treated like an array. The use of upvar and arrays is discussed further in Chapter 8 on page 92. The following procedure uses upvar to print the value of a variable given its name.

---

[*] Adapted from *Exploring Expect* by Don Libes, O'Reilly & Associates, Inc., 1995, and from *Numerical Recipes in C* by Press et al., Cambridge University Press, 1988.

Example 7–5 Print variable by name.

```
proc PrintByName { varName } {
    upvar 1 $varName var
    puts stdout "$varName = $var"
}
```

You can use upvar to fix the incr command. One drawback of the built-in
incr is that it raises an error if the variable does not exist. We can define a new
version of incr that initializes the variable if it does not already exist:

Example 7–6 Improved incr procedure.

```
proc incr { varName {amount 1}} {
    upvar 1 $varName var
    if {![info exists var]} {
        set var [expr $var + $amount]
    } else {
        set var $amount
    }
    return $var
}
```

Variable Aliases with upvar

The upvar command is useful in any situation where you have the name of a
variable stored in another variable. In Example 7–2 on page 82, the loop variable
param holds the names of other variables. Their value is obtained with this construct:

```
puts stdout "\t$param = [set $param]"
```

Another way to do this is to use upvar. It eliminates the need to use awkward constructs like [set $param]. If the variable is in the same scope, use zero
as the scope number with upvar. The following is equivalent:

```
upvar 0 $param x
puts stdout "\t$param = $x"
```

Associating State with Data

Suppose you have a program that maintains state about a set of objects like
files, URLs, or people. You can use the name of these objects as the name of a
variable that keeps state about the object. The upvar command makes this more
convenient:

```
upvar #0 $name state
```

Using the name directly like this is somewhat risky. If there were an object
named x, then this trick might conflict with an unrelated variable named x elsewhere in your program. You can modify the name to make this trick more robust:

```
upvar #0 state$name state
```

Your code can pass *name* around as a handle on an object, then use `upvar` to get access to the data associated with the object. Your code is just written to use the `state` variable, which is an alias to the state variable for the current object. This technique is illustrated in Example 17–7 on page 232.

Namespaces and `upvar`

You can use `upvar` to create aliases for namespace variables, too. Namespaces are described in Chapter 14. For example, as an alternative to reserving all global variables beginning with `state`, you can use a namespace to hide these variables:

```
upvar #0 state::$name state
```

Now `state` is an alias to the namespace variable. This `upvar` trick works from inside any namespace.

Commands That Take Variable Names

Several Tcl commands involve variable names. For example, the Tk widgets can be associated with a global Tcl variable. The `vwait` and `tkwait` commands also take variable names as arguments.

Upvar aliases do not work with text variables.

The aliases created with `upvar` do not work with these commands, nor do they work if you use `trace`, which is described on page 183. Instead, you must use the actual name of the global variable. To continue the above example where `state` is an alias, you cannot:

```
vwait state(foo)
button .b -textvariable state(foo)
```

Instead, you must

```
vwait state$name\(foo)
button .b -textvariable state$name\(foo)
```

The backslash turns off the array reference so Tcl does not try to access `name` as an array. You do not need to worry about special characters in $name, except parentheses. Once the name has been passed into the Tk widget it will be used directly as a variable name.

Tcl Arrays

This chapter describes Tcl arrays, which provide a flexible mechanism to build many other data structures in Tcl. Tcl command described is: `array`.

An array is a Tcl variable with a string-valued index. You can think of the index as a key, and the array as a collection of related data items identified by different keys. The index, or key, can be any string value. Internally, an array is implemented with a hash table, so the cost of accessing each array element is about the same. Before Tcl 8.0, arrays had a performance advantage over lists that took time to access proportional to the size of the list.

The flexibility of arrays makes them an important tool for the Tcl programmer. A common use of arrays is to manage a collection of variables, much as you use a C struct or Pascal record. This chapter shows how to create several simple data structures using Tcl arrays.

Array Syntax

The index of an array is delimited by parentheses. The index can have any string value, and it can be the result of variable or command substitution. Array elements are defined with `set`:

```
set arr(index) value
```

The value of an array element is obtained with $ substitution:

```
set foo $arr(index)
```

Example 8–1 uses the loop variable value `$i` as an array index. It sets `arr(x)` to the product of `1 * 2 * ... * x`:

Example 8–1 Using arrays.

```
set arr(0) 1
for {set i 1} {$i <= 10} {incr i} {
   set arr($i) [expr {$i * $arr([expr $i-1])}]
}
```

Complex Indices

An array index can be any string, like orange, 5, 3.1415, or foo,bar. The examples in this chapter, and in this book, often use indices that are pretty complex strings to create flexible data structures. As a rule of thumb, you can use any string for an index, but avoid using a string that contains spaces.

Parentheses are not a grouping mechanism.

The main Tcl parser does not know about array syntax. All the rules about grouping and substitution described in Chapter 1 are still the same in spite of the array syntax described here. Parentheses do not group like curly braces or quotes, which is why a space causes problems. If you have complex indices, use a comma to separate different parts of the index. If you use a space in an index instead, then you have a quoting problem. The space in the index needs to be quoted with a backslash, or the whole variable reference needs to be grouped:

```
set {arr(I'm asking for trouble)} {I told you so.}
set arr(I'm\ asking\ for\ trouble) {I told you so.}
```

If the array index is stored in a variable, then there is no problem with spaces in the variable's value. The following works well:

```
set index {I'm asking for trouble}
set arr($index) {I told you so.}
```

Array Variables

You can use an array element as you would a simple variable. For example, you can test for its existence with info exists, increment its value with incr, and append elements to it with lappend:

```
if {[info exists stats($event)]} {incr stats($event)}
```

You can delete an entire array, or just a single array element with unset. Using unset on an array is a convenient way to clear out a big data structure.

It is an error to use a variable as both an array and a normal variable. The following is an error:

```
set arr(0) 1
set arr 3
=> can't set "arr": variable is array
```

The name of the array can be the result of a substitution. This is a tricky situation, as shown in Example 8–2:

Example 8–2 Referencing an array indirectly.

```
set name TheArray
=> TheArray
set ${name}(xyz) {some value}
=> some value
set x $TheArray(xyz)
=> some value
set x ${name}(xyz)
=> TheArray(xyz)
set x [set ${name}(xyz)]
=> some value
```

A better way to deal with this situation is to use the `upvar` command, which is introduced on page 85. The previous example is much cleaner when `upvar` is used:

Example 8–3 Referencing an array indirectly using `upvar`.

```
set name TheArray
=> TheArray
upvar 0 $name a
set a(xyz) {some value}
=> some value
set x $TheArray(xyz)
=> some value
```

The `array` Command

The `array` command returns information about array variables. The `array names` command returns the index names that are defined in the array. If the array variable is not defined, then `array names` just returns an empty list. It allows easy iteration through an array with a `foreach` loop:

```
foreach index [array names arr pattern] {
    # use arr($index)
}
```

The order of the names returned by `array names` is arbitrary. It is essentially determined by the hash table implementation of the array. You can limit what names are returned by specifying a *pattern* that matches indices. The pattern is the kind supported by the `string match` command, which is described on page 48.

It is also possible to iterate through the elements of an array one at a time using the search-related commands listed in Table 8–1. The ordering is also random, and I find the `foreach` over the results of `array names` much more convenient. If your array has an extremely large number of elements, or if you need to manage an iteration over a long period of time, then the array search operations might be more appropriate. Frankly, I never use them. Table 8–1 summarizes the `array` command:

Table 8–1 The `array` command.

`array exists arr`	Returns 1 if *arr* is an array variable.
`array get arr ?pattern?`	Returns a list that alternates between an index and the corresponding array value. *pattern* selects matching indices. If not specified, all indices and values are returned.
`array names arr ?pattern?`	Returns the list of all indices defined for *arr*, or those that match the string match *pattern*.
`array set arr list`	Initializes the array *arr* from *list*, which has the same form as the list returned by `array get`.
`array size arr`	Returns the number of indices defined for *arr*.
`array startsearch arr`	Returns a search token for a search through *arr*.
`array nextelement arr id`	Returns the value of the next element in *array* in the search identified by the token *id*. Returns an empty string if no more elements remain in the search.
`array anymore arr id`	Returns 1 if more elements remain in the search.
`array donesearch arr id`	Ends the search identified by *id*.

Converting Between Arrays and Lists

The `array get` and `array set` operations are used to convert between an array and a list. The list returned by `array get` has an even number of elements. The first element is an index, and the next is the corresponding array value. The list elements continue to alternate between index and value. The list argument to `array set` must have the same structure.

```
array set fruit {
    best    kiwi
    worst   peach
    ok      banana
}
array get fruit
=> ok banana best kiwi worst peach
```

Another way to loop through the contents of an array is to use `array get` and the two-variable form of the `foreach` command.

```
foreach {key value} [array get fruit] {
    # key is ok, best, or worst
    # value is some fruit
}
```

Passing Arrays by Name

The `upvar` command works on arrays. You can pass an array name to a procedure and use the `upvar` command to get an indirect reference to the array variable in the caller's scope. This is illustrated in Example 8–4, which inverts an array. As with `array names`, you can specify a pattern to `array get` to limit what part of the array is returned. This example uses `upvar` because the array names are passed into the `ArrayInvert` procedure. The inverse array does not need to exist before you call `ArrayInvert`.

Example 8–4 `ArrayInvert` inverts an array.

```
proc ArrayInvert {arrName inverseName {pattern *}} {
    upvar $arrName array $inverseName inverse
    foreach {index value} [array get array $pattern] {
        set inverse($value) $index
    }
}
```

Building Data Structures with Arrays

This section describes several data structures you can build with Tcl arrays. These examples are presented as procedures that implement access functions to the data structure. Wrapping up your data structures in procedures is good practice. It shields the user of your data structure from the details of its implementation.

Use arrays to collect related variables.

A good use for arrays is to collect together a set of related variables for a module, much as one would use a record in other languages. By collecting these together in an array that has the same name as the module, name conflicts between different modules are avoided. Also, in each of the module's procedures, a single `global` statement will suffice to make all the state variables visible. You can also use `upvar` to manage a collection of arrays, as shown in Example 8–8 on page 95.

Simple Records

Suppose we have a database of information about people. One approach uses a different array for each class of information. The name of the person is the index into each array:

Example 8–5 Using arrays for records, version 1.

```
proc Emp_AddRecord {id name manager phone} {
    global employeeID employeeManager \
        employeePhone employeeName
    set employeeID($name) $id
    set employeeManager($name) $manager
    set employeePhone($name) $phone
    set employeeName($id) $name
}
proc Emp_Manager {name} {
```

```
    global employeeManager
    return $employeeManager($name)
}
```

Simple procedures are defined to return fields of the record, which hides the implementation so that you can change it more easily. The `employeeName` array provides a secondary key. It maps from the employee ID to the name so that the other information can be obtained if you have an ID instead of a name. Another way to implement the same little database is to use a single array with more complex indices:

Example 8–6 Using arrays for records, version 2.

```
proc Emp_AddRecord {id name manager phone} {
    global employee
    set employee(id,$name) $id
    set employee(manager,$name) $manager
    set employee(phone,$name) $phone
    set employee(name,$id) $name
}
proc Emp_Manager {name} {
    global employee
    return $employee(manager,$name)
}
```

The difference between these two approaches is partly a matter of taste. Using a single array can be more convenient because there are fewer variables to manage. In any case, you should hide the implementation in a small set of procedures.

A Stack

A stack can be implemented with either a list or an array. If you use a list, then the push and pop operations have a runtime cost that is proportional to the size of the stack. If the stack has a few elements this is fine. If there are a lot of items in a stack, you may wish to use arrays instead.

Example 8–7 Using a list to implement a stack.

```
proc Push { stack value } {
    upvar $stack list
    lappend list $value
}
proc Pop { stack } {
    upvar $stack list
    set value [lindex $list end]
    set list [lrange $list 0 [expr [llength $list]-2]]
    return $value
}
```

In these examples, the name of the stack is a parameter, and upvar is used to convert that into the data used for the stack. The variable is a list in Example 8–7 and an array in Example 8–8. The user of the stack module does not have to know.

The array implementation of a stack uses one array element to record the number of items in the stack. The other elements of the array have the stack values. The Push and Pop procedures both guard against a nonexistent array with the info exists command. When the first assignment to S(top) is done by Push, the array variable is created in the caller's scope. The example uses array indices in two ways. The top index records the depth of the stack. The other indices are numbers, so the construct $S($S(top)) is used to reference the top of the stack.

Example 8–8 Using an array to implement a stack.

```
proc Push { stack value } {
    upvar $stack S
    if {![info exists S(top)]} {
        set S(top) 0
    }
    set S($S(top)) $value
    incr S(top)
}
proc Pop { stack } {
    upvar $stack S
    if {![info exists S(top)]} {
        return {}
    }
    if {$S(top) == 0} {
        return {}
    } else {
        incr S(top) -1
        set x $S($S(top))
        unset S($S(top))
        return $x
    }
}
```

A List of Arrays

Suppose you have many arrays, each of which stores some data, and you want to maintain an overall ordering among the data sets. One approach is to keep a Tcl list with the name of each array in order. Example 8–9 defines RecordInsert to add an array to the list, and an iterator function, RecordIterate, that applies a script to each array in order. The iterator uses upvar to make data an alias for the current array. The script is executed with eval, which is described in detail in Chapter 10. The Tcl commands in script can reference the arrays with the name data:

Example 8–9 A list of arrays.

```
proc RecordAppend {listName arrayName} {
    upvar $listName list
    lappend list $arrayName
}
proc RecordIterate {listName script} {
    upvar $listName list
    foreach arrayName $list {
        upvar #0 $arrayName data
        eval $script
    }
}
```

Another way to implement this list-of-records structure is to keep references to the arrays that come before and after each record. Example 8–10 shows
the insert function and the iterator function when using this approach. Once
again, upvar is used to set up data as an alias for the current array in the iterator. In this case, the loop is terminated by testing for the existence of the next
array. It is perfectly all right to make an alias with upvar to a nonexistent variable. It is also all right to change the target of the upvar alias. One detail that is
missing from the example is the initialization of the very first record so that its
next element is the empty string:

Example 8–10 A list of arrays.

```
proc RecordInsert {recName afterThis} {
    upvar $recName record $afterThis after
    set record(next) $after(next)
    set after(next) $recName
}
proc RecordIterate {firstRecord body} {
    upvar #0 $firstRecord data
    while {[info exists data]} {
        eval $body
        upvar #0 $data(next) data
    }
}
```

A Simple In-Memory Database

Suppose you have to manage a lot of records, each of which contain a large
chunk of data and one or more key values you use to look up those values. The
procedure to add a record is called like this:

```
Db_Insert keylist datablob
```

The datablob might be a name, value list suitable for passing to array set,
or simply a large chunk of text or binary data. One implementation of Db_Insert
might just be:

```
    foreach key $keylist {
        lappend Db($key) $datablob
    }
```

The problem with this approach is that it duplicates the data chunks under each key. A better approach is to use two arrays. One stores all the data chunks under a simple ID that is generated automatically. The other array stores the association between the keys and the data chunks. Example 8–11, which uses the namespace syntax described in Chapter 14, illustrates this approach. The example also shows how you can easily dump data structures by writing array set commands to a file, and then load them later with a source command:

Example 8–11 A simple in-memory database.

```
namespace eval db {
    variable data        ;# Array of data blobs
    variable uid 0        ;# Index into data
    variable index        ;# Cross references into data
}
proc db::insert {keylist datablob} {
    variable data
    variable uid
    variable index
    set data([incr uid]) $datablob
    foreach key $keylist {
        lappend index($key) $uid
    }
}
proc db::get {key} {
    variable data
    variable index
    set result {}
    if {![info exist index($key)]} {
        return {}
    }
    foreach uid $index($key) {
        lappend result $data($uid)
    }
    return $result
}
proc db::save {filename} {
    variable uid
    set out [open $filename w]
    puts $out [list namespace eval db \
        [list variable uid $uid]]
    puts $out [list array set db::data [array get db::data]]
    puts $out [list array set db::index [array get db::index]]
    close $out
}
proc db::load {filename} {
    source $filename
}
```

## CHAPTER 9

Working with Files and Programs

This chapter describes how to run programs, examine the file system, and access environment variables through the env array. Tcl commands described are: exec, file, open, close, read, write, puts, gets, flush, seek, tell, glob, pwd, cd, exit, pid, **and** registry.

*T*his chapter describes how to run programs and access the file system from Tcl. These commands were designed for UNIX. In Tcl 7.5 they were implemented in the Tcl ports to Windows and Macintosh. There are facilities for naming files and manipulating file names in a platform-independent way, so you can write scripts that are portable across systems. These capabilities enable your Tcl script to be a general-purpose glue that assembles other programs into a tool that is customized for your needs.

Running Programs with exec

The exec command runs programs from your Tcl script.[*] For example:

```
set d [exec date]
```

The standard output of the program is returned as the value of the exec command. However, if the program writes to its standard error channel or exits with a nonzero status code, then exec raises an error. If you do not care about the exit status, or you use a program that insists on writing to standard error, then you can use catch to mask the errors:

```
catch {exec program arg arg} result
```

---

[*] Unlike other UNIX shell exec commands, the Tcl exec does not replace the current process with the new one. Instead, the Tcl library forks first and executes the program as a child process.

The `exec` command supports a full set of *I/O redirection* and *pipeline* syntax. Each process normally has three I/O channels associated with it: standard input, standard output, and standard error. With I/O redirection, you can divert these I/O channels to files or to I/O channels you have opened with the Tcl `open` command. A pipeline is a chain of processes that have the standard output of one command hooked up to the standard input of the next command in the pipeline. Any number of programs can be linked together into a pipeline.

Example 9–1 Using `exec` on a process pipeline.

```
set n [exec sort < /etc/passwd | uniq | wc -1 2> /dev/null]
```

Example 9–1 uses `exec` to run three programs in a pipeline. The first program is `sort`, which takes its input from the file `/etc/passwd`. The output of `sort` is piped into `uniq`, which suppresses duplicate lines. The output of `uniq` is piped into `wc`, which counts the lines. The error output of the command is diverted to the null device to suppress any error messages. Table 9–1 provides a summary of the syntax understood by the `exec` command.

Table 9–1 Summary of the `exec` syntax for I/O redirection.

`-keepnewline`	(First argument.) Do not discard trailing newline from the result.
`|`	Pipes standard output from one process into another.
`|&`	Pipes both standard output and standard error output.
`< fileName`	Takes input from the named file.
`<@ fileId`	Takes input from the I/O channel identified by `fileId`.
`<< value`	Takes input from the given `value`.
`> fileName`	Overwrites `fileName` with standard output.
`2> fileName`	Overwrites `fileName` with standard error output.
`>& fileName`	Overwrites `fileName` with both standard error and standard out.
`>> fileName`	Appends standard output to the named file.
`2>> fileName`	Appends standard error to the named file.
`>>& fileName`	Appends both standard error and standard output to the named file.
`>@ fileId`	Directs standard output to the I/O channel identified by `fileId`.
`2>@ fileId`	Directs standard error to the I/O channel identified by `fileId`.
`>&@ fileId`	Directs both standard error and standard output to the I/O channel.
`&`	As the last argument, indicates pipeline should run in background.

A trailing & causes the program to run in the background. In this case, the process identifier is returned by the exec command. Otherwise, the exec command blocks during execution of the program, and the standard output of the program is the return value of exec. The trailing newline in the output is trimmed off, unless you specify -keepnewline as the first argument to exec.

If you look closely at the I/O redirection syntax, you'll see that it is built up from a few basic building blocks. The basic idea is that | stands for pipeline, > for output, and < for input. The standard error is joined to the standard output by &. Standard error is diverted separately by using 2>. You can use your own I/O channels by using @.

The auto_noexec Variable

The Tcl shell programs are set up during interactive use to attempt to execute unknown Tcl commands as programs. For example, you can get a directory listing by typing:

```
ls
```

instead of:

```
exec ls
```

This is handy if you are using the Tcl interpreter as a general shell. It can also cause unexpected behavior when you are just playing around. To turn this off, define the auto_noexec variable:

```
set auto_noexec anything
```

Limitations of exec on Windows

Windows 3.1 has an unfortunate combination of special cases that stem from console-mode programs, 16-bit programs, and 32-bit programs. In addition, pipes are really just simulated by writing output from one process to a temporary file and then having the next process read from that file. If exec or a process pipeline fails, it is because of a fundamental limitation of Windows. The good news is that Windows 95 and Windows NT cleaned up most of the problems with exec. Windows NT 4.0 is the most robust.

Tcl 8.0p2 was the last release to officially support Windows 3.1. That release includes Tcl1680.dll, which is necessary to work with the win32s subsystem. If you copy that file into the same directory as the other Tcl DLLs, you may be able to use later releases of Tcl on Windows 3.1. However, there is no guarantee this trick will continue to work.

AppleScript on Macintosh

The exec command is not provided on the Macintosh. Tcl ships with an AppleScript extension that lets you control other Macintosh applications. You can find documentation in the AppleScript.html that goes with the distribution. You must use package require to load the AppleScript command:

```
package require Tclapplescript
AppleScript junk
=> bad option "junk": must be compile, decompile, delete,
execute, info, load, run, or store.
```

The `file` Command

The `file` command provides several ways to check the status of files in the file system. For example, you can find out if a file exists, what type of file it is, and other file attributes. There are facilities for manipulating files in a platform-independent manner. Table 9–2 provides a summary of the various forms of the `file` command. They are described in more detail later. Note that the `split`, `join`, and `pathtype` operations were added in Tcl 7.5. The `copy`, `delete`, `mkdir`, and `rename` operations were added in Tcl 7.6. The `attributes` operation was added in Tcl 8.0.

Table 9–2 The `file` command options.

`file atime` *name*	Returns access time as a decimal string.
`file attributes` *name* `?`*option*`? ?`*value*`?` ...	Queries or sets file attributes. (Tcl 8.0)
`file copy ?-force?` *source destination*	Copies file *source* to file *destination*. The *source* and *destination* can be directories. (Tcl 7.6)
`file delete ?-force?` *name*	Deletes the named file. (Tcl 7.6)
`file dirname` *name*	Returns parent directory of file *name*.
`file executable` *name*	Returns 1 if *name* has execute permission, else 0.
`file exists` *name*	Returns 1 if *name* exists, else 0.
`file extension` *name*	Returns the part of *name* from the last dot (i.e., .) to the end. The dot is included in the return value.
`file isdirectory` *name*	Returns 1 if *name* is a directory, else 0.
`file isfile` *name*	Returns 1 if *name* is not a directory, symbolic link, or device, else 0.
`file join` *path* *path*...	Joins pathname components into a new pathname. (Tcl 7.5)
`file lstat` *name var*	Places attributes of the link *name* into *var*.
`file mkdir` *name*	Creates directory *name*. (Tcl 7.6)
`file mtime` *name*	Returns modify time of *name* as a decimal string.

Table 9–2 The `file` command options. (Continued)

`file nativename` *name*	Returns the platform-native version of *name*. (Tk 8.0).
`file owned` *name*	Returns 1 if current user owns the file *name*, else 0.
`file pathtype` *name*	`relative`, `absolute`, or `driverelative`. (Tcl 7.5)
`file readable` *name*	Returns 1 if *name* has read permission, else 0.
`file readlink` *name*	Returns the contents of the symbolic link *name*.
`file rename ?-force?` *old new*	Changes the name of *old* to *new*. (Tcl 7.6)
`file rootname` *name*	Returns all but the extension of *name* (i.e., up to but not including the last `.` in *name*).
`file size` *name*	Returns the number of bytes in *name*.
`file split` *name*	Splits *name* into its pathname components. (Tcl 7.5)
`file stat` *name var*	Places attributes of *name* into array *var*. The elements defined for *var* are listed in Table 9–3.
`file tail` *name*	Returns the last pathname component of *name*.
`file type` *name*	Returns type identifier, which is one of: `file`, `directory`, `characterSpecial`, `blockSpecial`, `fifo`, `link`, or `socket`.
`file writable` *name*	Returns 1 if *name* has write permission, else 0.

Cross-Platform File Naming

Files are named differently on UNIX, Windows, and Macintosh. UNIX separates file name components with a forward slash (/), Macintosh separates components with a colon (:), and Windows separates components with a backslash (\). In addition, the way that absolute and relative names are distinguished is different. For example, these are absolute pathnames for the Tcl script library (i.e., `$tcl_library`) on Macintosh, Windows, and UNIX, respectively:

```
Disk:System Folder:Extensions:Tool Command Language:tcl7.6
c:\Program Files\Tcl\lib\Tcl7.6
/usr/local/tcl/lib/tcl7.6
```

The good news is that Tcl provides operations that let you deal with file pathnames in a platform-independent manner. The file operations described in this chapter allow either native format or the UNIX naming convention. The backslash used in Windows pathnames is especially awkward because the backslash is special to Tcl. Happily, you can use forward slashes instead:

```
c:/Program Files/Tcl/lib/Tcl7.6
```

There are some ambiguous cases that can be specified only with native pathnames. On my Macintosh, Tcl and Tk are installed in a directory that has a slash in it. You can name it only with the native Macintosh name:

```
Disk:Applications:Tcl/Tk 4.2
```

Another construct to watch out for is a leading `//` in a file name. This is the Windows syntax for network names that reference files on other computers. You can avoid accidentally constructing a network name by using the `file join` command described next. Of course, you can use network names to access remote files.

If you must communicate with external programs, you may need to construct a file name in the native syntax for the current platform. You can construct these names with `file join` described later. You can also convert a UNIX-like name to a native name with `file nativename`.

Several of the `file` operations operate on pathnames as opposed to returning information about the file itself. You can use the `dirname`, `extension`, `join`, `pathtype`, `rootname`, `split`, and `tail` operations on any string; there is no requirement that the pathnames refer to an existing file.

Building up Pathnames: `file join`

You can get into trouble if you try to construct file names by simply joining components with a slash. If part of the name is in native format, joining things with slashes will result in incorrect pathnames on Macintosh and Windows. The same problem arises when you accept user input. The user is likely to provide file names in native format. For example, this construct will not create a valid pathname on the Macintosh because `$tcl_library` is in native format:

```
set file $tcl_library/init.tcl
```

Use `file join` to construct file names.

The platform-independent way to construct file names is with `file join`. The following command returns the name of the `init.tcl` file in native format:

```
set file [file join $tcl_library init.tcl]
```

The `file join` operation can join any number of pathname components. In addition, it has the feature that an absolute pathname overrides any previous components. For example (on UNIX), `/b/c` is an absolute pathname, so it overrides any paths that come before it in the arguments to `file join`:

```
file join a b/c d
=> a/b/c/d
file join a /b/c d
=> /b/c/d
```

On Macintosh, a relative pathname starts with a colon, and an absolute pathname does not. To specify an absolute path, you put a trailing colon on the first component so that it is interpreted as a volume specifier. These relative components are joined into a relative pathname:

```
file join a :b:c d
=> :a:b:c:d
```

In the next case, `b:c` is an absolute pathname with `b:` as the volume specifier. The absolute name overrides the previous relative name:

```
file join a b:c d
=> b:c:d
```

The file join operation converts UNIX-style pathnames to native format. For example, on Macintosh you get this:

```
file join /usr/local/lib
=> usr:local:lib
```

Chopping Pathnames: `split`, `dirname`, `tail`

The `file split` command divides a pathname into components. It is the inverse of `file join`. The `split` operation detects automatically if the input is in native or UNIX format. The results of `file split` may contain some syntax to help resolve ambiguous cases when the results are passed back to `file join`. For example, on Macintosh a UNIX-style pathname is split on slash separators. The Macintosh syntax for a volume specifier (`Disk:`) is returned on the leading component:

```
file split "/Disk/System Folder/Extensions"
=> Disk: {System Folder} Extensions
```

A common reason to split up pathnames is to divide a pathname into the directory part and the file part. This task is handled directly by the `dirname` and `tail` operations. The `dirname` operation returns the parent directory of a pathname, while `tail` returns the trailing component of the pathname:

```
file dirname /a/b/c
=> /a/b
file tail /a/b/c
=> c
```

For a pathname with a single component, the `dirname` option returns ".", on UNIX and Windows, or ":" on Macintosh. This is the name of the current directory.

The `extension` and `root` options are also complementary. The `extension` option returns everything from the last period in the name to the end (i.e., the file suffix including the period.) The `root` option returns everything up to, but not including, the last period in the pathname:

```
file root /a/b.c
=> /a/b
file extension /a/b.c
=> .c
```

Manipulating Files and Directories

Tcl 7.6 added file operations to copy files, delete files, rename files, and create directories. In earlier versions it was necessary to `exec` other programs to do these things, except on Macintosh, where `cp`, `rm`, `mv`, `mkdir`, and `rmdir` were built in. These commands are no longer supported on the Macintosh. Your scripts should use the `file` command operations described below to manipulate files in a platform-independent way.

File name patterns are not directly supported by the `file` operations. Instead, you can use the `glob` command described on page 115 to get a list of file names that match a pattern.

Copying Files

The `file copy` operation copies files and directories. The following example copies *file1* to *file2*. If *file2* already exists, the operation raises an error unless the `-force` option is specified:

```
file copy ?-force? file1 file2
```

Several files can be copied into a destination directory. The names of the source files are preserved. The `-force` option indicates that files under *directory* can be replaced:

```
file copy ?-force? file1 file2 ... directory
```

Directories can be recursively copied. The `-force` option indicates that files under *dir2* can be replaced:

```
file copy ?-force? dir1 dir2
```

Creating Directories

The `file mkdir` operation creates one or more directories:

```
file mkdir dir dir ...
```

It is *not* an error if the directory already exists. Furthermore, intermediate directories are created if needed. This means that you can always make sure a directory exists with a single `mkdir` operation. Suppose `/tmp` has no subdirectories at all. The following command creates `/tmp/sub1` and `/tmp/sub1/sub2`:

```
file mkdir /tmp/sub1/sub2
```

The `-force` option is not understood by `file mkdir`, so the following command accidentally creates a folder named `-force`, as well as one named `oops`.

```
file mkdir -force oops
```

Deleting Files

The `file delete` operation deletes files and directories. It is *not* an error if the files do not exist. A non-empty directory is not deleted unless the `-force` option is specified, in which case it is recursively deleted:

```
file delete ?-force? name name ...
```

To delete a file or directory named `-force`, you must specify a nonexistent file before the `-force` to prevent it from being interpreted as a flag (`-force -force` won't work):

```
file delete xyzzy -force
```

Renaming Files and Directories

The `file rename` operation changes a file's name from *old* to *new*. The `-force` option causes *new* to be replaced if it already exists.

```
file rename ?-force? old new
```

Using `file rename` is the best way to update an existing file. First, generate the new version of the file in a temporary file. Then, use `file rename` to replace the old version with the new version. This ensures that any other programs that access the file will not see the new version until it is complete.

File Attributes

There are several file operations that return specific file attributes: `atime`, `executable`, `exists`, `isdirectory`, `isfile`, `mtime`, `owned`, `readable`, `readlink`, `size` and `type`. Refer to Table 9–2 on page 102 for their function. The following command uses `file mtime` to compare the modify times of two files. If you have ever resorted to piping the results of *ls -l* into *awk* in order to derive this information in other shell scripts, you will appreciate this example:

Example 9–2 Comparing file modify times.

```
proc newer { file1 file2 } {
    if ![file exists $file2] {
        return 1
    } else {
        # Assume file1 exists
        expr [file mtime $file1] > [file mtime $file2]
    }
}
```

The `stat` and `lstat` operations return a collection of file attributes. They take a third argument that is the name of an array variable, and they initialize that array with elements that contain the file attributes. If the file is a symbolic link, then the `lstat` operation returns information about the link itself and the `stat` operation returns information about the target of the link. The array elements are listed in Table 9–3. All the element values are decimal strings, except for `type`, which can have the values returned by the `type` option. The element names are based on the UNIX `stat` system call. Use the `file attributes` command described later to get other platform-specific attributes:

Table 9–3 Array elements defined by `file stat`.

atime	The last access time, in seconds.
ctime	The last change time (not the create time), in seconds.
dev	The device identifier, an integer.
gid	The group owner, an integer.
ino	The file number (i.e., inode number), an integer.
mode	The permission bits.
mtime	The last modify time, in seconds.
nlink	The number of links, or directory references, to the file.
size	The number of bytes in the file.
type	`file`, `directory`, `characterSpecial`, `blockSpecial`, `fifo`, `link`, or `socket`.
uid	The owner's user ID, an integer.

Example 9–3 uses the device (`dev`) and inode (`ino`) attributes of a file to determine whether two pathnames reference the same file. The attributes are UNIX specific; they are not well defined on Windows and Macintosh.

Example 9–3 Determining whether pathnames reference the same file.

```
proc fileeq { path1 path2 } {
    file stat $path1 stat1
    file stat $path2 stat2
    expr $stat1(ino) == $stat2(ino) && \
         $stat1(dev) == $stat2(dev)
}
```

The `file attributes` operation was added in Tcl 8.0 to provide access to platform-specific attributes. The `attributes` operation lets you set and query attributes. The interface uses option-value pairs. With no options, all the current values are returned.

```
file attributes book.doc
=> -creator FRAM -hidden 0 -readonly 0 -type MAKR
```

These Macintosh attributes are explained in Table 9–4. The four-character type codes used on Macintosh are illustrated on page 514. With a single option, only that value is returned:

```
file attributes book.doc -readonly
=> 0
```

The attributes are modified by specifying one or more option–value pairs. Setting attributes can raise an error if you do not have the right permissions:

```
file attributes book.doc -readonly 1 -hidden 0
```

Table 9–4 Platform-specific file attributes.

-permissions *mode*	File permission bits. *mode* is a number with bits defined by the chmod system call. (UNIX)
-group *ID*	The group owner of the file. (UNIX)
-owner *ID*	The owner of the file. (UNIX)
-archive *bool*	The archive bit, which is set by backup programs. (Windows)
-hidden *bool*	If set, then the file does not appear in listings. (Windows, Macintosh)
-readonly *bool*	If set, then you cannot write the file. (Windows, Macintosh)
-system *bool*	If set, then you cannot remove the file. (Windows)
-creator *type*	*type* is 4-character code of creating application. (Macintosh)
-type *type*	*type* is 4-character type code. (Macintosh)

Input/Output Command Summary

The following sections describe how to open, read, and write files. The basic model is that you open a file, read or write it, then close the file. Network sockets also use the commands described here. Socket programming is discussed in Chapter 17, and more advanced *event-driven* I/O is described in Chapter 16. Table 9–5 lists the basic commands associated with file I/O:

Table 9–5 Tcl commands used for file access.

open *what* ?*access*? ?*permissions*?	Returns channel ID for a file or pipeline.
puts ?-nonewline? ?*channel*? *string*	Writes a string.
gets *channel* ?*varname*?	Reads a line.
read *channel* ?*numBytes*?	Reads *numBytes* bytes, or all data.
read -nonewline *channel*	Reads all bytes and discard the last \n.
tell *channel*	Returns the seek offset.
seek *channel offset* ?*origin*?	Sets the seek offset. *origin* is one of start, current, or end.
eof *channel*	Queries end-of-file status.
flush *channel*	Writes buffers of a channel.
close *channel*	Closes an I/O channel.

Opening Files for I/O

The `open` command sets up an I/O channel to either a file or a pipeline of processes. The return value of `open` is an identifier for the I/O channel. Store the
result of `open` in a variable and use the variable as you used the `stdout`, `stdin`,
and `stderr` identifiers in the examples so far. The basic syntax is:

> `open` *what ?access? ?permissions?*

The *what* argument is either a file name or a pipeline specification similar
to that used by the `exec` command. The *access* argument can take two forms,
either a short character sequence that is compatible with the `fopen` library routine, or a list of POSIX access flags. Table 9–6 summarizes the first form, while
Table 9–7 summarizes the POSIX flags. If *access* is not specified, it defaults to
read.

Example 9–4 Opening a file for writing.

```
set fileId [open /tmp/foo w 0600]
puts $fileId "Hello, foo!"
close $fileId
```

Table 9–6 Summary of the `open` access arguments.

r	Opens for reading. The file must exist.
r+	Opens for reading and writing. The file must exist.
w	Opens for writing. Truncate if it exists. Create if it does not exist.
w+	Opens for reading and writing. Truncate or create.
a	Opens for writing. Data is appended to the file.
a+	Opens for reading and writing. Data is appended.

Table 9–7 Summary of `POSIX` flags for the access argument.

RDONLY	Opens for reading.
WRONLY	Opens for writing.
RDWR	Opens for reading and writing.
APPEND	Opens for append.
CREAT	Creates the file if it does not exist.
EXCL	If `CREAT` is also specified, then the file cannot already exist.
NOCTTY	Prevents terminal devices from becoming the controlling terminal.
NONBLOCK	Does not block during the open.
TRUNC	Truncates the file if it exists.

The *permissions* argument is a value used for the permission bits on a newly created file. UNIX uses three bits each for the owner, group, and everyone else. The bits specify read, write, and execute permission. These bits are usually specified with an octal number, which has a leading zero, so that there is one octal digit for each set of bits. The default permission bits are 0666, which grant read/write access to everybody. Example 9–4 specifies 0600 so that the file is readable and writable only by the owner. 0775 would grant read, write, and execute permissions to the owner and group, and read and execute permissions to everyone else. You can set other special properties with additional high-order bits. Consult the UNIX manual page on *chmod* command for more details.

The following example illustrates how to use a list of POSIX access flags to open a file for reading and writing, creating it if needed, and not truncating it. This is something you cannot do with the simpler form of the access argument:

```
set fileId [open /tmp/bar {RDWR CREAT}]
```

Catch errors from open.

In general, you should check for errors when opening files. The following example illustrates a catch phrase used to open files. Recall that catch returns 1 if it catches an error; otherwise, it returns zero. It treats its second argument as the name of a variable. In the error case, it puts the error message into the variable. In the normal case, it puts the result of the command into the variable:

Example 9–5 A more careful use of open.

```
if [catch {open /tmp/data r} fileId] {
    puts stderr "Cannot open /tmp/data: $fileId"
} else {
    # Read and process the file, then...
    close $fileId
}
```

Opening a Process Pipeline

You can open a process pipeline by specifying the pipe character, |, as the first character of the first argument. The remainder of the pipeline specification is interpreted just as with the exec command, including input and output redirection. The second argument determines which end of the pipeline open returns. The following example runs the UNIX *sort* program on the password file, and it uses the split command to separate the output lines into list elements:

Example 9–6 Opening a process pipeline.

```
set input [open "|sort /etc/passwd" r]
set contents [split [read $input] \n]
close $input
```

You can open a pipeline for both read and write by specifying the r+ access mode. In this case, you need to worry about buffering. After a puts, the data may still be in a buffer in the Tcl library. Use the `flush` command to force the data out to the spawned processes before you try to read any output from the pipeline. You can also use the `fconfigure` command described on page 223 to force line buffering. Remember that read-write pipes will not work at all with Windows 3.1 because pipes are simulated with files. Event-driven I/O is also very useful with pipes. It means you can do other processing while the pipeline executes, and simply respond when the pipe generates data. This is described in Chapter 16.

Expect

If you are trying to do sophisticated things with an external application, you will find that the *Expect* extension provides a much more powerful interface than a process pipeline. *Expect* adds Tcl commands that are used to control interactive applications. It is extremely useful for automating FTP, Telnet, and programs under test. It comes as a Tcl shell named *expect*, and it is also an extension that you can dynamically load into other Tcl shells. It was created by Don Libes at the National Institute of Standards and Technology (NIST). *Expect* is described in *Exploring Expect* (Libes, O'Reilly & Associates, Inc., 1995). You can find the software on the CD and on the web at:

```
http://expect.nist.gov/
```

Reading and Writing

The standard I/O channels are already open for you. There is a standard input channel, a standard output channel, and a standard error output channel. These channels are identified by `stdin`, `stdout`, and `stderr`, respectively. Other I/O channels are returned by the `open` command, and by the `socket` command described on page 226.

There may be cases when the standard I/O channels are not available. Windows has no standard error channel. Some UNIX window managers close the standard I/O channels when you start programs from window manager menus. You can also close the standard I/O channels with `close`.

The `puts` and `gets` Commands

The `puts` command writes a string and a newline to the output channel. There are a couple of details about the `puts` command that we have not yet used. It takes a `-nonewline` argument that prevents the newline character that is normally appended to the output channel. This is used in the prompt example below. The second feature is that the channel identifier is optional, defaulting to `stdout` if not specified. Note that you must use `flush` to force output of a partial line. This is illustrated in Example 9–7.

Example 9–7 Prompting for input.

```
puts -nonewline "Enter value: "
flush stdout  ;# Necessary to get partial line output
set answer [gets stdin]
```

The gets command reads a line of input, and it has two forms. In the previous example, with just a single argument, gets returns the line read from the specified I/O channel. It discards the trailing newline from the return value. If end of file is reached, an empty string is returned. You must use the eof command to tell the difference between a blank line and end-of-file. eof returns 1 if there is end of file. Given a second *varName* argument, gets stores the line into a named variable and returns the number of bytes read. It discards the trailing newline, which is not counted. A -1 is returned if the channel has reached the end of file.

Example 9–8 A read loop using gets.

```
while {[gets $channel line] >= 0} {
    # Process line
}
close $channel
```

The read Command

The read command reads blocks of data, and this capability is often more efficient. There are two forms for read: You can specify the -nonewline argument or the *numBytes* argument, but not both. Without *numBytes*, the whole file (or what is left in the I/O channel) is read and returned. The -nonewline argument causes the trailing newline to be discarded. Given a byte count argument, read returns that amount, or less if there is not enough data in the channel. The trailing newline is not discarded in this case.

Example 9–9 A read loop using read and split.

```
foreach line [split [read $channel] \n] {
    # Process line
}
close $channel
```

For moderate-sized files, it is about 10 percent faster to loop over the lines in a file using the read loop in the second example. In this case, read returns the whole file, and split chops the file into list elements, one for each line. For small files (less than 1K) it doesn't really matter. For large files (megabytes) you might induce paging with this approach.

Platform-Specific End of Line Characters

Tcl automatically detects different end of line conventions. On UNIX, text lines are ended with a newline character (\n). On Macintosh, they are terminated with a carriage return (\r). On Windows, they are terminated with a carriage return, newline sequence (\r\n). Tcl accepts any of these, and the line terminator can even change within a file. All these different conventions are converted to the UNIX style so that once read, text lines are always terminated with a newline character (\n). Both the read and gets commands do this conversion.

During output, text lines are generated in the platform-native format. The automatic handling of line formats means that it is easy to convert a file to native format. You just need to read it in and write it out:

```
puts -nonewline $out [read $in]
```

To suppress conversions, use the fconfigure command, which is described in more detail on page 223.

Example 9–10 demonstrates a File_Copy procedure that translates files to native format. It is complicated because it handles directories:

Example 9–10 Copy a file and translate to native format.

```
proc File_Copy {src dest} {
    if [file isdirectory $src] {
        file mkdir $dest
        foreach f [glob -nocomplain [file join $src *]] {
            File_Copy $f [file join $dest [file tail $f]]
        }
        return
    }
    if [file isdirectory $dest] {
        set dest [file join $dest [file tail $src]]
    }
    set in [open $src]
    set out [open $dest w]
    puts -nonewline $out [read $in]
    close $out ; close $in
}
```

Random Access I/O

The seek and tell commands provide random access to I/O channels. Each channel has a current position called the *seek offset*. Each read or write operation updates the seek offset by the number of bytes transferred. The current value of the offset is returned by the tell command. The seek command sets the seek offset by an amount, which can be positive or negative, from an origin which is either start, current, or end.

Closing I/O Channels

The `close` command is just as important as the others because it frees operating system resources associated with the I/O channel. If you forget to close a channel, it will be closed when your process exits. However, if you have a long-running program, like a Tk script, you might exhaust some operating system resources if you forget to close your I/O channels.

The `close` command can raise an error.

If the channel was a process pipeline and any of the processes wrote to their standard error channel, then Tcl believes this is an error. The error is raised when the channel to the pipeline is finally closed. Similarly, if any of the processes in the pipeline exit with a nonzero status, `close` raises an error.

The Current Directory — cd and pwd

Every process has a current directory that is used as the starting point when resolving a relative pathname. The `pwd` command returns the current directory, and the `cd` command changes the current directory. Example 9–11 uses these commands.

Matching File Names with glob

The `glob` command expands a pattern into the set of matching file names. The general form of the `glob` command is:

```
glob ?flags? pattern ?pattern? ...
```

The pattern syntax is similar to the `string match` patterns:

- `*` matches zero or more characters.
- `?` matches a single character.
- `[abc]` matches a set of characters.
- `{a,b,c}` matches any of *a*, *b*, or *c*.
- All other characters must match themselves.

The `-nocomplain` flag causes `glob` to return an empty list if no files match the pattern. Otherwise, `glob` raises an error if no files match.

The `--` flag must be used if the *pattern* begins with a `-`.

Unlike the glob matching in *csh*, the Tcl `glob` command matches only the names of existing files. In *csh*, the `{a,b}` construct can match nonexistent names. In addition, the results of `glob` are not sorted. Use the `lsort` command to sort its result if you find it important.

Example 9–11 shows the `FindFile` procedure, which traverses the file system hierarchy using recursion. At each iteration it saves its current directory and then attempts to change to the next subdirectory. A `catch` guards against bogus names. The `glob` command matches file names:

Example 9–11 Finding a file by name.

```
proc FindFile { startDir namePat } {
    set pwd [pwd]
    if [catch {cd $startDir} err] {
        puts stderr $err
        return
    }
    foreach match [glob -nocomplain -- $namePat] {
        puts stdout [file join $startDir $match]
    }
    foreach file [glob -nocomplain *] {
        if [file isdirectory $file] {
            FindFile [file join $startDir $file] $namePat
        }
    }
    cd $pwd
}
```

Expanding Tilde in File Names

The glob command also expands a leading tilde (~) in filenames. There are two cases:

- ~/ expands to the current user's home directory.
- ~user expands to the home directory of user.

If you have a file that starts with a literal tilde, you can avoid the tilde expansion by adding a leading ./ (e.g., ./~foobar).

The exit and pid Commands

The exit command terminates your script. Note that exit causes termination of the whole process that was running the script. If you supply an integer-valued argument to exit, then that becomes the exit status of the process.

The pid command returns the process ID of the current process. This can be useful as the seed for a random number generator because it changes each time you run your script. It is also common to embed the process ID in the name of temporary files.

You can also find out the process IDs associated with a process pipeline with pid:

```
set pipe [open "|command"]
set pids [pid $pipe]
```

There is no built-in mechanism to control processes in Tcl. On UNIX systems you can exec the *kill* program to terminate a process:

```
exec kill $pid
```

Environment Variables

Environment variables are a collection of string-valued variables associated with each process. The process's environment variables are available through the global array env. The name of the environment variable is the index, (e.g., env(PATH)), and the array element contains the current value of the environment variable. If assignments are made to env, they result in changes to the corresponding environment variable. Environment variables are inherited by child processes, so programs run with the exec command inherit the environment of the Tcl script. The following example prints the values of environment variables.

Example 9–12 Printing environment variable values.

```
proc printenv { args } {
    global env
    set maxl 0
    if {[llength $args] == 0} {
        set args [lsort [array names env]]
    }
    foreach x $args {
        if {[string length $x] > $maxl} {
            set maxl [string length $x]
        }
    }
    incr maxl 2
    foreach x $args {
        puts stdout [format "%*s = %s" $maxl $x $env($x)]
    }
}
printenv USER SHELL TERM
=>
USER    = welch
SHELL   = /bin/csh
TERM    = tx
```

Note: Environment variables can be initialized for Macintosh applications by editing a resource of type STR# whose name is Tcl Environment Variables. This resource is part of the *tclsh* and *wish* applications. Follow the directions on page 28 for using *ResEdit*. The format of the resource values is *NAME=VALUE*.

The registry Command

Windows uses the *registry* to store various system configuration information. The Windows tool to browse and edit the registry is called *regedit*. Tcl provides a registry command. It is a loadable package that you must load by using:

```
package require registry
```

The registry structure has keys, value names, and typed data. The value names are stored under a key, and each value name has data associated with it.

The keys are organized into a hierarchical naming system, so another way to think of the value names is as an extra level in the hierarchy. The main point is that you need to specify both a key name and a value name in order to get something out of the registry. The key names have one of the following formats:

```
\\hostname\rootname\keypath
rootname\keypath
rootname
```

The *rootname* is one of HKEY_LOCAL_MACHINE, HKEY_PERFORMANCE_DATA, HKEY_USERS, HKEY_CLASSES_ROOT, HKEY_CURRENT_USER, HKEY_CURRENT_CONFIG, or HKEY_DYN_DATA. Tables 9–8 and 9–9 summarize the registry command and data types:

Table 9–8 The registry command.

registry delete *key* ?*valueName*?	Deletes the *key* and the named value, or it deletes all values under the key if *valueName* is not specified.
registry get *key* *valueName*	Returns the value associated with *valueName* under *key*.
registry keys *key* ?*pat*?	Returns the list of keys or value names under *key* that match *pat*, which is a string match pattern.
registry set *key*	Creates *key*.
registry set *key* *valueName* *data* ?*type*?	Creates *valueName* under *key* with value *data* of the given *type*. Types are listed in Table 9–9.
registry type *key* *valueName*	Returns the type of *valueName* under *key*.
registry values *key* ?*pat*?	Returns the names of the values stored under *key* that match *pat*, which is a string match pattern.

Table 9–9 The registry data types.

binary	Arbitrary binary data.
none	Arbitrary binary data.
expand_sz	A string that contains references to environment variables with the %VARNAME% syntax.
dword	A 32-bit integer.
dword_big_endian	A 32-bit integer in the other byte order. It is represented in Tcl as a decimal string.
link	A symbolic link.
multi_sz	An array of strings, which are represented as a Tcl list.
resource_list	A device driver resource list.

P A R T   II

Advanced Tcl

Part II describes advanced programming techniques that support sophisticated applications. The Tcl interfaces remain simple, so you can quickly construct powerful applications.

Chapter 10 describes `eval`, which lets you create Tcl programs on the fly. There are tricks with using `eval` correctly, and a few rules of thumb to make your life easier.

Chapter 11 describes regular expressions. This is the most powerful string processing facility in Tcl. This chapter includes a cookbook of useful regular expressions.

Chapter 12 describes the library and package facility used to organize your code into reusable modules.

Chapter 13 describes introspection and debugging. Introspection provides information about the state of the Tcl interpreter.

Chapter 14 describes namespaces that partition the global scope for variables and procedures. Namespaces help you structure large Tcl applications.

Chapter 15 describes the features that support Internationalization, including Unicode, other character set encodings, and message catalogs.

Chapter 16 describes event-driven I/O programming. This lets you run process pipelines in the background. It is also very useful with network socket programming, which is the topic of Chapter 17.

Chapter 18 describes TclHttpd, a Web server built entirely in Tcl. You can build applications on top of TclHttpd, or integrate the server into existing applications to give them a web interface. TclHttpd also supports regular Web sites.

Chapter 19 describes Safe-Tcl and using multiple Tcl interpreters. You can create multiple Tcl interpreters for your application. If an interpreter is safe, then you can grant it restricted functionality. This is ideal for supporting network applets that are downloaded from untrusted sites.

Quoting Issues and Eval

This chapter describes explicit calls to the interpreter with the `eval` command. An extra round of substitutions is performed that results in some useful effects. The chapter describes the quoting problems with `eval` and the ways to avoid them. The `uplevel` command evaluates commands in a different scope. The `subst` command does substitutions but no command invocation.

Dynamic evaluation makes Tcl flexible and powerful, but it can be tricky to use properly. The basic idea is that you create a string and then use the `eval` command to interpret that string as a command or a series of commands. Creating program code on the fly is easy with an interpreted language like Tcl, and very hard, if not impossible, with a statically compiled language like C++ or Java. There are several ways that dynamic code evaluation is used in Tcl:

- In some cases, a simple procedure isn't quite good enough, and you need to glue together a command from a few different pieces and then execute the result using `eval`. This often occurs with *wrappers*, which provide a thin layer of functionality over existing commands.
- *Callbacks* are script fragments that are saved and evaluated later in response to some event. Examples include the commands associated with Tk buttons, `fileevent` I/O handlers, and `after` timer handlers. Callbacks are a flexible way to link different parts of an application together.
- You can add new control structures to Tcl using the `uplevel` command. For example, you can write a function that applies a command to each line in a file or each node in a tree.
- You can have a mixture of code and data, and just process the code part with the `subst` command. For example, this is useful in HTML templates described in Chapter 18. There are also some powerful combinations of `subst` and `regsub` described in Chapter 11.

Constructing Code with the `list` Command

It can be tricky to assemble a command so that it is evaluated properly by `eval`. The same difficulties apply to commands like `after`, `uplevel`, and the Tk `send` command, all of which have similar properties to `eval`, except that the command evaluation occurs later or in a different context. Constructing commands dynamically is a source of many problems. The worst part is that you can write code that works sometimes but not others, which can be very confusing.

Use `list` when constructing commands.

The root of the quoting problems is the internal use of `concat` by `eval` and similar commands to concatenate their arguments into one command string. The `concat` can lose some important list structure so that arguments are not passed through as you expect. The general strategy to avoid these problems is to use `list` and `lappend` to explicitly form the command callback as a single, well-structured list.

The `eval` Command

The `eval` command results in another call to the Tcl interpreter. If you construct a command dynamically, you must use `eval` to interpret it. For example, suppose we want to construct the following command now but execute it later:

```
puts stdout "Hello, World!"
```

In this case, it is sufficient to do the following:

```
set cmd {puts stdout "Hello, World!"}
=> puts stdout "Hello, World!"
# sometime later...
eval $cmd
=> Hello, World!
```

In this case, the value of `cmd` is passed to Tcl. All the standard grouping and substitution are done again on the value, which is a `puts` command.

However, suppose that part of the command is stored in a variable, but that variable will not be defined at the time `eval` is used. We can artificially create this situation like this:

```
set string "Hello, World!"
set cmd {puts stdout $string}
=> puts stdout $string
unset string
eval $cmd
=> can't read "string": no such variable
```

In this case, the command contains `$string`. When this is processed by `eval`, the interpreter looks for the current value of `string`, which is undefined. This example is contrived, but the same problem occurs if `string` is a local variable, and `cmd` will be evaluated later in the global scope.

A common mistake is to use double quotes to group the command. That will let `$string` be substituted now. However, this works only if string has a simple value, but it fails if the value of `string` contains spaces or other Tcl special characters:

```
set cmd "puts stdout $string"
=> puts stdout Hello, World!
eval $cmd
=> bad argument "World!": should be "nonewline"
```

The problem is that we have lost some important structure. The identity of `$string` as a single argument gets lost in the second round of parsing by `eval`. The solution to this problem is to construct the command using `list`, as shown in the following example:

Example 10–1 Using `list` to construct commands.

```
set string "Hello, World!"
set cmd [list puts stdout $string]
=> puts stdout {Hello, World!}
unset string
eval $cmd
=> Hello, World!
```

The trick is that `list` has formed a list containing three elements: `puts`, `stdout`, and the value of `string`. The substitution of `$string` occurs before `list` is called, and `list` takes care of grouping that value for us. In contrast, using double quotes is equivalent to:

```
set cmd [concat puts stdout $string]
```

Double quotes lose list structure.

The problem here is that `concat` does not preserve list structure. The main lesson is that you should use `list` to construct commands if they contain variable values or command results that must be substituted now. If you use double quotes, the values are substituted but you lose proper command structure. If you use curly braces, then values are not substituted until later, which may not be in the right context.

Commands That Concatenate Their Arguments

The `uplevel`, `after` and `send` commands concatenate their arguments into a command and execute it later in a different context. The `uplevel` command is described on page 130, `after` is described on page 218, and `send` is described on page 560. Whenever I discover such a command, I put it on my danger list and make sure I explicitly form a single command argument with `list` instead of letting the command `concat` items for me. Get in the habit now:

```
after 100 [list doCmd $param1 $param2]
send $interp [list doCmd $param1 $param2];# Safe!
```

The danger here is that `concat` and `list` can result in the same thing, so you can be led down the rosy garden path only to get errors later when values change. The two previous examples always work. The next two work only if `param1` and `param2` have values that are single list elements:

```
after 100 doCmd $param1 $param2
send $interp doCmd $param1 $param2 ;# Unsafe!
```

If you use other Tcl extensions that provide `eval`-like functionality, carefully check their documentation to see whether they contain commands that `concat` their arguments into a command. For example, Tcl-DP, which provides a network version of `send`, `dp_send`, also uses `concat`.

Commands That Use Callbacks

The general strategy of passing out a command or script to call later is a flexible way to assemble different parts of an application, and it is widely used by Tcl commands. Examples include commands that are called when users click on Tk buttons, commands that are called when I/O channels have data ready, or commands that are called when clients connect to network servers. It is also easy to write your own procedures or C extensions that accept scripts and call them later in response to some event.

These other callback situations may not appear to have the "`concat` problem" because they take a single script argument. However, as soon as you use double quotes to group that argument, you have created the `concat` problem all over again. So, all the caveats about using `list` to construct these commands still apply.

Command Prefix Callbacks

There is a variation on command callbacks called a *command prefix*. In this case, the command is given additional arguments when it is invoked. In other words, you provide only part of the command, the command prefix, and the module that invokes the callback adds additional arguments before using `eval` to invoke the command.

For example, when you create a network server, you supply a procedure that is called when a client makes a connection. That procedure is called with three additional arguments that indicate the client's socket, IP address, and port number. This is described in more detail on page 227. The tricky thing is that you can define your callback procedure to take four (or more) arguments. In this case you specify some of the parameters when you define the callback, and then the socket subsystem specifies the remaining arguments when it makes the callback. The following command creates the server side of a socket:

```
set virtualhost www.beedub.com
socket -server [list Accept $virtualhost] 8080
```

However, you define the `Accept` procedure like this:

```
proc Accept {myname sock ipaddr port} { ... }
```

The `myname` parameter is set when you construct the command prefix. The remaining parameters are set when the callback is invoked. The use of `list` in this example is not strictly necessary because "we know" that `virtualhost` will always be a single list element. However, using `list` is just a good habit when forming callbacks, so I always write the code this way.

There are many other examples of callback arguments that are really command prefixes. Some of these include the scrolling callbacks between Tk scrollbars and their widgets, the command aliases used with Safe Tcl, the sorting functions in `lsort`, and the completion callback used with `fcopy`. Example 13–6 on page 181 shows how to use `eval` to make callbacks from Tcl procedures.

Constructing Procedures Dynamically

The previous examples have all focused on creating single commands by using list operations. Suppose you want to create a whole procedure dynamically. Unfortunately, this can be particularly awkward because a procedure body is not a simple list. Instead, it is a sequence of commands that are each lists, but they are separated by newlines or semicolons. In turn, some of those commands may be loops and `if` commands that have their own command bodies. To further compound the problem, you typically have two kinds of variables in the procedure body: some that are to be used as values when constructing the body, and some that are to be used later when executing the procedure. The result can be very messy.

The main trick to this problem is to use either `format` or `regsub` to process a template for your dynamically generated procedure. If you use format, then you can put `%s` into your templates where you want to insert values. You may find the positional notation of the format string (e.g., `%1$s` and `%2$s`) useful if you need to repeat a value in several places within your procedure body. The following example is a procedure that generates a new version of other procedures. The new version includes code that counts the number of times the procedure was called and measures the time it takes to run:

Example 10–2 Generating procedures dynamically with a template.

```
proc TraceGen {procName} {
   rename $procName $procName-orig
   set arglist {}
   foreach arg [info args $procName-orig] {
      append arglist "\$$arg "
   }
   proc $procName [info args $procName-orig] [format {
      global _trace_count _trace_msec
      incr _trace_count(%1$s)
      incr _trace_msec(%1$s) [lindex [time {
         set result [%1$s-orig %2$s]
      } 1] 0]
      return $result
   } $procName $arglist]
}
```

Suppose that we have a trivial procedure `foo`:

```
proc foo {x y} {
    return [expr $x * $y]
}
```

If you run `TraceGen` on it and look at the results, you see this:

```
TraceGen foo
info body foo
=>
    global _trace_count _trace_msec
    incr _trace_count(foo)
    incr _trace_msec(foo) [lindex [time {
        set result [foo-orig $x $y]
    } 1] 0]
    return $result
```

Exploiting the `concat` inside `eval`

The previous section warns about the danger of concatenation when forming commands. However, there are times when concatenation is done for good reason. This section illustrates cases where the `concat` done by `eval` is useful in assembling a command by concatenating multiple lists into one list. A `concat` is done internally by `eval` when it gets more than one argument:

```
eval list1 list2 list3 ...
```

The effect of `concat` is to join all the lists into one list; a new level of list structure is *not* added. This is useful if the lists are fragments of a command. It is common to use this form of `eval` with the `args` construct in procedures. Use the `args` parameter to pass optional arguments through to another command. Invoke the other command with `eval`, and the values in `$args` get concatenated onto the command properly. The special args parameter is illustrated in Example 7–2 on page 82.

Using `eval` in a Wrapper Procedure.

Here, we illustrate the use of `eval` and `$args` with a simple Tk example. In Tk, the `button` command creates a button in the user interface. The `button` command can take many arguments, and commonly you simply specify the text of the button and the Tcl command that is executed when the user clicks on the button:

```
button .foo -text Foo -command foo
```

After a button is created, it is made visible by packing it into the display. The `pack` command can also take many arguments to control screen placement. Here, we just specify a side and let the packer take care of the rest of the details:

```
pack .foo -side left
```

Even though there are only two Tcl commands to create a user interface button, we will write a procedure that replaces the two commands with one. Our first version might be:

```
proc PackedButton {name txt cmd} {
    button $name -text $txt -command $cmd
    pack $name -side left
}
```

This is not a very flexible procedure. The main problem is that it hides the full power of the Tk `button` command, which can really take about 20 widget configuration options, such as `-background`, `-cursor`, `-relief`, and more. They are listed on page 391. For example, you can easily make a red button like this:

```
button .foo -text Foo -command foo -background red
```

A better version of `PackedButton` uses `args` to pass through extra configuration options to the `button` command. The `args` parameter is a list of all the extra arguments passed to the Tcl procedure. My first attempt to use `$args` looked like this, but it was not correct:

```
proc PackedButton {name txt cmd args} {
    button $name -text $txt -command $cmd $args
    pack $name -side left
}
PackedButton .foo "Hello, World!" {exit} -background red
=> unknown option "-background red"
```

The problem is that `$args` is a list value, and `button` gets the whole list as a single argument. Instead, `button` needs to get the elements of `$args` as individual arguments.

Use `eval` with `$args`

In this case, you can use `eval` because it concatenates its arguments to form a single list before evaluation. The single list is, by definition, the same as a single Tcl command, so the `button` command parses correctly. Here we give `eval` two lists, which it joins into one command:

```
eval {button $name -text $txt -command $cmd} $args
```

The use of the braces in this command is discussed in more detail below. We also generalize our procedure to take some options to the `pack` command. This argument, `pack`, must be a list of packing options. The final version of `Packed-Button` is shown in Example 10–3:

Example 10–3 Using `eval` with `$args`.

```
# PackedButton creates and packs a button.
proc PackedButton {path txt cmd {pack {-side right}} args} {
    eval {button $path -text $txt -command $cmd} $args
    eval {pack $path} $pack
}
```

In `PackedButton`, both `pack` and `args` are list-valued parameters that are used as parts of a command. The internal `concat` done by `eval` is perfect for this situation. The simplest call to `PackedButton` is:

```
PackedButton .new "New" { New }
```

The quotes and curly braces are redundant in this case but are retained to convey some type information. The quotes imply a string label, and the braces imply a command. The `pack` argument takes on its default value, and the `args` variable is an empty list. The two commands executed by `PackedButton` are:

```
button .new -text New -command New
pack .new -side right
```

`PackedButton` creates a horizontal stack of buttons by default. The packing can be controlled with a packing specification:

```
PackedButton .save "Save" { Save $file } {-side left}
```

The two commands executed by `PackedButton` are:

```
button .new -text Save -command { Save $file }
pack .new -side left
```

The remaining arguments, if any, are passed through to the button command. This lets the caller fine-tune some of the button attributes:

```
PackedButton .quit Quit { Exit } {-side left -padx 5} \
    -background red
```

The two commands executed by `PackedButton` are:

```
button .quit -text Quit -command { Exit } -background red
pack .quit -side left -padx 5
```

You can see a difference between the `pack` and `args` argument in the call to `PackedButton`. You need to group the packing options explicitly into a single argument. The `args` parameter is automatically made into a list of all remaining arguments. In fact, if you group the extra button parameters, it will be a mistake:

```
PackedButton .quit Quit { Exit } {-side left -padx 5} \
    {-background red}
=> unknown option "-background red"
```

Correct Quoting with `eval`

What about the peculiar placement of braces in `PackedButton`?

```
eval {button $path -text $txt -command $cmd} $args
```

By using braces, we control the number of times different parts of the command are seen by the Tcl evaluator. Without any braces, everything goes through two rounds of substitution. The braces prevent one of those rounds. In the above command, only `$args` is substituted twice. Before `eval` is called, the `$args` is replaced with its list value. Then, `eval` is invoked, and it concatenates its two list arguments into one list, which is now a properly formed command. The second round of substitutions done by `eval` replaces the `txt` and `cmd` values.

Do not use double quotes with `eval`.

You may be tempted to use double quotes instead of curly braces in your uses of `eval`. *Don't give in!* Using double quotes is, mostly likely, wrong. Suppose the first `eval` command is written like this:

```
eval "button $path -text $txt -command $cmd $args"
```

Incidentally, the previous is equivalent to:

```
eval button $path -text $txt -command $cmd $args
```

These versions happen to work with the following call because `txt` and `cmd` have one-word values with no special characters in them:

```
PackedButton .quit Quit { Exit }
```

The button command that is ultimately evaluated is:

```
button .quit -text Quit -command { Exit }
```

In the next call, an error is raised:

```
PackedButton .save "Save As" [list Save $file]
=> unknown option "As"
```

This is because the button command is this:

```
button .save -text Save As -command Save /a/b/c
```

But it should look like this instead:

```
button .save -text {Save As} -command {Save /a/b/c}
```

The problem is that the structure of the `button` command is now wrong. The value of `txt` and `cmd` are substituted first, before `eval` is even called, and then the whole command is parsed again. The worst part is that sometimes using double quotes works, and sometimes it fails. The success of using double quotes depends on the value of the parameters. When those values contain spaces or special characters, the command gets parsed incorrectly.

Braces: the one true way to group arguments to eval.

To repeat, the safe construct is:

```
eval {button $path -text $txt -command $cmd} $args
```

The following variations are also correct. The first uses `list` to do quoting automatically, and the others use backslashes or braces to prevent the extra round of substitutions:

```
eval [list button $path -text $txt -command $cmd] $args
eval button \$path -text \$txt -command \$cmd $args
eval button {$path} -text {$txt} -command {$cmd} $args
```

Finally, here is one more *incorrect* approach that tries to quote by hand:

```
eval "button {$path} -text {$txt} -command {$cmd} $args"
```

The problem above is that quoting is not always done with curly braces. If a value contains an unmatched curly brace, Tcl would have used backslashes to quote it, and the above command would raise an error:

```
set blob "foo\{bar space"
=> foo{bar space
eval "puts {$blob}"
=> missing close brace
eval puts {$blob}
=> foo{bar space
```

The `uplevel` Command

The `uplevel` command is similar to `eval`, except that it evaluates a command in a different scope than the current procedure. It is useful for defining new control structures entirely in Tcl. The syntax for `uplevel` is:

    uplevel ?*level*? *command* ?*list1 list2* ...?

As with `upvar`, the *level* parameter is optional and defaults to 1, which means to execute the command in the scope of the calling procedure. The other common use of level is `#0`, which means to evaluate the command in the global scope. You can count up farther than one (e.g., 2 or 3), or count down from the global level (e.g., `#1` or `#2`), but these cases rarely make sense.

When you specify the *command* argument, you must be aware of any substitutions that might be performed by the Tcl interpreter before `uplevel` is called. If you are entering the command directly, protect it with curly braces so that substitutions occur in the other scope. The following affects the variable `x` in the caller's scope:

    uplevel {set x [expr $x + 1]}

However, the following will use the value of `x` in the current scope to define the value of `x` in the calling scope, which is probably not what was intended:

    uplevel "set x [expr $x + 1]"

If you are constructing the command dynamically, again use `list`. This fragment is used later in Example 10–4:

    uplevel [list foreach $args $valueList {break}]

It is common to have the command in a variable. This is the case when the command has been passed into your new control flow procedure as an argument. In this case, you should evaluate the command one level up. Put the level in explicitly to avoid cases where `$cmd` looks like a number!

    uplevel 1 $cmd

Another common scenario is reading commands from users as part of an application. In this case, you should evaluate the command at the global scope. Example 16–2 on page 220 illustrates this use of `uplevel`:

    uplevel #0 $cmd

If you are assembling a command from a few different lists, such as the `args` parameter, then you can use `concat` to form the command:

    uplevel [concat $cmd $args]

The lists in `$cmd` and `$args` are concatenated into a single list, which is a valid Tcl command. Like `eval`, `uplevel` uses `concat` internally if it is given extra arguments, so you can leave out the explicit use of `concat`. The following commands are equivalent:

    uplevel [concat $cmd $args]
    uplevel "$cmd $args"
    uplevel $cmd $args

Example 10–4 shows list assignment using the `foreach` trick described on Page 75. List assignment is useful if a command returns several values in a list.

The `lassign` procedure assigns the list elements to several variables. The `lassign` procedure hides the `foreach` trick, but it must use the `uplevel` command so that the loop variables get assigned in the correct scope. The `list` command is used to construct the `foreach` command that is executed in the caller's scope. This is necessary so that `$variables` and `$values` get substituted before the command is evaluated in the other scope.

Example 10–4 `lassign`: list assignment with `foreach`.

```
# Assign a set of variables from a list of values.
# If there are more values than variables, they are returned.
# If there are fewer values than variables,
# the variables get the empty string.

proc lassign {valueList args} {
    if {[llength $args] == 0} {
        error "wrong # args: lassign list varname ?varname..?"
    }
    if {[llength $valueList] == 0} {
        # Ensure one trip through the foreach loop
        set valueList [list {}]
    }
    uplevel 1 [list foreach $args $valueList {break}]
    return [lrange $valueList [llength $args] end]
}
```

Example 10–5 illustrates a new control structure with the `File_Process` procedure that applies a callback to each line in a file. The call to `uplevel` allows the `callback` to be concatenated with the `line` to form the command. The `list` command is used to quote any special characters in `line`, so it appears as a single argument to the command.

Example 10–5 The File_Process procedure applies a command to each line of a file.

```
proc File_Process {file callback} {
    set in [open $file]
    while {[gets $file line] >= 0} {
        uplevel 1 $callback [list $line]
    }
    close $in
}
```

What is the difference between these two commands?

```
    uplevel 1 [list $callback $line]
    uplevel 1 $callback [list $line]
```

The first form limits `callback` to be the name of the command, while the second form allows `callback` to be a command prefix. Once again, what is the bug with this version?

```
    uplevel 1 $callback $line
```

The arbitrary value of $line is concatenated to the callback command, and it is likely to be a malformed command when executed.

The subst Command

The subst command is useful when you have a mixture of Tcl commands, Tcl variable references, and plain old data. The subst command looks through the data for square brackets, dollar signs, and backslashes, and it does substitutions on those. It leaves the rest of the data alone:

```
set a "foo bar"
subst {a=$a date=[exec date]}
=> a=foo bar date=Thu Dec 15 10:13:48 PST 1994
```

The subst command does not honor the quoting effect of curly braces. It does substitutions regardless of braces:

```
subst {a=$a date={[exec date]}}
=> a=foo bar date={Thu Dec 15 10:15:31 PST 1994}
```

You can use backslashes to prevent variable and command substitution.

```
subst {a=\$a date=\[exec date]}
=> a=$a date=[exec date]
```

You can use other backslash substitutions like \uXXXX to get Unicode characters, \n to get newlines, or \-newline to hide newlines.

The subst command takes flags that limit the substitutions it will perform. The flags are -nobackslashes, -nocommands, or -novariables. You can specify one or more of these flags before the string that needs to be substituted:

```
subst -novariables {a=$a date=[exec date]}
=> a=$a date=Thu Dec 15 10:15:31 PST 1994
```

String Processing with subst

The subst command can be used with the regsub command to do efficient, two-step string processing. In the first step, regsub is used to rewrite an input string into data with embedded Tcl commands. In the second step, subst or eval replaces the Tcl commands with their result. By artfully mapping the data into Tcl commands, you can dynamically construct a Tcl script that processes the data. The processing is efficient because the Tcl parser and the regular expression processor have been highly tuned. Chapter 11 has several examples that use this technique.

Regular Expressions

This chapter describes regular expression pattern matching and string processing based on regular expression substitutions. These features provide the most powerful string processing facilities in Tcl. Tcl commands described are: `regexp` and `regsub`.

*R*egular expressions are a formal way to describe string patterns. They provide a powerful and compact way to specify patterns in your data. Even better, there is a very efficient implementation of the regular expression mechanism due to Henry Spencer. If your script does much string processing, it is worth the effort to learn about the `regexp` command. Your Tcl scripts will be compact and efficient. This chapter uses many examples to show you the features of regular expressions.

Regular expression substitution is a mechanism that lets you rewrite a string based on regular expression matching. The `regsub` command is another powerful tool, and this chapter includes several examples that do a lot of work in just a few Tcl commands. Stephen Uhler has shown me several ways to transform input data into a Tcl script with `regsub` and then use `subst` or `eval` to process the data. The idea takes a moment to get used to, but it provides a very efficient way to process strings.

Tcl 8.1 added a new regular expression implementation that supports Unicode and *advanced regular expressions* (ARE). This implementation adds more syntax and escapes that makes it easier to write patterns, once you learn the new features! If you know Perl, then you are already familiar with these features. The Tcl advanced regular expressions are almost identical to the Perl 5 regular expressions. The new features include a few very minor incompatibilities with the regular expressions implemented in earlier versions of Tcl 8.0, but these rarely occur in practice. The new regular expression package supports Unicode, of course, so you can write patterns to match Japanese or Hindu documents!

When to Use Regular Expressions

Regular expressions can seem overly complex at first. They introduce their own syntax and their own rules, and you may be tempted to use simpler commands like `string first`, `string range`, or `string match` to process your strings. However, often a single regular expression command can replace a sequence of several `string` commands. Any time you can replace several Tcl commands with one, you get a performance improvement. Furthermore, the regular expression matcher is implemented in optimized C code, so pattern matching is fast.

The regular expression matcher does more than test for a match. It also tells you what part of your input string matches the pattern. This is useful for picking data out of a large input string. In fact, you can capture several pieces of data in just one match by using subexpressions. The `regexp` Tcl command makes this easy by assigning the matching data to Tcl variables. If you find yourself using `string first` and `string range` to pick out data, remember that `regexp` can do it in one step instead.

The regular expression matcher is structured so that patterns are first compiled into an form that is efficient to match. If you use the same pattern frequently, then the expensive compilation phase is done only once, and all your matching uses the efficient form. These details are completely hidden by the Tcl interface. If you use a pattern twice, Tcl will nearly always be able to retrieve the compiled form of the pattern. As you can see, the regular expression matcher is optimized for lots of heavy-duty string processing.

Avoiding a Common Problem

Group your patterns with curly braces.

One of the stumbling blocks with regular expressions is that they use some of the same special characters as Tcl. Any pattern that contains brackets, dollar signs, or spaces must be quoted when used in a Tcl command. In many cases you can group the regular expression with curly braces, so Tcl pays no attention to it. However, when using Tcl 8.0 (or earlier) you may need Tcl to do backslash substitutions on part of the pattern, and then you need to worry about quoting the special characters in the regular expression.

Advanced regular expressions eliminate this problem because backslash substitution is now done by the regular expression engine. Previously, to get `\n` to mean the newline character (or `\t` for tab) you had to let Tcl do the substitution. With Tcl 8.1, `\n` and `\t` inside a regular expression mean newline and tab. In fact, there are now about 20 backslash escapes you can use in patterns. Now more than ever, remember to group your patterns with curly braces to avoid conflicts between Tcl and the regular expression engine.

The patterns in the first sections of this Chapter ignore this problem. The sample expressions in Table 11–7 on page 151 are quoted for use within Tcl scripts. Most are quoted simply by putting the whole pattern in braces, but some are shown without braces for comparison.

Regular Expression Syntax

This section describes the basics of regular expression patterns, which are found in all versions of Tcl. There are occasional references to features added by advanced regular expressions, but they are covered in more detail starting on page 138. There is enough syntax in regular expressions that there are five tables that summarize all the options. These tables appear together starting at page 145.

A regular expression is a sequence of the following items:

- A literal character.
- A matching character, character set, or character class.
- A repetition quantifier.
- An alternation clause.
- A subpattern grouped with parentheses.

Matching Characters

Most characters simply match themselves. The following pattern matches an a followed by a b:

    ab

The general wild-card character is the period, "`.`". It matches any single character. The following pattern matches an a followed by any character:

    a.

Remember that matches can occur anywhere within a string; a pattern does not have to match the whole string. You can change that by using anchors, which are described on page 137.

Character Sets

The matching character can be restricted to a set of characters with the [xyz] syntax. Any of the characters between the two brackets is allowed to match. For example, the following matches either Hello or hello:

    [Hh]ello

The matching set can be specified as a range over the character set with the [x-y] syntax. The following matches any digit:

    [0-9]

There is also the ability to specify the complement of a set. That is, the matching character can be anything except what is in the set. This is achieved with the [^xyz] syntax. Ranges and complements can be combined. The following matches anything except the uppercase and lowercase letters:

    [^a-zA-Z]

Using special characters in character sets.

If you want a] in your character set, put it immediately after the initial opening bracket. You do not need to do anything special to include `[` in your character set. The following matches any square brackets or curly braces:

    []{}

Most regular expression syntax characters are no longer special inside character sets. This means you do not need to backslash anything inside a bracketed character set except for backslash itself. The following pattern matches several of the syntax characters used in regular expressions:

    [][+*?()|\\]

Advanced regular expressions add names and backslash escapes as shorthand for common sets of characters like white space, alpha, alphanumeric, and more. These are described on page 139 and listed in Table 11–3 on page 146.

Quantifiers

Repetition is specified with `*`, for zero or more, `+`, for one or more, and `?`, for zero or one. These *quantifiers* apply to the previous item, which is either a matching character, a character set, or a subpattern grouped with parentheses. The following matches a string that contains `b` followed by zero or more `a`'s:

    ba*

You can group part of the pattern with parentheses and then apply a quantifier to that part of the pattern. The following matches a string that has one or more sequences of `ab`:

    (ab)+

The pattern that matches anything, even the empty string, is:

    .*

These quantifiers have a *greedy* matching behavior: They match as many characters as possible. Advanced regular expressions add nongreedy matching, which is described on page 140. For example, a pattern to match a single line might look like this:

    .*\n

However, as a greedy match, this will match all the lines in the input, ending with the last newline in the input string. The following pattern matches up through the first newline.

    [^\n]*\n

We will shorten this pattern even further on page 140 by using nongreedy quantifiers. There are also special newline sensitive modes you can turn on with some options described on page 143.

Alternation

Alternation lets you test more than one pattern at the same time. The matching engine is designed to be able to test multiple patterns in parallel, so alternation is efficient. Alternation is specified with `|`, the pipe symbol. Another way to match either `Hello` or `hello` is:

```
hello|Hello
```

You can also write this pattern as:

```
(h|H)ello
```

or as:

```
[hH]ello
```

Anchoring a Match

By default a pattern does not have to match the whole string. There can be unmatched characters before and after the match. You can anchor the match to the beginning of the string by starting the pattern with ^, or to the end of the string by ending the pattern with $. You can force the pattern to match the whole string by using both. All strings that begin with spaces or tabs are matched with:

```
^[ \t]+
```

If you have many text lines in your input, you may be tempted to think of ^ as meaning "beginning of line" instead of "beginning of string." By default, the ^ and $ anchors are relative to the whole input, and embedded newlines are ignored. Advanced regular expressions support options that make the ^ and $ anchors line-oriented. They also add the \A and \Z anchors that always match the beginning and end of the string, respectively.

Backslash Quoting

Use the backslash character to turn off these special characters :

```
. * ? + [ ] ( ) ^ $ | \
```

For example, to match the plus character, you will need:

```
\+
```

Remember that this quoting is not necessary inside a bracketed expression (i.e., a character set definition.) For example, to match either plus or question mark, either of these patterns will work:

```
(\+|\?)
```

```
[+?]
```

To match a single backslash, you need two. You must do this everywhere, even inside a bracketed expression. Or you can use \B, which was added as part of advanced regular expressions. Both of these match a single backslash:

```
\\
```

```
\B
```

Unknown backslash sequences are an error.

Versions of Tcl before 8.1 ignored unknown backslash sequences in regular expressions. For example, \= was just =, and \w was just w. Even \n was just n, which was probably frustrating to many beginners trying to get a newline into their pattern. Advanced regular expressions add backslash sequences for tab, newline, character classes, and more. This is a convenient improvement, but in rare cases it may change the semantics of a pattern. Usually these cases are where an unneeded backslash suddenly takes on meaning, or causes an error because it is unknown.

Matching Precedence

If a pattern can match several parts of a string, the matcher takes the match that occurs earliest in the input string. Then, if there is more than one match from that same point because of alternation in the pattern, the matcher takes the longest possible match. The rule of thumb is: *first, then longest*. This rule gets changed by nongreedy quantifiers that prefer a shorter match.

Watch out for *, which means zero or more, because zero of anything is pretty easy to match. Suppose your pattern is:

```
[a-z]*
```

This pattern will match against `123abc`, but not how you expect. Instead of matching on the letters in the string, the pattern will match on the zero-length substring at the very beginning of the input string! This behavior can be seen by using the `-indices` option of the `regexp` command described on page 148. This option tells you the location of the matching string instead of the value of the matching string.

Capturing Subpatterns

Use parentheses to capture a subpattern. The string that matches the pattern within parentheses is remembered in a matching variable, which is a Tcl variable that gets assigned the string that matches the pattern. Using parentheses to capture subpatterns is very useful. Suppose we want to get everything between the `<td>` and `</td>` tags in some HTML. You can use this pattern:

```
<td>([^<]*)</td>
```

The matching variable gets assigned the part of the input string that matches the pattern inside the parentheses. You can capture many subpatterns in one match, which makes it a very efficient way to pick apart your data. Matching variables are explained in more detail on page 148 in the context of the `regexp` command.

Sometimes you need to introduce parentheses but you do not care about the match that occurs inside them. The pattern is slightly more efficient if the matcher does not need to remember the match. Advanced regular expressions add noncapturing parentheses with this syntax:

```
(?:pattern)
```

Advanced Regular Expressions

The syntax added by advanced regular expressions is mostly just shorthand notation for constructs you can make with the basic syntax already described. There are also some new features that add additional power: nongreedy quantifiers, back references, look-ahead patterns, and named character classes. If you are just starting out with regular expressions, you can ignore most of this section, except for the one about backslash sequences. Once you master the basics, of if you are already familiar with regular expressions in Tcl (or the UNIX *vi* editor or *grep* utility), then you may be interested in the new features of advanced regular expressions.

Compatibility with Patterns in Tcl 8.0

Advanced regular expressions add syntax in an upward compatible way. Old patterns continue to work with the new matcher, but advanced regular expressions will raise errors if given to old versions of Tcl. For example, the question mark is used in many of the new constructs, and it is artfully placed in locations that would not be legal in older versions of regular expressions. The added syntax is summarized in Table 11–2 on page 145.

If you have unbraced patterns from older code, they are very likely to be correct in Tcl 8.1 and later versions. For example, the following pattern picks out everything up to the next newline. The pattern is unbraced, so Tcl substitutes the newline character for each occurrence of \n. The square brackets are quoted so that Tcl does not think they delimit a nested command:

```
regexp "(\[^\n\]+)\n" $input
```

The above command behaves identically when using advanced regular expressions, although you can now also write it like this:

```
regexp {([^\n]+)\n} $input
```

The curly braces hide the brackets from the Tcl parser, so they do not need to be escaped with backslash. This saves us two characters and looks a bit cleaner.

Backslash Escape Sequences

The most significant change in advanced regular expression syntax is backslash substitutions. In Tcl 8.0 and earlier, a backslash is only used to turn off special characters such as: . + * ? [ ] . Otherwise it was ignored. For example, \n was simply n to the Tcl 8.0 regular expression engine. This was a source of confusion, and it meant you could not always quote patterns in braces to hide their special characters from Tcl's parser. In advanced regular expressions, \n now means the newline character to the regular expression engine, so you should never need to let Tcl do backslash processing.

Again, *always group your pattern with curly braces* to avoid confusion.

Advanced regular expressions add a lot of new backslash sequences. They are listed in Table 11–4 on page 146. Some of the more useful ones include \s, which matches space-like characters, \w, which matches letters, digit, and the underscore, \y, which matches the beginning or end of a word, and \B, which matches a backslash.

Character Classes

Character classes are names for sets of characters. The named character class syntax is valid only inside a bracketed character set. The syntax is

```
[:identifier:]
```

For example, `alpha` is the name for the set of uppercase and lowercase letters. The following two patterns are *almost* the same:

```
[A-Za-z]
[[:alpha:]]
```

The difference is that the alpha character class also includes accented characters like è. If you match data that contains nonASCII characters, the named character classes are more general than trying to name the characters explicitly.

There are also backslash sequences that are shorthand for some of the named character classes. The following patterns to match digits are equivalent:

```
[0-9]
[[:digit:]]
\d
```

The following patterns match space-like characters including backspace, form feed, newline, carriage return, tag, and vertical tab:

```
[ \b\f\n\r\t\v]
[:space:]
\s
```

The named character classes and the associated backslash sequence are listed in Table 11–3 on page 146.

You can use character classes in combination with other characters or character classes inside a character set definition. The following patterns match letters, digits, and underscore:

```
[[:digit:][:alpha:]_]
[\d[:alpha:]_]
[[:alnum:]_]
\w
```

Note that `\d`, `\s` and `\w` can be used either inside or outside character sets. When used outside a bracketed expression, they form their own character set. There are also `\D`, `\S`, and `\W`, which are the complement of `\d`, `\s`, and `\w`. These escapes (i.e., `\D` for not-a-digit) cannot be used inside a bracketed character set.

There are two special character classes, `[[:<:]]` and `[[:>:]]`, that match the beginning and end of a word, respectively. A word is defined as one or more characters that match `\w`.

Nongreedy Quantifiers

The *, +, and ? characters are *quantifiers* that specify repetition. By default these match as many characters as possible, which is called *greedy* matching. A *nongreedy* match will match as few characters as possible. You can specify nongreedy matching by putting a question mark after these quantifiers. Consider the pattern to match "one or more of not-a-newline followed by a newline." The not-a-newline must be explicit with the greedy quantifier, as in:

```
[^\n]+\n
```

Otherwise, if the pattern were just

```
.+\n
```

then the "." could well match newlines, so the pattern would greedily consume everything until the very last newline in the input. A nongreedy match would be satisfied with the very first newline instead:

```
.+?\n
```

By using the nongreedy quantifier we've cut the pattern from eight characters to five. Another example that is shorter with a nongreedy quantifier is the HTML example from page 138. The following pattern also matches everything between `<td>` and `</td>`:

```
<td>(.*?)</td>
```

Even ? can be made nongreedy, ??, which means it prefers to match zero instead of one. This only makes sense inside the context of a larger pattern. Send me e-mail if you have a compelling example for it!

Bound Quantifiers

The {m,n} syntax is a quantifier that means match at least m and at most n of the previous matching item. There are two variations on this syntax. A simple {m} means match exactly m of the previous matching item. A {m,} means match m or more of the previous matching item. All of these can be made nongreedy by adding a ? after them.

Back References

A back reference is a feature you cannot easily get with basic regular expressions. A back reference matches the value of a subpattern captured with parentheses. If you have several sets of parentheses you can refer back to different captured expressions with \1, \2, and so on. You count by left parentheses to determine the reference.

For example, suppose you want to match a quoted string, where you can use either single or double quotes. You need to use an alternation of two patterns to match strings that are enclosed in double quotes or in single quotes:

```
("[^"]*"|'[^']*')
```

With a back reference, \1, the pattern becomes simpler:

```
('|").*?\1
```

The first set of parenthesis matches the leading quote, and then the \1 refers back to that particular quote character. The nongreedy quantifier ensures that the pattern matches up to the first occurrence of the matching quote.

Look-ahead

Look-ahead patterns are subexpressions that are matched but do not consume any of the input. They act like constraints on the rest of the pattern, and they typically occur at the end of your pattern. A positive look-ahead causes the pattern to match if it also matches. A negative look-ahead causes the pattern to match if it would not match. These constraints make more sense in the context of matching variables and in regular expression substitutions done with the `regsub` command. For example, the following pattern matches a filename that begins with A and ends with `.txt`

```
^A.*\.txt$
```

The next version of the pattern adds parentheses to group the file name suffix.

```
^A.*(\.txt)$
```

The parentheses are not strictly necessary, but they are introduced so that we can compare the pattern to one that uses look-ahead. A version of the pattern that uses look-ahead looks like this:

```
^A.*(?=\.txt)$
```

The pattern with the look-ahead constraint matches only the part of the filename before the `.txt`, but only if the `.txt` is present. In other words, the `.txt` is not consumed by the match. This is visible in the value of the matching variables used with the `regexp` command. It would also affect the substitutions done in the `regsub` command.

There is negative look-ahead too. The following pattern matches a filename that begins with A and does not end with `.txt`.

```
^A.*(?!\.txt)$
```

Writing this pattern without negative look-ahead is awkward.

Character Codes

The $\backslash nn$ and $\backslash mmm$ syntax, where n and m are digits, can also mean an 8-bit character code corresponding to the octal value nn or mmm. This has priority over a back reference. However, I just wouldn't use this notation for character codes. Instead, use the Unicode escape sequence, $\backslash unnnn$, which specifies a 16-bit value. The $\backslash xnn$ sequence also specifies an 8-bit character code. Unfortunately, the $\backslash x$ escape consumes all hex digits after it (not just two!) and then truncates the hexadecimal value down to 8 bits. This misfeature of $\backslash x$ is not considered a bug and will probably not change even in future versions of Tcl.

The $\backslash Uyyyyyyyy$ syntax is reserved for 32-bit Unicode, but I don't expect to see that implemented anytime soon.

Collating Elements

Collating elements are characters or long names for characters that you can use inside character sets. Currently, Tcl only has some long names for various

ASCII punctuation characters. Potentially, it could support names for every Unicode character, but it doesn't because the mapping tables would be huge. This section will briefly mention the syntax so that you can understand it if you see it. But its usefulness is still limited.

Within a bracketed expression, the following syntax is used to specify a collating element:

```
[.identifier.]
```

The identifier can be a character or a long name. The supported long names can be found in the `generic/regc_locale.c` file in the Tcl source code distribution. A few examples are shown below:

```
[.c.]
[.#.]
[.number-sign.]
```

Equivalence Classes

An equivalence class is all characters that sort to the same position. This is another feature that has limited usefulness in the current version of Tcl. In Tcl, characters sort by their Unicode character value, so there are no equivalence classes that contain more than one character! However, you could imagine a character class for 'o', 'ò', and other accented versions of the letter o. The syntax for equivalence classes within bracketed expressions is:

```
[=char=]
```

where `char` is any one of the characters in the character class. This syntax is valid only inside a character class definition.

Newline Sensitive Matching

By default, the newline character is just an ordinary character to the matching engine. You can make the newline character special with two options: `lineanchor` and `linestop`. You can set these options with flags to the `regexp` and `regsub` Tcl commands, or you can use the embedded options described later in Table 11–5 on page 147.

The `lineanchor` option makes the ^ and $ anchors work relative to newlines. The ^ matches immediately after a newline, and $ matches immediately before a newline. These anchors continue to match the very beginning and end of the input, too. With or without the `lineanchor` option, you can use \A and \z to match the beginning and end of the string.

The `linestop` option prevents . (i.e., period) and character sets that begin with ^ from matching a newline character. In other words, unless you explicitly include \n in your pattern, it will not match across newlines.

Embedded Options

You can start a pattern with embedded options to turn on or off case sensitivity, newline sensitivity, and expanded syntax, which is explained in the next section. You can also switch from advanced regular expressions to a literal string, or to older forms of regular expressions. The syntax is a leading:

```
(?chars)
```

where *chars* is any number of option characters. The option characters are listed in Table 11–5 on page 147.

Expanded Syntax

Expanded syntax lets you include comments and extra white space in your patterns. This can greatly improve the readability of complex patterns. Expanded syntax is turned on with a `regexp` command option or an embedded option.

Comments start with a # and run until the end of line. Extra white space and comments can occur anywhere except inside bracketed expressions (i.e., character sets) or within multicharacter syntax elements like `(?=`. When you are in expanded mode, you can turn off the comment character or include an explicit space by preceding them with a backslash. Example 11–1 shows a pattern to match URLs. The leading `(?x)` turns on expanded syntax. The whole pattern is grouped in curly braces to hide it from Tcl. This example is considered again in more detail in Example 11–3 on page 150:

Example 11–1 Expanded regular expressions allow comments.

```
regexp {(?x)         # A pattern to match URLS
       ([^:]+):      # The protocol before the initial colon
       //([^:/]+)    # The server name
       (:([0-9]+))?  # The optional port number
       (/.*)         # The trailing pathname
} $input
```

Syntax Summary

Table 11–1 summarizes the syntax of regular expressions available in all versions of Tcl:

Table 11–1 Basic regular expression syntax.

.	Matches any character.
*	Matches zero or more instances of the previous pattern item.
+	Matches one or more instances of the previous pattern item.
?	Matches zero or one instances of the previous pattern item.
( )	Groups a subpattern. The repetition and alternation operators apply to the preceding subpattern.
|	Alternation.
[ ]	Delimit a set of characters. Ranges are specified as [x-y]. If the first character in the set is ^, then there is a match if the remaining characters in the set are *not* present.
^	Anchor the pattern to the beginning of the string. Only when first.
$	Anchor the pattern to the end of the string. Only when last.

Advanced regular expressions, which were introduced in Tcl 8.1, add more syntax that is summarized in Table 11–2:

Table 11–2 Additional advanced regular expression syntax.

{m}	Matches *m* instances of the previous pattern item.
{m}?	Matches *m* instances of the previous pattern item. Nongreedy.
{m,}	Matches *m* or more instances of the previous pattern item.
{m,}?	Matches *m* or more instances of the previous pattern item. Nongreedy.
{m,n}	Matches *m* through *n* instances of the previous pattern item.
{m,n}?	Matches *m* through *n* instances of the previous pattern item. Nongreedy.
*?	Matches zero or more instances of the previous pattern item. Nongreedy.
+?	Matches one or more instances of the previous pattern item. Nongreedy.
??	Matches zero or one instances of the previous pattern item. Nongreedy.
(?:re)	Groups a subpattern, re, but does not capture the result.
(?=re)	Positive look-ahead. Matches the point where re begins.
(?!re)	Negative look-ahead. Matches the point where re does not begin.
(?abc)	Embedded options, where abc is any number of option letters listed in Table 11–5.

II. Advanced Tcl

Table 11–2   Additional advanced regular expression syntax. (Continued)

\c	One of many backslash escapes listed in Table 11–4.
[: :]	Delimits a character class within a bracketed expression. See Table 11–3.
[. .]	Delimits a collating element within a bracketed expression.
[= =]	Delimits an equivalence class within a bracketed expression.

Table 11–3 lists the named character classes defined in advanced regular expressions and their associated backslash sequences, if any. Character class names are valid inside bracketed character sets with the [:*class*:] syntax.

Table 11–3   Character classes.

alnum	Upper and lower case letters and digits.
alpha	Upper and lower case letters.
blank	Space and tab.
cntrl	Control characters: \u0001 through \u001F.
digit	The digits zero through nine. Also \d.
graph	Printing characters that are not in cntrl or space.
lower	Lowercase letters.
print	The same as alnum.
punct	Punctuation characters.
space	Space, newline, carriage return, tab, vertical tab, form feed. Also \s.
upper	Uppercase letters.
xdigit	Hexadecimal digits: zero through nine, a-f, A-F.

Table 11–4 lists backslash sequences supported in Tcl 8.1.

Table 11–4   Backslash escapes in regular expressions.

\a	Alert, or "bell", character.
\A	Matches only at the beginning of the string.
\b	Backspace character, \u0008.
\B	Synonym for backslash.
\c*X*	Control-*X*.
\d	Digits. Same as [[:digit:]]
\D	Not a digit. Same as [^[:digit:]]

Table 11–4 Backslash escapes in regular expressions. (Continued)

\e	Escape character, \u001B.
\f	Form feed, \u000C.
\m	Matches the beginning of a word.
\M	Matches the end of a word.
\n	Newline, \u000A.
\r	Carriage return, \u000D.
\s	Space. Same as [[:space:]]
\S	Not a space. Same as [^[:space:]]
\t	Horizontal tab, \u0009.
\u*XXXX*	A 16-bit Unicode character code.
\v	Vertical tab, \u000B.
\w	Letters, digit, and underscore. Same as [[:alnum:]_]
\W	Not a letter, digit, or underscore. Same as [^[:alnum:]_]
\x*hh*	An 8-bit hexadecimal character code. Consumes all hex digits after \x.
\y	Matches the beginning or end of a word.
\Y	Matches a point that is not the beginning or end of a word.
\Z	Matches the end of the string.
\0	NULL, \u0000
x	Where *x* is a digit, this is a back-reference.
xy	Where *x* and *y* are digits, either a decimal back-reference, or an 8-bit octal character code.
xyz	Where *x*, *y* and *z* are digits, either a decimal back-reference or an 8-bit octal character code.

Table 11–5 lists the embedded option characters used with the (?*abc*) syntax.

Table 11–5 Embedded option characters used with the (?*x*) syntax.

b	The rest of the pattern is a basic regular expression (a la *vi* or *grep*).
c	Case sensitive matching. This is the default.
e	The rest of the pattern is an extended regular expression (*a la* Tcl 8.0).
i	Case insensitive matching.
m	Synonym for the n option.

II. Advanced Tcl

Table 11–5 Embedded option characters used with the (?x) syntax. (Continued)

n	Newline sensitive matching . Both `lineanchor` and `linestop` mode.
p	Partial newline sensitive matching. Only `linestop` mode.
q	The rest of the pattern is a literal string.
s	No newline sensitivity. This is the default.
t	Tight syntax; no embedded comments. This is the default.
w	Inverse partial newline-sensitive matching. Only `lineanchor` mode.
x	Expanded syntax with embedded white space and comments.

The `regexp` Command

The `regexp` command provides direct access to the regular expression matcher. Not only does it tell you whether a string matches a pattern, it can also extract one or more matching substrings. The return value is 1 if some part of the string matches the pattern; it is 0 otherwise. Its syntax is:

```
regexp ?flags? pattern string ?match sub1 sub2...?
```

The *flags* are described in Table 11–6:

Table 11–6 Options to the regexp command.

-nocase	Lowercase characters in *pattern* can match either lowercase or uppercase letters in *string*.
-indices	The match variables each contain a pair of numbers that are in indices delimiting the match within *string*. Otherwise, the matching string itself is copied into the match variables.
-expanded	The pattern uses the expanded syntax discussed on page 144.
-line	The same as specifying both -lineanchor and -linestop.
-lineanchor	Change the behavior of ^ and $ so they are line-oriented as discussed on page 143.
-linestop	Change matching so that . and character classes do not match newlines as discussed on page 143.
-about	Useful for debugging. It returns information about the pattern instead of trying to match it against the input.
--	Signals the end of the options. You must use this if your pattern begins with -.

The *pattern* argument is a regular expression as described earlier. If *string* matches *pattern*, then the results of the match are stored in the variables named in the command. These match variable arguments are optional. If present, *match* is set to be the part of the string that matched the pattern. The remaining variables are set to be the substrings of *string* that matched the corresponding subpatterns in *pattern*. The correspondence is based on the order of left parentheses in the pattern to avoid ambiguities that can arise from nested subpatterns.

Example 11–2 uses regexp to pick the hostname out of the DISPLAY environment variable, which has the form:

> *hostname:display.screen*

Example 11–2 Using regular expressions to parse a string.

```
set env(DISPLAY) sage:0.1
regexp {(([^:]*):} $env(DISPLAY) match host
=> 1
set match
=> sage:
set host
=> sage
```

The pattern involves a complementary set, [^:], to match anything except a colon. It uses repetition, *, to repeat that zero or more times. It groups that part into a subexpression with parentheses. The literal colon ensures that the DISPLAY value matches the format we expect. The part of the string that matches the complete pattern is stored into the match variable. The part that matches the subpattern is stored into host. The whole pattern has been grouped with braces to quote the square brackets. Without braces it would be:

> regexp (\[^:\]*): $env(DISPLAY) match host

With advanced regular expressions the nongreedy quantifier *? can replace the complementary set:

> regexp (.*?): $env(DISPLAY) match host

This is quite a powerful statement, and it is efficient. If we had only had the string command to work with, we would have needed to resort to the following, which takes roughly twice as long to interpret:

```
set i [string first : $env(DISPLAY)]
if {$i >= 0} {
    set host [string range $env(DISPLAY) 0 [expr $i-1]]
}
```

A Pattern to Match URLs

Example 11–3 demonstrates a pattern with several subpatterns that extract the different parts of a URL. There are lots of subpatterns, and you can determine which match variable is associated with which subpattern by counting the left parenthesis. The pattern will be discussed in more detail after the example:

Example 11–3 A pattern to match URLs.

```
set url http://www.beedub.com:80/index.html
regexp {(([^:]+)://([^:/]+)(:([0-9]+))?(/.*)} $url \
    match protocol x serverport path
=> 1
set match
=> http://www.beedub.com:80/index.html
set protocol
=> http
set server
=> www.beedub.com
set x
=> :80
set port
=> 80
set path
=> /index.html
```

Let's look at the pattern one piece at a time. The first part looks for the protocol, which is separated by a colon from the rest of the URL. The first part of the
pattern is one or more characters that are not a colon, followed by a colon. This
matches the `http:` part of the URL:

    `[^:]+:`

Using nongreedy `+?` quantifier, you could also write that as:

    `.+?:`

The next part of the pattern looks for the server name, which comes after
two slashes. The server name is followed either by a colon and a port number, or
by a slash. The pattern uses a complementary set that specifies one or more
characters that are *not* a colon or a slash. This matches the `//www.beedub.com`
part of the URL:

    `//[^:/]+`

The port number is optional, so a subpattern is delimited with parentheses
and followed by a question mark. An additional set of parentheses are added to
capture the port number without the leading colon. This matches the `:80` part of
the URL:

    `(:([0-9]+))?`

The last part of the pattern is everything else, starting with a slash. This
matches the `/index.html` part of the URL:

    `/.*`

Use subpatterns to parse strings.

To make this pattern really useful, we delimit several subpatterns with
parentheses:

    `([^:]+)://([^:/]+)(:([0-9]+))?(/.*)`

These parentheses do not change the way the pattern matches. Only the
optional port number really needs the parentheses in this example. However, the
`regexp` command gives us access to the strings that match these subpatterns. In

one step `regexp` can test for a valid URL and divide it into the protocol part, the server, the port, and the trailing path.

The parentheses around the port number include the : before the digits. We've used a dummy variable that gets the : and the port number, and another match variable that just gets the port number. By using noncapturing parentheses in advanced regular expressions, we can eliminate the unused match variable. We can also replace both complementary character sets with a nongreedy `.+?` match. Example 11–4 shows this variation:

Example 11–4 An advanced regular expression to match URLs.

```
set url http://www.beedub.com:80/book/
regexp {(.+?)://(.+?)(?::([0-9]+))?(/.*)} $url \
    match protocol server port path
=> 1
set match
=> http://www.beedub.com:80/book/
set protocol
=> http
set server
=> www.beedub.com
set port
=> 80
set path
=> /book/
```

Sample Regular Expressions

The table in this section lists regular expressions as you would use them in Tcl commands. Most are quoted with curly braces to turn off the special meaning of square brackets and dollar signs. Other patterns are grouped with double quotes and use backslash quoting because the patterns include backslash sequences like `\n` and `\t`. In Tcl 8.0 and earlier, these must be substituted by Tcl before the `regexp` command is called. In these cases, the equivalent advanced regular expression is also shown.

Table 11–7 Sample regular expressions.

`{^[yY]}`	Begins with y or Y, as in a Yes answer.
`{^(yes|YES|Yes)$}`	Exactly "yes", "Yes", or "YES".
`"^\[^ \t:\]+:"`	Begins with colon-delimited field that has no spaces or tabs.
`{^\S+:}`	Same as above, using `\S` for "not space".
`"^\[ \t]*$"`	A string of all spaces or tabs.
`{(?n)^\s*$}`	A blank line using newline sensitive mode.

Table 11-7 Sample regular expressions. (Continued)

`"(\n|^)\[^\n\]*(\n|$)"`	A blank line, the hard way.
`{^[A-Za-z]+$}`	Only letters.
`{^[[:alpha:]]+$}`	Only letters, the Unicode way.
`{[A-Za-z0-9_]+}`	Letters, digits, and the underscore.
`{\w+}`	Letters, digits, and the underscore using `\w`.
`{[][${}\\]}`	The set of Tcl special characters:] [$ { } \
`"\[^\n\]*\n"`	Everything up to a newline.
`{.*?\n}`	Everything up to a newline using nongreedy `*?`
`{\.}`	A period.
`{[][$^?+*()|\\]}`	The set of regular expression special characters:] [$ ^ ? + * ( ) | \
`<H1>(.*?)</H1>`	An `H1` HTML tag. The subpattern matches the string between the tags.
`<!--.*?-->`	HTML comments.
`{[0-9a-hA-H][0-9a-hA-H]}`	2 hex digits.
`{[[:xdigit:]]{2}}`	2 hex digits, using advanced regular expressions.
`{\d{1,3}}`	1 to 3 digits, using advanced regular expressions.

The `regsub` Command

The `regsub` command does string substitution based on pattern matching. It is very useful for processing your data. It can perform simple tasks like replacing sequences of spaces and tabs with a single space. It can perform complex data transforms, too, as described in the next section. Its syntax is:

```
regsub ?switches? pattern string subspec varname
```

The `regsub` command returns the number of matches and replacements, or 0 if there was no match. `regsub` copies *string* to *varname*, replacing occurrences of *pattern* with the substitution specified by *subspec*. If the pattern does not match, then *string* is copied to *varname* without modification. The optional switches include:

- `-all`, which means to replace all occurrences of the pattern. Otherwise, only the first occurrence is replaced.
- The `-nocase`, `-expanded`, `-line`, `-linestop`, and `-lineanchor` switches are the same as in the `regexp` command. They are described on page 148.
- The `--` switch separates the pattern from the switches, which is necessary if your pattern begins with a `-`.

The replacement pattern, *subspec*, can contain literal characters as well as the following special sequences:

- & is replaced with the string that matched the pattern.
- \ *x* , where *x* is a number, is replaced with the string that matched the corresponding subpattern in *pattern*. The correspondence is based on the order of left parentheses in the pattern specification.

II. Advanced Tcl

The following replaces a user's home directory with a ~:

```
regsub ^$env(HOME)/ $pathname ~/ newpath
```

The following constructs a C compile command line given a filename:

```
set file tclIO.c
regsub {(([^\.]*)\.c$} $file {cc -c & -o \1.o} ccCmd
```

The matching pattern captures everything before the trailing `.c` in the file name. The & is replaced with the complete match, `tclIO.c`, and `\1` is replaced with `tclIO`, which matches the pattern between the parentheses. The value assigned to `ccCmd` is:

```
cc -c tclIO.c -o tclIO.o
```

We could execute that with:

```
eval exec $ccCmd
```

The following replaces sequences of multiple space characters with a single space:

```
regsub -all {\s+} $string " " string
```

It is perfectly safe to specify the same variable as the input value and the result. Even if there is no match on the pattern, the input string is copied into the output variable.

The `regsub` command can count things for us. The following command counts the newlines in some text. In this case the substitution is not important:

```
set numLines [regsub -all \n $text {} ignore]
```

Transforming Data to Program with `regsub`

One of the most powerful combinations of Tcl commands is `regsub` and `subst`. This section describes a few examples that use `regsub` to transform data into Tcl commands, and then use `subst` to replace those commands with a new version of the data. This technique is very efficient because it relies on two subsystems that are written in highly optimized C code: the regular expression engine and the Tcl parser. These examples are primarily written by Stephen Uhler.

URL Decoding

When a URL is transmitted over the network, it is encoded by replacing special characters with a %*xx* sequence, where *xx* is the hexadecimal code for the character. In addition, spaces are replaced with a plus (+). It would be tedious and very inefficient to scan a URL one character at a time with Tcl statements to undo this encoding. It would be more efficient to do this with a custom C program, but still very tedious. Instead, a combination of `regsub` and `subst` can efficiently decode the URL in just a few Tcl commands.

Replacing the + with spaces requires quoting the + because it is the one-or-more special character in regular expressions:

```
regsub -all {\+} $url { } url
```

The %*xx* are replaced with a `format` command that will generate the right character:

```
regsub -all {%([0-9a-hA-H][0-9a-hA-H])} $url \
    {[format %c 0x\1]} url
```

The `%c` directive to `format` tells it to generate the character from a character code number. We force a hexadecimal interpretation with a leading `0x`. Advanced regular expressions let us write the "2 hex digits" pattern a bit more cleanly:

```
regsub -all {%([[:xdigit:]]{2})} $url \
    {[format %c 0x\1]} url
```

The resulting string is passed to `subst` to get the `format` commands substituted:

```
set url [subst $url]
```

For example, if the input is %7ewelch, the result of the `regsub` is:

```
[format %c 0x7e]welch
```

And then `subst` generates:

```
~welch
```

Example 11–5 encapsulates this trick in the `Url_Decode` procedure.

Example 11–5 The `Url_Decode` procedure.

```
proc Url_Decode {url} {
    regsub -all {\+} $url { } url
    regsub -all {%([[:xdigit:]]{2})} $url \
        {[format %c 0x\1]} url
    return [subst $url]
}
```

CGI Argument Parsing

Example 11–6 builds upon `Url_Decode` to decode the inputs to a CGI program that processes data from an HTML form. Each form element is identified by a name, and the value is URL encoded. All the names and encoded values are passed to the CGI program in the following format:

```
name1=value1&name2=value2&name3=value3
```

Example 11–6 shows `Cgi_List` and `Cgi_Query`. `Cgi_Query` receives the form data from the standard input or the `QUERY_STRING` environment variable, depending on whether the form data is transmitted with a POST or GET request. These HTTP operations are described in detail in Chapter 17. `Cgi_List` uses `split` to get back a list of names and values, and then it decodes them with `Url_Decode`. It returns a Tcl-friendly name, value list that you can either iterate through with a `foreach` command, or assign to an array with `array set`:

Example 11–6 The `Cgi_Parse` and `Cgi_Value` procedures.

```
proc Cgi_List {} {
    set query [Cgi_Query]
    regsub -all {\+} $query { } query
    set result {}
    foreach {x} [split $query &=] {
        lappend result [Url_Decode $x]
    }
    return $result
}
proc Cgi_Query {} {
    global env
    if {![info exists env(QUERY_STRING)] ||
            [string length $env(QUERY_STRING)] == 0} {
        if {[info exists env(CONTENT_LENGTH)] &&
                [string length $env(CONTENT_LENGTH)] != 0} {
            set query [read stdin $env(CONTENT_LENGTH)]
        } else {
            gets stdin query
        }
        set env(QUERY_STRING) $query
        set env(CONTENT_LENGTH) 0
    }
    return $env(QUERY_STRING)
}
```

An HTML form can have several form elements with the same name, and this can result in more than one value for each name. If you blindly use `array set` to map the results of `Cgi_List` into an array, you will lose the repeated values. Example 11–7 shows `Cgi_Parse` and `Cgi_Value` that store the query data in a global `cgi` array. `Cgi_Parse` adds list structure whenever it finds a repeated form value. The global `cgilist` array keeps a record of how many times a form value is repeated. The `Cgi_Value` procedure returns elements of the global `cgi` array, or the empty string if the requested value is not present.

Example 11–7 `Cgi_Parse` and `Cgi_Value` store query data in the `cgi` array.

```
proc Cgi_Parse {} {
    global cgi cgilist
    catch {unset cgi cgilist}
    set query [Cgi_Query]
    regsub -all {\+} $query { } query
    foreach {name value} [split $query &=] {
        set name [CgiDecode $name]
```

```
        if {[info exists cgilist($name)] &&
               ($cgilist($name) == 1)} {
           # Add second value and create list structure
           set cgi($name) [list $cgi($name) \
               [Url_Decode $value]]
        } elseif {[info exists cgi($name)]} {
           # Add additional list elements
           lappend cgi($name) [CgiDecode $value]
        } else {
           # Add first value without list structure
           set cgi($name) [CgiDecode $value]
           set cgilist($name) 0    ;# May need to listify
        }
        incr cgilist($name)
    }
    return [array names cgi]
}
proc Cgi_Value {key} {
    global cgi
    if {[info exists cgi($key)]} {
        return $cgi($key)
    } else {
        return {}
    }
}
proc Cgi_Length {key} {
    global cgilist
    if {[info exist cgilist($key)]} {
        return $cgilist($key)
    } else {
        return 0
    }
}
```

Decoding HTML Entities

The next example is a decoder for HTML *entities*. In HTML, special characters are encoded as entities. If you want a literal < or > in your document, you
encode them as the entities < and >, respectively, to avoid conflict with the
<tag> syntax used in HTML. HTML syntax is briefly described in Chapter 3 on
page 32. Characters with codes above 127 such as copyright © and egrave è are
also encoded. There are named entities, such as < for < and è for è.
You can also use decimal-valued entities such as © for ©. Finally, the trailing semicolon is optional, so &lt or < can both be used to encode <.

The entity decoder is similar to Url_Decode. In this case, however, we need
to be more careful with subst. The text passed to the decoder could contain special characters like a square bracket or dollar sign. With Url_Decode we can rely
on those special characters being encoded as, for example, %24. Entity encoding is
different (do not ask me why URLs and HTML have different encoding standards), and dollar signs and square brackets are not necessarily encoded. This

requires an additional pass to quote these characters. This `regsub` puts a back-slash in front of all the brackets, dollar signs, and backslashes.

```
regsub -all {[][$\\]} $text {\\&} new
```

The decimal encoding (e.g., `&#169;`) is also more awkward than the hexa-decimal encoding used in URLs. We cannot force a decimal interpretation of a number in Tcl. In particular, if the entity has a leading zero (e.g., `&#010;`) then Tcl interprets the value (e.g., `010`) as octal. The `scan` command is used to do a decimal interpretation. It scans into a temporary variable, and `set` is used to get that value:

```
regsub -all {&#([0-9][0-9]?[0-9]?);?}  $new \
    {[format %c [scan \1 %d tmp; set tmp]]} new
```

With advanced regular expressions, this could be written as follows using bound quantifiers to specify one to three digits:

```
regsub -all {&#(\d{1,3});?}  $new \
    {[format %c [scan \1 %d tmp;set tmp]]} new
```

The named entities are converted with an array that maps from the entity names to the special character. The only detail is that unknown entity names (e.g., `&foobar;`) are not converted. This mapping is done inside `HtmlMapEntity`, which guards against invalid entities.

```
regsub -all {&([a-zA-Z]+)(;?)} $new \
    {[HtmlMapEntity \1 \\\2 ]} new
```

If the input text contained:

```
[x &lt; y]
```

then the `regsub` would transform this into:

```
\[x [HtmlMapEntity lt \; ] y\]
```

Finally, `subst` will result in:

```
[x < y]
```

Example 11–8 `Html_DecodeEntity`.

```
proc Html_DecodeEntity {text} {
    if {![regexp & $text]} {return $text}
    regsub -all {[][$\\]} $text {\\&} new
    regsub -all {&#([0-9][0-9]?[0-9]?);?}  $new {\
        [format %c [scan \1 %d tmp;set tmp]]} new
    regsub -all {&([a-zA-Z]+)(;?)} $new \
        {[HtmlMapEntity \1 \\\2 ]} new
    return [subst $new]
}
proc HtmlMapEntity {text {semi {}}} {
    global htmlEntityMap
    if {[info exist htmlEntityMap($text)]} {
        return $htmlEntityMap($text)
    } else {
        return $text$semi
    }
}
```

```
# Some of the htmlEntityMap
array set htmlEntityMap {
    lt <   gt >   amp &
    aring \xe5  atilde \xe3
    copy  \xa9  ecirc  \xea   egrave \xe8
}
```

A Simple HTML Parser

The following example is the brainchild of Stephen Uhler. It uses `regsub` to transform HTML into a Tcl script. When it is evaluated the script calls a procedure to handle each tag in an HTML document. This provides a general framework for processing HTML. Different callback procedures can be applied to the tags to achieve different effects. For example, the `html_library-0.3` package on the CD-ROM uses `Html_Parse` to display HTML in a Tk text widget.

Example 11–9 `Html_Parse`.

```
proc Html_Parse {html cmd {start {}}} {

    # Map braces and backslashes into HTML entities
    regsub -all \{ $html {\&ob;} html
    regsub -all \} $html {\&cb;} html
    regsub -all {\\} $html {\&bsl;} html

    # This pattern matches the parts of an HTML tag
    set s" \t\r\n"    ;# white space
    set exp <(/?)(\[^$s>]+)\[$s]*(\[^>]*)>

    # This generates a call to cmd with HTML tag parts
    # \1 is the leading /, if any
    # \2 is the HTML tag name
    # \3 is the parameters to the tag, if any
    # The curly braces at either end group of all the text
    # after the HTML tag, which becomes the last arg to $cmd.
    set sub "\}\n$cmd {\\2} {\\1} {\\3} \{"
    regsub -all $exp $html $sub html

    # This balances the curly braces,
    # and calls $cmd with $start as a pseudo-tag
    # at the beginning and end of the script.
    eval "$cmd {$start} {} {} {$html}"
    eval "$cmd {$start} / {} {}"
}
```

The main `regsub` pattern can be written more simply with advanced regular expressions:

```
    set exp {<(/?)(\S+?)\s*(.*?)>}
```

An example will help visualize the transformation. Given this HTML:

```
<Title>My Home Page</Title>
<Body bgcolor=white text=black>
<H1>My Home</H1>
This is my <b>home</b> page.
```

and a call to `Html_Parse` that looks like this:

```
Html_Parse $html {Render .text} hmstart
```

then the generated program is this:

```
Render .text {hmstart} {} {} {}
Render .text {Title} {} {} {My Home Page}
Render .text {Title} {/} {} {
}
Render .text {Body} {} {bgcolor=white text=black} {
}
Render .text {H1} {} {} {My Home}
Render .text {H1} {/} {} {
This is my }
Render .text {b} {} {} {home}
Render .text {b} {/} {} { page.
}
Render .text {hmstart} / {} {}
```

One overall point to make about this example is the difference between using `eval` and `subst` with the generated script. The decoders shown in Examples 11–5 and 11–8 use `subst` to selectively replace encoded characters while ignoring the rest of the text. In `Html_Parse` we must process all the text. The main trick is to replace the matching text (e.g., the HTML tag) with some Tcl code that ends in an open curly brace and starts with a close curly brace. This effectively groups all the unmatched text.

When `eval` is used this way you must do something with any braces and backslashes in the unmatched text. Otherwise, the resulting script does not parse correctly. In this case, these special characters are encoded as HTML entities. We can afford to do this because the `cmd` that is called must deal with encoded entities already. It is not possible to quote these special characters with backslashes because all this text is inside curly braces, so no backslash substitution is performed. If you try that the backslashes will be seen by the `cmd` callback.

Finally, I must admit that I am always surprised that this works:

```
eval "$cmd {$start} {} {} {$html}"
```

I always forget that `$start` and `$html` are substituted in spite of the braces. This is because double quotes are being used to group the argument, so the quoting effect of braces is turned off. Try this:

```
set x hmstart
set y "foo {$x} bar"
=> foo {hmstart} bar
```

Stripping HTML Comments

The `Html_Parse` procedure does not correctly handle HTML comments. The problem is that the syntax for HTML commands allows tags inside comments, so there can be > characters inside the comment. HTML comments are also used to hide Javascript inside pages, which can also contain >. We can fix this with a pass that eliminates the comments.

The comment syntax is this:

```
<!-- HTML comment, could contain <markup> -->
```

Using nongreedy quantifiers, we can strip comments with a single `regsub`:

```
regsub -all <!--.*?--> $html {} html
```

Using only greedy quantifiers, it is awkward to match the closing `-->` without getting stuck on embedded > characters, or without matching too much and going all the way to the end of the last comment. Time for another trick:

```
regsub -all --> $html \x81 html
```

This replaces all the end comment sequences with a single character that is not allowed in HTML. Now you can delete the comments like this:

```
regsub -all "<!--\[^\x81\]*\x81" $html {} html
```

Other Commands That Use Regular Expressions

Several Tcl commands use regular expressions.

- `lsearch` takes a `-regexp` flag so that you can search for list items that match a regular expression. The `lsearch` command is described on page 64.
- `switch` takes a `-regexp` flag, so you can branch based on a regular expression match instead of an exact match or a `string match` style match. The `switch` command is described on page 71.
- The Tk text widget can search its contents based on a regular expression match. Searching in the text widget is described on page 461.
- The *Expect* Tcl extension can match the output of a program with regular expressions. *Expect* is the subject of its own book, *Exploring Expect* (O'Reilly, 1995) by Don Libes.

Script Libraries and Packages

Collections of Tcl commands are kept in libraries and organized into packages.
Tcl automatically loads libraries as an application uses their commands.
Tcl commands discussed are: `package`, `pkg_mkIndex`,
`auto_mkindex`, `unknown`, and `tcl_findLibrary`.

*L*ibraries group useful sets of Tcl proce-
dures so that they can be used by multiple applications. For example, you could
use any of the code examples that come with this book by creating a script
library and then directing your application to check in that library for missing
procedures. One way to structure a large application is to have a short main
script and a library of support scripts. The advantage of this approach is that not
all the Tcl code needs to be loaded to start the application. Applications start up
quickly, and as new features are accessed, the code that implements them is
loaded automatically.

The Tcl package facility supports version numbers and has a *provide/*
require model of use. Typically, each file in a library provides one package with a
particular version number. Packages also work with shared object libraries that
implement Tcl commands in compiled code, which are described in Chapter 44. A
package can be provided by a combination of script files and object files. Applications specify which packages they require and the libraries are loaded automatically. The package facility is an alternative to the auto loading scheme used in
earlier versions of Tcl. You can use either mechanism, and this chapter describes
them both.

If you create a package you may wish to use the namespace facility to avoid
conflicts between procedures and global variables used in different packages.
Namespaces are the topic of Chapter 14. Before Tcl 8.0 you had to use your own
conventions to avoid conflicts. This chapter explains a simple coding convention
for large Tcl programs. I use this convention in *exmh*, a mail user interface that

has grown from about 2,000 to over 35,000 lines of Tcl code. A majority of the code has been contributed by the *exmh* user community. Such growth might not have been possible without coding conventions.

Locating Packages: The `auto_path` Variable

The package facility assumes that Tcl libraries are kept in well-known directories. The list of well-known directories is kept in the `auto_path` Tcl variable. This is initialized by *tclsh* and *wish* to include the Tcl script library directory, the Tk script library directory (for *wish*), and the parent directory of the Tcl script library directory. For example, on my Macintosh `auto_path` is a list of these three directories:

```
Disk:System Folder:Extensions:Tool Command Language:tcl8.2
Disk:System Folder:Extensions:Tool Command Language
Disk:System Folder:Extensions:Tool Command Language:tk8.2
```

On my Windows 95 machine the `auto_path` lists these directories:

```
c:\Program Files\Tcl\lib\Tcl8.2
c:\Program Files\Tcl\lib
c:\Program Files\Tcl\lib\Tk8.2
```

On my UNIX workstation the `auto_path` lists these directories:

```
/usr/local/tcl/lib/tcl8.2
/usr/local/tcl/lib
/usr/local/tcl/lib/tk8.2
```

The package facility searches these directories and their subdirectories for packages. The easiest way to manage your own packages is to create a directory at the same level as the Tcl library:

```
/usr/local/tcl/lib/welchbook
```

Packages in this location, for example, will be found automatically because the `auto_path` list includes `/usr/local/tcl/lib`. You can also add directories to the `auto_path` explicitly:

```
lappend auto_path directory
```

One trick I often use is to put the directory containing the main script into the `auto_path`. The following command sets this up:

```
lappend auto_path [file dirname [info script]]
```

If your code is split into `bin` and `lib` directories, then scripts in the `bin` directory can add the adjacent `lib` directory to their `auto_path` with this command:

```
lappend auto_path \
    [file join [file dirname [info script]] ../lib]
```

Using Packages

Each script file in a library declares what package it implements with the `package provide` command:

```
package provide name version
```

The *name* identifies the package, and the *version* has a *major.minor* format. The convention is that the minor version number can change and the package implementation will still be compatible. If the package changes in an incompatible way, then the major version number should change. For example, Chapter 17 defines several procedures that use the HTTP network protocol. These include `Http_Open`, `Http_Get`, and `Http_Validate`. The file that contains the procedures starts with this command:

```
package provide Http 1.0
```

Case is significant in package names. In particular, the package that comes with Tcl is named `http` — all lowercase.

More than one file can contribute to the same package simply by specifying the same *name* and *version*. In addition, different versions of the same package can be kept in the same directory but in different files.

An application specifies the packages it needs with the `package require` command:

```
package require name ?version? ?-exact?
```

If the *version* is left off, then the highest available version is loaded. Otherwise the highest version with the same major number is loaded. For example, if the client requires version 1.1, version 1.2 could be loaded if it exists, but versions 1.0 and 2.0 would not be loaded. You can restrict the package to a specific version with the `-exact` flag. If no matching version can be found, then the `package require` command raises an error.

Loading Packages Automatically

The `package require` command depends on an index to record which files implement which packages. The index must be maintained by you, your project librarian, or your system administrator when packages change. The index is computed by the `pkg_mkIndex` command that puts the results into the `pkgIndex.tcl` file in each library directory. The `pkg_mkIndex` command takes the name of a directory and one or more *glob* patterns that specify files within that directory. File name patterns are described on page 115. The syntax is:

```
pkg_mkIndex ?options? directory pattern ?pattern ...?
```

For example:

```
pkg_mkIndex /usr/local/lib/welchbook *.tcl
pkg_mkIndex -direct /usr/local/lib/Sybtcl *.so
```

The `pkg_mkIndex` command sources or loads all the files matched by the pattern, detects what packages they provide, and computes the index. You should be aware of this behavior because it works well only for libraries. If the `pkg_mkIndex` command hangs or starts random applications, it is because it sourced an application file instead of a library file.

By default, the index created by `pkg_mkIndex` contains commands that set up the `auto_index` array used to automatically load commands when they are first used. This means that code does not get loaded when your script does a `package require`. If you want the package to be loaded right away, specify the `-direct` flag to `pkg_mkIndex` so that it creates an index file with `source` and `load` commands. The `pkg_mkIndex` options are summarized in Table 12–1.

Table 12–1 Options to the `pkg_mkIndex` command.

`-direct`	Generates an index with `source` and `load` commands in it. This results in packages being loaded directly as a result of `package require`.
`-load` *pattern*	Dynamically loads packages that match *pattern* into the slave interpreter used to compute the index. A common reason to need this is with the `tcbload` package needed to load `.tbc` files compiled with *TclPro Compiler*.
`-verbose`	Displays the name of each file processed and any errors that occur.

Packages Implemented in C Code

The files in a library can be either script files that define Tcl procedures or binary files in shared library format that define Tcl commands in compiled code (i.e., a Dynamic Link Library (DLL)). Chapter 44 describes how to implement Tcl commands in C. There is a C API to the package facility that you use to declare the package name for your commands. This is shown in Example 44–1 on page 608. Chapter 37 also describes the Tcl `load` command that is used instead of `source` to link in shared libraries. The `pkg_mkIndex` command also handles shared libraries:

```
pkg_mkIndex directory *.tcl *.so *.shlib *.dll
```

In this example, `.so`, `.shlib`, and `.dll` are file suffixes for shared libraries on UNIX, Macintosh, and Windows systems, respectively. You can have packages that have some of their commands implemented in C, and some implemented as Tcl procedures. The script files and the shared library must simply declare that they implement the same package. The `pkg_mkIndex` procedure will detect this and set up the `auto_index`, so some commands are defined by sourcing scripts, and some are defined by loading shared libraries.

If your file servers support more than one machine architecture, such as Solaris and Linux systems, you probably keep the shared library files in machine-specific directories. In this case the `auto_path` should also list the machine-specific directory so that the shared libraries there can be loaded automatically. If your system administrator configured the Tcl installation properly, this should already be set up. If not, or you have your shared libraries in a nonstandard place, you must append the location to the `auto_path` variable.

Summary of Package Loading

The basic structure of package loading works like this:

- An application does a `package require` command. If the package is already loaded, the command just returns the version number of the already loaded package. If is not loaded, the following steps occur.
- The package facility checks to see if it knows about the package. If it does, then it runs the Tcl scripts registered with the `package ifneeded` command. These commands either load the package or set it up to be loaded automatically when its commands are first used.
- If the package is unknown, the `tclPkgUnknown` procedure is called to find it. Actually, you can specify what procedure to call to do the lookup with the `package unknown` command, but the standard one is `tclPkgUnknown`.
- The `tclPkgUnknown` procedure looks through the `auto_path` directories and their subdirectories for `pkgIndex.tcl` files. It sources those to build an internal database of packages and version information. The `pkgIndex.tcl` files contain calls to `package ifneeded` that specify what to do to define the package. The standard action is to call the `tclPkgSetup` procedure that sets up the `auto_index` so that the commands in the package will be automatically loaded. If you use `-direct` with `pkg_mkIndex`, the script contains `source` and `load` commands instead.
- The `tclPkgSetup` procedure defines the `auto_index` array to contain the correct `source` or `load` commands to define each command in the package. Automatic loading and the `auto_index` array are described in more detail later.

As you can see, there are several levels of processing involved in finding packages. The system is flexible enough that you can change the way packages are located and how packages are loaded. The default scenario is complicated because it uses the delayed loading of source code that is described in the next section. Using the `-direct` flag to `pkg_mkIndex` simplifies the situation. In any case, it all boils down to three key steps:

- Use `pkg_mkIndex` to maintain your index files. Decide at this time whether or not to use direct package loading.
- Put the appropriate `package require` and `package provide` commands in your code.
- Ensure that your library directories, or their parent directories, are listed in the `auto_path` variable.

The `package` Command

The `package` command has several operations that are used primarily by the `pkg_mkIndex` procedure and the automatic loading facility. These operations are summarized in Table 12–2.

Table 12–2 The `package` command.

`package forget` *package*	Deletes registration information for package.
`package ifneeded` *package* ?*command*?	Queries or sets the command used to set up automatic loading of a package.
`package names`	Returns the set of registered packages.
`package provide` *package* *version*	Declares that a script file defines commands for *package* with the given *version*.
`package require` *package* ?*version*? ?*-exact*?	Declares that a script uses *package*. The `-exact` flag specifies that the exact `version` must be loaded. Otherwise, the highest matching version is loaded.
`package unknown` ?*command*?	Queries or sets the *command* used to locate packages.
`package vcompare` *v1 v2*	Compares version *v1* and *v2*. Returns 0 if they arc equal, -1 if *v1* is less than *v2*, or 1 if *v1* is greater than *v2*.
`package versions` *package*	Returns which versions of the package are registered.
`package vsatisfies` *v1 v2*	Returns 1 if *v1* is greater or equal to *v2* and still has the same major version number. Otherwise returns 0.

Libraries Based on the `tclIndex` File

You can create libraries without using the `package` command. The basic idea is that a directory has a library of script files, and an index of the Tcl commands defined in the library is kept in a `tclIndex` file. The drawback is that versions are not supported and you may need to adjust the `auto_path` to list your library directory. The main advantage of this approach is that this mechanism has been part of Tcl since the earliest versions. If you currently maintain a library using `tclIndex` files, it will still work.

You must generate the index that records what procedures are defined in the library. The `auto_mkindex` procedure creates the index, which is stored in a file named `tclIndex` that is kept in the script library directory. (Watch out for the difference in capitalization between `auto_mkindex` and `pkg_mkIndex`!) Suppose all the examples from this book are in the directory `/usr/local/tcl/welchbook`. You can make the examples into a script library by creating the `tclIndex` file:

```
auto_mkindex /usr/local/tcl/welchbook *.tcl
```

You will need to update the `tclIndex` file if you add procedures or change any of their names. A conservative approach to this is shown in the next example. It is conservative because it re-creates the index if anything in the library has changed since the `tclIndex` file was last generated, whether or not the change added or removed a Tcl procedure.

Example 12–1 Maintaining a `tclIndex` file.

```
proc Library_UpdateIndex { libdir } {
```

```
        set index [file join $libdir tclIndex]
        if {![file exists $index]} {
           set doit 1
        } else {
           set age [file mtime $index]
           set doit 0
           # Changes to directory may mean files were deleted
           if {[file mtime $libdir] > $age} {
              set doit 1
           } else {
              # Check each file for modification
              foreach file [glob [file join $libdir *.tcl]] {
                 if {[file mtime $file] > $age} {
                    set doit 1
                    break
                 }
              }
           }
        }
        if { $doit } {
           auto_mkindex $libdir *.tcl
        }
    }
```

Tcl uses the `auto_path` variable to record a list of directories to search for unknown commands. To continue our example, you can make the procedures in the book examples available by putting this command at the beginning of your scripts:

```
    lappend auto_path /usr/local/tcl/welchbook
```

This has no effect if you have not created the `tclIndex` file. If you want to be extra careful, you can call `Library_UpdateIndex`. This will update the index if you add new things to the library.

```
    lappend auto_path /usr/local/tcl/welchbook
    Library_UpdateIndex /usr/local/tcl/welchbook
```

This will not work if there is no `tclIndex` file at all because Tcl won't be able to find the implementation of `Library_UpdateIndex`. Once the `tclIndex` has been created for the first time, then this will ensure that any new procedures added to the library will be installed into `tclIndex`. In practice, if you want this sort of automatic update, it is wise to include something like the `Library_UpdateIndex` procedure directly into your application as opposed to loading it from the library it is supposed to be maintaining.

The unknown Command

Automatic loading of Tcl commands is implemented by the unknown command. Whenever the Tcl interpreter encounters a command that it does not know about, it calls the unknown command with the name of the missing command. The unknown command is implemented in Tcl, so you are free to provide your own mechanism to handle unknown commands. This chapter describes the behavior of the default implementation of unknown, which can be found in the init.tcl file in the Tcl library. The location of the library is returned by the info library command.

How Auto Loading Works

The unknown command uses an array named auto_index. One element of the array is defined for each procedure that can be automatically loaded. The auto_index array is initialized by the package mechanism or by tclIndex files. The value of an auto_index element is a command that defines the procedure. Typical commands are:

```
source [file join $dir bind_ui.tcl]
load [file join $dir mime.so] Mime
```

The $dir gets substituted with the name of the directory that contains the library file, so the result is a source or load command that defines the missing Tcl command. The substitution is done with eval, so you could initialize auto_index with any commands at all. Example 12–2 is a simplified version of the code that reads the tclIndex file.

Example 12–2 Loading a tclIndex file.

```
# This is a simplified part of the auto_load_index procedure.
# Go through auto_path from back to front.
set i [expr [llength $auto_path]-1]
for {} {$i >= 0} {incr i -1} {
    set dir [lindex $auto_path $i]
    if [catch {open [file join $dir tclIndex]} f] {
        # No index
        continue
    }
    # eval the file as a script. Because eval is
    # used instead of source, an extra round of
    # substitutions is performed and $dir gets expanded
    # The real code checks for errors here.
    eval [read $f]
    close $f
}
```

Disabling the Library Facility: auto_noload

If you do not want the unknown procedure to try and load procedures, you can set the auto_noload variable to disable the mechanism:

```
set auto_noload anything
```

Auto loading is quite fast. I use it regularly on applications both large and small. A large application will start faster if you only need to load the code necessary to start it up. As you access more features of your application, the code will load automatically. Even a small application benefits from auto loading because it encourages you to keep commonly used code in procedure libraries.

Interactive Conveniences

The unknown command provides a few other conveniences. These are used only when you are typing commands directly. They are disabled once execution enters a procedure or if the Tcl shell is not being used interactively. The convenience features are automatic execution of programs, command history, and command abbreviation. These options are tried, in order, if a command implementation cannot be loaded from a script library.

Auto Execute

The unknown procedure implements a second feature: automatic execution of external programs. This makes a Tcl shell behave more like other UNIX shells that are used to execute programs. The search for external programs is done using the standard PATH environment variable that is used by other shells to find programs. If you want to disable the feature all together, set the auto_noexec variable:

```
set auto_noexec anything
```

History

The history facility described in Chapter 13 is implemented by the unknown procedure.

Abbreviations

If you type a unique prefix of a command, unknown recognizes it and executes the matching command for you. This is done after automatic program execution is attempted and history substitutions are performed.

Tcl Shell Library Environment

Tcl searches for its script library directory when it starts up. In early versions of Tcl you had to compile in the correct location, set a Windows registry value, or set the TCL_LIBRARY environment variable to the correct location. Recent versions of Tcl use a standard searching scheme to locate the script library. The search understands the standard installation and build environments for Tcl, and it should eliminate the need to use the TCL_LIBRARY environment variable. On Windows the search for the library used to depend on registry values, but this has also been discontinued in favor of a standard search. In summary, "it should just work." However, this section explains how Tcl finds its script library so that you can troubleshoot problems.

Locating the Tcl Script Library

The default library location is defined when you configure the source distribution, which is explained on page 642. At this time an initial value for the `auto_path` variable is defined. (This default value appears in `tcl_pkgPath`, but changing this variable has no effect once Tcl has started. I just pretend `tcl_pkgPath` does not exist.) These values are just hints; Tcl may use other directories depending on what it finds in the file system.

When Tcl starts up, it searches for a directory that contains its `init.tcl` startup script. You can short-circuit the search by defining the `TCL_LIBRARY` environment variable. If this is defined, Tcl uses it only for its script library directory. However, you should not need to define this with normal installations of Tcl 8.0.5 or later. In my environment I'm often using several different versions of Tcl for various applications and testing purposes, so setting `TCL_LIBRARY` is never correct for all possibilities. If I find myself setting this environment variable, I know something is wrong with my Tcl installations!

The standard search starts with the default value that is compiled into Tcl (e.g., `/usr/local/lib/tcl8.1`.) After that, the following directories are examined for an `init.tcl` file. These example values assume Tcl version 8.1 and patch level 8.1.1:

```
../lib/tcl8.1
../../lib/tcl8.1
../library
../../tcl8.1.1/library
../../../tcl8.1.1/library
```

The first two directories correspond to the standard installation directories, while the last three correspond to the standard build environment for Tcl or Tk. The first directory in the list that contains a valid `init.tcl` file becomes the Tcl script library. This directory location is saved in the `tcl_library` global variable, and it is also returned by the `info library` command.

The primary thing defined by `init.tcl` is the implementation of the unknown procedure. It also initializes `auto_path` to contain `$tcl_library` and the parent directory of `$tcl_library`. There may be additional directories added to `auto_path` depending on the compiled in value of `tcl_pkgPath`.

tcl_findLibrary

A generalization of this search is implemented by `tcl_findLibrary`. This procedure is designed for use by extensions like Tk and [incr Tcl]. Of course, Tcl cannot use `tcl_findLibrary` itself because it is defined in `init.tcl`!

The `tcl_findLibrary` procedure searches relative to the location of the main program (e.g., *tclsh* or *wish)* and assumes a standard installation or a standard build environment. It also supports an override by an environment variable, and it takes care of sourcing an initialization script. The usage of `tcl_findLibrary` is:

```
tcl_findLibrary base version patch script enVar varName
```

The *base* is the prefix of the script library directory name. The *version* is the main version number (e.g., "8.0"). The *patch* is the full patch level (e.g., "8.0.3"). The *script* is the initialization script to source from the directory. The *enVar* names an environment variable that can be used to override the default search path. The *varName* is the name of a variable to set to name of the directory found by `tcl_findLibrary`. A side effect of `tcl_findLibrary` is to source the script from the directory. An example call is:

```
tcl_findLibrary tk 8.0 8.0.3 tk.tcl TK_LIBRARY tk_library
```

This call first checks to see whether `TK_LIBRARY` is defined in the environment. If so, it uses its value. Otherwise, it searches the following directories for a file named `tk.tcl`. It sources the script and sets the `tk_library` variable to the directory containing that file. The search is relative to the value returned by `info nameofexecutable`:

```
../lib/tk8.0
../../lib/tk8.0
../library
../../tk8.0.3/library
../../../tk8.0.3/library
```

Tk also adds `$tk_library` to the end of `auto_path`, so the other script files in that directory are available to the application:

```
lappend auto_path $tk_library
```

Coding Style

If you supply a package, you need to follow some simple coding conventions to make your library easier to use by other programmers. You can use the namespace facility introduced in Tcl 8.0. You can also use conventions to avoid name conflicts with other library packages and the main application. This section describes the conventions I developed before namespaces were added to Tcl.

A Module Prefix for Procedure Names

The first convention is to choose an identifying prefix for the procedures in your package. For example, the preferences package in Chapter 42 uses `Pref` as its prefix. All the procedures provided by the library begin with `Pref`. This convention is extended to distinguish between private and exported procedures. An exported procedure has an underscore after its prefix, and it is acceptable to call this procedure from the main application or other library packages. Examples include `Pref_Add`, `Pref_Init`, and `Pref_Dialog`. A private procedure is meant for use only by the other procedures in the same package. Its name does not have the underscore. Examples include `PrefDialogItem` and `PrefXres`.

This naming convention precludes casual names like doit, setup, layout, and so on. Without using namespaces, there is no way to hide procedure names, so you must maintain the naming convention for all procedures in a package.

A Global Array for State Variables

You should use the same prefix on the global variables used by your package. You can alter the capitalization; just keep the same prefix. I capitalize procedure names and use lowercase letters for variables. By sticking with the same prefix you identify what variables belong to the package and you avoid conflict with other packages.

Collect state in a global array.

In general, I try to use a single global array for a package. The array provides a convenient place to collect a set of related variables, much as a struct is used in C. For example, the preferences package uses the pref array to hold all its state information. It is also a good idea to keep the use of the array private. It is better coding practice to provide exported procedures than to let other modules access your data structures directly. This makes it easier to change the implementation of your package without affecting its clients.

If you do need to export a few key variables from your module, use the underscore convention to distinguish exported variables. If you need more than one global variable, just stick with the prefix convention to avoid conflicts.

The Official Tcl Style Guide

John Ousterhout has published two programming style guides, one for C programming known as *The Engineering Manual* and one for Tcl scripts known as *The Style Guide*. These describe details about file structure as well as naming conventions for modules, procedures, and variables. The *Tcl Style Guide* conventions use Tcl namespaces to separate packages. Namespaces automatically provide a way to avoid conflict between procedure names. Namespaces also support collections of variables without having to use arrays for grouping.

You can find these style guides on the CD-ROM and also in ftp:// ftp.scriptics.com/pub/tcl/doc. *The Engineering Manual* is distributed as a compressed tar file, engManual.tar.Z, that contains sample files as well as the main document. *The Style Guide* is distributed as styleGuide.ps (or .pdf).

Reflection and Debugging

This chapter describes commands that give you a view into the interpreter. The `history` command and a simple debugger are useful during development and debugging. The `info` command provides a variety of information about the internal state of the Tcl interpreter. The `time` command measures the time it takes to execute a command. Tcl commands discussed are: `clock`, `info`, `history`, and `time`.

*R*eflection provides feedback to a script about the internal state of the interpreter. This is useful in a variety of cases, from testing to see whether a variable exists to dumping the state of the interpreter. The `info` command provides lots of different information about the interpreter.

The `clock` command is useful for formatting dates as well as parsing date and time values. It also provides high-resolution timer information for precise measurements.

Interactive command history is the third topic of the chapter. The history facility can save you some typing if you spend a lot of time entering commands interactively.

Debugging is the last topic. The old-fashioned approach of adding `puts` commands to your code is often quite useful. For tough problems, however, a real debugger is invaluable. The *TclPro* tools from Scriptics include a high quality debugger and static code checker. The *thinspect* program is an inspector that lets you look into the state of a Tk application. It can hook up to any Tk application dynamically, so it proves quite useful.

The `clock` Command

The `clock` command has facilities for getting the current time, formatting time values, and scanning printed time strings to get an integer time value. The `clock` command was added in Tcl 7.5. Table 13–1 summarizes the `clock` command:

Table 13–1 The `clock` command.

`clock clicks`	A system-dependent high resolution counter.
`clock format` *value* `?-format` *str*?	Formats a clock value according to *str*.
`clock scan` *string* `?-base` *clock*? `?-gmt` *boolean*?	Parses date *string* and return seconds value. The *clock* value determines the date.
`clock seconds`	Returns the current time in seconds.

The following command prints the current time:

```
clock format [clock seconds]
=> Sun Nov 24 14:57:04  1996
```

The `clock seconds` command returns the current time, in seconds since a starting epoch. The `clock format` command formats an integer value into a date string. It takes an optional argument that controls the format. The format strings contains % keywords that are replaced with the year, month, day, date, hours, minutes, and seconds, in various formats. The default string is:

```
%a %b %d %H:%M:%S %Z %Y
```

Tables 13–2 and 13–3 summarize the `clock` formatting strings:

Table 13–2 Clock formatting keywords.

`%%`	Inserts a `%`.
`%a`	Abbreviated weekday name (Mon, Tue, etc.).
`%A`	Full weekday name (Monday, Tuesday, etc.).
`%b`	Abbreviated month name (Jan, Feb, etc.).
`%B`	Full month name.
`%c`	Locale specific date and time (e.g., `Nov 24 16:00:59 1996`).
`%d`	Day of month (01 – 31).
`%H`	Hour in 24-hour format (00 – 23).
`%I`	Hour in 12-hour format (01 – 12).
`%j`	Day of year (001 – 366).
`%m`	Month number (01 – 12).
`%M`	Minute (00 – 59).
`%p`	AM/PM indicator.
`%S`	Seconds (00 – 59).
`%U`	Week of year (00 – 52) when Sunday starts the week.
`%w`	Weekday number (Sunday = 0).

Table 13–2 Clock formatting keywords. (Continued)

%W	Week of year (01 – 52) when Monday starts the week.
%x	Locale specific date format (e.g., Feb 19 1997).
%X	Locale specific time format (e.g., 20:10:13).
%y	Year without century (00 – 99).
%Y	Year with century (e.g. 1997).
%Z	Time zone name.

Table 13–3 UNIX-specific clock formatting keywords.

%D	Date as %m/%d/%y (e.g., 02/19/97).
%e	Day of month (1 – 31), no leading zeros.
%h	Abbreviated month name.
%n	Inserts a newline.
%r	Time as %I:%M:%S %p (e.g., 02:39:29 PM).
%R	Time as %H:%M (e.g., 14:39).
%t	Inserts a tab.
%T	Time as %H:%M:%S (e.g., 14:34:29).

The `clock clicks` command returns the value of the system's highest resolution clock. The units of the clicks are not defined. The main use of this command is to measure the relative time of different performance tuning trials. The following command counts the clicks per second over 10 seconds, which will vary from system to system:

Example 13–1 Calculating clicks per second.

```
set t1 [clock clicks]
after 10000 ;# See page 218
set t2 [clock clicks]
puts "[expr ($t2 - $t1)/10] Clicks/second"
=> 1001313 Clicks/second
```

The `clock scan` command parses a date string and returns a seconds value. The command handles a variety of date formats. If you leave off the year, the current year is assumed.

Year 2000 Compliance

Tcl implements the standard interpretation of two-digit year values, which is that 70–99 are 1970–1999, 00–69 are 2000–2069. Versions of Tcl before 8.0 did not properly deal with two-digit years in all cases. Note, however, that Tcl is limited by your system's time epoch and the number of bits in an integer. On Windows, Macintosh, and most UNIX systems, the clock epoch is January 1, 1970. A 32-bit integer can count enough seconds to reach forward into the year 2037, and backward to the year 1903. If you try to `clock scan` a date outside that range, Tcl will raise an error because the seconds counter will overflow or underflow. In this case, Tcl is just reflecting limitations of the underlying system.

If you leave out a date, `clock scan` assumes the current date. You can also use the `-base` option to specify a date. The following example uses the current time as the base, which is redundant:

```
clock scan "10:30:44 PM" -base [clock seconds]
=> 2931690644
```

The date parser allows these modifiers: `year`, `month`, `fortnight` (two weeks), `week`, `day`, `hour`, `minute`, `second`. You can put a positive or negative number in front of a modifier as a multiplier. For example:

```
clock format [clock scan "10:30:44 PM 1 week"]
=> Sun Dec 01 22:30:44  1996
clock format [clock scan "10:30:44 PM -1 week"]
Sun Nov 17 22:30:44  1996
```

You can also use `tomorrow`, `yesterday`, `today`, `now`, `last`, `this`, `next`, and `ago`, as modifiers.

```
clock format [clock scan "3 years ago"]
=> Wed Nov 24 17:06:46  1993
```

Both `clock format` and `clock scan` take a `-gmt` option that uses Greenwich Mean Time. Otherwise, the local time zone is used.

```
clock format [clock seconds] -gmt true
=> Sun Nov 24 09:25:29  1996
clock format [clock seconds] -gmt false
=> Sun Nov 24 17:25:34  1996
```

The `info` Command

Table 13–4 summarizes the `info` command. The operations are described in more detail later.

Table 13–4 The `info` command.

`info args` *procedure*	A list of *procedure*'s arguments.
`info body` *procedure*	The commands in the body of *procedure*.
`info cmdcount`	The number of commands executed so far.
`info commands` *?pattern?*	A list of all commands, or those matching *pattern*. Includes built-ins and Tcl procedures.
`info complete` *string*	True if *string* contains a complete Tcl command.

Table 13–4 The `info` command. (Continued)

`info default proc arg var`	True if `arg` has a default parameter value in procedure `proc`. The default value is stored into `var`.
`info exists variable`	True if `variable` is defined.
`info globals ?pattern?`	A list of all global variables, or those matching `pattern`.
`info hostname`	The name of the machine. This may be the empty string if networking is not initialized.
`info level`	The stack level of the current procedure, or 0 for the global scope.
`info level number`	A list of the command and its arguments at the specified level of the stack.
`info library`	The pathname of the Tcl library directory.
`info loaded ?interp?`	A list of the libraries loaded into the interpreter named `interp`, which defaults to the current one.
`info locals ?pattern?`	A list of all local variables, or those matching `pattern`.
`info nameofexecutable`	The file name of the program (e.g., of *tclsh* or *wish*).
`info patchlevel`	The release patch level for Tcl.
`info procs ?pattern?`	A list of all Tcl procedures, or those that match `pattern`.
`info script`	The name of the file being processed, or the empty string.
`info sharedlibextension`	The file name suffix of shared libraries.
`info tclversion`	The version number of Tcl.
`info vars ?pattern?`	A list of all visible variables, or those matching `pattern`.

Variables

There are three categories of variables: *local*, *global*, and *visible*. Information about these categories is returned by the `locals`, `globals`, and `vars` operations, respectively. The local variables include procedure arguments as well as locally defined variables. The global variables include all variables defined at the global scope. The visible variables include locals, plus any variables made visible via `global` or `upvar` commands. A pattern can be specified to limit the returned list of variables to those that match the pattern. The pattern is interpreted according to the rules of `string match`, which is described on page 48:

```
info globals auto*
=> auto_index auto_noexec auto_path
```

Namespaces, which are the topic of the next chapter, partition global variables into different scopes. You query the variables visible in a namespace with:

```
info vars namespace::*
```

Remember that a variable may not be defined yet even though a `global` or `upvar` command has declared it visible in the current scope. Use the `info exists` command to test whether a variable or an array element is defined or not. An example is shown on page 90.

Procedures

You can find out everything about a Tcl procedure with the `args`, `body`, and `default` operations. This is illustrated in the following `Proc_Show` example. The `puts` commands use the `-nonewline` flag because the newlines in the procedure body, if any, are retained:

Example 13–2 Printing a procedure definition.

```
proc Proc_Show {{namepat *} {file stdout}} {
    foreach proc [info procs $namepat] {
        set space ""
        puts -nonewline $file "proc $proc {"
        foreach arg [info args $proc] {
            if [info default $proc $arg value] {
                puts -nonewline $file "$space{$arg $value}"
            } else {
                puts -nonewline $file $space$arg
            }
            set space " "
        }

        # No newline needed because info body may return a
        # value that starts with a newline

        puts -nonewline $file "} {"
        puts -nonewline $file [info body $proc]
        puts $file "}"
    }
}
```

Example 13–3 is a more elaborate example of procedure introspection that comes from the `direct.tcl` file, which is part of the Tcl Web Server described in Chapter 18. This code is used to map URL requests and the associated query data directly into Tcl procedure calls. This is discussed in more detail on page 247. The Web server collects Web form data into an array called `form`. Example 13–3 matches up elements of the `form` array with procedure arguments, and it collects extra elements into an `args` parameter. If a form value is missing, then the default argument value or the empty string is used:

Example 13–3 Mapping form data onto procedure arguments.

```
# cmd is the name of the procedure to invoke
# form is an array containing form values

set cmdOrig $cmd
set params [info args $cmdOrig]

# Match elements of the form array to parameters

foreach arg $params {
    if {![info exists form($arg)]} {
        if {[info default $cmdOrig $arg value]} {
            lappend cmd $value
        } elseif {[string compare $arg "args"] == 0} {
            set needargs yes
        } else {
            lappend cmd {}
        }
    } else {
        lappend cmd $form($arg)
    }
}
# If args is a parameter, then append the form data
# that does not match other parameters as extra parameters

if {[info exists needargs]} {
    foreach {name value} $valuelist {
        if {[lsearch $params $name] < 0} {
            lappend cmd $name $value
        }
    }
}
# Eval the command

set code [catch $cmd result]
```

The info commands operation returns a list of all commands, which includes both built-in commands defined in C and Tcl procedures. There is no operation that just returns the list of built-in commands. Example 13–4 finds the built-in commands by removing all the procedures from the list of commands.

Example 13–4 Finding built-in commands.

```
proc Command_Info {{pattern *}} {
    # Create a table of procedures for quick lookup

    foreach p [info procs $pattern] {
        set isproc($p) 1
    }

    # Look for command not in the procedure table
    set result {}
```

```
    foreach c [info commands $pattern] {
        if {![info exists isproc($c)]} {
            lappend result $c
        }
    }
    return [lsort $result]
}
```

The Call Stack

The `info level` operation returns information about the Tcl evaluation stack, or *call stack*. The global level is numbered zero. A procedure called from the global level is at level one in the call stack. A procedure it calls is at level two, and so on. The `info level` command returns the current level number of the stack if no level number is specified.

If a positive level number is specified (e.g., `info level 3`), then the command returns the procedure name and argument values at that level in the call stack. If a negative level is specified, then it is relative to the current call stack. Relative level -1 is the level of the current procedure's caller, and relative level 0 is the current procedure. The following example prints the call stack. The `Call_trace` procedure avoids printing information about itself by starting at one less than the current call stack level:

Example 13–5 Getting a trace of the Tcl call stack.

```
proc Call_Trace {{file stdout}} {
    puts $file "Tcl Call Trace"
    for {set x [expr [info level]-1]} {$x > 0} {incr x -1} {
        puts $file "$x: [info level $x]"
    }
}
```

Command Evaluation

If you want to know how many Tcl commands are executed, use the `info cmdcount` command. This counts all commands, not just top-level commands. The counter is never reset, so you need to sample it before and after a test run if you want to know how many commands are executed during a test.

The `info complete` operation figures out whether a string is a complete Tcl command. This is useful for command interpreters that need to wait until the user has typed in a complete Tcl command before passing it to `eval`. Example 13–6 defines `Command_Process` that gets a line of input and builds up a command. When the command is complete, the command is executed at the global scope. `Command_Process` takes two *callbacks* as arguments. The `inCmd` is evaluated to get the line of input, and the `outCmd` is evaluated to display the results. Chapter 10 describes callbacks why the curly braces are used with `eval` as they are in this example:

Example 13–6 A procedure to read and evaluate commands.

```
proc Command_Process {inCmd outCmd} {
    global command
    append command(line) [eval $inCmd]
    if [info complete $command(line)] {
        set code [catch {uplevel #0 $command(line)} result]
        eval $outCmd {$result $code}
        set command(line) {}
    }
}
proc Command_Read {{in stdin}} {
    if [eof $in] {
        if {$in != "stdin"} {
            close $in
        }
        return {}
    }
    return [gets $in]
}
proc Command_Display {file result code} {
    puts stdout $result
}
while {![eof stdin]} {
    Command_Process {Command_Read stdin} \
        {Command_Display stdout}
}
```

Scripts and the Library

The name of the current script file is returned with the info script command. For example, if you use the source command to read commands from a file, then info script returns the name of that file if it is called during execution of the commands in that script. This is true even if the info script command is called from a procedure that is not defined in the script.

Use info script to find related files.

I often use info script to source or process files stored in the same directory as the script that is running. A few examples are shown in Example 13–7.

Example 13–7 Using info script to find related files.

```
# Get the directory containing the current script.
set dir [file dirname [info script]]

# Source a file in the same directory
source [file join $dir helper.tcl]

# Add an adjacent script library directory to auto_path
# The use of ../lib with file join is cross-platform safe.
lappend auto_path [file join $dir ../lib]
```

The pathname of the Tcl library is stored in the `tcl_library` variable, and it is also returned by the `info library` command. While you could put scripts into this directory, it might be better to have a separate directory and use the script library facility described in Chapter 12. This makes it easier to deal with new releases of Tcl and to package up your code if you want other sites to use it.

Version Numbers

Each Tcl release has a version number such as 7.4 or 8.0. This number is returned by the `info tclversion` command. If you want your script to run on a variety of Tcl releases, you may need to test the version number and take different actions in the case of incompatibilities between releases.

The Tcl release cycle starts with one or two alpha and beta releases before the final release, and there may even be a patch release after that. The `info patchlevel` command returns a qualified version number, like 8.0b1 for the first beta release of 8.0. We switched from using "p" (e.g., 8.0p2) to a three-level scheme (e.g., 8.0.3) for patch releases. The patch level is zero for the final release (e.g., 8.2.0). In general, you should be prepared for feature changes during the beta cycle, but there should only be bug fixes in the patch releases. Another rule of thumb is that the Tcl script interface remains quite compatible between releases; feature additions are upward compatible.

Execution Environment

The file name of the program being executed is returned with `info nameofexecutable`. This is more precise than the name in the `argv0` variable, which could be a relative name or a name found in a command directory on your command search path. It is still possible for `info nameofexecutable` to return a relative pathname if the user runs your program as `./foo`, for example. The following construct always returns the absolute pathname of the current program. If `info nameofexecutable` returns an absolute pathname, then the value of the current directory is ignored. The `pwd` command is described on page 115:

```
file join [pwd] [info nameofexecutable]
```

A few operations support dynamic loading of shared libraries, which are described in Chapter 44. The `info sharedlibextension` returns the file name suffix of dynamic link libraries. The `info loaded` command returns a list of libraries that have been loaded into an interpreter. Multiple interpreters are described in Chapter 19.

Cross-Platform Support

Tcl is designed so that you can write scripts that run unchanged on UNIX, Macintosh, and Windows platforms. In practice, you may need a small amount of code that is specific to a particular platform. You can find out information about the platform via the `tcl_platform` variable. This is an array with these elements defined:

- `tcl_platform(platform)` is one of `unix`, `macintosh`, or `windows`.
- `tcl_platform(os)` identifies the operating system. Examples include `MacOS`, `Solaris`, `Linux`, `Win32s` (Windows 3.1 with the Win32 subsystem), `Windows 95`, `Windows NT`, and `SunOS`.
- `tcl_platform(osVersion)` gives the version number of the operating system.
- `tcl_platform(machine)` identifies the hardware. Examples include `ppc` (Power PC), `68k` (68000 family), `sparc`, `intel`, `mips`, and `alpha`.
- `tcl_platform(isWrapped)` indicates that the application has been wrapped up into a single executable with *TclPro Wrapper*. This is not defined in normal circumstances.
- `tcl_platform(user)` gives the login name of the current user.
- `tcl_platform(debug)` indicates that Tcl was compiled with debugging symbols.
- `tcl_platform(thread)` indicates that Tcl was compiled with thread support enabled.

On some platforms a *hostname* is defined. If available, it is returned with the `info hostname` command. This command may return an empty string.

One of the most significant areas affected by cross-platform portability is the file system and the way files are named. This topic is discussed on page 103.

Tracing Variable Values

The `trace` command registers a command to be called whenever a variable is accessed, modified, or unset. This form of the command is:

```
trace variable name ops command
```

The *name* is a Tcl variable name, which can be a simple variable, an array, or an array element. If a whole array is traced, the trace is invoked when any element is used according to *ops*. The *ops* argument is one or more of the letters `r`, for read traces, `w`, for write traces, and `u`, for unset traces. The *command* is executed when one of these events occurs. It is invoked as:

```
command name1 name2 op
```

The *name1* argument is the variable or array name. The *name2* argument is the name of the array index, or null if the trace is on a simple variable. If there is an unset trace on an entire array and the array is unset, *name2* is also null. The value of the variable is not passed to the procedure. The traced variable is one level up the Tcl call stack. The `upvar`, `uplevel`, or `global` commands need to be used to make the variable visible in the scope of *command*. These commands are described in more detail in Chapter 7.

A read trace is invoked before the value of the variable is returned, so if it changes the variable itself, the new value is returned. A write trace is called after the variable is modified. The unset trace is called after the variable is unset.

Read-Only Variables

Example 13–8 uses traces to implement a read-only variable. A variable is modified before the trace procedure is called, so the ReadOnly variable is needed to preserve the original value. When a variable is unset, the traces are automatically removed, so the unset trace action reestablishes the trace explicitly. Note that the upvar alias (e.g., var) cannot be used to set up the trace:

Example 13–8 Tracing variables.

```
proc ReadOnlyVar {varName} {
    upvar 1 $varName var
    global ReadOnly
    set ReadOnly($varName) $var
    trace variable $varName wu ReadOnlyTrace
}
proc ReadOnlyTrace { varName index op } {
    global ReadOnly
    upvar 1 $varName var
    switch $op {
        w {
            set var $ReadOnly($varName)
        }
        u {
            set var $ReadOnly($varName)
            # Re-establish the trace using the true name
            trace variable $varName wu ReadOnlyTrace
        }
    }
}
```

This example merely overrides the new value with the saved value. Another alternative is to raise an error with the error command. This will cause the command that modified the variable to return the error. Another common use of trace is to update a user interface widget in response to a variable change. Several of the Tk widgets have this feature built into them.

If more than one trace is set on a variable, then they are invoked in the reverse order; the most recent trace is executed first. If there is a trace on an array and on an array element, then the trace on the array is invoked first.

Creating an Array with Traces

Example 13–9 uses an array trace to dynamically create array elements:

Example 13–9 Creating array elements with array traces.

```
# make sure variable is an array
set dynamic() {}
trace variable dynamic r FixupDynamic
proc FixupDynamic {name index op} {
    upvar 1 $name dynArray
    if {![info exists dynArray($index)]} {
        set dynArray($index) 0
    }
}
```

Information about traces on a variable is returned with the `vinfo` option:

```
trace vinfo dynamic
=> {r FixupDynamic}
```

A trace is deleted with the `vdelete` option, which has the same form as the `variable` option. The trace in the previous example can be removed with the following command:

```
trace vdelete dynamic r FixupDynamic
```

Interactive Command History

The Tcl shell programs keep a log of the commands that you type by using a history facility. The log is controlled and accessed via the `history` command. The history facility uses the term *event* to mean an entry in its history log. The events are just commands, and they have an event ID that is their index in the log. You can also specify an event with a negative index that counts backwards from the end of the log. Event -1 is the previous event. Table 13–5 summarizes the Tcl `history` command. In the table, *event* defaults to -1.

In practice you will want to take advantage of the ability to abbreviate the history options and even the name of the `history` command itself. For the command, you need to type a unique prefix, and this depends on what other commands are already defined. For the options, there are unique one-letter abbreviations for all of them. For example, you could reuse the last word of the previous command with [hist w $]. This works because a $ that is not followed by alphanumerics or an open brace is treated as a literal $.

Several of the history operations update the history list. They remove the actual `history` command and replace it with the command that resulted from the history operation. The `event` and `redo` operations all behave in this manner. This makes perfect sense because you would rather have the actual command in the history, instead of the history command used to retrieve the command.

Table 13–5 The `history` command.

`history`	Short for `history info` with no *count*.
`history add command ?exec?`	Adds the command to the history list. If `exec` is specified, then execute the command.
`history change new ?event?`	Changes the command specified by *event* to *new* in the command history.
`history event ?event?`	Returns the command specified by *event*.
`history info ?count?`	Returns a formatted history list of the last *count* commands, or of all commands.
`history keep count`	Limits the history to the last *count* commands.
`history nextid`	Returns the number of the next event.
`history redo ?event?`	Repeats the specified command.

History Syntax

Some extra syntax is supported when running interactively to make the history facility more convenient to use. Table 13–6 shows the special history syntax supported by *tclsh* and *wish*.

Table 13–6 Special `history` syntax.

`!!`	Repeats the previous command.
`!n`	Repeats command number *n*. If *n* is negative it counts backward from the current command. The previous command is event -1.
`!prefix`	Repeats the last command that begins with *prefix*.
`!pattern`	Repeats the last command that matches *pattern*.
`^old^new`	Globally replaces *old* with *new* in the last command.

The next example shows how some of the history operations work:

Example 13–10 Interactive `history` usage.

```
% set a 5
5
% set a [expr $a+7]
12
% history
    1 set a 5
    2 set a [expr $a+7]
    3 history
% !2
19
% !!
```

```
26
% ^7^13
39
% !h
   1 set a 5
   2 set a [expr $a+7]
   3 history
   4 set a [expr $a+7]
   5 set a [expr $a+7]
   6 set a [expr $a+13]
   7 history
```

A Comparison to C Shell History Syntax

The history syntax shown in the previous example is simpler than the history syntax provided by the C shell. Not all of the history operations are supported with special syntax. The substitutions (using ^old^new) are performed globally on the previous command. This is different from the quick-history of the C shell. Instead, it is like the !:gs/old/new/ history command. So, for example, if the example had included ^a^b in an attempt to set b to 39, an error would have occurred because the command would have used b before it was defined:

```
set b [expr $b+7]
```

If you want to improve the history syntax, you will need to modify the unknown command, which is where it is implemented. This command is discussed in more detail in Chapter 12. Here is the code from the unknown command that implements the extra history syntax. The main limitation in comparison with the C shell history syntax is that the ! substitutions are performed only when ! is at the beginning of the command:

Example 13–11 Implementing special history syntax.

```
# Excerpts from the standard unknown command
# uplevel is used to run the command in the right context
if {$name == "!!"} {
    set newcmd [history event]
} elseif {[regexp {^!(.+)$} $name dummy event]} {
    set newcmd [history event $event]
} elseif {[regexp {^\^([^^]*)\^([^^]*)\^?$} $name x old new]} {
    set newcmd [history event -1]
    catch {regsub -all -- $old $newcmd $new newcmd}
}
if {[info exists newcmd]} {
    history change $newcmd 0
    return [uplevel $newcmd]
}
```

Debugging

The rapid turnaround with Tcl coding means that it is often sufficient to add a few puts statements to your script to gain some insight about its behavior. This solution doesn't scale too well, however. A slight improvement is to add a Debug procedure that can have its output controlled better. You can log the information to a file, or turn it off completely. In a Tk application, it is simple to create a text widget to hold the contents of the log so that you can view it from the application. Here is a simple Debug procedure. To enable it you need to set the debug(enable) variable. To have its output go to your terminal, set debug(file) to stderr.

Example 13–12 A Debug procedure.

```
proc Debug { args } {
    global debug
    if {![info exists debug(enabled)]} {
        # Default is to do nothing
        return
    }
    puts $debug(file) [join $args " "]
}
proc DebugOn {{file {}}} {
    global debug
    set debug(enabled) 1
    if {[string length $file] == 0} {
        set debug(file) stderr
    } else {
        if [catch {open $file w} fileID] {
            puts stderr "Cannot open $file: $fileID"
            set debug(file) stderr
        } else {
            puts stderr "Debug info to $file"
            set debug(file) $fileID
        }
    }
}
proc DebugOff {} {
    global debug
    if {[info exists debug(enabled)]} {
        unset debug(enabled)
        flush $debug(file)
        if {$debug(file) != "stderr" &&
            $debug(file) != "stdout"} {
            close $debug(file)
            unset debug(file)
        }
    }
}
```

Scriptics' TclPro

Scriptics offers a commercial development environment for Tcl called *TclPro*. *TclPro* features an extended Tcl platform and a set of development tools. The Tcl platform includes the popular [incr Tcl], Expect, and TclX extensions. These extensions and Tcl/Tk are distributed in source and binary form for Windows and a variety of UNIX platforms. There is an evaluation copy of TclPro on the CD-ROM. The *TclPro* distribution includes a copy of Tcl/Tk and the extensions that you can use for free. However, you will need to register at the Scriptics web site to obtain an evaluation license for the *TclPro* development tools. Please visit the following URL:

```
http://www.scriptics.com/registration/welchbook.html
```

The current version of TclPro contains these tools:

TclPro Debugger

TclPro Debugger provides a nice graphical user interface with all the features you expect from a traditional debugger. You can set breakpoints, single step, examine variables, and look at the call stack. It understands a subtle issue that can arise from using the `update` command: nested call stacks. It is possible to launch a new Tcl script as a side effect of the `update` command, which pushes the current state onto the execution stack. This shows up clearly in the debugger stack trace. It maintains project state, so it will remember breakpoint settings and other preference items between runs. One of the most interesting features is that it can debug remotely running applications. I use it regularly to debug Tcl code running inside the Tcl Web Server.

TclPro Checker

TclPro Checker is a static code checker. This is a real win for large program development. It examines every line of your program looking for syntax errors and dubious coding practices. It has detailed knowledge of Tcl, Tk, Expect, [incr Tcl], and TclX commands and validates your use of them. It checks that you call Tcl procedures with the correct number of arguments, and can cross-check large groups of Tcl files. It knows about changes between Tcl versions, and it can warn you about old code that needs to be updated.

TclPro Compiler

TclPro Compiler is really just a reader and writer for the byte codes that the Tcl byte-code compiler generates internally. It lets you precompile scripts and save the results, and then load the byte-code later instead of raw source. This provides a great way to hide your source code, if that is important to you. It turns out to save less time than you might think, however. By the time it reads the file from disk, decodes it, and builds the necessary Tcl data structures, it is not much faster than reading a source file and compiling it on the fly.

TclPro Wrapper

TclPro Wrapper assembles a collection of Tcl scripts, data files, and a Tcl/Tk interpreter into a single executable file. This makes distribution of your Tcl application as easy as giving out one file. The Tcl C library has been augmented with hooks in its file system access routines so that a wrapped application can look inside itself for files. The rule is that if you use a relative pathname (i.e., lib/myfile.dat), then the wrapped application will look first inside itself for the file. If the file is not found, or if the pathname is absolute (e.g., /usr/local/lib/myfile.dat), then Tcl looks on your hard disk for the file. The nice thing about *TclPro Wrapper* is that it handles all kinds of files, not just Tcl source files. It works by concatenating a ZIP file onto the end of a specially prepared Tcl interpreter. *TclPro* comes with pre-built interpreters that include Expect, [incr Tcl], and TclX, or you can build your own interpreter that contains custom C extensions.

Other Tools

The Tcl community has built many interesting and useful tools to help your Tcl development. Only two of them are mentioned below, but you can find many more at the Scriptics Tcl Resource Center:

```
http://www.scriptics.com/resource/
```

The *tkinspect* Program

The *tkinspect* program is a Tk application that lets you look at the state of other Tk applications. It displays procedures, variables, and the Tk widget hierarchy. With *tkinspect* you can issue commands to another application in order to change variables or test out commands. This turns out to be a very useful way to debug Tk applications. It was written by Sam Shen and is available on the CD-ROM. The current FTP address for this is:

```
ftp.neosoft.com:/pub/tcl/sorted/devel/tkinspect-5.1.6.tar.gz
```

The *Tuba* Debugger

Tuba is a debugger written purely in Tcl. It sets breakpoints by rewriting Tcl procedures to contain extra calls to the debugger. A small amount of support code is loaded into your application automatically, and the debugger application can set breakpoints, watch variables, and trace execution. It was written by John Stump and is available on the CD-ROM. The current URL for this package is:

```
http://www.geocities.com/SiliconValley/Ridge/2549/tuba/
```

The bgerror Command

When a Tcl script encounters an error during background processing, such as handling file events or during the command associated with a button, it signals the error by calling the bgerror procedure. A default implementation displays a dialog and gives you an opportunity to view the Tcl call stack at the point of the error. You can supply your own version of bgerror. For example, when my *exmh* mail application gets an error it offers to send mail to me with a few words of explanation from the user and a copy of the stack trace. I get interesting bug reports from all over the world!

The bgerror command is called with one argument that is the error message. The global variable errorInfo contains the stack trace information. There is an example tkerror implementation in the on-line sources associated with this book.

The tkerror Command

The bgerror command used to be called tkerror. When event processing shifted from Tk into Tcl with Tcl 7.5 and Tk 4.1, the name tkerror was changed to bgerror. Backwards compatibility is provided so that if tkerror is defined, then tkerror is called instead of bgerror. I have run into problems with the compatibility setup and have found it more reliable to update my applications to use bgerror instead of tkerror. If you have an application that runs under either Tk 4.0 or Tk 4.1, you can simply define both:

```
proc bgerror [info args tkerror] [info body tkerror]
```

Performance Tuning

The time command measures the execution time of a Tcl command. It takes an optional parameter that is a repetition count:

```
time {set a "Hello, World!"} 1000
=> 28 microseconds per iteration
```

If you need the result of the command being timed, use set to capture the result:

```
puts $log "command: [time {set result [command]}]"
```

Time stamps in a Log

Another way to gain insight into the performance of your script is to generate log records that contain time stamps. The clock seconds value is too coarse, but you can couple it with the clock clicks value to get higher resolution measurements. Use the code shown in Example 13–1 on page 175 to calibrate the clicks per second on your system. Example 13–13 writes log records that contain the current time and the number of clicks since the last record. There will be occasional glitches in the clicks value when the system counter wraps around or is reset by the system clock, but it will normally give pretty accurate results. The Log procedure adds overhead, too, so you should take several measurements in a tight loop to see how long each Log call takes:

II. Advanced Tcl

Example 13–13 Time Stamps in log records.

```
proc Log {args} {
    global log
    if [info exists log(file)] {
        set now [clock clicks]
        puts $log(file) [format "%s (%d)\t%s" \
            [clock format [clock seconds]] \
            [expr $now - $log(last)] \
            [join $args " "]]
        set log(last) $now
    }
}
proc Log_Open {file} {
    global log
    catch {close $log(file)}
    set log(file) [open $file w]
    set log(last) [clock clicks]
}
proc Log_Flush {} {
    global log
    catch {flush $log(file)}
}
proc Log_Close {} {
    global log
    catch {close $log(file)}
    catch {unset log(file)}
}
```

A more advanced `profile` command is part of the Extended Tcl (TclX) package, which is described in *Tcl/Tk Tools* (Mark Harrison, ed., O'Reilly & Associates, Inc., 1997). The TclX `profile` command monitors the number of calls, the CPU time, and the elapsed time spent in different procedures.

The Tcl Compiler

The built-in Tcl compiler improves performance in the following ways:

- Tcl scripts are converted into an internal byte-code format that is efficient to process. The byte codes are saved so that cost of compiling is paid only the first time you execute a procedure or loop. After that, execution proceeds much faster. Compilation is done as needed, so unused code is never compiled. If you redefine a procedure, it is recompiled the next time it is executed.

- Variables and command arguments are kept in a native format as long as possible and converted to strings only when necessary. There are several native types, including integers, floating point numbers, Tcl lists, byte codes, and arrays. There are C APIs for implementing new types. Tcl is still dynamically typed, so a variable can contain different types during its lifetime.

- Expressions and control structures are compiled into special byte codes, so they are executed more efficiently. Because `expr` does its own round of substitutions, the compiler generates better code if you group expressions with braces. This means that expressions go through only one round of substitutions. The compiler can generate efficient code because it does not have to worry about strange code like:

```
set subexpr {$x+$y}
expr 5 * $subexpr
```

The previous expression is not fully defined until runtime, so it has to be parsed and executed each time it is used. If the expression is grouped with braces, then the compiler knows in advance what operations will be used and can generate byte codes to implement the expression more efficiently.

The operation of the compiler is essentially transparent to scripts, but there are some differences in lists and expressions. These are described in Chapter 51. With lists, the good news is that large lists are more efficient. The problem is that lists are parsed more aggressively, so syntax errors at the end of a list will be detected even if you access only the beginning of the list. There were also some bugs in the code generator in the widely used Tcl 8.0p2 release. Most of these were corner cases like unbraced expressions in `if` and `while` commands. Most of these bugs were fixed in the 8.0.3 patch release, and the rest were cleaned up in Tcl 8.1 with the addition of a new internal parsing package.

II. Advanced Tcl

Namespaces

Namespaces group procedures and variables into separate name spaces.
Namespaces were added in Tcl 8.0. This chapter describes the
`namespace` and `variable` commands.

Namespaces provide new scopes for procedures and global variables. Originally Tcl had one global scope for shared variables, local scopes within procedures, and one global namespace for procedures. The single global scope for procedures and global variables can become unmanageable as your Tcl application grows. I describe some simple naming conventions on page 171 that I have used successfully in large programs. The namespace facility is a more elegant solution that partitions the global scope for procedure names and global variables.

Namespaces help structure large Tcl applications, but they add complexity. In particular, command callbacks may have to be handled specially so that they execute in the proper namespace. You choose whether or not you need the extra structure and learning curve of namespaces. If your applications are small, then you can ignore the namespace facility. If you are developing library packages that others will use, you should pick a namespace for your procedures and data so that they will not conflict with the applications in which they are used.

Using Namespaces

Namespaces add new syntax to procedure and variable names. A double colon, `::`, separates the namespace name from the variable or procedure name. You use this syntax to reference procedures and variables in a different namespace. The `namespace import` command lets you name things in other namespaces without the extra syntax. Namespaces can be nested, so you can create a hierarchy of scopes. These concepts are explained in more detail in the rest of this chapter.

One feature not provided by namespaces is any sort of protection, or a way to enforce access controls between different namespaces. This sort of thing is awkward, if not impossible, to provide in a dynamic language like Tcl. For example, you are always free to use `namespace eval` to reach into any other namespace. Instead of providing strict controls, namespaces are meant to provide structure that enables large scale programming.

The package facility described in Chapter 12 was designed before namespaces. This chapter illustrates a style that ties the two facilities together, but they are not strictly related. It is possible to create a package named A that implements a namespace B, or to use a package without namespaces, or a namespace without a package. However, it makes sense to use the facilities together.

Example 14–1 repeats the random number generator from Example 7–4 on page 85 using namespaces. The standard naming style conventions for namespaces use lowercase:

Example 14–1 Random number generator using namespaces.

```
package provide random 1.0

namespace eval random {
    # Create a variable inside the namespace
    variable seed [clock seconds]

    # Make the procedures visible to namespace import
    namespace export init random range

    # Create procedures inside the namespace
    proc init { value } {
        variable seed
        set seed $value
    }
    proc random {} {
        variable seed
        set seed [expr ($seed*9301 + 49297) % 233280]
        return [expr $seed/double(233280)]
    }
    proc range { range } {
        expr int([random]*$range)
    }
}
```

Example 14–1 defines three procedures and a variable inside the namespace `random`. From inside the namespace, you can use these procedures and variables directly. From outside the namespace, you use the `::` syntax for namespace qualifiers. For example, the state variable is just `seed` within the namespace, but you use `random::seed` to refer to the variable from outside the namespace. Using the procedures looks like this:

```
random::random
=> 0.3993355624142661
random::range 10
=> 4
```

If you use a package a lot you can *import* its procedures. A namespace declares what procedures can be imported with the `namespace export` command. Once you import a procedure, you can use it without a qualified name:

```
namespace import random::random
random
=> 0.54342849794238679
```

Importing and exporting are described in more detail later.

Namespace Variables

The `variable` command defines a variable inside a namespace. It is like the `set` command because it can define a value for the variable. You can declare several namespace variables with one `variable` command. The general form is:

```
variable name ?value? ?name value? ...
```

If you have an array, do not assign a value in the `variable` command. Instead, use regular Tcl commands after you declare the variable. You can put any commands inside a `namespace` block:

```
namespace eval foo {
    variable arr
    array set arr {name value name2 value2}
}
```

A namespace variable is similar to a global variable because it is outside the scope of any procedures. Procedures use the `variable` command or qualified names to reference namespace variables. For example, the `random` procedure has a `variable` command that brings the namespace variable into the current scope:

```
variable seed
```

If a procedure has a `variable` command that names a new variable, it is created in the namespace when it is first `set`.

Watch out for conflicts with global variables.

You need to be careful when you use variables inside a namespace block. If you declare them with a `variable` command, they are clearly namespace variables. However, if you forget to declare them, then they will either become namespace variables, or latch onto an existing global variable by the same name. Consider the following code:

```
namespace eval foo {
    variable table
    for {set i 1} {$i <= 256} {incr i} {
    set table($i) [format %c $i]
    }
}
```

If there is already a global variable i, then the `for` loop will use that variable. Otherwise, it will create the `foo::i` variable. I found this behavior surprising, but it does make it easier to access global variables like `env` without first declaring them with `global` inside the namespace block.

Qualified Names

A fully qualified name begins with `::`, which is the name for the global namespace. A fully qualified name unambiguously names a procedure or a variable. The fully qualified name works anywhere. If you use a fully qualified variable name, it is *not* necessary to use a `global` command. For example, suppose namespace `foo` has a namespace variable x, and there is also a global variable x. The global variable x can be named with this:

```
::x
```

The `::` syntax does not affect variable substitutions. You can get the value of the global variable x with `$::x`. Name the namespace variable x with this:

```
::foo::x
```

A partially qualified name does not have a leading `::`. In this case the name is resolved from the current namespace. For example, the following also names the namespace variable x:

```
foo::x
```

You can use qualified names with `global`. Once you do this, you can access the variable with its short name:

```
global ::foo::x
set x 5
```

Declaring variables is more efficient than using qualified names.

The Tcl byte-code compiler generates faster code when you declare namespace and global variables. Each procedure context has its own table of variables. The table can be accessed by a direct slot index, or by a hash table lookup of the variable name. The hash table lookup is slower than the direct slot access. When you use the `variable` or `global` command, then the compiler can use a direct slot access. If you use qualified names, the compiler uses the more general hash table lookup.

Command Lookup

A command is looked up first in the current name space. If it is not found there, then it is looked up in the global namespace. This means that you can use all the built-in Tcl commands inside a namespace with no special effort.

You can play games by redefining commands within a namespace. For example, a namespace could define a procedure named `set`. To get the built-in `set` you could use `::set`, while `set` referred to the `set` defined inside namespace. Obviously you need to be quite careful when you do this.

You can use qualified names when defining procedures. This eliminates the

need to put the `proc` commands inside a `namespace` block. However, you still
need to use `namespace eval` to create the namespace before you can create procedures inside it. Example 14–2 repeats the random number generator using qualified names. `random::init` does not need a `variable` command because it uses a
qualified name for `seed`:

Example 14–2 Random number generator using qualified names.

```
namespace eval random {
    # Create a variable inside the namespace
    variable seed [clock seconds]
}
# Create procedures inside the namespace
proc random::init { seed } {
    set ::random::seed $seed
}
proc random::random {} {
    variable seed
    set seed [expr ($seed*9301 + 49297) % 233280]
    return [expr $seed/double(233280)]
}
proc random::range { range } {
    expr int([random]*$range)
}
```

Nested Namespaces

Namespaces can be nested inside other namespaces. Example 14–3 shows three
namespaces that have their own specific variable x. The fully qualified names for
these variables are `::foo::x`, `::bar::x`, and `::bar::foo::x`.

Example 14–3 Nested namespaces.

```
namespace eval foo {
    variable x 1      ;# ::foo::x
}
namespace eval bar {
    variable x 2      ;# ::bar::x
    namespace eval foo {
        variable x 3  ;# ::bar::foo::x
    }
    puts $foo::x      ;# prints 3
}
puts $foo::x          ;# prints 1
```

Partially qualified names can refer to two different objects.

In Example 14–3 the partially qualified name `foo::x` can reference one of
two variables depending on the current namespace. From the global scope the
name `foo::x` refers to the namespace variable x inside `::foo`. From the `::bar`

namespace, `foo::x` refers to the variable `x` inside `::bar::foo`.

If you want to unambiguously name a variable in the current namespace, you have two choices. The simplest is to bring the variable into scope with the `variable` command:

```
variable x
set x something
```

If you need to give out the name of the variable, then you have two choices. The most general solution is to use the `namespace current` command to create a fully qualified name:

```
trace variable [namespace current]::x r \
    [namespace current]::traceproc
```

However, it is simpler to just explicitly write out the namespace as in:

```
trace variable ::myname::x r ::myname::traceproc
```

The drawback of this approach is that it litters your code with references to `::myname::`, which might be subject to change during program development.

Importing and Exporting Procedures

Commands can be imported from namespaces to make it easier to name them. An imported command can be used without its namespace qualifier. Each namespace specifies exported procedures that can be the target of an import. Variables cannot be imported. Note that importing is only a convenience; you can always use qualified names to access any procedure. As a matter of style, I avoid importing names, so I know what package a command belongs to when I'm reading code.

The `namespace export` command goes inside the namespace block, and it specifies what procedures a namespace exports. The specification is a list of `string match` patterns that are compared against the set of commands defined in a namespace. The export list can be defined before the procedures being exported. You can do more than one `namespace export` to add more procedures, or patterns, to the export list for a namespace. Use the `-clear` flag if you need to reset the export list.

```
namespace export ?-clear? ?pat? ?pat? ...
```
Only exported names appear in package indexes.

When you create the `pkgIndex.tcl` package index file with `pkg_mkIndex`, which is described Chapter 12, you should be aware that only exported names appear in the index. Because of this, I often resort to exporting everything. I never plan to import the names, but I do rely on automatic code loading based on the index files. This exports everything:

```
namespace export *
```

The `namespace import` command makes commands in another namespace visible in the current namespace. An `import` can cause conflicts with commands in the current namespace. The `namespace import` command raises an error if there is a conflict. You can override this with the `-force` option. The general form of the command is:

```
namespace import ?-force? namespace::pat ?namespace::pat?...
```

The *pat* is a `string match` type pattern that is matched against *exported* commands defined in *namespace*. You cannot use patterns to match *namespace*. The *namespace* can be a fully or partially qualified name of a namespace.

If you are lazy, you can import all procedures from a namespace:

```
namespace import random::*
```

The drawback of this approach is that `random` exports an `init` procedure, which might conflict with another module you import in the same way. It is safer to `import` just the procedures you plan on using:

```
namespace import random::random random::range
```

A namespace import takes a snapshot.

If the set of procedures in a namespace changes, or if its export list changes, then this has no effect on any imports that have already occurred from that namespace.

Callbacks and Namespaces

Commands like `after`, `bind`, and `button` take arguments that are Tcl scripts that are evaluated later. These *callback* commands execute later in the global scope by default. If you want a callback to be evaluated in a particular namespace, you can construct the callback with `namespace code`. This command does not execute the callback. Instead, it generates a Tcl command that will execute in the current namespace scope when it is evaluated later. For example, suppose `::current` is the current namespace. The `namespace code` command determines the current scope and adds that to the `namespace inscope` command it generates:

```
set callback [namespace code {set x 1}]
=> namespace inscope ::current {set x 1}
# sometime later ...
eval $callback
```

When you evaluate `$callback` later, it executes in the `::current` namespace because of the `namespace inscope` command. In particular, if there is a namespace variable `::current::x`, then that variable is modified. An alternative to using namespace code is to name the variable with a qualified name:

```
set callback {set ::current::x 1}
```

The drawback of this approach is that it makes it tedious to move the code to a different namespace.

If you need substitutions to occur on the command when you define it, use `list` to construct it. Using `list` is discussed in more detail on pages 123 and 387. Example 14–4 wraps up the `list` and the `namespace inscope` into the `code` procedure, which is handy because you almost always want to use `list` when constructing callbacks. The `uplevel` in `code` ensures that the correct namespace is captured; you can use `code` anywhere:

Example 14-4 The code procedure to wrap callbacks.

```
proc code {args} {
    set namespace [uplevel {namespace current}]
    return [list namespace inscope $namespace $args]
}
namespace eval foo {
    variable y "y value" x {}
    set callback [code set x $y]
    => namespace inscope ::foo {set x {y value}}
}
```

The example defines a callback that will set `::foo::x` to `y value`. If you want to set `x` to the value that `y` has at the time of the callback, then you do not want to do any substitutions. In that case, the original `namespace code` is what you want:

```
    set callback [namespace code {set x $y}]
    => namespace inscope ::foo {set x $y}
```

If the callback.has additional arguments added by the caller, `namespace inscope` correctly adds them. For example, the scrollbar protocol described on page 429 adds parameters to the callback that controls a scrollbar.

Introspection

The `info commands` operation returns all the commands that are currently visible. It is described in more detail on page 179. You can limit the information returned with a `string match` pattern. You can also include a namespace specifier in the pattern to see what is visible in a namespace. Remember that global commands and imported commands are visible, so `info commands` returns more than just what is defined by the namespace. Example 14-5 uses `namespace origin`, which returns the original name of imported commands, to sort out the commands that are really defined in a namespace:

Example 14-5 Listing commands defined by a namespace.

```
proc Namespace_List {{namespace {}}} {
    if {[string length $namespace] == 0} {
        # Determine the namespace of our caller
        set namespace [uplevel {namespace current}]
    }
    set result {}
    foreach cmd [info commands ${namespace}::*] {
        if {[namespace origin $cmd] == $cmd} {
            lappend result $cmd
        }
    }
    return [lsort $result]
}
```

The namespace Command

Table 14–1 summarizes the namespace operations:

Table 14–1 The namespace command.

namespace current	Returns the current namespace.
namespace children ?*name*? ?*pat*?	Returns names of nested namespaces. *name* defaults to current namespace. *pat* is a string match pattern that limits what is returned.
namespace code *script*	Generates a namespace inscope command that will eval *script* in the current namespace.
namespace delete *name* ?*name*? ...	Deletes the variables and commands from the specified namespaces.
namespace eval *name cmd* ?*args*? ...	Concatenates *args*, if present, onto *cmd* and evaluates it in *name* namespace.
namespace export ?-clear? ?*pat*? ?*pat*? ...	Adds patterns to the export list for current namespace. Returns export list if no patterns.
namespace forget *pat* ?*pat*? ...	Undoes the import of names matching patterns.
namespace import ?-force? *pat* ?*pat*? ...	Adds the names matching the patterns to the current namespace.
namespace inscope *name cmd* ?*args*? ...	Appends *args*, if present, onto *cmd* as list elements and evaluates it in *name* namespace.
namespace origin *cmd*	Returns the original name of *cmd*.
namespace parent ?*name*?	Returns the parent namespace of *name*, or of the current namespace.
namespace qualifiers *name*	Returns the part of *name* up to the last : : in it.
namespace which ?*flag*? *name*	Returns the fully qualified version of *name*. The *flag* is one of -command, -variable, or -namespace.
namespace tail *name*	Returns the last component of *name*.

Converting Existing Packages to use Namespaces

Suppose you have an existing set of Tcl procedures that you want to wrap in a namespace. Obviously, you start by surrounding your existing code in a namespace eval block. However, you need to consider three things: global variables, exported procedures, and callbacks.

* Global variables remain global until you change your code to use variable instead of global. Some variables may make sense to leave at the global scope. Remember that the variables that Tcl defines are global, including

env, `tcl_platform`, and the others listed in Table 2–2 on page 30. If you use the `upvar #0` trick described on page 86, you can adapt this to namespaces by doing this instead:

```
upvar #0 [namespace current]::$instance state
```

- Exporting procedures makes it more convenient for users of your package. It is not strictly necessary because they can always use qualified names to reference your procedures. An export list is a good hint about which procedures are expected to be used by other packages. Remember that the export list determines what procedures are visible in the index created by `pkg_mkIndex`.

- Callbacks execute at the global scope. If you use variable traces and variables associated with Tk widgets, these are also treated as global variables. If you want a callback to invoke a namespace procedure, or if you give out the name of a namespace variable, then you must construct fully qualified variable and procedure names. You can hardwire the current namespace:

```
button .foo -command ::myname::callback \
    -textvariable ::myname::textvar
```

or you can use `namespace current`:

```
button .foo -command [namespace current]::callback \
    -textvariable [namespace current]::textvar
```

[incr Tcl] Object System

The Tcl namespace facility does not provide classes and inheritance. It just provides new scopes and a way to hide procedures and variables inside a scope. There are Tcl C APIs that support hooks in variable name and command lookup for object systems so that they can implement classes and inheritance. By exploiting these interfaces, various object systems can be added to Tcl as shared libraries.

The Tcl namespace facility was proposed by Michael McLennan based on his experiences with [incr Tcl], which is the most widely used object-oriented extension for Tcl. [incr Tcl] provides classes, inheritance, and protected variables and commands. If you are familiar with C++, [incr Tcl] should feel similar. A complete treatment of [incr Tcl] is not made in this book. *Tcl/Tk Tools* (Mark Harrison, O'Reilly & Associates, Inc., 1997) is an excellent source of information. You can find a version of [incr Tcl] on the CD-ROM. The [incr Tcl] home page is:

```
http://www.tcltk.com/itcl/
```

Notes

The final section of this chapter touches on a variety of features of the namespace facility.

Names for Widgets, Images, and Interpreters

There are a number of Tcl extensions that are not affected by the namespaces described in this chapter, which apply only to commands and variable names. For example, when you create a Tk widget, a Tcl command is also created that corresponds to the Tk widget. This command is always created in the global command namespace even when you create the Tk widget from inside a `namespace eval` block. Other examples include Tcl interpreters, which are described in Chapter 19, and Tk images, which are described in Chapter 38.

The `variable` command at the global scope

It turns out that you can use `variable` like the `global` command if your procedures are not inside a namespace. This is consistent because it means "this variable belongs to the current namespace," which might be the global namespace.

Auto Loading and `auto_import`

The following sequence of commands can be used to import commands from the `foo` package:

```
package require foo
namespace import foo::*
```

However, because of the default behavior of packages, there may not be anything that matches `foo::*` after the `package require`. Instead, there are entries in the `auto_index` array that will be used to load those procedures when you first use them. The auto loading mechanism is described in Chapter 12. To account for this, Tcl calls out to a hook procedure called `auto_import`. This default implementation of this procedure searches `auto_index` and forcibly loads any pending procedures that match the import pattern. Packages like [incr Tcl] exploit this hook to implement more elaborate schemes. The `auto_import` hook was first introduced in Tcl 8.0.3.

Namespaces and `uplevel`

Namespaces affect the Tcl call frames just like procedures do. If you walk the call stack with `info level`, the namespace frames are visible. This means that you can get access to all variables with `uplevel` and `upvar`. Level #0 is still the absolute global scope, outside any namespace or procedure. Try out `Call_Trace` from Example 13–5 on page 180 on your code that uses namespaces to see the effect.

Naming Quirks

When you name a namespace, you are allowed to have extra colons at the end. You can also have two or more colons as the separator between namespace name components. These rules make it easier to assemble names by adding to the value returned from `namespace current`. These all name the same namespace:

```
::foo::bar
::foo::bar::
::foo:::::::bar
```

The name of the global namespace can be either `::` or the empty string. This follows from the treatment of `::` in namespace names.

When you name a variable or command, a trailing `::` is significant. In the following command a variable inside the `::foo::bar` namespace is modified. The variable has an empty string for its name!

```
set ::foo::bar:: 3
namespace eval ::foo::bar { set {} }
=> 3
```

If you want to embed a reference to a variable just before two colons, use a backslash to turn off the variable name parsing before the colons:

```
set x xval
set y $x\::foo
=> xval::foo
```

Miscellaneous

You can remove names you have imported:

```
namespace forget random::init
```

You can `rename` imported procedures to modify their names:

```
rename range Range
```

You can even move a procedure into another namespace with `rename`:

```
rename random::init myspace::init
```

Internationalization

This chapter describes features that support text processing for different character sets such as ASCII and Japanese. Tcl can read and write data in various character set encodings, but it processes data in a standard character set called Unicode. Tcl has a message catalog that lets you generate different versions of an application for different languages. Tcl commands described are: `encoding` and `msgcat`.

*D*ifferent languages use different alphabets, or *character sets*. An *encoding* is a standard way to represent a character set. Tcl hides most of the issues associated with encodings and character sets, but you need to be aware of them when you write applications that are used in different countries. You can also write an application using a *message catalog* so that the strings you display to users can be in the language of their choice. Using a message catalog is more work, but Tcl makes it as easy as possible.

Most of the hard work in dealing with character set encodings is done "under the covers" by the Tcl C library. The Tcl C library underwent substantial changes to support international character sets. Instead of using 8-bit bytes to store characters, Tcl uses a 16-bit character set called Unicode, which is large enough to encode the alphabets of all languages. There is also plenty of room left over to represent special characters like ♥ and ⊗.

In spite of all the changes to support Unicode, there are few changes visible to the Tcl script writer. Scripts written for Tcl 8.0 and earlier continue to work fine with Tcl 8.1 and later versions. You only need to modify scripts if you want to take advantage of the features added to support internationalization.

This chapter begins with a discussion of what a character set is and why different codings are used to represent them. It concludes with a discussion of message catalogs.

Character Sets and Encodings

If you are from the United States, you've probably never thought twice about character sets. Most computers use the ASCII encoding, which has 127 characters. That is enough for the 26 letters in the English alphabet, upper case and lower case, plus numbers, various punctuation characters, and control characters like tab and newline. ASCII fits easily in 8-bit characters, which can represent 256 different values.

European alphabets include accented characters like è, ñ, and ä. The ISO Latin-1 encoding is a superset of ASCII that encodes 256 characters. It shares the ASCII encoding in values 0 through 127 and uses the "high half" of the encoding space to represent accented characters as well as special characters like ©. There are several ISO Latin encodings to handle different alphabets, and these share the trick of encoding ASCII in the lower half and other characters in the high half. You might see these encodings referred to as `iso8859-1`, `iso8859-2`, and so on.

Asian character sets are simply too large to fit into 8-bit encodings. There are a number of 16-bit encodings for these languages. If you work with these, you are probably familiar with the "Big 5" or ShiftJIS encodings.

Unicode is an international standard character set encoding. There are both 16-bit Unicode and 32-bit Unicode standards, but Tcl and just about everyone else just use the 16-bit standard. Unicode has the important property that it can encode all the important character sets without conflicts and overlap. By converting all characters to the Unicode encoding, Tcl can work with different character sets simultaneously.

The System Encoding

Computer systems are set up with a standard system encoding for their files. If you always work with this encoding, then you can ignore character set issues. Tcl will read files and automatically convert them from the system encoding to Unicode. When Tcl writes files, it automatically converts from Unicode to the system encoding. If you are curious, you can find out the system encoding with:

```
encoding system
=> cp1252
```

The "cp" is short for "code page," the term that Windows uses to refer to different encodings. On my Unix system, the system encoding is `iso8859-1`.

Do not change the system encoding.

You could also change the system encoding with:

```
encoding system encoding
```

But this is not a good idea. It immediately changes how Tcl passes strings to your operating system, and it is likely to leave Tcl in an unusable state. Tcl automatically determines the system encoding for you. Don't bother trying to set it yourself.

The `encoding names` command lists all the encodings that Tcl knows about. The encodings are kept in files stored in the `encoding` directory under the Tcl script library. They are loaded automatically the first time you use an encoding.

```
lsort [encoding names]
=> ascii big5 cp1250 cp1251 cp1252 cp1253 cp1254 cp1255
cp1256 cp1257 cp1258 cp437 cp737 cp775 cp850 cp852 cp855
cp857 cp860 cp861 cp862 cp863 cp864 cp865 cp866 cp869
cp874 cp932 cp936 cp949 cp950 dingbats euc-cn euc-jp euc-
kr gb12345 gb1988 gb2312 identity iso2022 iso2022-jp
iso2022-kr iso8859-1 iso8859-2 iso8859-3 iso8859-4
iso8859-5 iso8859-6 iso8859-7 iso8859-8 iso8859-9
jis0201 jis0208 jis0212 ksc5601 macCentEuro macCroatian
macCyrillic macDingbats macGreek macIceland macJapan
macRoman macRomania macThai macTurkish macUkraine
shiftjis symbol unicode utf-8
```

The encoding names reflect their origin. The "cp" refers to the "code pages" that Windows uses to manage encodings. The "mac" encodings come from the Macintosh. The "iso," "euc," "gb," and "jis" encodings come from various standards bodies.

File Encodings and `fconfigure`

The conversion to Unicode happens automatically in the Tcl C library. When Tcl reads and writes files, it translates from the current system encoding into Unicode. If you have files in different encodings, you can use the `fconfigure` command to set the encoding. For example, to read a file in the standard Russian encoding (`iso8859-7`):

```
set in [open README.russian]
fconfigure $in -encoding iso8859-7
```

Example 15–1 shows a simple utility I use in *exmh*,[*] a MIME-aware mail reader. MIME has its own convention for specifying the character set encoding of a mail message that differs slightly from Tcl's naming convention. The procedure launders the name and then sets the encoding. Exmh was already aware of MIME character sets, so it could choose fonts for message display. Adding this procedure and adding two calls to it was all I had to do to adapt *exmh* to Unicode.

Example 15–1 MIME character sets and file encodings.

```
proc Mime_SetEncoding {file charset} {
    regsub -all {(iso|jis|us)-} $charset {\1} charset
    set charset [string tolower charset]
    regsub usascii $charset ascii charset
    fconfigure $file -encoding $charset
}
```

[*] The *exmh* home page is http://www.beedub.com/exmh/. It is a wonderful tool that helps me manage tons of e-mail. It is written in Tcl/Tk, of course, and relies on the MH mail system, which limits it to UNIX.

Scripts in Different Encodings

If you have scripts that are not in the system encoding, then you cannot use
source to load them. However, it is easy to read the files yourself under the
proper encoding and use eval to process them. Example 15–2 adds a -encoding
flag to the source command. This is likely to become a built-in feature in future
versions of Tcl so that commands like info script will work properly:

Example 15–2 Using scripts in nonstandard encodings.

```
proc Source {args} {
    set file [lindex $args end]
    if {[llength $args] == 3 &&
            [string equal -encoding [lindex $args 0]]} {
        set encoding [lindex $args 1]
        set in [open $file]
        fconfigure $in -encoding $encoding
        set script [read $in]
        close $in
        return [uplevel 1 $script]
    } elseif {[llength $args] == 1} {
        return [uplevel 1 [list source $file]]
    } else {
        return -code error \
            "Usage: Source ?-encoding encoding? file?"
    }
}
```

Unicode and UTF-8

UTF-8 is an encoding for Unicode. While Unicode represents all characters
with 16 bits, the UTF-8 encoding uses either 8, 16, or 24 bits to represent one
Unicode character. This variable-width encoding is useful because it uses 8 bits
to represent ASCII characters. This means that a pure ASCII string, one with
character codes all fewer than 128, is also a UTF-8 string. Tcl uses UTF-8 internally to make the transition to Unicode easier. It allows interoperability with Tcl
extensions that have not been made Unicode-aware. They can continue to pass
ASCII strings to Tcl, and Tcl will interpret them correctly.

As a Tcl script writer, you can mostly ignore UTF-8 and just think of Tcl as
being built on Unicode (i.e., full 16-bit character set support). If you write Tcl
extensions in C or C++, however, the impact of UTF-8 and Unicode is quite visible. This is explained in more detail in Chapter 44.

Tcl lets you read and write files in UTF-8 encoding or directly in Unicode.
This is useful if you need to use the same file on systems that have different system encodings. These files might be scripts, message catalogs, or documentation.
Instead of using a particular native format, you can use Unicode or UTF-8 and
read the files the same way on any of your systems. Of course, you will have to
set the encoding properly by using fconfigure as shown earlier.

The Binary Encoding

If you want to read a data file and suppress all character set transformations, use the `binary` encoding:

```
fconfigure $in -encoding binary
```

Under the binary encoding, Tcl reads in each 8-bit byte and stores it into the lower half of a 16-bit Unicode character with the high half set to zero. During binary output, Tcl writes out the lower byte of each Unicode character. You can see that reading in binary and then writing it out doesn't change any bits. Watch out if you read something in one encoding and then write it out in binary. Any information in the high byte of the Unicode character gets lost!

Tcl actually handles the binary encoding more efficiently than just described, but logically the previous description is still accurate. As described in Chapter 44, Tcl can manage data in several forms, not just strings. When you read a file in binary format, Tcl stores the data as a `ByteArray` that is simply 8 bits of data in each byte. However, if you ask for this data as a string (e.g., with the `puts` command), Tcl automatically converts from 8-bit bytes to 16-bit Unicode characters by setting the high byte to all zeros.

The `binary` command also manipulates data in `ByteArray` format. If you read a file with the binary encoding and then use the `binary` command to process the data, Tcl will keep the data in an efficient form.

The string command also understands the `ByteArray` format, so you can do operations like `string length`, `string range`, and `string index` on binary data without suffering the conversion cost from a `ByteArray` to a UTF-8 string.

Conversions Between Encodings

The `encoding` command lets you convert strings between encodings. The `encoding convertfrom` command converts data in some other encoding into a Unicode string. The `encoding convertto` command converts a Unicode string into some other encoding. For example, the following two sequences of commands are equivalent. They both read data from a file that is in Big5 encoding and convert it to Unicode:

```
fconfigure $input -encoding gb12345
set unicode [read $input]
```

or

```
fconfigure $input -encoding binary
set unicode [encoding convertfrom gb12345 [read $input]]
```

In general, you can lose information when you go from Unicode to any other encoding, so you ought to be aware of the limitations of the encodings you are using. In particular, the `binary` encoding may not preserve your data if it starts out from an arbitrary Unicode string. Similarly, an encoding like `iso-8859-2` may simply not have a representation of a given Unicode character.

The encoding Command

Table 15–1 summarizes the encoding command:

Table 15–1 The encoding command.

encoding convert-from ?*encoding*? *data*	Converts binary *data* from the specified *encoding*, which defaults to the system encoding, into Unicode.
encoding convertto ?*encoding*? *string*	Converts *string* from Unicode into data in the *encoding* format, which defaults to the system encoding.
encoding names	Returns the names of known encodings.
encoding system ?*encoding*?	Queries or change the system encoding.

Message Catalogs

A message catalog is a list of messages that your application will display. The main idea is that you can maintain several catalogs, one for each language you support. Unfortunately, you have to be explicit about using message catalogs. Everywhere you generate output or display strings in Tk widgets, you need to change your code to go through a message catalog. Fortunately, Tcl uses a nice trick to make this fairly easy and to keep your code readable. Instead of using keys like "message42" to get messages out of the catalog, Tcl just uses the strings you would use by default. For example, instead of this code:

```
puts "Hello, World!"
```

A version that uses message catalogs looks like this:

```
puts [msgcat::mc "Hello, World!"]
```

If you have not already loaded your message catalog, or if your catalog doesn't contain a mapping for "Hello, World!", then msgcat::mc just returns its argument. Actually, you can define just what happens in the case of unknown inputs by defining your own msgcat::mcunknown procedure, but the default behavior is quite good.

The message catalog is implemented in Tcl in the msgcat package. You need to use package require to make it available to your scripts:

```
package require msgcat
```

In addition, all the procedures in the package begin with "mc," so you can use namespace import to shorten their names further. I am not a big fan of namespace import, but if you use message catalogs, you will be calling the msgcat::mc function a lot, so it may be worthwhile to import it:

```
namespace import msgcat::mc
puts [mc "Hello, World!"]
```

Specifying a Locale

A *locale* identifies a language or language dialect to use in your output. A three-level scheme is used in the locale identifier:

```
language_country_dialect
```

The language codes are defined by the ISO-3166 standard. For example, "en" is English and "es" is Spanish. The country codes are defined by the ISO-639 standard. For example, US is for the United States and UK is for the United Kingdom. The dialect is up to you. The country and dialect parts are optional. Finally, the locale specifier is case insensitive. The following examples are all valid locale specifiers:

```
es
en
en_US
en_us
en_UK
en_UK_Scottish
en_uk_scottish
```

Users can set their initial locale with the LANG and LOCALE environment variables. If there is no locale information in the environment, then the "c" locale is used (i.e., the C programming language.) You can also set and query the locale with the msgcat::mclocale procedure:

```
msgcat::mclocale
=> c
msgcat::mclocale en_US
```

The msgcat::mcpreferences procedure returns a list of the user's locale preferences from most specific (i.e., including the dialect) to most general (i.e., only the language). For example:

```
msgcat::mclocale en_UK_Scottish
msgcat::mcpreferences
=> en_UK_Scottish en_UK en
```

Managing Message Catalog Files

A message catalog is simply a Tcl source file that contains a series of msgcat::mcset commands that define entries in the catalog. The syntax of the msgcat::mcset procedure is:

```
msgcat::mcset locale src-string ?dest-string?
```

The *locale* is a locale description like es or en_US_Scottish. The *src-string* is the string used as the key when calling msgcat::mc. The *dest-string* is the result of msgcat::mc when the *locale* is in force.

The msgcat::mcload procedure should be used to load your message catalog files. It expects the files to be named according to their locale (e.g., en_US_Scottish.msg), and it binds the message catalog to the current namespace.

The `msgcat::mcload` procedure loads files that match the `msgcat::mcpref-`
`erences` and have the `.msg` suffix. For example, with a locale of `en_UK_Scottish`,
`msgcat::mcload` would look for these files:

```
en_UK_Scottish.msg en_UK.msg en.msg
```

The standard place for message catalog files is in the `msgs` directory below
the directory containing a package. With this arrangement you can call `msg-`
`cat::mcload` as shown below. The use of `info script` to find related files is
explained on page 181.

```
msgcat::mcload [file join [file dirname [info script]] msgs]
```

The message catalog file is sourced, so it can contain any Tcl commands.
You might find it convenient to import the `msgcat::mcset` procedure. Be sure to
use `-force` with `namespace import` because that command might already have
been imported as a result of loading other message catalog files. Example 15–3
shows three trivial message catalog files:

Example 15–3 Three sample message catalog files.

```
## en.msg
namespace import -force msgcat::mcset

mcset en Hello Hello_en
mcset en Goodbye Goodbye_en
mcset en String String_en
# end of en.msg

## en_US.msg
namespace import -force msgcat::mcset

mcset en_US Hello Hello_en_US
mcset en_US Goodbye Goodbye_en_US
# end of en_US.msg

## en_US_Texan.msg
namespace import -force msgcat::mcset

mcset en_US_Texan Hello Howdy!
# end of en_US_Texan.msg
```

Assuming the files from Example 15–3 are all in the `msgs` directory below
your script, you can load all these files with these commands:

```
msgcat::mclocale en_US_Texan
msgcat::mcload [file join [file dirname [info script]] msgs]
```

The dialect has the highest priority:

```
msgcat::mc Hello
=> Howdy!
```

If the dialect does not specify a mapping, then the country mapping is
checked:

```
msgcat::mc Goodbye
```
=> Goodbye_en_US

Finally, the lowest priority is the language mapping:

```
msgcat::mc String
```
=> String_en

Message Catalogs and Namespaces

What happens if two different library packages have conflicting message catalogs? Suppose the `foo` package contains this call:

```
msgcat::set fr Hello Bonjour
```

But the `bar` package contains this conflicting definition:

```
msgcat::mcset fr Hello Ello
```

What happens is that `msgcat::mcset` and `msgcat::mc` are sensitive to the current Tcl namespace. Namespaces are described in detail in Chapter 14. If the `foo` package loads its message catalog while inside the `foo` namespace, then any calls to `msgcat::mc` from inside the `foo` namespace will see those definitions. In fact, if you call `msgcat::mc` from inside any namespace, it will find only message catalog definitions defined from within that namespace.

If you want to share message catalogs between namespaces, you will need to implement your own version of `msgcat::mcunknown` that looks in the shared location. Example 15–4 shows a version that looks in the global namespace before returning the default string.

Example 15–4 Using `msgcat::mcunknown` to share message catalogs.

```
proc msgcat::mcunknown {local src} {
    variable insideUnknown
    if {![info exist insideUnknown]} {

        # Try the global namespace, being careful to note
        # that we are already inside this procedure.

        set insideUnknown true
        set result [namespace eval :: [list \
            msgcat::mc $src \
        ]]
        unset insideUnknown
        return $result
    } else {

        # Being called because the message isn't found
        # in the global namespace

        return $src
    }
}
```

The `msgcat` package

Table 15–2 summarizes the `msgcat` package.

Table 15–2 The msgcat package

`msgcat::mc` *src*	Returns the translation of *src* according to the current locale and namespace.
`msgcat::mclocale` *?locale?*	Queries or set the current *locale*.
`msgcat::mcpreferences`	Returns a list of locale preferences ordered from the most specific to the most general.
`msgcat::mcload` *directory*	Loads message files for the current locale from *directory*.
`msgcat::mcset` *locale src translation*	Defines a mapping for the *src* string in *locale* to the *translation* string.
`msgcat::mcunknown` *locale src*	This procedure is called to resolve unknown translations. Applications can provide their own implementations.

Event-Driven Programming

II. Advanced Tcl

This chapter describes event-driven programming using timers and asynchronous I/O facilities. The `after` command causes Tcl commands to occur at a time in the future, and the `fileevent` command registers a command to occur in response to file input/output (I/O). Tcl commands discussed are: `after`, `fblocked`, `fconfigure`, `fileevent`, and `vwait`.

Event-driven programming is used in long-running programs like network servers and graphical user interfaces. This chapter introduces event-driven programming in Tcl. Tcl provides an easy model in which you register Tcl commands, and the system then calls those commands when a particular event occurs. The `after` command is used to execute Tcl commands at a later time, and the `fileevent` command is used to execute Tcl commands when the system is ready for I/O. The `vwait` command is used to wait for events. During the wait, Tcl automatically calls Tcl commands that are associated with different events.

The event model is also used when programming user interfaces using Tk. Originally, event processing was associated only with Tk. The event loop moved from Tk to Tcl in the Tcl 7.5/Tk 4.1 release.

The Tcl Event Loop

An event loop is built into Tcl. Tcl checks for events and calls out to handlers that have been registered for different types of events. Some of the events are processed internally to Tcl. You can register Tcl commands to be called in response to events. There are also C APIs to event loop, which are described on page 689. Event processing is active all the time in Tk applications. If you do not use Tk, you can start the event loop with the `vwait` command as shown in Example 16–2 on page 220. The four event classes are handled in the following order:

- Window events. These include keystrokes and button clicks. Handlers are set up for these automatically by the Tk widgets, and you can register window event handlers with the `bind` command described in Chapter 26.
- File events. The `fileevent` command registers handlers for these events.
- Timer events. The `after` command registers commands to occur at specific times.
- Idle events. These events are processed when there is nothing else to do. The Tk widgets use idle events to display themselves. The `after idle` command registers a command to run at the next idle time.

The `after` Command

The `after` command sets up commands to happen in the future. In its simplest form, it pauses the application for a specified time, in milliseconds. The example below waits for half a second:

```
after 500
```

During this time, the application *does not* process events. You can use the `vwait` command as shown on page 220 to keep the Tcl event loop active during the waiting period. The `after` command can register a Tcl command to occur after a period of time, in milliseconds:

```
after milliseconds cmd arg arg...
```

The `after` command treats its arguments like `eval`; if you give it extra arguments, it concatenates them to form a single command. If your argument structure is important, use `list` to build the command. The following example always works, no matter what the value of `myvariable` is:

```
after 500 [list puts $myvariable]
```

The return value of `after` is an identifier for the registered command. You can cancel this command with the `after cancel` operation. You specify either the identifier returned from `after`, or the command string. In the latter case, the event that matches the command string exactly is canceled.

Table 16–1 summarizes the `after` command:

Table 16–1 The `after` command.

after *milliseconds*	Pauses for *milliseconds*.
after *ms arg* ?*arg*...?	Concatenates the *args* into a command and executes it after *ms* milliseconds. Immediately returns an ID.
after cancel *id*	Cancels the command registered under *id*.
after cancel *command*	Cancels the registered *command*.
after idle *command*	Runs *command* at the next idle moment.
after info ?*id*?	Returns a list of IDs for outstanding `after` events, or the command associated with *id*.

The `fileevent` Command

The `fileevent` command registers a procedure that is called when an I/O channel is ready for read or write events. For example, you can open a pipeline or network socket for reading, and then process the data from the pipeline or socket using a command registered with `fileevent`. The advantage of this approach is that your application can do other things, like update the user interface, while waiting for data from the pipeline or socket. Network servers use `fileevent` to manage connections to many clients. You can use `fileevent` on `stdin` and `stdout`, too. Using network sockets is described in Chapter 17.

The command registered with `fileevent` uses the regular Tcl commands to read or write data on the I/O channel. For example, if the pipeline generates line-oriented output, you should use `gets` to read a line of input. If you try and read more data than is available, your application may block waiting for more input. For this reason, you should read one line in your `fileevent` handler, assuming the data is line-oriented. If you know the pipeline will generate data in fixed-sized blocks, then you can use the `read` command to read one block.

The `fconfigure` command, which is described on page 221, can put a channel into nonblocking mode. This is not strictly necessary when using `fileevent`. The pros and cons of nonblocking I/O are discussed later.

End of file makes a channel readable.

You should check for end of file in your read handler because it will be called when end of file occurs. It is important to close the channel inside the handler because closing the channel automatically unregisters the handler. If you forget to close the channel, your read event handler will be called repeatedly.

Example 16–1 shows a read event handler. A pipeline is opened for reading and its command executes in the background. The `Reader` command is invoked when data is available on the pipe. When end of file is detected a variable is set, which signals the application waiting with `vwait`. Otherwise, a single line of input is read and processed. The `vwait` command is described on the next page. Example 22–1 on page 316 also uses `fileevent` to read from a pipeline.

Example 16–1 A read event file handler.

```
proc Reader { pipe } {
    global done
    if {[eof $pipe]} {
        catch {close $pipe}
        set done 1
        return
    }
    gets $pipe line
    # Process the line here...
}
set pipe [open "|some command"]
fileevent $pipe readable [list Reader $pipe]
vwait done
```

There can be at most one read handler and one write handler for an I/O channel. If you register a handler and one is already registered, then the old registration is removed. If you call `fileevent` without a command argument, it returns the currently registered command, or it returns the empty string if there is none. If you register the empty string, it deletes the current file handler. Table 16–2 summarizes the `fileevent` command.

Table 16–2 The `fileevent` command.

`fileevent` *fileId* `readable` *?command?*	Queries or registers *command* to be called when *fileId* is readable.
`fileevent` *fileId* `writable` *?command?*	Queries or registers *command* to be called when *fileId* is writable.

The `vwait` Command

The `vwait` command waits until a variable is modified. For example, you can set variable x at a future time, and then wait for that variable to be set with `vwait`.

```
set x 0
after 500 {set x 1}
vwait x
```

Waiting with `vwait` causes Tcl to enter the event loop. Tcl will process events until the variable x is modified. The `vwait` command completes when some Tcl code runs in response to an event and modifies the variable. In this case the event is a timer event, and the Tcl code is simply:

```
set x 1
```

In some cases `vwait` is used only to start the event loop. Example 16–2 sets up a file event handler for `stdin` that will read and execute commands. Once this is set up, `vwait` is used to enter the event loop and process commands until the input channel is closed. The process exits at that point, so the `vwait` variable `Stdin(wait)` is not used:

Example 16–2 Using `vwait` to activate the event loop.

```
proc Stdin_Start {prompt} {
    global Stdin
    set Stdin(line) ""
    puts -nonewline $prompt
    flush stdout
    fileevent stdin readable [list StdinRead $prompt]
    vwait Stdin(wait)
}
proc StdinRead {prompt} {
    global Stdin
    if {[eof stdin]} {
        exit
```

```
    }
    append Stdin(line) [gets stdin]
    if {[info complete $Stdin(line)]} {
        catch {uplevel #0 $Stdin(line)} result
        puts $result
        puts -nonewline $prompt
        flush stdout
        set Stdin(line) {}
    } else {
        append Stdin(line) \n
    }
}
```

The fconfigure Command

The fconfigure command sets and queries several properties of I/O channels. The default settings for channels are suitable for most cases. If you do event-driven I/O you may want to set your channel into nonblocking mode. If you handle binary data, you should turn off end of line and character set translations. You can query the channel parameters like this:

```
fconfigure stdin
-blocking 1 -buffering none -buffersize 4096 -encoding
iso8859-1 -eofchar {} -translation lf
```

Table 16–3 summarizes the properties controlled by fconfigure. They are discussed in more detail below.

Table 16–3 I/O channel properties controlled by fconfigure.

-blocking	Blocks until I/O channel is ready: 0 or 1.
-buffering	Buffer mode: none, line, or full.
-buffersize	Number of characters in the buffer.
-eofchar	Special end of file character. Control-z (\x1a) for DOS. Null otherwise.
-encoding	The character set encoding.
-error	Returns the last POSIX error message associated with a channel.
-translation	End of line translation: auto, lf, cr, crlf, binary.
-mode	Serial devices only. Format: *baud,parity,data,stop*
-peername	Sockets only. IP address of remote host.
-peerport	Sockets only. Port number of remote host.

Nonblocking I/O

By default, I/O channels are *blocking*. A gets or read will wait until data is available before returning. A puts may also wait if the I/O channel is not ready to accept data. This behavior is all right if you are using disk files, which are essentially always ready. If you use pipelines or network sockets, however, the blocking behavior can hang up your application.

The fconfigure command can set a channel into *nonblocking mode*. A gets or read command may return immediately with no data. This occurs when there is no data available on a socket or pipeline. A puts to a nonblocking channel will accept all the data and buffer it internally. When the underlying device (i.e., a pipeline or socket) is ready, then Tcl automatically writes out the buffered data. Nonblocking channels are useful because your application can do something else while waiting for the I/O channel. You can also manage several nonblocking I/O channels at once. Nonblocking channels should be used with the fileevent command described earlier. The following command puts a channel into nonblocking mode:

```
fconfigure fileID -blocking 0
```

It is not strictly necessary to put a channel into nonblocking mode if you use fileevent. However, if the channel is in blocking mode, then it is still possible for the gets or read done by your fileevent procedure to block. For example, an I/O channel might have some data ready, but not a complete line. In this case, a gets would block, unless the channel is nonblocking. Perhaps the best motivation for a nonblocking channel is the buffering behavior of a nonblocking puts. You can even close a channel that has buffered data, and Tcl will automatically write out the buffers as the channel becomes ready. For these reasons, it is common to use a nonblocking channel with fileevent. Example 16–3 shows a fileevent handler for a nonblocking channel. As described above, the gets may not find a complete line, in which case it doesn't read anything and returns -1.

Example 16–3 A read event file handler for a nonblocking channel.

```
set pipe [open "|some command"]
fileevent $pipe readable [list Reader $pipe]
fconfigure $pipe -blocking 0
proc Reader { pipe } {
    global done
    if {[eof $pipe]} {
        catch {close $pipe}
        set done 1
        return
    }
    if {[gets $pipe line] < 0} {
        # We blocked anyway because only part of a line
        # was available for input
    } else {
        # Process one line
    }
}
vwait done
```

The `fblocked` Command

The `fblocked` command returns 1 if a channel does not have data ready. Normally the `fileevent` command takes care of waiting for data, so I have seen `fblocked` useful only in testing channel implementations.

Buffering

By default, Tcl buffers data, so I/O is more efficient. The underlying device is accessed less frequently, so there is less overhead. In some cases you may want data to be visible immediately and buffering gets in the way. The following turns off all buffering:

```
fconfigure fileID -buffering none
```

Full buffering means that output data is accumulated until a buffer fills; then a write is performed. For reading, Tcl attempts to read a whole buffer each time more data is needed. The read-ahead for buffering will not block. The `-buffersize` parameter controls the buffer size:

```
fconfigure fileID -buffering full -buffersize 8192
```

Line buffering is used by default on `stdin` and `stdout`. Each newline in an output channel causes a write operation. Read buffering is the same as full buffering. The following command turns on line buffering:

```
fconfigure fileID -buffering line
```

End of Line Translations

On UNIX, text lines end with a newline character ($\n$). On Macintosh they end with a carriage return ($\r$). On Windows they end with a carriage return, newline sequence ($\r\n$). Network sockets also use the carriage return, newline sequence. By default, Tcl accepts any of these, and the line terminator can even change within a channel. All of these different conventions are converted to the UNIX style so that once read, text lines always end with a newline character ($\n$). Both the `read` and `gets` commands do this conversion. By default, text lines are generated in the platform-native format during output.

The default behavior is almost always what you want, but you can control the translation with `fconfigure`. Table 16–4 shows settings for `-translation`:

Table 16–4 End of line translation modes.

`binary`	No translation at all.
`lf`	UNIX-style, which also means no translations.
`cr`	Macintosh style. On input, carriage returns are converted to newlines. On output, newlines are converted to carriage returns.
`crlf`	Windows and Network style. On input, carriage return, newline is converted to a newline. On output, a newline is converted to a carriage return, newline.
`auto`	The default behavior. On input, all end of line conventions are converted to a newline. Output is in native format.

II. Advanced Tcl

End of File Character

In DOS file systems, there may be a Control-z character (`\x1a`) at the end of a text file. By default, this character is ignored on the Windows platform if it occurs at the end of the file, and this character is output when you close the file. You can turn this off by specifying an empty string for the end of file character:

```
fconfigure fileID -eofchar {}
```

Serial Devices

The `-mode` attribute specifies the baud rate, parity mode, the number of data bits, and the number of stop bits:

```
set tty [open /dev/ttya]
fconfigure $tty -mode
=> 9600,0,8,2
```

If you need to set additional attributes of the serial channel, you will have to write a command in C that makes the system calls you need. If you are familiar with serial devices, you know there are quite a few possibilities!

Windows has some special device names that always connect you to the serial line devices when you use `open`. They are `com1` through `com8`. The system console is named `con`. The null device is `nul`.

UNIX has names for serial devices in `/dev`. The serial devices are `/dev/ttya`, `/dev/ttyb`, and so on. The system console is `/dev/console`. The current terminal is `/dev/tty`. The null device is `/dev/null`.

Macintosh needs a special command to open serial devices. This is provided by a third-party extension that you can find at the Tcl Resource Center under:

```
http://www.scriptics.com/resource/software/extensions/macintosh/
```

Character Set Encodings

Tcl automatically converts various character set encodings into Unicode internally. It cannot automatically detect the encoding for a file or network socket, however, so you need to use `fconfigure -encoding` if you are reading data that is not in the system's default encoding. Character set issues are explained in more detail in Chapter 15.

Configuring Read-Write Channels

If you have a channel that is used for both input and output, you can set the channel parameters independently for input and output. In this case, you can specify a two-element list for the parameter value. The first element is for the input side of the channel, and the second element is for the output side of the channel. If you specify only a single element, it applies to both input and output. For example, the following command forces output end of line translations to be `crlf` mode, leaves the input channel on automatic, and sets the buffer size for both input and output:

```
fconfigure pipe -translation {auto crlf} -buffersize 4096
```

Socket Programming

This chapter shows how to use sockets for programming network clients and servers. Advanced I/O techniques for sockets are described, including nonblocking I/O and control over I/O buffering. Tcl commands discussed are: `socket`, `fconfigure`, and `http::geturl`.

Sockets are network communication channels. The sockets described in this chapter use the TCP network protocol, although you can find Tcl extensions that create sockets using other protocols. TCP provides a reliable byte stream between two hosts connected to a network. TCP handles all the issues about routing information across the network, and it automatically recovers if data is lost or corrupted along the way. TCP is the basis for other protocols like Telnet, FTP, and HTTP.

A Tcl script can use a network socket just like an open file or pipeline. Instead of using the Tcl `open` command, you use the `socket` command to open a socket. Then you use `gets`, `puts`, and `read` to transfer data. The `close` command closes a network socket.

Network programming distinguishes between clients and servers. A server is a process or program that runs for long periods of time and controls access to some resource. For example, an FTP server governs access to files, and an HTTP server provides access to hypertext pages on the World Wide Web. A client typically connects to the server for a limited time in order to gain access to the resource. For example, when a Web browser fetches a hypertext page, it is acting as a client. The extended examples in this chapter show how to program the client side of the HTTP protocol.

The Scotty extension supports many network protocols.

The Scotty Tcl extension provides access to other network protocols like UDP, DNS, and RPC. It also supports the SNMP network management protocol and the MIB database associated with SNMP. Scotty is a great extension pack-

225

age that is widely used for network management applications. Its home page is:

```
http://wwwsnmp.cs.utwente.nl/~schoenw/scotty/
```

Client Sockets

A client opens a socket by specifying the *host address* and *port number* for the server of the socket. The host address gives the network location (i.e., which computer), and the port selects a particular server from all the possible servers that may be running on that host. For example, HTTP servers typically use port 80, while FTP servers use port 20. The following example shows how to open a client socket to a Web server:

```
set s [socket www.scriptics.com 80]
```

There are two forms for host names. The previous example uses a *domain name*: www.scriptics.com. You can also specify raw IP addresses, which are specified with four dot-separated integers (e.g., 128.15.115.32). A domain name is mapped into a raw IP address by the system software, and it is almost always a better idea to use a domain name in case the IP address assignment for the host changes. This can happen when hosts are upgraded or they move to a different part of the network. As of Tcl 8.2, there is no direct access from Tcl to the DNS service that maps host names to IP addresses. You'll need to use Scotty to get DNS access.

Some systems also provide symbolic names for well-known port numbers. For example, instead of using 20 for the FTP service, you can use ftp. On UNIX systems, the well-known port numbers are listed in the file named /etc/services.

Client Socket Options

The socket command accepts some optional arguments when opening the client-side socket. The general form of the command is:

```
socket ?-async? ?-myaddr address? ?-myport myport? host port
```

Ordinarily the address and port on the client side are chosen automatically. If your computer has multiple network interfaces, you can select one with the -myaddr option. The address value can be a domain name or an IP address. If your application needs a specific client port, it can choose one with the -myport option. If the port is in use, the socket command will raise an error.

The -async option causes connection to happen in the background, and the socket command returns immediately. The socket becomes writable when the connection completes, or fails. You can use fileevent to get a callback when this occurs. This is shown in Example 17–1. If you use the socket before the connection completes, and the socket is in blocking mode, then Tcl automatically blocks and waits for the connection to complete. If the socket is in nonblocking mode, attempts to use the socket return immediately. The gets and read commands would return -1, and fblocked would return 1 in this situation.

In some cases, it can take a long time to open the connection to the server. Usually this occurs when the server host is down, and it may take longer than you want for the connection to time out. The following example sets up a timer with `after` so that you can choose your own timeout limit on the connection:

Example 17–1 Opening a client socket with a timeout.

```
proc Socket_Client {host port timeout} {
    global connected
    after $timeout {set connected timeout}
    set sock [socket -async $host $port]
    fileevent $sock w {set connected ok}
    vwait connected
    if {$connected == "timeout"} {
        return -code error timeout
    } else {
        return $sock
    }
}
```

Server Sockets

A TCP server socket allows multiple clients. The way this works is that the `socket` command creates a *listening socket*, and then new sockets are created when clients make connections to the server. Tcl takes care of all the details and makes this easy to use. You simply specify a port number and give the socket command a *callback* to execute when a client connects to your server socket. The callback is just a Tcl command. A simple example is shown below:

Example 17–2 Opening a server socket.

```
set listenSocket [socket -server Accept 2540]
proc Accept {newSock addr port} {
    puts "Accepted $newSock from $addr port $port"
}
vwait forever
```

The `Accept` command is the callback. With server sockets, Tcl adds additional arguments to the callback before it calls it. The arguments are the new socket connection, and the host and port number of the remote client. In this simple example, `Accept` just prints out its arguments.

The `vwait` command puts Tcl into its event loop so that it can do the background processing necessary to accept connections. The `vwait` command will wait until the `forever` variable is modified, which won't happen in this simple example. The key point is that Tcl processes other events (e.g., network connections and other file I/O) while it waits. If you have a Tk application (e.g., *wish*), then it already has an event loop to handle window system events, so you do not need to use `vwait`. The Tcl event loop is discussed on page 217.

Server Socket Options

By default, Tcl lets the operating system choose the network interface used for the server socket, and you simply supply the port number. If your computer has multiple interfaces, you may want to specify a particular one. Use the `-myaddr` option for this. The general form of the command to open server sockets is:

```
socket -server callback ?-myaddr address? port
```

The last argument to the `socket` command is the server's port number. For your own unofficial servers, you'll need to pick port numbers higher than 1024 to avoid conflicts with existing services. UNIX systems prevent user programs from opening server sockets with port numbers less than 1024. If you use 0 as the port number, then the operating system will pick the listening port number for you. You must use `fconfigure` to find out what port you have:

```
fconfigure $sock -sockname
=> ipaddr hostname port
```

The Echo Service

Example 17–3 The echo service.

```
proc Echo_Server {port} {
    global echo
    set echo(main) [socket -server EchoAccept $port]
}
proc EchoAccept {sock addr port} {
    global echo
    puts "Accept $sock from $addr port $port"
    set echo(addr,$sock) [list $addr $port]
    fconfigure $sock -buffering line
    fileevent $sock readable [list Echo $sock]
}
proc Echo {sock} {
    global echo
    if {[eof $sock] || [catch {gets $sock line}]} {
        # end of file or abnormal connection drop
        close $sock
        puts "Close $echo(addr,$sock)"
        unset echo(addr,$sock)
    } else {
        if {[string compare $line "quit"] == 0} {
            # Prevent new connections.
            # Existing connections stay open.
            close $echo(main)
        }
        puts $sock $line
    }
}
```

The echo server accepts connections from clients. It reads data from the clients and writes that data back. The example uses `fileevent` to wait for data from the client, and it uses `fconfigure` to adjust the buffering behavior of the network socket. You can use Example 17–3 as a template for more interesting services.

The `Echo_Server` procedure opens the socket and saves the result in `echo(main)`. When this socket is closed later, the server stops accepting new connections but existing connections won't be affected. If you want to experiment with this server, start it and wait for connections like this:

```
Echo_Server 2540
vwait forever
```

The `EchoAccept` procedure uses the `fconfigure` command to set up line buffering. This means that each `puts` by the server results in a network transmission to the client. The importance of this will be described in more detail later. A complete description of the `fconfigure` command is given in Chapter 16. The `EchoAccept` procedure uses the `fileevent` command to register a procedure that handles I/O on the socket. In this example, the `Echo` procedure will be called whenever the socket is readable. Note that it is not necessary to put the socket into nonblocking mode when using the `fileevent` callback. The effects of nonblocking mode are discussed on page 221.

`EchoAccept` saves information about each client in the `echo` array. This is used only to print out a message when a client closes its connection. In a more sophisticated server, however, you may need to keep more interesting state about each client. The name of the socket provides a convenient handle on the client. In this case, it is used as part of the array index.

The `Echo` procedure first checks to see whether the socket has been closed by the client or there is an error when reading the socket. The `if` expression only performs the `gets` if the `eof` does not return true:

```
if {[eof $sock] || [catch {gets $sock line}]} {
```

Closing the socket automatically clears the `fileevent` registration. If you forget to close the socket upon the end of file condition, the Tcl event loop will invoke your callback repeatedly. It is important to close it when you detect end of file.

Example 17–4 A client of the echo service.

```
proc Echo_Client {host port} {
    set s [socket $host $port]
    fconfigure $s -buffering line
    return $s
}
set s [Echo_Client localhost 2540]
puts $s "Hello!"
gets $s
=> Hello!
```

II. Advanced Tcl

In the normal case, the server simply reads a line with `gets` and then writes it back to the client with `puts`. If the line is "quit," then the server closes its main socket. This prevents any more connections by new clients, but it doesn't affect any clients that are already connected.

Example 17–4 shows a sample client of the `Echo` service. The main point is to ensure that the socket is line buffered so that each `puts` by the client results in a network transmission. (Or, more precisely, each newline character results in a network transmission.) If you forget to set line buffering with `fconfigure`, the client's `gets` command will probably hang because the server will not get any data; it will be stuck in buffers on the client.

Fetching a URL with HTTP

The HyperText Transport Protocol (HTTP) is the protocol used on the World Wide Web. This section presents a procedure to fetch pages or images from a server on the Web. Items in the Web are identified with a Universal Resource Location (URL) that specifies a host, port, and location on the host. The basic outline of HTTP is that a client sends a URL to a server, and the server responds with some header information and some content data. The header information describes the content, which can be hypertext, images, postscript, and more.

Example 17–5 Opening a connection to an HTTP server.

```
proc Http_Open {url} {
    global http
    if {![regexp -nocase {^(http://)?([^:/]+)(:([0-9])+)?(/.*)} \
            $url x protocol server y port path]} {
        error "bogus URL: $url"
    }
    if {[string length $port] == 0} {
        set port 80
    }
    set sock [socket $server $port]
    puts $sock "GET $path HTTP/1.0"
    puts $sock "Host: $server"
    puts $sock "User-Agent: Tcl/Tk Http_Open"
    puts $sock ""
    flush $sock
    return $sock
}
```

The `Http_Open` procedure uses `regexp` to pick out the server and port from the URL. This regular expression is described in detail on page 149. The leading `http://` is optional, and so is the port number. If the port is left off, then the standard port 80 is used. If the regular expression matches, then a `socket` command opens the network connection.

The protocol begins with the client sending a line that identifies the command (GET), the path, and the protocol version. The path is the part of the URL after the server and port specification. The rest of the request is lines in the following format:

```
key: value
```

The Host identifies the server, which supports servers that implement more than one server name. The User-Agent identifies the client program, which is often a browser like *Netscape Navigator* or *Internet Explorer*. The key-value lines are terminated with a blank line. This data is flushed out of the Tcl buffering system with the flush command. The server will respond by sending the URL contents back over the socket. This is described shortly, but first we consider proxies.

Proxy Servers

A *proxy* is used to get through firewalls that many organizations set up to isolate their network from the Internet. The proxy accepts HTTP requests from clients inside the firewall and then forwards the requests outside the firewall. It also relays the server's response back to the client. The protocol is nearly the same when using the proxy. The difference is that the complete URL is passed to the GET command so that the proxy can locate the server. Example 17–6 uses a proxy if one is defined:

Example 17–6 Opening a connection to an HTTP server.

```
# Http_Proxy sets or queries the proxy
proc Http_Proxy {{new {}}} {
   global http
   if ![info exists http(proxy)] {
      return {}
   }
   if {[string length $new] == 0} {
      return $http(proxy):$http(proxyPort)
   } else {
      regexp {^([^:]+):([0-9]+)$} $new x \
         http(proxy) http(proxyPort)
   }
}

proc Http_Open {url {cmd GET} {query {}}} {
   global http
   if {![regexp -nocase {^(http://)?([^:/]+)(:([0-9]+))?(/.*)} \
         $url x protocol server y port path]} {
      error "bogus URL: $url"
   }
   if {[string length $port] == 0} {
      set port 80
   }
   if {[info exists http(proxy)] &&
         [string length $http(proxy)]} {
      set sock [socket $http(proxy) $http(proxyPort)]
```

```
          puts $sock "$cmd http://$server:$port$path HTTP/1.0"
    } else {
          set sock [socket $server $port]
          puts $sock "$cmd $path HTTP/1.0"
    }
    puts $sock "User-Agent: Tcl/Tk Http_Open"
    puts $sock "Host: $server"
    if {[string length $query] > 0} {
          puts $sock "Content-Length: [string length $query]"
          puts $sock ""
          puts $sock $query
    }
    puts $sock ""
    flush $sock
    fconfigure $sock -blocking 0
    return $sock
}
```

The HEAD Request

In Example 17–6, the Http_Open procedure takes a cmd parameter so that
the user of Http_Open can perform different operations. The GET operation
fetches the contents of a URL. The HEAD operation just fetches the description of
a URL, which is useful to validate a URL. The POST operation transmits query
data to the server (e.g., values from a form) and also fetches the contents of the
URL. All of these operations follow a similar protocol. The reply from the server
is a status line followed by lines that have key-value pairs. This format is similar
to the client's request. The reply header is followed by content data with GET and
POST operations. Example 17–7 implements the HEAD command, which does not
involve any reply data:

Example 17–7 Http_Head validates a URL.

```
proc Http_Head {url} {
    upvar #0 $url state
    catch {unset state}
    set state(sock) [Http_Open $url HEAD]
    fileevent $state(sock) readable [list HttpHeader $url]
    # Specify the real name, not the upvar alias, to vwait
    vwait $url\(status)
    catch {close $state(sock)}
    return $state(status)
}
proc HttpHeader {url} {
    upvar #0 $url state
    if {[eof $state(sock)]} {
        set state(status) eof
        close $state(sock)
        return
    }
    if {[catch {gets $state(sock) line} nbytes]} {
```

```
            set state(status) error
            lappend state(headers) [list error $nbytes]
            close $state(sock)
            return
        }
        if {$nbytes < 0} {
            # Read would block
            return
        } elseif {$nbytes == 0} {
            # Header complete
            set state(status) head
        } elseif {![info exists state(headers)]} {
            # Initial status reply from the server
            set state(headers) [list http $line]
        } else {
            # Process key-value pairs
            regexp {^([^:]+): *(.*)$} $line x key value
            lappend state(headers) [string tolower $key] $value
        }
    }
}
```

The `Http_Head` procedure uses `Http_Open` to contact the server. The `HttpHeader` procedure is registered as a `fileevent` handler to read the server's reply. A global array keeps state about each operation. The URL is used in the array name, and `upvar` is used to create an alias to the name (`upvar` is described on page 86):

```
upvar #0 $url state
```

You cannot use the `upvar` alias as the variable specified to `vwait`. Instead, you must use the actual name. The backslash turns off the array reference in order to pass the name of the array element to `vwait`, otherwise Tcl tries to reference `url` as an array:

```
vwait $url\(status)
```

The `HttpHeader` procedure checks for special cases: end of file, an error on the `gets`, or a short read on a nonblocking socket. The very first reply line contains a status code from the server that is in a different format than the rest of the header lines:

```
code message
```

The code is a three-digit numeric code. `200` is OK. Codes in the `400`'s and `500`'s indicate an error. The codes are explained fully in RFC 1945 that specifies HTTP 1.0. The first line is saved with the key `http`:

```
set state(headers) [list http $line]
```

The rest of the header lines are parsed into key-value pairs and appended onto `state(headers)`. This format can be used to initialize an array:

```
array set header $state(headers)
```

When `HttpHeader` gets an empty line, the header is complete and it sets the `state(status)` variable, which signals `Http_Head`. Finally, `Http_Head` returns the status to its caller. The complete information about the request is still in the global array named by the URL. Example 17–8 illustrates the use of `Http_Head`:

Example 17–8 Using `Http_Head`.

```
set url http://www.sun.com/
set status [Http_Head $url]
=> eof
upvar #0 $url state
array set info $state(headers)
parray info
info(http)              HTTP/1.0 200 OK
info(server)            Apache/1.1.1
info(last-modified)  Nov ...
info(content-type)   text/html
```

The GET and POST Requests

Example 17–9 shows `Http_Get`, which implements the GET and POST
requests. The difference between these is that POST sends query data to the
server after the request header. Both operations get a reply from the server that
is divided into a descriptive header and the content data. The `Http_Open` procedure sends the request and the query, if present, and reads the reply header.
`Http_Get` reads the content.

The descriptive header returned by the server is in the same format as the
client's request. One of the key-value pairs returned by the server specifies the
`Content-Type` of the URL. The content-types come from the MIME standard,
which is described in RFC 1521. Typical content-types are:

- `text/html` — HyperText Markup Language (HTML), which is introduced in
  Chapter 3.
- `text/plain` — plain text with no markup.
- `image/gif` — image data in GIF format.
- `image/jpeg` — image data in JPEG format.
- `application/postscript` — a postscript document.
- `application/x-tcl` — a Tcl program! This type is discussed in Chapter 20.

Example 17–9 `Http_Get` fetches the contents of a URL.

```
proc Http_Get {url {query {}}} {
    upvar #0 $url state         ;# Alias to global array
    catch {unset state}         ;# Aliases still valid.
    if {[string length $query] > 0} {
       set state(sock) [Http_Open $url POST $query]
    } else {
       set state(sock) [Http_Open $url GET]
    }
    set sock $state(sock)
    fileevent $sock readable [list HttpHeader $url]

    # Specify the real name, not the upvar alias, to vwait
    vwait $url\(status)
```

```
    set header(content-type) {}
    set header(http) "500 unknown error"
    array set header $state(headers)

    # Check return status.
    # 200 is OK, other codes indicate a problem.
    regsub "HTTP/1.. " $header(http) {} header(http)
    if {![string match 2* $header(http)]} {
        catch {close $sock}
        if {[info exists header(location)] &&
                [string match 3* $header(http)]} {
            # 3xx is a redirection to another URL
            set state(link) $header(location)
            return [Http_Get $header(location) $query]
        }
        return -code error $header(http)
    }
    # Set up to read the content data
    switch -glob -- $header(content-type) {
        text/*      {
            # Read HTML into memory
            fileevent $sock readable [list HttpGetText $url]
        }
        default     {
            # Copy content data to a file
            fconfigure $sock -translation binary
            set state(filename) [File_TempName http]
            if [catch {open $state(filename) w} out] {
                set state(status) error
                set state(error) $out
                close $sock
                return $header(content-type)
            }
            set state(fd) $out
            fcopy $sock $out -command [list HttpCopyDone $url]
        }
    }
    vwait $url\(status)
    return $header(content-type)
}
```

Http_Get uses Http_Open to initiate the request, and then it looks for errors. It handles redirection errors that occur if a URL has changed. These have error codes that begin with 3. A common case of this error is when a user omits the trailing slash on a URL (e.g., http://www.scriptics.com). Most servers respond with:

```
302 Document has moved

Location: http://www.scriptics.com/
```

If the content-type is text, then Http_Get sets up a fileevent handler to read this data into memory. The socket is in nonblocking mode, so the read handler can read as much data as possible each time it is called. This is more efficient than using gets to read a line at a time. The text will be stored in the

state(body) variable for use by the caller of Http_Get. Example 17–10 shows
the HttpGetText fileevent handler:

Example 17–10 HttpGetText reads text URLs.

```
proc HttpGetText {url} {
    upvar #0 $url state
    if {[eof $state(sock)]} {
        # Content complete
        set state(status) done
        close $state(sock)
    } elseif {[catch {read $state(sock)} block]} {
        set state(status) error
        lappend state(headers) [list error $block]
        close $state(sock)
    } else {
        append state(body) $block
    }
}
```

The content may be in binary format. This poses a problem for Tcl 7.6 and
earlier. A null character will terminate the value, so values with embedded nulls
cannot be processed safely by Tcl scripts. Tcl 8.0 supports strings and variable
values with arbitrary binary data. Example 17–9 uses fcopy to copy data from
the socket to a file without storing it in Tcl variables. This command was introduced in Tcl 7.5 as unsupported0, and became fcopy in Tcl 8.0. It takes a callback argument that is invoked when the copy is complete. The callback gets
additional arguments that are the bytes transferred and an optional error string.
In this case, these arguments are added to the url argument specified in the
fcopy command. Example 17–11 shows the HttpCopyDone callback:

Example 17–11 HttpCopyDone is used with fcopy.

```
proc HttpCopyDone {url bytes {error {}}} {
    upvar #0 $url state
    if {[string length $error]} {
        set state(status) error
        lappend state(headers) [list error $error]
    } else {
        set state(status) ok
    }
    close $state(sock)
    close $state(fd)
}
```

The user of Http_Get uses the information in the state array to determine
the status of the fetch and where to find the content. There are four cases to deal
with:

- There was an error, which is indicated by the `state(error)` element.
- There was a redirection, in which case, the new URL is in `state(link)`. The client of `Http_Get` should change the URL and look at its state instead. You can use `upvar` to redefine the alias for the `state` array:

```
upvar #0 $state(link) state
```

- There was text content. The content is in `state(body)`.
- There was another content-type that was copied to `state(filename)`.

The `fcopy` Command

The `fcopy` command can do a complete copy in the background. It automatically sets up `fileevent` handlers, so you do not have to use `fileevent` yourself. It also manages its buffers efficiently. The general form of the command is:

```
fcopy input output ?-size size? ?-command callback?
```

The `-command` argument makes `fcopy` work in the background. When the copy is complete or an error occurs, the `callback` is invoked with one or two additional arguments: the number of bytes copied, and, in the case of an error, it is also passed an error string:

```
fcopy $in $out -command [list CopyDone $in $out]
proc CopyDone {in out bytes {error {}} {
    close $in ; close $out
}
```

With a background copy, the `fcopy` command transfers data from *input* until end of file or *size* bytes have been transferred. If no `-size` argument is given, then the copy goes until end of file. It is not safe to do other I/O operations with *input* or *output* during a background `fcopy`. If either *input* or *output* gets closed while the copy is in progress, the current copy is stopped. If the *input* is closed, then all data already queued for *output* is written out.

Without a `-command` argument, the `fcopy` command reads as much as possible depending on the blocking mode of *input* and the optional *size* parameter. Everything it reads is queued for output before `fcopy` returns. If *output* is blocking, then `fcopy` returns after the data is written out. If *input* is blocking, then `fcopy` can block attempting to read *size* bytes or until end of file.

The `http` Package

The standard Tcl library includes an `http` package that is based on the code I wrote for this chapter. This section documents the package, which has a slightly different interface. The library version uses namespaces and combines the `Http_Get`, `Http_Head`, and `Http_Post` procedures into a single `http::geturl` procedure. The examples in this chapter are still interesting, but you should look at `http.tcl` in the Tcl library, which I also wrote. Definitely use the standard `http` package for your production code.

http::config

The `http::config` command is used to set the proxy information, time-outs, and the `User-Agent` and `Accept` headers that are generated in the HTTP request. You can specify the proxy host and port, or you can specify a Tcl command that is run to determine the proxy. With no arguments, `http::config` returns the current settings:

```
http::config
=> -accept */* -proxyfilter httpProxyRequired -proxyhost
{} -proxyport {} -timeout unlimited
-useragent {Tcl http client package 2.0}
```

If you specify just one option, its value is returned:

```
http::config -proxyfilter
=> httpProxyRequired
```

You can set one or more options:

```
http::config -proxyhost webcache.eng -proxyport 8080
```

The default proxy filter just returns the `-proxyhost` and `-proxyport` values if they are set. You can supply a smarter filter that picks a proxy based on the host in the URL. The proxy filter is called with the hostname and should return a list of two elements, the proxy host and port. If no proxy is required, return an empty list.

The `-timeout` value limits the time the transaction can take. Its value is `unlimited` for no timeout, or a milliseconds value. You can specify 500, for example, to have a half-second timeout.

http::geturl

The `http::geturl` procedure does a GET, POST, or HEAD transaction depending on its arguments. By default, `http::geturl` blocks until the request completes and it returns a token that represents the transaction. As described below, you use the token to get the results of the transaction. If you supply a `-command` *callback* option, then `http::geturl` returns immediately and invokes *callback* when the transaction completes. The callback is passed the token that represents the transaction. Table 17–1 lists the options to `http::geturl`:

Table 17–1 Options to the `http::geturl` command.

`-blocksize` *num*	Block size when copying to a channel.
`-channel` *fileID*	The *fileID* is an open file or socket. The URL data is copied to this channel instead of saving it in memory.
`-command` *callback*	Calls *callback* when the transaction completes. The token from `http::geturl` is passed to *callback*.
`-handler` *command*	Called from the event handler to read data from the URL.

Table 17–1 Options to the http::geturl command. (Continued)

-headers *list*	The *list* specifies a set of headers that are included in the HTTP request. The list alternates between header keys and values.
-progress *command*	Calls *command* after each block is copied to a channel. It gets called with three parameters: *command token totalsize currentsize*
-query *codedstring*	Issues a POST request with the *codedstring* form data.
-timeout *msec*	Aborts the request after *msec* milliseconds have elapsed.
-validate *bool*	If *bool* is true, a HEAD request is made.

For simple applications you can simply block on the transaction:

```
set token [http::geturl www.beedub.com/index.html]
=> http::1
```

The leading http:// in the URL is optional. The return value is a token that is also the name of a global array that contains state about the transaction. Names like http::1 are used instead of using the URL as the array name. You can use upvar to convert the return value from http::geturl to an array variable:

```
upvar #0 $token state
```

By default, the URL data is saved in state(body). The elements of the state array are described in Table 17–2:

Table 17–2 Elements of the http::geturl state array.

body	The contents of the URL.
currentsize	The current number of bytes transferred.
error	An explanation of why the transaction was aborted.
http	The HTTP reply status.
meta	A list of the keys and values in the reply header.
status	The current status: pending, ok, eof, or reset.
totalsize	The expected size of the returned data.
type	The content type of the returned data.
url	The URL of the request.

A handful of access functions are provided so that you can avoid using the state array directly. These are listed in Table 17–3:

Table 17-3 The `http` support procedures.

`http::data $token`	Returns `state(body)`.
`http::status $token`	Returns `state(status)`.
`http::error $token`	Returns `state(error)`.
`http::code $token`	Returns `state(http)`.
`http::wait $token`	Blocks until the transaction completes.
`http::cleanup $token`	Unsets the state array named by `$token`.

You can take advantage of the asynchronous interface by specifying a command that is called when the transaction completes. The callback is passed the token returned from `http::geturl` so that it can access the transaction state:

```
http::geturl $url -command [list Url_Display $text $url]
proc Url_Display {text url token} {
    upvar #0 $token state
    # Display the url in text
}
```

You can have `http::geturl` copy the URL to a file or socket with the `-channel` option. This is useful for downloading large files or images. In this case, you can get a progress callback so that you can provide user feedback during the transaction. Example 17-12 shows a simple downloading script:

Example 17-12 Downloading files with `http::geturl`.

```
#!/usr/local/tclsh8.0
if {$argc < 2} {
    puts stderr "Usage: $argv0 url file"
    exit 1
}
package require http
set url [lindex $argv 0]
set file [lindex $argv 1]
set out [open $file w]
proc progress {token total current} {
    puts -nonewline "."
}
http::config -proxyhost webcache.eng -proxyport 8080
set token [http::geturl $url -progress progress \
    -headers {Pragma no-cache} -channel $out]
close $out
# Print out the return header information
puts ""
upvar #0 $token state
puts $state(http)
foreach {key value} $state(meta) {
    puts "$key: $value"
}
exit 0
```

`http::formatQuery`

If you specify form data with the `-query` option, then `http::geturl` does a POST transaction. You need to encode the form data for safe transmission. The `http::formatQuery` procedure takes a list of keys and values and encodes them in `x-www-url-encoded` format. Pass this result as the query data:

```
http::formatQuery name "Brent Welch" title "Tcl Programmer"
=> name=Brent+Welch&title=Tcl+Programmer
```

`http::reset`

You can cancel an outstanding transaction with `http::reset`:

```
http::reset $token
```

This is done automatically when you setup a `-timeout` with `http::config`.

`http::cleanup`

When you are done with the data returned from `http::geturl`, use the `http::cleanup` procedure to unset the state variable used to store the data.

Basic Authentication

Web pages are often password protected. The most common form of this uses a protocol called Basic Authentication, which is not very strong, but easy to implement. With this scheme, the server responds to an HTTP request with a 401 error status and a `Www-Authenticate` header, which specifies the authentication protocol the server wants to use. For example, the server response can contain the following information:

```
HTTP/1.0 401 Authorization Required
Www-Authenticate: Basic realm="My Pages"
```

The *realm* is meant to be an authentication domain. In practice, it is used in the string that gets displayed to the user as part of the password prompt. For example, a Web browser will display this prompt:

```
Enter the password for My Pages at www.beedub.com
```

After getting the user name and password from the user, the Web browser tries its HTTP request again. This time it includes an `Authorization` header that contains the user name and password encoded with *base64 encoding*. There is no encryption at all — anyone can decode the string, which is why this is not a strong form of protection. The Tcl Web Server includes a `base64.tcl` file that has `Base64_Encode` and `Base64_Decode` procedures. Example 17–13 illustrates the Basic Authentication protocol. `http::geturl` takes a `-headers` option that lets you pass additional headers in the request.

Example 17–13 Basic Authentication using `http::geturl`.

```
proc BasicAuthentication {url promptProc} {
    set token [http::geturl $url]
    http::wait $token
    if {[string match *401* [http::code $token]]} {
        upvar #0 $token data

        # Extract the realm from the Www-Authenticate line

        array set reply $data(meta)
        if {[regexp {realm=(.*)} $reply(Www-Authenticate) \
                x realm]} {

            # Call back to prompt for username, password

            set answer [$promptProc $realm]
            http::cleanup $token

            # Encode username:password and pass this in
            # the Authorization header

            set auth [Base64_Encode \
                [lindex $answer 0]:[lindex $answer 1]]
            set token [http::geturl $url -headers \
                [list Authorization "Basic $auth"]]
            http::wait $token
        }
    }
    return $token
}
```

Example 17–13 takes a `promptProc` argument that is the name of a procedure to call to get the username and password. This procedure could display a Tk
dialog box, or prompt for user input from the terminal. In practice, you probably
already know the username and password. In this case, you can skip the initial
challenge–response steps and simply supply the `Authorization` header on the
first request:

```
http::geturl $url -headers \
    [list Authorization \
        "Basic [Base64_Encode $username:$password]"]
```

TclHttpd Web Server

This chapter describes TclHttpd, a Web server built entirely in Tcl. The Web
server can be used as a standalone server, or it can be embedded into
applications to Web-enable them. TclHttpd provides a Tcl+HTML
template facility that is useful for maintaining site-wide look and feel, and
an application-direct URL that invokes a Tcl procedure in an application.

TclHttpd started out as about 175 lines of
Tcl that could serve up HTML pages and images. The Tcl `socket` and I/O commands make this easy. Of course, there are lots of features in Web servers like
Apache or Netscape that were not present in the first prototype. Steve Uhler
took my prototype, refined the HTTP handling, and aimed to keep the basic
server under 250 lines. I went the other direction, setting up a modular architecture, adding in features found in other Web servers, and adding some interesting
ways to connect TclHttpd to Tcl applications.

Today TclHttpd is used both as a general-purpose Web server, and as a
framework for building server applications. It implements www.scriptics.com,
including the Tcl Resource Center and Scriptics' electronic commerce facilities. It
is also built into several commercial applications such as license servers and
mail spam filters. Instructions for setting up the TclHttpd on your platform are
given toward the end of the chapter, on page 266. It works on Unix, Windows,
and Macintosh. Using TclHttpd, you can have your own Web server up and running quickly.

This chapter provides an overview of the server and several examples of
how you can use it. The chapter is not an exhaustive reference to every feature.
Instead, it concentrates on a very useful subset of server features that I use the
most. There are references to Tcl files in the server's implementation, which are
all found in the `lib` directory of the distribution. You may find it helpful to read
the code to learn more about the implementation. You can find the source on the
CD-ROM.

Integrating TclHttpd with your Application

The bulk of this chapter describes the various ways you can extend the server and integrate it into your application. TclHttpd is interesting because, as a Tcl script, it is easy to add to your application. Suddenly your application has an interface that is accessible to Web browsers in your company's intranet or the global Internet. The Web server provides several ways you can connect it to your application:

- *Static pages* — As a "normal" Web server, you can serve static documents that describe your application.
- *Domain handlers* — You can arrange for all URL requests in a section of your Web site to be handled by your application. This is a very general interface where you interpret what the URL means and what sort of pages to return to each request. For example, `http://www.scriptics.com/resource` is implemented this way. The URL past `/resource` selects an index in a simple database, and the server returns a page describing the pages under that index.
- *Application-Direct URLs* — This is a domain handler that maps URLs onto Tcl procedures. The form query data that is part of the HTTP GET or POST request is automatically mapped onto the parameters of the application-direct procedure. The procedure simply computes the page as its return value. This is an elegant and efficient alternative to the CGI interface. For example, in TclHttpd the URLs under `/status` report various statistics about the Web server's operation.
- *Document handlers* — You can define a Tcl procedure that handles all files of a particular type. For example, the server has a handler for CGI scripts, HTML files, image maps, and HTML+Tcl template files.
- *HTML+Tcl Templates* — These are Web pages that mix Tcl and HTML markup. The server replaces the Tcl using the `subst` command and returns the result. The server can cache the result in a regular HTML file to avoid the overhead of template processing on future requests. Templates are a great way to maintain common look and feel to a family of Web pages, as well as to implement more advanced dynamic HTML features like self-checking forms.

TclHttpd Architecture

Figure 18–1 shows the basic components of the server. At the core is the `Httpd` module (`httpd.tcl`), which implements the server side of the `HTTP` protocol. The "d" in Httpd stands for *daemon*, which is the name given to system servers on `UNIX`. This module manages network requests, dispatches them to the `Url` module, and provides routines used to return the results to requests.

The `Url` module (`url.tcl`) divides the Web site into *domains*, which are subtrees of the URL hierarchy provided by the server. The idea is that different domains may have completely different implementations. For example, the Docu-

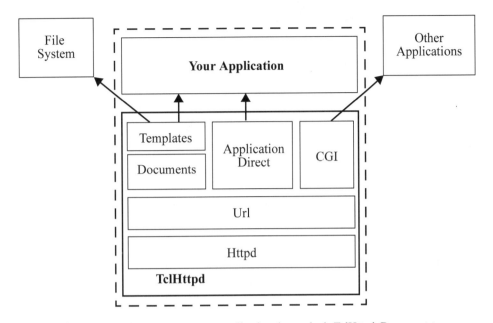

Fig. 18–1 The dotted box represents one application that embeds TclHttpd. Document templates and Application Direct URLs provide direct connections from an HTTP request to your application.

ment domain (doc.tcl) maps its URLs into files and directories on your hard disk, while the Application-Direct domain (direct.tcl) maps URLs into Tcl procedure calls within your application. The CGI domain (cgi.tcl) maps URLs onto other programs that compute Web pages.

Domain Handlers

You can implement new kinds of domains that provide your own interpretation of a URL. This is the most flexible interface available to extend the Web server. You provide a callback that is invoked to handle every request in a domain, or subtree, of the URL hierarchy. The callback interprets the URL, computes the page content, and returns the data using routines from the Httpd module.

Example 18–1 defines a simple domain that always returns the same page to every request. The domain is registered with the Url_PrefixInstall command. The arguments to Url_PrefixInstall are the URL prefix and a callback that is called to handle all URLs that match that prefix. In the example, all URLs that have the prefix /simple are dispatched to the SimpleDomain procedure.

Example 18–1 A simple URL domain.

```
Url_PrefixInstall /simple [list SimpleDomain /simple]

proc SimpleDomain {prefix sock suffix} {
    upvar #0 Httpd$sock data

    # Generate page header

    set html "<title>A simple page</title>\n"
    append html "<h1>$prefix$suffix</h1>\n"
    append html "<h1>Date and Time</h1>\n"
    append html [clock format [clock seconds]]
    # Display query data

    if {[info exist data(query)]} {
        append html "<h1>Query Data</h1>\n"
        append html "<table>\n"
        foreach {name value} [Url_DecodeQuery $data(query)] {
            append html "<tr><td>$name</td>\n"
            append html "<td>$value</td></tr>\n"
        }
        append html "</table>\n"
    }
    Httpd_ReturnData $sock text/html $html
}
```

The `SimpleDomain` handler illustrates several properties of domain handlers. The `sock` and `suffix` arguments to `SimpleDomain` are appended by `Url_Dispatch` when it invokes the domain handler. The `suffix` parameter is the part of the URL after the prefix. The `prefix` is passed in as part of the callback definition so the domain handler can recreate the complete URL. For example, if the server receives a request for the URL `/simple/page`, then the prefix is `/simple`, the suffix is `/request`.

Connection State and Query Data

The `sock` parameter is a handle on the socket connection to the remote client. This variable is also used to name a state variable that the `Httpd` module maintains about the connection. The name of the state array is `Httpd$sock`, and `SimpleDomain` uses `upvar` to get a more convenient name for this array (i.e., `data`):

```
upvar #0 Httpd$sock data
```

An important element of the state array is the query data, `data(query)`. This is the information that comes from HTML forms. The query data arrives in an encoded format, and the `Url_DecodeQuery` procedure is used to decode the data into a list of names and values. `Url_DecodeQuery` is similar to `Cgi_List` from Example 11–5 on page 154 and is a standard function provided by `url.tcl`.

Returning Results

Finally, once the page has been computed, the `Httpd_ReturnData` procedure is used to return the page to the client. This takes care of the HTTP protocol as well as returning the data. There are three related procedures, `Httpd_ReturnFile`, `Httpd_Error`, and `Httpd_Redirect`. These are summarized in Table 18–1 on page 259.

Application Direct URLs

The Application Direct domain implementation provides the simplest way to extend the Web server. It hides the details associated with query data, decoding URL paths, and returning results. All you do is define Tcl procedures that correspond to URLs. Their arguments are automatically matched up to the query data as shown in Example 13–3 on page 179. The Tcl procedures compute a string that is the result data, which is usually HTML. That's all there is to it.

The `Direct_Url` procedure defines a URL prefix and a corresponding Tcl command prefix. Any URL that begins with the URL prefix will be handled by a corresponding Tcl procedure that starts with the Tcl command prefix. This is shown in Example 18–2:

Example 18–2 Application Direct URLs.

```tcl
Direct_Url /demo Demo

proc Demo {} {
    return "<html><head><title>Demo page</title></head>\n\
        <body><h1>Demo page</h1>\n\
        <a href=/demo/time>What time is it?</a>\n\
        <form action=/demo/echo>\n\
        Data: <input type=text name=data>\n\
        <br>\n\
        <input type=submit name=echo value='Echo Data'>\n\
        </form>\n\
        </body></html>"
}
proc Demo/time {{format "%H:%M:%S"}} {
    return [clock format [clock seconds] -format $format]
}
proc Demo/echo {args} {
    # Compute a page that echoes the query data

    set html "<head><title>Echo</title></head>\n"
    append html "<body><table>\n"
    foreach {name value} $args {
        append html "<tr><td>$name</td><td>$value</td></tr>\n"
    }
    append html "</tr></table>\n"
    return $html
}
```

Example 18–2 defines /demo as an Application Direct URL domain that is implemented by procedures that begin with Demo. There are just three URLs defined:

```
/demo
/demo/time
/demo/echo
```

The /demo page displays a hypertext link to the /demo/time page and a simple form that will be handled by the /demo/echo page. This page is static, and so there is just one return command in the procedure body. Each line of the string ends with:

```
\n\
```

This is just a formatting trick to let me indent each line in the procedure, but not have the line indented in the resulting string. Actually, the \-newline will be replaced by one space, so each line will be indented one space. You can leave those off and the page will display the same in the browser, but when you view the page source you'll see the indenting. Or you could not indent the lines in the string, but then your code looks somewhat odd.

The /demo/time procedure just returns the result of clock format. It doesn't even bother adding <html>, <head>, or <body> tags, which you can get away with in today's browsers. A simple result like this is also useful if you are using programs to fetch information via HTTP requests.

Using Query Data

The /demo/time procedure is defined with an optional format argument. If a format value is present in the query data, then it overrides the default value given in the procedure definition.

The /demo/echo procedure creates a table that shows its query data. Its args parameter gets filled in with a name-value list of all query data. You can have named parameters, named parameters with default values, and the args parameter in your application-direct URL procedures. The server automatically matches up incoming form values with the procedure declaration. For example, suppose you have an application direct procedure declared like this:

```
proc Demo/param { a b {c cdef} args} { body }
```

You could create an HTML form that had elements named a, b, and c, and specified /demo/param for the ACTION parameter of the FORM tag. Or you could type the following into your browser to embed the query data right into the URL:

```
/demo/param?a=5&b=7&c=red&d=%7ewelch&e=two+words
```

In this case, when your procedure is called, a is 5, b is 7, c is red, and the args parameter becomes a list of:

```
d ~welch e {two words}
```

The %7e and the + are special codes for nonalphanumeric characters in the query data. Normally, this encoding is taken care of automatically by the Web browser when it gets data from a form and passes it to the Web server. However, if you type query data directly or format URLs with complex query data in them, then you need to think about the encoding. Use the `Url_Encode` procedure to encode URLs that you put into Web pages.

If parameters are missing from the query data, they either get the default values from the procedure definition or the empty string. Consider this example:

```
/demo/param?b=5
```

In this case `a` is `" "`, `b` is 5, `c` is `cdef`, and `args` is an empty list.

Returning Other Content Types

The default content type for application direct URLs is `text/html`. You can specify other content types by using a global variable with the same name as your procedure. (Yes, this is a crude way to craft an interface.) Example 18–3 shows part of the `faces.tcl` file that implements an interface to a database of picons — personal icons — that is organized by user and domain names. The idea is that the database contains images corresponding to your e-mail correspondents. The `Faces_ByEmail` procedure, which is not shown, looks up an appropriate image file. The application direct procedure is `Faces/byemail`, and it sets the global variable `Faces/byemail` to the correct value based on the file-name extension. This value is used for the `Content-Type` header in the result part of the `HTTP` protocol.

Example 18–3 Alternate types for Application Direct URLs.

```
Direct_Url /faces Faces
proc Faces/byemail {email} {
    global Faces/byemail
    set filename [Faces_ByEmail $email]
    set Faces/byemail [Mtype $filename]
    set in [open $filename]
    fconfigure $in -translation binary
    set X [read $in]
    close $in
    return $X
}
```

Document Types

The Document domain (`doc.tcl`) maps URLs onto files and directories. It provides more ways to extend the server by registering different document type handlers. This occurs in a two-step process. First, the type of a file is determined by its suffix. The `mime.types` file contains a map from suffixes to MIME types such as `text/html` or `image/gif`. This map is controlled by the `Mtype` module in `mtype.tcl`. Second, the server checks for a Tcl procedure with the appropriate name:

```
Doc_mimetype
```

The matching procedure, if any, is called to handle the URL request. The procedure should use routines in the Httpd module to return data for the request. If there is no matching Doc_*mimetype* procedure, then the default document handler uses Httpd_ReturnFile and specifies the Content Type based on the file extension:

```
Httpd_ReturnFile $sock [Mtype $path] $path
```

You can make up new types to support your application. Example 18–4 shows the pieces needed to create a handler for a fictitious document type application/myjunk that is invoked to handle files with the .junk suffix. You need to edit the mime.types file and add a document handler procedure to the server:

Example 18–4 A sample document type handler.

```
# Add this line to mime.types
application/myjunk      .junk

# Define the document handler procedure
#   path is the name of the file on disk
#   suffix is part of the URL after the domain prefix
#   sock is the handle on the client connection

proc Doc_application/myjunk {path suffix sock} {
    upvar #0 Httpd$sock data
    # data(url) is more useful than the suffix parameter.

    # Use the contents of file $path to compute a page
    set contents [somefunc $path]

    # Determine your content type
    set type text/html

    # Return the page
    Httpd_ReturnData $sock $type $data
}
```

As another example, the HTML+Tcl templates use the .tml suffix that is mapped to the application/x-tcl-template type. The TclHttpd distribution also includes support for files with a .snmp extension that implements a template-based Web interface to the Scotty SNMP Tcl extension.

HTML + Tcl Templates

The template system uses HTML pages that embed Tcl commands and Tcl variable references. The server replaces these using the subst command and returns the results. The server comes with a general template system, but using subst is so easy you could create your own template system. The general template framework has these components:

- Each `.html` file has a corresponding `.tml` template file. This feature is enabled with the `Doc_CheckTemplates` command in the server's configuration file. Normally, the server returns the `.html` file unless the corresponding `.tml` file has been modified more recently. In this case, the server processes the template, caches the result in the `.html` file, and returns the result.

- A dynamic template (e.g., a form handler) must be processed each time it is requested. If you put the `Doc_Dynamic` command into your page, it turns off the caching of the result in the `.html` page. The server responds to a request for a `.html` page by processing the `.tml` page. Or you can just reference the `.tml` file directly. If you do this, the server always processes the template.

- The server creates a `page` global Tcl variable that has context about the page being processed. Table 18–7 lists the elements of the page array.

- The server initializes the `env` global Tcl variable with similar information, but in the standard way for CGI scripts. Table 18–8 lists the elements of the `env` array that are set by `Cgi_SetEnv` in `cgi.tcl`.

- The server supports per-directory ".tml" files that contain Tcl source code. These files are designed to contain procedure definitions and variable settings that are shared among pages. The name of the file is simply ".tml", with nothing before the period. This is a standard way to hide files in UNIX, but it can be confusing to talk about the per-directory ".tml" files and the *file*.tml templates that correspond to *file*.html pages. The server will source the ".tml" files in all directories leading down to the directory containing the template file. The server compares the modify time of these files against the template file and will process the template if these ".tml" files are newer than the cached `.html` file. So, by modifying the ".tml" file in the root of your URL hierarchy, you invalidate all the cached `.html` files.

- The server supports a script library for the procedures called from templates. The `Doc_TemplateLibrary` procedure registers this directory. The server adds the directory to its `auto_path`, which assumes you have a `tclIndex` or `pkgIndex.tcl` file in the directory so that the procedures are loaded when needed.

Where to put your Tcl Code

There are three places you can put the code of your application: directly in your template pages, in the per-directory ".tml" files, or in the library directory.

The advantage of putting procedure definitions in the library is that they are defined one time but executed many times. This works well with the Tcl bytecode compiler. The disadvantage is that if you modify procedures in these files, you have to explicitly source them into the server for these changes to take effect. The `/debug/source` URL described on page 264 is handy for this chore.

The advantage of putting code into the per-directory ".tml" files is that changes are picked up immediately with no effort on your part. The server automatically checks if these files are modified and sources them each time it processes your templates. However, that code is run only one time, so the byte-code compiler just adds overhead.

I try to put as little code as possible in my *file*.tml template files. It is awkward to put lots of code there, and you cannot share procedures and variable definitions easily with other pages. Instead, my goal is to have just procedure calls in the template files, and put the procedure definitions elsewhere. I also avoid putting if and foreach commands directly into the page.

Templates for Site Structure

The next few examples show a simple template system used to maintain a common look at feel across the pages of a site. Example 18–5 shows a simple one-level site definition that is kept in the root .tml file. This structure lists the title and URL of each page in the site:

Example 18–5 A one-level site structure.

```
set site(pages) {
    Home                   /index.html
    "Ordering Computers"/ordering.html
    "New Machine Setup" /setup.html
    "Adding a New User" /newuser.html
    "Network Addresses" /network.html
}
```

Each page includes two commands, SitePage and SiteFooter, that generate HTML for the navigational part of the page. Between these commands is regular HTML for the page content. Example 18–6 shows a sample template file:

Example 18–6 A HTML + Tcl template file.

```
[SitePage "New Machine Setup"]
This page describes the steps to take when setting up a new
computer in our environment. See
<a href=/ordering.html>Ordering Computers</a>
for instructions on ordering machines.
<ol>
<li>Unpack and setup the machine.
<li>Use the Network control panel to set the IP address
and hostname.
<!-- Several steps omitted -->
<li>Reboot for the last time.
</ol>
[SiteFooter]
```

The SitePage procedure takes the page title as an argument. It generates HTML to implement a standard navigational structure. Example 18–7 has a simple implementation of SitePage:

Example 18–7 SitePage template procedure.

```tcl
proc SitePage {title} {
    global site
    set html "<html><head><title>$title</title></head>\n"
    append html "<body bgcolor=white text=black>\n"
    append html "<h1>$title</h1>\n"
    set sep ""
    foreach {label url} $site(pages) {
        append html $sep
        if {[string compare $label $title] == 0} {
            append html "$label"
        } else {
            append html "<a href='$url'>$label</a>"
        }
        set sep " | "
    }
    return $html
}
```

II. Advanced Tcl

The foreach loop that computes the simple menu of links turns out to be useful in many places. Example 18–8 splits out the loop and uses it in the Site-Page and SiteFooter procedures. This version of the templates creates a left column for the navigation and a right column for the page content:

Example 18–8 SiteMenu and SiteFooter template procedures.

```tcl
proc SitePage {title} {
    global site
    set html "<html><head><title>$title</title></head>\n\
        <body bgcolor=$site(bg) text=$site(fg)>\n\
        <!-- Two Column Layout -->\n\
        <table cellpadding=0>\n\
        <tr><td>\n\
        <!-- Left Column -->\n\
        <img src='$site(mainlogo)'>\n\
        <font size=+1>\n\
        [SiteMenu <br> $site(pages)]\n\
        </font>\n\
        </td><td>\n\
        <!-- Right Column -->\n\
        <h1>$title</h1>\n\
        <p>\n"
    return $html
}
proc SiteFooter {} {
    global site
    set html "<p><hr>\n\
        <font size=-1>[SiteMenu | $site(pages)]</font>\n\
        </td></tr></table>\n"
    return $html
}
proc SiteMenu {sep list} {
```

```
    global page
    set s ""
    set html ""
    foreach {label url} $list {
        if {[string compare $page(url) $url] == 0} {
            append html $s$label
        } else {
            append html "$s<a href='$url'>$label</a>"
        }
        set s $sep
    }
    return $html
}
```

Of course, a real site will have more elaborate graphics and probably a two-level, three-level, or more complex tree structure that describes its structure. You can also define a family of templates so that each page doesn't have to fit the same mold. Once you start using templates, it is fairly easy to change both the template implementation and to move pages around among different sections of your Web site.

There are many other applications for "macros" that make repetitive HTML coding chores easy. Take, for example, the link to /ordering.html in Example 18–6. The proper label for this is already defined in $site(pages), so we could introduce a SiteLink procedure that uses this:

Example 18–9 The SiteLink procedure.

```
proc SiteLink {label} {
    global site
    array set map $site(pages)
    if {[info exist map($label)]} {
        return "<a href='$map($label)'>$label</a>"
    } else {
        return $label
    }
}
```

If your pages embed calls to SiteLink, then you can change the URL associated with the page name by changing the value of site(pages). If this is stored in the top-level ".tml" file, the templates will automatically track the changes.

Form Handlers

HTML forms and form-handling programs go together. The form is presented to the user on the client machine. The form handler runs on the server after the user fills out the form and presses the submit button. The form presents input widgets like radiobuttons, checkbuttons, selection lists, and text entry fields. Each of these widgets is assigned a name, and each widget gets a value based on the user's input. The form handler is a program that looks at the names and values from the form and computes the next page for the user to read.

CGI is a standard way to hook external programs to Web servers for the purpose of processing form data. CGI has a special encoding for values so that they can be transported safely. The encoded data is either read from standard input or taken from the command line. The CGI program decodes the data, processes it, and writes a new HTML page on its standard output. Chapter 3 describes writing CGI scripts in Tcl.

TclHttpd provides alternatives to CGI that are more efficient because they are built right into the server. This eliminates the overhead that comes from running an external program to compute the page. Another advantage is that the Web server can maintain state between client requests in Tcl variables. If you use CGI, you must use some sort of database or file storage to maintain information between requests.

Application Direct Handlers

The server comes with several built-in form handlers that you can use with little effort. The /mail/forminfo URL will package up the query data and mail it to you. You use form fields to set various mail headers, and the rest of the data is packaged up into a Tcl-readable mail message. Example 18–10 shows a form that uses this handler. Other built-in handlers are described starting at page 263.

Example 18–10 Mail form results with /mail/forminfo.

```
<form action=/mail/forminfo method=post>
    <input type=hidden name=sendto value=mailreader@my.com>
    <input type=hidden name=subject value="Name and Address">
    <table>
        <tr><td>Name</td><td><input name=name></td></tr>
        <tr><td>Address</td><td><input name=addr1></td></tr>
        <tr><td> </td><td><input name=addr2></td></tr>
        <tr><td>City</td><td><input name=city></td></tr>
        <tr><td>State</td><td><input name=state></td></tr>
        <tr><td>Zip/Postal</td><td><input name=zip></td></tr>
        <tr><td>Country</td><td><input name=country></td></tr>
    </table>
</form>
```

The mail message sent by /mail/forminfo is shown in Example 18–11.

Example 18–11 Mail message sent by /mail/forminfo.

```
To: mailreader@my.com
Subject: Name and Address

data {
    name    {Joe Visitor}
```

```
addr1  {Acme Company}
addr2  {100 Main Street}
city   {Mountain View}
state  California
zip    12345
country  USA
}
```

It is easy to write a script that strips the headers, defines a `data` procedure, and uses `eval` to process the message body. Whenever you send data via e-mail, if you format it with Tcl list structure, you can process it quite easily. The basic structure of such a mail reader procedure is shown in Example 18–12:

Example 18–12 Processing mail sent by /mail/forminfo.

```
# Assume the mail message is on standard input

set X [read stdin]

# Strip off the mail headers, when end with a blank line
if {[regsub {.*?\n\ndata} $X {data} X] != 1} {
    error "Malformed mail message"
}
proc data {fields} {
    foreach {name value} $fields {
        # Do something
    }
}
# Process the message. For added security, you may want
# do this part in a safe interpreter.
eval $X
```

Template Form Handlers

The drawback of using application-direct URL form handlers is that you must modify their Tcl implementation to change the resulting page. Another approach is to use templates for the result page that embed a command that handles the form data. The `Mail_FormInfo` procedure, for example, mails form data. It takes no arguments. Instead, it looks in the query data for `sendto` and `subject` values, and if they are present, it sends the rest of the data in an e-mail. It returns an HTML comment that flags that mail was sent.

When you use templates to process form data, you need to turn off result caching because the server must process the template each time the form is submitted. To turn off caching, embed the `Doc_Dynamic` command into your form handler pages, or set the `page(dynamic)` variable to 1. Alternatively, you can simply post directly to the `file`.tml page instead of to the `file`.html page.

Self Posting Forms

This section illustrates a self-posting form. This is a form on a page that posts the form data to back to the same page. The page embeds a Tcl command to check its own form data. Once the data is correct, the page triggers a redirect to the next page in the flow. This is a powerful technique that I use to create complex page flows using templates. Of course, you need to save the form data at each step. You can put the data in Tcl variables, use the data to control your application, or store it into a database. TclHttpd comes with a `Session` module, which is one way to manage this information. For details you should scan the `session.tcl` file in the distribution.

Example 18–13 shows the `Form_Simple` procedure that generates a simple self-checking form. Its arguments are a unique ID for the form, a description of the form fields, and the URL of the next page in the flow. The field description is a list with three elements for each field: a required flag, a form element name, and a label to display with the form element. You can see this structure in the template shown in Example 18–14 on page 258. The procedure does two things at once. It computes the HTML form, and it also checks if the required fields are present. It uses some procedures from the `form` module to generate form elements that retain values from the previous page. If all the required fields are present, it discards the HTML, saves the data, and triggers a redirect by calling `Doc_Redirect`.

Example 18–13 A self-checking form procedure.

```
proc Form_Simple {id fields nextpage} {
    global page
    if {![form::empty formid]} {
        # Incoming form values, check them
        set check 1
    } else {
        # First time through the page
        set check 0
    }
    set html "<!-- Self-posting. Next page is $nextpage -->\n"
    append html "<form action=\"$page(url)\" method=post>\n"
    append html "<input type=hidden name=formid value=$id>\n"
    append html "<table border=1>\n"
    foreach {required key label} $fields {
        append html "<tr><td>"
        if {$check && $required && [form::empty $key]} {
            lappend missing $label
            append html "<font color=red>*</font>"
        }
        append html "</td><td>$label</td>\n"
        append html "<td><input [form::value $key]></td>\n"
        append html "</tr>\n"
    }
    append html "</table>\n"
    if {$check} {
        if {![info exist missing]} {
```

```
        # No missing fields, so advance to the next page.
        # In practice, you must save the existing fields
        # at this point before redirecting to the next page.

        Doc_Redirect $nextpage
    } else {
        set msg "<font color=red>Please fill in "
        append msg [join $missing ", "]
        append msg "</font>"
        set html <p>$msg\n$html
    }
}
append html "<input type=submit>\n</form>\n"
return $html
}
```

Example 18–14 shows a page template that calls `Form_Simple` with the required field description.

Example 18–14 A page with a self-checking form.

```
<html><head>
    <title>Name and Address Form</title>
</head>
<body bgcolor=white text=black>
    <h1>Name and Address</h1>
    Please enter your name and address.
    [myform::simple nameaddr {
        1 name     "Name"
        1 addr1    "Address"
        0 addr2"   "Address"
        1 city     "City"
        0 state    "State"
        1 zip      "Zip Code"
        0 country "Country"
    } nameok.html]
</body></html>
```

The form package

TclHttpd comes with a `form` package (`form.tcl`) that is designed to support self-posting forms. The `Form_Simple` procedure uses `form::empty` to test if particular form values are present in the query data. For example, it tests to see whether the `formid` field is present so that the procedure knows whether or not to check for the rest of the fields. The `form::value` procedure is useful for constructing form elements on self-posting form pages. It returns:

```
name="name" value="value"
```

The *value* is the value of form element *name* based on incoming query data, or just the empty string if the query value for *name* is undefined. As a result, the form can post to itself and retain values from the previous version of the page. It is used like this:

```
<input type=text [form::value name]>
```

The `form::checkvalue` and `form::radiovalue` procedures are similar to `form::value` but designed for checkbuttons and radio buttons. The `form::select` procedure formats a selection list and highlights the selected values. The `form::data` procedure simply returns the value of a given form element. These are summarized in Table 18–6 on page 261.

Programming Reference

This section summarizes many of the more useful functions defined by the server. These tables are not complete, however. You are encouraged to read through the code to learn more about the features offered by the server.

Table 18–1 summarizes the `Httpd` functions used when returning pages to the client.

Table 18–1 `Httpd` support procedures.

`Httpd_Error sock code`	Returns a simple error page to the client. The `code` is a numeric error code like 404 or 500.
`Httpd_ReturnData sock type data`	Returns a page with Content-Type `type` and content `data`.
`Httpd_ReturnFile sock type file`	Returns a `file` with Content-Type `type`.
`Httpd_Redirect newurl sock`	Generates a 302 error return with a Location of `newurl`.
`Httpd_SelfUrl url`	Expands `url` to include the proper `http://` `server:port` prefix to reference the current server.

Table 18–2 summarizes a few useful procedures provided by the `Url` module (`url.tcl`). The `Url_DecodeQuery` is used to decode query data into a Tcl-friendly list. The `Url_Encode` procedure is useful when encoding values directly into URLs. URL encoding is discussed in more detail on page 247.

Table 18–2 `Url` support procedures.

`Url_DecodeQuery query`	Decodes a `www-url-encoded` query string and return a name, value list.
`Url_Encode value`	Returns `value` encoded according to the www-url-encoded standard.
`Url_PrefxInstall prefix callback`	Registers `callback` as the handler for all URLs that begin with `prefix`. The callback is invoked with two additional arguments: `sock`, the handle to the client, and `suffix`, the part of the URL after `prefix`.

The `Doc` module provides procedures for configuration and generating responses, which are summarized in Tables 18–3 and 18–4, respectively.

Table 18–3 `Doc` procedures for configuration.

`Doc_Root ?directory?`	Sets or queries the *directory* that corresponds to the root of the URL hierarchy.
`Doc_AddRoot virtual directory`	Maps the file system *directory* into the URL subtree starting at *virtual*.
`Doc_ErrorPage file`	Specifies a *file* relative to the document root used as a simple template for error messages. This is processed by `DocSubstSystem` file in `doc.tcl`.
`Doc_CheckTemplates how`	If *how* is 1, then `.html` files are compared against corresponding `.tml` files and regenerated if necessary.
`Doc_IndexFile pattern`	Registers a file name *pattern* that will be searched for the default index file in directories.
`Doc_NotFoundPage file`	Specifies a *file* relative to the document root used as a simple template for page not found messages. This is processed by `DocSubstSystem` file in `doc.tcl`.
`Doc_PublicHtml dirname`	Defines the directory used for each users home directory. When a URL like ~*user* is specified, the *dirname* under their home directory is accessed.
`Doc_TemplateLibrary directory`	Adds *directory* to the `auto_path` so the source files in it are available to the server.
`Doc_TemplateInterp interp`	Specifies an alternate interpreter in which to process document templates (i.e., `.tml` files.)
`Doc_Webmaster ?email?`	Sets or queries the *email* for the Webmaster.

Table 18–4 `Doc` procedures for generating responses.

`Doc_Error sock errorInfo`	Generates a 500 response on *sock* based on the template registered with `Doc_ErrorPage`. *errorInfo* is a copy of the Tcl error trace after the error.
`Doc_NotFound sock`	Generates a 404 response on *sock* by using the template registered with `Doc_NotFoundPage`.
`Doc_Subst sock file ?interp?`	Performs a `subst` on the file and return the resulting page on *sock*. *interp* specifies an alternate Tcl interpreter.

The `Doc` module also provides procedures for cookies and redirects that are useful in document templates. These are described in Table 18–5.

Table 18–5 Doc procedures that support template processing.

Doc_Coookie *name*	Returns the cookie *name* passed to the server for this request, or the empty string if it is not present.
Doc_Dynamic	Turns off caching of the HTML result. Meant to be called from inside a page template.
Doc_IsLinkToSelf *url*	Returns 1 if the *url* is a link to the current page.
Doc_Redirect *newurl*	Raises a special error that aborts template processing and triggers a page redirect to *newurl*.
Doc_SetCookie -name *name* -value *value* -path *path* -domain *domain* -expires *date*	Sets cookie *name* with the given *value* that will be returned to the client as part of the response. The *path* and *domain* restrict the scope of the cooke. The *date* sets an expiration date.

Table 18–6 describes the form module that is useful for self-posting forms, which are discussed on page 257.

Table 18–6 The form package.

form::data *name*	Returns the value of the form value *name*, or the empty string.
form::empty *name*	Returns 1 if the form value *name* is missing or zero length.
form::value *name*	Returns name="*name*" value="*value*", where *value* comes from the query data, if any.
form::checkvalue *name value*	Returns name="*name*" value="*value*" CHECKED, if *value* is present in the query data for *name*. Otherwise, it just returns name="*name*" value="*value*".
form::radiovalue *name value*	Returns name="*name*" value="*value*" CHECKED, if the query data for *name* is equal to *value*. Otherwise, it just returns name="*name*" value="*value*".
form::select *name valuelist args*	Generates a select form element with name *name*. The *valuelist* determines the option tags and values, and *args* are optional parameters to the main select tag.

Table 18–7 shows the initial elements of the page array that is defined during the processing of a template.

Table 18–7 Elements of the page array.

query	The decoded query data in a name, value list.
dynamic	If 1, the results of processing the template are not cached in the corresponding .html file.
filename	The file system pathname of the requested file (e.g., /usr/local/ htdocs/tclhttpd/index.html).

Table 18–7 Elements of the `page` array. (Continued)

`template`	The file system pathname of the template file (e.g., `/usr/local/htdocs/tclhttpd/index.tml`).
`url`	The part of the url after the server name (e.g., `/tclhttpd/index.html`).
`root`	A relative path from the template file back to the root of the URL tree. This is useful for creating relative links between pages in different directories.

Table 18–8 shows the elements of the `env` array. These are defined during CGI requests, application-direct URL handlers, and page template processing:

Table 18–8 Elements of the `env` array.

`AUTH_TYPE`	Authentication protocol (e.g., `Basic`).
`CONTENT_LENGTH`	The size of the query data.
`CONTENT_TYPE`	The type of the query data.
`DOCUMENT_ROOT`	File system pathname of the document root.
`GATEWAY_INTERFACE`	Protocol version, which is `CGI/1.1`.
`HTTP_ACCEPT`	The Accept headers from the request.
`HTTP_AUTHORIZATION`	The Authorization challenge from the request.
`HTTP_COOKIE`	The cookie from the request.
`HTTP_FROM`	The From: header of the request.
`HTTP_REFERER`	The Referer indicates the previous page.
`HTTP_USER_AGENT`	An ID string for the Web browser.
`PATH_INFO`	Extra path information after the template file.
`PATH_TRANSLATED`	The extra path information appended to the document root.
`QUERY_STRING`	The form query data.
`REMOTE_ADDR`	The client's IP address.
`REMOTE_USER`	The remote user name specified by Basic authentication.
`REQUEST_METHOD`	GET, POST, or HEAD.
`REQUEST_URI`	The complete URL that was requested.
`SCRIPT_NAME`	The name of the current file relative to the document root.
`SERVER_NAME`	The server name, e.g., `www.beedub.com`.
`SERVER_PORT`	The server's port, e.g., 80.
`SERVER_PROTOCOL`	The protocol (e.g., `http` or `https`).
`SERVER_SOFTWARE`	A software version string for the server.

Standard Application-Direct URLs

The server has several modules that provide application-direct URLs. These application-direct URLs lets you control the server or examine its state from any Web browser. You can look at the implementation of these modules as examples for your own application.

Status

The /status URL is implemented in the status.tcl file. The status module implements the display of hit counts, document hits, and document misses (i.e., documents not found). The Status_Url command enables the application-direct URLs and assigns the top-level URL for the status module. The default configuration file contains this command:

```
Status_Url /status
```

Assuming this configuration, the following URLs are implemented:

Table 18–9 Status application-direct URLs.

/status	Main status page showing summary counters and hit count histograms.
/status/doc	Shows hit counts for each page. This page lets you sort by name or hit count, and limit files by patterns.
/status/hello	A trivial URL that returns "hello".
/status/notfound	Shows miss counts for URLs that users tried to fetch.
/status/size	Displays an estimated size of Tcl code and Tcl data used by the TclHttpd program.
/status/text	This is a version of the main status page that doesn't use the graphical histograms of hit counts.

Debugging

The /debug URL is implemented in the debug.tcl file. The debug module has several useful URLs that let you examine variable values and other internal state. It is turned on with this command in the default configuration file:

```
Debug_Url /debug
```

Table 18–10 lists the /debug URLs. These URLs often require parameters that you can specify directly in the URL. For example, the /debug/echo URL echoes its query parameters:

```
http://yourserver:port/debug/echo?name=value&name2=val2
```

II. Advanced Tcl

Table 18–10 Debug application-direct URLs.

/debug/after	Lists the outstanding after events.
/debug/dbg	Connects to *TclPro Debugger*. This takes a host and port parameter. You need to install prodebug.tcl from *TclPro* into the server's script library directory.
/debug/echo	Echoes its query parameters. Accepts a title parameter.
/debug/errorInfo	Displays the errorInfo variable along with the server's version number and Webmaster e-mail. Accepts title and errorInfo arguments.
/debug/parray	Displays a global array variable. The name of the variable is specified with the aname parameter.
/debug/pvalue	A more general value display function. The name of the variable is specified with the aname parameter. This can be a variable name, an array name, or a pattern that matches several variable names.
/debug/raise	Raises an error (to test error handling). Any parameters become the error string.
/debug/source	Sources a file from either the server's main library directory or the Doc_TemplateLibrary directory. The file is specified with the source parameter.

The sample URL tree that is included in the distribution includes the file htdocs/hacks.html. This file has several small forms that use the /debug URLs to examine variables and source files. Example 18–15 shows the implementation of /debug/source. You can see that it limits the files to the main script library and to the script library associated with document templates. It may seem dangerous to have these facilities, but I reason that because my source directories are under my control, it cannot hurt to reload any source files. In general, the library scripts contain only procedure definitions and no global code that might reset state inappropriately. In practice, the ability to tune (i.e., fix bugs) in the running server has proven useful to me on many occasions. It lets you evolve your application without restarting it!

Example 18–15 The /debug/source application-direct URL implementation.

```
proc Debug/source {source} {
    global Httpd Doc
    set source [file tail $source]
    set dirlist $Httpd(library)
    if {[info exists Doc(templateLibrary)]} {
        lappend dirlist $Doc(templateLibrary)
    }
    foreach dir $dirlist {
        set file [file join $dir $source]
        if [file exists $file] {
            break
```

```
        }
    }
    set error [catch {uplevel #0 [list source $file]} result]
    set html "<title>Source $source</title>\n"
    if {$error} {
        global errorInfo
        append html "<H1>Error in $source</H1>\n"
        append html "<pre>$result<p>$errorInfo</pre>"
    } else {
        append html "<H1>Reloaded $source</H1>\n"
        append html "<pre>$result</pre>"
    }
    return $html
}
```

Administration

The /admin URL is implemented in the admin.tcl file. The admin module lets you load URL redirect tables, and it provides URLs that reset some of the counters maintained by the server. It is turned on with this command in the default configuration file:

```
Admin_Url /admin
```

Currently, there is only one useful admin URL. The /admin/redirect/ reload URL sources the file named redirect in the document root. This file is expected to contain a number of Url_Redirect commands that establish URL redirects. These are useful if you change the names of pages and want the old names to still work.

The administration module has a limited set of application-direct URLs because the simple application-direct mechanism doesn't provide the right hooks to check authentication credentials. The HTML+Tcl templates work better with the authentication schemes.

Sending Email

The /mail URL is implemented in the mail.tcl file. The mail module implements various form handlers that e-mail form data. Currently, it is UNIX-specific because it uses /usr/lib/sendmail to send the mail. It is turned on with this command in the default configuration file:

```
Mail_Url /mail
```

The application-direct URLs shown in Table 18–11 are useful form handlers. You can specify them as the ACTION parameter in your <FORM> tags. The mail module provides two Tcl procedures that are generally useful. The MailInner procedure is the one that sends mail. It is called like this:

```
MailInner sendto subject from type body
```

The sendto and from arguments are e-mail addresses. The type is the Mime type (e.g., text/plain or text/html) and appears in a Content-Type header. The body contains the mail message without any headers.

Table 18–11 Application-direct URLS that e-mail form results.

/mail/bugreport	Sends e-mail with the errorInfo from a server error. It takes an email parameter for the destination address and an error-Info parameter. Any additional arguments get included into the message.
/mail/forminfo	Sends e-mail containing form results. It requires these parameters: sendto for the destination address, subject for the mail subject, href and label for a link to display on the results page. Any additional arguments are formatted with the Tcl list command for easy processing by programs that read the mail.
/mail/formdata	This is an older form of /mail/forminfo that doesn't format the data into Tcl lists. It requires only the email and subject parameters. The rest are formatted into the message body.

The Mail_FormInfo procedure is designed for use in HTML+Tcl template files. It takes no arguments but instead looks in current query data for its parameters. It expects to find the same arguments as the /mail/forminfo direct URL. Using a template with Mail_FormInfo gives you more control over the result page than posting directly to /mail/forminfo, and is illustrated in Example 18–10 on page 255.

The TclHttpd Distribution

Get the TclHttpd distribution from the CD-ROM, or find it on the Internet at:

```
ftp://ftp.scriptics.com/pub/tcl/httpd/
http://www.scriptics.com/tclhttpd/
```

Quick Start

Unpack the tar file or the zip file, and you can run the server from the httpd.tcl script in the bin directory. On UNIX:

```
tclsh httpd.tcl -port 80
```

This command will start the Web server on the standard port (80). By default it uses port 8015 instead. If you run it with the -help flag, it will tell you what command line options are available. If you use *wish* instead of *tclsh,* then a simple Tk user interface is displayed that shows how many hits the server is getting.

On Windows you can double-click the httpd.tcl script to start the server. It will use *wish* and display the user interface. Again it will start on port 8015. You will need to create a shortcut that passes the -port argument, or edit the associated configuration file to change this. Configuring the server is described later.

Once you have the server running, you can connect to it from your Web browser. Use this URL if you are running on the default (nonstandard) port:

```
http://hostname:8015/
```

If you are running without a network connection, you may need to specify 127.0.0.1 for the hostname. This is the "localhost" address and will bypass the network subsystem.

```
http://127.0.0.1:8015/
```

Inside the Distribution

The TclHttpd distribution is organized into the following directories:

- bin — This has sample start-up scripts and configuration files. The httpd.tcl script runs the server. The tclhttpd.rc file is the standard configuration file. The minihttpd.tcl file is the 250-line version. The torture.tcl file has some scripts that you can use to fetch many URLs at once from a server.
- lib — This has all the Tcl sources. In general, each file provides a package. You will see the package require commands partly in bin/httpd.tcl and partly in bin/tclhttpd.rc. The idea is that only the core packages are required by httpd.tcl, and different applications can tune what packages are needed by adjusting the contents of tclhttpd.rc.
- htdocs — This is a sample URL tree that demonstrates the features of the Web server. There is also some documentation there. One directory to note is htdocs/libtml, which is the standard place to put site-specific Tcl scripts used with the Tcl+HTML template facility.
- src — There are a few C source files for a some optional packages. These have been precompiled for some platforms, and you can find the compiled libraries back under lib/Binaries in platform-specific subdirectories.

Server Configuration

TclHttpd configures itself with three main steps. The first step is to process the command line arguments described in Table 18–12. The arguments are copied into the Config Tcl array. Anything not specified on the command line gets a default value. The next configuration step is to source the configuration file. The default configuration file is named tclhttpd.rc in the same directory as the start-up script (i.e., bin/tclhttpd.rc). This file can override command line arguments by setting the Config array itself. This file also has application-specific package require commands and other Tcl commands to initialize the application. Most of the Tcl commands used during initialization are described in the rest of this section. The final step is to actually start up the server. This is done back in the main httpd.tcl script. For example, to start the server for the document tree under /usr/local/htdocs and your own e-mail address as Webmaster, you can execute this command to start the server:

```
tclsh httpd.tcl -docRoot /usr/local/htdocs -webmaster welch
```

Alternatively, you can put these settings into a configuration file, and start the server with that configuration file:

II. Advanced Tcl

```
tclsh httpd.tcl -config mytclhttpd.rc
```

In this case, the `mytclhttpd.rc` file could contain these commands to hard-wire the document root and Webmaster e-mail. In this case, the command line arguments *cannot* override these settings:

```
set Config(docRoot) /usr/local/htdocs
set Config(webmaster) welch
```

Command Line Arguments

There are several parameters you may need to set for a standard Web server. These are shown below in Table 18–12. The command line values are mapped into the `Config` array by the `httpd.tcl` start-up script.

Table 18–12 Basic TclHttpd Parameters.

Parameter	Command Option	Config Variable
Port number. The default is 8015.	`-port number`	`Config(port)`
Server name. The default is `[info hostname]`.	`-name name`	`Config(name)`
IP address. The default is 0, for "any address".	`-ipaddr address`	`Config(ipaddr)`
Directory of the root of the URL tree. The default is the `htdocs` directory.	`-docRoot directory`	`Config(docRoot)`
User ID of the TclHttpd process. The default is 50. (UNIX only.)	`-uid uid`	`Config(uid)`
Group ID of the TclHttpd process. The default is 100. (UNIX only.)	`-gid gid`	`Config(gid)`
Webmaster e-mail. The default is `webmaster`.	`-webmaster email`	`Config(webmaster)`
Configuration file. The default is `tclhttpd.rc`.	`-config filename`	`Config(file)`
Additional directory to add to the `auto_path`.	`-library directory`	`Config(library)`

Server Name and Port

The name and port parameters define how your server is known to Web browsers. The URLs that access your server begin with:

```
http://name:port/
```

If the port number is 80, you can leave out the port specification. The call that starts the server using these parameters is found in `httpd.tcl` as:

```
Httpd_Server $Config(name) $Config(port) $Config(ipaddr)
```

Specifying the IP address is necessary only if you have several network interfaces (or several IP addresses assigned to one network interface) and want the server to listen to requests on a particular network address. Otherwise, by default, server accepts requests from any network interface.

User and Group ID

The user and group IDs are used on UNIX systems with the `setuid` and `setgid` system calls. This lets you start the server as root, which is necessary to listen on port 80, and then switch to a less privileged user account. If you use Tcl+HTML templates that cache the results in HTML files, then you need to pick an account that can write those files. Otherwise, you may want to pick a very unprivileged account.

The `setuid` function is available through the TclX (Extended Tcl) `id` command, or through a `setuid` extension distributed with TclHttpd under the src directory. If do not have either of these facilities available, then the attempt to change user ID gracefully fails. See the `README` file in the `src` directory for instructions on compiling and installing the extensions found there.

Webmaster Email

The Webmaster e-mail address is used for automatic error reporting in the case of server errors. This is defined in the configuration file with the following command:

```
Doc_Webmaster $Config(webmaster)
```

If you call `Doc_Webmaster` with no arguments, it returns the e-mail address you previously defined. This is useful when generating pages that contain `mailto:` URLs with the Webmaster address.

Document Root

The document root is the directory that contains the static files, templates, CGI scripts, and so on that make up your Web site. By default the httpd.tcl script uses the *htdocs* directory next to the directory containing *httpd.tcl*. It is worth noting the trick used to locate this directory:

```
file join [file dirname [info script]] ../htdocs
```

The `info script` command returns the full name of the `http.tcl` script, `file dirname` computes its directory, and `file join` finds the adjacent directory. The path `../htdocs` works with `file join` on any platform. The default location of the configuration file is found in a similar way:

```
file join [file dirname [info script]] tclhttpd.rc
```

The configuration file initializes the document root with this call:

```
Doc_Root $Config(docRoot)
```

If you need to find out what the document root is, you can call Doc_Root with no arguments and it returns the directory of the document root. If you want to add additional document trees into your Web site, you can do that with a call like this in your configuration file:

```
Doc_AddRoot directory urlprefix
```

Other Document Settings

The Doc_IndexFile command sets a pattern used to find the index file in a directory. The command used in the default configuration file is:

```
Doc_IndexFile index.{htm,html,tml,subst}
```

If you invent other file types with different file suffixes, you can alter this pattern to include them. This pattern will be used by the Tcl glob command.

The Doc_PublicHtml command is used to define "home directories" on your HTML site. If the URL begins with ~username, then the Web server will look under the home directory of username for a particular directory. The command in the default configuration file is:

```
Doc_PublicHtml public_html
```

For example, if my home directory is /home/welch, then the URL ~welch maps to the directory /home/welch/public_html. If there is no Doc_PublicHtml command, then this mapping does not occur.

You can register two special pages that are used when the server encounters an error and when a user specifies an unknown URL. The default configuration file has these commands:

```
Doc_ErrorPage error.html

Doc_NotFoundPage notfound.html
```

These files are treated like templates in that they are passed through subst in order to include the error information or the URL of the missing page. These are pretty crude templates compared to the templates described earlier. You can count only on the Doc and Httpd arrays being defined. Look at the Doc_SubstSystemFile in doc.tcl for the truth about how these files are processed.

Document Templates

The template mechanism has two main configuration options. The first specifies an additional library directory that contains your application-specific scripts. This lets you keep your application-specific files separate from the TclHttpd implementation. The command in the default configuration file specifies the libtml directory of the document tree:

```
Doc_TemplateLibrary [file join $Config(docRoot) libtml]
```

You can also specify an alternate Tcl interpreter in which to process the templates. The default is to use the main interpreter, which is named {} according to the conventions described in Chapter 19.

```
Doc_TemplateInterp {}
```

Log Files

The server keeps standard format log files. The `Log_SetFile` command defines the base name of the log file. The default configuration file uses this command:

```
Log_SetFile /tmp/log$Config(port)_
```

By default the server rotates the log file each night at midnight. Each day's log file is suffixed with the current date (e.g., `/tmp/logport_990218.`) The error log, however, is not rotated, and all errors are accumulated in `/tmp/logport_error`.

The log records are normally flushed every few minutes to eliminate an extra I/O operation on each HTTP transaction. You can set this period with `Log_FlushMinutes`. If minutes is 0, the log is flushed on every HTTP transaction. The default configuration file contains:

```
Log_FlushMinutes 1
```

CGI Directories

You can register a directory that contains CGI programs with the `Cgi_Directory` command. This command has the interesting effect of forcing all files in the directory to be executed as CGI scripts, so you cannot put normal HTML files there. The default configuration file contains:

```
Cgi_Directory /cgi-bin
```

This means that the `cgi-bin` directory under the document root is a CGI directory. If you supply another argument to `Cgi_Directory`, then this is a file system directory that gets mapped into the URL defined by the first argument. You can also put CGI scripts into other directories and use the `.cgi` suffix to indicate that they should be executed as CGI scripts.

The `cgi.tcl` file has some additional parameters that you can tune only by setting some elements of the `Cgi` Tcl array. See the comments in the beginning of that file for details.

Multiple Interpreters and Safe-Tcl

This chapter describes how to create more than one Tcl interpreter in your application. A child interpreter can be made safe so that it can execute untrusted scripts without compromising your application or your computer. Command aliases, hidden commands, and shared I/O channels enable communication among interpreters. Tcl command described is: `interp`.

Safe-Tcl was invented by Nathaniel Borenstein and Marshall Rose so that they could send Tcl scripts via e-mail and have the recipient safely execute the script without worry of viruses or other attacks. Safe-Tcl works by removing dangerous commands like `exec` and `open` that would let an untrusted script damage the host computer. You can think of this restricted interpreter as a "padded cell" in which it is safe to execute untrusted scripts. To continue the analogy, if the untrusted code wants to do anything potentially unsafe, it must ask permission. This works by adding additional commands, or *aliases*, that are implemented by a different Tcl interpreter. For example, a `safeopen` command could be implemented by limiting file space to a temporary directory that is deleted when the untrusted code terminates.

The key concept of Safe-Tcl is that there are two Tcl interpreters in the application, a trusted one and an untrusted (or "safe") one. The trusted interpreter can do anything, and it is used for the main application (e.g., the Web browser or e-mail user interface). When the main application receives a message containing an untrusted script, it evaluates that script in the context of the untrusted interpreter. The restricted nature of the untrusted interpreter means that the application is safe from attack. This model is much like user mode and kernel mode in a multiuser operating system like UNIX or Windows/NT. In these systems, applications run in user mode and trap into the kernel to access resources like files and the network. The kernel implements access controls so that users cannot read and write each other's files, or hijack network services. In Safe-Tcl the application implements access controls for untrusted scripts.

The dual interpreter model of Safe-Tcl has been generalized in Tcl 7.5 and made accessible to Tcl scripts. A Tcl script can create other interpreters, destroy them, create command aliases among them, share I/O channels among them, and evaluate scripts in them.

The `interp` Command

The `interp` command is used to create and manipulate interpreters. The interpreter being created is called a *slave*, and the interpreter that creates it is called the *master*. The master has complete control over the slave. The `interp` command is summarized in Table 19–1.

Table 19–1 The `interp` command.

`interp aliases slave`	Lists aliases that are defined in `slave`.
`interp alias slave cmd1`	Returns target command and arguments for the alias `cmd1` in `slave`.
`interp alias slave cmd1 master` `    cmd2 arg ...`	Defines `cmd1` in `slave` that is an alias to `cmd2` in `master` with additional `args`.
`interp create ?-safe? slave`	Creates an interpreter named `slave`.
`interp delete slave`	Destroys interpreter `slave`.
`interp eval slave cmd args ...`	Evaluates `cmd` and `args` in `slave`.
`interp exists slave`	Returns 1 if `slave` is an interpreter, else 0.
`interp expose slave cmd`	Exposes hidden command `cmd` in `slave`.
`interp hide slave cmd`	Hides `cmd` from `slave`.
`interp hidden slave`	Returns the commands hidden from `slave`.
`interp invokehidden slave cmd` `    arg ...`	Invokes hidden command `cmd` and `args` in `slave`.
`interp issafe slave`	Returns 1 if `slave` was created with `-safe` flag.
`interp marktrusted slave`	Clears the `issafe` property of `slave`.
`interp share master file slave`	Shares the I/O descriptor named `file` in `master` with `slave`.
`interp slaves master`	Returns the list of slave interpreters of `master`.
`interp target slave cmd`	Returns the name of the interpreter that is the target of alias `cmd` in `slave`.
`interp transfer master file` `    slave`	Transfers the I/O descriptor named `file` from `master` to `slave`.

Creating Interpreters

Here is a simple example that creates an interpreter, evaluates a couple of commands in it, and then deletes the interpreter:

Example 19–1 Creating and deleting an interpreter.

```
interp create foo
=> foo
interp eval foo {set a 5}
=> 5
set sum [interp eval foo {expr $a + $a}]
=> 10
interp delete foo
```

In Example 19–1 the interpreter is named `foo`. Two commands are evaluated in the `foo` interpreter:

```
set a 5
expr $a + $a
```

Note that curly braces are used to protect the commands from any interpretation by the main interpreter. The variable `a` is defined in the `foo` interpreter and does not conflict with variables in the main interpreter. The set of variables and procedures in each interpreter is completely independent.

The Interpreter Hierarchy

A slave interpreter can itself create interpreters, resulting in a hierarchy. The next examples illustrates this, and it shows how the grandparent of an interpreter can reference the grandchild by name. The example uses `interp slaves` to query the existence of child interpreters.

Example 19–2 Creating a hierarchy of interpreters.

```
interp create foo
=> foo
interp eval foo {interp create bar}
=> bar
interp create {foo bar2}
=> foo bar2
interp slaves
=> foo
interp slaves foo
=> bar bar2
interp delete bar
=> interpreter named "bar" not found
interp delete {foo bar}
```

The example creates `foo`, and then it creates two children of `foo`. The first one is created by `foo` with this command:

```
interp eval foo {interp create bar}
```

The second child is created by the main interpreter. In this case, the grand-child must be named by a two-element list to indicate that it is a child of a child. The same naming convention is used when the grandchild is deleted:

```
interp create {foo bar2}
interp delete {foo bar2}
```

The `interp slaves` operation returns the names of child (i.e., slave) inter-preters. The names are relative to their parent, so the slaves of `foo` are reported simply as `bar` and `bar2`. The name for the current interpreter is the empty list, or `{}`. This is useful in command aliases and file sharing described later. For secu-rity reasons, it is not possible to name the master interpreter from within the slave.

The Interpreter Name as a Command

After interpreter *slave* is created, a new command is available in the main interpreter, also called *slave*, that operates on the child interpreter. The follow-ing two forms are equivalent most operations:

```
slave operation args ...
interp operation slave args ...
```

For example, the following are equivalent commands:

```
foo eval {set a 5}
interp eval foo {set a 5}
```

And so are these:

```
foo issafe
interp issafe foo
```

However, the operations `delete`, `exists`, `share`, `slaves`, `target`, and `trans-fer` cannot be used with the per interpreter command. In particular, there is no `foo delete` operation; you must use `interp delete foo`.

If you have a deep hierarchy of interpreters, the command corresponding to the slave is defined only in the parent. For example, if a master creates `foo`, and `foo` creates `bar`, then the master must operate on `bar` with the `interp` command. There is no `"foo bar"` command defined in the master.

Use `list` with `interp eval`

The `interp eval` command treats its arguments like `eval`. If there are extra arguments, they are all concatenated together first. This can lose important structure, as described in Chapter 10. To be safe, use `list` to construct your com-mands. For example, to safely define a variable in the slave, you should do this:

```
interp eval slave [list set var $value]
```

Safe Interpreters

A child can be created either safe (i.e., untrusted) or fully functional. In the examples so far, the children have been trusted and fully functional; they have all the basic Tcl commands available to them. An interpreter is made safe by eliminating certain commands. Table 19–2 lists the commands removed from safe interpreters. As described later, these commands can be used by the master on behalf of the safe interpreter. To create a safe interpreter, use the -safe flag:

```
interp create -safe untrusted
```

Table 19–2 Commands hidden from safe interpreters.

cd	Changes directory.
exec	Executes another program.
exit	Terminates the process.
fconfigure	Sets modes of an I/O stream.
file	Queries file attributes.
glob	Matches on file name patterns.
load	Dynamically loads object code.
open	Opens files and process pipelines.
pwd	Determines the current directory.
socket	Opens network sockets.
source	Loads scripts.

A safe interpreter does not have commands to manipulate the file system and other programs (e.g., cd, open, and exec). This ensures that untrusted scripts cannot harm the host computer. The socket command is removed so that untrusted scripts cannot access the network. The exit, source, and load commands are removed so that an untrusted script cannot harm the hosting application. Note that commands like puts and gets are *not* removed. A safe interpreter can still do I/O, but it cannot create an I/O channel. We will show how to pass an I/O channel to a child interpreter on page 281.

The initial state of a safe interpreter is very safe, but it is too limited. The only thing a safe interpreter can do is compute a string and return that value to the parent. By creating command aliases, a master can give a safe interpreter controlled access to resources. A *security policy* implements a set of command aliases that add controlled capabilities to a safe interpreter. We will show, for example, how to provide limited network and file system access to untrusted slaves. Tcl provides a framework to manage several security policies, which is described in Chapter 20.

Command Aliases

A *command alias* is a command in one interpreter that is implemented by a command in another interpreter. The master interpreter installs command aliases in its slaves. The command to create an alias has the following general form:

```
interp alias slave cmd1 target cmd2 ?arg arg ...?
```

This creates *cmd1* in *slave* that is an alias for *cmd2* in *target*. When *cmd1* is invoked in *slave*, *cmd2* is invoked in *target*. The alias mechanism is transparent to the slave. Whatever *cmd2* returns, the slave sees as the return value of *cmd1*. If *cmd2* raises an error, the error is propagated to the slave.

Name the current interpreter with {}.

If *target* is the current interpreter, name it with {}. The empty list is the way to name yourself as the interpreter. This is the most common case, although *target* can be a different slave. The *slave* and *target* can even be the same interpreter.

The arguments to *cmd1* are passed to *cmd2*, after any additional arguments to *cmd2* that were specified when the alias was created. These hidden arguments provide a safe way to pass extra arguments to an alias. For example, it is quite common to pass the name of the slave to the alias. In Example 19–3, exit in the interpreter foo is an alias that is implemented in the current interpreter (i.e., {}). When the slave executes exit, the master executes:

```
interp delete foo
```

Example 19–3 A command alias for exit.

```
interp create foo
interp alias foo exit {} interp delete foo
interp eval foo exit
# Child foo is gone.
```

Alias Introspection

You can query what aliases are defined for a child interpreter. The interp aliases command lists the aliases; the interp alias command can also return the value of an alias, and the interp target command tells you what interpreter implements an alias. These are illustrated in the following examples:

Example 19–4 Querying aliases.

```
proc Interp_ListAliases {name out} {
    puts $out "Aliases for $name"
    foreach alias [interp aliases $name] {
        puts $out [format "%-20s => (%s) %s" $alias \
                [interp target $name $alias] \
                [interp alias $name $alias]]
    }
}
```

Example 19–4 generates output in a human readable format. Example 19–5 generates the aliases as Tcl commands that can be used to re-create them later:

Example 19–5 Dumping aliases as Tcl commands.

```
proc Interp_DumpAliases {name out} {
    puts $out "# Aliases for $name"
    foreach alias [interp aliases $name] {
        puts $out [format "interp alias %s %s %s %s" \
            $name $alias [list [interp target $name $alias]] \
            [interp alias $name $alias]]
    }
}
```

II. Advanced Tcl

Hidden Commands

The commands listed in Table 19–2 are *hidden* instead of being completely removed. A hidden command can be invoked in a slave by its master. For example, a master can load Tcl scripts into a slave by using its hidden source command:

```
interp create -safe slave
interp invokehidden slave source filename
```

Without hidden commands, the master has to do a bit more work to achieve the same thing. It must open and read the file and eval the contents of the file in the slave. File operations are described in Chapter 9.

```
interp create -safe slave
set in [open filename]
interp eval slave [read $in]
close $in
```

Hidden commands were added in Tcl 7.7 in order to better support the Tcl/Tk browser plug-in described in Chapter 20. In some cases, hidden commands are strictly necessary; it is not possible to simulate them any other way. The best examples are in the context of Safe-Tk, where the master creates widgets or does potentially dangerous things on behalf of the slave. These will be discussed in more detail later.

A master can hide and expose commands using the interp hide and interp expose operations, respectively. You can even hide Tcl procedures. However, the commands inside the procedure run with the same privilege as that of the slave. For example, if you are really paranoid, you might not want an untrusted interpreter to read the clock or get timing information. You can hide the clock and time commands:

```
interp create -safe slave
interp hide slave clock
interp hide slave time
```

You can remove commands from the slave entirely like this:

```
interp eval slave [list rename clock {}]
interp eval slave [list rename time {}]
```

Substitutions

You must be aware of Tcl parsing and substitutions when commands are invoked in other interpreters. There are three cases corresponding to `interp eval`, `interp invokehidden`, and command aliases.

With `interp eval` the command is subject to a complete round of parsing and substitutions in the target interpreter. This occurs after the parsing and substitutions for the `interp eval` command itself. In addition, if you pass several arguments to `interp eval`, those are concatenated before evaluation. This is similar to the way the `eval` command works as described in Chapter 19. The most reliable way to use `interp eval` is to construct a list to ensure the command is well structured:

```
interp eval slave [list cmd arg1 arg2]
```

With hidden commands, the command and arguments are taken directly from the arguments to `interp invokehidden`, and there are no substitutions done in the target interpreter. This means that the master has complete control over the command structure, and nothing funny can happen in the other interpreter. For this reason you should not create a list. If you do that, the whole list will be interpreted as the command name! Instead, just pass separate arguments to `interp invokehidden` and they are passed straight through to the target:

```
interp invokehidden slave command arg1 arg2
```

Never `eval` alias arguments.

With aliases, all the parsing and substitutions occur in the slave before the alias is invoked in the master. The alias implementation should never `eval` or `subst` any values it gets from the slave to avoid executing arbitrary code.

For example, suppose there is an alias to open files. The alias does some checking and then invokes the hidden `open` command. An untrusted script might pass `[exit]` as the name of the file to open in order to create mischief. The untrusted code is hoping that the master will accidentally `eval` the filename and cause the application to exit. This attack has nothing to do with opening files; it just hopes for a poor alias implementation. Example 19–6 shows an alias that is not subject to this attack:

Example 19–6 Substitutions and hidden commands.

```
interp alias slave open {} safeopen slave
proc safeopen {slave filename {mode r}} {
    # do some checks, then...
    interp invokehidden $slave open $filename $mode
}
interp eval slave {open \[exit\]}
```

The command in the slave starts out as:

```
open \[exit\]
```

The master has to quote the brackets in its `interp eval` command or else the slave will try to invoke `exit` because of command substitution. Presumably `exit` isn't defined, or it is defined to terminate the slave. Once this quoting is done, the value of `filename` is `[exit]` and it is not subject to substitutions. It is safe to use `$filename` in the `interp invokehidden` command because it is only substituted once, in the master. The hidden `open` command also gets `[exit]` as its filename argument, which is never evaluated as a Tcl command.

I/O from Safe Interpreters

A safe child interpreter cannot open files or network sockets directly. An alias can create an I/O channel (i.e., open a file or socket) and give the child access to it. The parent can share the I/O channel with the child, or it can transfer the I/O channel to the child. If the channel is shared, both the parent and the child can use it. If the channel is transferred, the parent no longer has access to the channel. In general, transferring an I/O channel is simpler, but sharing an I/O channel gives the parent more control over an unsafe child. The differences are illustrated in Example 19–7 and Example 19–9.

There are three properties of I/O channels that are important to consider when choosing between sharing and transferring: the name, the seek offset, and the reference count.

- The name of the I/O channel (e.g., `file4`) is the same in all interpreters. If a parent transfers a channel to a child, it can close the channel by evaluating a `close` command in the child. Although names are shared, an interpreter cannot attempt I/O on a channel to which it has not been given access.
- The seek offset of the I/O channel is shared by all interpreters that share the I/O channel. An I/O operation on the channel updates the seek offset for all interpreters that share the channel. This means that if two interpreters share an I/O channel, their output will be cleanly interleaved in the channel. If they both read from the I/O channel, they will get different data. Seek offsets are explained in more detail on page 114.
- A channel has a reference count of all interpreters that share the I/O channel. The channel remains open until all references are closed. When a parent transfers an I/O channel, the reference count stays the same. When a parent shares an I/O channel, the reference count increments by one. When an interpreter closes a channel with `close`, the reference count is decremented by one. When an interpreter is deleted, all of its references to I/O channels are removed.

The syntax of commands to share or transfer an I/O channel is:

```
interp share interp1 chanName interp2
interp transfer interp1 chanName interp2
```

In these commands, *chanName* exists in *interp1* and is being shared or transferred to *interp2*. As with command aliases, if *interp1* is the current interpreter, name it with {}.

The following example creates a temporary file for an unsafe interpreter. The file is opened for reading and writing, and the slave can use it to store data temporarily.

Example 19–7 Opening a file for an unsafe interpreter.

```
proc TempfileAlias {slave} {
    set i 0
    while {[file exists Temp$slave$i]} {
        incr i
    }
    set out [open Temp$slave$i w+]
    interp transfer {} $out $slave
    return $out
}
proc TempfileExitAlias {slave} {
    foreach file [glob -nocomplain Temp$slave*] {
        file delete -force $file
    }
    interp delete $slave
}
interp create -safe foo
interp alias foo Tempfile {} TempfileAlias foo
interp alias foo exit {} TempfileExitAlias foo
```

The `TempfileAlias` procedure is invoked in the parent when the child interpreter invokes `Tempfile`. `TempfileAlias` returns the name of the open channel, which becomes the return value from `Tempfile`. `TempfileAlias` uses `interp transfer` to pass the I/O channel to the child so that the child has permission to access the I/O channel. In this example, it would also work to invoke the hidden `open` command to create the I/O channel directly in the slave.

Example 19–7 is not fully safe because the unsafe interpreter can still overflow the disk or create a million files. Because the parent has transferred the I/O channel to the child, it cannot easily monitor the I/O activity by the child. Example 19–9 addresses these issues.

The Safe Base

An safe interpreter created with `interp create -safe` has no script library environment and no way to source scripts. Tcl provides a *safe base* that extends a raw safe interpreter with the ability to source scripts and packages which are described in Chapter 12. The safe base also defines an `exit` alias that terminates the slave like the one in Example 19–7. The safe base is implemented as Tcl scripts that are part of the standard Tcl script library. Create an interpreter that uses the safe base with `safe::interpCreate`:

```
safe::interpCreate foo
```

The safe base has `source` and `load` aliases that only access directories on an *access path* defined by the master interpreter. The master has complete control over what files can be loaded into a slave. In general, it would be all right to source any Tcl program into an untrusted interpreter. However, untrusted scripts might learn things from the error messages they get by sourcing arbitrary files. The safe base also has versions of the `package` and unknown commands that support the library facility. Table 19–3 lists the Tcl procedures in the safe base:

Table 19–3 The safe base master interface.

`safe::interpCreate ?`*slave*`?` `?`*options*`?`	Creates a safe interpreter and initialize the security policy mechanism.
`safe::interpInit` *slave* `?`*options*`?`	Initializes a safe interpreter so it can use security policies.
`safe::interpConfigure` *slave* `?`*options*`?`	Options are `-accessPath`*pathlist*, `-nostatics`, `-deleteHook` *script*, `-nestedLoadOk`.
`safe::interpDelete` *slave*	Deletes a safe interpreter.
`safe::interpAddToAccessPath` *slave directory*	Adds a directory to the slave's access path.
`safe::interpFindInAccessPath`	Maps from a directory to the token visible in the slave for that directory.
`safe::setLogCmd ?`*cmd arg* `... ?`	Sets or queries the logging command used by the safe base.

Table 19–4 lists the aliases defined in a safe interpreter by the safe base.

Table 19–4 The safe base slave aliases.

`source`	Loads scripts from directories in the access path.
`load`	Loads binary extensions from the slaves access path.
`file`	Only the `dirname`, `join`, `extension`, `root`, `tail`, `pathname`, and `split` operations are allowed.
`exit`	Destroys the slave interpreter.

Security Policies

A *security policy* defines what a safe interpreter can do. Designing security policies that are secure is difficult. If you design your own, make sure to have your colleagues review the code. Give out prizes to folks who can break your policy. Good policy implementations are proven with lots of review and trial attacks.

The good news is that Safe-Tcl security policies can be implemented in relatively small amounts of Tcl code. This makes them easier to analyze and get correct. Here are a number of rules of thumb:

- Small policies are better than big, complex policies. If you do a lot of complex processing to allow or disallow access to resources, chances are there are holes in your policy. Keep it simple.
- Never `eval` arguments to aliases. If an alias accepts arguments that are passed by the slave, you must avoid being tricked into executing arbitrary Tcl code. The primary way to avoid this is never to `eval` arguments that are passed into an alias. Watch your expressions, too. The `expr` command does an extra round of substitutions, so brace all your expressions so that an attacker cannot pass `[exit]` where you expect a number!
- Security policies do not compose. Each time you add a new alias to a security policy, it changes the nature of the policy. Even if *alias1* and *alias2* are safe in isolation, there is no guarantee that they cannot be used together to mount an attack. Each addition to a security policy requires careful review.

Limited Socket Access

The `Safesock` security policy provides limited socket access. The policy is designed around a simple table of allowed hosts and ports. An untrusted interpreter can connect only to addresses listed in the table. For example, I would never let untrusted code connect to the *sendmail*, *ftp*, or *telnet* ports on my hosts. There are just too many attacks possible on these ports. On the other hand, I might want to let untrusted code fetch a URL from certain hosts, or connect to a database server for an intranet application. The goal of this policy is to have a simple way to specify exactly what hosts and ports a slave can access. Example 19–8 shows a simplified version of the `Safesock` security policy that is distributed with Tcl 8.0.

Example 19–8 The `Safesock` security policy.

```
# The index is a host name, and the
# value is a list of port specifications, which can be
# an exact port number
# a lower bound on port number: N-
# a range of port numbers, inclusive: N-M
array set safesock {
    sage.eng        3000-4000
    www.sun.com     80
    webcache.eng    {80 8080}
    bisque.eng      {80 1025-}
}
proc Safesock_PolicyInit {slave} {
    interp alias $slave socket {} SafesockAlias $slave
}
```

```
proc SafesockAlias {slave host port} {
    global safesock
    if ![info exists safesock($host)] {
        error "unknown host: $host"
    }

    foreach portspec $safesock($host) {
        set low [set high ""]
        if {[regexp {^([0-9]+)-([0-9]*)$} $portspec x low high]} {
            if {($low <= $port && $high == "") ||
                    ($low <= $port && $high >= $port)} {
                set good $port
                break
            }
        } elseif {$port == $portspec} {
            set good $port
        }
    }

    if [info exists good] {
        set sock [interp invokehidden $slave socket $host $good]
        interp invokehidden $slave fconfigure $sock \
            -blocking 0
        return $sock
    }
    error "bad port: $port"
}
```

The policy is initialized with `Safesock_PolicyInit`. The name of this procedure follows a naming convention used by the safe base. In this case, a single alias is installed. The alias gives the slave a `socket` command that is implemented by `SafesockAlias` in the master.

The alias checks for a port that matches one of the port specifications for the host. If a match is found, then the `invokehidden` operation is used to invoke two commands in the slave. The `socket` command creates the network connection, and the `fconfigure` command puts the socket into nonblocking mode so that `read` and `gets` by the slave do not block the application:

```
set sock [interp invokehidden $slave socket $host $good]
interp invokehidden $slave fconfigure $sock -blocking 0
```

The `socket` alias in the slave does not conflict with the hidden `socket` command. There are two distinct sets of commands, hidden and exposed. It is quite common for the alias implementation to invoke the hidden command after various permission checks are made.

The Tcl Web browser plug-in ships with a slightly improved version of the `Safesock` policy. It adds an alias for `fconfigure` so that the `http` package can set end of line translations and buffering modes. The `fconfigure` alias does not let you change the blocking behavior of the socket. The policy has also been extended to classify hosts into trusted and untrusted hosts based on their address. A different table of allowed ports is used for the two classes of hosts. The classification is done with two tables: One table lists patterns that match trusted hosts, and the other table lists hosts that should not be trusted even though they match the first table. The improved version also lets a downloaded script connect to the Web server that it came from. The Web browser plug-in is described in Chapter 20.

Limited Temporary Files

Example 19–9 improves on Example 19–7 by limiting the number of temporary files and the size of the files. It is written to work with the safe base, so it has a `Tempfile_PolicyInit` that takes the name of the slave as an argument. `TempfileOpenAlias` lets the child specify a file by name, yet it limits the files to a single directory.

The example demonstrates a shared I/O channel that gives the master control over output. `TempfilePutsAlias` restricts the amount of data that can be written to a file. By sharing the I/O channel for the temporary file, the slave can use commands like `gets`, `eof`, and `close`, while the master does the `puts`. The need for shared I/O channels is somewhat reduced by hidden commands, which were added to Safe-Tcl more recently than shared I/O channels. For example, the `puts` alias can either write to a shared channel after checking the file size, or it can invoke the hidden `puts` in the slave. This alternative is shown in Example 19–10.

Example 19–9 The `Tempfile` security policy.

```
# Policy parameters:
#   directory is the location for the files
#   maxfile is the number of files allowed in the directory
#   maxsize is the max size for any single file.

array set tempfile {
    maxfile      4
    maxsize      65536
}
# tempfile(directory) is computed dynamically based on
# the source of the script

proc Tempfile_PolicyInit {slave} {
    global tempfile
    interp alias $slave open {} \
        TempfileOpenAlias $slave $tempfile(directory) \
            $tempfile(maxfile)
    interp alias $slave puts {} TempfilePutsAlias $slave \
        $tempfile(maxsize)
    interp alias $slave exit {} TempfileExitAlias $slave
}
proc TempfileOpenAlias {slave dir maxfile name {m r} {p 0777}} {
    global tempfile
    # remove sneaky characters
    regsub -all {|/:} [file tail $name] {} real
    set real [file join $dir $real]
```

```tcl
        # Limit the number of files
        set files [glob -nocomplain [file join $dir *]]
        set N [llength $files]
        if {($N >= $maxfile) && (\
                [lsearch -exact $files $real] < 0)} {
            error "permission denied"
        }
        if [catch {open $real $m $p} out] {
            return -code error "$name: permission denied"
        }
        lappend tempfile(channels,$slave) $out
        interp share {} $out $slave
        return $out
}
proc TempfileExitAlias {slave} {
    global tempfile
    interp delete $slave
    if [info exists tempfile(channels,$slave)] {
        foreach out $tempfile(channels,$slave) {
            catch {close $out}
        }
        unset tempfile(channels,$slave)
    }
}
# See also the puts alias in Example 22-4 on page 327
proc TempfilePutsAlias {slave max chan args} {
    # max is the file size limit, in bytes
    # chan is the I/O channel
    # args is either a single string argument,
    # or the -nonewline flag plus the string.

    if {[llength $args] > 2} {
        error "invalid arguments"
    }
    if {[llength $args] == 2} {
        if {![string match -n* [lindex $argv 0]]} {
            error "invalid arguments"
        }
        set string [lindex $args 1]
    } else {
        set string [lindex $args 0]\n
    }
    set size [expr [tell $chan] + [string length $string]]
    if {$size > $max} {
        error "File size exceeded"
    } else {
        puts -nonewline $chan $string
    }
}
```

The `TempfileAlias` procedure is generalized in Example 19–9 to have parameters that specify the directory, name, and a limit to the number of files allowed. The `directory` and `maxfile` limit are part of the alias definition. Their existence is transparent to the slave. The slave specifies only the name and access mode (i.e., for reading or writing.) The `Tempfile` policy can be used by different slave interpreters with different parameters.

The master is careful to restrict the files to the specified directory. It uses `file tail` to strip off any leading pathname components that the slave might specify. The `tempfile(directory)` definition is not shown in the example. The application must choose a directory when it creates the safe interpreter. The `Browser` security policy described on page 300 chooses a directory based on the name of the URL containing the untrusted script.

The `TempfilePutsAlias` procedure implements a limited form of `puts`. It checks the size of the file with `tell` and measures the output string to see if the total exceeds the limit. The limit comes from a parameter defined when the alias is created. The file cannot grow past the limit, at least not by any action of the child interpreter. The `args` parameter is used to allow an optional `-nonewline` flag to `puts`. The value of `args` is checked explicitly instead of using the `eval` trick described in Example 10–3 on page 127. Never `eval` arguments to aliases or else a slave can attack you with arguments that contain embedded Tcl commands.

The master and slave share the I/O channel. The name of the I/O channel is recorded in `tempfile`, and `TempfileExitAlias` uses this information to close the channel when the child interpreter is deleted. This is necessary because both parent and child have a reference to the channel when it is shared. The child's reference is automatically removed when the interpreter is deleted, but the parent must close its own reference.

The shared I/O channel lets the master use `puts` and `tell`. It is also possible to implement this policy by using hidden `puts` and `tell` commands. The reason `tell` must be hidden is to prevent the slave from implementing its own version of `tell` that lies about the seek offset value. One advantage of using hidden commands is that there is no need to clean up the tempfile state about open channels. You can also layer the puts alias on top of any existing puts implementation. For example, a script may define `puts` to be a procedure that inserts data into a text widget. Example 19–10 shows the difference when using hidden commands.

Example 19–10 Restricted `puts` using hidden commands.

```
proc Tempfile_PolicyInit {slave} {
    global tempfile
    interp alias $slave open {} \
        TempfileOpenAlias $slave $tempfile(directory) \
            $tempfile(maxfile)
    interp hide $slave tell
    interp alias $slave tell {} TempfileTellAlias $slave
    interp hide $slave puts
    interp alias $slave puts {} TempfilePutsAlias $slave \
        $tempfile(maxsize)
    # no special exit alias required
}
proc TempfileOpenAlias {slave dir maxfile name {m r} {p 0777}} {
```

```
    # remove sneaky characters
    regsub -all {|/:} [file tail $name] {} real
    set real [file join $dir $real]
    # Limit the number of files
    set files [glob -nocomplain [file join $dir *]]
    set N [llength $files]
    if {($N >= $maxfile) && (\
            [lsearch -exact $files $real] < 0)} {
        error "permission denied"
    }
    if [catch {interp invokehidden $slave \
            open $real $m $p} out] {
        return -code error "$name: permission denied"
    }
    return $out
}
proc TempfileTellAlias {slave chan} {
    interp invokehidden $slave tell $chan
}
proc TempfilePutsAlias {slave max chan args} {
    if {[llength $args] > 2} {
        error "invalid arguments"
    }
    if {[llength $args] == 2} {
        if {![string match -n* [lindex $args 0]]} {
            error "invalid arguments"
        }
        set string [lindex $args 1]
    } else {
        set string [lindex $args 0]\n
    }
    set size [interp invokehidden $slave tell $chan]
    incr size [string length $string]
    if {$size > $max} {
        error "File size exceeded"
    } else {
        interp invokehidden $slave \
            puts -nonewline $chan $string
    }
}
```

Safe `after` Command

The `after` command is unsafe because it can block the application for an arbitrary amount of time. This happens if you only specify a time but do not specify a command. In this case, Tcl just waits for the time period and processes no events. This will stop all interpreters, not just the one doing the `after` command. This is a kind of *resource attack*. It doesn't leak information or damage anything, but it disrupts the main application.

Example 19–11 defines an alias that implements `after` on behalf of safe interpreters. The basic idea is to carefully check the arguments, and then do the `after` in the parent interpreter. As an additional feature, the number of outstanding `after` events is limited. The master keeps a record of each `after` event scheduled. Two IDs are associated with each event: one chosen by the master (i.e., `myid`), and the other chosen by the `after` command (i.e., `id`). The master keeps a map from `myid` to `id`. The map serves two purposes: The number of map entries counts the number of outstanding events. The map also hides the real `after` ID from the slave, which prevents a slave from attempting mischief by specifying invalid after IDs to `after cancel`. The `SafeAfterCallback` is the procedure scheduled. It maintains state and then invokes the original callback in the slave.

Example 19–11 A safe `after` command.

```
# SafeAfter_PolicyInit creates a child with
# a safe after command

proc SafeAfter_PolicyInit {slave max} {
    # max limits the number of outstanding after events
    global after
    interp alias $slave after {} SafeAfterAlias $slave $max
    interp alias $slave exit {} SafeAfterExitAlias $slave
    # This is used to generate after IDs for the slave.
    set after(id,$slave) 0
}

# SafeAfterAlias is an alias for after. It disallows after
# with only a time argument and no command.

proc SafeAfterAlias {slave max args} {
    global after
    set argc [llength $args]
    if {$argc == 0} {
        error "Usage: after option args"
    }
    switch -- [lindex $args 0] {
        cancel {
            # A naive implementation would just
            # eval after cancel $args
            # but something dangerous could be hiding in args.
            set myid [lindex $args 1]
            if {[info exists after(id,$slave,$myid)]} {
                set id $after(id,$slave,$myid)
                unset after(id,$slave,$myid)
                after cancel $id
            }
            return ""
        }
        default {
            if {$argc == 1} {
                error "Usage: after time command args..."
            }
            if {[llength [array names after id,$slave,*]]\
                    >= $max} {
                error "Too many after events"
```

```
            }
            # Maintain concat semantics
            set command [concat [lrange $args 1 end]]
            # Compute our own id to pass the callback.
            set myid after#[incr after(id,$slave)]
            set id [after [lindex $args 0] \
                [list SafeAfterCallback $slave $myid $command]]
            set after(id,$slave,$myid) $id
            return $myid
        }
    }
}

# SafeAfterCallback is the after callback in the master.
# It evaluates its command in the safe interpreter.

proc SafeAfterCallback {slave myid cmd} {
    global after
    unset after(id,$slave,$myid)
    if [catch {
        interp eval $slave $cmd
    } err] {
        catch {interp eval $slave bgerror $error}
    }
}

# SafeAfterExitAlias is an alias for exit that does cleanup.

proc SafeAfterExitAlias {slave} {
    global after
    foreach id [array names after id,$slave,*] {
        after cancel $after($id)
        unset after($id)
    }
    interp delete $slave
}
```

II. Advanced Tcl

Safe-Tk and the Browser Plugin

This chapter describes Safe-Tk that lets untrusted scripts display and manipulate graphical user interfaces. The main application of Safe-Tk is the Tcl/Tk plugin for Web browsers like Netscape Navigator and Internet Explorer.

II. Advanced Tcl

$\mathcal{S}$afe-Tk supports network applets that display user interfaces. The main vehicle for Safe-Tk is a plugin for Netscape Navigator and Internet Explorer. The plugin supports Tcl applets, or *Tclets*, that are downloaded from the Web server and execute inside a window in a Web browser. For the most part, Tcl/Tk applications can run unchanged in the plugin. However, security policies place some restrictions on Tclets. The plugin supports multiple security policies, so Tclets can do a variety of interesting things in a safe manner.

The current version of the plugin uses Tcl/Tk 8.0. You can configure the plugin to use an existing *wish* application to host the Tcl applets, or the plugin can load the Tcl/Tk shared libraries and everything runs in the browser process. You can use a custom *wish* that has extensions built in or dynamically loaded. This gives intranet applications of the plugin the ability to access databases and other services that are not provided by the Tcl/Tk core. With the security policy mechanism you can still provide mediated access to these resources. This chapter describes how to set up the plugin.

The source code of the plugin is freely available. You can recompile the plugin against newer versions of Tcl/Tk, or build custom plugins that have your own Tcl extensions built in. One particularly active plugin user is NASA, which maintains and distributes an enhanced version of the plugin. You can find them from the main plugin Web site at:

```
http://www.scriptics.com/plugin/
```

Tk in Child Interpreters

A child interpreter starts out with just the core Tcl commands. It does not include Tk or any other extensions that might be available to the parent interpreter. This is true whether or not the child interpreter is declared safe. You add extensions to child interpreters by using a form of the `load` command that specifies an interpreter:

```
load {} Tk child
```

Normally, `load` takes the name of the library file that contains the extension. In this case, the Tk package is a *static package* that is already linked into the program (e.g., *wish* or the plugin), so the file name is the empty string. The `load` command calls the Tk initialization procedure to register all the Tcl commands provided by Tk.

Embedding Tk Windows

By default, a slave interpreter that loads Tk gets a new top-level window. *Wish* supports a `-use` command line option that directs Tk to use an existing window as dot. You can use this to embed an application within another. For example, the following commands run a copy of *Wish* that uses the `.embed` toplevel as its main window:

```
toplevel .embed
exec wish -use [winfo id .embed] somescript.tcl &
```

More often, embedding is used with child interpreters. If the interpreter is *not* safe, you can set the `argv` and `argc` variables in the slave before loading Tk:

```
interp create trustedTk
interp eval trustedTk \
    [list set argv [list -use [winfo id .embed]]]
interp eval trustedTk [list set argc 2]
load {} Tk trustedTk
```

If the child interpreter is safe, then you cannot set `argv` and `argc` directly. The easiest way to pass `-use` to a safe interpreter is with the `safe::loadTk` command:

```
safe::interpCreate safeTk
safe::loadTk safeTk -use [winfo id .embed]
```

When Tk is loaded into a safe interpreter, it calls back into the master interpreter and evaluates the `safe::TkInit` procedure. The job of this procedure is to return the appropriate `argv` value for the slave. The `safe::loadTk` procedure stores its additional arguments in the `safe::tkInit` variable, and this value is retrieved by the `safe::TkInit` procedure and returned to the slave. This protocol is used so that a safe interpreter cannot attempt to hijack the windows of its master by constructing its own `argv` variable!

Safe-Tk Restrictions

When Tk is loaded into a safe interpreter, it hides several Tk commands. Primarily these are hidden to prevent *denial of service* attacks against the main process. For example, if a child interpreter did a global `grab` and never released it, all input would be forever directed to the child. Table 20–1 lists the Tk commands hidden by default from a safe interpreter. The Tcl commands that are hidden in safe interpreters are listed on page 277.

Table 20–1 Tk commands omitted from safe interpreters.

`bell`	Rings the terminal bell.
`clipboard`	Accesses the CLIPBOARD selection.
`grab`	Directs input to a specified widget.
`menu`	Creates and manipulates menus, because menus need `grab`.
`selection`	Manipulates the selection.
`send`	Executes a command in another Tk application.
`tk`	Sets the application name.
`tk_chooseolor`	Color choice dialog.
`tk_getOpenFile`	File open dialog.
`tk_getSaveFile`	File save dialog.
`tk_messageBox`	Simple dialog boxes.
`toplevel`	Creates a detached window.
`wm`	Controls the window manager.

If you find these restrictions limiting, you can restore commands to safe interpreters with the `interp expose` command. For example, to get menus and toplevels working, you could do:

```
interp create -safe safeTk
foreach cmd {grab menu menubutton toplevel wm} {
    interp expose safeTk $cmd
}
```

Instead of exposing the command directly, you can also construct aliases that provide a subset of the features. For example, you could disable the `-global` option to grab. Aliases are described in detail in Chapter 19.

The Browser plugin defines a more elaborate configuration system to control what commands are available to slave interpreters. You can have lots of control, but you need to distribute the *security policies* that define what Tclets can do in the plugin. Configuring security policies for the plugin is described later.

II. Advanced Tcl

The Browser Plugin

The HTML EMBED tag is used to put various objects into a Web page, including a Tcl program. For example:

```
<EMBED src=eval.tcl width=400 height=300>
```

The width and height are interpreted by the plugin as the size of the embedded window. The src specifies the URL of the program. These parameter names (e.g., width) are case sensitive and should be lowercase. In the above example, eval.tcl is a relative URL, so it should be in the same directory as the HTML file that has the EMBED tag. The window size is fixed in the browser, which is different from normal toplevels in Tk. The plugin turns off geometry propagation on your main window so that your Tclet stays the size allocated.

There are also "full window" Tclets that do not use an EMBED tag at all. Instead, you just specify the .tcl file directly in the URL. For example, you can type this into your browser, or use it as the HREF parameter in a URL link:

```
http://www.beedub.com/plugin/bike.tcl
```

In this case, the plugin occupies the whole browser window and will resize as you resize the browser window.

The embed_args and plugin Variables

The parameters in the EMBED tag are available to the Tcl program in the embed_args variable, which is an array with the parameter names as the index values. For example, the string for a ticker-tape Tclet can be passed in the EMBED tag as the string parameter, and the Tclet will use $embed_args(string) as the value to display:

```
<EMBED src=ticker.tcl width=400 height=50 string="Hello World">
```

Note that HTML tag parameters are case sensitive. Your Tclet may want to map all the parameter names to lowercase for convenience:

```
foreach {name value} [array get embed_args] {
    set embed_args([string tolower $name]) $value
}
```

The plugin array has version, patchLevel, and release elements that identify the version and release date of the plugin implementation.

Example Plugins

The plugin home page is a great place to find Tclet examples. There are several plugins done by the Tcl/Tk team at Sunlabs, plus links to a wide variety of Tclets done on the Net.

```
http://www.scriptics.com/plugin/
```

I wrote a cute little plugin that calculates the effective wheel diameter of multigear bicycles. Brian Lewis, who built the Tcl 8.0 byte-code compiler, explained to me the concept and how important this information is to bicycle enthusiasts. I put together a Tclet that displays the gear combinations on a Tk canvas and lets you change the number of gears and their size. You can find the result at:

```
http://www.beedub.com/plugin/bike.html
```

Setting Up the plugin

There are plugin versions for UNIX, Windows, and Macintosh. The installation scripts take care of installing the plugin in the correct locations, which are described in the next sections about each platform. The plugin and the security policies that are distributed with it will continue to be updated. You can get the latest version from the Tcl/Tk Web site, `http://www.scriptics.com/plugin/`. If that URL changes, you can find an up-to-date pointer under `http://www.beedub.com/book/`. The plugin may already be installed at your site. Bring up the `About Plugins` dialog under `Help` in your browser to see if the Tcl/Tk plugin is listed.

The plugin is composed of the following parts, although the location of these files varies somewhat among platforms:

- The plugin shared libraries (i.e., DLLs). The Web browser dynamically loads the plugin implementation when it needs to execute a Tclet embedded in a Web page. There is a standard directory that the browser scans for the libraries that implement plugins.
- The Tcl/Tk script libraries. The plugin needs the standard script libraries that come with Tcl and Tk, plus it has its own scripts that complete its implementation. Each platform has a plugin script directory with these subdirectories: `tcl`, `tk`, `plugin`, `config`, `safetcl`, and `utils`. The plugin implementation is in the `plugin` directory.
- The security policies. These are kept in a `safetcl` directory that is a peer of the Tcl script library.
- The trust configuration. This defines what Tclets can use which security policies. This is in a `config` directory that is a peer of the Tcl script library.
- Local hooks. Local customization is supported by two hooks, `siteInit` and `siteSafeInit`. The `siteInit` procedure is called from the plugin when it first loads, and `siteSafeInit` is called when each applet is initialized. It is called with the name of the slave interpreter and the list of arguments from the `<EMBED>` tag. You can provide these as scripts that get loaded from the `auto_path` of the master interpreter. Chapter 12 describes how to manage script libraries found in the `auto_path`. The plugin also sources a personal start up script in which you can define `siteInit` and `siteSafeInit`. This script is `~/.pluginrc` on UNIX and `plugin/tclplugin.rc` on Windows and Macintosh.

Plugin Environment Variables

The plugin can be configured to run Tcl/Tk directly in the browser process, or to run with a small library in the browser that communicates with an external *wish* application. The default is to run in process. The advantage of the external process is that you can use custom *wish* shells that can load various extensions. Table 20–2 shows the environment variables used to control the plugin configuration.

Table 20–2 Plugin Environment Variables

TCL_PLUGIN_INPROCESS	If this is defined and 1, then Tcl/Tk is loaded directly into the browser. Otherwise, the plugin forks *wish*.
TCL_PLUGIN_WISH	This names the *wish* executable used to run Tclets. This must be version 8.0 or higher to properly support embedding.
TCL_PLUGIN_CONSOLE	If this is set to 1, then a console is opened when a Tclet is loaded. The console prompts for Tcl commands that are evaluated in the master interpreter. If the value is something other than 1, then it is taken to be a script (e.g., *TkCon*) that implements a console.
TCL_PLUGIN_LOGWINDOW	If 1, various status messages from the plugin are displayed.
TCL_PLUGIN_LOGFILE	If defined, this file captures the log output.

UNIX Configuration

Netscape looks in each user's ~/.netscape/plugins for the shared libraries that implement plugins. It also looks in a plugins directory under its main directory, which will vary from site to site. You can define a search path for plugins with the NXP_PLUGIN_PATH environment variable. The plugin script library is in ~/.tclplug/2.0/plugin. You can change this default location by setting the TCL_PLUGIN_DIR environment variable. Once the plugin finds its script library, it assumes that the Tcl and Tk script directories, the security policies, and the trust map are in peer directories.

Windows Configuration

The default location for plugins is in the PLUGINS directory of the Netscape installation. The Tcl/Tk plugin also works in Internet Explorer from the same location. The script libraries are found under C:\TCLPLUG\2.0. You can change this location by setting the registry variable:

        Software\Sun\Tcl Plugin\2.0\Directory

Macintosh Configuration

Installing the plugin on the Macintosh is a three-step process. In step one, you unpack the initial download file, which creates another installer file. In step two, you run that installer, which puts files into two locations. You specify one folder that will hold the documentation and the Netscape plugin. The rest of the plugin goes into a plugin folder under the Tool Command Language folder in your system's `Extensions` folder. It does not conflict with any existing Tcl/Tk installations you may already have. In step three, you complete the process by moving the `Tcl Plugin` file into the `Plugins` directory of your Netscape installation.

The current version of the Macintosh plugin is limited to Netscape. Version 4 works better than Netscape 3, and Internet Explorer is not supported at all.

Security Policies and Browser Plugin

Tclets run in a safe interpreter that is set up with the *safe base* facilities described on page 282. This limits a Tclet to a display-only application. To do something more interesting, you must grant the Tclet more privilege. The extra functions are bundled together into a *security policy*, which is implemented as a set of command aliases. Unlike a Java applet, a Tclet can choose from different security policies. A few standard security policies are distributed with the plugin, and these are described below. You can also create custom security policies to support intranet applications. You can even choose to grant certain Tclets the full power of Tcl/Tk. The `policy` command is used to request a security policy:

    policy *name*

The policies that are part of the standard plugin distribution are described below. The `home`, `inside`, and `outside` policies all provide limited network access. They differ in what set of hosts are accessible. The default trust configuration lets any Tclet request the `home`, `inside`, or `outside` policy.

- `home`. This provides a `socket` and `fconfigure` commands that are limited to connecting to the host from which the Tclet was downloaded. You can specify an empty string for the host argument to `socket` to connect back to the home host. This policy also supports `open` and `file delete` that are similar to the `Tempfile` policy shown in Example 19–9 on page 286. This provides limited local storage that is inside a directory that is, by default, private to the Tclet. Files in the private directory persist after the Tclet exits, so it can maintain long term state. Tclets from the same server can share the directory by putting the same `prefix=partialurl` argument in their EMBED tag. The `partialurl` must be a prefix of the Tclet's URL. Finally, the `home` policy automatically provides a `browser` package that is described later.
- `inside`. This is just like the `home` policy, except that the site administrator controls a table of hosts and ports to which untrusted slaves can connect with `socket`. A similar set of tables control what URLs can be accessed with the `browser` package. This is similar to the `Safesock` policy shown in Example 19–8 on page 284. The set of hosts is supposed to be inside the firewall. The local file storage used by this policy is distinct from that used by the `home` and `outside` policies. This is true even if Tclets try to share by using the `prefix=partialurl` parameter.
- `outside`. This is just like the `home` and `inside` policies, except that the set of hosts is configured to be outside the firewall. The local file storage used by

this policy is distinct from that used by the `home` and `inside` policies.

- `trusted`. This policy restores all features of Tcl and Tk. This policy lets you launch all your Tcl and Tk applications from the Web browser. The default trust map settings do not allow this for any Tclet. The trust map configuration is described later.

- `javascript`. This policy provides a superset of the `browser` package that lets you invoke arbitrary Javascript and to write HTML directly to frames. This does not have the limited socket or temporary file access that the `home`, `inside`, and `outside` policies have. However, the `javascript` policy places no restrictions on the URLs you can fetch, plus it lets Tclets execute Javascript, which may have its own security risks. The default trust map settings do not allow this for any Tclet.

The Browser Package

The `browser` package is bundled with several of the security policies. It makes many features of the Web browser accessible to Tclets. They can fetch URLs and display HTML in frames. However, the `browser` package has some risks associated with it. HTTP requests can be used to transmit information, so a Tclet using the policy could leak sensitive information if it can fetch a URL outside the firewall. To avoid information leakage, the `inside`, `outside`, and `home` policies restrict the URL that can be fetched with `browser::getURL`. Table 20–3 lists the aliases defined by the `browser` package.

Table 20–3 Aliases defined by the `browser` package.

`browser::status` *string*	Displays *string* in the browser status window.
`browser::getURL` *url* *?timeout? ?newcallback?* *?writecallback?* *?endcallback?*	Fetches *url*, if allowed by the security policy. The *callbacks* occur before, during, and after the *url* data is returned.
`browser::displayURL` *url* *frame*	Causes the browser to display *url* in *frame*.
`browser::getForm` *url data* *?raw? ?timeout?* *?newcallback?* *?writecallback?* *?endcallback?*	Posts data to url. The callbacks are the same as for browser::getURL. If *raw* is 0, then data is a name value list that gets encoded automatically. Otherwise, it is assumed to be encoded already.
`browser::displayForm` *url* *frame data ?raw?*	Posts *data* to *url* and displays the result in *frame*. The *raw* argument is the same as in `browser::getForm`.

The `browser::getURL` function uses the browser's built-in functions, so it understands proxies and supports `ftp:`, `http:`, and `file:` urls. Unfortunately, the `browser::getURL` interface is different from the `http::geturl` interface. It uses a more complex callback scheme that is due to the nature of the browser's built-in functions. If you do not specify any callbacks, then the call blocks until all the data is received, and then that data is returned. The callback functions are described in Table 20–4.

Table 20–4 The browser::getURL callbacks.

`newcallback` *name stream url mimetype datemodified size*	This is called when data starts to arrive from *url*. The *name* identifies the requesting Tclet, and the *stream* identifies the connection. The *mimetype*, *datemodified*, and *size* parameters are attributes of the returned data.
`writecallback` *name stream size data*	This is called when *size* bytes of *data* arrive for Tcllet *name* over *stream*.
`endcallback` *name stream reason data*	This is called when the request has completed, although there may be some final bytes in *data*. The reason is one of: EOF, NETWOR_ERROR, USER_BREAK, or TIMEOUT.

Configuring Security Policies

There are three aspects to the plugin security policy mechanism: *policies, features*, and *trust maps*. A policy is an umbrella for a set of features that are allowed for certain Tclets based on the trust map. A feature is a set of commands and aliases that are defined for a safe interpreter that requests a policy. The trust map is a filter based on the URL of the Tclet. In the future, trust may bet determined by digital signatures instead of URLs. The trust map determines whether a Tclet can request a given policy.

Security Policies are configured for each client.

Remember that the configuration files affect the client machine, which is the workstation that runs the Web browser. If you create Tclets that require custom security policies, you have the burden of distributing the configuration files to clients that will use your Tclets. You also have the burden of convincing them that your security policy is safe!

The `config/plugin.cfg` File

The main configuration file is the `config/plugin.cfg` file in the plugin distribution. This file lists what features are supported by the plugin, and it defines the URL filters for the trust map.

The configuration file is defined into sections with a `section` command. The policies section defines which Tclets can use which security policies. For example, the default configuration file contains these lines in the policies section:

```
section policies
    allow home
    disallow intercom
    disallow inside
```

```
disallow outside
disallow trusted
allow javascript ifallowed trustedJavaScriptURLS \
     $originURL
```

This configuration grants all Tclets the right to use the `home` policy, disallows all Tclets from using the `intercom, inside, outside,` and `trusted` policies, and grants limited access to the `javascript` policy.

If you are curious, the configuration files are almost Tcl, but not quite. I lost an argument about that one, so these are stylized configuration files that follow their own rules. For example, the `originURL` variable is not defined in the configuration file but is a value that is tested later when the Tclet is loaded. I'll just give examples here and you can peer under the covers if you want to learn how they are parsed.

The `ifallowed` clause depends on another section to describe the trust mapping for that policy. For the `javascript` policy, the `config/plugin.cfg` file contains:

```
section trustedJavascriptURLs
     allow http://sunscript.sun.com:80/plugin/javascript/*
```

Unfortunately, this server isn't running anymore, so you may want to add the Scriptics Web server to your own configuration:

```
allow http://www.scriptics.com:80/plugin/javascript/*
```

You can use a combination of `allow` and `disallow` rules in a section. The arguments to `allow` and `disallow` are URL `string match` patterns, and they are processed in order. For example, you could put a liberal `allow` rule followed by `disallow` rules that restrict access, or vice versa. It is probably safest to explicitly list each server that you trust.

Policy Configuration Files

Each security policy has a configuration file associated with it. For example, the `outside` policy uses the file `outside.cfg` file in the `config` directory. This file specifies what hosts and ports are accessible to Tclets using the outside policy. For the `inside` and `outside` policies, the configuration files are similar in spirit to the `safesock` array used to configure the `Safesock` security policy shown on page 284. There are a set of allowed hosts and ports, and a set of excluded hosts. The excluded hosts are an exception list. If a host matches the included set but also matches the excluded set, it is not accessible. There is an included and excluded set for URLs that affect `browser::geturl`. The settings from the `Tempfile` policy shown on page 286 are also part of the `home, inside,` and `outside` configuration files. The configuration files are well commented, and you should read through them to learn about the configuration options for each security policy.

Security Policy Features

The aliases that make up a security policy are organized into sets called *features*. The features are listed in the main `config/plugin.cfg` configuration file:

```
variable featuresList {url stream network persist unsafe}
```

In turn, each security policy configuration file lists what features are part of the policy. For example, the `config/home.cfg` file lists these features:

```
section features
    allow url
    allow network
    allow persist unless {[string match {UNKNOWN *} \
        [getattr originURL]]}
```

Each feature is implemented in a file in the `safetcl` directory of the distribution. For example, the url feature is implemented in `safetcl/url.tcl`. The code in these files follows some conventions in order to work with the configuration mechanism. Each one is implemented inside a namespace that is a child of the `safefeature` namespace (e.g., `safefeature::url`). It must implement an `install` procedure that is called to initialize the feature for a new Tclet. It is inside this procedure that the various allow/disallow rules are checked. The `cfg::allowed` command supports the rule language used in the `.cfg` files.

Creating New Security Policies

This book does not describe the details of the configuration language or the steps necessary to create a new security policy. There are several manual pages distributed with the plugin that explain these details. They can be found on the Web at:

```
http://www.scriptics.com/plugin/man/
```

If you are serious about tuning the existing security policies or creating new ones, you should read the existing feature implementations in detail. As usual, modifying a working example is the best way to proceed! I think it is a very nice property of the plugin that its security policies are implemented in Tcl source code that is clearly factored out from the rest of the Tcl/Tk and plugin implementation. With a relatively small amount of code, you can create custom security policies that grant interesting abilities to Tclets.

Tk Basics

Part III introduces Tk, the toolkit for building graphical user interfaces. The Tcl command interface to Tk makes it quick and easy to build powerful user interfaces. Tk is portable and your user interface code can work unchanged on UNIX, Windows, and the Macintosh.

Chapter 21 describes the basic concepts of Tk and provides an overview of its facilities.

Chapter 22 illustrates Tk with three example programs including a browser for the examples from this book. These examples use facilities that are described in more detail in later chapters.

Geometry managers implement the layout of a user interface. Chapters Chapter 23, Chapter 24, and Chapter 25 describe the `pack`, `grid`, and `place` geometry managers. The packer and gridder are general-purpose managers that use constraints to create flexible layouts with a small amount of code. The placer is a special purpose geometry manager that can be used for special effects.

Chapter 26 describes event bindings that associate Tcl commands with events like keystrokes and mouse motion.

Tk Fundamentals

This chapter introduces the basic concepts used in the Tk graphical user interface toolkit. Tk adds about 35 Tcl commands that let you create and manipulate widgets in a graphical user interface. Tk works with the X window system, Windows, and Macintosh. The same script can run unchanged on all of these major platforms.

Tk is a toolkit for programming graphical user interfaces. It was designed for the X window system used on UNIX systems, and it was ported later to the Macintosh and Windows environments. Tk shares many concepts with other windowing toolkits, but you do not need to know much about graphical user interfaces to get started with Tk.

Tk provides a set of Tcl commands that create and manipulate *widgets*. A widget is a window in a graphical user interface that has a particular appearance and behavior. The terms *widget* and *window* are often used interchangeably. Widget types include buttons, scrollbars, menus, and text windows. Tk also has a general-purpose drawing widget called a *canvas* that lets you create lighter-weight items such as lines, boxes, and bitmaps. The Tcl commands added by Tk are summarized at the end of this chapter.

Tk widgets are organized in a hierarchy. To an application, the window hierarchy means that there is a primary window, and inside that window there can be a number of children windows. The children windows can contain more windows, and so on. Just as a hierarchical file system has directories (i.e., folders) that are containers for files and directories, a hierarchical window system uses windows as containers for other windows. The hierarchy affects the naming scheme used for Tk widgets as described later, and it is used to help arrange widgets on the screen.

Widgets are under the control of a *geometry manager* that controls their size and location on the screen. Until a geometry manager learns about a widget, it will not be mapped onto the screen and you will not see it. Tk has powerful geometry managers that make it very easy to create nice screen layouts. The main trick with any geometry manager is that you use *frame* widgets as containers for other widgets. One or more widgets are created and then arranged in a frame by a geometry manager. By putting frames within frames you can create complex layouts. There are three different geometry managers you can use in Tk: grid, pack, and place. The Tk geometry managers are discussed in detail in Chapters 23, 24, and 25.

A Tk-based application has an *event-driven* control flow, like most window system toolkits. The Tk widgets handle most events automatically, so programming your application remains simple. For specialized behaviors, you use the bind command to register a Tcl command that runs when an event occurs. There are lots of events, including mouse motion, keystrokes, window resize, and window destruction. You can also define *virtual events*, like Cut and Paste, that are caused by different events on different platforms. Bindings are discussed in detail in Chapter 26. Chapter 16 describes I/O events and the Tcl event loop, while Chapter 47 describes C programming and the event loop.

Event bindings are grouped into classes, which are called *bindtags*. The bindtags command associates a widget with an ordered set of bindtags. The level of indirection between the event bindings and the widgets creates a flexible and powerful system for managing events. You can create your own bindtags and dynamically change the bindtags for a widget to support mode changes in your application.

A concept related to binding is *focus*. At any given time, one of the widgets has the input focus, and keyboard events are directed to it. There are two general approaches to focusing: give focus to the widget under the mouse, or explicitly set the focus to a particular widget. Tk provides commands to change focus so you can implement either style of focus management. To support modal dialog boxes, you can forcibly *grab* the focus away from other widgets. Chapter 36 describes focus, grabs, and dialogs.

The basic structure of a Tk script begins by creating widgets and arranging them with a geometry manager, and then binding actions to the widgets. After the interpreter processes the commands that initialize the user interface, the event loop is entered and your application begins running.

If you use *wish* interactively, it creates and displays an empty main window and gives you a command-line prompt. With this interface, your keyboard commands are handled by the event loop, so you can build your Tk interface gradually. As we will see, you will be able to change virtually all aspects of your application interactively.

Hello, World! in Tk

Our first Tk script is very simple. It creates a button that prints "Hello, World!" to standard output when you press it. Above the button widget is a title bar that is provided by the window manager, which in this case is *twm* under X windows:

Example 21–1 "Hello, World!" Tk program.

```
#!/usr/local/bin/wish
button .hello -text Hello \
    -command {puts stdout "Hello, World!"}
pack .hello -padx 20 -pady 10
```

The first line identifies the interpreter for the script:

```
#!/usr/local/bin/wish
```

This special line is necessary if the script is in a file that will be used like other UNIX command files. Chapter 2 describes how to set up scripts on different platforms.

There are two Tcl commands in the script: one to create the button, and one to make it visible on the display. The button command creates an instance of a button:

```
button .hello -text Hello \
    -command {puts stdout "Hello, World!"}
=> .hello
```

The name of the button is .hello. The label on the button is Hello, and the command associated with the button is:

```
puts stdout "Hello, World!"
```

The pack command maps the button onto the screen. Some padding parameters are supplied, so there is space around the button:

```
pack .hello -padx 20 -pady 10
```

If you type these two commands into wish, you will not see anything happen when the button command is given. After the pack command, though, you will see the empty main window shrink to be just big enough to contain the button and its padding. The behavior of the packer will be discussed further in Chapters 22 and 23.

Tk uses an object-based system for creating and naming widgets. Associated with each class of widget (e.g., Button) is a command that creates instances of that class of widget. As the widget is created, a new Tcl command is defined that operates on that instance of the widget. Example 21–1 creates a button named .hello, and we can operate on the button using its name as a Tcl command. For example, we can cause the button to highlight a few times:

```
.hello flash
```

Or we can run the command associated with the button:

```
.hello invoke
=> Hello, World!
```

Tk has widget classes and instances, but it is not fully object oriented. It is not possible to subclass a widget class and use inheritance. Instead, Tk provides very flexible widgets that can be configured in many different ways to tune their appearance. The resource database can store configuration information that is shared by many widgets, and new classes can be introduced to group resources. Widget behavior is shared by using binding tags that group bindings. Instead of building class hierarchies, Tk uses composition to assemble widgets with shared behavior and attributes.

Naming Tk Widgets

The period in the name of the button instance, .hello, is required. Tk uses a naming system for the widgets that reflects their position in a hierarchy of widgets. The root of the hierarchy is the main window of the application, and its name is simply a dot (i.e., .). This is similar to the naming convention for directories in UNIX where the root directory is named /, and then / is used to separate components of a file name. Tk uses a dot in the same way. Each widget that is a child of the main window is named something like .foo. A child widget of .foo would be .foo.bar, and so on. Just as file systems have directories that are containers for files and other directories, the Tk window hierarchy uses frame widgets that are containers for widgets and other frames.

Each component of a Tk pathname must start with a lowercase letter or a number. Obviously, a component cannot include a period, either. The lower case restriction avoids a conflict with resource class names that begin with an upper case letter. A resource name can include Tk pathname components and Tk widget classes, and case is used to distinguish them. Chapter 28 describes resources in detail.

Store widget names in variables.

There is one drawback to the Tk widget naming system. If your interface changes enough it can result in some widgets changing their position in the widget hierarchy. In that case they may need to change their name. You can insulate yourself from this programming nuisance by using variables to hold the names of important widgets. Use a variable reference instead of widget pathnames in case you need to change things, or if you want to reuse your code in a different interface.

Configuring Tk Widgets

Example 21–1 illustrates a style of named parameter passing that is prevalent in the Tk commands. Pairs of arguments specify the attributes of a widget. The attribute names begin with -, such as -text, and the next argument is the value of that attribute. Even the simplest Tk widget can have a dozen or more attributes that can be specified this way, and complex widgets can have 20 or more attributes. However, the beauty of Tk is that you need to specify only the attributes for which the default value is not good enough. This is illustrated by the simplicity of the `Hello, World` example.

Finally, each widget instance supports a `configure` operation, which can be abbreviated to `config`, that can query and change these attributes. The syntax for `config` uses the same named argument pairs used when you create the widget. For example, we can change the background color of the button to red even after it has been created and mapped onto the screen:

```
.hello config -background red
```

Widget attributes can be redefined any time, even the `text` and `command` that were set when the button was created. The following command changes `.hello` into a goodbye button:

```
.hello config -text Goodbye! -command exit
```

Widgets have a `cget` operation to query the current value of an attribute:

```
.hello cget -background
=> red
```

You can find out more details about a widget attribute by using `configure` without a value:

```
.hello config -background
=> -background background Background #ffe4c4 red
```

The returned information includes the command-line switch, the resource name, the class name, the default value, and the current value, which is last. The class and resource name have to do with the resource mechanism described in Chapter 28. If you only specify `configure` and no attribute, then a list of the configuration information for all widget attributes is returned. Example 21–2 uses this to print out all the information about a widget:

Example 21–2 Looking at all widget attributes.

```
proc Widget_Attributes {w {out stdout}} {
    puts $out [format "%-20s %-10s %s" Attribute Default Value]
    foreach item [$w configure] {
        puts $out [format "%-20s %-10s %s" \
            [lindex $item 0] [lindex $item 3] \
            [lindex $item 4]]
    }
}
```

Tk Widget Attributes and the Resource Database

A widget attribute can be named three different ways: by its command-line option, by its resource name, and by its resource class. The command-line option is the format you use in Tcl scripts. This form is always all lowercase and prefixed with a hyphen (e.g., `-offvalue`). The resource name for the attribute has no leading hyphen, and it has uppercase letters at internal word boundaries (e.g., offValue). The resource class begins with an uppercase letter and has uppercase letters at internal word boundaries. (e.g., OffValue).

The tables in this book list widget attributes by their resource name.

You need to know these naming conventions if you specify widget attributes via the resource mechanism. The command-line option can be derived from the resource name by mapping it to all lowercase. The primary advantage of using resources to specify attributes is that you do not have to litter your code with attribute specifications. With just a few resource database entries you can specify attributes for all your widgets. In addition, if attributes are specified with resources, users can provide alternate resource specifications in order to override the values supplied by the application. For attributes like colors and fonts, this feature can be important to users. Resource specifications are described in detail in Chapter 28.

The Tk Manual Pages

This book provides summaries for all the Tk commands, the widget attributes, and the default bindings. However, for the absolute truth, you may need to read the on-line manual pages that come with Tk. They provide a complete reference source for the Tk commands. You should be able to use the UNIX *man* program to read them:

```
% man button
```

The *tkman* program provides a very nice graphical user interface to the UNIX manual pages. On the Macintosh platform, the manual pages are formatted into HTML documents that you can find in the HTML Docs folder of the Tcl/Tk distribution. On Windows, the manual pages are formatted into Help documents. You can find the manual pages on the web at:

```
http://www.scriptics.com/man/
```

There are a large number of attributes that are common across most of the Tk widgets. These are described in a separate man page under the name options. Each man page begins with a STANDARD OPTIONS section that lists which of these standard attributes apply, but you have to look at the options man page for the description. In contrast, the tables in this book always list all widget attributes.

Summary of the Tk Commands

The following tables list the Tcl commands added by Tk. Table 21–1 lists commands that create widgets. There are 15 different widgets in Tk, although 4 of them are variations on a button, and 5 are devoted to different flavors of text display. Table 21–2 lists commands that manipulate widgets and provide associated functions like input focus, event binding, and geometry management. Table 21–3 lists several support procedures that implement standard dialogs, option menus, and other facilities. The page number in the table is the primary reference for the command, and there are other references in the index.

Table 21–1 Tk widget-creation commands.

Command	Pg.	Description
button	386	Create a command button.
checkbutton	390	Create a toggle button that is linked to a Tcl variable.
radiobutton	390	Create one of a set of radio buttons linked to one variable.
menubutton	394	Create a button that posts a menu.
menu	394	Create a menu.
canvas	473	Create a canvas, which supports lines, boxes, bitmaps, images, arcs, text, polygons, and embedded widgets.
label	418	Create a read-only, one-line text label.
entry	435	Create a one-line text entry widget.
message	420	Create a read-only, multiline text message.
listbox	441	Create a line-oriented, scrolling text widget.
text	451	Create a general-purpose, editable text widget.
scrollbar	427	Create a scrollbar that can be linked to another widget.
scale	423	Create a scale widget that adjusts the value of a variable.
frame	415	Create a container widget used with geometry managers.
toplevel	415	Create a frame that is a new top level window.

Table 21–2 Tk widget-manipulation commands.

Command	Pg.	Description
bell	426	Ring the terminal bell device.
bind	367	Bind a Tcl command to an event.
bindtags	369	Create binding classes and control binding inheritance.
clipboard	508	Manipulate the clipboard.
destroy	519	Delete a widget.
event	378	Define and generate virtual events.
focus	516	Control the input focus.
font	553	Set and query font attributes and measurements.
grab	518	Steal the input focus from other widgets.
grid	356	Arrange widgets into a grid with constraints.
image	540	Create and manipulate images.
lower	347	Lower a window in the stacking order.

III. Tk Basics

Table 21–2 Tk widget-manipulation commands. (Continued)

option	407	Set and query the resources database.
pack	346	Pack a widget in the display with constraints.
place	365	Place a widget in the display with positions.
raise	347	Raise a window in the stacking order.
selection	507	Manipulate the selection.
send	560	Send a Tcl command to another Tk application.
tk	580	Query or set the application name.
tkerror	190	Handler for background errors.
tkwait	518	Wait for an event.
update	522	Update the display by going through the event loop.
winfo	574	Query window state.
wm	569	Interact with the window manager.

Table 21–3 Tk support procedures.

Command	Pg.	Description
tk_bisque	535	Install bisque family of colors.
tk_chooseColor	515	Dialog to select a color. (Tk 4.2)
tk_dialog	513	Create simple dialogs.
tk_focusFollowsMouse	516	Install mouse-tracking focus model.
tk_focusNext	517	Focus on next widget in tab order.
tk_focusPrev	517	Focus on previous widget in tab order.
tk_getOpenFile	514	Dialog to open an existing file. (Tk 4.2)
tk_getSaveFile	514	Dialog to open a new file. (Tk 4.2)
tk_messageBox	514	Message dialog. (Tk 4.2)
tk_optionMenu	396	Create an option menu.
tk_popup	396	Create a pop-up menu.
tk_setPalette	535	Set the standard color palette. (Tk 4.2)

Tk by Example

This chapter introduces Tk through a series of short examples. The ExecLog
runs a program in the background and displays its output. The Example
Browser displays the Tcl examples from the book. The Tcl Shell lets you
type Tcl commands and execute them in a slave interpreter.

Tk provides a quick and fun way to gen-
erate user interfaces. In this chapter we will go through a series of short example
programs to give you a feel for what you can do. Some details are glossed over in
this chapter and considered in more detail later. In particular, the `pack` geometry
manager is covered in Chapter 23 and event bindings are discussed in Chapter
26. The Tk widgets are discussed in more detail in later chapters.

ExecLog

Our first example provides a simple user interface to running another program
with the `exec` command. The interface consists of two buttons, Run it and Quit,
an entry widget in which to enter a command, and a text widget in which to log
the results of running the program. The script runs the program in a pipeline
and uses the `fileevent` command to wait for output. This structure lets the user
interface remain responsive while the program executes. You could use this to
run *make*, for example, and it would save the results in the log. The complete
example is given first, and then its commands are discussed in more detail.

315

Example 22–1 Logging the output of a program run with exec.

```
#!/usr/local/bin/wish
# execlog - run a program with exec and log the output
# Set window title
wm title . ExecLog

# Create a frame for buttons and entry.

frame .top -borderwidth 10
pack .top -side top -fill x

# Create the command buttons.

button .top.quit -text Quit -command exit
set but [button .top.run -text "Run it" -command Run]
pack .top.quit .top.run -side right

# Create a labeled entry for the command

label .top.l -text Command: -padx 0
entry .top.cmd -width 20 -relief sunken \
    -textvariable command
pack .top.l -side left
pack .top.cmd -side left -fill x -expand true

# Set up key binding equivalents to the buttons

bind .top.cmd <Return> Run
bind .top.cmd <Control-c> Stop
focus .top.cmd

# Create a text widget to log the output

frame .t
set log [text .t.log -width 80 -height 10 \
    -borderwidth 2 -relief raised -setgrid true \
```

```
        -yscrollcommand {.t.scroll set}]
scrollbar .t.scroll -command {.t.log yview}
pack .t.scroll -side right -fill y
pack .t.log -side left -fill both -expand true
pack .t -side top -fill both -expand true

# Run the program and arrange to read its input

proc Run {} {
    global command input log but
    if [catch {open "|$command |& cat"} input] {
        $log insert end $input\n
    } else {
        fileevent $input readable Log
        $log insert end $command\n
        $but config -text Stop -command Stop
    }
}

# Read and log output from the program

proc Log {} {
    global input log
    if [eof $input] {
        Stop
    } else {
        gets $input line
        $log insert end $line\n
        $log see end
    }
}

# Stop the program and fix up the button

proc Stop {} {
    global input but
    catch {close $input}
    $but config -text "Run it" -command Run
}
```

Window Title

The first command sets the title that appears in the title bar implemented by the window manager. Recall that dot (i.e., .) is the name of the main window:

```
wm title . ExecLog
```

The wm command communicates with the window manager. The window manager is the program that lets you open, close, and resize windows. It implements the title bar for the window and probably some small buttons to close or resize the window. Different window managers have a distinctive look; the figure shows a title bar from *twm*, a window manager for X.

A Frame for Buttons

A frame is created to hold the widgets that appear along the top of the interface. The frame has a border to provide some space around the widgets:

```
frame .top -borderwidth 10
```

The frame is positioned in the main window. The default packing side is the top, so -side top is redundant here, but it is used for clarity. The -fill x packing option makes the frame fill out to the whole width of the main window:

```
pack .top -side top -fill x
```

Command Buttons

Two buttons are created: one to run the command, the other to quit the program. Their names, .top.quit and .top.run, imply that they are children of the .top frame. This affects the pack command, which positions widgets inside their parent by default:

```
button .top.quit -text Quit -command exit
set but [button .top.run -text "Run it" \
    -command Run]
pack .top.quit .top.run -side right
```

A Label and an Entry

The label and entry are also created as children of the .top frame. The label is created with no padding in the X direction so that it can be positioned right next to the entry. The size of the entry is specified in terms of characters. The relief attribute gives the entry some looks to set it apart visually on the display. The contents of the entry widget are linked to the Tcl variable command:

```
label .top.l -text Command: -padx 0
entry .top.cmd -width 20 -relief sunken \
    -textvariable command
```

The label and entry are positioned to the left inside the .top frame. The additional packing parameters to the entry allow it to expand its packing space and fill up that extra area with its display. The difference between packing space and display space is discussed in Chapter 23 on page 337:

```
pack .top.l -side left
pack .top.cmd -side left -fill x -expand true
```

Key Bindings and Focus

Key bindings on the entry widget provide an additional way to invoke the functions of the application. The bind command associates a Tcl command with an event in a particular widget. The <Return> event is generated when the user presses the Return key on the keyboard. The <Control-c> event is generated when the letter c is typed while the Control key is already held down. For the events to go to the entry widget, `.top.cmd`, input focus must be given to the widget. By default, an entry widget gets the focus when you click the left mouse button in it. The explicit `focus` command is helpful for users with the focus-follows-mouse model. As soon as the mouse is over the main window the user can type into the entry:

```
bind .top.cmd <Return> Run
bind .top.cmd <Control-c> Stop
focus .top.cmd
```

A Resizable Text and Scrollbar

A text widget is created and packed into a frame with a scrollbar. The width and height of the text widget are specified in characters and lines, respectively. The `setgrid` attribute of the text widget is turned on. This restricts the resize so that only a whole number of lines and average-sized characters can be displayed.

The scrollbar is a separate widget in Tk, and it can be connected to different widgets using the same setup as is used here. The text's `yscrollcommand` updates the display of the scrollbar when the text widget is modified, and the scrollbar's `command` scrolls the associated widget when the user manipulates the scrollbar:

```
frame .t
set log [text .t.log -width 80 -height 10 \
    -borderwidth 2 -relief raised -setgrid true\
    -yscrollcommand {.t.scroll set}]
scrollbar .t.scroll -command {.t.log yview}
pack .t.scroll -side right -fill y
pack .t.log -side left -fill both -expand true
pack .t -side top -fill both -expand true
```

A side effect of creating a Tk widget is the creation of a new Tcl command that operates on that widget. The name of the Tcl command is the same as the Tk pathname of the widget. In this script, the text widget command, `.t.log`, is needed in several places. However, it is a good idea to put the Tk pathname of an important widget into a variable because that pathname can change if you reorganize your user interface. The disadvantage of this is that you must declare the variable with `global` inside procedures. The variable `log` is used for this purpose in this example to demonstrate this style.

The Run Procedure

The `Run` procedure starts the program specified in the command entry. That value is available in the global `command` variable because of the `textvariable` attribute of the entry. The command is run in a pipeline so that it executes in the background. The leading `|` in the argument to `open` indicates that a pipeline is being created. The `catch` command guards against bogus commands. The variable `input` is set to an error message, or to the normal `open` return that is a file descriptor. The program is started like this:

```
if [catch {open "|$command |& cat"} input] {
```

Trapping errors from pipelines.

The pipeline diverts error output from the command through the *cat* program. If you do not use *cat* like this, then the error output from the pipeline, if any, shows up as an error message when the pipeline is closed. In this example it turns out to be awkward to distinguish between errors generated from the program and errors generated because of the way the Stop procedure is implemented. Furthermore, some programs interleave output and error output, and you might want to see the error output in order instead of all at the end.

If the pipeline is opened successfully, then a callback is set up using the fileevent command. Whenever the pipeline generates output, then the script can read data from it. The Log procedure is registered to be called whenever the pipeline is readable:

```
fileevent $input readable Log
```

The command (or the error message) is inserted into the log. This is done using the name of the text widget, which is stored in the log variable, as a Tcl command. The value of the command is appended to the log, and a newline is added so that its output will appear on the next line.

```
$log insert end $command\n
```

The text widget's insert function takes two parameters: a *mark* and a string to insert at that mark. The symbolic mark end represents the end of the contents of the text widget.

The run button is changed into a stop button after the program begins. This avoids a cluttered interface and demonstrates the dynamic nature of a Tk interface. Again, because this button is used in a few different places in the script, its pathname has been stored in the variable but:

```
$but config -text Stop -command Stop
```

The Log Procedure

The Log procedure is invoked whenever data can be read from the pipeline, and when end of file has been reached. This condition is checked first, and the Stop procedure is called to clean things up. Otherwise, one line of data is read and inserted into the log. The text widget's see operation is used to position the view on the text so that the new line is visible to the user:

```
if [eof $input] {
    Stop
} else {
    gets $input line
    $log insert end $line\n
    $log see end
}
```

The Stop Procedure

The stop procedure terminates the program by closing the pipeline. The close is wrapped up with a catch. This suppresses the errors that can occur when the pipeline is closed prematurely on the process. Finally, the button is restored to its run state so that the user can run another command:

```
catch {close $input}
$but config -text "Run it" -command Run
```

In most cases, closing the pipeline is adequate to kill the job. On UNIX, this results in a signal, SIGPIPE, being delivered to the program the next time it does a write to its standard output. There is no built-in way to kill a process, but you can exec the UNIX *kill* program. The pid command returns the process IDs from the pipeline:

```
foreach pid [pid $input] {
    catch {exec kill $pid}
}
```

If you need more sophisticated control over another process, you should check out the *expect* Tcl extension, which is described in the book *Exploring Expect* (Don Libes, O'Reilly & Associates, Inc., 1995). *Expect* provides powerful control over interactive programs. You can write Tcl scripts that send input to interactive programs and pattern match on their output. *Expect* is designed to automate the use of programs that were designed for interactive use.

Cross-Platform Issues

This script will run on UNIX and Windows, but not on Macintosh because there is no exec command. One other problem is the binding for <Control-c> to cancel the job. This is UNIX-like, while Windows users expect <Escape> to cancel a job, and Macintosh users expect <Command-period>. Platform_CancelEvent defines a virtual event, <<Cancel>>, and Stop is bound to it:

Example 22–2 A platform-specific cancel event.

```
proc Platform_CancelEvent {} {
    global tcl_platform
    switch $tcl_platform(platform) {
        unix {
            event add <<Cancel>> <Control-c>
        }
        windows {
            event add <<Cancel>> <Escape>
        }
        macintosh {
            event add <<Cancel>> <Command-period>
        }
    }
}
bind .top.entry <<Cancel>> Stop
```

There are other virtual events already defined by Tk. The `event` command
and virtual events are described on page 378.

The Example Browser

Example 22–3 is a browser for the code examples that appear in this book. The
basic idea is to provide a menu that selects the examples, and a text window to
display the examples. Before you can use this sample program, you need to edit
it to set the proper location of the `exsource` directory that contains all the example sources from the book. Example 22–4 on page 327 extends the browser with a
shell that is used to test the examples.

Example 22–3 A browser for the code examples in the book.

```
#!/usr/local/bin/wish
#   Browser for the Tcl and Tk examples in the book.

# browse(dir) is the directory containing all the tcl files
# Please edit to match your system configuration.

switch $tcl_platform(platform) {
    "unix" {set browse(dir) /cdrom/tclbook2/exsource}
    "windows" {set browse(dir) D:/exsource}
    "macintosh" {set browse(dir) /tclbook2/exsource}
}

wm minsize . 30 5
wm title . "Tcl Example Browser"

# Create a row of buttons along the top

set f [frame .menubar]
pack $f -fill x
button $f.quit -text Quit -command exit
button $f.next -text Next -command Next
button $f.prev -text Previous -command Previous

# The Run and Reset buttons use EvalEcho that
# is defined by the Tcl shell in Example 22-4 on page 327

button $f.load -text Run -command Run
button $f.reset -text Reset -command Reset
pack $f.quit $f.reset $f.load $f.next $f.prev -side right

# A label identifies the current example

label $f.label -textvariable browse(current)
pack $f.label -side right -fill x -expand true

# Create the menubutton and menu
```

```tcl
menubutton $f.ex -text Examples -menu $f.ex.m
pack $f.ex -side left
set m [menu $f.ex.m]

# Create the text to display the example
# Scrolled_Text is defined in Example 30-1 on page 428

set browse(text) [Scrolled_Text .body \
    -width 80 -height 10\
    -setgrid true]
pack .body -fill both -expand true

# Look through the example files for their ID number.

foreach f [lsort -dictionary [glob [file join $browse(dir) *]]] {
    if [catch {open $f} in] {
        puts stderr "Cannot open $f: $in"
        continue
    }
    while {[gets $in line] >= 0} {
        if [regexp {^# Example ([0-9]+)-([0-9]+)} $line \
                x chap ex] {
            lappend examples($chap) $ex
            lappend browse(list) $f
            # Read example title
            gets $in line
            set title($chap-$ex) [string trim $line "# "]
            set file($chap-$ex) $f
            close $in
            break
        }
    }
}

# Create two levels of cascaded menus.
# The first level divides up the chapters into chunks.
# The second level has an entry for each example.

option add *Menu.tearOff 0
set limit 8
set c 0; set i 0
foreach chap [lsort -integer [array names examples]] {
    if {$i == 0} {
        $m add cascade -label "Chapter $chap..." \
            -menu $m.$c
        set sub1 [menu $m.$c]
        incr c
    }
    set i [expr ($i +1) % $limit]
    $sub1 add cascade -label "Chapter $chap" -menu $sub1.sub$i
    set sub2 [menu $sub1.sub$i ]
    foreach ex [lsort -integer $examples($chap)] {
        $sub2 add command -label "$chap-$ex $title($chap-$ex)" \
            -command [list Browse $file($chap-$ex)]
```

```
        }
}

# Display a specified file. The label is updated to
# reflect what is displayed, and the text is left
# in a read-only mode after the example is inserted.

proc Browse { file } {
    global browse
    set browse(current) [file tail $file]
    set browse(curix) [lsearch $browse(list) $file]
    set t $browse(text)
    $t config -state normal
    $t delete 1.0 end
    if [catch {open $file} in] {
        $t insert end $in
    } else {
        $t insert end [read $in]
        close $in
    }
    $t config -state disabled
}

# Browse the next and previous files in the list

set browse(curix) -1
proc Next {} {
    global browse
    if {$browse(curix) < [llength $browse(list)] - 1} {
        incr browse(curix)
    }
    Browse [lindex $browse(list) $browse(curix)]
}
proc Previous {} {
    global browse
    if {$browse(curix) > 0} {
        incr browse(curix) -1
    }
    Browse [lindex $browse(list) $browse(curix)]
}

# Run the example in the shell

proc Run {} {
    global browse
    EvalEcho [list source \
        [file join $browse(dir) $browse(current)]]
}

# Reset the slave in the eval server

proc Reset {} {
    EvalEcho reset
}
```

More about Resizing Windows

This example uses the `wm minsize` command to put a constraint on the minimum size of the window. The arguments specify the minimum width and height. These values can be interpreted in two ways. By default they are pixel values. However, if an internal widget has enabled *geometry gridding*, then the dimensions are in grid units of that widget. In this case the text widget enables gridding with its `setgrid` attribute, so the minimum size of the window is set so that the text window is at least 30 characters wide by five lines high:

```
wm minsize . 30 5
```

In older versions of Tk, Tk 3.6, gridding also enabled interactive resizing of the window. Interactive resizing is enabled by default in Tk 4.0 and later.

Managing Global State

The example uses the `browse` array to collect its global variables. This makes it simpler to reference the state from inside procedures because only the array needs to be declared global. As the application grows over time and new features are added, that `global` command won't have to be adjusted. This style also serves to emphasize what variables are important. The `browse` array holds the name of the example directory (`dir`), the Tk pathname of the text display (`text`), and the name of the current file (`current`). The `list` and `curix` elements are used to implement the `Next` and `Previous` procedures.

Searching through Files

The browser searches the file system to determine what it can display. The `tcl_platform(platform)` variable is used to select a different example directory on different platforms. You may need to edit the on-line example to match your system. The example uses `glob` to find all the files in the `exsource` directory. The `file join` command is used to create the file name pattern in a platform-independent way. The result of `glob` is sorted explicitly so the menu entries are in the right order. Each file is read one line at a time with `gets`, and then `regexp` is used to scan for keywords. The loop is repeated here for reference:

```
foreach f [lsort -dictionary [glob [file join $browse(dir) *]]] {
    if [catch {open $f} in] {
        puts stderr "Cannot open $f: $in"
        continue
    }
    while {[gets $in line] >= 0} {
        if [regexp {^# Example ([0-9]+)-([0-9]+)} $line \
               x chap ex] {
            lappend examples($chap) $ex
            lappend browse(list) $f
            # Read example title
            gets $in line
            set title($chap-$ex) [string trim $line "# "]
            set file($chap-$ex) $f
```

```
                close $in
                break
            }
        }
    }
```

The example files contain lines like this:

```
# Example 1-1
# The Hello, World! program
```

The `regexp` picks out the example numbers with the `([0-9]+)-([0-9]+)` part of the pattern, and these are assigned to the `chap` and `ex` variables. The `x` variable is assigned the value of the whole match, which is more than we are interested in. Once the example number is found, the next line is read to get the description of the example. At the end of the `foreach` loop the `examples` array has an element defined for each chapter, and the value of each element is a list of the examples for that chapter.

Cascaded Menus

The values in the `examples` array are used to build up a cascaded menu structure. First a menubutton is created that will post the main menu. It is associated with the main menu with its `menu` attribute. The menu must be a child of the menubutton for its display to work properly:

```
menubutton $f.ex -text Examples -menu $f.ex.m
set m [menu $f.ex.m]
```

There are too many chapters to put them all into one menu. The main menu has a `cascade` entry for each group of eight chapters. Each of these submenus has a `cascade` entry for each chapter in the group, and each chapter has a menu of all its examples. Once again, the submenus are defined as a child of their parent menu. Note the inconsistency between menu entries and buttons. Their text is defined with the `-label` option, not `-text`. Other than this they are much like buttons. Chapter 27 describes menus in more detail. The code is repeated here:

```
set limit 8 ; set c 0 ; set i 0
foreach key [lsort -integer [array names examples]] {
    if {$i == 0} {
        $m add cascade -label "Chapter $key..." \
            -menu $m.$c
        set sub1 [menu $m.$c]
        incr c
    }
    set i [expr ($i +1) % $limit]
    $sub1 add cascade -label "Chapter $key" -menu $sub1.sub$i
    set sub2 [menu $sub1.sub$i]
    foreach ex [lsort -integer $examples($key)] {
        $sub2 add command -label "$key-$ex $title($key-$ex)" \
            -command [list Browse $file($key-$ex)]
    }
}
```

A Read-Only Text Widget

The `Browse` procedure is fairly simple. It sets `browse(current)` to be the name of the file. This changes the main label because of its `textvariable` attribute that links it to this variable. The `state` attribute of the text widget is manipulated so that the text is read-only after the text is inserted. You have to set the `state` to `normal` before inserting the text; otherwise, the `insert` has no effect. Here are a few commands from the body of `Browse`:

```
global browse
set browse(current) [file tail $file]
$t config -state normal
$t insert end [read $in]
$t config -state disabled
```

A Tcl Shell

This section demonstrates the text widget with a simple Tcl shell application. It uses a text widget to prompt for commands and display their results. It uses a second Tcl interpreter to evaluate the commands you type. This dual interpreter structure is used by the console built into the Windows and Macintosh versions of *wish*. The *TkCon* application written by Jeff Hobbs is an even more elaborate console that has many features to support interactive Tcl use.

Example 22–4 is written to be used with the browser from Example 22–3 in the same application. The browser's `Run` button runs the current example in the shell. An alternative is to have the shell run as a separate process and use the `send` command to communicate Tcl commands between separate applications. That alternative is shown in Example 40–2 on page 563.

Example 22–4 A Tcl shell in a text widget.

```
#!/usr/local/bin/wish
# Simple evaluator. It executes Tcl in a slave interpreter

set t [Scrolled_Text .eval -width 80 -height 10]
pack .eval -fill both -expand true

# Text tags give script output, command errors, command
# results, and the prompt a different appearance

$t tag configure prompt -underline true
$t tag configure result -foreground purple
$t tag configure error -foreground red
$t tag configure output -foreground blue

# Insert the prompt and initialize the limit mark

set eval(prompt) "tcl> "
$t insert insert $eval(prompt) prompt
$t mark set limit insert
```

III. Tk Basics

```
$t mark gravity limit left
focus $t
set eval(text) $t

# Key bindings that limit input and eval things. The break in
# the bindings skips the default Text binding for the event.

bind $t <Return> {EvalTypein ; break}
bind $t <BackSpace> {
    if {[%W tag nextrange sel 1.0 end] != ""} {
       %W delete sel.first sel.last
    } elseif {[%W compare insert > limit]} {
       %W delete insert-1c
       %W see insert
    }
    break
}
bind $t <Key> {
    if [%W compare insert < limit] {
       %W mark set insert end
    }
}

# Evaluate everything between limit and end as a Tcl command

proc EvalTypein {} {
    global eval
    $eval(text) insert insert \n
    set command [$eval(text) get limit end]
    if [info complete $command] {
       $eval(text) mark set limit insert
       Eval $command
    }
}

# Echo the command and evaluate it

proc EvalEcho {command} {
    global eval
    $eval(text) mark set insert end
    $eval(text) insert insert $command\n
    Eval $command
}

# Evaluate a command and display its result

proc Eval {command} {
    global eval
    $eval(text) mark set insert end
    if [catch {$eval(slave) eval $command} result] {
       $eval(text) insert insert $result error
    } else {
       $eval(text) insert insert $result result
    }
    if {[$eval(text) compare insert != "insert linestart"]} {
```

```
            $eval(text) insert insert \n
        }
        $eval(text) insert insert $eval(prompt) prompt
        $eval(text) see insert
        $eval(text) mark set limit insert
        return
    }

    # Create and initialize the slave interpreter

    proc SlaveInit {slave} {
        interp create $slave
        load {} Tk $slave
        interp alias $slave reset {} ResetAlias $slave
        interp alias $slave puts {} PutsAlias $slave
        return $slave
    }

    # The reset alias deletes the slave and starts a new one

    proc ResetAlias {slave} {
        interp delete $slave
        SlaveInit $slave
    }

    # The puts alias puts stdout and stderr into the text widget

    proc PutsAlias {slave args} {
        if {[llength $args] > 3} {
            error "invalid arguments"
        }
        set newline "\n"
        if {[string match "-nonewline" [lindex $args 0]]} {
            set newline ""
            set args [lreplace $args 0 0]
        }
        if {[llength $args] == 1} {
            set chan stdout
            set string [lindex $args 0]$newline
        } else {
            set chan [lindex $args 0]
            set string [lindex $args 1]$newline
        }
        if [regexp (stdout|stderr) $chan] {
            global eval
            $eval(text) mark gravity limit right
            $eval(text) insert limit $string output
            $eval(text) see limit
            $eval(text) mark gravity limit left
        } else {
            puts -nonewline $chan $string
        }
    }
    set eval(slave) [SlaveInit shell]
```

Text Marks, Tags, and Bindings

The shell uses a text *mark* and some extra bindings to ensure that users only type new text into the end of the text widget. A mark represents a position in the text that is updated as characters are inserted and deleted. The `limit` mark keeps track of the boundary between the read-only area and the editable area. The `insert` mark is where the cursor is displayed. The `end` mark is always the end of the text. The `EvalTypein` procedure looks at all the text between `limit` and `end` to see if it is a complete Tcl command. If it is, it evaluates the command in the slave interpreter.

The `<Key>` binding checks to see where the `insert` mark is and bounces it to the `end` if the user tries to input text before the `limit` mark. The `puts` alias sets `right` gravity on `limit`, so the mark is pushed along when program output is inserted right at `limit`. Otherwise, the `left` gravity on limit means that the mark does not move when the user inserts right at `limit`.

Text *tags* are used to give different regions of text difference appearances. A tag applies to a range of text. The tags are configured at the beginning of the script and they are applied when text is inserted.

Chapter 33 describes the text widget in more detail.

Multiple Interpreters

The `SlaveInit` procedure creates another interpreter to evaluate the commands. This prevents conflicts with the procedures and variables used to implement the shell. Initially, the slave interpreter only has access to Tcl commands. The `load` command installs the Tk commands, and it creates a new top-level window that is "." for the slave interpreter. Chapter 20 describes how you can embed the window of the slave within other frames.

The `shell` interpreter is not created with the `-safe` flag, so it can do anything. For example, if you type `exit`, it will exit the whole application. The `SlaveInit` procedure installs an alias, `reset`, that just deletes the slave interpreter and creates a new one. You can use this to clean up after working in the shell for a while. Chapter 19 describes the `interp` command in detail.

Native Look and Feel

When you run a Tk script on different platforms, it uses native buttons, menus, and scrollbars. The text and entry widgets are tuned to give the application the native look and feel. The following screen shots show the combined browser and shell as it looks on Macintosh, Windows, and UNIX.

Example 22–5 Macintosh look and feel.

Example 22–6 Windows look and feel.

Example 22–7 UNIX look and feel.

The Pack Geometry Manager

This chapter explores the `pack` geometry manager that positions widgets on the screen.

Geometry managers arrange widgets on the screen. This chapter describes the `pack` geometry manager, which is a constraint-based system. The next two chapters describe the `grid` and `place` geometry managers. The `pack` and `grid` geometry managers are quite general, while `place` is used for special-purpose applications. This book uses `pack` a lot because it was the original geometry manager for Tk. The `grid` geometry manager was added in Tk 4.1.

A geometry manager uses one widget as a parent, and it arranges multiple children (also called slaves) inside the parent. The parent is almost always a frame, but this is not strictly necessary. A widget can only be managed by one geometry manager at a time, but you can use different managers to control different widgets in your user interface. If a widget is not managed, then it doesn't appear on your display at all.

The packer is a powerful constraint-based geometry manager. Instead of specifying in detail the placement of each window, the programmer defines some constraints about how windows should be positioned, and the packer works out the details. It is important to understand the algorithm the packer uses; otherwise, the constraint-based results may not be what you expect.

This chapter explores the packer through a series of examples. The background of the main window is set to black, and the other frames are given different colors so you can identify frames and observe the effect of the different packing parameters. When consecutive examples differ by a small amount, the added command or option is printed in **bold courier** to highlight the addition.

Packing toward a Side

The following example creates two frames and packs them toward the top side of
the main window. The upper frame, .one, is not as big and the main window
shows through on either side. The children are packed toward the specified side
in order, so .one is on top. The four possible sides are: top, right, bottom, and
left. The top side is the default.

Example 23–1 Two frames packed inside the main frame.

```
# Make the main window black
. config -bg black
# Create and pack two frames
frame .one -width 40 -height 40 -bg white
frame .two -width 100 -height 50 -bg grey50
pack .one .two -side top
```

Shrinking Frames and pack propagate

In the previous example, the main window shrank down to be just large
enough to hold its two children. In most cases this is the desired behavior. If not,
you can turn it off with the pack propagate command. Apply this to the parent
frame, and it will not adjust its size to fit its children:

Example 23–2 Turning off geometry propagation.

```
frame .one -width 40 -height 40 -bg white
frame .two -width 100 -height 50 -bg grey50
pack propagate . false
pack .one .two -side top
```

Horizontal and Vertical Stacking

In general, you use either horizontal or vertical stacking within a frame. If you mix sides such as left and top, the effect might not be what you expect. Instead, you should introduce more frames to pack a set of widgets into a stack of a different orientation. For example, suppose we want to put a row of buttons inside the upper frame in the examples we have given so far:

Example 23–3 A horizontal stack inside a vertical stack.

```
frame .one -bg white
frame .two -width 100 -height 50 -bg grey50
# Create a row of buttons
foreach b {alpha beta gamma} {
    button .one.$b -text $b
    pack .one.$b -side left
}
pack .one .two -side top
```

Example 23–4 Even more nesting of horizontal and vertical stacks.

```
frame .one -bg white
frame .two -width 100 -height 50 -bg grey50
foreach b {alpha beta} {
    button .one.$b -text $b
    pack .one.$b -side left
}
# Create a frame for two more buttons
frame .one.right
foreach b {delta epsilon} {
    button .one.right.$b -text $b
    pack .one.right.$b -side bottom
}
pack .one.right -side right
pack .one .two -side top
```

You can build more complex arrangements by introducing nested frames and switching between horizontal and vertical stacking as you go. Within each frame pack all the children with either a combination of `-side left` and `-side right`, or `-side top` and `-side bottom`.

Example 23–4 replaces the `.one.gamma` button with a vertical stack of two buttons, `.one.right.delta` and `.one.right.epsilon`. These are packed toward the bottom of `.one.right`, so the first one packed is on the bottom.

The frame `.one.right` was packed to the right, and in the previous example, the button `.one.gamma` was packed to the left. Despite the difference, they ended up in the same position relative to the other two widgets packed inside the `.one` frame. The next section explains why.

The Cavity Model

The packing algorithm is based on a *cavity model* for the available space inside a frame. For example, when the main *wish* window is created, the main frame is empty and there is an obvious space, or cavity, in which to place widgets. The primary rule about the packing cavity is *a widget occupies one whole side of the cavity*. To demonstrate this, pack three widgets into the main frame. Put the first two on the bottom, and the third one on the right:

Example 23–5 Mixing bottom and right packing sides.

```
# pack two frames on the bottom.
frame .one -width 100 -height 50 -bg grey50
frame .two -width 40 -height 40 -bg white
pack .one .two -side bottom
# pack another frame to the right
frame .three -width 20 -height 20 -bg grey75
pack .three -side right
```

When we pack a third frame into the main window with `-side left` or `-side right`, the new frame is positioned inside the cavity, which is above the two frames already packed toward the bottom side. The frame does not appear to the right of the existing frames as you might have expected. This is because the `.two` frame occupies the whole bottom side of the packing cavity, even though its display does not fill up that side.

Can you tell where the packing cavity is after this example? It is to the left of the frame `.three`, which is the last frame packed toward the right, and it is above the frame `.two`, which is the last frame packed toward the bottom. This explains why there was no difference between the previous two examples when .one.gamma was packed to the left, but .one.right was packed to the right. At that point, packing to the left or right of the cavity had the same effect. However, it will affect what happens if another widget is packed into those two configurations. Try out the following commands after running Example 23–3 and Example 23–4 and compare the difference.[*]

```
button .one.omega -text omega
pack .one.omega -side right
```

Each packing parent has its own cavity, which is why introducing nested frames can help. If you use a horizontal or vertical arrangement inside any given frame, you can more easily simulate the packer's behavior in your head!

Packing Space and Display Space

The packer distinguishes between *packing* space and *display* space when it arranges the widgets. The display space is the area requested by a widget for the purposes of painting itself. The packing space is the area the packer allows for the placement of the widget. Because of geometry constraints, a widget may be allocated more (or less) packing space than it needs to display itself. The extra space, if any, is along the side of the cavity against which the widget was packed.

The -fill Option

The -fill packing option causes a widget to fill up the allocated packing space with its display. A widget can fill in the X or Y direction, or both. The default is not to fill, which is why the black background of the main window has shown through in the examples so far:

Example 23–6 Filling the display into extra packing space.

```
frame .one -width 100 -height 50 -bg grey50
frame .two -width 40 -height 40 -bg white
# Pack with fill enabled
pack .one .two -side bottom -fill x
frame .three -width 20 -height 20 -bg red
pack .three -side right -fill x
```

---

[*] Answer: After Example 23–3 the new button is to the right of all buttons. After Example 23–4 the new button is between .one.beta and .one.right.

This is just like Example 23–5, except that -fill x has been specified for all the frames. The .two frame fills, but the .three frame does not. This is because the fill does not expand into the packing cavity. In fact, after this example, the packing cavity is the part that shows through in black. Another way to look at this is that the .two frame was allocated the whole bottom side of the packing cavity, so its fill can expand the frame to occupy that space. The .three frame has only been allocated the right side, so a fill in the X direction will not have any effect.

Another use of fill is for a menu bar that has buttons at either end and some empty space between them. The frame that holds the buttons is packed toward the top. The buttons are packed into the left and right sides of the menu bar frame. Without fill, the menu bar shrinks to be just large enough to hold all the buttons, and the buttons are squeezed together. When fill is enabled in the X direction, the menu bar fills out the top edge of the display:

Example 23–7 Using horizontal fill in a menu bar.

```
frame .menubar -bg white
frame .body -width 150 -height 50 -bg grey50
# Create buttons at either end of the menubar
foreach b {alpha beta} {
    button .menubar.$b -text $b
}
pack .menubar.alpha -side left
pack .menubar.beta -side right
# Let the menu bar fill along the top
pack .menubar -side top -fill x
pack .body
```

Internal Padding with -ipadx and -ipady

Another way to get more fill space is with the -ipadx and -ipady packing options that request more display space in the X and Y directions, respectively. Due to other constraints the request might not be offered, but in general you can use this to give a widget more display space. The next example is just like the previous one except that some internal padding has been added:

Example 23–8 The effects of internal padding (-ipady).

```
# Create and pack two frames
frame .menubar -bg white
frame .body -width 150 -height 50 -bg grey50
# Create buttons at either end of the menubar
foreach b {alpha beta} {
    button .menubar.$b -text $b
}
pack .menubar.alpha -side left -ipady 10
pack .menubar.beta -side right -ipadx 10
# Let the menu bar fill along the top
pack .menubar -side top -fill x -ipady 5
pack .body
```

The alpha button is taller and the beta button is wider because of the internal padding. The frame has internal padding, which reduces the space available for the packing cavity, so the .menubar frame shows through above and below the buttons.

Some widgets have attributes that result in more display space. For example, it would be hard to distinguish a frame with width 50 and no internal padding from a frame with width 40 and a -ipadx 5 packing option. The packer would give the frame 5 more pixels of display space on either side for a total width of 50.

Buttons have their own -padx and -pady options that give them more display space, too. This padding provided by the button is used to keep its text away from the edge of the button. The following example illustrates the difference. The -anchor e button option positions the text as far to the right as possible. Example 37–5 on page 531 provides another comparison of these options:

Example 23–9 Button padding vs. packer padding.

```
# Foo has internal padding from the packer
button .foo -text Foo -anchor e -padx 0 -pady 0
pack .foo -side right -ipadx 10 -ipady 10
# Bar has its own padding
button .bar -text Bar -anchor e -pady 10 -padx 10
pack .bar -side right -ipadx 0 -ipady 0
```

III. Tk Basics

External Padding with -padx and -pady

The packer can provide external padding that allocates packing space that cannot be filled. The space is outside of the border that widgets use to implement their 3D reliefs. Example 37–2 on page 528 shows the different reliefs. The look of a default button is achieved with an extra frame and some padding:

Example 23–10 The look of a default button.

```
. config -borderwidth 10
# OK is the default button
frame .ok -borderwidth 2 -relief sunken
button .ok.b -text OK
pack .ok.b -padx 5 -pady 5
# Cancel is not
button .cancel -text Cancel
pack .ok .cancel -side left -padx 5 -pady 5
```

Even if the .ok.b button were packed with -fill both, it would look the same. The external padding provided by the packer will not be filled by the child widgets.

Example 23–10 handcrafts the look of a default button. Tk 8.0 has a -default attribute for buttons that gives them the right appearance for the default button on the current platform. It looks somewhat like this on UNIX, but the appearance is different on Macintosh and Windows.

Resizing and -expand

The -expand true packing option lets a widget expand its packing space into unclaimed space in the packing cavity. Example 23–6 could use this on the small frame on top to get it to expand across the top of the display, even though it is packed to the right side. The more common case occurs when you have a resizable window. When the user makes the window larger, the widgets have to be told to take advantage of the extra space. Suppose you have a main widget like a text, listbox, or canvas that is in a frame with a scrollbar. That frame has to be told to expand into the extra space in its parent (e.g., the main window) and then the main widget (e.g., the canvas) has to be told to expand into its parent frame. Example 22–1 on page 316 does this.

In nearly all cases the -fill both option is used along with -expand true so that the widget actually uses its extra packing space for its own display. The converse is not true. There are many cases where a widget should fill extra space but not attempt to expand into the packing cavity. The examples below show the difference.

Now we can investigate what happens when the window is made larger. The next example starts like Example 23–7 on page 338, but the size of the main window is increased:

Example 23–11 Resizing without the expand option.

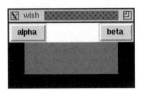

```
# Make the main window black
. config -bg black
# Create and pack two frames
frame .menubar -bg white
frame .body -width 150 -height 50 -bg grey50
# Create buttons at either end of the menubar
foreach b {alpha beta} {
    button .menubar.$b -text $b
}
pack .menubar.alpha -side left
pack .menubar.beta -side right
# Let the menu bar fill along the top
pack .menubar -side top -fill x
pack .body
# Resize the main window to be bigger
wm geometry . 200x100
# Allow interactive resizing
wm minsize . 100 50
```

The only widget that claims any of the new space is .menubar because of its -fill x packing option. The .body frame needs to be packed properly:

Example 23–12 Resizing with expand turned on.

```
# Use all of Example 23-11 then repack .body
pack .body -expand true -fill both
```

If more than one widget inside the same parent is allowed to expand, then the packer shares the extra space between them proportionally. This is probably not the effect you want in the examples we have built so far. The `.menubar`, for example, is not a good candidate for expansion.

Example 23–13 More than one expanding widget.

```
# Use all of Example 23-11 then repack .menubar and .body
pack .menubar -expand true -fill x
pack .body -expand true -fill both
```

Anchoring

If a widget is left with more packing space than display space, you can position it within its packing space using the `-anchor` packing option. The default anchor position is `center`. The other options correspond to points on a compass: n, ne, e, se, s, sw, w, and nw:

Example 23–14 Setup for anchor experiments.

```
# Make the main window black
. config -bg black
# Create two frames to hold open the cavity
frame .prop -bg white -height 80 -width 20
frame .base -width 120 -height 20 -bg grey50
pack .base -side bottom
# Float a label and the prop in the cavity
label .foo -text Foo
pack .prop .foo -side right -expand true
```

The `.base` frame is packed on the bottom. Then the `.prop` frame and the `.foo` label are packed to the right with expand set but no fill. Instead of being pressed up against the right side, the expand gives each of these widgets half of the extra space in the X direction. Their default anchor of `center` results in the positions shown. The next example shows some different anchor positions:

Example 23–15 The effects of noncenter anchors.

```
. config -bg black
# Create two frames to hold open the cavity
frame .prop -bg white -height 80 -width 20
frame .base -width 120 -height 20 -bg grey50
pack .base -side bottom
# Float the label and prop
# Change their position with anchors
label .foo -text Foo
pack .prop -side right -expand true -anchor sw
pack .foo -side right -expand true -anchor ne
```

The `label` has room on all sides, so each of the different anchors will position it differently. The `.prop` frame only has room in the X direction, so it can only be moved into three different positions: left, center, and right. Any of the anchors w, nw, and sw result in the left position. The anchors center, n, and s result in the center position. The anchors e, se, and ne result in the right position.

If you want to see all the variations, type in the following commands to animate the different packing anchors. The `update idletasks` forces any pending display operations. The `after 500` causes the script to wait for `500` milliseconds:

Example 23–16 Animating the packing anchors.

```
foreach anchor {center n ne e se s sw w nw center} {
    pack .foo .prop -anchor $anchor
    # Update the display
    update idletasks
    # Wait half a second
    after 500
}
```

Packing Order

The packer maintains an order among the children that are packed into a frame. By default, each new child is appended to the end of the packing order. The most obvious effect of the order is that the children first in the packing order are closest to the side they are packed against. You can control the packing order with the -before and -after packing options, and you can reorganize widgets after they have already been packed:

Example 23–17 Controlling the packing order.

```
# Create five labels in order
foreach label {one two three four five} {
    label .$label -text $label
    pack .$label -side left -padx 5
}
# ShuffleUp moves a widget to the beginning of the order
proc ShuffleUp { parent child } {
    set first [lindex [pack slaves $parent] 0]
    pack $child -in $parent -before $first
}
# ShuffleDown moves a widget to the end of the order
proc ShuffleDown { parent child } {
    pack $child -in $parent
}
ShuffleUp . .five
ShuffleDown . .three
```

Introspection

The pack slaves command returns the list of children in their packing order. The ShuffleUp procedure uses this to find out the first child so that it can insert another child before it. The ShuffleDown procedure is simpler because the default is to append the child to the end of the packing order.

When a widget is repacked, then it retains all its packing parameters that have already been set. If you need to examine the current packing parameters for a widget, use the pack info command.

```
pack info .five
=> -in . -anchor center -expand 0 -fill none -ipadx 0 \
    -ipady 0 -padx 0 -pady 0 -side left
```

Pack the Scrollbar First

The packing order also determines what happens when the window is made too small. If the window is made small enough the packer will clip children that come later in the packing order. This is why, when you pack a scrollbar and a text widget into a frame, you should pack the scrollbar first. Otherwise, when the window is made smaller the text widget takes up all the space and the scrollbar is clipped.

Choosing the Parent for Packing

In nearly all of the examples in this chapter, a widget is packed into its parent frame. In general, it is possible to pack a widget into any descendent of its parent. For example, the `.a.b` widget could be packed into `.a`, `.a.c` or `.a.d.e.f`. The `-in` packing option lets you specify an alternate packing parent. One motivation for this is that the frames introduced to get the arrangement right can cause cluttered names for important widgets. In Example 23–4 on page 335, the buttons have names like `.one.alpha` and `.one.right.delta`, which is not consistent. Here is an alternate implementation of the same example that simplifies the button names and gives the same result:

Example 23–18 Packing into other relatives.

```
# Create and pack two frames
frame .one -bg white
frame .two -width 100 -height 50 -bg grey50
# Create a row of buttons
foreach b {alpha beta} {
    button .$b -text $b
    pack .$b -in .one -side left
}
# Create a frame for two more buttons
frame .one.right
foreach b {delta epsilon} {
    button .$b -text $b
    pack .$b -in .one.right -side bottom
}
pack .one.right -side right
pack .one .two -side top
```

When you do this, remember that the order in which you create widgets is important. Create the frames first, then create the widgets. The stacking order for windows will cause the later windows to obscure the windows created first. The following is a common mistake because the frame obscures the button:

```
button .a -text hello
frame .b
pack .a -in .b
```

If you cannot avoid this problem scenario, then you can use the `raise` command to fix things up. Stacking order is also discussed on page 347.

```
raise .a
```

Unpacking a Widget

The `pack forget` command removes a widget from the packing order. The widget gets unmapped, so it is not visible. If you unpack a parent frame, the packing

III. Tk Basics

structure inside it is maintained, but all the widgets inside the frame get unmapped. Unpacking a widget is useful if you want to suppress extra features of your interface. You can create all the parts of the interface, and just delay packing them in until the user requests to see them. Then you can pack and unpack them dynamically.

Packer Summary

Keep these rules in mind about the packer:

- Pack vertically (-side top and -side bottom) or horizontally (-side left and -side right) within a frame. Only rarely will a different mixture of packing directions work out the way you want. Add frames to build more complex structures.
- By default, the packer puts widgets into their parent frame, and the parent frame must be created before the children that are packed into it.
- If you put widgets into other relatives, remember to create the frames first so the frames stay underneath the widgets packed into them.
- By default, the packer ignores -width and -height attributes of frames that have widgets packed inside them. It shrinks frames to be just big enough to allow for its border width and to hold the widgets inside them. Use pack propagate to turn off the shrink-wrap behavior.
- The packer distinguishes between packing space and display space. A widget's display might not take up all the packing space allocated to it.
- The -fill option causes the display to fill up the packing space in the X or Y directions, or both.
- The -expand true option causes the packing space to expand into any room in the packing cavity that is otherwise unclaimed. If more than one widget in the same frame wants to expand, then they share the extra space.
- The -ipadx and -ipady options allocate more display space inside the border, if possible.
- The -padx and -pady options allocate more packing space outside the border, if possible. This space is never filled by the widget's display.

The pack Command

Table 23–1 summarizes the pack command. Table 23–2 summarizes the packing options for a widget. These are set with the pack configure command, and the current settings are returned by the pack info command:

Table 23–1 The `pack` command.

`pack win ?win ..? ?options?`	This is just like `pack configure`.
`pack configure win ?win ...? ?options?`	Packs one or more widgets according to the `options,` which are given in Table 23–2.
`pack forget win ?win...?`	Unpacks the specified windows.
`pack info win`	Returns the packing parameters of `win`.
`pack propagate win ?bool?`	Queries or sets the geometry propagation of `win`, which has other widgets packed inside it.
`pack slaves win`	Returns the list of widgets managed by `win`.

Table 23–2 Packing options.

`-after win`	Packs after `win` in the packing order.
`-anchor anchor`	Anchors: `center`, n, ne, e, se, s, sw, w, or nw.
`-before win`	Packs before `win` in the packing order.
`-expand boolean`	Controls expansion into the unclaimed packing cavity.
`-fill style`	Controls fill of packing space. Style: x, y, `both`, or `none`.
`-in win`	Packs inside `win`.
`-ipadx amount`	Horizontal internal padding, in screen units.
`-ipady amount`	Vertical internal padding, in screen units.
`-padx amount`	Horizontal external padding, in screen units.
`-pady amount`	Vertical external padding, in screen units.
`-side side`	Sides: `top`, `right`, `bottom`, or `left`.

III. Tk Basics

Window Stacking Order

The `raise` and `lower` commands control the window stacking order. The stacking order controls the display of windows. Windows higher in the stacking order obscure windows lower in the stacking order. By default, new windows are created at the top of the stacking order so they obscure older windows. Consider this sequence of commands:

```
button .one
frame .two
pack .one -in .two
```

If you do this, you do not see the button. The problem is that the frame is higher in the stacking order so it obscures the button. You can change the stacking order with the `raise` command:

```
raise .one .two
```

This puts `.one` just above `.two` in the stacking order. If `.two` was not specified, then `.one` would be put at the top of the stacking order.

The `lower` command has a similar form. With one argument, it puts that window at the bottom of the stacking order. Otherwise, it puts it just below another window in the stacking order.

You can use `raise` and `lower` on top-level windows to control their stacking order among all other top-level windows. For example, if a user requests a dialog that is already displayed, use `raise` to make it pop to the foreground of their cluttered desktop.

The Grid Geometry Manager

This chapter explores the `grid` geometry manager that positions widgets on a grid that automatically adjusts its size. Grid was added in Tk 4.1.

The `grid` geometry manager arranges widgets on a grid with variable-sized rows and columns. You specify the rows and columns occupied by each widget, and the grid is adjusted to accommodate all the widgets it contains. This is ideal for creating table-like layouts. The manager also has sophisticated facilities for controlling row and column sizes and the dynamic resize behavior. By introducing subframes with grids of their own, you can create arbitrary layouts.

A Basic Grid

Example 24–1 uses `grid` to lay out a set of labels and frames in two parallel columns. It takes advantage of the relative placement feature of `grid`. You do not necessarily have to specify rows and columns. Instead, the order of `grid` commands and their arguments implies the layout. Each `grid` command starts a new row, and the order of the widgets in the `grid` command determines the column. In the example, there are two columns, and iteration of the loop adds a new row. `Grid` makes each column just wide enough to hold the biggest widget. Widgets that are smaller are centered in their cell. That's why the labels appear centered in their column:

Example 24–1 A basic grid.

```
foreach color {red orange yellow green blue purple} {
    label .l$color -text $color -bg white
    frame .f$color -background $color -width 100 -height 2
    grid .l$color .f$color
}
```

The -sticky Setting

If a grid cell is larger than the widget inside it, you can control the size and position of the widget with the -sticky option. The -sticky option combines the functions of -fill and -anchor used with the pack geometry manager. You specify to which sides of its cell a widget sticks. You can specify any combination of n, e, w, and s to stick a widget to the top, right, left, and bottom sides of its cell. You can concatenate these letters together (e.g., news) or uses spaces or commas to separate them (e.g., n,e,w,s). Example 24–2 uses -sticky w to left justify the labels, and -sticky ns to stretch the color frames to the full height of their row:

Example 24–2 A grid with sticky settings.

```
foreach color {red orange yellow green blue purple} {
    label .l$color -text $color -bg white
    frame .f$color -background $color -width 100 -height 2
    grid .l$color .f$color
    grid .l$color -sticky w
    grid .f$color -sticky ns
}
```

Example 24–2 uses `grid` in two ways. The first `grid` in the loop fixes the positions of the widgets because it is the first time they are assigned to the master. The next `grid` commands modify the existing parameters; they just adjust the `-sticky` setting because their row and column positions are already known.

You can specify row and column positions explicitly with the `-row` and `-column` attribute. This is generally more work than using the relative placement, but it is necessary if you need to dynamically move a widget into a different cell. Example 24–3 keeps track of rows and columns explicitly and achieves the same layout as Example 24–2:

Example 24–3 A grid with row and column specifications.

```
set row 0
foreach color {red orange yellow green blue purple} {
    label .l$color -text $color -bg white
    frame .f$color -background $color -width 100
    grid .l$color -row $row -column 0 -sticky w
    grid .f$color -row $row -column 1 -sticky ns
    incr row
}
```

External Padding with -padx and -pady

You can keep a widget away from the edge of its cell with the `-padx` and `-pady` settings. Example 24–4 uses external padding to shift the labels away from the left edge, and to keep some blank space between the color bars:

Example 24–4 A grid with external padding.

```
foreach color {red orange yellow green blue purple} {
    label .l$color -text $color -bg white
    frame .f$color -background $color -width 100 -height 2
    grid .l$color .f$color
    grid .l$color -sticky w -padx 3
    grid .f$color -sticky ns -pady 1
}
```

Internal Padding with -ipadx and -ipady

You can give a widget more display space than it normally needs with internal padding. The internal padding increases the size of the grid. In contrast, a -sticky setting might stretch a widget, but it will not change the size of the grid. Example 24–5 makes the labels taller with -ipady:

Example 24–5 A grid with internal padding.

```
foreach color {red orange yellow green blue purple} {
    label .l$color -text $color -bg white
    frame .f$color -background $color -width 100 -height 2
    grid .l$color .f$color
    grid .l$color -sticky w -padx 3 -ipady 5
    grid .f$color -sticky ns -pady 1
}
```

Multiple Widgets in a Cell

Example 24–6 shows all possible -sticky settings. It uses the ability to put more than one widget into a grid cell. A large square frame is put in each cell, and then a label is put into the same cell with a different -sticky setting. It is important to create the frame first so it is below the label. Window stacking is discussed on page 347. External padding is used to keep the labels away from the edge so that they do not hide the -ridge relief of the frames.

Example 24–6 All combinations of -sticky settings.

```
set index 0
foreach x {news ns ew  " " new sew wsn esn nw ne sw se n s w e} {
    frame .f$x -borderwidth 2 -relief ridge -width 40 -height 40
    grid .f$x -sticky news \
        -row [expr $index/4] -column [expr $index%4]
    label .l$x -text $x -background white
    grid .l$x -sticky $x -padx 2 -pady 2 \
        -row [expr $index/4] -column [expr $index%4]
    incr index
}
```

Spanning Rows and Columns

A widget can occupy more than one cell. The -rowspan and -columnspan attributes indicate how many rows and columns are occupied by a widget. Example 24–7 uses explicit row, column, rowspan, and columnspan specifications:

Example 24–7 Explicit row and column span.

```
. config -bg white
foreach color {888 999 aaa bbb ccc fff} {
    frame .$color -bg #$color -width 40 -height 40
}
grid .888 -row 0 -column 0 -columnspan 3 -sticky news
grid .999 -row 1 -column 0 -rowspan 2 -sticky news
grid .aaa -row 1 -column 1 -columnspan 2 -sticky news
grid .bbb -row 2 -column 2 -rowspan 2 -sticky news
grid .ccc -row 3 -column 0 -columnspan 2 -sticky news
grid .fff -row 2 -column 1 -sticky news
```

You can also use special syntax in grid commands that imply row and column placement. Special characters represent a cell that is spanned or skipped:

- represents a spanned column.
^ represents a spanned row.
x represents a skipped cell.

A nice feature of the implicit row and column assignments is that it is easy to make minor changes to your layout. Example 24–8 achieves the same layout:

III. Tk Basics

Example 24–8 Grid syntax row and column span.

```
. config -bg white
foreach color {888 999 aaa bbb ccc ddd fff} {
    frame .$color -bg #$color -width 40 -height 40
}
grid .888 -       -       -sticky news
grid .999 .aaa    -       -sticky news
grid ^    .fff    .bbb    -sticky news
grid .ccc -       ^       -sticky news
```

Row and Column Constraints

The grid manager supports attributes on whole rows and columns. You can control the row and column sizes with a -pad and -minsize attribute. The -weight attribute controls resize behavior. The grid command has a rowconfigure and columnconfigure operation to set and query these attributes:

> grid columnconfigure *master col* ?*attributes*?
> grid rowconfigure *master row* ?*attributes*?

With no *attributes*, the current settings are returned. The *row* and *col* specifications can be lists instead of simple indices, so you can configure several rows or columns at once.

Row and Column Padding

The -pad attribute increases a row or column size. The initial size of a row or column is determined by the largest widget, and -pad adds to this size. This padding can be filled by the widget by using the -sticky attribute. Row and column padding works like internal padding because it is extra space that can be occupied by the widget's display. In contrast, the -pad attribute on an individual widget acts like a spacer that keeps the widget away from the edge of the cell. Example 24–9 shows the difference. The row padding increases the height of the row, but the padding on .f1 keeps it away from the edge of the cell:

Example 24–9 Row padding compared to widget padding.

```
. config -bg black
label .f1 -text left -bg #ccc
label .f2 -text right -bg #aaa
grid .f1 .f2 -sticky news
grid .f1 -padx 10 -pady 10
grid rowconfigure . 0 -pad 20
```

Minimum Size

The `-minsize` attribute restricts a column or row to be a minimum size. The row or column can grow bigger if its widget requests it, but they will not get smaller than the minimum. One useful application of `-minsize` is to create empty rows or columns, which is more efficient than creating an extra frame.

Managing Resize Behavior

If the master frame is bigger than the required size of the grid, it shrinks to be just large enough to contain the grid. You can turn off the shrink-wrap behavior with `grid propagate`. If geometry propagation is off, then the grid is centered inside the master. If the master frame is too small to fit the grid, then the grid is anchored to the upper-left corner of the master and clipped on the bottom-right.

By default, rows and columns do not resize when you grow the master frame. You enable resizing by specifying a `-weight` for a row or column that is an integer value greater than zero. Example 24–10 grids a text widget and two scrollbars. The protocol between the scrollbar and the text widget is described on page 429. The text widget is in row 0, column 0, and both of these can expand. The vertical scrollbar is in row 0, column 1, so it only grows in the Y direction. The horizontal scrollbar is in row 1, column 0, so it only grows in the X direction:

Example 24–10 Gridding a text widget and scrollbar.

```
text .text -yscrollcommand ".yscroll set" \
    -xscrollcommand ".xscroll set"-width 40 -height 10
scrollbar .yscroll -command ".text yview" -orient vertical
scrollbar .xscroll -command ".text xview" -orient horizontal
grid .text .yscroll -sticky news
grid .xscroll -sticky ew
grid rowconfigure . 0 -weight 1
grid columnconfigure . 0 -weight 1
```

You can use different weights to let different rows and columns grow at different rates. However, there are some tricky issues because the resize behavior applies to extra space, not total space. For example, suppose there are four columns that have widths 10, 20, 30, and 40 pixels, for a total of 100. If the master frame is grown to 140 pixels wide, then there are 40 extra pixels. If each column has weight 1, then each column gets an equal share of the extra space, or 10 more pixels. Now suppose column 0 has weight 0, columns 1 and 2 have weight 1, and column 3 has weight 2. Column 0 will not grow, columns 1 and 2 will get 10 more pixels, and column 3 will get 20 more pixels. In most cases, weights of 0 or 1 make the most sense.

Weight works in reverse when shrinking.

If a row or column has to shrink, the weights are applied in reverse. A row or column with a higher weight will shrink more. For example, put two equal sized frames in columns with different weights. When the user makes the window bigger, the frame in the column with more weight gets larger more quickly. When the window is made smaller, that frame gets smaller more quickly.

The grid Command

Table 24–1 summarizes the usage of the grid command.

Table 24–1 The grid command.

grid bbox *master* ?*c1 r1*? ?*c2 r2*?	Returns the bounding box, of the whole grid, the cell at *c1*, *r1*, or the cells from *c1*, *r1* to *c2*, *r2*.
grid columnconfigure *master col* ?*options*?	Sets or queries the configuration of *col*. Options are -minsize, -weight, and -pad.
grid configure *win* ?*win* ...? ?*options*?	Grids one or more widgets according to the *options,* which are given in Table 24–2.
grid forget *win* ?*win*...?	Unmaps the specified windows.
grid info *win*	Returns the grid parameters of *win*.
grid location *master x y*	Returns the cell column and row under the point *x, y* in *master.*
grid propagate *master* ?*boolean*?	Enables or disables shrink-wrapping of *master.*
grid rowconfigure *master row* ?*options*?	Sets or queries the configuration of *row.* Options are -minsize, -weight, and -pad.
grid remove *slave*	Unmaps *slave,* but remember its configuration.
grid size master	Returns the number of columns and rows.
grid slaves *win* ?-row *r*? ?-column *c*?	Returns the list of widgets managed by *win*, or just those in the specified row or column.

Table 24–2 summarizes the grid options for a widget. These are set with the `grid configure` command, and the current settings are returned by the `grid info` command.

Table 24–2 Grid widget options.

`-in` *win*	Places inside *win*.
`-column` *col*	Column position. Columns count from zero.
`-columnspan` *n*	Spans *n* columns.
`-ipadx` *pixels*	Internal widget padding in the X direction, in screen units.
`-ipady` *pixels*	Internal widget padding in the Y direction, in screen units.
`-padx` *pixels*	External widget padding in the X direction, in screen units.
`-pady` *pixels*	External widget padding in the Y direction, in screen units.
`-row` *row*	Row position. Rows count from zero.
`-rowspan` *n*	Spans *n* rows.
`-sticky` *how*	Positions widget next to any combination of north (n), south (s), east (w), and west (e) sides of the cell. Use { } for center.

III. Tk Basics

The Place Geometry Manager

This chapter explores the `place` geometry manager that positions widgets on the screen.

The `place` geometry manager is much simpler than `pack` and `grid`. You specify the exact position and size of a window, or you specify the relative position and relative size of a widget. This is useful in a few situations, but it rapidly becomes tedious if you have to position lots of windows. The best application of `place` is to create special-purpose geometry managers using its relative constraints. A standard application of `place` is to adjust the boundary between two adjacent windows.

place **Basics**

The `place` command lets you specify the width and height of a window, and the X and Y locations of the window's anchor point. The size and location can be specified in absolute or relative terms. Relative specifications are more powerful. Example 25–1 uses `place` to center a window in its parent. You can use this command to position dialogs that you do not want to be detached top-level windows:

Example 25–1 Centering a window with `place`.

```
place $w -in $parent -relx 0.5 -rely 0.5 -anchor center
```

The `-relx` and `-rely` specify the relative X and Y positions of the anchor point of the widget `$w` in `$parent`. A relative X (or Y) value of zero corresponds to the left (or top) edge of $parent. A value of one corresponds to the right (or bottom) edge of $parent. A value of 0.5 specifies the middle. The anchor point determines what point in $w is positioned according to the specifications. In Example 25–1 the center anchor point is used so that the center of $w is centered in $parent.

The relative height and width settings are used to base a widget's size on another widget. Example 25–2 completely covers one window with another window. It uses the default anchor point for windows, which is their upper-left hand corner (nw):

Example 25–2 Covering a window with place.

```
place $w -in $parent -relwidth 1 -relheight 1 -x 0 -y 0
```

The absolute and relative size and position parameters are additive (e.g., -width and -relwidth). You can make a window slightly larger or smaller than the parent by specifying both parameters. In Example 25–3, a negative width and height are used to make a window smaller than another one:

Example 25–3 Combining relative and absolute sizes.

```
place $w -in $parent -relwidth 1 -relheight 1 -x 0 -y 0 \
    -width -4 -height -4
```

It is not necessary for $parent to actually be the parent widget of $w. The requirement is that $parent be the parent, or a descendant of the parent, of $w. It also has to be in the same top-level window. This guarantees that $w is visible whenever $parent is visible. These are the same restrictions imposed by the pack geometry manager.

It is not necessary to position a widget inside another widget, either. Example 25–4 positions a window five pixels above a sibling widget. If $sibling is repositioned, then $w moves with it. This approach is useful when you decorate a resizable window by placing other widgets at its corners or edges. When the window is resized, the decorations automatically move into place:

Example 25–4 Positioning a window above a sibling with place.

```
place $w -in $sibling -relx 0.5 -y -5 -anchor s \
    -bordermode outside
```

The -bordermode outside option is specified so that any decorative border in $sibling is ignored when positioning $w. In this case the position is relative to the outside edge of $sibling. By default, the border is taken into account to make it easy to position widgets inside their parent's border.

The parent widget does not have to be a frame. Example 25–1 can be used to place a dialog in the middle of a text widget. In Example 25–4, $sibling and $w can both be label widgets.

The Pane Manager

The relative size and placement parameters of the place command can be used to create custom geometry managers. Example 25–5 shows a paned layout manager. Two frames, or panes, are placed inside another frame. A small third frame represents a grip that is used to adjust the boundary between the two panes:

Example 25–5 Pane_Create sets up vertical or horizontal panes.

```
proc Pane_Create {f1 f2 args} {

    # Map optional arguments into array values
    set t(-orient) vertical
    set t(-percent) 0.5
    set t(-in) [winfo parent $f1]
    array set t $args

    # Keep state in an array associated with the master frame
    set master $t(-in)
    upvar #0 Pane$master pane
    array set pane [array get t]

    # Create the grip and set placement attributes that
    # will not change. A thin divider line is achieved by
    # making the two frames one pixel smaller in the
    # adjustable dimension and making the main frame black.

    set pane(1) $f1
    set pane(2) $f2
    set pane(grip) [frame $master.grip -background gray50 \
        -width 10 -height 10 -bd 1 -relief raised \
        -cursor crosshair]
    if {[string match vert* $pane(-orient)]} {
        set pane(D) Y;# Adjust boundary in Y direction
        place $pane(1) -in $master -x 0 -rely 0.0 -anchor nw \
            -relwidth 1.0 -height -1
        place $pane(2) -in $master -x 0 -rely 1.0 -anchor sw \
            -relwidth 1.0 -height -1
        place $pane(grip) -in $master -anchor c -relx 0.8
    } else {
        set pane(D) X ;# Adjust boundary in X direction
        place $pane(1) -in $master -relx 0.0 -y 0 -anchor nw \
            -relheight 1.0 -width -1
        place $pane(2) -in $master -relx 1.0 -y 0 -anchor ne \
```

```
                   -relheight 1.0 -width -1
        place $pane(grip) -in $master -anchor c -rely 0.8
    }
    $master configure -background black

    # Set up bindings for resize, <Configure>, and
    # for dragging the grip.

    bind $master <Configure> [list PaneGeometry $master]
    bind $pane(grip) <ButtonPress-1> \
        [list PaneDrag $master %$pane(D)]
    bind $pane(grip) <B1-Motion> \
        [list PaneDrag $master %$pane(D)]
    bind $pane(grip) <ButtonRelease-1> \
        [list PaneStop $master]

    # Do the initial layout

    PaneGeometry $master
}
```

Parsing Arguments and Maintaining State

The `Pane_Create` procedure is given two widgets to manage, and an optional set of parameters. The general syntax of `Pane_Create` is:

```
    Pane_Create f1 f2 ?-orient xy? ?-percent p? ?-in master?
```

All the optional arguments are available in `$args`. Its attribute-value structure is used to initialize a temporary array `t`. Default values are set before the assignment from `$args`. The following code is compact but doesn't check errors in the optional arguments.

```
    set t(-orient) vertical
    set t(-percent) 0.5
    set t(-in) [winfo parent $f1]
    array set t $args
```

Global state about the layout is kept in an array whose name is based on the master frame. The name of the master frame isn't known until after arguments are parsed, which is why `t` is used. After the `upvar` the argument values are copied from the temporary array into the global state array:

```
    set master $t(-in)
    upvar #0 Pane$master pane
    array set pane [array get t]
```

Sticky Geometry Settings

Example 25–5 sets several `place` parameters on the frames when they are created. These are remembered, and other parameters are adjusted later to dynamically adjust the boundary between the frames. All Tk geometry managers retain settings like this. The initial settings for the vertical layout is shown here:

```
place $pane(1) -in $parent -x 0 -rely 0.0 -anchor nw \
    -relwidth 1.0 -height -1
place $pane(2) -in $parent -x 0 -rely 1.0 -anchor sw \
    -relwidth 1.0 -height -1
place $pane(grip) -in $parent -anchor c -relx 0.8
```

The position of the upper and lower frames is specified with an absolute X and a relative Y position, and the anchor setting is chosen to keep the frame visible inside the main frame. For example, the lower frame is positioned at the bottom-left corner of the container with -x 0 and -rely 1.0. The -anchor sw attaches the lower-left corner of the frame to this position.

The size of the contained frames is also a combination of absolute and relative values. The width is set to the full width of the container with -relwidth 1.0. The height is set to minus one with -height -1. This value gets added to a relative height that is determined later. It will leave a little space between the two contained frames.

The resize grip is just a small frame positioned at the boundary. Initially it is just placed over toward one size with -relx 0.8. It gets positioned on the boundary with a -rely setting later. It has a different cursor to indicate it is active.

Event Bindings

The example uses some event bindings that are described in more detail in Chapter 26. The <Configure> event occurs when the containing frame is resized by the user. When the user presses the mouse button over the grip and drags it, there is a <ButtonPress-1> event, one or more <B1-Motion> events, and finally a <ButtonRelease-1> event. Tcl commands are bound to these events:

```
bind $parent <Configure> [list PaneGeometry $parent]
bind $pane(grip) <ButtonPress-1> \
    [list PaneDrag $parent %$pane(D)]
bind $pane(grip) <B1-Motion> \
    [list PaneDrag $parent %$pane(D)]
bind $pane(grip) <ButtonRelease-1> [list PaneStop $parent]
```

Managing the Layout

The code is set up to work with either horizontal or vertical layouts. The pane(D) variable is either X, for a horizontal layout, or Y, for a vertical layout. This value is used in the bindings to get %X or %Y, which are replaced with the X and Y screen positions of the mouse when the bindings fire. This value is passed to PaneDrag as the parameter D. The PaneDrag procedure remembers the previous position in pane(lastD) and uses that to update the percentage split between the two contained panes:

III. Tk Basics

Example 25–6 PaneDrag adjusts the percentage.

```
proc PaneDrag {master D} {
    upvar #0 Pane$master pane
    if [info exists pane(lastD)] {
        set delta [expr double($pane(lastD) - $D) \
                                    / $pane(size)]
        set pane(-percent) [expr $pane(-percent) - $delta]
        if {$pane(-percent) < 0.0} {
            set pane(-percent) 0.0
        } elseif {$pane(-percent) > 1.0} {
            set pane(-percent) 1.0
        }
        PaneGeometry $master
    }
    set pane(lastD) $D
}
proc PaneStop {master} {
    upvar #0 Pane$master pane
    catch {unset pane(lastD)}
}
```

The PaneGeometry procedure adjusts the positions of the frames. It is called when the main window is resized, so it updates pane(size). It is also called as the user drags the grip. For a vertical layout, the grip is moved by setting its relative Y position. The size of the two contained frames is set with a relative height. Remember that this is combined with the fixed height of -1 to get some space between the two frames:

Example 25–7 PaneGeometry updates the layout.

```
proc PaneGeometry {master} {
    upvar #0 Pane$master pane
    if {$pane(D) == "X"} {
        place $pane(1) -relwidth $pane(-percent)
        place $pane(2) -relwidth [expr 1.0 - $pane(-percent)]
        place $pane(grip) -relx $pane(-percent)
        set pane(size) [winfo width $master]
    } else {
        place $pane(1) -relheight $pane(-percent)
        place $pane(2) -relheight [expr 1.0 - $pane(-percent)]
        place $pane(grip) -rely $pane(-percent)
        set pane(size) [winfo height $master]
    }
}
proc PaneTest {{p .p} {orient vert}} {
    catch {destroy $p}
    frame $p -width 200 -height 200
    label $p.1 -bg blue -text foo
    label $p.2 -bg green -text bar
    pack $p -expand true -fill both
```

```
        pack propagate $p off
        Pane_Create $p.1 $p.2 -in $p -orient $orient -percent 0.3
}
```

The place Command

Table 25–1 summarizes the usage of the place command.

Table 25–1 The place command.

place *win* ?*win* ..? ?*options*?	This is just like place configure.
place configure *win* ?*win* ...? ?*options*?	Places one or more widgets according to the *options*, which are given Table 25–2.
place forget *win* ?*win*...?	Unmaps the specified windows.
place info *win*	Returns the placement parameters of *win*.
place slaves *win*	Returns the list of widgets managed by *win*.

Table 25–2 summarizes the placement options for a widget. These are set with the place configure command, and the current settings are returned by the place info command.

Table 25–2 Placement options.

-in *win*	Places inside (or relative to) *win*.
-anchor *where*	Anchors: center, n, ne, e, se, s, sw, w, or nw. Default: nw.
-x *coord*	X position, in screen units, of the anchor point.
-relx *offset*	Relative X position. 0.0 is the left edge. 1.0 is the right edge.
-y *coord*	Y position, in screen units, of the anchor point.
-rely *offset*	Relative Y position. 0.0 is the top edge. 1.0 is the bottom edge.
-width size	Width of the window, in screen units.
-relwidth size	Width relative to parent's width. 1.0 is full width.
-height size	Height of the window, in screen units.
-relheight size	Height relative to the parent's height. 1.0 is full height.
-bordermode mode	If mode is inside, then size and position are inside the parent's border. If mode is outside, then size and position are relative to the outer edge of the parent. The default is inside.

Binding Commands to Events

This chapter introduces the event binding mechanism in Tk. Bindings associate a Tcl command with an event like a mouse click or a key stroke. There are also facilities to define virtual events like <<Cut>> and <<Paste>> that are associated with different keystrokes on different platforms. Tcl commands discussed are: bind, bindtags, and event.

*B*indings associate a Tcl command with a sequence of events from the window system. Events include key press, key release, button press, button release, mouse entering a window, mouse leaving, window changing size, window open, window close, focus in, focus out, and widget destroyed. The bindings are defined on *binding tags*, and each widget is associated with an ordered set of binding tags. The binding tags provide a level of indirection between bindings and widgets that creates a flexible and powerful system.

Virtual events are used to support a different look and feel on different platforms. A virtual event is a higher-level name, like <<Copy>>, for a lower-level event name like <Control-c> or <Key-F6>. A virtual event hides the different keystrokes used on different platforms for the same logical operation. Tk defines a few virtual events, and applications can define their own.

The bind Command

The bind command creates event bindings, and it returns information about current bindings. The general form of the command is:

    bind *bindingTag* ?*eventSequence*? ?*command*?

If all arguments are present, a binding from *eventSequence* to *command* is defined for *bindingTag*. The *bindingTag* is typically a widget class name (e.g., Button) or a widget instance name (e.g., .buttons.foo). Binding tags are

described in more detail later. Called with a single argument, a binding tag, `bind`
returns the events for which there are command bindings:

```
bind Menubutton
=> <Key-Return> <Key-space> <ButtonRelease-1>
   <B1-Motion> <Motion> <Button-1> <Leave> <Enter>
```

The events in this example are keystroke and mouse events. `<Button-1>` is
the event generated when the user presses the first, or left-hand, mouse button.
`<B1-Motion>` is generated when the user moves the mouse while holding down
the first mouse button. The `<Key-space>` event occurs when the user presses the
space bar. The surrounding angle brackets delimit a single event, and you can
define bindings for a sequence of events. The event syntax is described on page
371, and event sequences are described on page 377.

If `bind` is given a binding tag and an event sequence, it returns the Tcl command bound to that event sequence:

```
bind Menubutton <B1-Motion>
=> tkMbMotion %W down %X %Y
```

The Tcl commands in event bindings support an additional syntax for event
keywords. These keywords begin with a percent sign and have one more character that identifies some attribute of the event. The keywords are substituted
with event-specific data before the Tcl command is evaluated. For example, `%W` is
replaced with the widget's pathname. The `%X` and `%Y` keywords are replaced with
the coordinates of the event relative to the screen. The `%x` and `%y` keywords are
replaced with the coordinates of the event relative to the widget. The event keywords are summarized on page 379.

The `%` substitutions are performed throughout the entire command bound to
an event, without regard to other quoting schemes. You must use `%%` to obtain a
single percent sign. For this reason you should make your binding commands
short, adding a new procedure if necessary (e.g., `tkMbMotion`), instead of littering
percent signs throughout your code.

A new binding is created by specifying a binding tag, an event sequence,
and a command:

```
bind Menubutton <B1-Motion> {tkMbMotion %W down %X %Y}
```

If the first character of the binding command is +, the command (without
the +) is added to the commands, if any, for that event and binding tag:

```
bind bindingTag event {+ command args}
```

To delete a binding for an event, bind the event to the null string:

```
bind bindingTag event {}
```

Bindings execute in the global scope.

When a binding is triggered, the command is evaluated at the global scope.
A very common mistake is to confuse the scope that is active when the `bind` command creates a binding, and the scope that is active when the binding is triggered. The same problem crops up with the commands associated with buttons,
and it is discussed in more detail at the beginning of Chapter 27.

The `bindtags` Command

A binding tag groups related bindings, and each widget is associated with an ordered set of binding tags. The level of indirection between widgets and bindings lets you group functionality on binding tags and compose widget behavior from different binding tags.

For example, the `all` binding tag has bindings on `<Tab>` that change focus among widgets. The `Text` binding tag has bindings on keystrokes that insert and edit text. Only text widgets use the `Text` binding tag, but all widgets share the `all` binding tag. You can introduce new binding tags and change the association of widgets to binding tags dynamically. The result is a powerful and flexible way to manage bindings.

The `bindtags` command sets or queries the binding tags for a widget. The general form of the `bindtags` command is:

```
bindtags widget ?tagList?
```

The following command returns the binding tags for text widget `.t`:

```
bindtags .t
=> .t Text . all
```

You can change the binding tags and their order. The `tagList` argument to `bindtags` must be a proper Tcl list. The following command reorders the binding tags for `.t` and eliminates the `.` binding tag:

```
bindtags .t [list all Text .t]
```

By default, all the Tk widgets, except a top-level, have four binding tags in the following order:

- The widget's Tk pathname (e.g., `.t`). Use this binding tag to provide special behavior to a particular widget. There are no bindings on this bindtag by default.
- The widget's class (e.g., `Text`). The class for a widget is derived from the name of the command that creates it. A button widget has the class `Button`, a text has the class `Text`, and so on. The Tk widgets define their default behavior with bindings on their class.
- The Tk pathname of the widget's top-level window (e.g., `.`). This is redundant in the case of a top-level widget, so it is not used twice. There are no bindings on this bindtag by default. The bindings on a top-level window can be used in dialog boxes to handle keyboard accelerators.
- The global binding tag `all`. The default bindings on `all` are used to change focus among widgets. They are described on page 517.

When there is more than one binding tag on a widget, then one binding from each binding tag can match an event. The bindings are processed in the order of the binding tags. By default, the most specific binding tag comes first, and the most general binding tag comes last.

Example 26–1 has two frame widgets that have the following behavior. When the mouse enters them, they turn red. They turn white when the mouse leaves. When the user types `<Control-c>`, the frame under the mouse is destroyed. One of the frames, `.two`, reports the coordinates of mouse clicks:

Example 26–1 Bindings on different binding tags.

```
frame .one -width 30 -height 30
frame .two -width 30 -height 30
bind Frame <Enter> {%W config -bg red}
bind Frame <Leave> {%W config -bg white}
bind .two <Button> {puts "Button %b at %x %y"}
pack .one .two -side left
bind all <Control-c> {destroy %W}
bind all <Enter> {focus %W}
```

The `Frame` class has a binding on `<Enter>` and `<Leave>` that changes a frame's background color when the mouse moves in and out of the window. This binding is shared by all the frames. There is also a binding on `all` for `<Enter>` that sets the keyboard focus. Both bindings will trigger when the mouse enters a frame.

Focus and Key Events

The binding on `<Control-c>` is shared by all widgets. The binding destroys the target widget. Because this is a keystroke, it is important to get the keyboard *focus* directed at the proper widget. By default, focus is on the main window, and destroying it terminates the entire application. The global binding for `<Enter>` gives focus to a widget when you move the mouse over the widget. In this example, moving the mouse into a widget and then typing `<Control-c>` destroys the widget. Bind the `focus` command to `<Button>` instead of `<Enter>` if you prefer a click-to-type focus model. Focus is described in Chapter 36.

Using `break` and `continue` in Bindings

The `break` and `continue` commands control the progression through the set of binding tags. The `break` command stops the current binding and suppresses the bindings from any remaining tags in the binding set order. The `continue` command in a binding stops the current binding and continues with the command from the next binding tag.

For example, the `Entry` binding tag has bindings that insert and edit text in a one-line entry widget. You can put a binding on `<Return>` that executes a Tcl command using the value of the widget. The following example runs *Some Command* before the \r character is added to the entry widget. The binding is on the name of the widget, which is first in the set of binding tags, so the `break` suppresses the `Entry` binding that inserts the character:

```
bind .entry <Return> {Some Command ; break}
```

Note that you cannot use the `break` or `continue` commands inside a procedure that is called by the binding. This is because the procedure mechanism will not propagate the `break` or `continue` signal. Instead, you could use the `-code` option to `return`, which is described on page 80:

```
return -code break
```

Defining New Binding Tags

You introduce new binding tags just by using them in a `bind` or `bindtags` command. Binding tags are useful for grouping bindings into different sets, such as specialized bindings for different modes of an editor. One way to emulate the *vi* editor, for example, is to use two bind tags, one for insert mode and one for command mode. The user types i to enter insert mode, and they type `<Escape>` to enter command mode:

```
bindtags $t [list ViInsert Text $t all]
bind ViInsert <Escape> {bindtags %W {ViCmd %W all}}
bind ViCmd <Key-i> {bindtags %W {ViInsert Text %W all}}
```

The `Text` class bindings are used in insert mode. The command to put the widget into command mode is put on a new binding tag, `ViInsert`, instead of changing the default `Text` bindings. The `bindtag` command changes the mode by changing the set of binding tags for the widget. The `%W` is replaced with the name of the widget, which is the same as `$t` in this example. Of course, you need to define many more bindings to fully implement all the *vi* commands.

Event Syntax

The `bind` command uses the following syntax to describe events:

```
<modifier-modifier-type-detail>
<<Event>>
```

The first form is for physical events like keystrokes and mouse motion. The second form is for *virtual events* like Cut and Paste, which correspond to different physical events on different platforms. Physical events are described in this section. Virtual events are described in more detail on page 378.

The primary part of the description is the *type*, (e.g., `Button` or `Motion`). The *detail* is used in some events to identify keys or buttons, (.e.g., `Key-a` or `Button-1`). A *modifier* is another key or button that is already pressed when the event occurs, (e.g., `Control-Key-a` or `B2-Motion`). There can be multiple modifiers (e.g., `Control-Shift-x`) . The < and > delimit a single event.

Table 26–1 on the next page lists all physical event types. When two event types are listed together (e.g., `ButtonPress` and `Button`) they are equivalent.

Keyboard Events

The `KeyPress` type is distinguished from `KeyRelease` so that you can have different bindings for each of these events. `KeyPress` can be abbreviated `Key`, and `Key` can be left off altogether if a detail is given to indicate what key. Finally, as a special case for `KeyPress` events, the angle brackets can also be left out. The following are all equivalent event specifications:

```
<KeyPress-a>
<Key-a>
<a>
a
```

The detail for a key is also known as the *keysym*, which refers to the graphic printed on the key of the keyboard. For punctuation and non-printing characters, special keysyms are defined. Case is significant in keysyms, but unfortunately there is no consistent scheme. In particular BackSpace has a capital B and a capital S. Commonly encountered keysyms include:

```
Return, Escape, BackSpace, Tab, Up, Down, Left, Right, comma,
period, dollar, asciicircum, numbersign, exclam.
```

Table 26–1 Event types.

Activate	The application has been activated. (Macintosh)
ButtonPress, Button	A button is pressed (down).
ButtonRelease	A button is released (up).
Circulate	The stacking order of the window changed.
Colormap	The color map has changed.
Configure	The window changed size, position, border, or stacking order.
Deactivate	The application has been deactivated. (Macintosh)
Destroy	The window has been destroyed.
Enter	The mouse has entered the window.
Expose	The window has been exposed.
FocusIn	The window has received focus.
FocusOut	The window has lost focus.
Gravity	The window has moved because of a change in size of its parent window.
KeyPress, Key	A key is pressed (down).
KeyRelease	A key is released (up).
MouseWheel	The scrolling mouse wheel has moved.
Motion	The mouse is moving in the window.
Leave	The mouse is leaving the window.
Map	The window has been mapped (opened).
Property	A property on the window has been changed or deleted.
Reparent	A window has been reparented.
Unmap	The window has been unmapped (iconified).
Visibility	The window has changed visibility.

Finding out what keysyms are generated by your keyboard.

There are times when you do not know what keysym is generated by a special key on your keyboard. The keysyms are defined by the window system implementation, and on UNIX systems they are affected by a dynamic keyboard map, the X modmap. You may find the next binding useful to determine just what the keysym for a particular key is on your system:

```
bind $w <KeyPress> {puts stdout {%%K=%K %%A=%A}}
```

The %K keyword is replaced with the keysym from the event. The %A is replaced with the printing character that results from the event and any modifiers like Shift. The %% is replaced with a single percent sign. Note that these substitutions occur in spite of the curly braces used for grouping. If the user types a capital Q, there are two KeyPress events, one for the Shift key, and one for the q key. The output is:

```
%K=Shift_R %A={}
%K=Q %A=Q
```

The Shift_R keysym indicates the right-hand shift key was pressed. The %A keyword is replaced with {} when modifier keys are pressed. You can check for this in <KeyPress> bindings to avoid doing anything if only a modifier key is pressed. On Macintosh, there is no event at all when the modifier keys are pressed. The following can be used with a text widget. The double quotes are necessary to force a string comparison:

```
bind $w <KeyPress> {
    if {"%A" != "{}"} {%W insert insert %A}
}
```

Mouse Events

Button events also distinguish between ButtonPress, (or Button), and ButtonRelease. Button can be left off if a detail specifies a button by number. The following are equivalent:

```
<ButtonPress-1>
<Button-1>
<1>
```

Note: The event <1> implies a ButtonPress event, while the event 1 implies a KeyPress event. To avoid confusion, always specify the Key or Button type.

The mouse is tracked by binding to the Enter, Leave, and Motion events. Enter and Leave are triggered when the mouse comes into and exits out of the widget, respectively. A Motion event is generated when the mouse moves within a widget.

The coordinates of the mouse event are represented by the %x and %y keywords in the binding command. The coordinates are widget-relative, with the origin at the upper-left hand corner of a widget's window. The keywords %X and %Y represent the coordinates relative to the screen:

```
bind $w <Enter>  {puts stdout "Entered %W at %x %y"}
```

III. Tk Basics

```
bind $w <Leave>  {puts stdout "Left %W at %x %y"}
bind $w <Motion> {puts stdout "%W %x %y"}
```

A mouse drag event is a `Motion` event that occurs when the user holds down a mouse button. In this case the mouse button is a modifier, which is discussed in more detail on page 375. The binding looks like this:

```
bind $w <B1-Motion> {puts stdout "%W %x %y"}
```

Other Events

The `<Map>` and `<Unmap>` events are generated when a window is opened and closed, or when a widget is packed or unpacked by its geometry manager.

The `<Activate>` and `<Deactivate>` events are generated when an application is activated by the operating system. This applies to Macintosh systems, and it occurs when the user clicks in the application window.

The `<Configure>` event is generated when the window changes size. A canvas that computes its display based on its size can bind a redisplay procedure to the `<Configure>` event, for example. The `<Configure>` event can be caused by interactive resizing. It can also be caused by a `configure` widget command that changes the size of the widget. You should not reconfigure a widget's size while processing a `<Configure>` event to avoid an indefinite sequence of these events.

The `<Destroy>` event is generated when a widget is destroyed. You can intercept requests to delete windows, too. See also the description of the wm command on page 569.

The `<MouseWheel>` event is generated on Windows by the small scrolling wheel built into the Microsoft Mouse. It reports a delta value using the %D keyword. Currently the delta is an integer multiple of 120, where positive values indicate a scroll up, and negative values indicate a scroll down.

Chapter 33 presents some examples that use the `<FocusIn>` and `<FocusOut>` events. The remaining events in Table 26–1 have to do with dark corners of the X protocol, and they are seldom used. More information can be found on these events in the Event Reference section of the *Xlib Reference Manual* (Adrian Nye, O'Reilly & Associates, Inc., 1992).

Bindings on Top-level Windows

Bindings on toplevels are shared by widgets they contain.

Be careful when binding events to top-level windows because their name is used as a binding tag on all the widgets contained in them. For example, the following binding fires when the user destroys the main window, which means the application is about to exit:

```
bind . <Destroy> {puts "goodbye"}
```

Unfortunately, all widgets inside the main window are destroyed as a side effect, and they all share the name of their toplevel widget as a binding tag. So this binding fires when every widget inside the main window is destroyed. Typically you only want to do something one time. The following binding checks the identity of the widget before doing anything:

```
bind . <Destroy> {if {"%W" == "."} {puts "goodbye"}}
```

Modifiers

A modifier indicates that another key or button is being held down at the time of the event. Typical modifiers are the `Shift` and `Control` keys. The mouse buttons can also be used as modifiers. If an event does not specify any modifiers, the presence of a modifier key is ignored by the event dispatcher. However, if there are two possible matching events, the more accurate match will be used. For example, consider these three bindings:

```
bind $w <KeyPress> {puts "key=%A"}
bind $w <Key-c> {puts "just a c"}
bind $w <Control-Key-c> {exit}
```

The last event is more specific than the others. Its binding will be triggered when the user types c with the `Control` key held down. If the user types c with the `Meta` key held down, the second binding will be triggered. The `Meta` key is ignored because it does not match any binding. If the user types something other than a c, the first binding is triggered. If the user presses the `Shift` key, then the keysym that is generated is C, not c, so the last two events do not match.

There are eight possible modifier keys. The `Control`, `Shift`, and `Lock` modifiers are found on nearly all keyboards. The `Meta` and `Alt` modifiers tend to vary from system to system, and they may not be defined at all. They are commonly mapped to be the same as `Mod1` or `Mod2`, and Tk will try to determine how the mappings are set. The Macintosh has a `Command` modifier that corresponds to the clover-leaf or apple key. The remaining modifiers, `Mod3` through `Mod5`, are sometimes mapped to other special keys. In OpenLook environments, for example, the `Paste` function key is also mapped to the `Mod5` modifier.

The button modifiers, `B1` through `B5`, are most commonly used with the `Motion` event to distinguish different mouse dragging operations. For example, `<B1-Motion>` is the event generated when the user drags the mouse with the first mouse button held down.

Double-click warning.

The `Double` and `Triple` events match on repetitions of an event within a short period of time. These are commonly used with mouse events. Be careful: The binding for the regular press event will match on the first press of the `Double`. Then the command bound to the `Double` event will match on the second press. Similarly, a `Double` event will match on the first two presses of a `Triple` event. Verify this by trying out the following bindings:

```
bind . <1> {puts stdout 1}
bind . <Double-1> {puts stdout 2}
bind . <Triple-1> {puts stdout 3}
```

If you click the first mouse button several times quickly, you will see a 1, 2, and then a few 3's output. Your bindings must take into consideration that more than one binding might match a `Double` or `Triple` event. This effect is compatible with an interface that selects an object with the first click, and then operates on the selected object with a `Double` event. In an editor, character, word, and line selection on a single, double, and triple click, respectively, is a good example.[*]

Table 26–2 summarizes the modifiers.

Table 26–2 Event modifiers.

`Control`	The control key.
`Shift`	The shift key.
`Lock`	The caps-lock key.
`Command`	The command key. (Macintosh)
`Meta, M`	Defined to be what ever modifier (`M1` through `M5`) is mapped to the `Meta_L` and `Meta_R` keysyms.
`Alt`	Defined to be the modifier mapped to `Alt_L` and `Alt_R`.
`Mod1, M1`	The first modifier.
`Mod2, M2, Alt`	The second modifier.
`Mod3, M3`	Another modifier.
`Mod4, M4`	Another modifier.
`Mod5, M5`	Another modifier.
`Button1, B1`	The first mouse button (left).
`Button2, B2`	The second mouse button (middle).
`Button3, B3`	The third mouse button (right).
`Button4, B4`	The fourth mouse button.
`Button5, B5`	The fifth mouse button.
`Double`	Matches double-press event.
`Triple`	Matches triple-press event.
`Any`	Matches any combination of modifiers. (Before Tk 4.0)

The UNIX *xmodmap* program returns the current mappings from keys to these modifiers. The first column of its output lists the modifier. The rest of each line identifies the keysym(s) and low-level keycodes that are mapped to each

---

[*] If you really want to disable this, you can experiment with using `after` to postpone processing of one event. The time constant in the bind implementation of `<Double>` is 500 milliseconds. At the single-click event, schedule its action to occur after 600 milliseconds, and verify at that time that the `<Double>` event has not occurred.

modifier. The *xmodmap* program can also be used to change mappings. The following example shows the mappings on my system. Your setup may be different.

Example 26–2 Output from the UNIX *xmodmap* program.

```
xmodmap: up to 3 keys per modifier,
        (keycodes in parentheses):
shift Shift_L (0x6a), Shift_R (0x75)
lock Caps_Lock (0x7e)
control Control_L (0x53)
mod1 Meta_L (0x7f), Meta_R (0x81)
mod2 Mode_switch (0x14)
mod3 Num_Lock (0x69)
mod4 Alt_L (0x1a)
mod5 F13 (0x20), F18 (0x50), F20 (0x68)
```

Event Sequences

The `bind` command accepts a sequence of events in a specification, and most commonly this is a sequence of key events. In the following examples, the `Key` events are abbreviated to just the character detail, and so `abc` is a sequence of three `Key` events:

```
bind . a {puts stdout A}
bind . abc {puts stdout C}
```

With these bindings in effect, both bindings are executed when the user types `abc`. The binding for `a` is executed when `a` is pressed, even though this event is also part of a longer sequence. This is similar to the behavior with `Double` and `Triple` event modifiers. For this reason you must be careful when binding sequences. You can use `break` in the binding for the prefix to ensure that it does not do anything:

```
bindtags $w [list $w Text [winfo toplevel $w] all]
bind $w <Control-x> break
bind $w <Control-x><Control-s> {Save ; break}
bind $w <Control-x><Control-c> {Quit ; break}
```

The `break` ensures that the default `Text` binding that inserts characters does not trigger. This trick is embodied by `BindSequence` in the next example. If a sequence is detected, then a `break` binding is added for the prefix. The procedure also supports the *emacs* convention that `<Meta-x>` is equivalent to `<Escape>x`. This convention arose because `Meta` is not that standard across keyboards. There is no meta key at all on Windows and Macintosh keyboards. The `regexp` command is used to pick out the detail from the `<Meta>` event.

III. Tk Basics

Example 26–3 Emacs-like binding convention for `Meta` and `Escape`.

```
proc BindSequence { w seq cmd } {
    bind $w $seq $cmd
    # Double-bind Meta-key and Escape-key
    if [regexp {<Meta-(.*)>} $seq match letter] {
        bind $w <Escape><$letter> $cmd
    }
    # Make leading keystroke harmless
    if [regexp {(<.+>)<.+>} $seq match prefix] {
        bind $w $prefix break
    }
}
```

The use of `break` and `continue` in bindings is not supported in Tk 3.6 and earlier. This is because only a single binding tag can match an event. To make a prefix of a sequence harmless in Tk 3.6, bind a space to it:

```
bind $w $prefix { }
```

This installs a binding for the widget, which suppresses the class binding in Tk 3.6. The space is different than a null string, `{}`. Binding to a null string deletes the current binding instead of replacing it with a harmless one.

Virtual Events

A virtual event corresponds to one or more event sequences. When any of the event sequences occurs, then the virtual event occurs. The next example shows the default virtual events for each platform:

Example 26–4 Virtual events for cut, copy, and paste.

```
switch $tcl_platform(platform) {
    "unix" {
        event add <<Cut>> <Control-Key-x> <Key-F20>
        event add <<Copy>> <Control-Key-c> <Key-F16>
        event add <<Paste>> <Control-Key-v> <Key-F18>
    }
    "windows" {
        event add <<Cut>> <Control-Key-x> <Shift-Key-Delete>
        event add <<Copy>> <Control-Key-c> <Control-Key-Insert>
        event add <<Paste>> <Control-Key-v> <Shift-Key-Insert>
    }
    "macintosh" {
        event add <<Cut>> <Control-Key-x> <Key-F2>
        event add <<Copy>> <Control-Key-c> <Key-F3>
        event add <<Paste>> <Control-Key-v> <Key-F4>
    }
}
```

You can define more than one physical event that maps to the same virtual event:

```
event add <<Cancel>> <Control-c> <Escape> <Command-.>
```

With this definition any of the physical events will trigger a <<Cancel>>. This would be convenient if the same user commonly used your application on different platforms. However, it is also possible that the physical bindings on different platforms overlap in conflicting ways.

By default, virtual event definitions add to existing definitions for the same virtual event. The previous command could be replaced with these three:

```
event add <<Cancel>> <Control-c>
event add <<Cancel>> <Escape>
event add <<Cancel>> <Command-.>
```

The event command is summarized in Table 26–3.

Table 26–3 The event command.

event add *virt phys1 phy2 ...*	Adds a mapping from one or more physical events to virtual event *virt*.
event delete *virt*	Deletes virtual event *virt*.
event info	Returns the defined virtual events.
event info *virt*	Returns the physical events that map to *virt*.
event generate *win event ?opt val? ...*	Generates *event* for window *win*. The options are listed in Table 26–4.

Event Keywords

Table 26–4 lists the percent keywords and the corresponding option to the event generate command. Remember that keyword substitutions occur throughout the command, regardless of other Tcl quoting conventions. Keep your binding commands short, introducing procedures if needed. For the details about various event fields, consult the *Xlib Reference Manual* (O'Reilly & Associates, Inc.). The string values for the keyword substitutions are listed after a short description of the keyword. If no string values are listed, the keyword has an integer value like a coordinate or a window ID.

Table 26–4 A summary of the event keywords.

%%		Use this to get a single percent sign. All events.
%#	-serial *num*	The serial number for the event. All events.
%a	-above *win*	The above field from the event. Configure event.
%b	-button *num*	Button number. Events: ButtonPress and ButtonRelease.
%c	-count *num*	The count field. Events: Expose and Map.

III. Tk Basics

Table 26–4 A summary of the event keywords. (Continued)

%d	-detail *value*	The detail field. Values: NotifyAncestor, NotifyNon-linearVirtual, NotifyDetailNone, Notify-Pointer, NotifyInferior, NotifyPointerRoot, NotifyNonlinear, or NotifyVirtual. Events: Enter, Leave, FocusIn, and FocusOut.
%f	-focus *boolean*	The focus field (0 or 1). Events: Enter and Leave.
%h	-height *num*	The height field. Events: Configure and Expose.
%k	-keycode *num*	The keycode field. Events: KeyPress and KeyRelease.
%m	-mode *value*	The mode field. Values: NotifyNormal, NotifyGrab, NotifyUngrab, or NotifyWhileGrabbed. Events: Enter, Leave, FocusIn, and FocusOut.
%o	-override *bool-ean*	The override_redirect field. Events: Map, Reparent, and Configure.
%p	-place *value*	The place field. Values: PlaceOnTop, PlaceOnBottom. Circulate event.
%s	-state *value*	The state field. A decimal string for events: ButtonPress, ButtonRelease, Enter, Leave, KeyPress, KeyRelease, and Motion. Values for the Visibility event: VisibilityUnobscured, VisibilityPartiallyObscured, or VisibilityFullyObscured.
%t	-time *num*	The time field. All events.
%v		The value_mask field. Configure event.
%w	-width *num*	The width field. Events: Configure and Expose.
%x	-x *pixel*	The X coordinate, widget relative. Mouse events.
%y	-y *pixel*	The Y coordinate, widget relative. Mouse events.
%A		The printing character from the event, or { }. Events: KeyPress and KeyRelease.
%B	-borderwidth *num*	The border width. Configure event.
%D	-delta value	The delta value. MouseWheel event.
%E	-sendevent *bool*	The send_event field. All events.
%K	-keysym *symbol*	The keysym from the event. Events: KeyPress and KeyRelease.
%N		The keysym as a decimal number. Events: KeyPress and KeyRelease.
%R	-root *win*	The root window ID. All events.
%S	-subwindow *win*	The subwindow ID. All events.
%T		The type field. All events.

Table 26–4 A summary of the event keywords. (Continued)

%W		The Tk pathname of the widget receiving the event. All events.
%X	-rootx *pixel*	The x_root field. Relative to the (virtual) root window. Events: ButtonPress, ButtonRelease, KeyPress, KeyRelease, and Motion.
%Y	-rooty *pixel*	The y_root field. Relative to the (virtual) root window. Events: ButtonPress, ButtonRelease, KeyPress, KeyRelease, and Motion.

III. Tk Basics

Tk Widgets

Part IV describes the Tk widgets. These are the components you use to build up your graphical user interface. Tk widgets are simple to use, so you can rapidly develop your interface. At the same time, they have sophisticated features that you can use to fine-tune your interface in response to user feedback.

Chapter 27 describes buttons and menus. Tk 8.0 adds native look and feel to these widgets, so a single script will look different depending on the platform it is running on.

Associated with the widgets is a resource database that stores settings like colors and fonts. Chapter 28 describes the resource database and generalizes it to store button and menu configurations.

Chapter 29 describes a few simple widgets. The frame and toplevel are containers for other widgets. The label displays a text string. The message formats a long text string onto multiple lines. The scale represents a numeric value. The bell command rings the terminal bell.

Chapter 30 describes scrollbars, which can be attached in a general way to other widgets.

Chapter 31 describes entry widgets that provide one line of editable text.

Chapter 32 describes the listbox widget that displays several lines of text. The lines are manipulated as units.

Chapter 33 describes the general-purpose text widget. It can display multiple fonts and have binding tags on ranges of text.

Chapter 34 describes the canvas widget. The canvas manages objects like lines, boxes, images, arcs, and text labels. You can have binding tags on these objects and classes of objects.

IV. Tk Widgets

## CHAPTER 27

Buttons and Menus

Buttons and menus are the primary way that applications expose functions to users. This chapter describes how to create and manipulate buttons and menus.

A button widget is associated with a Tcl command that invokes an action in the application. The checkbutton and radiobutton widgets affect an application indirectly by controlling a Tcl variable. A menu elaborates on this concept by organizing button-like items into related sets, including cascaded menus. The menubutton widget is a special kind of button that displays a menu when you click on it.

Tk 8.0 provides a cross-platform menu bar facility. The menu bar is really just a menu that is displayed horizontally along the top of your application's main window. On the Macintosh, the menu bar appears at the top of the screen. You define the menu bar the same on all platforms. Tk 8.0 also uses native button and menu widgets on the Windows and Macintosh platforms. This contributes to a native look and feel for your application. In earlier versions, Tk displayed the widgets identically on all platforms.

Associating a command to a button is usually quite simple, as illustrated by the Tk "Hello, World!" example:

```
button .hello -command {puts stdout "Hello, World!"}
```

This chapter describes a few useful techniques for setting up the commands in more general cases. If you use variables inside button commands, you have to understand the scoping rules that apply. This is the first topic of the chapter. Once you get scoping figured out, then the other aspects of buttons and menus are quite straightforward.

IV. Tk Widgets

Button Commands and Scope Issues

Perhaps the trickiest issue with button commands has to do with variable scoping. A button command is executed at the global scope, which is outside of any procedure. If you create a button while inside a procedure, then the button command executes in a different scope later. The commands used in event bindings also execute later at the global scope.

I think of this as the "now" (i.e., button definition) and "later" (i.e., button use) scope problem. For example, you may want to use the values of some variables when you define a button command but use the value of other variables when the button command is used. When these two contexts are mixed, it can be confusing. The next example illustrates the problem. The button's command involves two variables: x and val. The global variable x is needed later, when the button's command executes. The local variable val is needed now, in order to define the command. Example 27–1 shows this awkward mixture of scopes:

Example 27–1 A troublesome button command.

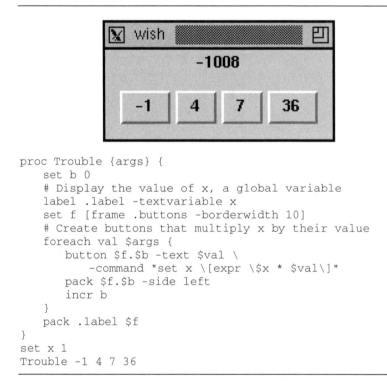

```
proc Trouble {args} {
    set b 0
    # Display the value of x, a global variable
    label .label -textvariable x
    set f [frame .buttons -borderwidth 10]
    # Create buttons that multiply x by their value
    foreach val $args {
        button $f.$b -text $val \
            -command "set x \[expr \$x * $val\]"
        pack $f.$b -side left
        incr b
    }
    pack .label $f
}
set x 1
Trouble -1 4 7 36
```

The example uses a label widget to display the current value of x. The `textvariable` attribute is used so that the label displays the current value of the variable, which is always a global variable. It is not necessary to have a `global` command inside `Trouble` because the value of x is not used there. The button's command is executed later at the global scope.

The definition of the button's command is ugly, though. The value of the loop variable `val` is needed when the button is defined, but the rest of the substitutions need to be deferred until later. The variable substitution of `$x` and the command substitution of `expr` are suppressed by quoting with backslashes:

```
set x \[expr \$x * $val\]
```

In contrast, the following command assigns a constant expression to x each time the button is clicked, and it depends on the current value of x, which is not defined the first time through the loop. Clearly, this is incorrect:

```
button $f.$b -text $val \
    -command "set x [expr $x * $val]"
```

Another incorrect approach is to quote the whole command with braces. This defers too much, preventing the value of `val` from being used at the correct time.

Use procedures for button commands.

The general technique for dealing with these sorts of scoping problems is to introduce Tcl procedures for use as the button commands. Example 27–2 introduces a little procedure to encapsulate the expression:

Example 27–2 Fixing the troublesome situation.

```
proc LessTrouble { args } {
    set b 0
    label .label -textvariable x
    set f [frame .buttons -borderwidth 10]
    foreach val $args {
        button $f.$b -text $val \
            -command "UpdateX $val"
        pack $f.$b -side left
        incr b
    }
    pack .label $f
}
proc UpdateX { val } {
    global x
    set x [expr $x * $val]
}
set x 1
LessTrouble -1 4 7 36
```

It may seem just like extra work to introduce the helper procedure, `UpdateX`. However, it makes the code clearer in two ways. First, you do not have to struggle with backslashes to get the button command defined correctly. Second, the code is much clearer about the function of the button. Its job is to update the global variable x.

You can generalize `UpdateX` to work on any variable by passing the name of the variable to update. Now it becomes much like the `incr` command:

```
button $f.$b -text $val -command "Update x $val"
```

The definition of Update uses upvar, which is explained on page 85, to manipulate the named variable in the global scope:

```
proc Update {varname val} {
    upvar #0 $varname x
    set x [expr $x * $val]
}
```

Double quotes are used in the button command to allow $val to be substituted. Whenever you use quotes like this, you have to be aware of the possible values for the substitutions. If you are not careful, the command you create may not be parsed correctly. The safest way to generate the command is with list:

```
button $f.$b -text $val -command [list UpdateX $val]
```

Using list ensures that the command is a list of two elements, UpdateX and the value of val. This is important because UpdateX takes only a single argument. If val contained white space, then the resulting command would be parsed into more words than you expected. Of course, in this case we plan to always call LessTrouble with an integer value, which does not contain white space.

Example 27–3 provides a more straightforward application of procedures for button commands. In this case the advantage of the procedure MaxLine-Length is that it creates a scope for the local variables used during the button action. This ensures that the local variables do not accidentally conflict with global variables used elsewhere in the program. There is also the standard advantage of a procedure, which is that you may find another use for the action in another part of your program.

Example 27–3 A button associated with a Tcl procedure.

```
proc MaxLineLength { file } {
    set max 0
    if [catch {open $file} in] {
        return $in
    }
    foreach line [split [read $in] \n] {
        set len [string length $line]
```

```
        if {$len > $max} {
            set max $len
        }
    }
    return "Longest line is $max characters"
}
# Create an entry to accept the file name,
# a label to display the result
# and a button to invoke the action
. config -borderwidth 10
entry .e -width 30 -bg white -relief sunken
button .doit -text "Max Line Length" \
    -command {.label config -text [MaxLineLength [.e get]]}
label .label -text "Enter file name"
pack .e .doit .label -side top -pady 5
```

The example is centered around the MaxLineLength procedure. This opens a file and loops over the lines finding the longest one. The file open is protected with catch in case the user enters a bogus file name. In that case, the procedure returns the error message from open. Otherwise, the procedure returns a message about the longest line in the file. The local variables in, max, and len are hidden inside the scope of the procedure.

The user interface has three widgets: an entry for user input, the button, and a label to display the result. These are packed into a vertical stack, and the main window is given a border. Obviously, this simple interface can be improved in several ways. There is no Quit button, for example.

All the action happens in the button command:

```
.label config -text [MaxLineLength [.e get]]
```

Braces are used when defining the button command so that the command substitutions all happen when the button is clicked. The value of the entry widget is obtained with .e get. This value is passed into MaxLineLength, and the result is configured as the text for the label. This command is still a little complex for a button command. For example, suppose you wanted to invoke the same command when the user pressed <Return> in the entry. You would end up repeating this command in the entry binding. It might be better to introduce a one-line procedure to capture this action so that it is easy to bind the action to more than one user action. Here is how that might look:

```
proc Doit {} {
    .label config -text [MaxLineLength [.e get]]
}
button .doit -text "Max Line Length" -command Doit
bind .e <Return> Doit
```

Chapter 26 describes the bind command in detail, Chapter 29 describes the label widget, and Chapter 32 describes the entry widget.

IV. Tk Widgets

Buttons Associated with Tcl Variables

The checkbutton and radiobutton widgets are associated with a global Tcl variable. When one of these buttons is clicked, a value is assigned to the Tcl variable. In addition, if the variable is assigned a value elsewhere in the program, the appearance of the checkbutton or radiobutton is updated to reflect the new value. A set of radiobuttons all share the same global variable. The set represents a choice among mutually exclusive options. In contrast, each checkbutton has its own global variable.

The ShowChoices example uses a set of radiobuttons to display a set of mutually exclusive choices in a user interface. The ShowBooleans example uses checkbutton widgets:

Example 27–4 Radiobuttons and checkbuttons.

```
proc ShowChoices { parent varname args } {
    set f [frame $parent.choices -borderwidth 5]
    set b 0
    foreach item $args {
        radiobutton $f.$b -variable $varname \
            -text $item -value $item
        pack $f.$b -side left
        incr b
    }
    pack $f -side top
}
proc ShowBooleans { parent args } {
    set f [frame $parent.booleans -borderwidth 5]
    set b 0
    foreach item $args {
        checkbutton $f.$b -text $item -variable $item
        pack $f.$b -side left
        incr b
    }
    pack $f -side top
}
set choice kiwi
ShowChoices {} choice apple orange peach kiwi strawberry
set Bold 1 ; set Italic 1
ShowBooleans {} Bold Italic Underline
```

The ShowChoices procedure takes as arguments the parent frame, the name of a variable, and a set of possible values for that variable. If the parent frame is null, {}, then the interface is packed into the main window. ShowChoices creates a radiobutton for each value, and it puts the value into the text of the button. It also has to specify the value to assign to the variable when the button is clicked because the default value associated with a radiobutton is the empty string.

The ShowBooleans procedure is similar to ShowChoices. It takes a set of variable names as arguments, and it creates a checkbutton for each variable. The default values for the variable associated with a checkbutton are zero and one, which is fine for this example. If you need particular values, you can specify them with the -onvalue and -offvalue options.

Radiobuttons and checkbuttons can have commands associated with them, just like ordinary buttons. The command is invoked after the associated Tcl variable has been updated. Remember that the Tcl variable associated with the button is defined in the global scope. For example, you could log the changes to variables as shown in the next example.

Example 27–5 A command on a radiobutton or checkbutton.

```
proc PrintByName { varname } {
    upvar #0 $varname var
    puts stdout "$varname = $var"
}
checkbutton $f.$b -text $item -variable $item \
    -command [list PrintByName $item]
radiobutton $f.$b -variable $varname \
    -text $item -value $item \
    -command [list PrintByName $varname]
```

Button Attributes

Table 27–1 lists the attributes for the button, checkbutton, menubutton, and radiobutton widgets. Unless otherwise indicated, the attributes apply to all of these widget types. Chapters 37, 38, and 39 discuss many of these attributes in more detail. Some attributes are ignored on the Windows and Macintosh platforms because they are not supported by the native button widgets.

The table uses the resource name for the attributes, which has capitals at internal word boundaries. In Tcl commands, the attributes are specified with a dash and they are all lowercase. Compare:

```
option add *Menubutton.activeBackground: red
.mb configure -activebackground red
```

The first command defines a resource database entry that covers all menubuttons and gives them a red active background. This only affects menubuttons created after the database entry is added. The second command changes an existing menubutton (`.mb`) to have a red active background. Note the difference in capitalization of `background` in the two commands. The resource database is introduced on page 311, and Chapter 28 explains how to use the resource database in more detail.

Table 27–1 Resource names of attributes for all button widgets.

`activeBackground`	Background color when the mouse is over the button.
`activeForeground`	Text color when the mouse is over the button.
`anchor`	Anchor point for positioning the text.
`background`	The normal background color.
`bitmap`	A bitmap to display instead of text.
`borderWidth`	Width of the border around the button.
`command`	Tcl command to invoke when button is clicked.
`cursor`	Cursor to display when mouse is over the widget.
`default`	`active` displays as a default button. `normal` and `disabled` display as normal button. See page 715 (Tk 8.0).
`direction`	`up`, `down`, `left`, `right`, `active`. Offset direction for posting menus. `menubutton`. (Tk 8.0).
`disabledForeground`	Foreground (text) color when button is disabled.
`font`	Font for the text.
`foreground`	Foreground (text) color. (Also `fg`).
`height`	Height, in lines for text, or screen units for images.
`highlightBack-` `ground`	Focus highlight color when widget does not have focus.
`highlightColor`	Focus highlight color when widget has focus.
`highlightThickness`	Width of highlight border.
`image`	Image to display instead of text or bitmap.
`indicatorOn`	Boolean that controls if the indicator is displayed: `checkbutton`, `menubutton`, or `radiobutton`.
`justify`	Text justification: `center`, `left`, or `right`.
`menu`	Menu posted when `menubutton` is clicked.
`offValue`	Value for Tcl variable when `checkbutton` is not selected.
`onValue`	Value for Tcl variable when `checkbutton` is selected.
`padX`	Extra space to the left and right of the button text.
`padY`	Extra space above and below the button text.

Table 27-1 Resource names of attributes for all button widgets. (Continued)

relief	flat, sunken, raised, groove, solid or ridge.
selectColor	Color for selector. checkbutton or radiobutton.
selectImage	Alternate graphic image for selector: checkbutton or radiobutton.
state	Enabled (normal) or deactivated (disabled).
takeFocus	Control focus changes from keyboard traversal.
text	Text to display in the button.
textVariable	Tcl variable that has the value of the text.
underline	Index of text character to underline.
value	Value for Tcl variable when radiobutton is selected.
variable	Tcl variable associated with the button: checkbutton or radiobutton.
width	Width in characters for text, or screen units for image.
wrapLength	Maximum character length before text is wrapped, *in screen units.*

Button Operations

Table 27-2 summarizes the operations on button widgets. In the table, $w is a button, checkbutton, radiobutton, or menubutton, except when noted. For the most part, these operations are used by the script libraries that implement the bindings for buttons. The cget and configure operations are the most commonly used by applications.

Table 27-2 Button operations.

$w cget *option*	Returns the value of the specified attribute.
$w configure ?*option*? ?*value*? ...	Queries or manipulates the configuration information for the widget.
$w deselect	Deselects the radiobutton or checkbutton. Set the radiobutton variable to the null string. Set the checkbutton variable to the off value.
$w flash	Redisplays the button several times in alternate colors.
$w invoke	Invokes the command associated with the button.
$w select	Selects the radiobutton or checkbutton, setting the associated variable appropriately.

Menus and Menubuttons

A menu presents a set of button-like *menu entries* to users. A menu entry is not a full fledged Tk widget. Instead, you create a menu widget and then add entries to the menu as shown in the following examples. There are several kinds of menu entries:

- Command entries are like buttons.
- Check entries are like checkbuttons.
- Radio entries are like radiobuttons.
- Separator entries are used to visually set apart entries.
- Cascade entries are used to post submenus.
- Tear-off entries are used to detach a menu from its menu button so that it becomes a new top-level window.

A menubutton is a special kind of button that posts (i.e., displays) a menu when you press it. If you click on a menubutton, then the menu is posted and remains posted until you click on a menu entry to select it, or click outside the menu to dismiss it. If you press and hold the menubutton, then the menu is unposted when you release the mouse. If you release the mouse over the menu, it selects the menu entry that was under the mouse.

You can have a command associated with a menubutton, too. The command is invoked *before* the menu is posted, which means you can compute the menu contents when the user presses the menubutton.

Our first menu example creates a sampler of the different entry types:

Example 27–6 A menu sampler.

```
menubutton .mb -text Sampler -menu .mb.menu
pack .mb -padx 10 -pady 10
set m [menu .mb.menu -tearoff 1]
```

```
$m add command -label Hello! -command {puts "Hello, World!"}
$m add check -label Boolean -variable foo \
    -command {puts "foo = $foo"}
$m add separator
$m add cascade -label Fruit -menu $m.sub1
set m2 [menu $m.sub1 -tearoff 0]
$m2 add radio -label apple -variable fruit -value apple
$m2 add radio -label orange -variable fruit -value orange
$m2 add radio -label kiwi -variable fruit -value kiwi
```

The example creates a menubutton and two menus. The main menu .mb.menu is a child of the menubutton .mb. This relationship is necessary so that the menu displays correctly when the menubutton is selected. Similarly, the cascaded submenu .mb.menu.sub1 is a child of the main menu. The first menu entry is represented by the dashed line. This is a tear-off entry that, when selected, makes a copy of the menu in a new top-level window. This is useful if the menu operations are invoked frequently. The -tearoff 0 argument is used when creating the submenu to eliminate its tear-off entry.

The command, radio, and check entries are similar to the corresponding button types. The configuration options for menu entries are similar to those for buttons. The main difference is that the text string in the menu entry is defined with the -label option, not -text. Table 27–6 gives the complete set of options for menu entries.

The cascade menu entry is associated with another menu. It is distinguished by the small right arrow in the entry. When you select the entry, the submenu is posted. It is possible to have several levels of cascaded menus. There is no limit to the number of levels, except that your users will complain if you nest too many menus.

A Menu Bar

You can create a menu bar manually by packing several menubuttons into a frame. The default bindings on menubuttons are such that you can drag your mouse over the menu bar and the different menus will display as you drag over their menubutton.

Tk 8.0 lets you create a menu bar as a horizontal menu that is associated with a top-level window. On Windows and UNIX the menu is displayed along the top of the window. On Macintosh this menu replaces the main menu along the top of the screen when the window is activated. The menu bar menu should have all cascade entries so that when you select an entry, another menu is displayed. This is illustrated in Example 27–7. It defines variables that store the names of the menu widgets:

```
set $m [menu .menubar.m$m]
```

This creates a variable named File, Edit, and Help that store the names of the menu widgets. This trick is generalized on page 400 in a package that hides the menu widget names.

Example 27–7 A menu bar in Tk 8.0.

```
menu .menubar
# attach it to the main window
. config -menu .menubar
# Create more cascade menus
foreach m {File Edit Help} {
    set $m [menu .menubar.m$m]
    .menubar add cascade -label $m -menu .menubar.m$m
}
$File add command -label Quit -command exit
# add more menu items...
```

System Menus

The Tk 8.0 menu bar implementation can add entries to the Windows system menu, the Macintosh Apple menu, and the Help menu on all platforms. This works by recognizing special names. For example, if the menu bar is .menubar, then the special names are .menubar.system, .menubar.apple, and .menubar.help. The Help menu is right justified on all platforms. The Apple menu is normally used by applications for their About... entry. The entries you add to the Apple menu are added to the top of the menu. The System menu appears in the Windows title bar and has entries such as Close and Minimize.

Pop-Up Menus

A pop-up menu is not associated with a menubutton. Instead, it is posted in response to a keystroke or other event in the application. The tk_popup command posts a pop-up menu:

```
tk_popup menu x y ?entry?
```

The last argument specifies the entry to activate when the menu is posted. It is an optional parameter that defaults to 1, which avoids the tear-off entry in position zero. The menu is posted at the specified X and Y coordinates in its parent widget.

Option Menus

An option menu represents a choice with a set of radio entries, and it displays the current choice in the text of the menubutton. The tk_optionMenu command creates a menubutton and a menu full of radio entries:

```
tk_optionMenu w varname firstValue ?value value ...?
```

The first argument is the pathname of the menubutton to create. The second is the variable name. The third is the initial value for the variable, and the rest are the other choices for the value. The menubutton displays the current choice and a small symbol, the indicator, to indicate it is an option menu.

Multicolumn Palette Menus

Tk 8.0 adds a -columnbreak menu entry attribute that puts the entry at the top of a new column. This is most useful when the menu consists of several images that are arranged as a palette. Set the entry's image with the -image attribute. You can create checkbutton and radiobutton entries that have images and no indicator by using the -hidemargin attribute. In this case, a selected entry is indicated by drawing a solid rectangle around it.

Keyboard Traversal

The default bindings for menus allow for keyboard selection of menu entries. The selection process is started by pressing <Alt-x>, where x is the distinguishing letter for a menubutton. The underline attribute of a menubutton is used to highlight the appropriate letter. The underline value is a number that specifies a character position, and the count starts at zero. For example, a File menu with a highlighted F is created like this:

```
menubutton .menubar.file -text File -underline 0 \
    -menu .menubar.file.m
```

When the user types <Alt-f> over the main window, the menu is posted. The case of the highlighted letter is not important.

After a menu is posted, the arrow keys change the selected entry. The <Up> and <Down> keys move within a menu, and the <Left> and <Right> keys move between adjacent menus. The bindings assume that you create your menus from left to right.

If any of the menu entries have a letter highlighted with the -underline option, typing that letter invokes that menu entry. For example, an Export entry that is invoked by typing x can be created like this:

```
.menubar.file.m add command -label Export -underline 1 \
    -command File_Export
```

The <space> and <Return> keys invoke the menu entry that is currently selected. The <Escape> key aborts the menu selection and removes the menu.

Manipulating Menus and Menu Entries

There are a number of operations that apply to menu entries. We have already introduced the add operation. The entryconfigure operation is similar to the configure operation for widgets. It accepts the same attribute-value pairs used when the menu entry was added. The delete operation removes a range of menu entries. The rest of the operations are used by the library scripts that implement the standard bindings for menus.

A menu entry is referred to by an *index*. The index can be numerical, counting from zero, or symbolic. Table 27–3 summarizes the index formats. One of the most useful indices is a pattern that matches the label in the menu entry. The

pattern matching is done with the rules of `string match`. Using a pattern eliminates the need to keep track of the numerical indices.

Table 27–3 Menu entry index keywords

`index`	A numerical index counting from zero.
`active`	The activated entry, either because it is under the mouse or has been activated by keyboard traversal.
`end`	The last menu entry.
`last`	The same as `end`.
`none`	No entry at all.
`@ycoord`	The entry under the given Y coordinate. Use `@%y` in bindings.
`pattern`	A `string match` pattern to match the label of a menu entry.

Table 27–4 summarizes the complete set of menu operations. In the table, `$w` is a
menu widget.

Table 27–4 Menu operations.

`$w activate index`	Highlights the specified entry.
`$w add type ?option value? ...`	Adds a new menu entry of the specified type with the given values for various attributes.
`$w cget option`	Returns the value for the configuration `option`.
`$w clone`	Makes a linked copy of the menu. This is used to implement tear-offs and menu bars.
`$w configure ?option? ?value? ...`	Returns the configuration information for the menu.
`$w delete i1 ?i2?`	Deletes the menu entries from index `i1` to `i2`.
`$w entrycget index option`	Returns the value of `option` for the specified entry.
`$w entryconfigure index ?option? ?value? ...`	Queries or modifies the configuration information for the specified menu entry.
`$w index index`	Returns the numerical value of `index`.
`$w insert type index ?option value? ...`	Like `add`, but inserts the new entry after the specified `index`.
`$w invoke index`	Invokes the command associated with the entry.
`$w post x y`	Displays the menu at the specified coordinates.
`$w postcascade index`	Displays the cascade menu from entry `index`.
`$w type index`	Returns the type of the entry at `index`.

Table 27–4 Menu operations. (Continued)

| `$w unpost` | Unmaps the menu. |
| `$w yposition` *index* | Returns the Y coordinate of the top of the entry. |

Menu Attributes

A menu has a few global attributes, and then each menu entry has many button-like attributes that describe its appearance and behavior. Table 27–5 specifies the attributes that apply globally to the menu, unless overridden by a per-entry attribute. The table uses the X resource names, which may have a capital at interior word boundaries. In Tcl commands, use all lowercase and a leading dash.

Table 27–5 Menu attribute resource names.

`activeBackground`	Background color when the mouse is over a menu entry.
`activeForeground`	Text color when the mouse is over a menu entry.
`activeBorderWidth`	Width of the raised border around active entries.
`background`	The normal background color for menu entries.
`borderWidth`	Width of the border around all the menu entries.
`cursor`	Cursor to display when mouse is over the menu.
`disabledForeground`	Foreground (text) color when menu entries are disabled.
`font`	Default font for the text.
`foreground`	Foreground color. (Also `fg`).
`postCommand`	Tcl command to run just before the menu is posted.
`selectColor`	Color for selector in check and radio type entries.
`takeFocus`	Control focus changes from keyboard traversal.
`tearOff`	True if menu should contain a tear-off entry.
`tearOffCommand`	Command to execute when menu is torn off. Two arguments are added: the original menu and the new tear-off.
`type`	(Read-only) `normal`, `menubar`, or `tearoff`. (Tk 8.0).

Table 27–6 describes the attributes for menu entries, as you would use them in a Tcl command (i.e., all lowercase with a leading dash.) The attributes for menu entries are not supported directly by the resource database. However, Example 28–6 on page 411 describes how you can use the resource database for menu entries.

IV. Tk Widgets

Table 27–6 Attributes for menu entries.

-activebackground	Background color when the mouse is over the entry.
-activeforeground	Foreground (text) color with mouse is over the entry.
-accelerator	Text to display as a reminder about keystroke binding.
-background	The normal background color.
-bitmap	A bitmap to display instead of text.
-columnbreak	Puts the entry at the start of a new column. (Tk 8.0).
-command	Tcl command to invoke when entry is invoked.
-font	Default font for the text.
-foreground	Foreground color. (Also fg).
-hidemargin	Suppresses the margin reserved for button indicators. (Tk 8.0).
-image	Image to display instead of text or bitmap.
-label	Text to display in the menu entry.
-justify	Text justification: center, left, or right.
-menu	Menu posted when cascade entry is invoked.
-offvalue	Variable value when check entry is not selected.
-onvalue	Value for Tcl variable when check entry is selected.
-selectcolor	Color for selector: check and radio entries.
-state	The state: normal, active, or disabled
-underline	Index of text character to underline.
-value	Value for Tcl variable when radiobutton entry is selected.
-variable	Tcl variable associated with the check or radio entry.

A Menu by Name Package

If your application supports extensible or user-defined menus, then it can be tedious to expose all the details of the Tk menus. The examples in this section create a little package that lets users refer to menus and entries by name. In addition, the package keeps keystroke accelerators for menus consistent with bindings.

The Menu_Setup procedure initializes the package. It creates a frame to hold the set of menu buttons, and it initializes some state variables: the frame for the menubuttons and a counter used to generate widget pathnames. All the global state for the package is kept in the array called menu.

The Menu procedure creates a menubutton and a menu. It records the association between the text label of the menubutton and the menu that was created for it. This mapping is used throughout the rest of the package so that the client of the package can refer to the menu by its label (e.g., File) as opposed to the internal Tk pathname, (e.g., .top.menubar.file.menu).

Example 27–8 A simple menu by name package.

```
proc Menu_Setup { menubar } {
    global menu
    frame $menubar
    pack $menubar -side top -fill x
    set menu(menubar) $menubar
    set menu(uid) 0
}
proc Menu { label } {
    global menu
    if [info exists menu(menu,$label)] {
        error "Menu $label already defined"
    }
    # Create the menubutton and its menu
    set name $menu(menubar).mb$menu(uid)
    set menuName $name.menu
    incr menu(uid)
    set mb [menubutton $name -text $label -menu $menuName]
    pack $mb -side left
    menu $menuName -tearoff 1
    # Remember the name to menu mapping
    set menu(menu,$label) $menuName
}
```

These procedures are repeated in Example 27–9, except that they use the Tk 8.0 menu bar mechanism. The rest of the procedures in the package are the same with either version of menu bars.

Example 27–9 Using the Tk 8.0 menu bar facility.

```
proc Menu_Setup { menubar } {
    global menu
    menu $menubar
    # Associated menu with its main window
    set top [winfo parent $menubar]
    $top config -menu $menubar
    set menu(menubar) $menubar
    set menu(uid) 0
}
proc Menu { label } {
    global menu
    if [info exists menu(menu,$label)] {
        error "Menu $label already defined"
    }
    # Create the cascade menu
    set menuName $menu(menubar).mb$menu(uid)
```

IV. Tk Widgets

```
    incr menu(uid)
    menu $menuName -tearoff 1
    $menu(menubar) add cascade -label $label -menu $menuName
    # Remember the name to menu mapping
    set menu(menu,$label) $menuName
}
```

Once the menu is set up, the `menu` array is used to map from a menu name, like `File`, to the Tk widget name such as `.menubar.mb3`. Even though this can be done with a couple of lines of Tcl code, the mapping is put inside the `MenuGet` procedure to hide the implementation. `MenuGet` uses `return -code error` if the menu name is unknown, which changes the error reporting slightly as shown in Example 6–19 on page 80. If the user specifies a bogus menu name, the undefined variable error is caught and a more informative error is raised instead. `MenuGet` is private to the package, so it does not have an underscore in its name.

Example 27–10 `MenuGet` maps from name to menu.

```
proc MenuGet {menuName} {
    global menu
    if [catch {set menu(menu,$menuName)} m] {
        return -code error "No such menu: $menuName"
    }
    return $m
}
```

The procedures `Menu_Command`, `Menu_Check`, `Menu_Radio`, and `Menu_Separator` are simple wrappers around the basic menu commands. They use `MenuGet` to map from the menu label to the Tk widget name.

Example 27–11 Adding menu entries.

```
proc Menu_Command { menuName label command } {
    set m [MenuGet $menuName]
    $m add command -label $label -command $command
}

proc Menu_Check { menuName label var { command {} } } {
    set m [MenuGet $menuName]
    $m add check -label $label -command $command \
        -variable $var
}

proc Menu_Radio { menuName label var {val {}} {command {}} }
{
    set m [MenuGet $menuName]
    if {[string length $val] == 0} {
        set val $label
    }
    $m add radio -label $label -command $command \
        -value $val -variable $var
```

```
}

proc Menu_Separator { menuName } {
    [MenuGet $menuName] add separator
}
```

Creating a cascaded menu also requires saving the mapping between the label in the cascade entry and the Tk pathname for the submenu. This package imposes a restriction that different menus, including submenus, cannot have the same label.

Example 27–12 A wrapper for cascade entries.

```
proc Menu_Cascade { menuName label } {
    global menu
    set m [MenuGet $menuName]
    if [info exists menu(menu,$label)] {
        error "Menu $label already defined"
    }
    set sub $m.sub$menu(uid)
    incr menu(uid)
    menu $sub -tearoff 0
    $m add cascade -label $label -menu $sub
    set menu(menu,$label) $sub
}
```

Creating the sampler menu with this package looks like this:

Example 27–13 Using the menu by name package.

```
Menu_Setup .menubar
Menu Sampler
Menu_Command Sampler Hello! {puts "Hello, World!"}
Menu_Check Sampler Boolean foo {puts "foo = $foo"}
Menu_Separator Sampler
Menu_Cascade Sampler Fruit
Menu_Radio Fruit apple fruit
Menu_Radio Fruit orange fruit
Menu_Radio Fruit kiwi fruit
```

Menu Accelerators

The final touch on the menu package is to support accelerators in a consistent way. A menu entry can display another column of information that is assumed to be a keystroke identifier to remind users of a binding that also invokes the menu entry. However, there is no guarantee that this string is correct, or that if the user changes the binding that the menu will be updated. Example 27–14 shows the `Menu_Bind` procedure that takes care of this.

Example 27–14 Keeping the accelerator display up to date.

```
proc Menu_Bind { what sequence menuName label } {
    global menu
    set m [MenuGet $menuName]
    if [catch {$m index $label} index] {
        error "$label not in menu $menuName"
    }
    set command [$m entrycget $index -command]
    bind $what $sequence $command
    $m entryconfigure $index -accelerator $sequence
}
```

The Menu_Bind command uses the index operation to find out what menu entry has the given label. It gets the command for that entry with entrycget and uses this command in a binding. It updates the display of the accelerator using the entryconfigure operation. This approach has the advantage of keeping the keystroke command consistent with the menu command, as well as updating the display. To try Menu_Bind, add an empty frame to the sampler example, and bind a keystroke to it and one of the menu commands, like this:

```
frame .body -width 100 -height 50
pack .body ; focus .body
Menu_Bind .body <space> Sampler Hello!
```

## CHAPTER 28

The Resource Database

This chapter describes the use of the resource database, and how users can define buttons and menus via resource specifications. This chapter describes the `option` command.

Tk supports a resource database that holds specifications of widget attributes such as fonts and colors. You can control all attributes of the Tk widgets through the resource database. It can also be used as a more general database of application-specific parameter settings.

Because a Tk application can use Tcl for customization, it might not seem necessary to use the resource database. The resource database is, however, a useful tool for your Tk application. A developer can make global changes with just a few database entries. In addition, it lets users and site administrators customize applications without modifying the code.

An Introduction to Resources

When a Tk widget is created, its attributes are set by one of three sources. It is important to note that Tcl command specifications have priority over resource database specifications:

- The most evident source of attributes are the options in Tcl commands, such as the `-text quit` attribute specification for a button.
- If an attribute is not specified on the command line, then the resource database is queried as described later.
- If there is nothing in the resource database, then a hard-coded value from the widget implementation is used.

The resource database consists of a set of keys and values. Unlike many other databases, however, the keys are patterns that are matched against the names of widgets and attributes. This makes it possible to specify attribute values for a large number of widgets with just a few database entries. In addition, the resource database can be shared by many applications, so users and administrators can define common attributes for their whole set of applications.

The resource database is maintained in main memory by the Tk toolkit. On UNIX the database is initialized from the RESOURCE_MANAGER property on the root window, or the .Xdefaults file in your home directory. On Windows and Macintosh, there are a few resources added by the tk.tcl library file. Additional files can be explicitly loaded with the option readfile command, and individual database entries are added with the option add Tcl command.

The initialization of the database is different from the Xt toolkit, which loads specifications from as many as five different files to allow per-user, per-site, per-application, per-machine, and per-user-per-application specifications. You can achieve the same effect in Tk, but you must do it yourself. Example 42–1 on page 582 gives a partial solution.

Resource Patterns

The pattern language for the keys is related to the naming convention for Tk widgets. Recall that a widget name reflects its position in the hierarchy of windows. You can think of the resource names as extending the hierarchy one more level at the bottom to account for all the attributes of each individual widget. There is also a new level of the hierarchy at the top to specify the application by name. For example, the database could contain an entry like the following in order to define a font for the quit button in a frame called .buttons:

```
Tk.buttons.quit.font: fixed
```

The leading Tk. matches the default class name for Tcl/Tk applications. You could also specify a more specific application name, such as exmh, or an asterisk to match any application:

```
*buttons.quit.font: fixed
```

Resource keys can also specify *classes* of widgets and attributes as opposed to individual instances. The quit button, for example, is an instance of the Button class. Class names for widgets are the same as the Tcl command used to create them, except for a leading capital letter. A class-oriented specification that would set the font for all buttons in the .buttons frame would be:

```
Tk.buttons.Button.font: fixed
```

Patterns let you replace one or more components of the resource name with an asterisk (*). For example, to set the font for all the widgets packed into the .buttons frame, you can use the resource name *buttons*font, or you can specify the font for all buttons with the pattern *Button.font. In these examples, we have replaced the leading Tk. with an asterisk as well. It is the ability to collapse several layers of the hierarchical name with a single asterisk that makes it easy to specify attributes for many widgets with just a few database entries.

The tables in this book list attributes by their resource name. The resource names use a capital letter at the internal word boundaries. For example, if the command line switch is `-offvalue`, then the corresponding resource name is `offValue`. There are also class names for attributes, which are distinguished with a leading capital (e.g., `OffValue`).

Warning: Order is Important!

The matching between a widget name and the patterns in the database can be ambiguous. It is possible that multiple patterns can match the same widget. The way this is resolved in Tk is by the ordering of database entries, with later entries taking precedence. (This is different from the Xt toolkit, in which longer matching patterns have precedence, and instance specifications have priority over class specifications.) Suppose the database contained just two entries, in this order:

```
*Text*foreground: blue
*foreground: red
```

Despite the more specific `*Text*foreground` entry, all widgets will have a red foreground, even `text` widgets. For this reason you should list your most general patterns early in your resource files and give the more specific patterns later.

Tk also supports different priorities among resources, as described in the next section. The ordering precedence described here applies to all resources with the same priority.

Loading Option Database Files

The `option` command manipulates the resource database. The first form of the command loads a file containing database entries:

```
option readfile filename ?priority?
```

The *priority* distinguishes different sources of resource information and gives them different priorities. Priority levels are numeric, from 0 to 100. However, symbolic names are defined for standard priorities. From lowest to highest, the standard priorities are `widgetDefault` (20), `startupFile` (40), `userDefault` (60), and `interactive` (80). These names can be abbreviated. The default priority is `interactive`.

Example 28–1 Reading an option database file.

```
if [file exists $appdefaults] {
    if [catch {option readfile $appdefaults startup} err] {
        puts stderr "error in $appdefaults: $err"
    }
}
```

The format of the entries in the file is:

```
key: value
```

The key has the pattern format previously described. The value can be anything, and there is no need to group multiword values with any quoting characters. In fact, quotes will be picked up as part of the value.

Comment lines are introduced by the exclamation mark (!).

Example 28–2 A file containing resource specifications.

```
!
! Grey color set
! These values match those used by the Tk widgets on UNIX
!
*background:          #d9d9d9
*foreground:          black
*activeBackground:    #ececec
*activeForeground:    black
*selectColor:         #b03060
*selectBackground:    #c3c3c3
*troughColor:         #c3c3c3
*disabledforeground:#a3a3a3
```

The example resource file specifies the color scheme for the Tk widget set on UNIX that is based on a family of gray levels. Color highlighting shows up well against this backdrop. These colors are applied generically to all the widgets. The hexadecimal values for the colors specify two digits (eight bits) each for red, green, and blue. Chapter 38 describes the use of color in detail.

Adding Individual Database Entries

You can enter individual database entries with the `option add` Tcl command. This is appropriate to handle special cases, or if you do not want to manage a separate per application resource specification file. The command syntax is:

```
option add pattern value ?priority?
```

The *priority* is the same as that used with `option readfile`. The *pattern* and *value* are the same as in the file entries, except that the key does not have a trailing colon when specified in an `option add` command. If *value* contains spaces or special characters, you will need to group it like any other argument to a Tcl command. Some of the specifications from the last example could be added as follows:

```
option add *foreground black
option add *selectBackground #bfdfff
```

You can clear the option database:

```
option clear
```

However, on UNIX the database will be initialized from your `~/.Xdefaults` file, or the `RESOURCE_MANAGER` property on the root window, the next time the database is accessed.

Accessing the Database

Often, it is sufficient just to set up the database and let the widget implementations use the values. However, it is also possible to record application-specific information in the database. To fetch a resource value, use `option get`:

```
option get window name class
```

The *window* is a Tk widget pathname. The *name* is a resource name. In this case, it is not a pattern or a full name. Instead, it is the resource name as specified in the tables in this book. Similarly, the *class* is a simple class name. It is possible to specify a null name or class. If there is no matching database entry, `option get` returns the empty string.

It is not possible to enumerate the database, nor can you detect the difference between a value that is the empty string and the absence of a value. You can work around this by introducing well-known resource names that list other resources. This trick is used in the next section.

User-Defined Buttons

Suppose you want users to be able to define a set of their own buttons for frequently executed commands. Or perhaps users can augment the application with their own Tcl code. The following scheme, which is based on an idea from John LoVerso, lets them define buttons to invoke their own code or their favorite commands.

The application creates a special frame to hold the user-defined buttons and places it appropriately. Assume the frame is created like this:

```
frame .user -class User
```

The class specification for the frame means that we can name resources for the widgets inside the frame relative to *User. Users specify the buttons that go in the frame via a personal file containing resource specifications.

The first problem is that there is no means to enumerate the database, so we must create a resource that lists the names of the user-defined buttons. We use the name `buttonlist` and make an entry for `*User.buttonlist` that specifies which buttons are being defined. It is possible to use artificial resource names (e.g., `buttonlist`), but they must be relative to an existing Tk widget.

Example 28–3 Using resources to specify user-defined buttons.

```
*User.buttonlist: save search justify quit
*User.save.text: Save
*User.save.command: File_Save
*User.search.text: Search
*User.search.command: Edit_Search
*User.justify.text: Justify
*User.justify.command: Edit_Justify
*user.quit.text: Quit
*User.quit.command: File_Quit
*User.quit.background: red
```

In Example 28–3, we have listed four buttons and specified some of the attributes for each, most importantly the `text` and `command` attributes. We are assuming, of course, that the application manual publishes a set of commands that users can invoke safely. In this simple example, the commands are all one word, but there is no problem with multiword commands. There is no interpretation done of the value, so it can include references to Tcl variables and nested command calls. Example 28–4 uses these resource specifications to define the buttons:

Example 28–4 `Resource_ButtonFrame` defines buttons based on resources.

```
proc Resource_ButtonFrame { f class } {
    frame $f -class $class -borderwidth 2
    pack $f -side top -fill x
    foreach b [option get $f buttonlist {}] {
        if [catch {button $f.$b}] {
            button $f.$b -font fixed
        }
        pack $f.$b -side right
    }
}
```

The `catch` phrase is introduced to handle a common problem with fonts and widget creation. If the user's resources specify a bogus or missing font, then the widget creation command will fail. The `catch` phrase guards against this case by falling back to the `fixed` font, which is guaranteed to exist. This problem is fixed in Tk 8.0 because the font mechanism will search for alternate fonts.

Example 28–5 assumes that the resource specifications from Example 28–2 are in the file `button.resources`. It creates the user-defined buttons in the `.users` frame.

Example 28–5 Using `Resource_ButtonFrame`.

```
option readfile button.resources
Resource_ButtonFrame .user User
```

User-Defined Menus

User-defined menus can be set up with a similar scheme. However, it is more complex because there are no resources for specific menu entries. We must use more artificial resources to emulate this. We use `menulist` to name the set of menus. Then, for each of these, we define an `entrylist` resource. Finally, for each entry we define a few more resources. The name of the entry has to be combined with some type information, which leads to the following convention:

- `l_entry` is the label for the entry.
- `t_entry` is the type of the entry.
- `c_entry` is the command associated with the entry.
- `v_entry` is the variable associated with the entry.
- `m_entry` is the menu associated with the entry.

Example 28-6 Specifying menu entries via resources.

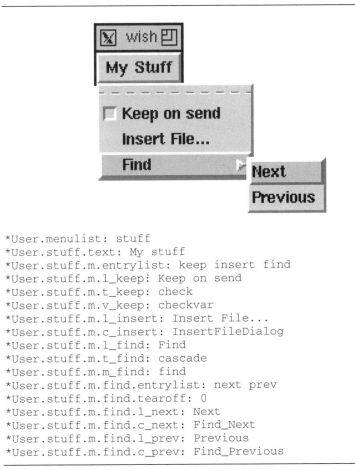

```
*User.menulist: stuff
*User.stuff.text: My stuff
*User.stuff.m.entrylist: keep insert find
*User.stuff.m.l_keep: Keep on send
*User.stuff.m.t_keep: check
*User.stuff.m.v_keep: checkvar
*User.stuff.m.l_insert: Insert File...
*User.stuff.m.c_insert: InsertFileDialog
*User.stuff.m.l_find: Find
*User.stuff.m.t_find: cascade
*User.stuff.m.m_find: find
*User.stuff.m.find.entrylist: next prev
*User.stuff.m.find.tearoff: 0
*User.stuff.m.find.l_next: Next
*User.stuff.m.find.c_next: Find_Next
*User.stuff.m.find.l_prev: Previous
*User.stuff.m.find.c_prev: Find_Previous
```

In Example 28–6, `.user.stuff` is a Tk menubutton. It has a menu as its child, `.user.stuff.m`, where the menu `.m` is set by convention. You will see this later in the code for `Resource_Menubar`. The `entrylist` for the menu is similar in spirit to the `buttonlist` resource. For each entry, however, we have to be a little creative with the next level of resource names. The following does not work:

```
*User.stuff.m.keep.label: Keep on send
```

The problem is that Tk does not directly support resources for menu entries, so it assumes `.stuff.m.keep` is a widget pathname, but it is not. You can add the resource, but you cannot retrieve it with `option get`. Instead, we must combine the attribute information (i.e., label) with the name of the entry:

```
*User.stuff.m.l_keep: Keep on send
```

You must do something similar if you want to define resources for items on a canvas, too, because that is not supported directly by Tk. The code to support menu definition by resources is shown in the next example:

Example 28–7 Defining menus from resource specifications.

```
proc Resource_Menubar { f class } {
    set f [frame $f -class $class]
    pack $f -side top
    foreach b [option get $f menulist {}] {
        set cmd [list menubutton $f.$b -menu $f.$b.m \
                      -relief raised]
        if [catch $cmd t] {
            eval $cmd {-font fixed}
        }
        if [catch {menu $f.$b.m}] {
            menu $f.$b.m -font fixed
        }
        pack $f.$b -side left
        ResourceMenu $f.$b.m
    }
}
proc ResourceMenu { menu } {
    foreach e [option get $menu entrylist {}] {
        set l [option get $menu l_$e {}]
        set c [option get $menu c_$e {}]
        set v [option get $menu v_$e {}]
        switch -- [option get $menu t_$e {}] {
            check {
                $menu add checkbutton -label $l -command $c \
                    -variable $v
            }
            radio {
                $menu add radiobutton -label $l -command $c \
                    -variable $v -value $l
            }
            separator {
                $menu add separator
            }
            cascade {
                set sub [option get $menu m_$e {}]
```

```
                    if {[string length $sub] != 0} {
                        set submenu [menu $menu.$sub]
                        $menu add cascade -label $l -command $c \
                            -menu $submenu
                        ResourceMenu $submenu
                    }
                }
                default {
                    $menu add command -label $l -command $c
                }
            }
        }
    }
}
```

Application and User Resources

The examples presented here are a subset of a package I use in some large applications, *exmh* and *webtk*. The applications define nearly every button and menu via resources, so users and site administrators can redefine them. The buttonlist, menulist, and entrylist resources are generalized into user, site, and application lists. The application uses the application lists for the initial configuration. The site and user lists can add and remove widgets. For example:

- buttonlist – the application list of buttons
- l-buttonlist – the site-specific list of buttons to remove
- lbuttonlist – the site-specific list of buttons to add
- u-buttonlist – the per-user list of buttons to remove
- ubuttonlist – the per-user list of buttons to add

This idea and the initial implementation was contributed to *exmh* by Achim Bonet. The Resource_GetFamily procedure merges five sets of resources shown above. It can replace the option get commands for the buttonlist, menulist, and entrylist resources in Examples 28–4 and 28–7:

Example 28–8 Resource_GetFamily merges user and application resources.

```
proc Resource_GetFamily { w resname } {
    set res   [option get $w $resname {}]
    set lres  [option get $w l$resname {}]
    set ures  [option get $w u$resname {}]
    set l-res [option get $w l-$resname {}]
    set u-res [option get $w u-$resname {}]
    # Site-local deletions from application resources
    set list [lsubtract $res ${l-res}]
    # Site-local additions
    set list [concat $list $lres]
    # Per-user deletions
    set list [lsubtract $list ${u-res}]
    # Per-user additions
    return [concat $list $ures]
```

IV. Tk Widgets

```
    }
proc lsubtract { orig nuke } {
    # Remove elements in $nuke from $orig
    foreach x $nuke {
        set ix [lsearch $orig $x]
        if {$ix >= 0} {
            set orig [lreplace $orig $ix $ix]
        }
    }
    return $orig
}
```

Expanding Variables

If the command resource contains substitution syntax like $ and [], then these are evaluated later when the command is invoked by the button or menu. This is because there is no interpretation of the command value when the widgets are created. However, it may be that you want variables substituted when the buttons and menus are defined. You can use the subst command to do this:

```
    set cmd [$button cget -command]
    $button config -command [subst $cmd]
```

Choosing the scope for the subst can be tricky. The previous command does the subst in the current scope. If this is the Resource_ButtonFrame procedure, then there are no interesting application-specific variables defined. The next command uses uplevel to do the subst in the scope of the caller of Resource_ButtonFrame. The list is necessary so that uplevel preserves the structure of the original subst command.

```
    $button config -command [uplevel [list subst $cmd]]
```

If you do a subst in ResourceMenu, then you need to keep track of the recursion level to get back to the scope of the caller of Resource_Menubar. The next few lines show what changes in ResourceMenu:

```
    proc ResourceMenu { menu {level 1} } {
        foreach e [option get $menu entrylist {}] {
            # code omitted
            set c [option get $menu c_$e {}]
            set c [uplevel $level [list subst $c]]
            # And the recursive call is
            ResourceMenu $submenu [expr $level+1]
            # more code omitted
        }
    }
```

If you want the subst to occur in the global scope, use this:

```
    $button config -command [uplevel #0 [list subst $cmd]]
```

However, the global scope may not be much different when you define the button than when the button is invoked. In practice, I have used subst to capture variables defined in the procedure that calls Resource_Menubar.

Simple Tk Widgets

This chapter describes several simple Tk widgets: the `frame`, `label`, `message`, and `scale`. In general, these widgets require minimal setup to be useful in your application. The `bell` command rings the terminal bell.

*T*his chapter describes four simple widgets and the `bell` command.

- The `frame` is a building block for widget layout. A `toplevel` is a frame that is detached from the main window.
- The `label` provides a line of read-only text.
- The `message` provides a read-only block of text that gets formatted onto several lines.
- The `scale` is a slider-like widget used to set a numeric value.
- The `bell` command rings the terminal bell.

Chapters 37, 38, and 39 go into more detail about some of the generic widget attributes shared by the widgets presented in this chapter. The examples in this chapter use the default widget attributes in most cases.

Frames and Toplevel Windows

Frames have been introduced before for use with the geometry managers. There is not much to a frame, except for its background color and border. You can also specify a colormap and visual type for a frame. Chapter 38 describes visual types and colormaps on page 538.

A toplevel widget is like a frame, except that it is created as a new main window. That is, it is not positioned inside the main window of the application.

This is useful for dialog boxes, for example. A toplevel has the same attributes as a frame, plus `screen` and `menu` attributes. The `menu` attribute is used to create menubars along the top edge of a toplevel. This feature was added in Tk 8.0, and it is described on page 395. On UNIX, the `screen` option lets you put the toplevel on any X display. The value of the `screen` option has the following format:

> `host:display.screenNum`

For example, I have one X server on my workstation `sage` that controls two screens. My two screens are named `sage:0.0` and `sage:0.1`. If the `screenNum` specifier is left off, it defaults to `0`.

Attributes for Frames and Toplevels

Table 29–1 lists the attributes for the frame and toplevel widgets. The attributes are named according to their resource name, which includes a capital letter at internal word boundaries. When you specify an attribute in a Tcl command when creating or reconfiguring a widget, however, you specify the attribute with a dash and all lowercase letters. Chapter 28 explains how to use resource specifications for attributes. Chapters 37, 38, and 39 discuss many of these attributes in more detail.

Table 29–1 Attributes for frame and toplevel widgets.

background	Background color (also `bg`).
borderWidth	Extra space around the edge of the frame.
class	Resource class and binding class name.
colormap	The value is `new` or the name of a window.
container	If `true`, frame embeds another application.
cursor	Cursor to display when mouse is over the frame.
height	Height, in screen units.
highlightBackground	Focus highlight color when widget does not have focus.
highlightColor	Focus highlight color when widget has focus.
highlightThickness	Thickness of focus highlight rectangle.
menu	The menu to use for the menubar. Toplevel only.
relief	`flat`, `sunken`, `raised`, `groove`, `solid` or `ridge`.
screen	An X display specification. (Toplevel only, and this cannot be specified in the resource database).
takeFocus	Controls focus changes from keyboard traversal.
use	A window ID from `winfo id`. This embeds the frame or toplevel into the specified window.

Table 29–1 Attributes for frame and toplevel widgets. (Continued)

visual	Type: staticgrey, greyscale, staticcolor, pseudocolor, directcolor, or truecolor.
width	Width, in screen units.

You cannot change the class, colormap, visual, or screen attributes after the frame or toplevel has been created. These settings are so fundamental that you need to destroy the frame and start over if you must change them.

Embedding Other Applications

The container and use attributes support application embedding. Embedding puts another application's window into a Tk frame or puts a Tk frame into another application. The use attribute specifies the ID of a window that will contain a Tk frame. *Wish* supports a -use command line argument that is used for the same purpose. Set the container attribute if you want to embed another window. For example, here is how to run another *wish* application and embed its window in one of your frames:

```
frame .embed -container 1 -bd 4 -bg red
exec wish somescript.tcl -use [winfo id .embed] &
```

Toplevel Window Styles

On Windows and Macintosh there are several styles of toplevel windows. They differ in their appearance and their behavior. On UNIX, toplevel windows are usually decorated by the window manager, which is a separate application. Chapter 41 describes how to interact with the window manager.

On Macintosh, Tk has an unsupported1 command that you can use to set the window style:

```
unsupported1 style window style
```

The possible values for *style* include documentProc, dBoxProc, plainDBox, altDBoxProc, movableDBoxProc, zoomDocProc, rDocProc, floatProc, floatZoomProc, floatSideProc, or floatSideZoomProc. The dBoxProc, plainDBox, and altDBoxProc styles have no title bar, so there is no close box on them. The other styles have different title bars, a close box, and possibly a full-sized zoom box. The default style is documentProc. I used the following code to see what each looked like:

Example 29–1 Macintosh window styles.

```
set x {documentProc dBoxProc plainDBox altDBoxProc \
   movableDBoxProc zoomDocProc rDocProc floatProc \
   floatZoomProc floatSideProc floatSideZoomProc}
foreach y $x {
   toplevel .$y
```

IV. Tk Widgets

```
label .$y.1 -text $y
pack .$y.1 -padx 40 -pady 20
if [catch {unsupported1 style .$y $y} err] {
    puts "$y: $err"
}
}
```

This feature may appear as part of the wm command in future releases of Tk. On Windows you can get a couple different styles by using transient and overrideredirect windows, which are described on page 574.

The Label Widget

The label widget provides a read-only text label, and it has attributes that let you control the position of the label within the display space. Most commonly, however, you just need to specify the text for the label:

```
label .version -text "MyApp v1.0"
```

The text can be specified indirectly by using a Tcl variable to hold the text. In this case the label is updated whenever the value of the Tcl variable changes. The variable is used from the global scope, even if there happens to be a local variable by the same name when you create the widget inside a procedure:

```
set version "MyApp v1.0"
```

```
label .version -textvariable version
```

You can change the appearance of a label dynamically by using the configure widget operation. If you change the text or font of a label, you are liable to change the size of the widget, and this causes the packer to shuffle window positions. You can avoid this by specifying a width for the label that is large enough to hold all the strings you plan to display in it. The width is specified in characters, not screen coordinates:

Example 29–2 A label that displays different strings.

```
proc FixedWidthLabel { name values } {
    # name is a widget name to be created
    # values is a list of strings
    set maxWidth 0
    foreach value $values {
        if {[string length $value] > $maxWidth} {
            set maxWidth [string length $value]
        }
    }
    # Use -anchor w to left-justify short strings
    label $name -width $maxWidth -anchor w \
        -text [lindex $values 0]
    return $name
}
```

The `FixedWidthLabel` example is used to create a label with a width big enough to hold a set of different strings. It uses the `-anchor w` attribute to left-justify strings that are shorter than the maximum. You can change the text for the label later by using the `configure` widget operation, which can be abbreviated to `config`:

```
FixedWidthLabel .status {OK Busy Error}
.status config -text Busy
```

A label can display a bitmap or image instead of a text string, which is described in Chapter 38 and the section on *Bitmaps and Images*.

This example could use the font metrics facilities of Tk 8.0 to get more accurate sizes of the text for different strings. It is possible, for example, that a three-character string like **OOO** is wider than a four-character string like **llll** in a variable-width font. The `font metrics` command is described on page 552.

Label Width and Wrap Length

When a label is displaying text, its `width` attribute is interpreted as a number of characters. The label is made wide enough to hold this number of averaged width characters in the label's font. However, if the label is holding a bitmap or an image, then the `width` is in pixels or another screen unit.

The `wrapLength` attribute determines when a label's text is wrapped onto multiple lines. *The wrap length is always screen units.* If you need to compute a `wrapLength` based on the font metrics, then you can use the `font metrics` command. If you use Tk 4.2 or earlier, then you have to measure text using a `text` widget with the same font. Chapter 33 describes the `text` widget operations that return size information for characters.

You can force line breaks by including newlines (`\n`) in the label's text. This lets you create labels that have multiple lines of text.

Label Attributes

Table 29–2 lists the widget attributes for the label widget. The attributes are named according to their resource name, which includes a capital letter at internal word boundaries. When you specify an attribute as an option in a Tcl command when creating or reconfiguring a widget, however, you specify the attribute with a dash and all lowercase letters. Chapter 28 explains how to use resource specifications for attributes. Chapters 37, 38, and 39 discuss many of these attributes in more detail.

Table 29–2 Label Attributes.

anchor	Relative position of the label within its packing space.
background	Background color (also bg).
bitmap	Name of a bitmap to display instead of a text string.

IV. Tk Widgets

Table 29–2 Label Attributes. (Continued)

borderWidth	Extra space around the edge of the label.
cursor	Cursor to display when mouse is over the label.
font	Font for the label's text.
foreground	Foreground color (also fg).
height	In screen units for bitmaps, in lines for text.
highlightBackground	Focus highlight color when widget does not have focus.
highlightColor	Focus highlight color when widget has focus.
highlightThickness	Thickness of focus highlight rectangle.
image	Specifies image to display instead of bitmap or text.
justify	Text justification: left, right, or center.
padX	Extra space to the left and right of the label.
padY	Extra space above and below the label.
relief	flat, sunken, raised, groove, solid or ridge.
takeFocus	Controls focus changes from keyboard traversal.
text	Text to display.
textVariable	Name of Tcl variable. Its value is displayed.
underline	Index of character to underline.
width	Width. In characters for text labels.
wrapLength	Length at which text is wrapped *in screen units*.

The Message Widget

The message widget displays a long text string by formatting it onto several lines. It is designed for use in dialog boxes. It can format the text into a box of a given width, in screen units, or a given *aspect ratio*. The aspect ratio is defined to be the ratio of the width to the height, times 100. The default is 150, which means that the text will be one and a half times as wide as it is high.

Example 29–3 creates a message widget with one long line of text. Backslashes are used to continue the text string without embedding any newlines. (You can also just type a long line into your script.) Note that backslash-newline collapses white space after the newline into a single space.

Example 29–3 The message widget formats long lines of text.

```
message .msg -justify center -text "This is a very long text\
    line that will be broken into many lines by the\
    message widget"
pack .msg
```

A newline in the string forces a line break in the message display. You can retain exact control over the formatting by putting newlines into your string and specifying a very large aspect ratio. In Example 29–4, grouping with double quotes is used to continue the string over more than one line. The newline character between the quotes is included in the string, and it causes a line break:

Example 29–4 Controlling the text layout in a message widget.

```
message .msg -aspect 1000 -justify left -text \
"This is the first long line of text,
and this is the second line."
pack .msg
```

One disadvantage of a message widget is that, by default, you cannot select the text it displays. Chapter 35 describes how to define custom selection handlers, so you could define one that returned the message string. The message widget predates the text widget, which has many more features and can emulate the message widget. If selections, multiple fonts, and other formatting are important, use a text widget instead of a message widget. Text widgets are described in Chapter 33.

IV. Tk Widgets

Message Attributes

Table 29–3 lists the attributes for the message widget. The table lists the resource name, which has capitals at internal word boundaries. In Tcl commands these options are specified with a dash and all lowercase:

Table 29–3 Message Attributes

anchor	Relative position of the text within its packing space.
aspect	100 * width / height. Default 150.
background	Background color (also bg).
borderWidth	Extra space around the edge of the text.
cursor	Cursor to display when mouse is over the widget.
font	Font for the message's text.
foreground	Foreground color (also fg).
highlightBackground	Focus highlight color when widget does not have focus.
highlightColor	Focus highlight color when widget has focus.
highlightThickness	Thickness of focus highlight rectangle.
justify	Justification: left, center, or right.
padX	Extra space to the left and right of the text.
padY	Extra space above and below the text.
relief	flat, sunken, raised, groove, solid or ridge.
takeFocus	Controls focus changes from keyboard traversal.
text	Text to display.
textVariable	Name of Tcl variable. Its value is displayed.
width	Width, in screen units.

Arranging Labels and Messages

Both the label and message widgets have attributes that control the position of their text in much the same way that the packer controls the position of widgets within a frame. These attributes are padX, padY, anchor, and border-Width. The anchor takes effect when the size of the widget is larger than the space needed to display its text. This happens when you specify the -width attribute or if you pack the widget with fill enabled and there is extra room. See Chapter 37 and the section on *Padding and Anchors* for more details.

The Scale Widget

The scale widget displays a *slider* in a *trough*. The trough represents a range of numeric values, and the slider position represents the current value. The scale can have an associated label, and it can display its current value next to the slider. The value of the scale can be used in three different ways:

- Explicitly get and set the value with widget commands.
- Associate the scale with a Tcl variable. The variable is kept in sync with the value of the scale, and changing the variable affects the scale.
- Register a Tcl command to be executed after the scale value changes. You specify the initial part of the Tcl command, and the scale implementation adds the current value as another argument to the command.

Example 29–5 A scale widget.

```
scale .scale -from -10 -to 20 -length 200 -variable x \
    -orient horizontal -label "The value of X" \
    -tickinterval 5 -showvalue true
pack .scale
```

Example 29–5 shows a scale for a variable that ranges in value from -10 to +20. The variable x is defined at the global scope. The tickinterval option results in the labels across the bottom, and the showvalue option causes the current value to be displayed. The length of the scale is in screen units (i.e., pixels).

Scale Bindings

Table 29–4 lists the bindings for scale widgets. You must direct focus to a scale explicitly for the key bindings like <Up> and <Down> to take effect.

Table 29–4 Bindings for scale widgets.

<Button-1>	Clicking on the trough moves the slider by one unit of resolution toward the mouse click.
<Control-Button-1>	Clicking on the trough moves the slider all the way to the end of the trough toward the mouse click.

Table 29–4 Bindings for scale widgets. (Continued)

`<Left> <Up>`	Moves the slider toward the left (top) by one unit.
`<Control-Left>` `<Control-Up>`	Moves the slider toward the left (top) by the value of the `bigIncrement` attribute.
`<Right> <Down>`	Moves the slider toward the right (bottom) one unit.
`<Control-Right>` `<Control-Down>`	Moves the slider toward the right (bottom) by the value of the `bigIncrement` attribute.
`<Home>`	Moves the slider all the way to the left (top).
`<End>`	Moves the slider all the way to the right (bottom).

Scale Attributes

Table 29–5 lists the scale widget attributes. The table uses the resource name, which has capitals at internal word boundaries. In Tcl commands the attributes are specified with a dash and all lowercase.

Table 29–5 Attributes for scale widgets.

`activeBackground`	Background color when the mouse is over the slider.
`background`	The background color (also `bg` in commands).
`bigIncrement`	Coarse grain slider adjustment value.
`borderWidth`	Extra space around the edge of the widget.
`command`	Command to invoke when the value changes. The current value is appended as another argument
`cursor`	Cursor to display when mouse is over the widget.
`digits`	Number of significant digits in scale value.
`from`	Minimum value. The left or top end of the scale.
`font`	Font for the label.
`foreground`	Foreground color (also `fg`).
`highlightBackground`	Focus highlight color when widget does not have focus.
`highlightColor`	Focus highlight color when widget has focus.
`highlightThickness`	Thickness of focus highlight rectangle.
`label`	A string to display with the scale.
`length`	The length, in screen units, of the long axis of the scale.
`orient`	`horizontal` or `vertical`.
`relief`	`flat, sunken, raised, groove, solid` or `ridge`.

Table 29–5 Attributes for scale widgets. (Continued)

repeatDelay	Delay before keyboard auto-repeat starts. Auto-repeat is used when pressing `<Button-1>` on the trough.
repeatInterval	Time period between auto-repeat events.
resolution	The value is rounded to a multiple of this value.
showValue	If true, value is displayed next to the slider.
sliderLength	The length, in screen units, of the slider.
sliderRelief	The relief of the slider.
state	`normal`, `active`, or `disabled`.
takeFocus	Controls focus changes from keyboard traversal.
tickInterval	Spacing between tick marks. Zero means no marks.
to	Maximum value. Right or bottom end of the scale.
troughColor	The color of the bar on which the slider sits.
variable	Name of Tcl variable. Changes to the scale widget are reflected in the Tcl variable value, and changes in the Tcl variable are reflected in the scale display.
width	Width of the trough, or slider bar.

Programming Scales

The scale operations are primarily used by the default bindings and you do not need to program the scale directly. Table 29–6 lists the operations supported by the scale. In the table, $w is a scale widget.

Table 29–6 Operations on the scale widget.

$w cget *option*	Returns the value of the configuration option.
$w configure ...	Queries or modifies the widget configuration.
$w coords ?*value*?	Returns the coordinates of the point in the trough that corresponds to *value*, or the scale's value.
$w get ?x y?	Returns the value of the scale, or the value that corresponds to the position given by x and y.
$w identify x y	Returns `trough1`, `slider`, or `trough2` to indicate what is under the position given by x and y.
$w set *value*	Sets the value of the scale.

IV. Tk Widgets

The `bell` Command

The `bell` command rings the terminal bell. The bell is associated with the display; even if you are executing your program on a remote machine, the bell is heard by the user. If your application has windows on multiple displays, you can direct the bell to the display of a particular window with the `-displayof` option. The syntax for the `bell` command is given below:

```
bell ?-displayof window?
```

UNIX has an *xset* program that controls the bell's duration, pitch, and volume. The volume is in percent of a maximum, for example, 50. In practice, many keyboard bells only support a variable duration; the pitch and volume are fixed. The arguments of *xset* that control the bell are shown below.

```
exec xset b ?volume? ?hertz? ?milliseconds?
```

The `b` argument by itself resets the bell to the default parameters. You can turn the bell off with `-b`, or you can use the `on` or `off` arguments.

```
exec xset -b
exec xset b ?on? ?off?
```

Scrollbars

This chapter describes the Tk `scrollbar`. Scrollbars have a general protocol
that is used to attach them to one or more other widgets.

Scrollbars control other widgets through a
standard protocol based around Tcl commands. A scrollbar uses a Tcl command
to ask a widget to display part of its contents. The scrollable widget uses a Tcl
command to tell the scrollbar what part of its contents are visible. The Tk widgets designed to work with scrollbars are: entry, listbox, text, and canvas. The
scrollbar protocol is general enough to use with new widgets, or collections of
widgets. This chapter explains the protocol between scrollbars and the widgets
they control, but you don't need to know the details to use a scrollbar. All you
need to know is how to set things up, and then these widgets take care of themselves.

Using Scrollbars

The following commands create a text widget and two scrollbars that scroll it
horizontally and vertically:

```
scrollbar .yscroll -command {.text yview} -orient vertical
scrollbar .xscroll -command {.text xview} -orient horizontal
text .text -yscrollcommand {.yscroll set} \
    -xscrollcommand {.xscroll set}
```

The scrollbar's `set` operation is designed to be called from other widgets
when their display changes. The scrollable widget's `xview` and `yview` operations
are designed to be called by the scrollbar when the user manipulates them. Addi-

tional parameters are passed to these operations as described later. In most cases you can ignore the details of the protocol and just set up the connection between the scrollbar and the widget.

Example 30–1 A text widget and two scrollbars.

```
proc Scrolled_Text { f args } {
    frame $f
    eval {text $f.text -wrap none \
        -xscrollcommand [list $f.xscroll set] \
        -yscrollcommand [list $f.yscroll set]} $args
    scrollbar $f.xscroll -orient horizontal \
        -command [list $f.text xview]
    scrollbar $f.yscroll -orient vertical \
        -command [list $f.text yview]
    grid $f.text $f.yscroll -sticky news
    grid $f.xscroll -sticky news
    grid rowconfigure $f 0 -weight 1
    grid columnconfigure $f 0 -weight 1
    return $f.text
}
set t [Scrolled_Text .f -width 40 -height 8]
pack .f -side top -fill both -expand true
set in [open /etc/passwd]
$t insert end [read $in]
close $in
```

Example 30–1 defines `Scrolled_Text` that creates a text widget with two scrollbars. It reads and inserts the password file into the text widget. There is not enough room to display all the text, and the scrollbars indicate how much text is visible. Chapter 33 describes the text widget in more detail.

The `list` command constructs the `-command` and `-xscrollcommand` values. Even though one could use double quotes here, you should make a habit of using `list` when constructing values that are used later as Tcl commands. Example

30–1 uses `args` to pass through extra options to the text widget. The use of `eval` and `args` is explained in Example 10–3 on page 127. The scrollbars and the text widget are lined up with the `grid` geometry manager as explained in Example 24–10 on page 355.

The Scrollbar Protocol

When the user manipulates the scrollbar, it calls its registered `command` with some additional parameters that indicate what the user said to do. The associated widget responds to this command (e.g., its `xview` operation) by changing its display. After the widget changes its display, it calls the scrollbar by using its registered `xscrollcommand` or `yscrollcommand` (e.g., the `set` operation) with some parameters that indicate the new relative size and position of the display. The scrollbar updates its appearance to reflect this information.

The protocol supports widgets that change their display by themselves, such as when more information is added to the widget. Scrollable widgets also support a binding to `<B2-Motion>` (i.e., "middle drag") that scrolls the widget. When anything happens to change the view on a widget, the scrollable widgets use their scroll commands to update the scrollbar.

The Scrollbar `set` Operation

The scrollbar `set` operation takes two floating point values between zero and one, *first* and *last*, that indicate the relative position of the top and bottom (or left and right) of the widget's display. The scrollable widget adds these values when they use their `yscrollcommand` or `xscrollcommand`. For example, the text widget would issue the following command to indicate that the first quarter of the widget is displayed:

```
.yscroll set 0.0 0.25
```

If the two values are 0.0 and 1.0, it means that the widget's contents are fully visible, and a scrollbar is not necessary. You can monitor the protocol by using a Tcl wrapper, `Scroll_Set`, instead of the `set` operation directly. `Scroll_Set` waits for the scrollbar to be necessary before mapping it with a geometry manager command. It is not safe to unmap the scrollbar because that can change the size of the widget and create the need for a scrollbar. That leads to an infinite loop.

Example 30–2 `Scroll_Set` manages optional scrollbars.

```
proc Scroll_Set {scrollbar geoCmd offset size} {
    if {$offset != 0.0 || $size != 1.0} {
        eval $geoCmd     ;# Make sure it is visible
    }
    $scrollbar set $offset $size
}
```

Scroll_Set takes a geometry management command as an argument, which it uses to make the scrollbar visible. Example 30–3 uses Scroll_Set with a listbox. Note that it does not grid the scrollbars directly. Instead, it lets Scroll_Set do the geometry command the first time it is necessary.

Example 30–3 Listbox with optional scrollbars.

```
proc Scrolled_Listbox { f args } {
    frame $f
    listbox $f.list \
        -xscrollcommand [list Scroll_Set $f.xscroll \
            [list grid $f.xscroll -row 1 -column 0 -sticky we]] \
        -yscrollcommand [list Scroll_Set $f.yscroll \
            [list grid $f.yscroll -row 0 -column 1 -sticky ns]]
    eval {$f.list configure} $args
    scrollbar $f.xscroll -orient horizontal \
        -command [list $f.list xview]
    scrollbar $f.yscroll -orient vertical \
        -command [list $f.list yview]
    grid $f.list -sticky news
    grid rowconfigure $f 0 -weight 1
    grid columnconfigure $f 0 -weight 1
    return $f.list
}
```

Scrolled_Listbox takes optional parameters for the listbox. It uses eval to configure the listbox with these arguments. The style of using eval shown here is explained in Example 10–3 on page 127. Example 43–4 on page 596 associates two listboxes with one scrollbar.

The **xview** and **yview** Operations

The `xview` and `yview` operations are designed to be called from scrollbars, and they work the same for all scrollable widgets. You can use them to scroll the widgets for any reason, not just when the scrollbar is used. The following examples use a text widget named `.text` for illustration.

The `xview` and `yview` operations return the current *first* and *last* values that would be passed to a scrollbar `set` command:

```
.text yview
=> 0.2 0.55
```

When the user clicks on the arrows at either end of the scrollbar, the scrollbar adds `scroll` *num* units to its command, where *num* is positive to scroll down, and negative to scroll up. Scrolling up one line is indicated with this command:

```
.text yview scroll -1 units
```

When the user clicks above or below the elevator of the scrollbar, the scrollbar adds `scroll` *num* pages to its command. Scrolling down one page is indicated with this command:

```
.text yview scroll 1 pages
```

You can position a widget so that the top (or left) edge is at a particular offset from the beginning of the widget's contents. The offset is expressed as a floating point value between zero and one. To view the beginning of the contents:

```
.text yview moveto 0.0
```

If the offset is 1.0, the last part of the widget content's is displayed. The Tk widgets always keep the end of the widget contents at the bottom (or right) edge of the widget, unless the widget is larger than necessary to display all the contents. You can exploit this with the one-line entry widget to view the end of long strings:

```
.entry xview moveto 1.0
```

The Tk 3.6 Protocol

The protocol between the scrollbar and its associated widget changed in Tk 4.0. The scrollbar is backward compatible. The Tk 3.6 protocol had four parameters in the `set` operation: *totalUnits*, *windowUnits*, *firstUnit*, and *lastUnit*. If a scrollbar is updated with this form of a `set` command, then the `get` operation also changes to return this information. When the scrollbar makes the callback to the other widget (e.g., an `xview` or `yview` operation), it passes a single extra parameter that specifies what *unit* to display at the top (left) of the associated widget. The Tk widgets' `xview` and `yview` operations are also backward compatible with this interface.

IV. Tk Widgets

The Scrollbar Widget

Tk 8.0 uses native scrollbar widgets on Macintosh and Windows. While the use of scrollbars with other widgets is identical on all platforms, the interpretation of the attributes and the details of the bindings vary across platforms. This section describes the Tk scrollbar on UNIX. The default bindings and attributes are fine on all platforms, so the differences should not be important.

The scrollbar is made up of five components: arrow1, trough1, slider, trough2, and arrow2. The arrows are on either end, with arrow1 being the arrow to the left for horizontal scrollbars, or the arrow on top for vertical scrollbars. The slider represents the relative position of the information displayed in the associated widget, and the size of the slider represents the relative amount of the information displayed. The two trough regions are the areas between the slider and the arrows. If the slider covers all of the trough area, you can see all the information in the associated widget.

Scrollbar Bindings

Table 30–1 lists the default bindings for scrollbars on UNIX. Button 1 and button 2 of the mouse have the same bindings. You must direct focus to a scrollbar explicitly for the key bindings like `<Up>` and `<Down>` to take effect.

Table 30–1 Bindings for the scrollbar widget.

`<Button-1>` `<Button-2>`	Clicking on the arrows scrolls by one unit. Clicking on the trough moves by one screenful.
`<B1-Motion>` `<B2-Motion>`	Dragging the slider scrolls dynamically.
`<Control-Button-1>` `<Control-Button-2>`	Clicking on the trough or arrow scrolls all the way to the beginning (end) of the widget.
`<Up>` `<Down>`	Scrolls up (down) by one unit.
`<Control-Up>` `<Control-Down>`	Scrolls up (down) by one screenful.
`<Left>` `<Right>`	Scrolls left (right) by one unit.
`<Control-Left>` `<Control-Right>`	Scrolls left (right) by one screenful.
`<Prior>` `<Next>`	Scrolls back (forward) by one screenful.
`<Home>`	Scrolls all the way to the left (top).
`<End>`	Scrolls all the way to the right (bottom).

Scrollbar Attributes

Table 30–2 lists the scrollbar attributes. The table uses the resource name for the attribute, which has capitals at internal word boundaries. In Tcl commands, the attributes are specified with a dash and all lowercase.

There is no `length` attribute for a scrollbar. Instead, a scrollbar is designed to be packed next to another widget with a fill option that lets the `scrollbar` display grow to the right size. Only the relief of the active element can be set. The `background` color is used for the slider, the arrows, and the border. The slider and arrows are displayed in the `activeBackground` color when the mouse is over them. The trough is always displayed in the `troughColor`.

Table 30–2 Attributes for the scrollbar widget.

`activeBackground`	Color when the mouse is over the slider or arrows.
`activeRelief`	Relief of slider and arrows when mouse is over them.
`background`	The background color (also `bg` in commands).
`borderWidth`	Extra space around the edge of the scrollbar.
`command`	Prefix of the command to invoke when the scrollbar changes. Typically this is a `xview` or `yview` operation.
`cursor`	Cursor to display when mouse is over the widget.
`elementBorderWidth`	Border width of arrow and slider elements.
`highlightBackground`	Focus highlight color when widget does not have focus.
`highlightColor`	Focus highlight color when widget has focus.
`highlightThickness`	Thickness of focus highlight rectangle.
`elementBorderWidth`	Width of 3D border on arrows and slider.
`jump`	If true, dragging the elevator does not scroll dynamically. Instead, the display jumps to the new position.
`orient`	Orientation: `horizontal` or `vertical`.
`repeatDelay`	Milliseconds before auto-repeat starts. Auto-repeat is used when pressing `<Button-1>` on the trough or arrows.
`repeatInterval`	Milliseconds between auto-repeat events.
`troughColor`	The color of the bar on which the slider sits.
`width`	Width of the narrow dimension of the scrollbar.

Programming Scrollbars

The scrollbar operations are primarily used by the default bindings. Table 30–3 lists the operations supported by the scrollbar. In the table, `$w` is a scrollbar widget.

Table 30–3 Operations on the scrollbar widget.

`$w activate ?element?`	Queries or sets the active element, which can be `arrow1`, `arrow2`, or `slider`.
`$w cget option`	Returns the value of the configuration option.
`$w configure ...`	Queries or modifies the widget configuration.
`$w delta dx dy`	Returns the change in the *first* argument to `set` required to move the scrollbar slider by *dx* or *dy*.
`$w fraction x y`	Returns a number between 0 and 1 that indicates the relative location of the point in the trough.
`$s get`	Returns *first* and *last* from the `set` operation.
`$w identify x y`	Returns `arrow1`, `trough1`, `slider`, `trough2`, or `arrow2`, to indicate what is under the point.
`$w set first last`	Sets the scrollbar parameters. *first* is the relative position of the top (left) of the display. *last* is the relative position of the bottom (right) of the display.

The Entry Widget

The entry widget provides a single line of text for use as a data entry field. The string in the entry can be linked to a Tcl variable.

*E*ntry widgets are specialized text widgets that display a single line of editable text. They have a subset of the functionality of the general-purpose text widget described in Chapter 33. The entry is commonly used in dialog boxes when values need to be filled in, or as a simple command entry widget. A very useful feature of the entry is the ability to link it to a Tcl variable. The entry displays that variable's value, and editing the contents of the entry changes the Tcl variable.

Using Entry Widgets

The entry widget supports editing, scrolling, and selections, which make it more complex than label or message widgets. Fortunately, the default settings for an entry widget make it usable right away. You click with the left button to set the insert point and then type in text. Text is selected by dragging out a selection with the left button. The entry can be scrolled horizontally by dragging with the middle mouse button.

One common use of an entry widget is to associate a label with it, and a command to execute when `<Return>` is pressed in the entry. The grid geometry manager is ideal for lining up several entries and their labels. This is implemented in the following example:

Example 31–1 A command entry.

```
foreach field {Name Address1 Address2 Phone} {
    label .l$field -text $field -anchor w
    entry .e$field -textvariable address($field) -relief sunken
    grid .l$field .e$field -sticky news
    bind .e$field <Return> UpdateAddress
}
```

Example 31–1 creates four entries that are linked to variables with the `textvariable` attribute. The variables are elements of the `address` array. The `-relief sunken` for the entry widget sets them apart visually. Widget relief is described in more detail on page 528. The Tcl command `UpdateAddress` is bound to the `<Return>` keystroke. The `UpdateAddress` procedure, which is not shown, can get the current values of the entry widgets through the global array `address`.

Tips for Using Entry Widgets

If you are displaying long strings in an entry, you can use the following command to keep the end of the string in view. The command requests that all the string be off screen to the left, but the widget implementation fills up the display; the scrolling is limited so that the tail of the string is visible:

```
$entry xview moveto 1.0
```

The `show` attribute is useful for entries that accept passwords or other sensitive information. If `show` is not empty, it is used as the character to display instead of the real value:

```
$entry config -show *
```

The `state` attribute determines if the contents of an entry can be modified. Set the `state` to `disabled` to prevent modification and set it to `normal` to allow modification.

```
$entry config -state disabled ;# read-only

$entry config -state normal   ;# editable
```

The middle mouse button (`<Button-2>`) is overloaded with two functions. If you click and release the middle button, the selection is inserted at the insert cursor. The location of the middle click does not matter. If you press and hold the middle button, you can scroll the contents of the entry by dragging the mouse to the left or right.

The Entry Widget

Table 31–1 gives the bindings for entry widgets. When the table lists two sequences, they are equivalent. The table does not list all the right arrow key bindings; there are corresponding bindings for the left and right arrow keys.

Table 31–1 Entry bindings.

`<Button-1>`	Sets the insert point and starts a selection.
`<B1-Motion>`	Drags out a selection.
`<Double-Button-1>`	Selects a word.
`<Triple-Button-1>`	Selects all text in the entry.
`<Shift-B1-Motion>`	Adjusts the ends of the selection.
`<Control-Button-1>`	Sets insert point, leaving selection as is.
`<Button-2>`	Pastes selection at the insert cursor.
`<B2-Motion>`	Scrolls horizontally.
`<Left> <Control-b>`	Moves insert cursor one character left and starts the selection.
`<Shift-Left>`	Moves cursor left and extends the selection.
`<Control-Left>`	Moves cursor left one word and starts the selection.
`<Meta-b>`	Same as `<Control-Left>`.
`<Control-Shift-Left>`	Moves cursor left one word and extends the selection.
`<Right> <Control-f>`	Moves right one character.
`<Meta-f> <Control-Right>`	Moves right one word.
`<Home> <Control-a>`	Moves cursor to beginning of entry.
`<Shift-Home>`	Moves cursor to beginning and extends the selection.
`<End> <Control-e>`	Moves cursor to end of entry.
`<Shift-End>`	Moves cursor to end and extends the selection.
`<Select> <Control-Space>`	Anchors the selection at the insert cursor.
`<Shift-Select>` `<Control-Shift-Space>`	Adjusts the selection to the insert cursor.
`<Control-slash>`	Selects all the text in the entry.
`<Control-backslash>`	Clears the selection in the entry.

IV. Tk Widgets

Table 31–1 Entry bindings. (Continued)

`<Delete>`	Deletes the selection or deletes next character.
`<Backspace>` `<Control-h>`	Deletes the selection or deletes previous character.
`<Control-d>`	Deletes next character.
`<Meta-d>`	Deletes next word.
`<Control-k>`	Deletes to the end of the entry.
`<Control-w>`	Deletes previous word.
`<Control-x>`	Deletes the section, if it exists.
`<Control-t>`	Transposes characters.

Entry Attributes

Table 31–2 lists the entry widget attributes. The table lists the resource name, which has capitals at internal word boundaries. In Tcl commands these options are specified with a dash and are all lowercase.

Table 31–2 Entry attribute resource names.

`background`	Background color (also `bg`).
`borderWidth`	Extra space around the edge of the text (also `bd`).
`cursor`	Cursor to display when mouse is over the widget.
`exportSelection`	If true, selected text is exported via the X selection mechanism.
`font`	Font for the text.
`foreground`	Foreground color (also `fg`).
`highlightBackground`	Focus highlight color when widget does not have focus.
`highlightColor`	Focus highlight color when widget has focus.
`highlightThickness`	Thickness of focus highlight rectangle.
`insertBackground`	Background for area covered by insert cursor.
`insertBorderWidth`	Width of cursor border. Non-zero for 3D effect.
`insertOffTime`	Time, in milliseconds the insert cursor blinks off.
`insertOnTime`	Time, in milliseconds the insert cursor blinks on.
`insertWidth`	Width of insert cursor. Default is 2.
`justify`	Text justification: `left`, `right`, `center`.
`relief`	`flat`, `sunken`, `raised`, `groove`, `solid` or `ridge`.
`selectBackground`	Background color of selection.

Table 31–2 Entry attribute resource names. (Continued)

selectForeground	Foreground color of selection.
selectBorderWidth	Width of selection border. Nonzero for 3D effect.
show	A character (e.g., `*`) to display instead of contents.
state	State: `disabled` (read-only) or `normal`.
takeFocus	Controls focus changes from keyboard traversal.
textVariable	Name of Tcl variable.
width	Width, in characters.
xScrollCommand	Connects entry to a scrollbar.

Programming Entry Widgets

The default bindings for entry widgets are fairly good. However, you can completely control the entry with a set of widget operations for inserting, deleting, selecting, and scrolling. The operations involve addressing character positions called *indices*. The indices count from zero. The entry defines some symbolic indices such as `end`. The index corresponding to an X coordinate is specified with `@xcoord`, such as `@26`. Table 31–3 lists the formats for indices.

Table 31–3 Entry indices.

0	Index of the first character.
anchor	The index of the anchor point of the selection.
end	Index just after the last character.
number	Index a character, counting from zero.
insert	The character right after the insertion cursor.
sel.first	The first character in the selection.
sel.last	The character just after the last character in the selection.
@xcoord	The character under the specified X coordinate.

Table 31–4 summarizes the operations on entry widgets. In the table, `$w` is an entry widget.

Table 31–4 Entry operations.

$w cget *option*	Returns the value of the configuration option.
$w configure ...	Queries or modifies the widget configuration.

Table 31–4 Entry operations.

`$w delete first ?last?`	Deletes the characters from `first` to `last`, not including the character at `last`. The character at `first` is deleted if `last` is not specified.
`$w get`	Returns the string in the entry.
`$w icursor index`	Moves the insert cursor.
`$w index index`	Returns the numerical index corresponding to `index`.
`$w insert index string`	Inserts the `string` at the given `index`.
`$w scan mark x`	Starts a scroll operation. `x` is a screen coordinate.
`$w scan dragto x`	Scrolls from previous mark position.
`$w select adjust index`	Moves the boundary of an existing selection.
`$w select clear`	Clears the selection.
`$w select from index`	Sets the anchor position for the selection.
`$w select present`	Returns 1 if there is a selection in the entry.
`$w select range start end`	Selects the characters from `start` to the one just before `end`.
`$w select to index`	Extends the selection.
`$w xview`	Returns the offset and span of visible contents. These are both real numbers between 0 and 1.0.
`$w xview index`	Shifts the display so the character at `index` is at the left edge of the display.
`$w xview moveto fraction`	Shifts the display so that `fraction` of the contents are off the left edge of the display.
`$w xview scroll num what`	Scrolls the contents by the specified number of `what`, which can be `units` or `pages`.

For example, the binding for `<Button-1>` includes the following commands:

```
%W icursor @%x
%W select from @%x
if {%W cget -state] == "normal"} {focus %W}
```

Recall that the `%` triggers substitutions in binding commands, and that `%W` is replaced with the widget pathname and `%x` is replaced with the X coordinate of the mouse event. Chapter 26 describes bindings and these substitutions in detail. These commands set the insert point to the point of the mouse click by using the `@%x` index, which will be turned into something like `@17` when the binding is invoked. The binding also starts a selection. If the entry is not in the disabled state, then keyboard focus is given to the entry so that it gets `KeyPress` events.

The Listbox Widget

The listbox provides a scrollable list of text lines. The listbox supports
selections of one or more lines.

*L*istbox widgets display a set of text lines
in a scrollable display. The basic text unit is a line. There are operations to
insert, select, and delete lines, but there are no operations to modify the characters in a line. As such, the listbox is suitable for displaying a set of choices, such
as in a file selection dialog. By default a user can select one item from a listbox,
but you can select multiple items by setting the selection mode attribute.

Using Listboxes

The lines in a listbox are indexed from zero. The keyword index `end` addresses
the last line. Other indices are described on page 443. The most common programming task for a listbox is to insert text. If your data is in a list, you can loop
through the list and insert each element at the end:

```
foreach item $list {
    $listbox insert end $item
}
```

You can insert several items at once. The next command uses `eval` to concatenate the list onto a single `insert` command:

```
eval {$listbox insert end} $list
```

It is also common to react to mouse clicks on a listbox, although the default
bindings handle most of the details of selecting items. The `nearest` operation
finds the listbox entry that is closest to a mouse event. If the mouse is clicked

beyond the last element, the index of the last element is returned:

```
set index [$list nearest $y]
```

Example 32–1 displays two listboxes. The `Scrolled_Listbox` procedure on page 430 is used to put scrollbars on the listboxes. When the user clicks on an item in the first listbox, it is copied into the second listbox. When an item in the second listbox is selected, it is removed. This example shows how to manipulate items selected from a listbox:

Example 32–1 Choosing items from a listbox.

```
proc List_Select { parent values } {
    # Create two lists side by side
    frame $parent
    set choices [Scrolled_Listbox $parent.choices \
        -width 20 -height 5 ]
    set picked [Scrolled_Listbox $parent.picked \
        -width 20 -height 5]
    pack $parent.choices $parent.picked -side left \
        -expand true -fill both

    # Selecting in choices moves items into picked
    bind $choices <ButtonRelease-1> \
        [list ListTransferSel %W $picked]

    # Selecting in picked deletes items
    bind $picked <ButtonRelease-1> \
        {ListDeleteSel %W %y}

    # Insert all the choices
    foreach x $values {
        $choices insert end $x
    }
}
proc ListTransferSel {src dst} {
    foreach i [$src curselection] {
        $dst insert end [$src get $i]
    }
```

```
    }
proc ListDeleteSel {w y} {
    foreach i [lsort -integer -decreasing [$w curselection]] {
        $w delete $i
    }
}
proc List_SelectValues {parent} {
    set picked $parent.picked.list
    set result {}
    foreach i [$w curselection] {
        lappend result [$w get $i]
    }
}
List_Select .f {apples oranges bananas \
            grapes mangos peaches pears}
pack .f -expand true -fill both
```

Bindings are created to move items from $choices to $picked, and to delete items from $picked. Most of the work of selecting things in the listbox is done by the built-in bindings on the Listbox binding tag. The different selection models are described on page 446. Those bindings are on <ButtonPress-1> and <B1-Motion>. The selection is complete by the time the <ButtonRelease-1> event occurs. Consider the <ButtonRelease-1> binding for $choices:

```
    bind $choices <ButtonRelease-1> \
        [list ListTransferSel %W $picked]
```

The list command is used to construct the Tcl command because we need to expand the value of $picked at the time the binding is created. The command will be evaluated later at the global scope, and picked will not be defined after the List_Select procedure returns. Or, worse yet, an existing global variable named picked will be used, which is unlikely to be correct!

Short procedures are used to implement the binding commands. This style has two advantages. First, it confines the % substitutions done by bind to a single command. Second, if there are any temporary variables, such as the loop counter i, they are hidden within the scope of the procedure.

The ListTransferSel gets the list of all the selected items and loops over this list to insert them into the other list. The ListDeleteSel procedure is similar. However, it sorts the selection indices in reverse order. It deletes items from the bottom up so the indices remain valid throughout the process.

Programming Listboxes

The listbox operations use indices to reference lines in the listbox. The lines are numbered starting at zero. Keyword indices are also used for some special lines. The listbox keeps track of an *active* element, which is displayed with underlined text. There is also a selection *anchor* that is used when adjusting selections. Table 32–1 summarizes the keywords used for indices.

IV. Tk Widgets

Table 32–1 Listbox indices.

0	Index of the first line.
active	The index of the activated line.
anchor	The index of the anchor point of the selection.
end	Index of the last line.
number	Index a line, counting from zero.
@*x*,*y*	The line closest to the specified X and Y coordinates.

Table 32–2 presents the operations for programming a listbox. In the table, $w is a listbox widget. Most of the operations have to do with the selection, and these operations are already programmed by the default bindings for the List-box widget class:

Table 32–2 Listbox operations.

$w activate *index*	Activates the specified line.
$w bbox *index*	Returns the bounding box of the text in the specified line in the form: *xoff yoff width height*.
$w cget *option*	Returns the value of the configuration option.
$w configure ...	Queries or modifies the widget configuration.
$w curselection	Returns a list of indices of the selected lines.
$w delete *first* ?*last*?	Deletes the lines from *first* to *last*, including the line at *last*. The line at *first* is deleted if *last* is not given.
$w get *first* ?*last*?	Returns the lines from *first* to *last* as a list.
$w index *index*	Returns the numerical index corresponding to *index*.
$w insert *index* ?*string* *string string* ...?	Inserts the *string* items before the line at *index*. If *index* is end, then append the items.
$w nearest *y*	Returns the index of the line closest to the widget-relative Y coordinate.
$w scan mark *x y*	Starts a scroll operation. *x* and *y* are widget-relative screen coordinates.
$w scan dragto *x y*	Scrolls from previous mark position.
$w see *index*	Adjusts the display so the line at *index* is visible.
$w selection anchor *index*	Anchors the selection at the specified line.
$w selection clear *start* ?*end*?	Clears the selection.

Table 32–2 Listbox operations. (Continued)

`$w selection includes index`	Returns 1 if the line at *index* is in the selection.
`$w selection set start ?end?`	Selects the lines from *start* to *end*.
`$w xview`	Returns the offset and span of visible contents. These are both real numbers between 0 and 1.
`$w xview index`	Shifts the display so the character at *index* is at the left edge of the display.
`$w xview moveto fraction`	Shifts the display so that *fraction* of the contents are off the left edge of the display.
`$w xview scroll num what`	Scrolls the contents horizontally by the specified number of *what*, which can be `units` or `pages`.
`$w yview`	Returns the offset and span of visible contents. These are both real numbers between 0 and 1.
`$w yview index`	Shifts the display so the line at *index* is at the top edge of the display.
`$w yview moveto fraction`	Shifts the display so that *fraction* of the contents are off the top of the display.
`$w yview scroll num what`	Scrolls the contents vertically by the specified number of *what*, which can be `units` or `pages`.

IV. Tk Widgets

Listbox Bindings

A listbox has an *active* element and it may have one or more *selected* elements. The active element is highlighted with an underline, and the selected elements are highlighted with a different color. There are a large number of key bindings for listboxes. You must set the input focus to the listbox for the key bindings to work. Chapter 36 describes focus. There are four selection modes for a listbox, and the bindings vary depending what mode the listbox is in. Table 32–3 lists the four possible `selectMode` settings:

Table 32–3 The values for the `selectMode` of a listbox.

`single`	A single element can be selected.
`browse`	A single element can be selected, and the selection can be dragged with the mouse. This is the default.
`multiple`	More than one element can be selected by toggling the selection state of items, but you only select or deselect one line at a time.
`extended`	More than one element can be selected by dragging out a selection with the shift or control keys.

Browse Select Mode

In `browse` selection mode, `<Button-1>` selects the item under the mouse and dragging with the mouse moves the selection, too. Table 32–4 gives the bindings for `browse` mode.

Table 32–4 Bindings for `browse` selection mode.

`<Button-1>`	Selects the item under the mouse. This becomes the active element, too.
`<B1-Motion>`	Same as `<Button-1>`, the selection moves with the mouse.
`<Shift-Button-1>`	Activates the item under the mouse. The selection is not changed.
`<Key-Up> <Key-Down>`	Moves the active item up (down) one line, and selects it.
`<Control-Home>`	Activates and select the first element of the listbox.
`<Control-End>`	Activates and select the last element of the listbox.
`<space> <Select>` `<Control-slash>`	Selects the active element.

Single Select Mode

In `single` selection mode, `<Button-1>` selects the item under the mouse, but dragging the mouse does not change the selection. When you release the mouse, the item under that point is activated. Table 32–5 specifies the bindings for `single` mode:

Table 32–5 Bindings for `single` selection mode.

`<ButtonPress-1>`	Selects the item under the mouse.
`<ButtonRelease-1>`	Activates the item under the mouse.
`<Shift-Button-1>`	Activates the item under the mouse. The selection is not changed.
`<Key-Up> <Key-Down>`	Moves the active item up (down) one line. The selection is not changed.
`<Control-Home>`	Activates and selects the first element of the listbox.
`<Control-End>`	Activates and selects the last element of the listbox.
`<space> <Select>` `<Control-slash>`	Selects the active element.
`<Control-backslash>`	Clears the selection.

Extended Select Mode

In `extended` selection mode, multiple items are selected by dragging out a selection with the first mouse button. Hold down the `Shift` key to adjust the ends of the selection. Use the `Control` key to make a disjoint selection. The `Control` key works in a toggle fashion, changing the selection state of the item under the mouse. If this starts a new part of the selection, then dragging the mouse extends the new part of the selection. If the toggle action cleared the selected item, then dragging the mouse continues to clear the selection. The extended mode is quite intuitive once you try it. Table 32–6 specifies the complete set of bindings for `extended` mode:

Table 32–6 Bindings for `extended` selection mode.

`<Button-1>`	Selects the item under the mouse. This becomes the anchor point for adjusting the selection.
`<B1-Motion>`	Sweeps out a selection from the anchor point.
`<ButtonRelease-1>`	Activates the item under the mouse.
`<Shift-Button-1>`	Adjusts the selection from the anchor item to the item under the mouse.
`<Shift-B1-Motion>`	Continues to adjust the selection from the anchor.
`<Control-Button-1>`	Toggles the selection state of the item under the mouse, and makes this the anchor point.
`<Control-B1-Motion>`	Sets the selection state of the items from the anchor point to the item under the mouse to be the same as the selection state of the anchor point.
`<Key-Up>` `<Key-Down>`	Moves the active item up (down) one line, and starts a new selection with this item as the anchor point.
`<Shift-Up>` `<Shift-Down>`	Moves the active element up (down) and extends the selection to include this element.
`<Control-Home>`	Activates and selects the first element of the listbox.
`<Control-Shift-Home>`	Extends the selection to the first element.
`<Control-End>`	Activates and selects the last element of the listbox.
`<Control-Shift-End>`	Extends the selection to the last element.
`<space>` `<Select>`	Selects the active element.
`<Escape>`	Cancels the previous selection action.
`<Control-slash>`	Selects everything in the listbox.
`<Control-backslash>`	Clears the selection.

IV. Tk Widgets

Multiple Select Mode

In `multiple` selection mode you can select more than one item, but you can add or remove only one item at a time. Dragging the mouse does not sweep out a selection. If you click on a selected item it is deselected. Table 32–7 specifies the complete set of bindings for `multiple` selection mode.

Table 32–7 Bindings for `multiple` selection mode.

`<Button-1>`	Selects the item under the mouse.
`<ButtonRelease-1>`	Activates the item under the mouse.
`<Key-Up> <Key-Down>`	Moves the active item up (down) one line, and starts a new selection with this item as the anchor point.
`<Shift-Up> <Shift-Down>`	Moves the active element up (down).
`<Control-Home>`	Activates and selects the first element of the listbox.
`<Control-Shift-Home>`	Activates the first element of the listbox.
`<Control-End>`	Activates and selects the last element of the listbox.
`<Control-Shift-End>`	Activates the last element of the listbox.
`<space> <Select>`	Selects the active element.
`<Control-slash>`	Selects everything in the listbox.
`<Control-backslash>`	Clears the selection.

Scroll Bindings

There are a number of bindings that scroll the display of the listbox. In addition to the standard middle-drag scrolling, there are some additional key bindings for scrolling. Table 32–8 summarizes the the scroll-related bindings:

Table 32–8 Listbox scroll bindings.

`<Button-2>`	Marks the start of a scroll operation.
`<B2-Motion>`	Scrolls vertically *and* horizontally.
`<Left> <Right>`	Scrolls horizontally by one character.
`<Control-Left> <Control-Right>` `<Control-Prior> <Control-Next>`	Scrolls horizontally by one screen width.
`<Prior> <Next>`	Scrolls vertically by one screen height.
`<Home> <End>`	Scrolls to left and right edges of the screen, respectively.

Listbox Attributes

Table 32–9 lists the listbox widget attributes. The table uses the resource name for the attribute, which has capitals at internal word boundaries. In Tcl commands these options are specified with a dash and all lowercase.

Table 32–9 Listbox attribute resource names.

`background`	Background color (also `bg`).
`borderWidth`	Extra space around the edge of the text.
`cursor`	Cursor to display when mouse is over the widget.
`exportSelection`	If `true`, then the selected text is exported via the X selection mechanism.
`font`	Font for the text.
`foreground`	Foreground color (also `fg`).
`height`	Number of lines in the listbox.
`highlightBackground`	Focus highlight color when widget does not have focus.
`highlightColor`	Focus highlight color when widget has focus.
`highlightThickness`	Thickness of focus highlight rectangle.
`relief`	`flat`, `sunken`, `raised`, `groove`, `solid`, or `ridge`.
`selectBackground`	Background color of selection.
`selectForeground`	Foreground color of selection.
`selectBorderWidth`	Width of selection border. Nonzero for 3D effect.
`selectMode`	Mode: `browse`, `single`, `extended`, or `multiple`.
`setGrid`	Boolean. Set gridding attribute.
`takeFocus`	Controls focus changes from keyboard traversal.
`width`	Width, in average character sizes.
`xScrollCommand`	Connects listbox to a horizontal scrollbar.
`yScrollCommand`	Connects listbox to a vertical scrollbar.

IV. Tk Widgets

Geometry Gridding

The `setGrid` attribute affects interactive resizing of the window containing the listbox. By default, a window can be resized to any size. If gridding is turned on, the size is restricted so that a whole number of lines and a whole number of average-width characters is displayed. Gridding affects the user feedback during an interactive resize. Without gridding the size is reported in pixel dimensions. When gridding is turned on, then the size is reported in grided units.

## CHAPTER 33

The Text Widget

Tk text widget is a general-purpose editable text widget with features for line
spacing, justification, tags, marks, and embedded windows.

*T*he Tk text widget is versatile, simple to
use for basic text display and manipulation, and has many advanced features to
support sophisticated applications. The line spacing and justification can be controlled on a line-by-line basis. Fonts, sizes, and colors are controlled with *tags*
that apply to ranges of text. Edit operations use positional *marks* that keep track
of locations in text, even as text is inserted and deleted.

Tags are the most important feature of the text widget. You can define
attributes like font and justification for a tag. When that tag is applied to a range
of text, the text uses those attributes. Text can pick up attributes from any number of tags, so you can compose different tags for justification, font, line spacing,
and more. You can also define bindings for tags so that ranges of text can respond
to the mouse. Any interesting application of the text widget uses tags exten-
sively.

Text Indices

The characters in a text widget are addressed by their line number and the character position within the line. Lines are numbered starting at one, while characters are numbered starting at zero. The numbering for lines was chosen to be
compatible with other programs that number lines starting at one, like compilers
that generate line-oriented error messages. Here are some examples of text indices:

`1.0`	The first character.
`1.1`	The second character on the first line.
`2.end`	The newline character on the second line.

There are also symbolic indices. The `insert` index is the position at which new characters are normally inserted when the user types in characters. You can define new indices called *marks*, too, as described later. Table 33–1 summarizes the various forms for a text index.

Table 33–1 Text indices.

line.char	Lines count from 1. Characters count from 0.
`@`*x,y*	The character under the specified screen position.
`current`	The character currently under the mouse.
`end`	Just after the very last character.
image	The position of the embedded *image*.
`insert`	The position right after the insert cursor.
mark	Just after the named *mark*.
tag`.first`	The first character in the range tagged with *tag*.
tag`.last`	Just after the last character tagged with *tag*.
window	The position of the embedded *window*.

Inserting and Deleting Text

You add text with the `insert` operation (`$t` is a text widget):

```
$t insert index string ?tagList? ?string tagList? ...
```

The *index* can be any of the forms listed in the table, or it can be an index expression as described in a moment. The tags, if any, are added to the newly inserted text. Otherwise, *string* picks up any tags present on both sides of *index*. Tags are described on page 455. Multiple strings with different tags can be inserted with one command.

The most common index at which to insert text is the `insert` index, which is where the insert cursor is displayed. The default bindings insert text at `insert` when you type. You must include a newline character explicitly to force a line break:

```
$t insert insert "Hello, World\n"
```

The `delete` operation takes one or two indices. If only one index is given, the character at that position is deleted. If there are two indices, all the characters up to the second index are deleted. The character at the second index is not deleted. For example, you can delete the first line with this command:

```
$t delete 1.0 2.0
```

Index Arithmetic

The text widget supports a simple sort of arithmetic on indices. You can specify "the end of the line with this index" and "three characters before this index," and so on. This is done by grouping a modifying expression with the index. For example, the `insert` index can be modified like this:

```
"insert lineend"
"insert -3 chars"
```

The interpretation of indices and their modifiers is designed to operate well with the `delete` and `tag add` operations of the `text` widget. These operations apply to a range of text defined by two indices. The second index refers to the character just after the end of the range. For example, the following command deletes the word containing the insert cursor:

```
$t delete "insert wordstart" "insert wordend"
```

If you want to delete a whole line, including the trailing newline, you need to use a `"lineend +1 char"` modifier. Otherwise, the newline remains and you are left with a blank line. If you supply several modifiers to an index, they are applied in left to right order:

```
$t delete "insert linestart" "insert lineend +1 char"
```

Table 33–2 summarizes the set of index modifiers.

Table 33–2 Index modifiers for text widgets.

+ *count* chars	*count* characters past the index.
- *count* chars	*count* characters before the index.
+ *count* lines	*count* lines past the index, retaining character position.
- *count* lines	*count* lines before the index, retaining character position.
linestart	The beginning of the line.
lineend	The end of the line (i.e., the newline character).
wordstart	The first character of a word.
wordend	Just after the last character of a word.

Comparing Indices

The `compare` operation compares two text indices and index expressions. You must use `compare` for reliable comparisons because, for example, index 1.3 is less than index 1.13. If you try to compare indices as numbers, you get the wrong answer. The general form of the `compare` operation is:

```
$t compare ix1 op ix2
```

The comparison operator can be one of `<`, `<=`, `==`, `=>`, `>`, or `!=`. The indices can be simple indices in the forms listed in Table 33–1, and they can be index expressions. Example 33–6 on page 465 uses the `compare` operation.

Text Marks

A mark is a symbolic name for a position between two characters. Marks have the property that when text is inserted or deleted they retain their logical position, not their numerical index position. Marks are persistent: If you delete the text surrounding a mark, it remains intact. Marks are created with the mark set operation and must be explicitly deleted with the mark unset operation. Once defined, a mark can be used in operations that require indices. The following commands define a mark at the beginning of the word containing the insert cursor and delete from there up to the end of the line:

```
$t mark set foobar "insert wordstart"
$t delete foobar "foobar lineend"
$t mark unset foobar
```

When a mark is defined, it is set to be just before the character specified by the index expression. In the previous example, this is just before the first character of the word where the insert cursor is. When a mark is used in an operation that requires an index, it refers to the character just after the mark. So, in many ways the mark seems associated with the character right after it, except that the mark remains even if that character is deleted.

You can use almost any string for the name of a mark. However, do not use pure numbers and do not include spaces, plus (+) or minus (-). These characters are used in the mark arithmetic and may cause problems if you put them into mark names. The mark names operation returns a list of all defined marks.

The insert mark defines where the insert cursor is displayed. The insert mark is treated specially: you cannot remove it with the mark unset operation. Attempting to do so does not raise an error, though, so the following is a quick way to unset all marks. The eval is necessary to join the list of mark names into the mark unset command:

```
eval {$t mark unset} [$t mark names]
```

Mark Gravity

Each mark has a *gravity* that determines what happens when characters are inserted at the mark. The default gravity is right, which means that the mark sticks to the character that is to its right. Inserting text at a mark with right gravity causes the mark to be pushed along so it is always after the inserted text. With left gravity the mark stays with the character to its left, so inserted text goes after the mark and the mark does not move. In versions of Tk before 4.0, marks had only right gravity, which made some uses of marks awkward. The mark gravity operation is used to query and modify the gravity of a mark:

```
$t mark gravity foobar
=> right
$t mark gravity foobar left
```

Text Tags

A tag is a symbolic name that is associated with one or more ranges of characters. A tag has attributes that affect the display of text that is tagged with it. These attributes include fonts, colors, tab stops, line spacing and justification. A tag can have event bindings so you can create hypertext. A tag can also be used to represent application-specific information. The `tag names` and `tag ranges` operations described later tell you what tags are defined and where they are applied.

You can use almost any string for the name of a tag. However, do not use pure numbers, and do not include spaces, plus (+) or minus (-). These characters are used in the mark arithmetic and may cause problems if you use them in tag names.

A tag is added to a range with the `tag add` operation. The following command applies the tag `everywhere` to all the text in the widget:

```
$t tag add everywhere 1.0 end
```

You can add one or more tags when text is inserted, too:

```
$t insert insert "new text" {someTag someOtherTag}
```

If you do not specify tags when text is inserted, then the text picks up any tags that are present on the characters on both sides of the insertion point. (Before Tk 4.0, tags from the left-hand character were picked up.) If you specify tags in the `insert` operation, only those tags are applied to the text.

A tag is removed from a range of text with the `tag remove` operation. However, even if there is no text labeled with a tag, its attribute settings are remembered. All information about a tag can be removed with the `tag delete` operation:

```
$t tag remove everywhere 3.0 6.end
$t tag delete everywhere
```

Tag Attributes

The attributes for a tag are defined with the `tag configure` operation. For example, a tag for blue text is defined with the following command:

```
$t tag configure blue -foreground blue
```

Table 33–3 specifies the set of attributes for tags. Some attributes can only be applied with tags; there is no global attribute for `-bgstipple`, `-fgstipple`, `-justify`, `-lmargin1`, `-lmargin2`, `-offset`, `-overstrike`, `-rmargin`, and `-underline`. Table 33–10 on page 472 lists the attributes for the text widget as a whole.

The `-relief` and `-borderwidth` attributes go together. If you only specify a relief, there is no visible effect. The default relief is `flat`, too, so if you specify a border width without a relief you won't see any effect either.

The stipple attributes require a bitmap argument. Bitmaps and colors are explained in more detail in Chapter 38. For example, to "grey out" text you could use a foreground stipple of `gray50`:

```
$t tag configure disabled -fgstipple gray50
```

Table 33–3 Attributes for text tags.

`-background` *color*	The background color for text.
`-bgstipple` *bitmap*	A stipple pattern for the background color.
`-borderwidth` *pixels*	The width for 3D border effects.
`-fgstipple` *bitmap*	A stipple pattern for the foreground color.
`-font` *font*	The font for the text.
`-foreground` *color*	The foreground color for text.
`-justify` *how*	Justification: `left`, `right`, or `center`.
`-lmargin1` *pixels*	Normal left indent for a line.
`-lmargin2` *pixels*	Indent for the part of a line that gets wrapped.
`-offset` *pixels*	Baseline offset. Positive for superscripts.
`-overstrike` *boolean*	Draw text with a horizontal line through it.
`-relief` *what*	`flat`, `sunken`, `raised`, `groove`, `solid` or `ridge`.
`-rmargin` *pixels*	Right-hand margin.
`-spacing1` *pixels*	Additional space above a line.
`-spacing2` *pixels*	Additional space above wrapped part of line.
`-spacing3` *pixels*	Additional space below a line.
`-tabs` *tabstops*	Specifies tab stops.
`-underline` *boolean*	If true, the text is underlined.
`-wrap` *mode*	Line wrap: `none`, `char`, or `word`.

Configure tags early.

You can set up the appearance (and bindings) for tags once in your application, even before you have labeled any text with the tags. The attributes are retained until you explicitly delete the tag. If you are going to use the same appearance over and over again, then it is more efficient to do the setup once so that Tk can retain the graphics context.

On the other hand, if you change the configuration of a tag, any text with that tag will be redrawn with the new attributes. Similarly, if you change a binding on a tag, all tagged characters are affected immediately.

Example 33–1 defines a few tags for character styles you might see in an editor. The example is uses the font naming system added in Tk 8.0, which is described on page 548.

Example 33–1 Tag configurations for basic character styles.

```
proc TextStyles { t } {
    $t tag configure bold -font {times 12 bold}
    $t tag configure italic -font {times 12 italic}
    $t tag configure fixed -font {courier 12}
    $t tag configure underline -underline true
    $t tag configure super -offset 6 -font {helvetica 8}
    $t tag configure sub -offset -6 -font {helvetica 8}
}
```

Mixing Attributes from Different Tags

A character can be labeled with more than one tag. For example, one tag could determine the font, another could determine the background color, and so on. If different tags try to supply the same attribute, a priority ordering is taken into account. The latest tag added to a range of text has the highest priority. The ordering of tags can be controlled explicitly with the tag raise and tag lower commands.

You can achieve interesting effects by composing attributes from different tags. In a mail reader, for example, the listing of messages in a mail folder can use one color to indicate messages that are marked for delete, and it can use another color for messages that are marked to be moved into another folder. The tags might be defined like this:

```
$t tag configure deleted -background grey75
$t tag configure moved -background yellow
```

These tags conflict, but they are never used on the same message. However, a selection could be indicated with an underline, for example:

```
$t tag configure select -underline true
```

You can add and remove the select tag to indicate what messages have been selected, and the underline is independent of the background color determined by the moved or deleted tag. If you look at the *exmh* implementation, the ftocColor.tcl file defines several text tags that are composed like this.

Line Spacing and Justification

The spacing and justification for text have several attributes. These settings are complicated by wrapped text lines. The text widget distinguishes between the first *display line* and the remaining display lines for a given text line. For example, if a line in the text widget has 80 characters but the window is only wide enough for 30, then the line may be wrapped onto three display lines. See Table 33–10 on page 472 for a description of the text widget's wrap attribute that controls this behavior.

Spacing is controlled with three attributes, and there are global spacing attributes as well as per-tag spacing attributes. The -spacing1 attribute adds space above the first display line, while -spacing2 adds space above the subsequent display lines that exist because of wrapping. The -spacing3 attribute adds space below the last display line, which could be the same as the first display line if the line is not wrapped.

The margin settings also distinguish between the first and remaining display lines. The -lmargin1 attribute specifies the indent for the first display line, while the -lmargin2 attribute specifies the indent for the rest of the display lines, if any. There is only a single attribute, -rmargin, for the right indent. These margin attributes are only tag attributes. The closest thing for the text widget as a whole is the -padx attribute, but this adds an equal amount of spacing on both sides:

Example 33–2 Line spacing and justification in the text widget.

```
proc TextExample { f } {
    frame $f
    pack $f -side top -fill both -expand true
    set t [text $f.t -setgrid true -wrap word \
        -width 42 -height 14 \
        -yscrollcommand "$f.sy set"]
    scrollbar $f.sy -orient vert -command "$f.t yview"
    pack $f.sy -side right -fill y
    pack $f.t -side left -fill both -expand true

    $t tag configure para -spacing1 0.25i -spacing2 0.1i \
        -lmargin1 0.5i -lmargin2 0.1i -rmargin 0.5i
    $t tag configure hang -lmargin1 0.1i -lmargin2 0.5i

    $t insert end "Here is a line with no special settings\n"
    $t insert end "Now is the time for all good women and men
to come to the aid of their country. In this great time of
```

```
        need, no one can avoid their responsibility.\n"
            $t insert end "The quick brown fox jumps over the lazy dog."

            $t tag add para 2.0 2.end
            $t tag add hang 3.0 3.end
        }
```

The example defines two tags, para and hang, that have different spacing and margins. The -spacing1 setting for para causes the white space before the second line. The -spacing2 setting causes the white space between the wrapped portions of the second paragraph. The hang tag has no spacing attributes, so the last paragraph starts right below the previous paragraph. You can also see the difference between the -lmargin1 and -lmargin2 settings.

The newline characters are inserted explicitly. Each newline character defines a new line for the purposes of indexing, but not necessarily for display, as this example shows. In the third line there is no newline. This means that if more text is inserted at the end mark, it will be on line three.

The values for the spacing and margin parameters are in screen units. Because different fonts are different sizes, you may need to compute the spacings as a function of the character sizes. The bbox operation returns the bounding box (x, y, width, height) for a given character:

```
        $t insert 1.0 "ABCDE"
        $t bbox 1.0
        => 4 4 8 12
```

The Tk 8.0 font metrics command, which is described on page 552, also gives detailed measurements:

```
        font metrics {times 12}
        -ascent 9 -descent 3 -linespace 12 -fixed 0
```

Text justification is limited to three styles: left, right, or center. There is no setting that causes the text to line up on both margins, which would have to be achieved by introducing variable spacing between words.

Tab Stops

Text widgets have adjustable tab stops. The tabs attribute is a list of tab stops, which are specified with a screen unit and optionally a keyword that indicates justification. The tab justification keywords are left, right, center, and numeric, and these can be abbreviated. The default is left. The following resource specification defines tab stops at 2-centimeter intervals with different justification:

```
        *Text.tabs: 2c left 4c right 6c center 8c numeric
```

The tabs attribute applies to the whole text widget or to a tag. The last tab stop is extrapolated as needed. The following command defines a tag that has left justified tab stops every half inch:

```
        $t tag configure foo -tabs ".5i left"
```

IV. Tk Widgets

The Selection

The selection is implemented with a predefined tag named sel. If the application tags characters with sel, those characters are added to the selection. This is done as part of the default bindings on the text widget.

The exportSelection attribute of a text widget controls whether or not selected text is exported by the selection mechanism to other applications. By default the selection is exported. In this case, when another widget or application asserts ownership of the selection then the sel tag is removed from any characters that are tagged with it. Chapter 35 describes the selection mechanism in more detail.

You cannot delete the sel tag with the tag delete operation. However, it is not an error to do so. You can delete all the tags on the text widget with the following command. The eval command is used to join the list of tag names into the tag delete command:

```
eval {$t tag delete} [$t tag names]
```

Tag Bindings

You can associate a tag with bindings so that when the user clicks on different areas of the text display, different things happen. The syntax for the tag bind command is similar to that of the main Tk bind command. You can both query and set the bindings for a tag. Chapter 26 describes the bind command and the syntax for events in detail.

The only events supported by the tag bind command are Enter, Leave, ButtonPress, ButtonRelease, Motion, KeyPress, and KeyRelease. ButtonPress and KeyPress can be shorted to Button and Key as in the regular bind command. The Enter and Leave events are triggered when the mouse moves in and out of characters with a tag, which is different from when the mouse moves in and out of the window.

If a character has multiple tags, then the bindings associated with all the tags will be invoked, in the order from lowest priority tag to highest priority tag. After all the tag bindings have run, the binding associated with the main widget is run, if any. The continue and break commands work inside tag bindings in a similar fashion as they work with regular command bindings. See Chapter 26 for the details.

Example 33–3 defines a text button that has a highlighted relief and an action associated with it. The example generates a new tag name so that each text button is unique. The relief and background are set for the tag to set it apart visually. The winfo visual command is used to find out if the display supports color before adding a colored background to the tag. On a black and white display, the button is displayed in reverse video (i.e., white on black.) The command is bound to <Button-1>, which is the same as <ButtonPress-1>.

The cursor is changed when the mouse is over the tagged area by binding to the <Enter> and <Leave> events. Upon leaving the tagged area, the cursor is restored. Another tag is used to remember the previous setting for the cursor. You could also use a global variable, but it is often useful to decorate the text with tags for your own purposes.

Example 33–3 An active text button.

```
proc TextButton { t start end command } {
    global textbutton
    if ![info exists textbutton(uid)] {
        set textbutton(uid) 0
    } else {
        incr textbutton(uid)
    }
    set tag button$textbutton(uid)
    $t tag configure $tag -relief raised -borderwidth 2
    if {[regexp color [winfo visual $t]]} {
        $t tag configure $tag -background thistle
    } else {
        $t tag configure $tag -background [$t cget -fg]
        $t tag configure $tag -foreground [$t cget -bg]
    }
    # Bind the command to the tag
    $t tag bind $tag <Button-1> $command
    $t tag add $tag $start $end
    # use another tag to remember the cursor
    $t tag bind $tag <Enter> \
        [list TextButtonChangeCursor %W $start $end tcross]
    $t tag bind $tag <Leave> {TextButtonRestoreCursor %W}
}
proc TextButtonChangeCursor {t start end cursor} {
    $t tag add cursor=[$t cget -cursor] $start $end
    $t config -cursor $cursor
}
proc TextButtonRestoreCursor {t} {
    regexp {cursor=([^ ]*)} [$t tag names] x cursor
    $t config -cursor $cursor
}
```

To behave even more like a button, the action should trigger upon `<Button-Release-1>`, and the appearance should change upon `<ButtonPress-1>`. If this is important to you, you can always embed a real Tk button. Embedding widgets is described later.

Searching Text

The `search` operation scans the text widget for a string that matches a pattern. The index of the text that matches the pattern is returned. The search starts at an index and covers all the text widget unless a stop index is supplied. You can use `end` as the stop index to prevent the search from wrapping back to the beginning of the document. The general form of the search operation is this:

IV. Tk Widgets

```
$t search ?options? pattern index ?stopIndex?
```

Table 33–4 summarizes the *options* to the search operation:

Table 33–4 Options to the search operation.

-forward	Searches forward from *index*. This is the default.
-backward	Searches backward from *index*.
-exact	Matches *pattern* exactly. This is the default.
-regexp	Uses regular expression pattern matching.
-nocase	Lowercase letters in *pattern* can match upper case letters.
-count *varName*	Returns in *varName* the number of characters that matched *pattern*.
--	Ends the options. Necessary if *pattern* begins with -.

If you use a regular expression to match a pattern, you may be interested in how much text matched so you can highlight the match. The -count option specifies a variable that gets the number of matching characters:

```
set start [$t search -count cnt -regexp -- $pattern 1.0 end]
$t tag add sel $start "$start +$cnt chars"
```

Embedded Widgets

The text widget can display embedded widgets as well as text. You can include a picture, for example, by constructing it in a canvas and then inserting the canvas into the text widget. An embedded widget takes up one character in terms of indices. You can address the widget by its index position or by the Tk pathname of the widget.

For example, suppose $t names a text widget. The following commands create a button and insert it into the text widget. The button behaves normally, and in this case it invokes the Help command when the user clicks on it:

```
button $t.help -bitmap questhead -command Help
$t window create end -window $t.help
```

By default an embedded widget is centered vertically on its text line. You can adjust this with the -align option to the window create command. This setting only takes effect if the window is smaller than the text in the line. I find that windows are usually larger than the text line, and in that case the -align setting has no effect. This setting is also used with images, however, where it is more common to have small images (e.g., for special bullets). Table 33–5 describes the window and image alignment settings:

Table 33–5 Window and image alignment options.

top	Top lines up with top of text line.
center	Center lines up with center of text line.
baseline	Bottom lines up with text baseline.
bottom	Bottom lines up with bottom of text line.

You can postpone the creation of the embedded widget by specifying a Tcl command that creates the window, instead of specifying the -window option. The delayed creation is useful if you have lots of widgets embedded in your text. In this case the Tcl command is evaluated just before the text widget needs to display the widget. In other words, when the user scrolls the text so the widget will appear, the Tcl command is run to create the widget:

Example 33–4 Delayed creation of embedded widgets.

```
$t window create end -create [list MakeGoBack $t]
proc MakeGoBack { t } {
    button $t.goback -text "Go to Line 1" \
        -command [list $t see 1.0]
}
```

The MakeGoBack procedure is introduced to eliminate potential quoting problems. If you need to execute more than one Tcl command to create the widget or if the embedded button has a complex command, the quoting can quickly get out of hand.

Table 33–6 gives the complete set of options for creating embedded widgets. You can change these later with the window configure operation. For example:

```
$t window configure $t.goback -padx 2
```

Table 33–6 Options to the window create operation.

-align *where*	Alignment: top, center, bottom, or baseline.
-create *command*	Tcl command to create the widget.
-padx *pixels*	Padding on either side of the widget.
-pady *pixels*	Padding above and below the widget.
-stretch *boolean*	If true, the widget is stretched vertically to match the spacing of the text line.
-window *pathname*	Tk pathname of the widget to embed.

You can specify the window to reconfigure by its pathname or the index where the window is located. In practice, naming the widget by its pathname is much more useful. Note that end is not useful for identifying an embedded win-

IV. Tk Widgets

dow because the text widget treats end specially. You can insert a window at end, but end is always updated to be after the last item in the widget. Thus end will never name the position of an existing window.

Embedded Images

Tk 8.0 added embedded images that are much like embedded windows. They provide a more efficient way to add images than creating a canvas or label widget to hold the image. You can also put the same image into a text widget many times. Example 33–5 uses an image for the bullets in a bulleted list:

Example 33–5 Using embedded images for a bulleted list.

```
proc BList_Setup { t imagefile } {
    global blist
    set blist(image) [image create photo -file $imagefile]
    $t tag configure bulletlist -tabs ".5c center 1c left" \
        -lmargin1 0 -lmargin2 1c
}
proc BList_Item { t text {mark insert}} {
    global blist
    # Assume we are at the beginning of the line
    $t insert $mark \t bulletlist
    $t image create $mark -image $blist(image)
    $t insert $mark \t$text bulletlist
}
```

In Example 33–5, tabs are used to line up the bullet and the left edges of the text. The first tab centers the bullet over a point 0.5 centimeters from left margin. The second tab stop is the same as the -lmargin2 setting so the text on the first line lines up with the text that wraps onto more lines.

If you update the image dynamically, all the instances of that image in the text widget are updated, too. This follows from the image model used in Tk, which is described in Chapter 38 on page 539.

The options for embedded images are mostly the same as those for embedded windows. One difference is that images have a -name option so you can reference an image without remembering its position in the text widget. You cannot use the image name directly because the same image can be embedded many times in the text widget. If you do not choose a name, the text widget assigns a name for you. The image create operation returns this name:

```
$t image create 1.0 -image image1
=> image1
$t image create end -image image1
=> image1#1
```

Table 33–7 gives the complete set of options for creating embedded images. You can change these later with the image configure operation.

Table 33–7 Options to the `image create` operation.

`-align` *where*	Alignment: `top`, `center`, `bottom`, or `baseline`. Only has effect if *image* is shorter than the line height. See Table 33–5.
`-image` *image*	The Tk image to add to the text widget.
`-name` *name*	A name for this instance of the image. A #*num* may be appended to generate a unique name.
`-padx` *pixels*	Padding on either side of the image.
`-pady` *pixels*	Padding above and below the image.

Looking inside the Text Widget

The text widget has several operations that let you examine its contents. The simplest is `get`, which returns a range of text from the widget. You can get all the text with this command:

```
$t get 1.0 end
```

Looking at Tags

The `tag names` command returns all the tag names, or the names of the tags at a specified index:

```
$t tag names ?index?
```

A text tag can be applied to many different ranges of text. The `tag ranges` operation returns a list of indices that alternate between the start and end of tag ranges. The `foreach` command with two loop variables makes it easy to iterate through all the ranges:

```
foreach {start end} [$t tag ranges $tag] {
    # start is the beginning of a range
    # end is the end of a range
}
```

The `tag nextrange` and `tag prevrange` operations return two indices that delimit the next and previous range of a tag. They take a starting index and an optional ending index. The `tag nextrange` operation skips to the next range if the tag is present at the starting index, unless the starting index is right at the start of a range. The `tag prevrange` operation is complementary. It does not skip the current range, unless the starting index is at the beginning of the range. These rules are used in Example 33–6 that defines a procedure to return the current range:

Example 33–6 Finding the current range of a text tag.

```
proc Text_CurrentRange { t tag mark } {
    set range [$t tag prevrange $tag $mark]
    set end [lindex $range 1]
```

```
    if {[llength $range] == 0 || [$t compare $end < $mark]} {
        # This occurs when the mark is at the
        # very beginning of the node
        set range [$t tag nextrange $tag $mark]
        if {[llength $range] == 0 ||
                [$t compare $mark < [lindex $range 0]]} {
            return {}
        }
    }
    return $range
}
```

Looking at Marks

The mark names operation returns the names of all the marks. Unlike tag names, you cannot supply an index to find out if there are marks there. You must use the dump operation described later. The mark next and mark previous operations search from a given index for a mark. The mark next operation will find a mark if it is at the starting index.

Dumping the Contents

The dump operation provides the most general way to examine the contents of the text widget. The general form of the command is:

    $t dump ?*options*? *ix1* ?*ix2*?

The dump operation returns information for the elements from *ix1* to *ix2*, or just for the elements at *ix1* if *ix2* is not specified. You can limit what information is returned with options that indicate what to return: -text, -mark, -tag, -image, -window, or -all.

Three pieces of information are returned for each element of the text widget: the type, the value, and the index. The possible types are text, tagon, tagoff, mark, image, and window. The information reflects the way the text widget represents its contents. Tags are represented as tagon and tagoff elements. Text is stored in segments that do not include any marks, tag elements, windows, or images. In addition, a newline ends a text segment.

Example 33–7 prints out the contents of the text widget:

Example 33–7 Dumping the text widget.

```
proc Text_Dump {t {start 1.0} {end end}} {
    foreach {key value index} [$t dump $start $end] {
        if {$key == "text"} {
            puts "$index \"$value\""
        } else {
            puts "$index $key $value"
        }
    }
}
```

Instead of having `dump` return all the information, you can have it call a Tcl command to process each element. The command gets passed three pieces of information for each element: the type, the value, and the index. Example 33–8 shows another way to print out the text widget contents:

Example 33–8 Dumping the text widget with a command callback.

```
proc Text_Dump {t {start 1.0} {end end}} {
    $t dump -command TextDump $start $end
}
proc TextDump {key value index} {
    if {$key == "text"} {
        puts "$index \"$value\""
    } else {
        puts "$index $key $value"
    }
}
```

Text Bindings

There is an extensive set of default bindings for text widgets. In general, the commands that move the insertion cursor also clear the selection. Often you can hold the Shift key down to extend the selection, or hold the Control key down to move the insertion cursor without affecting the selection. Table 33–8 lists the default bindings for the text widget:

Table 33–8 Bindings for the text widget.

`<Any-Key>`	Inserts normal printing characters.
`<Button-1>`	Sets the insert point, clears the selection, sets focus.
`<Control-Button-1>`	Sets the insert point without affecting the selection.
`<B1-Motion>`	Sweeps out a selection from the insert point.
`<Double-Button-1>`	Selects the word under the mouse.
`<Triple-Button-1>`	Selects the line under the mouse.
`<Shift-Button-1>`	Adjusts the end of selection closest to the mouse.
`<Shift-B1-Motion>`	Continues to adjust the selection.
`<Button-2>`	Pastes the selection, or sets the scrolling anchor.
`<B2-Motion>`	Scrolls the window.
`<Key-Left> <Control-b>`	Moves the cursor left one character and clears the selection.
`<Shift-Left>`	Moves the cursor and extends the selection.

IV. Tk Widgets

Table 33–8 Bindings for the text widget. (Continued)

`<Control-Left>`	Moves the cursor by words. Clears the selection.
`<Control-Shift-Left>`	Moves the cursor by words. Extends selection.
`<Key-Right>` `<Control-f>`	`Right` bindings are analogous to `Left` bindings.
`<Meta-b>` `<Meta-f>`	Same as `<Control-Left>`, `<Control-Right>`.
`<Key-Up>` `<Control-p>`	Moves the cursor up one line. Clears the selection.
`<Shift-Up>`	Moves the cursor up one line. Extends the selection.
`<Control-Up>`	Moves the cursor up by paragraphs, which are a group of lines separated by a blank line.
`<Control-Shift-Up>`	Moves the cursor up by paragraph. Extends the selection.
`<Key-Down>` `<Control-n>`	All `Down` bindings are analogous to `Up` bindings.
`<Next>` `<Prior>`	Moves the cursor by one screen. Clears the selection.
`<Shift-Next>` `<Shift-Prior>`	Moves the cursor by one screen. Extends the selection.
`<Home>` `<Control-a>`	Moves the cursor to line start. Clears the selection.
`<Shift-Home>`	Moves the cursor to line start. Extends the selection.
`<End>` `<Control-e>`	Moves the cursor to line end. Clears the selection.
`<Shift-End>`	Moves the cursor to line end. Extends the selection.
`<Control-Home>` `<Meta-less>`	Moves the cursor to the beginning of text. Clears the selection.
`<Control-End>` `<Meta-greater>`	Moves the cursor to the end of text. Clears the selection.
`<Select>` `<Control-space>`	Sets the selection anchor to the position of the cursor.
`<Shift-Select>` `<Control-Shift-space>`	Adjusts the selection to the position of the cursor.
`<Control-slash>`	Selects everything in the text widget.
`<Control-backslash>`	Clears the selection.
`<Delete>`	Deletes the selection, if any. Otherwise, deletes the character to the right of the cursor.
`<BackSpace>` `<Control-h>`	Deletes the selection, if any. Otherwise, deletes the character to the left of the cursor.
`<Control-d>`	Deletes character to the right of the cursor.
`<Meta-d>`	Deletes word to the right of the cursor.

Table 33–8 Bindings for the text widget. (Continued)

`<Control-k>`	Deletes from cursor to end of the line. If you are at the end of line, deletes the newline character.
`<Control-o>`	Inserts a newline but does not advance the cursor.
`<Meta-Delete>` `<Meta-BackSpace>`	Deletes the word to the left of the cursor.
`<Control-t>`	Transposes the characters on either side of the cursor.
`<<Copy>> <Meta-w>`	Copies the selection to the clipboard.
`<<Cut>> <Control-w>`	Cuts the selection and saves it on the clipboard.
`<<Paste>> <Control-y>`	Pastes from the clipboard.

Text Operations

Table 33–9 describes the text widget operations, including some that are not discussed in this chapter. In the table, $t is a text widget:

Table 33–9 Operations for the text widget.

`$t bbox` *index*	Returns the bounding box of the character at *index*. Four numbers are returned: *x y width height*.
`$t cget` *option*	Returns the value of the configuration option.
`$t compare` *i1 op i2*	Performs index comparison. *i1* and *i2* are indexes. *op* is one of `<` `<=` `==` `>=` `>` `!=`
`$t configure ...`	Queries or sets configuration options.
`$t debug` *boolean*	Enables consistency checking for B-tree code.
`$t delete` *i1* ?*i2*?	Deletes from *i1* up to, but not including *i2*. Just deletes the character at *i1* if *i2* is not specified.
`$t dlineinfo` *index*	Returns the bounding box, in pixels, of the display for the line containing index. Five numbers are returned: *x y width height baseline*.
`$t dump` ?*options*? *i1* ?*i2*?	Returns the marks, tags, windows, images, and text contained in the widget. Options are `-all`, `-command` *command*, `-image`, `-mark`, `-tag`, `-text`, and `-window`.
`$t get` *i1* ?*i2*?	Returns the text from *i1* to *i2*, or just the character at *i1* if *i2* is not specified.
`$t image cget` *option*	Returns the value of the image *option*.

Table 33–9 Operations for the text widget. (Continued)

`$t image configure ?options?`	Queries or sets the configuration of an embedded image.
`$t image create option value ...`	Creates an embedded image. Options are described in Table 33–7 on page 465.
`$t image names`	Returns the names of all embedded images.
`$t index index`	Returns the numerical value of *index*.
`$t insert index chars ?tags? ?chars tags? ...`	Inserts *chars* at the specified *index*. If *tags* are specified, they are added to the new characters.
`$t mark gravity name ?direction?`	Queries or assigns a gravity direction to the mark *name*. *direction*, if specified, is `left` or `right`.
`$t mark names`	Returns a list of defined marks.
`$t mark next index`	Returns the mark after *index*.
`$t mark previous index`	Returns the mark before *index*.
`$t mark set name index`	Defines a mark *name* at the given *index*.
`$t mark unset name1 ?name2 ...?`	Deletes the named mark, or marks.
`$t scan mark x y`	Anchors a scrolling operation.
`$t scan dragto x y`	Scrolls based on a new position.
`$t search ?switches? pattern index ?stopIndex?`	Searches for *pattern* starting at *index*. The index of the start of the match is returned. Switches are described in Table 33–4 on page 462.
`$t see index`	Positions the display to view *index*.
`$t tag add name i1 ?i2? ?i1 i2? ?i1 i2? ...`	Adds the tag to *i1* through, but not including *i2*, or just the character at *i1* if *i2* is not given.
`$t tag bind name ?sequence? ?script?`	Queries or defines bindings for the tag *name*.
`$t tag configure name ...`	Sets or queries the configuration of tag *name*.
`$t tag cget name option`	Returns the value of *option* for tag *name*.
`$t tag delete tag1 ?tag2 ...?`	Deletes information for the named tags.
`$t tag lower tag ?below?`	Lowers the priority of *tag* to the lowest priority or to just below tag *below*
`$t tag names ?index?`	Returns the names of the tags at the specified *index*, or in the whole widget, sorted from lowest to highest priority.

Table 33–9 Operations for the text widget. (Continued)

`$t tag nextrange tag i1 ?i2?`	Returns a list of two indices that are the next range of text with tag that starts at or after `i1` and before index `i2`, or the end.
`$t tag prevrange tag i1 ?i2?`	Returns a list of two indices that are the previous range of text with tag that ends at or before `i1` and at or after index `i2`, or 1.0.
`$t tag raise tag ?above?`	Raises the priority of `tag` to the highest priority, or to just above the priority of tag `above`.
`$t tag ranges tag`	Returns a list describing all the ranges of tag.
`$t tag remove tag i1 ?i2? ?i1 i2? ?i1 i2? ...`	Removes `tag` from the range `i1` up to, but not including `i2`, or just at `i1` if `i2` is not specified.
`$t window config win ...`	Queries or modifies the configuration of the embedded window. `win` is a Tk pathname or an index.
`$t window cget win option`	Returns the value of `option` for `win`.
`$t window create ix args`	Creates an embedded window at `ix`.
`$t window names`	Returns a list of windows embedded in `$t`.
`$t xview`	Returns two fractions between zero and one that describe the amount of text off-screen to the left and the amount of text displayed.
`$t xview moveto fraction`	Positions the text so `fraction` of the text is off screen to the left.
`$t xview scroll num what`	Scrolls `num` of `what`, which is `units` or `pages`.
`$t yview`	Returns two fractions between zero and one that describe the amount of text off-screen toward the beginning and the amount of text displayed.
`$t yview moveto fraction`	Positions the text so `fraction` of the text is off-screen toward the beginning.
`$t yview scroll num what`	Scrolls `num` of `what`, which is `units` or `pages`.
`$t yview ?-pickplace? ix`	Obsolete. Use the `see` operation, which is similar.
`$t yview num`	Obsolete. Position line `num` at the top of screen.

Text Attributes

Table 33–10 lists the attributes for the text widget. The table uses the resource name, which has capitals at internal word boundaries. In Tcl commands, the attributes are specified with a dash and all lowercase:

IV. Tk Widgets

Table 33–10 Text attribute resource names.

background	Background color (also `bg`).
borderWidth	Extra space around the edge of the text.
cursor	Cursor to display when mouse is over the widget.
exportSelection	If true, selected text is exported to the selection.
font	Default font for the text.
foreground	Foreground color (also `fg`).
height	Height, in text lines.
highlightBackground	Focus highlight color when widget does not have focus.
highlightColor	Color for input focus highlight border.
highlightThickness	Width of highlight border.
insertBackground	Color for the insert cursor.
insertBorderWidth	Size of 3D border for insert cursor.
insertOffTime	Milliseconds insert cursor blinks off.
insertOnTime	Milliseconds insert cursor blinks on.
insertWidth	Width of the insert cursor.
padX	Extra space to the left and right of the text.
padY	Extra space above and below the text.
relief	`flat`, `sunken`, `raised`, `groove`, `ridge`, or `solid`.
selectBackground	Background color of selected text.
selectForeground	Foreground color of selected text.
selectBorderWidth	Size of 3D border for selection highlight.
setGrid	Enable/disable geometry gridding.
spacing1	Extra space above each unwrapped line.
spacing2	Space between parts of a line that have wrapped.
spacing3	Extra space below an unwrapped line.
state	Editable (`normal`) or read-only (`disabled`).
tabs	Tab stops.
takeFocus	Control focus changes from keyboard traversal.
width	Width, in characters, of the text display.
wrap	Line wrap mode: `none`, `char`, or `word`.
xScrollCommand	Tcl command prefix for horizontal scrolling.
yScrollCommand	Tcl command prefix for vertical scrolling.

The Canvas Widget

The canvas widget is a general-purpose widget that you can program to display a variety of objects including arcs, images, lines, ovals, polygons, rectangles, text, and embedded windows.

Canvas widgets display objects such as lines and images, and each object can have bindings that respond to user input, or be animated under program control. The objects can be labeled with *tags*, and the tags can be configured with display attributes and event bindings. This chapter describes all the predefined canvas object types. Chapter 47 outlines the C programming interface for creating new canvas objects.

Canvas Coordinates

The coordinate space of the canvas has 0, 0 at the top left corner. Larger X coordinates are to the right, and larger Y coordinates are downward. The position and possibly the size of a canvas object is determined by a set of coordinates. Different objects are characterized by different numbers of coordinates. For example, text objects have two coordinates, *x1 y1*, that specify their anchor point. A line can have many pairs of coordinates that specify the end points of its segments. The coordinates are set when the object is created, and they can be updated later with the `coords` operation. By default, coordinates are in pixels. Append a coordinate with one of the following letters to change the units:

```
c    centimeters
i    inches
m    millimeters
p    printer points (1/72 inches)
```

The `tk scale` command, which is described on page 580, changes the mapping from pixels to other screen measures. Use it before creating the canvas.

The `width` and `height` attributes of the canvas determine the size of the viewable area. The `scrollRegion` attribute of the canvas determines the boundaries of the canvas. Its value is four numbers that specify the upper-left and lower-right coordinates of the canvas. If you do not specify a scroll region, it defaults to the size of the viewable area. Example 34–1 creates a canvas that has a 1000 by 400 scrolling region, and a 300 by 200 viewing area. The canvas is connected to two scrollbars to provide horizontal and vertical scrolling:

Example 34–1 A large scrolling canvas.

```
proc Scrolled_Canvas { c args } {
    frame $c
    eval {canvas $c.canvas \
        -xscrollcommand [list $c.xscroll set] \
        -yscrollcommand [list $c.yscroll set] \
        -highlightthickness 0 \
        -borderwidth 0} $args
    scrollbar $c.xscroll -orient horizontal \
        -command [list $c.canvas xview]
    scrollbar $c.yscroll -orient vertical \
        -command [list $c.canvas yview]
    grid $c.canvas $c.yscroll -sticky news
    grid $c.xscroll -sticky ew
    grid rowconfigure $c 0 -weight 1
    grid columnconfigure $c 0 -weight 1
    return $c.canvas
}
Scrolled_Canvas .c -width 300 -height 200 \
    -scrollregion {0 0 1000 400}
=> .c.canvas
pack .c -fill both -expand true
```

Borders are drawn in the canvas.

The highlight thickness and border width are set to 0 in Example 34–1. Otherwise, these features occupy some of the canvas viewable area. If you want a raised border for your canvas, either use another frame, or remember to offset your positions to avoid having objects clipped by the borders.

Hello, World!

Example 34–2 creates an object that you can drag around with the mouse. It introduces the use of tags to classify objects. In this case the `movable` tag gets bindings that let you drag the item, so any item with the `movable` tag shares this behavior. The example uses `Scrolled_Canvas` from Example 34–1. When you use a scrolled canvas, you must map from the view coordinates reported by bindings to the canvas coordinates used to locate objects:

Example 34–2 The canvas "Hello, World!" example.

```
proc CanvasHello {} {
    set can [Scrolled_Canvas .c -width 400 -height 100 \
        -scrollregion {0 0 800 400}]
    pack .c -fill both -expand true
    # Create a text object on the canvas
    $can create text 50 50 -text "Hello, World!" -tag movable
    # Bind actions to objects with the movable tag
    $can bind movable <Button-1> {CanvasMark %x %y %W}
    $can bind movable <B1-Motion> {CanvasDrag %x %y %W}
}
proc CanvasMark { x y can} {
    global canvas
    # Map from view coordinates to canvas coordinates
    set x [$can canvasx $x]
    set y [$can canvasy $y]
    # Remember the object and its location
    set canvas($can,obj) [$can find closest $x $y]
    set canvas($can,x) $x
    set canvas($can,y) $y
}
proc CanvasDrag { x y can} {
    global canvas
    # Map from view coordinates to canvas coordinates
    set x [$can canvasx $x]
    set y [$can canvasy $y]
    # Move the current object
    set dx [expr $x - $canvas($can,x)]
    set dy [expr $y - $canvas($can,y)]
    $can move $canvas($can,obj) $dx $dy
    set canvas($can,x) $x
    set canvas($can,y) $y
}
```

Example 34–2 creates a text object and gives it a tag named movable:

```
.c create text 50 50 -text "Hello, World!" -tag movable
```

The first argument after create specifies the type, and the remaining arguments depend on the type of object being created. Each canvas object requires some coordinates, optionally followed by attribute value pairs. The complete set of attributes for canvas objects are presented later in this chapter. A text object needs two coordinates for its location.

Canvas Tags

The create operation returns an ID for the object being created, which would have been 1 in this case. However, the code manipulates the canvas objects by specifying a *tag* instead of an object ID. A tag is a more general handle on canvas objects. Many objects can have the same tag, and an object can have more than one tag. You can define bindings on tags, and you can define attributes for tags that will be picked up by objects with those tags.

IV. Tk Widgets

A tag name can be almost any string, but you should avoid spaces that can cause parsing problems and pure numbers that get confused with object IDs. There are two predefined tags: current and all. The current tag applies to whatever object is under the mouse. The all tag applies to all the objects on the canvas.

The example defines behavior for objects with the movable tag. Pressing button 1 starts a drag, and dragging with the mouse button down moves the object. The pathname of the canvas (%W) is passed to CanvasMark and CanvasDrag so these procedures can be used on different canvases. The %x and %y keywords get substituted with the X and Y coordinate of the event:

```
$can bind movable <Button-1> {CanvasMark %x %y %W}
$can bind movable <B1-Motion> {CanvasDrag %x %y %W}
```

The CanvasMark and CanvasDrag procedures let you drag the object around the canvas. Because CanvasMark is applied to any object with the movable tag, it must first find the object that was clicked on. First, the view coordinates are mapped into the canvas coordinates with the canvasx and canvasy operations:

```
set x [$can canvasx x]
set y [$can canvasy y]
```

Once you do this, you can use the find operation:

```
set canvas($can,obj) [$can find closest $x $y]
```

The actual moving is done in CanvasDrag with the move operation:

```
$can move $canvas($can,obj) $dx $dy
```

Try creating a few other object types and dragging them around, too:

```
$can create rect 10 10 30 30 -fill red -tag movable
$can create line 1 1 40 40 90 60 -width 2 -tag movable
$can create poly 1 1 40 40 90 60 -fill blue -tag movable
```

The CanvasMark and CanvasDrag procedures can be used with any canvas. They use the global array canvas to keep their state, and they parameterize the indices with the canvas pathname to avoid conflict if there is more that one canvas in the application. If you get into this coding habit early, then you will find it easy to write reusable code.

Canvas tags are not persistent.

Canvas tags do not work exactly like tags in the text widget. In the text widget, a tag is completely independent of the text. You can configure a text tag before it is applied to text, and the tag configuration is remembered even if you remove it from the text. A canvas tag, in contrast, must be applied to an object before you can configure it. If you configure a canvas tag that is not applied to any objects, those settings are forgotten. If you remove all the objects that share a tag, any settings associated with those tags are forgotten.

The Min Max Scale Example

This section presents Example 34–3 that constructs a scale-like object with two sliders. The sliders represent the minimum and maximum values for some parameter. Clearly, the minimum cannot be greater than the maximum, and vice versa. The example creates three rectangles on the canvas. One rectangle forms the long axis of the slider that represents the range of possible values. The other two rectangles are markers that represent the values. Two text objects float below the markers to give the current values of the minimum and maximum.

The example introduces four canvas operations: `bbox`, `coords`, `scale`, and `move`. The `bbox` operation returns the bounding box of an object or of all objects with a given tag. The `coords` operation sets or queries the coordinates of an object. The `scale` operation stretches an object, and the `move` operation translates the position of an object.

Use tags instead of object IDs.

Many of the canvas operations take an argument that identifies objects. The value can be a tag name, or it can be the numerical object identifier returned by the `create` operation. Example 34–3 does not use object IDs. Instead, it gives each object a symbolic identifier with a tag, plus it introduces more tags to represent classes of objects. The example uses the `all` tag to move all the items and to find out the bounding box of the image. The left box and the left hanging text both have the `left` tag. They can be moved together, and they share the same bindings. Similarly, the `right` tag is shared by the right box and the right hanging text. Each item has its own unique tag, so it can be manipulated individually, too. Those tags are `slider`, `lbox`, `lnum`, `rbox`, and `rnum`:

Example 34–3 A min max scale canvas example.

```
proc Scale2 {w min max {width {}} } {
    global scale2
    if {$width == {}} {
        # Set the long dimension, in pixels
        set width [expr $max - $min]
    }
    # Save parameters
    set scale2($w,scale) [expr ($max-$min)/$width.0]
    set scale2($w,min) $min;# Current minimum
    set scale2($w,max) $max
    set scale2($w,Min) $min ;# Lower bound to the scale
    set scale2($w,Max) $max
    set scale2($w,L) 10
```

```
set scale2($w,R) [expr $width+10]

# Build from 0 to 100, then scale and move it later.
# Distance between left edges of boxes is 100.
# The box is 10 wide, therefore the slider is 110 long.
# The left box sticks up, and the right one hangs down.

canvas $w
$w create rect 0 0 110 10 -fill grey -tag slider
$w create rect 0 -4 10 10 -fill black -tag {left lbox}
$w create rect 100 0 110 14 -fill red -tag {right rbox}
$w create text 5 16 -anchor n -text $min -tag {left lnum}
$w create text 105 16 -anchor n -text $max \
    -tag {right rnum} -fill red

# Stretch/shrink the slider to the right length
set scale [expr ($width+10) / 110.0]
$w scale slider 0 0 $scale 1.0

# move the right box and text to match new length
set nx [lindex [$w coords slider] 2]
$w move right [expr $nx-110] 0
# Move everything into view
$w move all 10 10

# Make the canvas fit comfortably around the image
set bbox [$w bbox all]
set height [expr [lindex $bbox 3]+4]
$w config -height $height -width [expr $width+30]

# Bind drag actions
$w bind left  <Button-1> {Scale2Mark %W %x lbox}
$w bind right <Button-1> {Scale2Mark %W %x rbox}
$w bind left  <B1-Motion> {Scale2Drag %W %x lbox}
$w bind right <B1-Motion> {Scale2Drag %W %x rbox}
}
```

The slider is constructed with absolute coordinates, and then it is scaled to the desired width. The alternative is to compute the coordinates based on the desired width. I have found it clearer to use numbers when creating the initial layout as opposed to using expr or introducing more variables. The scale operation stretches the slider bar to the correct length. The scale operation takes a reference point, which in our case is (0, 0), and independent scale factors for the X and Y dimensions. The scale factor is computed from the width parameter, taking into account the extra length added (10) so that the distance between the left edge of the slider boxes is $width:

```
set scale [expr ($width+10) / 110.0]
$w scale slider 0 0 $scale 1.0
```

The move operation repositions the right box and right hanging text. If the marker boxes are scaled, their shape gets distorted. The coords operation returns a list of four numbers: *x1 y1 x2 y2*. The distance to move is just the difference between the new right coordinate and the value used when constructing the slider initially. The box and text share the same tag, right, so they are both moved with a single move operation:

```
set nx [lindex [$w coords slider] 2]
$w move right [expr $nx-110] 0
```

After the slider is constructed, it is shifted away from (0, 0), which is the upper-left corner of the canvas. The bbox operation returns four coordinates: *x1 y1 x2 y2*, that define the bounding box of the items with the given tag. In the example, *y1* is zero, so *y2* gives us the height of the image. The information returned by bbox can be off by a few pixels, and the example needs a few more pixels of height to avoid clipping the text. The width is computed based on the extra length added for the marker box, the 10 pixels the whole image was shifted, and 10 more for the same amount of space on the right side:

```
set bbox [$w bbox all]
set height [expr [lindex $bbox 3]+4]
$w config -height $height -width [expr $width+30]
```

Bindings are defined for the box and hanging text. The general tags left and right are used for the bindings. This means that you can drag either the box or the text to move the slider. The pathname of the canvas is passed into these procedures so that you could have more than one double slider in your interface:

```
$w bind left   <Button-1>  {Scale2Mark %W %x lbox}
$w bind right  <Button-1>  {Scale2Mark %W %x rbox}
$w bind left   <B1-Motion> {Scale2Drag %W %x lbox}
$w bind right  <B1-Motion> {Scale2Drag %W %x rbox}
```

Example 34–4 Moving the markers for the min max scale.

```
proc Scale2Mark { w x what } {
    global scale2
    # Remember the anchor point for the drag
    set scale2($w,$what) $x
}
proc Scale2Drag { w x what } {
    global scale2

    # Compute delta and update anchor point
    set x1 $scale2($w,$what)
    set scale2($w,$what) $x
    set dx [expr $x - $x1]

    # Find out where the boxes are currently
    set rx [lindex [$w coords rbox] 0]
    set lx [lindex [$w coords lbox] 0]

    if {$what == "lbox"} {
        # Constrain the movement to be between the
        # left edge and the right marker.
        if {$lx + $dx > $rx} {
```

```
            set dx [expr $rx - $lx]
            set scale2($w,$what) $rx
        } elseif {$lx + $dx < $scale2($w,L)} {
            set dx [expr $scale2($w,L) - $lx]
            set scale2($w,$what) $scale2($w,L)
        }
        $w move left $dx 0

        # Update the minimum value and the hanging text
        set lx [lindex [$w coords lbox] 0]
        set scale2($w,min) [expr int($scale2($w,Min) + \
            ($lx-$scale2($w,L)) * $scale2($w,scale))]
        $w itemconfigure lnum -text $scale2($w,min)
    } else {
        # Constrain the movement to be between the
        # right edge and the left marker
        if {$rx + $dx < $lx} {
            set dx [expr $lx - $rx]
            set scale2($w,$what) $lx
        } elseif {$rx + $dx > $scale2($w,R)} {
            set dx [expr $scale2($w,R) - $rx]
            set scale2($w,$what) $scale2($w,R)
        }
        $w move right $dx 0

        # Update the maximum value and the hanging text
        set rx [lindex [$w coords right] 0]
        set scale2($w,max) [expr int($scale2($w,Min) + \
            ($rx-$scale2($w,L)) * $scale2($w,scale))]
        $w itemconfigure rnum -text $scale2($w,max)
    }
}
proc Scale2Value {w} {
    global scale2
    # Return the current values of the double slider
    return [list $scale2($w,min) $scale2($w,max)]
}
```

The Scale2Mark procedure initializes an anchor position, scale2($w,$what), and Scale2Drag uses this to detect how far the mouse has moved. The change in position, dx, is constrained so that the markers cannot move outside their bounds. The anchor is updated if a constraint was used, and this means that the marker will not move until the mouse is moved back over the marker. (Try commenting out the assignments to scale2($w,$what) inside the if statement.) After the marker and hanging text are moved, the value of the associated parameter is computed based on the parameters of the scale. The Scale2Value procedure queries the current values of the double slider.

Canvas Objects

The next several sections describe the built-in object types for the canvas: `arc`, `bitmap`, `image`, `line`, `oval`, `polygon`, `rectangle`, `text`, and `window`. Each object has its own set of attributes, and some attributes are found on most or all object types. Every object has a `-tags` attribute used to label the object with a list of symbolic names. Most objects, even `text`, specify their color with the `-fill` attribute. Only the `bitmap` uses `-foreground` and `-background`. If the object has a border, the color of the border is specified with `-outline`, and the thickness of the outline is specified with `-width`.

Arc Items

An arc is a section of an oval. The dimensions of the oval are determined by four coordinates that are its bounding box. The arc is then determined by two angles, the `start` angle and the `extent`. The region of the oval can be filled or unfilled, and there are three different ways to define the fill region. The `pieslice` style connects the arc with the center point of the oval. The `chord` style connects the two end points of the arc. The `arc` style just draws the arc itself and there is no fill. Example 34–5 shows three arcs with the same bounding box but different styles and angles:

Example 34–5 Canvas `arc` items.

```
# $c is a canvas
$c create arc 10 10 100 100 -start 45 -extent -90 \
    -style pieslice -fill orange -outline black
$c create arc 10 10 100 100 -start 135 -extent 90 \
    -style chord -fill blue -outline white -width 4
$c create arc 10 10 100 100 -start 255 -extent 45 \
    -style arc -outline black -width 3
```

Table 34–1 specifies the complete set of `arc` attributes.

IV. Tk Widgets

Table 34–1 Arc attributes.

`-extent degrees`	The length of the arc in the counter-clockwise direction.
`-fill color`	The color of the interior of the arc region.
`-outline color`	The color of the arc itself.
`-outlinestipple bmap`	The stipple pattern for the outline of the arc.
`-start degrees`	The starting angle of the arc.
`-stipple bitmap`	A stipple pattern for the fill.
`-style style`	`pieslice`, `chord`, `arc`.
`-tags tagList`	List of tags for the arc item.
`-width num`	Width, in canvas coordinates, of the arc and outline.

Bitmap Items

A bitmap is a simple graphic with a foreground and background color. One bit per pixel is used to choose between the foreground and the background. If you do not specify a background color, the background bits are clear and the canvas background shows through. A canvas `bitmap` item is positioned with two coordinates and an anchor position. Its size is determined by the bitmap data. The `bitmap` itself is specified with a symbolic name or by the name of a file that contains its definition. If the name begins with an @, it indicates a file name. The bitmaps built into wish are shown in the example below. Chapter 47 outlines the C interface for registering bitmaps under a name.

Example 34–6 Canvas `bitmap` items.

```
set o [$c create bitmap 10 10 -bitmap @candle.xbm -anchor nw\
    -background white -foreground blue]
set x [lindex [$c bbox $o] 2] ;# Right edge of bitmap
foreach builtin {error gray12 gray50 hourglass \
            info questhead question warning} {
    incr x 20
    set o [$c create bitmap $x 30 -bitmap $builtin -anchor c]
    set x [lindex [$c bbox $o] 2]
}
```

Table 34–2 specifies the complete set of `bitmap` attributes.

Table 34–2 Bitmap attributes.

`-anchor` *position*	Anchor: c, n, ne, e, se, s, sw, w, or nw.
`-background` *color*	The background color (for zero bits).
`-bitmap` *name*	A built-in bitmap.
`-bitmap` `@`*filename*	A bitmap defined by a file.
`-foreground` *color*	The foreground color (for one bits).
`-tags` *tagList*	List of tags for the bitmap item.

Image Items

The canvas `image` objects use the general image mechanism of Tk. You must first define an image using the `image` command, which is described in Chapter 38 in the section *Bitmaps and Images*. Once you have defined an image, all you need to specify for the canvas is its position, anchor point, and any tags. The size and color information is set when the image is defined. If an image is redefined, anything displaying that image automatically gets updated. Example 34–7 creates one image and puts six instances of it on a canvas:

Example 34–7 Canvas `image` items.

```
image create bitmap hourglass2 \
    -file hourglass.bitmap -maskfile hourglass.mask \
    -background white -foreground blue
for {set x 20} {$x < 300} {incr x 20} {
    $c create image $x 10 -image hourglass2 -anchor nw
    incr x [image width hourglass2]
}
```

Table 34–3 specifies the attributes for canvas `image` items.

Table 34–3 Image attributes.

`-anchor` *position*	Anchor: c, n, ne, e, se, s, sw, w, or nw.
`-image` *name*	The name of an image.
`-tags` *tagList*	List of tags for the image item.

Line Items

A line has two or more sets of coordinates, where each set of coordinates defines an end point of a line segment. The segments can be joined in several different styles, and the whole line can be drawn with a spline fit as opposed to straight-line segments. The next example draws a line in two steps. In the first pass, single-segment lines are drawn. When the stroke completes, these are replaced with a single line segment that is drawn with a spline curve.

Example 34–8 A canvas stroke drawing example.

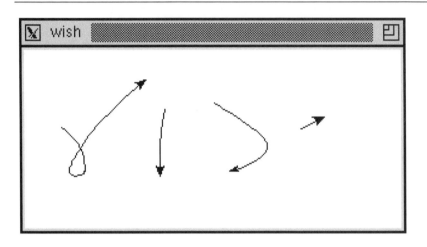

```
proc StrokeInit {} {
    canvas .c ; pack .c
    bind .c <Button-1> {StrokeBegin %W %x %y}
    bind .c <B1-Motion> {Stroke %W %x %y}
    bind .c <ButtonRelease-1> {StrokeEnd %W %x %y}
}
proc StrokeBegin { w x y } {
    global stroke
    catch {unset stroke}
    set stroke(N) 0
    set stroke(0) [list $x $y]
}
proc Stroke { w x y } {
    global stroke
    set coords $stroke($stroke(N))
    lappend coords $x $y
    incr stroke(N)
    set stroke($stroke(N)) [list $x $y]
    # eval gets the coordinates into individual arguments
    eval {$w create line} $coords {-tag segments}
}
proc StrokeEnd { w x y } {
    global stroke
    set coords {}
```

```
    for {set i 0} {$i <= $stroke(N)} {incr i} {
        append coords $stroke($i) " "
    }
    $w delete segments
    eval {$w create line} $coords \
        {-tag line -joinstyle round -smooth true -arrow last}
}
```

Example 34–8 uses the `stroke` array to hold the points of the line as it builds up the stroke. At the end of the stroke it assembles the points into a list. The `eval` command concatenates this list of points onto the `create line` command. Recall that `eval` uses `concat` if it gets multiple arguments. The other parts of the `create line` command are protected by braces so they get evaluated only once. Chapter 10 describes this trick in more detail on page 126.

The arrow attribute adds an arrow head to the end of the stroke. If you try this example you will notice that the arrow is not always aimed as you expect. This is because there are often many points generated close together as you release the mouse button. In fact, the X and Y coordinates seen by `StrokeEnd` are always the same as those seen by the last `Stroke` call. If you add this duplicate point to the end of the list of points, no arrowhead is drawn at all. In practice you might want to make `Stroke` filter out points that are too close together.

Table 34–4 specifies the complete set of line attributes. The `capstyle` affects the way the ends of the line are drawn. The `joinstyle` affects the way line segments are joined together. The `capstyle` and `joinstyle` attributes are from the X window system and may not be implemented on the Macintosh and Windows platforms. Future versions of Tk may support dashed and dotted lines, too.

Table 34–4 Line attributes.

`-arrow` *where*	Arrow location: `none`, `first`, `last`, or `both`.
`-arrowshape` *{a b c}*	Three parameters that describe the shape of the arrow. `c` is the width and `b` is the overall length. `a` is the length of the part that touches the line (e.g., 8 10 3).
`-capstyle` *what*	Line ends: `butt`, `projecting`, or `round`.
`-fill` *color*	The color of the line.
`-joinstyle` *what*	Line joints: `bevel`, `miter`, or `round`.
`-smooth` *boolean*	If `true`, a spline curve is drawn.
`-splinesteps` *num*	Number of line segments that approximate the spline.
`-stipple` *bitmap*	Stipple pattern for line fill.
`-tags` *tagList*	Set of tags for the line item.
`-width` *width*	Width of the line, in screen units.

IV. Tk Widgets

Oval Items

An `oval` is defined by two sets of coordinates that define its bounding box. If the box is square, a circle is drawn. You can set the color of the interior of the oval as well as the outline of the oval. A sampler of ovals is shown in Example 34–9.

Example 34–9 Canvas `oval` items.

```
$c create oval 10 10 80 80 -fill red -width 4
$c create oval 100 10 150 80 -fill blue -width 0
$c create oval 170 10 250 40 -fill black -stipple gray12
```

Table 34–5 specifies the complete set of `oval` attributes.

Table 34–5 Oval attributes.

`-fill color`	The color of the interior of the oval.
`-outline color`	The color for the outline of the oval.
`-stipple bitmap`	Stipple pattern for oval fill.
`-tags tagList`	Set of tags for the oval item.
`-width width`	The thickness of the outline.

Polygon Items

A `polygon` is a closed shape specified by sets of points, one for each vertex of the polygon. The vertices can be connected with smooth or straight lines. Example 34–10 creates a stop sign. The picture is centered at (0, 0) and then moved fully onto the canvas:

Example 34–10 Canvas `polygon` items.

```
$c create poly 20 -40 40 -20 40 20 20 40 -20 40 \
    -40 20 -40 -20 -20 -40 -fill red \
    -outline white -width 5
$c create text 0 0 -text STOP -fill white \
    -font {helvetica 18 bold}
$c move all 50 50
```

Table 34–6 specifies the `polygon` attributes.

Table 34–6 Polygon attributes.

`-fill color`	The color of the polygon.
`-outline color`	The color of the polygon's outline.
`-smooth boolean`	If `true`, a spline curve is drawn around the points.
`-splinesteps num`	Number of line segments that approximate the spline.
`-stipple bitmap`	Stipple pattern for polygon fill.
`-tags tagList`	Set of tags for the line item.
`-width width`	The thickness of the outline.

Rectangle Items

A `rectangle` is specified with two coordinates that are its opposite corners. A rectangle can have a fill color and an outline color. If you do not specify a fill, then the background of the canvas (or other objects) shows through. If you stipple the fill, the background also shows through the clear bits of the stipple pattern. You must use a second rectangle if you want the stippled fill to completely hide what is behind it. Example 34–11 drags out a box as the user drags the mouse. All it requires is remembering the last rectangle drawn so that it can be deleted when the next box is drawn:

Example 34–11 Dragging out a box.

```
proc BoxInit {} {
    canvas .c -bg white ; pack .c
    bind .c <Button-1> {BoxBegin %W %x %y}
    bind .c <B1-Motion> {BoxDrag %W %x %y}
}
proc BoxBegin { w x y } {
    global box
    set box($w,anchor) [list $x $y]
    catch {unset box($w,last)}
}
proc BoxDrag { w x y } {
    global box
    catch {$w delete $box($w,last)}
    set box($w,last) [eval {$w create rect} $box($w,anchor) \
        {$x $y -tag box}]
}
```

The example uses box($w,anchor) to record the start of the box. This is a list with the X and Y coordinates. The eval command is used so that this list can be spliced into the create rect command. Table 34–7 specifies the complete set of rectangle attributes:

Table 34–7 Rectangle attributes.

-fill *color*	The color of the interior of the rectangle.
-outline *color*	The color for the outline of the rectangle.
-stipple *bitmap*	Stipple pattern for rectangle fill.
-tags *tagList*	Set of tags for the rectangle item.
-width *width*	The thickness of the outline.

Text Items

The canvas text item provides yet another way to display and edit text. It supports selection, editing, and it can extend onto multiple lines. The position of a text item is specified by one set of coordinates and an anchor position. The size of the text is determined by the number of lines and the length of each line. A new line is started if there is a newline in the text string. If a width is specified, in screen units, then any line that is longer than this is wrapped onto multiple lines. The wrap occurs before a space character.

The editing and selection operations for text items use indices to specify positions within a given text item. These are very similar to those used in the entry widget. Table 34–8 summarizes the indices for canvas text items.

There are several canvas operations that manipulate text items. These are similar to some of the operations of the entry widget. The dchars and select to operations treat the second index differently than the corresponding operations

Table 34–8 Indices for canvas text items.

0	Index of the first character.
end	Index just past the last character.
number	Index a character, where *number* counts from zero.
insert	Index of the character right after the insertion cursor.
sel.first	Index of the first character in the selection.
sel.last	Index of the last character in the selection.
@*x*,*y*	Index of the character under the specified X and Y coordinate.

in the entry and text widget. The character at the second index *is* included in the operation (e.g., deleted), while in the entry and text widget it is not.

The canvas text operations are parameterized by the tag or ID of the canvas object being manipulated. If the tag refers to more than one object, then the operations apply to the first object in the display list that supports an insert cursor. The display list is described on page 494. Table 34–9 summarizes the operations on text items. In the table $t is a text item or tag and $c is a canvas.

Table 34–9 Canvas operations that apply to text items.

$c dchars $t *first ?last?*	Deletes the characters from *first* through *last*, or just the character at *first*.
$c focus ?$t?	Sets input focus to the specified item, or returns the ID of the item with the focus if it is not given.
$c icursor $t *index*	Sets the insert cursor to just before *index*.
$c index $t *index*	Returns the numerical value of *index*.
$c insert $t *index string*	Inserts the string just before *index*.
$c select adjust $t *index*	Moves the boundary of an existing selection.
$c select clear	Clears the selection.
$c select from $t *index*	Starts a selection.
$c select item	Returns the ID of the selected item, if any.
$c select to $t *index*	Extends the selection to the specified *index*.

There are no default bindings for canvas text items. Example 34–12 sets up some basic bindings for canvas text items. The <Button-1> and <Button-2> bindings are on the canvas as a whole. The rest of the bindings are on items with the text tag. You must add the text tag to text items that should share the editable text behavior. Small procedures are introduced for each binding to hide the details and any local variables needed in the operations.

Canvas find overlapping *vs.* find closest.

The CanvasFocus procedure uses the canvas find overlapping operation to see if a text object has been clicked. This must be used because find closest finds an object no matter how far away it is. It also uses the type operation to make sure only text objects are given the focus. If you want other object types to respond to key events, you should change that.

The CanvasPaste procedure does one of two things. It pastes the selection into the canvas item that has the focus. If no item has the focus, then a new text item is created with the selection as its value:

Example 34–12 Simple edit bindings for canvas text items.

```
proc Canvas_EditBind { c } {
    bind $c <Button-1> \
        {CanvasFocus %W [%W canvasx %x] [%W canvasy %y]}
    bind $c <Button-2> \
        {CanvasPaste %W [%W canvasx %x] [%W canvasy %y]}
    bind $c <<Cut>> {CanvasTextCopy %W; CanvasDelete %W}
    bind $c <<Copy>> {CanvasTextCopy %W}
    bind $c <<Paste>> {CanvasPaste %W}
    $c bind text <Button-1> \
        {CanvasTextHit %W [%W canvasx %x] [%W canvasy %y]}
    $c bind text <B1-Motion> \
        {CanvasTextDrag %W [%W canvasx %x] [%W canvasy %y]}
    $c bind text <Delete> {CanvasDelete %W}
    $c bind text <Control-d> {CanvasDelChar %W}
    $c bind text <Control-h> {CanvasBackSpace %W}
    $c bind text <BackSpace> {CanvasBackSpace %W}
    $c bind text <Control-Delete> {CanvasErase %W}
    $c bind text <Return> {CanvasNewline %W}
    $c bind text <Any-Key> {CanvasInsert %W %A}
    $c bind text <Key-Right> {CanvasMoveRight %W}
    $c bind text <Control-f> {CanvasMoveRight %W}
    $c bind text <Key-Left> {CanvasMoveLeft %W}
    $c bind text <Control-b> {CanvasMoveLeft %W}
}
proc CanvasFocus {c x y} {
    focus $c
    set id [$c find overlapping [expr $x-2] [expr $y-2] \
            [expr $x+2] [expr $y+2]]
    if {($id == {}) || ([$c type $id] != "text")} {
        set t [$c create text $x $y -text "" \
            -tags text -anchor nw]
        $c focus $t
        $c select clear
        $c icursor $t 0
    }
}
proc CanvasTextHit {c x y {select 1}} {
    $c focus current
    $c icursor current @$x,$y
    $c select clear
```

```
        $c select from current @$x,$y
}
proc CanvasTextDrag {c x y} {
    $c select to current @$x,$y
}
proc CanvasDelete {c} {
    if {[$c select item] != {}} {
        $c dchars [$c select item] sel.first sel.last
    } elseif {[$c focus] != {}} {
        $c dchars [$c focus] insert
    }
}
proc CanvasTextCopy {c} {
    if {[$c select item] != {}} {
        clipboard clear
        set t [$c select item]
        set text [$c itemcget $t -text]
        set start [$c index $t sel.first]
        set end [$c index $t sel.last]
        clipboard append [string range $text $start $end]
    } elseif {[$c focus] != {}} {
        clipboard clear
        set t [$c focus]
        set text [$c itemcget $t -text]
        clipboard append $text
    }
}
proc CanvasDelChar {c} {
    if {[$c focus] != {}} {
        $c dchars [$c focus] insert
    }
}
proc CanvasBackSpace {c} {
    if {[$c select item] != {}} {
        $c dchars [$c select item] sel.first sel.last
    } elseif {[$c focus] != {}} {
        set _t [$c focus]
        $c icursor $_t [expr [$c index $_t insert]-1]
        $c dchars $_t insert
    }
}
proc CanvasErase {c} {
    $c delete [$c focus]
}
proc CanvasNewline {c} {
    $c insert [$c focus] insert \n
}
proc CanvasInsert {c char} {
    $c insert [$c focus] insert $char
}
proc CanvasPaste {c {x {}} {y {}}} {
    if {[catch {selection get} _s] &&
        [catch {selection get -selection CLIPBOARD} _s]} {
        return ;# No selection
    }
```

```
    set id [$c focus]
    if {[string length $id] == 0 } {
        set id [$c find withtag current]
    }
    if {[string length $id] == 0 } {
        # No object under the mouse
        if {[string length $x] == 0} {
            # Keyboard paste
            set x [expr [winfo pointerx $c] - [winfo rootx $c]]
            set y [expr [winfo pointery $c] - [winfo rooty $c]]
        }
        CanvasFocus $c $x $y
    } else {
        $c focus $id
    }
    $c insert [$c focus] insert $_s
}

proc CanvasMoveRight {c} {
    $c icursor [$c focus] [expr [$c index current insert]+1]
}
proc CanvasMoveLeft {c} {
    $c icursor [$c focus] [expr [$c index current insert]-1]
}
```

Table 34–10 specifies the complete set of attributes for text items. Note that there are no foreground and background attributes. Instead, the fill color specifies the color for the text. It is possible to stipple the text as well.

Table 34–10 Text attributes

-anchor *position*	Anchor: c, n, ne, e, se, s, sw, w, or nw.
-fill *color*	The foreground color for the text.
-font *font*	The font for the text.
-justify *how*	Justification: left, right, or center.
-stipple *bitmap*	Stipple pattern for the text fill.
-tags *tagList*	Set of tags for the rectangle item.
-text *string*	The string to display.
-width *width*	The width, in screen units, before text is wrapped

Window Items

A window item lets you position other Tk widgets on a canvas. The position is specified by one set of coordinates and an anchor position. You can also specify the width and height, or you can let the widget determine its own size. The following example uses a canvas to provide a scrolling surface for a large set of

labeled entries. A frame is created and a set of labeled entry widgets are packed
into it. This main frame is put onto the canvas as a single window item. This way
we let grid take care of arranging all the labeled entries. The size of the canvas
is set up so that a whole number of labeled entries are displayed. The scroll
region and scroll increment are set up so that clicking on the scrollbar arrows
brings one new labeled entry completely into view.

Example 34–13 Using a canvas to scroll a set of widgets.

```
proc Example34-13 { top title labels } {
    # Create a resizable toplevel window
    toplevel $top
    wm minsize $top 200 100
    wm title $top $title

    # Create a frame for buttons,
    # Only Dismiss does anything useful
    set f [frame $top.buttons -bd 4]
    button $f.quit -text Dismiss -command "destroy $top"
    button $f.save -text Save
    button $f.reset -text Reset
    pack $f.quit $f.save $f.reset -side right
    pack $f -side top -fill x

    # Create a scrolling canvas
    frame $top.c
    canvas $top.c.canvas -width 10 -height 10 \
        -yscrollcommand [list $top.c.yscroll set]
    scrollbar $top.c.yscroll -orient vertical \
        -command [list $top.c.canvas yview]
    pack $top.c.yscroll -side right -fill y
    pack $top.c.canvas -side left -fill both -expand true
    pack $top.c -side top -fill both -expand true

    Scrolled_EntrySet $top.c.canvas $labels
}
proc Scrolled_EntrySet { canvas labels } {
    # Create one frame to hold everything
    # and position it on the canvas
    set f [frame $canvas.f -bd 0]
    $canvas create window 0 0 -anchor nw -window $f

    # Create and grid the labeled entries
    set i 0
    foreach label $labels {
        label $f.label$i -text $label
        entry $f.entry$i
        grid $f.label$i $f.entry$i
        grid $f.label$i -sticky w
        grid $f.entry$i -sticky we
        incr i
    }
    set child $f.entry0
```

```
# Wait for the window to become visible and then
# set up the scroll region based on
# the requested size of the frame, and set
# the scroll increment based on the
# requested height of the widgets

tkwait visibility $child
set bbox [grid bbox $f 0 0]
set incr [lindex $bbox 3]
set width [winfo reqwidth $f]
set height [winfo reqheight $f]
$canvas config -scrollregion "0 0 $width $height"
$canvas config -yscrollincrement $incr
set max [llength $labels]
if {$max > 10} {
    set max 10
}
set height [expr $incr * $max]
$canvas config -width $width -height $height
}
Example34-13 .ex "An example" {
    alpha beta gamma delta epsilon zeta eta theta iota kappa
    lambda mu nu xi omicron pi rho sigma tau upsilon
    phi chi psi omega}
```

The `tkwait visibility` command is important to the example. It causes the script to suspend execution until the top-level window, `$top`, is displayed on the screen. The `tkwait` is necessary so the right information gets returned by the `grid bbox` commands. By waiting for a subframe of the main frame, `$child`, we ensure that grid has gone through all its processing to position the interior widgets. The canvas's scroll region is set to be just large enough to hold the complete frame. The scroll increment is set to the height of one of the grid cells. Each click on the scrollbar arrows brings one new grid row completely into view.

Canvas Operations

Table 34–11 summarizes the operations on canvas widgets. In the table, `$c` is a canvas and `$t` represents a canvas tag or numerical object ID. In some cases, an operation only applies to a single object. In these cases, if a tag identifies several objects, the first object in the display list is operated on.

The canvas *display list* refers to the global order among canvas objects. New objects are put at the end of the display list. Objects later in the display list obscure objects earlier in the list. The term *above* refers to objects later in the display list.

Table 34–9 describes several of the canvas operations that only apply to `text` objects. They are `dchars`, `focus`, `index`, `icursor`, `insert`, and `select`. Table 34–11 does not repeat those operations.

Table 34–11 Operations on a `canvas` widget.

`$c addtag tag above $t`	Adds *tag* to the item just above `$t` in the display list.
`$c addtag tag all`	Adds *tag* to all objects in the canvas.
`$c addtag tag below $t`	Adds *tag* to the item just below `$t` in the display list.
`$c addtag tag closest x y ?halo? ?start?`	Adds *tag* to the item closest to the *x y* position. If more than one object is the same distance away, or if more than one object is within *halo* pixels, then the last one in the display list (uppermost) is returned. If *start* is specified, the closest object after *start* in the display list is returned.
`$c addtag tag enclosed x1 y1 x2 y2`	Adds *tag* to the items completely enclosed in the specified region. *x1 <= x2, y1 <= y2*.
`$c addtag tag withtag $t`	Adds *tag* to the items identified by `$t`.
`$c bbox $t ?tag tag ...?`	Returns the bounding box of the items identified by the tag(s) in the form *x1 y1 x2 y2*
`$c bind $t ?sequence? ?command?`	Sets or queries the bindings of canvas items.
`$c canvasx screenx ?grid?`	Maps from the X screen coordinate *screenx* to the X coordinate in canvas space, rounded to multiples of *grid* if specified.
`$c canvasy screeny ?grid?`	Maps from screen Y to canvas Y.
`$c cget option`	Returns the value of *option* for the canvas.
`$c configure ...`	Queries or updates the attributes of the canvas.
`$c coords $t ?x1 y1 ...?`	Queries or modifies the coordinates of the item.
`$c create type x y ?x2 y2 ...? ?opt value ...?`	Creates a canvas object of the specified *type* at the specified coordinates.
`$c delete $t ?tag ...?`	Deletes the item(s) specified by the tag(s) or ID(s).
`$c dtag $t ?deltag?`	Removes the specified tags from the items identified by `$t`. If *deltag* is omitted, it defaults to `$t`.
`$c find addtagSearch ...`	Returns the IDs of the tags that match the search specification: `above`, `all`, `below`, `closest`, `enclosed`, and `withtag`, as for `addtag`.
`$c gettags $t`	Returns the tags associated with the first item identified by `$t`.
`$c itemcget $t option`	Returns the value of *option* for item `$t`.
`$c itemconfigure $t ...`	Queries or reconfigures item `$t`.
`$c lower $t ?belowThis?`	Moves the items identified by `$t` to the beginning of the display list, or just before *belowThis*.

Table 34–11 Operations on a `canvas` widget. (Continued)

`$c move $t dx dy`	Moves `$t` by the specified amount.
`$c postscript ...`	Generates postscript. Table 34–12 lists options.
`$c raise $t ?aboveThis?`	Moves the items identified by `$t` to the end of the display list, or just after *aboveThis*.
`$c scale $t x0 y0 xS yS`	Scales the coordinates of the items identified by `$t`. The distance between *x0* and a given X coordinate changes by a factor of *xS*. Similarly for Y.
`$c scan mark x y`	Sets a mark for a scrolling operation.
`$c scan dragto x y`	Scrolls the canvas from the previous mark.
`$c type $t`	Returns the type of the first item identified by `$t`.
`$t xview`	Returns two fractions between zero and one that describes the amount of the canvas off-screen to the left and the amount of the canvas displayed.
`$t xview moveto fraction`	Positions the canvas so that *fraction* of the scroll region is off screen to the left.
`$t xview scroll num what`	Scrolls *num* of *what*, which is *units* or *pages*.
`$t yview`	Returns two fractions between zero and one that describes the amount of the canvas off screen to the top and the amount of the canvas displayed.
`$t yview moveto fraction`	Positions the text so that *fraction* of the canvas scroll region is off screen toward the top.
`$t yview scroll num what`	Scrolls *num* of *what*, which is *units* or *pages*.

Generating Postscript

The `postscript` operation generates postscript based on the contents of a canvas. One limitation to note is that embedded windows are not captured in the postscript output. Table 34–12 summarizes all the options for generating postscript:

Table 34–12 Canvas `postscript` options.

`-colormap varName`	The index of *varName* is a named color, and the contents of each element is the postscript code to generate the RGB values for that color.
`-colormode mode`	*mode* is one of `color`, `grey`, or `mono`.
`-file name`	The file in which to write the postscript. If not specified, the postscript is returned as the result of the command.

Table 34–12 Canvas `postscript` options. (Continued)

`-fontmap varName`	The index of *varName* is an X font name. Each element contains a list of two items: a postscript font name and a point size.
`-height size`	Height of the area to print.
`-pageanchor anchor`	Anchor: c, n, ne, e, se, s, sw, w, or nw.
`-pageheight size`	Height of image on the output. A floating point number followed by c (centimeters), i (inches), m (millimeters), or p (printer points).
`-pagewidth size`	Width of image on the output.
`-pagex position`	The output X coordinate of the anchor point.
`-pagey position`	The output Y coordinate of the anchor point.
`-rotate boolean`	If true, rotates so that X axis is the long direction of the page (landscape orientation).
`-width size`	Width of the area to print.
`-x position`	Canvas X coordinate of left edge of the image.
`-y position`	Canvas Y coordinate of top edge of the image.

You control what region of the canvas is printed with the `-width`, `-height`, `-x`, and `-y` options. You control the size and location of this in the output with the `-pageanchor`, `-pagex`, `-pagey`, `-pagewidth`, and `-pageheight` options. The postscript is written to the file named by the `-file` option, or it is returned as the value of the postscript canvas operation.

You control fonts with a mapping from X screen fonts to postscript fonts. Define an array where the index is the name of the X font and the contents are the name and pointsize of a postscript font.

The next example positions a number of text objects with different fonts onto a canvas. For each different X font used, it records a mapping to a postscript font. The example has a fairly simple font mapping, and in fact the canvas would probably have guessed the same font mapping itself. If you use more exotic screen fonts, you may need to help the canvas widget with an explicit font map.

The example positions the output at the upper-left corner of the printed page by using the `-pagex`, `-pagey`, and `-pageanchor` options. Recall that postscript has its origin at the lower-left corner of the page.

Example 34–14 Generating postscript from a canvas.

```
proc Setup {} {
    global fontMap
    canvas .c
    pack .c -fill both -expand true
    set x 10
    set y 10
```

```
    set last [.c create text $x $y -text "Font sampler" \
        -font fixed -anchor nw]

    # Create several strings in different fonts and sizes

    foreach family {times courier helvetica} {
        set weight bold
        switch -- $family {
            times { set fill blue; set psfont Times}
            courier { set fill green; set psfont Courier }
            helvetica { set fill red; set psfont Helvetica }
        }
        foreach size {10 14 24} {
            set y [expr 4+[lindex [.c bbox $last] 3]]

            # Guard against missing fonts
            if {[catch {.c create text $x $y \
                    -text $family-$weight-$size \
                    -anchor nw -fill $fill \
                    -font -*-$family-$weight-*-*-*-$size-*} \
                it] == 0} {
                set fontMap(-*-$family-$weight-*-*-*-$size-*)\
                    [list $psfont $size]
                set last $it
            }
        }
    }
    set fontMap(fixed) [list Courier 12]
}
proc Postscript { c file } {
    global fontMap
    # Tweak the output color
    set colorMap(blue) {0.1 0.1 0.9 setrgbcolor}
    set colorMap(green) {0.0 0.9 0.1 setrgbcolor}
    # Position the text at the upper-left corner of
    # an 8.5 by 11 inch sheet of paper
    $c postscript -fontmap fontMap -colormap colorMap \
        -file $file \
        -pagex 0.i -pagey 11.i -pageanchor nw
}
```

Canvas Attributes

Table 34–13 lists the attributes for the canvas widget. The table uses the resource name, which has capitals at internal word boundaries. In Tcl commands, the attributes are specified with a dash and are all lowercase.

Table 34–13 Canvas attribute resource names.

background	The normal background color.
borderWidth	The width of the border around the canvas.
closeEnough	Distance from mouse to an overlapping object.
confine	Boolean. True constrains the view to the scroll region.
cursor	Cursor to display when mouse is over the widget.
height	Height, in screen units, of canvas display.
highlightBackground	Focus highlight color when widget does not have focus.
highlightColor	Color for input focus highlight border.
highlightThickness	Width of highlight border.
insertBackground	Background for area covered by insert cursor.
insertBorderwidth	Width of cursor border. Nonzero for 3D effect.
insertOffTime	Time, in milliseconds the insert cursor blinks off.
insertOnTime	Time, in milliseconds the insert cursor blinks on.
insertWidth	Width of insert cursor. Default is 2.
relief	flat, sunken, raised, groove, solid, or ridge.
scrollIncrement	The minimum scrolling distance.
scrollRegion	Left, top, right, and bottom coordinates of the canvas.
selectBackground	Background color of selection.
selectForeground	Foreground color of selection.
selectBorderWidth	Width of selection border. Nonzero for 3D effect.
takeFocus	Controls focus changes from keyboard traversal.
width	Width in screen units for viewable area.
xScrollCommand	Tcl command prefix for horizontal scrolling.
xScrollIncrement	Distance for one scrolling unit in the X direction.
yScrollCommand	Tcl command prefix for vertical scrolling.
yScrollIncrement	Distance for one scrolling unit in the Y direction.

IV. Tk Widgets

The scroll region of a canvas defines the boundaries of the canvas coordinate space. It is specified as four coordinates, $x1\ y1\ x2\ y2$ where $(x1,\ y1)$ is the top-left corner and $(x2,\ y2)$ is the lower-right corner. If the confine attribute is true, then the canvas cannot be scrolled outside this region. It is OK to position canvas objects partially or totally off the scroll region; they just may not be visible. The scroll increment attributes determine how much the canvas is scrolled when the user clicks on the arrows in the scrollbar.

The `closeEnough` attribute indicates how far away a position can be from an object and still be considered to overlap it. This applies to the `overlapping` search criteria.

Hints

Screen Coordinates vs. Canvas Coordinates

The `canvasx` and `canvasy` operations map from a screen coordinate to a canvas coordinate. If the scroll region is larger than the display area, then you need to use these operations to map from the X and Y in an event (i.e., `%x` and `%y`) and the canvas coordinates. The typical use is:

```
set id [$c find closest [$c canvasx %x] [$c canvasy %y]]
```

Large Coordinate Spaces

Coordinates for canvas items are stored internally as floating point numbers, so the values returned by the `coords` operation will be floating point numbers. If you have a very large canvas, you may need to adjust the precision with which you see coordinates by setting the `tcl_precision` variable. This is an issue if you query coordinates, perform a computation on them, and then update the coordinates. (Tcl 8.0 changed the default `tcl_precision` from 6 to 12.)

Scaling and Rotation

The `scale` operation scales the coordinates of one or more canvas items. It is not possible to scale the whole coordinate space. The main problem with this is that you can lose precision when scaling and unscaling objects because their internal coordinates are actually changed by the scale operation. For simple cases this is not a problem, but in extreme cases it can show up.

The canvas does not support rotation.

Resources

There is no resource database support built into the canvas and its items. You can, however, define resources and query them yourself. For example, you could define:

```
*Canvas.foreground:    blue
```

This would have no effect by default. However, your code could look for this resource with `option get`, and specify this color directly for the `-fill` attribute of your objects:

```
set fg [option get $c foreground {}]
$c create rect 0 0 10 10 -fill $fg
```

The main reason to take this approach is to let your users customize the appearance of canvas objects without changing your code.

Objects with Many Points

The canvas implementation seems well optimized to handle lots of canvas objects. However, if an object like a line or a polygon has many points that define it, the implementation ends up scanning through these points linearly. This can adversely affect the time it takes to process mouse events in the area of the canvas containing such an item. Apparently any object in the vicinity of a mouse click is scanned to see if the mouse has hit it so that any bindings can be fired.

Selecting Canvas Items

Example 35–5 on page 510 implements cut and paste of canvas objects. The example exchanges the logical description of canvas objects with the selection mechanism.

IV. Tk Widgets

Tk Details

Part V describes the rest of the Tk toolkit.

Chapter 35 describes the selection mechanism that is used for cut and paste between applications. It includes an example that implements cut and paste of graphical objects on a canvas.

Chapter 36 describes dialogs. Tk has several built-in dialogs that use the native platform look and feel. The chapter also describes how to build your own dialogs.

Chapter 37 is the first of three chapters that explain widget attributes in more detail. It describes size and layout attributes. Chapter 38 describes colors, images, and cursors. It explains how to use the bitmap and color photo image types. The chapter includes a complete map of the cursor font. Chapter 39 describes fonts and other text-related attributes. The extended example is a font selection application.

Chapter 40 describes the Tk `send` command that lets you send commands among Tk applications. It also presents a socket-based alternative that can be used among applications on different hosts and with the Safe-Tcl mechanism to limit the power of remotely invoked commands.

Chapter 41 explains how to interact with the window manager using the `wm` command. The chapter describes all the information available through the `winfo` command.

Chapter 42 builds upon Chapter 28 to create a user preferences package and an associated user interface. The preference package links a Tcl variable used in your application to a resource specification.

Chapter 43 presents a user interface to the binding mechanism. You can browse and edit bindings for widgets and classes with the interface.

Selections and the Clipboard

Cut and paste allows information exchange between applications, and it is built upon a general purpose selection mechanism. The CLIPBOARD selection is used to implement cut and paste on all platforms. X Windows applications may also use the PRIMARY selection. This chapter describes the selection and clipboard commands.

Copy and paste is a basic way to transfer data between just about any two applications. In Tk, copy and paste is based on a general selection mechanism where the selection has a name, type, format, and value. For the most part you can ignore these details because they are handled by the Tk widgets. However, you can also control the selection explicitly. This chapter describes the selection model and the selection and clipboard commands. The last section of this chapter presents an example that implements copy and paste of graphical objects in a canvas.

The Selection Model

The Windows and Macintosh selection model is simpler than the selection model used in X windows. In the Macintosh and Windows there is one selection, although that selection may store different types of data like text or images. Users copy data from an application into a clipboard, and later they paste it into another application.

In X windows the selection model is generalized to support more than one selection, and they are identified by names like PRIMARY and CLIPBOARD. The CLIPBOARD selection is used for copy and paste as in Macintosh and Windows. The PRIMARY selection is described later. You could use other selection names, like SECONDARY or FOOBAR, but that only works if the other applications know about that selection name. The selection data has both a type and a format. These are described briefly later.

Data is not copied into a selection. Instead, an application asserts owner-ship of a selection, and other applications request the value of the selection from that owner. This model is used on all platforms. The window system keeps track of ownership, and applications are informed when some other application takes away ownership. Several of the Tk widgets implement selections and take care of asserting ownership and returning its value.

The X PRIMARY selection is used in a way that eliminates the explicit copy step in copy and paste user actions. Whenever you select an object in your appli-cation, your application automatically puts that value into the PRIMARY selection. The Tk entry, listbox, and text widgets do this with their text selections, although you can turn this off with the exportSelection widget attribute. Users typically insert the value of the PRIMARY selection by clicking with the middle mouse button. There is only one instance of the PRIMARY selection across all wid-gets and all applications. If the user makes a new selection it automatically over-writes the previous value of the PRIMARY selection.

The CLIPBOARD *is cross-platform.*

If you want a mechanism that works on all platforms, use the CLIPBOARD selection. The PRIMARY selection is implemented by Tk on all platforms, and you can use it within an application, but on Windows and Macintosh the non-Tk applications do not know about the PRIMARY selection. The main goal of copy and paste is to provide general interoperability among all applications, so stick with the CLIPBOARD.

Tk 3.6 and earlier only supported the PRIMARY selection. When Tk 4.0 added support for the CLIPBOARD, I tried to merge the two selections to "simplify" things for my users. Example 35–1 implements a Paste function that inserts either the PRIMARY or CLIPBOARD selection into a text widget. The selection get command is used to retrieve the selection value:

Example 35–1 Paste the PRIMARY or CLIPBOARD selection.

```
proc Paste { text } {
    if [catch {selection get} sel] {
        if [catch {selection get -selection CLIPBOARD} sel] {
            # no selection or clipboard data
            return
        }
    }
    $text insert insert $sel
}
```

This Paste function can be convenient, but it turns out that users still need to keep track of the difference between the two selections. If a user only under-stands the CLIPBOARD, then the use of PRIMARY is only surprising. I learned that it is best to have a separate paste user action for the two selections. The conven-tion is that <ButtonRelease-2> sets the insert point and inserts the PRIMARY selection. (This convention is awkward with the one- and two-button mice on Macintosh and Windows.) The <<Paste>> event (e.g., the Paste key) simply inserts the CLIPBOARD selection at the current insert point. This convention is shown in Example 35–2, although these bindings are defined automatically for the text and entry widgets:

Example 35–2 Separate paste actions.

```
bind Text <<Paste>> {
    catch {%W insert insert \
        [selection get -selection CLIPBOARD]
    }
}
bind Text <ButtonRelease-2> {
    %W mark set insert @%x,%y
    catch {%W insert insert \
        [selection get -selection PRIMARY]
    }
}
```

The `selection` Command

There are two Tcl commands that deal with selections. The `selection` command is a general-purpose command that can set and get different selections. By default it manipulates the PRIMARY selection. The `clipboard` command stores data for later retrieval using the CLIPBOARD selection.

The `selection` command exposes the fully general selection model of different selections, types, and formats. You can define selection handlers that return selection values, and you can assert ownership of a selection and find out when you lose ownership to another application. Example 35–5 on page 510 shows a selection handler for a canvas.

A selection can have a type. The default is STRING. The type is different than the name of the selection (e.g., PRIMARY or CLIPBOARD). Each type can have a format, and the default format is also STRING. Ordinarily these defaults are fine. If you are dealing with non-Tk applications, however, you may need to ask for their selections by the right type (e.g., FILE_NAME). Formats include STRING, ATOM, and INTEGER. An ATOM is a name that is registered with the X server and identified by number. It is probably not a good idea to use non-STRING types and formats because it limits what other applications can use the information. The details about X selection types and formats are specified in the *Inter-Client Communication Conventions Manual* (David Rosenthal, Stuart Marks, X Consortium Standard). This is distributed with the X11 sources and can be found on the web at http://tronche.lri.fr:8000/gui/x/icccm/.

All of the `selection` operations take a `-selection` option that specifies the name of the selection being manipulated. This defaults to PRIMARY. Some of the operations take a `-displayof` option that specifies what display the selection is on. The value for this option is a Tk pathname of a window, and the selection on that window's display is manipulated. This is useful in X where applications can have their windows on remote displays. The default is to manipulate the selec-

V. Tk Details

tion on the display of the main window. Table 35–1 summarizes the `selection` command:

Table 35–1 The `selection` command.

`selection clear ?-displayof` `win? ?-selection sel?`	Clears the specified selection.

`selection get ?displayof win?`
`?-selection sel? ?-type`
`type?`
	Returns the specified selection. The `type` defaults to STRING.

`selection handle ?-selection`
`sel? ?-type type? ?-format`
`format? window command`
	Defines `command` to be the handler for selection requests when `window` owns the selection.

`selection own ?-displayof` `window? ?-selection sel?`	Returns the Tk pathname of the window that owns the selection, if it is in this application.

`selection own ?-command com-`
`mand? ?-selection sel? win-`
`dow`
	Asserts that `window` owns the `sel` selection. The `command` is called when ownership of the selection is taken away from `window`.

The `clipboard` Command

The `clipboard` command installs values into the CLIPBOARD selection. The CLIP-BOARD is meant for values that have been recently or temporarily deleted. It is use for the copy and paste model of selections. You must use the `selection` command to retrieve values from the CLIPBOARD selection:

```
selection get -selection CLIPBOARD
```

Table 35–2 summarizes the `clipboard` command:

Table 35–2 The `clipboard` command.

`clipboard clear ?-displayof` `win?`	Clears the CLIPBOARD selection.

`clipboard append ?-displayof`
`win? ?-format format?`
`?-type type? ?--? data`
	Appends `data` to the CLIPBOARD with the specified `type` and `format`, which both default to STRING.

Selection Handlers

The `selection handle` command registers a Tcl command to handle selection requests. The command is called to return the value of the selection to a requesting application. If the selection value is large, the command might be called several times to return the selection in pieces. The command gets two parameters that indicate the offset within the selection to start returning data, and the maximum number of bytes to return. If the command returns fewer than that many bytes, the selection request is assumed to be completed. Otherwise, the command is called again to get the rest of the data, and the offset parameter is adjusted accordingly.

You can also get a callback when you lose ownership of the selection. At that time it is appropriate to unhighlight the selected object in your interface. The selection own command sets ownership and registers a callback for when you lose ownership.

A Canvas Selection Handler

Example 35–3 through Example 35–7 implement cut and paste for a canvas. The CanvasSelect_Demo procedure creates a canvas and sets up some bindings for cut and paste:

Example 35–3 Bindings for canvas selection.

```
proc CanvasSelect_Demo { c } {
    # Create a canvas with a couple of objects
    canvas $c
    pack $c
    $c create rect 10 10 50 50 -fill red -tag object
    $c create poly 100 100 100 30 140 50 -fill orange \
        -tag object
    # Set up cut and paste bindings
    $c bind object <Button-1> [list CanvasSelect $c %x %y]
    bind $c <Key-Delete> [list CanvasDelete $c]
    bind $c <<Cut>> [list CanvasCut $c]
    bind $c <<Copy>> [list CanvasCopy $c]
    bind $c <<Paste>> [list CanvasPaste $c]
    bind $c <Button-2> [list CanvasPaste $c %x %y]
    # Register the handler for selection requests
    selection handle $c [list CanvasSelectHandle $c]
}
```

The CanvasSelect procedure selects an object. It uses the find closest canvas operation to find out what object is under the mouse, which works because the binding is on canvas items with the object tag. If the binding were on the canvas as a whole, you would use the find overlapping operation to limit selection to objects near the mouse click. The CanvasHighlight procedure is used to highlight the selected object. It displays small boxes at the corners of the object's bounding box. Finally, the CanvasSelectLose procedure is registered to be called when another application asserts ownership of the PRIMARY selection.

Example 35–4 Selecting objects.

```
proc CanvasSelect { w x y } {
    # Select an item on the canvas.
    global canvas
    set id [$w find closest $x $y]
    set canvas(select,$w) $id
    CanvasHighlight $w $id
    # Claim ownership of the PRIMARY selection
    selection own -command [list CanvasSelectLose $w] $w
    focus $w
}
proc CanvasHighlight {w id {clear clear}} {
    if {$clear == "clear"} {
        $w delete highlight
    }
    foreach {x1 y1 x2 y2} [$w bbox $id] { # lassign }
    foreach x [list $x1 $x2] {
        foreach y [list $y1 $y2] {
            $w create rectangle [expr $x-2] [expr $y-2] \
                [expr $x+2] [expr $y+2] -fill black \
                -tag highlight
        }
    }
}
proc CanvasSelectLose { w } {
    # Some other app has claimed the selection
    global canvas
    $w delete highlight
    unset canvas(select,$w)
}
```

Once you claim ownership, Tk calls back to the CanvasSelectHandle procedure when another application, even yours, requests the selection. This uses
CanvasDescription to compute a description of the canvas object. It uses canvas
operations to query the object's configuration and store that as a command that
will create the object:

Example 35–5 A canvas selection handler.

```
proc CanvasSelectHandle { w offset maxbytes } {
    # Handle a selection request
    global canvas
    if ![info exists canvas(select,$w)] {
        error "No selected item"
    }
    set id $canvas(select,$w)
    # Return the requested chunk of data.
    return [string range [CanvasDescription $w $id] \
        $offset [expr $offset+$maxbytes]]
}
proc CanvasDescription { w id } {
    # Generate a description of the object that can
```

```
    # be used to recreate it later.
    set type [$w type $id]
    set coords [$w coords $id]
    set config {}
    # Bundle up non-default configuration settings
    foreach conf [$w itemconfigure $id] {
        # itemconfigure returns a list like
        # -fill {} {} {} red
        set default [lindex $conf 3]
        set value [lindex $conf 4]
        if {[string compare $default $value] != 0} {
            lappend config [lindex $conf 0] $value
        }
    }
    return [concat CanvasObject $type $coords $config]
}
```

The `CanvasCopy` procedure puts the description of the selected item onto the clipboard with the `clipboard append` command. The `CanvasDelete` deletes an object and the highlighting, and `CanvasCut` is built from `CanvasCopy` and `CanvasDelete`:

Example 35–6 The copy and cut operations.

```
proc CanvasCopy { w } {
    global canvas
    if [info exists canvas(select,$w)] {
        set id $canvas(select,$w)
        clipboard clear
        clipboard append [CanvasDescription $w $id]
    }
}
proc CanvasDelete {w} {
    global canvas
    catch {
        $w delete highlight
        $w delete $canvas(select,$w)
        unset canvas(select,$w)
    }
}
proc CanvasCut { w } {
    CanvasCopy $w
    CanvasDelete $w
}
```

The `CanvasPaste` operation gets the value from the CLIPBOARD selection. The selection value has all the parameters needed for a canvas `create` operation. It gets the position of the new object from the `<Button-2>` event, or from the current mouse position if the `<<Paste>>` event is generated. If the mouse is out of the window, then the object is just put into the middle of the canvas. The original position and the new position are used to compute values for a canvas `move`:

V. Tk Details

Example 35–7 Pasting onto the canvas.

```
proc CanvasPaste { w {x {}} {y {}}} {
    # Paste the selection from the CLIPBOARD
    if [catch {selection get -selection CLIPBOARD} sel] {
        # no clipboard data
        return
    }
    if {[string length $x] == 0} {
        # <<Paste>>, get the current mouse coordinates
        set x [expr [winfo pointerx $w] - [winfo rootx $w]]
        set y [expr [winfo pointery $w] - [winfo rooty $w]]
        if {$x < 0 || $y < 0 ||
                $x > [winfo width $w] ||
                $y > [winfo height $w]} {
            # Mouse outside the window - center object
            set x [expr [winfo width $w]/2]
            set y [expr [winfo height $w]/2]
        }
    }
    if [regexp {^CanvasObject} $sel] {
        if [catch {eval {$w create} [lrange $sel 1 end]} id] {
            return;
        }
        # look at the first coordinate to see where to
        # move the object. Element 1 is the type, the
        # next two are the first coordinate
        set x1 [lindex $sel 2]
        set y1 [lindex $sel 3]
        $w move $id [expr $x-$x1] [expr $y-$y1]
    }
}
```

There is more you can do for a drawing program, of course. You'd like to be able to select multiple objects, create new ones, and more. The *canvas_ui* program on the CD-ROM was my first little effort at a canvas drawing program. The *ImPress* application by Christopher Cox is a full-featured page layout application based on the Tk canvas. You can find it on the CD-ROM and on the Web at:

```
http://www.ntlug.org/~ccox/impress/
```

## CHAPTER 36

Focus, Grabs, and Dialogs

Dialog boxes are a standard part of any user interface. Several dialog boxes are built into Tk. This chapter also describes how to build dialogs from scratch, which involves keyboard focus and grabs. Input focus directs keyboard events to different widgets. The grab mechanism lets a widget capture the input focus. This chapter describes the `focus`, `grab`, `tk_dialog`, and `tkwait` commands. Tk 4.2 adds `tk_getOpenFile`, `tk_getSaveFile`, `tk_chooseColor`, and `tk_messageBox`.

Dialog boxes are a common feature in a user interface. The application needs some user response before it can continue. A dialog box displays some information and some controls, and the user must interact with it before the application can continue. To implement this, the application *grabs* the input focus so that the user can only interact with the dialog box. Tk has several built-in dialog boxes, including standard dialogs for finding files and selecting colors. A standard dialog has the same Tcl interface on all platforms, but it is implemented with platform-specific library routines to provide native look and feel. This chapter describes the dialogs built into Tk and then goes into the details of focus and grabs.

Standard Dialogs

The `tk_dialog` command presents a choice of buttons and returns a number indicating which one was clicked by the user. The general form of the command is:

```
tk_dialog win title text bitmap default ?label? ?label? ...
```

The *title* appears in the title bar, and the *text* appears in the dialog. The *bitmap* appears to the left of the text. Specify {} for the bitmap if you do not want one. The set of built-in bitmaps is given on page 541. The *label* arguments give labels that appear on buttons along the bottom of the dialog. The `default` argument gives the index of the default button, counting from zero. If there is no default, specify {} or -1.

513

Message Box

The `tk_messageBox` dialog is a limited form of `tk_dialog` that has native implementations on the different platforms. Like `tk_dialog`, it allows for a message, bitmap, and a set of buttons. However, the button sets are predefined, and the bitmaps are limited. The `yesno` button set, for example, displays a `Yes` and a `No` button. The `abortretryignore` button set displays `Abort`, `Retry`, and `Ignore` buttons. The `tk_messageBox` command returns the symbolic name of the selected button (e.g., `yes` or `retry`.) The `yesnocancel` message box could be used when trying to quit with unsaved changes:

```
set choice [tk_messageBox -type yesnocancel -default yes \
    -message "Save changes before quitting?" \
    -icon question]
```

The complete set of options to `tk_messageBox` is listed in Table 36–1:

Table 36–1 Options to `tk_messageBox`.

`-default` *name*	Default button name (e.g., `yes`)
`-icon` *name*	Name: `error`, `info`, `question`, or `warning`.
`-message` *string*	Message to display.
`-parent` *window*	Embeds dialog in *window.*
`-title` *title*	Dialog title (UNIX and Windows)
`-type` *type*	Type: `abortretrycancel`, `ok`, `okcancel`, `retrycancel`, `yesno`, or `yesnocancel`

File Dialogs

There are two standard file dialogs, `tk_getOpenFile` and `tk_getSaveFile`. The `tk_getOpenFile` dialog is used to find an existing file, while `tk_getSaveFile` can be used to find a new file. These procedures return the selected file name, or the empty string if the user cancels the operation. These procedures take several options that are listed in Table 36–2:

Table 36–2 Options to the standard file dialogs.

`-defaultextension` *ext*	Appends *ext* if an extension is not specified.
`-filetypes` *typelist*	*typelist* defines a set of file types that the user can select to limit the files displayed in the dialog.
`-initialdir` *dir*	Lists contents of *dir* in the initial display.
`-initialfile` *file*	Default *file*, for `tk_getSaveFile` only.
`-parent` *window*	Creates the dialog as an embedded child of *window.*
`-title` *string*	Displays *string* in the title (UNIX and Windows).

The file dialogs can include a listbox that lists different file types. The file types are used to limit the directory listing to match only those types. The *typelist* option specifies a set of file extensions and Macintosh file types that correspond to a named file type. If you do not specify a *typelist*, users just see all the files in a directory. Each item in *typelist* is itself a list of three values:

> *name extensions ?mactypes?*

The *name* is displayed in the list of file types. The *extensions* is a list of file extensions corresponding to that type. The empty extension "" matches files without an extension, and the extension * matches all files. The *mactypes* is an optional list of four-character Macintosh file types, which are ignored on other platforms. On the Macintosh, if you give both *extensions* and *mactypes*, the files must match both. If the *extensions* is an empty list, only the *mactypes* are considered. However, you can repeat *name* in the *typelist* and give *extensions* in one set and *mactypes* in another set. If you do this, then files that match either the *extensions* or *mactypes* are listed.

The following *typelist* matches Framemaker Interchange Files that have both a .mif extension *and* a MIF type:

```
set typelist {
    {"Maker Interchange Files" {".mif"} {"MIF "}}
}
```

The following typelist matches GIF image files that have either a .gif extension *or* the GIFF file type. Note that the *mactypes* are optional:

```
set typelist {
    {"GIF Image" {".gif"}}
    {"GIF Image" {} {"GIFF"}}}
}
```

The following typelist puts all these together, along with an entry for all files. The entry that comes first is displayed first:

```
set typelist {
    {"All Files" {*}}
    {"GIF Image" {".gif"}}
    {"GIF Image" {} {"GIFF"}}
    {"Maker Interchange Files" {".mif"} {"MIF "}}
}
```

Color Dialog

The tk_chooseColor dialog displays a color selection dialog. It returns a color, or the empty string if the user cancels the operation. The options to tk_chooseColor are listed in Table 36–3:

Table 36-3 Options to `tk_chooseColor`.

`-initialcolor` *color*	Initial color to display.
`-parent` *window*	Creates the dialog as an embedded child of *window.*
`-title` *string*	Displays *string* in the title (UNIX and Windows).

Custom Dialogs

When you create your own dialogs, you need to understand keyboard focus, focus grabs, and how to wait for the user to finish with a dialog. Here is the general structure of your code when creating a dialog:

```
# Create widgets, then
focus $toplevel
grab $toplevel
tkwait window $toplevel
```

This sequence of commands directs keyboard focus to the toplevel containing your dialog. The `grab` forces the user to interact with the dialog before using other windows in your application. The `tkwait` command returns when the toplevel window is destroyed, and this automatically releases the grab. This assumes that the button commands in the dialog destroy the toplevel. The following sections explain these steps in more detail, and Example 36–1 on page 519 illustrates a more robust sequence.

Input Focus

The window system directs keyboard events to the toplevel window that currently has the input focus. The application, in turn, directs the keyboard events to one of the widgets within that toplevel window. The `focus` command sets focus to a particular widget, and it is used by the default bindings for Tk widgets. Tk remembers what widget has focus within a toplevel window and automatically gives focus to that widget when the system gives focus to a toplevel window.

On Windows and Macintosh, the focus is given to an application when you click in its window. On UNIX, the window manager application gives focus to different windows, and window managers allow different conventions to shift focus. The click-to-type model is similar to Windows and Macintosh. There is also focus-follows-mouse, which gives focus to the window under the mouse. One thing to note about click-to-type is that the application does not see the mouse click that gives the window focus.

Once the application has focus, you can manage the focus changes among your widgets any way you like. By default, Tk uses a click-to-type model. Text and entry widgets set focus to themselves when you click on them with the left mouse button. You can get the focus-follows-mouse model within your widgets by calling the `tk_focusFollowsMouse` procedure. However, in many cases you will find that an explicit focus model is actually more convenient for users. Carefully positioning the mouse over a small widget can be tedious.

The `focus` Command

Table 36–4 summarizes the `focus` command. The focus implementation supports multiple displays with a separate focus window on each display. This is useful on UNIX where X supports multiple displays. The `-displayof` option can be used to query the focus on a particular display. The `-lastfor` option finds out what widget last had the focus within the same toplevel as another window. Tk will restore focus to that window if the widget that has the focus is destroyed. The toplevel widget gets the focus if no widget claims it.

Table 36–4 The `focus` command.

`focus`	Returns the widget that currently has the focus on the display of the application's main window.
`focus ?-force? window`	Sets the focus to *window*. The `-force` option ignores the window manger, so use it sparingly.
`focus -displayof win`	Returns the focus widget on the same display as *win*.
`focus -lastfor win`	Returns the name of the last widget to have the focus in the same toplevel as *win*.

Keyboard Focus Traversal

Users can change focus among widgets with `<Tab>` and `<Shift-Tab>`. The creation order of widgets determines a traversal order for focus that is used by the `tk_focusNext` and `tk_focusPrev` procedures. There are global bindings for `<Tab>` and `<Shift-Tab>` that call these procedures:

```
bind all <Tab> {tk_focusNext %W}
bind all <Shift-Tab> {tk_focusPrev %W}
```

The Tk widgets highlight themselves when they have the focus. The highlight size is controlled with the `highlightThickness` attribute, and the color of the highlight is set with the `highlightColor` attribute. The Tk widgets, even buttons and scrollbars, have bindings that support keyboard interaction. A `<space>` invokes the command associated with a button, if the button has the input focus.

All widgets have a `takeFocus` attribute that the `tk_focusNext` and `tk_focusPrev` procedures use to determine if a widget will take the focus during keyboard traversal. There are four possible values to the attribute:

- `0` indicates the widget should not take focus.
- `1` indicates the widget should always take focus.
- An empty string means the traversal procedures `tk_focusNext` and `tk_focusPrev` should decide based on the widget's state and bindings.

V. Tk Details

- Otherwise the value is a Tcl command prefix. The command is called with the widget name as an argument, and it should return either 0, 1, or the empty string.

Grabbing the Focus

An input *grab* overrides the normal focus mechanism. For example, a dialog box can grab the focus so that the user cannot interact with other windows in the application. The typical scenario is that the application is performing some task but it needs user input. The grab restricts the user's actions so it cannot drive the application into an inconsistent state. A *global grab* prevents the user from interacting with other applications, too, even the window manager. Tk menus use a global grab, for example, which is how they unpost themselves no matter where you click the mouse. When an application prompts for a password, a global grab is also a good idea. This prevents the user from accidentally typing their password into a random window. Table 36–5 summarizes the grab command.

Table 36–5 The grab command.

grab ?-global? *window*	Sets a grab to a particular window.
grab current ?*window*?	Queries the grabs on the display of *window*, or on all displays if *window* is omitted.
grab release *window*	Releases a grab on *window*.
grab set ?-global? *win*	Sets a grab to a particular window.
grab status *window*	Returns none, local, or global.

In most cases you only need to use the grab and grab release commands. Note that the grab set command is equivalent to the grab command. The next section includes examples that use the grab command.

The tkwait Command

You wait for the user to interact with the dialog by using the tkwait command. The tkwait waits for something to happen, and while waiting it allows events to be processed. Like vwait, you can use tkwait to wait for a Tcl variable to change value. You can also wait for a window to become visible, or wait for a window to be destroyed. Table 36–6 summarizes the tkwait command.

Table 36–6 The tkwait command.

tkwait variable *varname*	Waits for the global variable *varname* to be set. This is just like the vwait command.
tkwait visibility *win*	Waits for the window *win* to become visible.
tkwait window *win*	Waits for the window *win* to be destroyed.

Use `tkwait` *with global variables.*

The variable specified in the `tkwait variable` command must be a global variable. Remember this if you use procedures to modify the variable. They must declare it global or the `tkwait` command will not notice the assignments.

The `tkwait visibility` waits for the visibility state of the window to change. Most commonly this is used to wait for a newly created window to become visible. For example, if you have any sort of animation in a complex dialog, you could wait until the dialog is displayed before starting the animation.

Destroying Widgets

The `destroy` command deletes one or more widgets. If the widget has children, all the children are destroyed, too. Chapter 41 describes a protocol on page 572 to handle destroy events that come from the window manager. You wait for a window to be deleted with the `tkwait window` command.

The `focus`, `grab`, `tkwait` sequence

In practice, I use a slightly more complex command sequence than just `focus`, `grab`, and `tkwait`. You can remember what widget had focus before the dialog is created so that focus can be restored after the dialog completes. When you do this, it is more reliable to restore focus before destroying the dialog. This prevents a tug of war between your application and the window manager. This sequence looks like:

```
set old [focus]
focus $toplevel
grab $toplevel
tkwait variable doneVar
grab release $toplevel
focus $old
destroy $toplevel
```

This sequence supports another trick I use, which is to unmap dialogs instead of destroying them. This way the dialogs appear more quickly the next time they are used. This makes creating the dialogs a little more complex because you need to see if the toplevel already exists. Chapter 41 describes the window manager commands used to map and unmap windows on page 572. Example 36–1 shows `Dialog_Create`, `Dialog_Wait`, and `Dialog_Dismiss` that capture all of these tricks:

Example 36–1 Procedures to help build dialogs.

```
proc Dialog_Create {top title args} {
    global dialog
    if [winfo exists $top] {
        switch -- [wm state $top] {
            normal {
                # Raise a buried window
```

V. Tk Details

```
                raise $top
            }
            withdrawn -
            iconic {
                # Open and restore geometry
                wm deiconify $top
                catch {wm geometry $top $dialog(geo,$top)}
            }
        }
        return 0
    } else {
        eval {toplevel $top} $args
        wm title $top $title
        return 1
    }
}
proc Dialog_Wait {top varName {focus {}}} {
    upvar $varName var

    # Poke the variable if the user nukes the window
    bind $top <Destroy> [list set $varName cancel]

    # Grab focus for the dialog
    if {[string length $focus] == 0} {
        set focus $top
    }
    set old [focus -displayof $top]
    focus $focus
    catch {tkwait visibility $top}
    catch {grab $top}

    # Wait for the dialog to complete
    tkwait variable $varName
    catch {grab release $top}
    focus $old
}
proc Dialog_Dismiss {top} {
    global dialog
    # Save current size and position
    catch {
        # window may have been deleted
        set dialog(geo,$top) [wm geometry $top]
        wm withdraw $top
    }
}
```

The Dialog_Wait procedure allows a different focus widget than the toplevel. The idea is that you can start the focus out in the appropriate widget within the dialog, such as the first entry widget. Otherwise, the user has to click in the dialog first.

Grab can fail.

The catch statements in Dialog_Wait come from my experiences on different platforms. The tkwait visibility is sometimes required because grab can fail if the dialog is not yet visible. However, on other systems, the `tkwait visibility` itself can fail in some circumstances. Tk reflects these errors, but in this case all that can go wrong is no grab. The user can still interact with the dialog without a grab, so I just ignore these errors.

Prompter Dialog

Example 36–2 A simple dialog.

```
proc Dialog_Prompt { string } {
    global prompt
    set f .prompt
    if [Dialog_Create $f "Prompt" -borderwidth 10] {
        message $f.msg -text $string -aspect 1000
        entry $f.entry -textvariable prompt(result)
        set b [frame $f.buttons]
        pack $f.msg $f.entry $f.buttons -side top -fill x
        pack $f.entry -pady 5
        button $b.ok -text OK -command {set prompt(ok) 1}
        button $b.cancel -text Cancel \
            -command {set prompt(ok) 0}
        pack $b.ok -side left
        pack $b.cancel -side right
        bind $f.entry <Return> {set prompt(ok) 1 ; break}
        bind $f.entry <Control-c> {set prompt(ok) 0 ; break}
    }
    set prompt(ok) 0
    Dialog_Wait $f prompt(ok) $f.entry
    Dialog_Dismiss $f
    if {$prompt(ok)} {
        return $prompt(result)
    } else {
        return {}
    }
}
Dialog_Prompt "Please enter a name"
```

The `Dialog_Prompt` dialog gets a value from the user, returning the value entered, or the empty string if the user cancels the operation. `Dialog_Prompt` uses the Tcl variable `prompt(ok)` to indicate the dialog is complete. The variable is set if the user presses the `OK` or `Cancel` buttons, or if the user presses `<Return>` or `<Control-c>` in the entry widget. The `Dialog_Wait` procedure waits on `prompt(ok)`, and it grabs and restores focus. If the `Dialog_Create` procedure returns 1, then the dialog is built: otherwise, it already existed.

Keyboard Shortcuts and Focus

Focus is set on the entry widget in the dialog with `Dialog_Wait`, and it is convenient if users can use special key bindings to complete the dialog. Otherwise, they need to take their hands off the keyboard and use the mouse. The example defines bindings for `<Return>` and `<Control-c>` that invoke the `OK` and `Cancel` buttons, respectively. The bindings override all other bindings by including a `break` command. Otherwise, the `Entry` class bindings insert the short-cut keystroke into the entry widget.

Animation with the `update` Command

Suppose you want to entertain your user while your application is busy. By default, the user interface hangs until your processing completes. Even if you change a label or entry widget in the middle of processing, the updates to that widget are deferred until an idle moment. The user does not see your feedback, and the window is not refreshed if it gets obscured and uncovered. The solution is to use the `update` command that forces Tk to go through its event loop and update the display.

The next example shows a `Feedback` procedure that displays status messages. A read-only entry widget displays the messages, and the `update` command ensures that the user sees each new message. An entry widget is used because it won't change size based on the message length, and it can be scrolled by dragging with the middle mouse button. Entry widgets also work better with `update idletasks` as described later:

Example 36–3 A feedback procedure.

```
proc Feedback { message } {
    global feedback
    set e $feedback(entry)
    $e config -state normal
    $e delete 0 end
    $e insert 0 $message
    # Leave the entry in a read-only state
    $e config -state disabled
    # Force a display update
    update idletasks
}
```

The Tk widgets update their display at idle moments, which basically means after everything else is taken care of. This lets them collapse updates into one interaction with the window system. On UNIX, this improves the batching effects that are part of the X protocol. A call to `update idletasks` causes any pending display updates to be processed. Chapter 16 describes the Tk event loop in more detail.

Use `update idletasks` if possible.

The safest way to use `update` is with its `idletasks` option. If you use the `update` command with no options, then all events are processed. In particular, user input events are processed. If you are not careful, it can have unexpected effects because another thread of execution is launched into your Tcl interpreter. The current thread is suspended and any callbacks that result from input events are executed. It is usually better to use the `tkwait` command if you need to process input because it pauses the main application at a well-defined point.

One drawback of `update idletasks` is that in some cases a widget's redisplay is triggered by window system events. In particular, when you change the text of a label, it can cause the size of the label to change. The widget is too clever for us in this case. Instead of scheduling a redisplay at idle time, it requests a different size and then waits for the `<Configure>` event from the window system. The `<Configure>` event indicates a size has been chosen by the geometry manager, and it is at that point that the label schedules its redisplay. So, changing the label's text and doing `update idletasks` do not work as expected.

Tk Widget Attributes

Each Tk widget has a number of attributes that affect its appearance and behavior. This chapter describes attributes in general, and covers some of the size and appearance-related attributes. The next two chapters cover the attributes associated with colors, images, and text.

This chapter describes some of the attributes that are in common among many Tk widgets. A widget always provides a default value for its attributes, so you can avoid specifying most of them. If you want to fine-tune things, however, you'll need to know about all the widget attributes.

The native widgets used in Tk 8.0 ignore some of the original Tk attributes. This is because there is no support for them in the system widgets. For example, the buttons on Macintosh do not honor the borderWidth attribute, and they do not display a highlight focus. The native scrollbars on Windows and Macintosh have similar limitations. This chapter notes these limitations in the discussion of each attribute.

Configuring Attributes

You specify attributes for Tk widgets when you create them. You can also change them dynamically at any time after that. In both cases the syntax uses pairs of arguments. The first item in the pair identifies the attribute, the second provides the value. For example, a button can be created like this:

```
button .doit -text Doit -command DoSomething
```

The name of the button is .doit, and two attributes are specified: the text and the command. You can change the .doit button later with the configure widget operation:

```
.doit configure -text Stop -command StopIt
```

V. Tk Details

525

The current configuration of a widget can be queried with another form of the `configure` operation. If you just supply an attribute, the settings associated with that attribute are returned:

```
.doit configure -text
=> -text text Text { } Stop
```

This command returns several pieces of information: the command line switch, the resource name, the resource class, the default value, and the current value. If you don't give any options to configure, then the configuration information for all the attributes is returned. The following loop formats the information:

```
foreach item [$w configure] {
    puts "[lindex $item 0] [lindex $item 4]"
}
```

If you just want the current value, use the `cget` operation:

```
.doit cget -text
=> Stop
```

You can also configure widget attributes indirectly by using the resource database. An advantage of using the resource database is that users can reconfigure your application without touching the code. Otherwise, if you specify attribute values explicitly in the code, they cannot be overridden by resource settings. This is especially important for attributes like fonts and colors.

The tables in this chapter list the attributes by their resource name, which may have a capital letter at an internal word boundary (e.g., `activeBackground`). When you specify attributes in a Tcl command, use all lowercase instead, plus a leading dash. Compare:

```
option add *Button.activeBackground red
$button configure -activebackground red
```

The first command defines a resource that affects all buttons created after that point, and the second command changes an existing button. Command-line settings override resource database specifications. Chapter 28 describes the use of resources in detail.

Size

Most widgets have a `width` and `height` attribute that specifies their desired size, although there are some special cases. In all cases, the geometry manager for a widget might modify the size to some degree. The `winfo` operations described on page 571 return the current size of a widget.

Most of the text-related widgets interpret their sizes in units of characters for width and lines for height. All other widgets, including the `message` widget, interpret their dimensions in screen units, which are pixels by default. The `tk scale` command, which is described on page 580, controls the scale between pixels and the other measures. You can suffix the dimension with a unit specifier to get a particular measurement unit:

```
c    centimeters
```

```
i    inch
m    millimeters
p    printer points (1/72 inches)
```

Scales and scrollbars can have two orientations as specified by the `orient` attribute, so width and height are somewhat ambiguous. These widgets do not support a `height` attribute, and they interpret their `width` attribute to mean the size of their narrow dimension. The `scale` has a `length` attribute that determines its long dimension. Scrollbars do not even have a `length`. Instead, a `scrollbar` is assumed to be packed next to the widget it controls, and the `fill` packing attribute is used to extend the scrollbar to match the length of its adjacent widget. Example 30–1 on page 428 shows how to arrange scrollbars with another widget.

The `message` widget displays a fixed string on multiple lines, and it uses one of two attributes to constrain its size: its `aspect` or its `width`. The aspect ratio is defined to be 100*width/height, and it formats its text to honor this constraint. However, if a `width` is specified, it just uses that and uses as many lines (i.e., as much height) as needed. Example 29–3 on page 421 shows how message widgets display text. Table 37–1 summarizes the attributes used to specify the size for widgets:

Table 37–1 Size attribute resource names.

aspect	The aspect ratio of a `message` widget, which is 100 times the ratio of width divided by height.
height	Height, in text lines or screen units. Widgets: `button`, `canvas`, `checkbutton`, `frame`, `label`, `listbox`, `menubutton`, `radiobutton`, `text`, and `toplevel`.
length	The long dimension of a `scale`.
orient	Orientation for long and narrow widgets: `horizontal` or `vertical`. Widgets: `scale` and `scrollbar`.
width	Width, in characters or screen units. Widgets: `button`, `canvas`, `checkbutton`, `entry`, `frame`, `label`, `listbox`, `menubutton`, `message`, `radiobutton`, `scale`, `scrollbar`, `text`, and `toplevel`.

It is somewhat unfortunate that text-oriented widgets only take character- and line-oriented dimensions. These sizes change with the font used, and if you want a precise size you might be frustrated. Both `pack` and `grid` let the widgets decide how big to be. One trick is to put each widget, such as a label, in its own frame. Specify the size you want for the frame, and then pack the label and turn off size propagation. For example:

V. Tk Details

Example 37–1 Equal-sized labels.

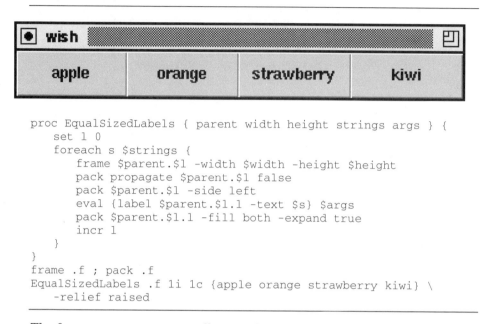

```
proc EqualSizedLabels { parent width height strings args } {
    set l 0
    foreach s $strings {
        frame $parent.$l -width $width -height $height
        pack propagate $parent.$l false
        pack $parent.$l -side left
        eval {label $parent.$l.l -text $s} $args
        pack $parent.$l.l -fill both -expand true
        incr l
    }
}
frame .f ; pack .f
EqualSizedLabels .f 1i 1c {apple orange strawberry kiwi} \
    -relief raised
```

The frames `$parent.$l` are all created with the same size. The `pack` propagate command prevents these frames from changing size when the labels are packed into them later. The labels are packed with `fill` and `expand` turned on so that they fill up the fixed-sized frames around them.

Borders and Relief

Example 37–2 illustrates the different reliefs:

Example 37–2 3D relief sampler.

```
frame .f -borderwidth 10
pack .f
foreach relief {raised sunken flat ridge groove solid} {
    label .f.$relief -text $relief -relief $relief \
        -bd 2 -padx 3
    pack .f.$relief -side left -padx 4
}
```

The three-dimensional appearance of widgets is determined by two attributes: `borderWidth` and `relief`. The `borderWidth` adds extra space around the edge of a widget's display, and this area can be displayed in a number of ways according to the `relief` attribute. The `solid` relief was added in Tk 8.0 to support the Macintosh look for entry widget, and it works well against white backgrounds. Macintosh and Windows buttons do not support different reliefs, and the Macintosh buttons do not honor border width.

The `activeBorderWidth` attribute is a special case for menus. It defines the border width for the menu entries. The relief of a menu is not configurable. It probably is not worth adjusting the menu border width attributes because the default looks OK. The native menus on Windows and Macintosh do not honor this attribute.

The `activeRelief` applies to the elements of a scrollbar (the elevator and two arrows) when the mouse is over them. The `elementBorderWidth` sets the size of the relief on these elements. Changing the `activeRelief` does not look good. The native scrollbars on Macintosh and Windows do not honor this attribute. Table 37–2 lists the attributes for borders and relief.

Table 37–2 Border and relief attribute resource names.

`borderWidth`	The width of the border around a widget, in screen units. Widgets: `button, canvas, checkbutton, entry, frame, label, listbox, menu, menubutton, message, radiobutton, scale, scrollbar, text,` and `toplevel`.
`bd`	Short for `borderwidth`. Tcl commands only.
`elementBorderWidth`	The width of the border on `scrollbar` and `scale` elements.
`relief`	The appearance of the border. Values: `flat, raised, sunken, ridge, groove,` or `solid`. Widgets: `button, canvas, checkbutton, entry, frame, label, listbox, menubutton, message, radiobutton, scale, scrollbar, text,` and `toplevel`.
`activeBorderWidth`	The border width for `menu` entries. UNIX only.
`activeRelief`	The relief for active `scrollbar` elements. UNIX only.

V. Tk Details

The Focus Highlight

Each widget can have a focus highlight indicating which widget currently has the input focus. This is a thin rectangle around each widget that is displayed in the highlight background color by default. When the widget gets the input focus, the highlight rectangle is displayed in an alternate color. The addition of the highlight adds a small amount of space outside the border described in the previous section. The attributes in Table 37–3 control the width and color of this rectangle. If the width is zero, no highlight is displayed.

By default, only the widgets that normally expect input focus have a non-zero width highlight border. This includes the `text`, `entry`, and `listbox` widgets. It also includes the `button` and `menu` widgets because there is a set of keyboard traversal bindings that focus input on these widgets, too. You can define nonzero highlight thicknesses for all widgets except Macintosh buttons.

Table 37–3 Highlight attribute resource names.

`highlightColor`	The color of the highlight when the widget has focus.
`highlightBackground`	The highlight color when the widget does not have focus.
`highlightThickness`	The width of the highlight border.

Padding and Anchors

Table 37–4 lists padding and anchor attributes that are similar in spirit to some packing attributes described in Chapter 23. However, they are distinct from the packing attributes, and this section explains how they work together with the packer.

Table 37–4 Layout attribute resource names.

`anchor`	The anchor position of the widget. Values: n, ne, e, se, s, sw, w, nw, or `center`. Widgets: `button, checkbutton, label, menubutton, message,` or `radiobutton`.
`padX, padY`	Padding space in the X or Y direction, in screen units. Widgets: `button, checkbutton, label, menubutton, message, radiobutton,` or `text`.

The padding attributes for a widget define space that is never occupied by the display of the widget's contents. For example, if you create a `label` with the following attributes and pack it into a frame by itself, you will see the text is still centered, despite the `anchor` attribute.

Example 37–3 Padding provided by labels and buttons.

```
label .foo -text Foo -padx 20 -anchor e
pack .foo
```

The `anchor` attribute only affects the display if there is extra room for another reason. One way to get extra room is to specify a `width` attribute that is longer than the text. The following label has right-justified text. You can see the default `padX` value for labels, which is one pixel:

Example 37–4 Anchoring text in a label or button.

```
label .foo -text Foo -width 10 -anchor e
pack .foo
```

Another way to get extra display space is with the `-ipadx` and `-ipady` packing parameters. The example in the next section illustrates this effect. Chapter 23 has several more examples of the packing parameters.

Putting It All Together

The number of different attributes that contribute to the size and appearance can be confusing. The example in this section uses a label to demonstrate the difference among size, borders, padding, and the highlight. Padding can come from the geometry manager, and it can come from widget attributes:

Example 37–5 Borders and padding.

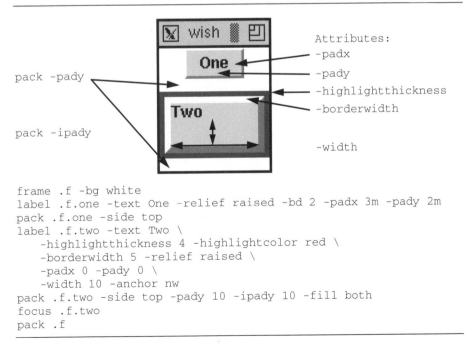

```
frame .f -bg white
label .f.one -text One -relief raised -bd 2 -padx 3m -pady 2m
pack .f.one -side top
label .f.two -text Two \
    -highlightthickness 4 -highlightcolor red \
    -borderwidth 5 -relief raised \
    -padx 0 -pady 0 \
    -width 10 -anchor nw
pack .f.two -side top -pady 10 -ipady 10 -fill both
focus .f.two
pack .f
```

The first label in the example uses a raised relief, so you can see the two-pixel border. (The default border size changed in Tk 8.0 to one pixel to match the CDE look and feel.) There is no highlight on a label by default. There is internal padding so that the text is spaced away from the edge of the label. The second label adds a highlight rectangle by specifying a nonzero thickness. Widgets like buttons, entries, listboxes, and text have a highlight rectangle by default. The second label's padding attributes are reduced to zero. The anchor positions the text right next to the border in the upper-left (nw) corner. However, note the effect of the padding provided by the packer. There is both external and internal padding in the Y direction. The external padding (from `pack -pady`) results in unfilled space. The internal packing (`pack -ipady`) is used by the label for its display. This is different from the label's own `-pady` attribute, which keeps the text away from the top edge of the widget.

Color, Images, and Cursors

This chapter describes the color attributes shared by the Tk widgets. Images and bitmaps can be displayed instead of text by several widgets. This chapter describes commands that create and manipulate images. The cursor attribute controls the shape and color of the mouse cursor when it is over a particular widget. This chapter includes a figure that shows all the cursors available in Tk.

Color is one of the most fun things to play with in a user interface. However, this chapter makes no attempt to improve your taste in color choices; it just describes the attributes that affect color. The tradition of having users change application colors is stronger in UNIX than on the other platforms. This is because all the X toolkits support color tuning via the resource database. Tk carries this tradition to Windows and Macintosh. However, if native look and feel is important, you should not change the default widget colors. On the other hand, tuning colors can provide a flair to your applications, and knowledge of colors is useful for canvas applications.

This chapter describes images, too. The image facility in Tk lets you create an image and then have other Tk widgets display it. The same image can be displayed by many different widgets, multiple times on a canvas, and multiple times within the text widget. If you redefine an image, its display is updated in whatever widgets are displaying it.

The last topic of the chapter is cursors. All widgets can control what the mouse cursor looks like when it is over them. In addition, the widgets that support text input define another cursor, the insert cursor. Its appearance is controlled with a few related attributes.

Colors

Table 38–1 lists the resource names for color attributes. The table indicates what widgets use the different color attributes. Remember to use all lowercase and a leading dash when specifying attributes in a Tcl command.

Table 38–1 Color attribute resource names.

background	The normal background color. All widgets.
bg	Short for background. Command line only.
foreground	The normal foreground color. Widgets: button, checkbutton, entry, label, listbox, menu, menubutton, message, radiobutton, scale, and text.
fg	Short for foreground. Command line only.
activeBackground	The background when a mouse button will take an action. Widgets: button, checkbutton, menu, menubutton, radiobutton, scale, and scrollbar.
activeForeground	The foreground when the mouse is over an active widget. Widgets: button, checkbutton, menu, menubutton, and radiobutton.
disabledForeground	The foreground when a widget is disabled. Widgets: button, checkbutton, menu, menubutton, and radiobutton.
highlightBackground	The highlight color when widget does not have focus. All widgets.
highlightColor	The highlight color when the widget has focus. All widgets.
insertBackground	The color of the insert cursor. Widgets: canvas, entry, and text.
selectBackground	The background of selected text. Widgets: canvas, entry, listbox, and text.
selectColor	The color of the selector indicator. Widgets: checkbutton, and radiobutton.
selectForeground	The foreground of selected text. Widgets: canvas, entry, listbox, and text.
troughColor	The trough part of scales and scrollbars.

The foreground color is used to draw an element, while the background color is used for the blank area behind the element. Text, for example, is painted with the foreground color. There are several variations on foreground and background that reflect different states for widgets or items they are displaying.

Each attribute also has a resource class. This is most useful for the variations on foreground and background colors. For example, Tk does not have a reverse video mode. However, with a couple of resource specifications you can convert a monochrome display into reverse video. The definitions are given in Example 38–1. The Foreground and Background resource class names are used, and the various foreground and background colors (e.g., activeBackground) have the correct resource class so these settings work. You have to set these resources before you create any widgets:

Example 38–1 Resources for reverse video.

```
proc ReverseVideo {} {
    option add *Foreground white
    option add *Background black
}
```

Color Palettes

The tk_setPalette command changes colors of existing widgets and installs resource values so new widgets have matching colors. If you give it a single argument, it treats this as the background and then computes new values for the other color resources. For example, if you do not like the standard Tk grey, you can lighten your spirits with a cool blue background:

```
tk_setPalette #0088cc
```

If you liked the light brown color scheme of Tk 3.6, you can restore that palette with the tk_bisque command:

```
tk_bisque
```

The tk_setPalette command can be used to change any of the color attributes. You can specify a set of name-value pairs, where the names are color resource names and the values are new color values:

```
tk_setPalette activeBackground red activeForeground white
```

Color Values

Color values are specified in two ways: symbolically (e.g., red), or by hexadecimal numbers (e.g., #ff0000). The leading # distinguishes the hexadecimal representation from the symbolic one. The number is divided into three equal-sized fields that give the red, green, and blue values, respectively. The fields can specify 4, 8, 12, or 16 bits of a color:

```
#RGB             4 bits per color
#RRGGBB          8 bits per color
#RRRGGGBBB       12 bits per color
#RRRRGGGGBBBB    16 bits per color
```

If you specify more resolution than is supported by the display, the low-order bits of each field are discarded. The different display types supported by Tk are described in the next section. Each field ranges from 0, which means no color, to a maximum, which is all ones in binary, or all f in hex, that means full color saturation. For example, pure red can be specified four ways:

#f00 #ff0000 #fff000000 #ffff00000000

There is a large collection of symbolic color names like "red," "blue," "green," "thistle," "medium sea green," and "yellow4." These names originate from X and UNIX, and Tk supports these colors on all platforms. You can find the list in the Tk sources in the xlib/xcolor.c file. Or, run the *xcolors* program that comes with the standard X distribution.

The Windows and Macintosh platforms have a small set of colors that are guaranteed to exist, and Tk defines names for these. The advantage of using these colors is that they are shared by all applications, so the system can manage colors efficiently. Table 38–2 lists the system colors on Windows. Several of these colors map to the same RGB value. Table 38–3 lists the system colors on Macintosh.

Table 38–2 Windows system colors.

system3dDarkShadow	Dark part of button 3D-relief.
system3dLight	Light part of button 3D-relief.
systemActiveBorder	Window border when activated.
systemActiveCaption	Caption (i.e., title bar) when activated.
systemAppWorkspace	Background for MDI workspaces.
systemBackground	Widget background.
systemButtonFace	Button background.
systemButtonHighlight	Lightest part of button 3D-relief.
systemButtonShadow	Darkest part of button 3D-relief.
systemButtonText	Button foreground.
systemCaptionText	Caption (i.e., title bar) text.
systemDisabledText	Text when disabled.
systemGrayText	Grey text color.
systemHighlight	Selection background.
systemHighlightText	Selection foreground.
systemInactiveBorder	Window border when not activated.
systemInactiveCaption	Caption background when not activated.
systemInactiveCaptionText	Caption text when not activated.
systemInfoBackground	Help pop-up background.
systemInfoText	Help pop-up text.

Table 38–2 Windows system colors. (Continued)

systemMenu	Menu background.
systemMenuText	Menu foreground.
systemScrollbar	Scrollbar background.
systemWindow	Text window background.
systemWindowFrame	Text window frame.
systemWindowText	Text window text color.

Table 38–3 Macintosh system colors.

systemHighlight	Selection background.
systemHighlightText	Selection foreground.
systemButtonFace	Button background.
systemButtonFrame	Button frame.
systemButtonText	Button foreground.
systemWindowBody	Widget background.
systemMenuActive	Selected menu item background.
systemMenuActiveText	Selected menu item foreground.
systemMenu	Menu background.
systemMenuDisabled	Disabled menu item background.
systemMenuText	Menu foreground.

Getting RGB values.

The `winfo rgb` command maps from a color name (or value) to three numbers that are its red, green, and blue values. You can use this to compute variations on a color. The `ColorDarken` procedure shown below uses the `winfo rgb` command to get the red, green, and blue components of the input color. It reduces these amounts by 5 percent, and reconstructs the color specification using the `format` command.

Example 38–2 Computing a darker color.

```
proc ColorDarken { win color } {
    set rgb [winfo rgb $win $color]
    return [format "#%03x%03x%03x" \
        [expr round([lindex $rgb 0] * 0.95)] \
        [expr round([lindex $rgb 1] * 0.95)] \
        [expr round([lindex $rgb 2] * 0.95)]]
}
```

V. Tk Details

Colormaps and Visuals

Computer screens can display only a fixed number of different colors at one time. The best monitors can display 24 million colors, but it is common to find 256 color displays. Really old VGA displays only display 16 colors. If you run several applications at once, it is possible that more colors are requested than can be displayed. The Windows and Macintosh platforms manage this scenario automatically. X provides lower-level facilities that Tk uses on UNIX to do the management. So, for the most part you don't have to worry. However, if you need more control, especially under X, then you need to understand *colormaps* and the different *visual* types.

Each pixel on the screen is represented by one or more bits of memory. There are a number of ways to map from a value stored at a pixel to the color that appears on the screen at that pixel. The mapping is a function of the number of bits at each pixel, which is called the *depth* of the display, and the style of interpretation, or *visual class*. The six visual classes defined by X are listed in the following table. Some of the visuals use a *colormap* that maps from the value stored at a pixel to a value used by the hardware to generate a color. A colormap enables a compact encoding for a much richer color. For example, a 256-entry colormap can be indexed with 8 bits, but it may contain 24 bits of color information. The UNIX *xdpyinfo* program reports the different visual classes supported by your display. Table 38–4 lists the visual classes:

Table 38–4 Visual classes for displays.

staticgrey	Greyscale with a fixed colormap defined by the system.
greyscale	Greyscale with a writable colormap.
staticcolor	Color with a fixed colormap defined by the system.
pseudocolor	Color values determined by single writable colormap.
truecolor	Color values determined by three colormaps defined by the system: one each for red, green, and blue.
directcolor	Color values determined by three writable colormaps: one each for red, green, and blue.
best	Use the best visual for a given depth.

The frame and toplevel widgets support a `colormap` and `visual` attribute. You can query these attributes on all platforms. On Windows and Macintosh there is only one `visual` type at a time, and users may be able to change it for their whole system. On UNIX, the X server typically supports more than one visual class on the same display, and you can create frames and toplevels that use a particular visual class. The value of the `visual` attribute has two parts, a visual type and the desired depth of the display. The following example requests a greyscale visual with a depth of 4 bits per pixel:

```
toplevel .grey -visual "greyscale 4"
```

You can start *wish* with a `-visual` command line argument:

```
wish -visual "truecolor 24"
```

A visual is associated with a colormap. Windows and Macintosh have a single colormap that is shared by all applications. UNIX allows for private colormaps, which can be useful if you absolutely must have lots of colors. However, the drawback of a private colormap is that the display flashes as the mouse enters windows with their own colormap. This is because the monitor hardware really only has one colormap, so the X server must swap colormaps. Macintosh and Windows manage their colormap more gracefully, although if you use too many colors some flashing can occur. Tk can simulate private colormaps on Windows, but it is probably better to let the system manage the colormap. Tk on the Macintosh always uses a 24-bit `truecolor` visual, which is basically unlimited colors, and lets the operating system dither colors if necessary.

By default a widget inherits the colormap and visual from its parent widget. The value of the `colormap` attribute can be the keyword `new`, in which case the frame or toplevel gets a new private colormap, or it can be the name of another widget, in which case the frame or toplevel shares the colormap of that widget. When sharing colormaps, the other widget must be on the same screen and using the same visual class.

Bitmaps and Images

The label and all the button widgets have an `image` attribute that specifies a graphic image to display. Using an image takes two steps. In the first step the image is created via the `image create` command. This command returns an identifier for the image, and it is this identifier that is passed to widgets as the value of their image attribute.

Example 38–3 Specifying an image for a widget.

```
set im [image create bitmap \
    -file glyph.bitmap -maskfile glyph.mask \
    -background white -foreground blue]
button .foo -image $im
```

There are three things that can be displayed by labels and all the buttons: text, bitmaps, and images. If more than one of these attributes are specified, then the image has priority over the bitmap, and the bitmap has priority over the text. You can remove the image or bitmap attribute by specifying a null string for its value:

```
.foo config -image {}
```

V. Tk Details

The image Command

Table 38–5 summarizes the image command.

Table 38–5 Summary of the image command.

image create *type* ?*name*? ?*options*?	Creates an image of the specified type. If *name* is not specified, one is made up. The remaining arguments depend on the *type* of image being created.
image delete *name*	Deletes the named image.
image height *name*	Returns the height of the image, in pixels.
image names	Returns the list of defined images.
image type *name*	Returns the type of the named image.
image types	Returns the list of possible image types.
image width *name*	Returns the width of the image, in pixels.

The exact set of options for image create depend on the image type. There are two built-in image types: bitmap and photo. Chapter 47 describes the C interface for defining new image types.

Bitmap Images

A bitmap image has a main image and an optional mask image. The main image is drawn in the foreground color. The mask image is drawn in the background color, unless the corresponding bit is set in the main image. The remaining bits are "clear" and the widget's normal background color shows through. Table 38–6 lists the options supported by the bitmap image type:

Table 38–6 Bitmap image options.

-background *color*	The background color (*no* -bg *equivalent*).
-data *string*	The contents of the bitmap as a string.
-file *name*	The name of the file containing a bitmap definition.
-foreground *color*	The foreground color (*no* -fg *equivalent*).
-maskdata *string*	The contents of the mask as a string.
-maskfile *name*	The name of the file containing the mask data.

The bitmap definition files are stylized C structure definitions that the Tk library parses. The files usually have a .xbm file name extension. These are generated by bitmap editors such as *bitmap* program, which comes with the standard X distribution. The -file and -maskfile options name a file that contains such a definition. The `-data` and `-maskdata` options specify a string in the same format as the contents of one of those files.

The `bitmap` Attribute

The label and all the button widgets also support a `bitmap` attribute, which is a special case of an image. This attribute is a little more convenient than the image attribute because the extra step of creating an image is not required. However, there are some power and flexibility with the `image` command, such as the ability to reconfigure a named image (e.g., for animation) that is not possible with a bitmap.

Example 38–4 Specifying a bitmap for a widget.

```
button .foo -bitmap @glyph.xbm -fg blue
```

The `@` syntax for the bitmap attribute signals that a file containing the bitmap is being specified. It is also possible to name built-in bitmaps. The predefined bitmaps are shown in the next figure along with their symbolic name. Chapter 47 describes the C interface for defining built in bitmaps.

Example 38–5 The built-in bitmaps.

```
frame .f -bd 4; frame .g -bd 4 ; pack .f .g -side left
set parent .f ; set next .g
foreach name {error gray12 gray50 hourglass \
              info questhead question warning} {
    frame $parent.$name
    label $parent.$name.l -text $name -width 9 -anchor w
    label $parent.$name.b -bitmap $name
    pack $parent.$name.l -side right
    pack $parent.$name.b -side top
    pack $parent.$name -side top -expand true -fill x
    set tmp $parent ; set parent $next ; set next $tmp
}
```

V. Tk Details

Photo Images

The `photo` image type was contributed to Tk by Paul Mackerras. It displays full color images and can do dithering and gamma correction. Table 38–7 lists the attributes for photo images. These are specified in the `image create photo` command.

Table 38–7 Photo image attributes.

`-format` *format*	Specifies the data format for the file or data string.
`-data` *string*	The contents of the photo as a base64 coded string.
`-file` *name*	The name of the file containing a photo definition.
`-gamma` *value*	A gamma correction factor, which must be greater than zero. A value greater than one brightens an image.
`-height` *value*	The height, in screen units.
`-width` *value*	The width of the image, in screen units.
`-palette` *spec*	The number of shades of gray or color for the image.

The `format` indicates what format the data are in. The `photo` image supports different image formats. Tk 4.0 supports the PPM, PGM, and GIF formats. There is a C interface to define new photo formats. The CD-ROM has a "plus-patch" version of Tk that supports pixmaps and JPEG files. Normally you do not need to specify the format because the photo implementation will try all format handlers until it find one that accepts the data. An explicit format limits what handlers are tried. The format name is treated as a prefix that is compared against the names of handlers. Case is not significant in the format name.

The `palette` setting determines how many colors or graylevels are used when rendering an image. If a single number is specified, the image is rendered in greyscale with that many shades of gray. For full color, three numbers separated by slashes specify the number of shades of red, green, and blue, respectively. The more shades you specify the more room you take up in your colormap. The photo widget will switch to a private colormap if necessary. Multiply the number of red, green, and blue shades to determine how many different colors you use. If you have an 8-bit display, there are only 256 colors available. Reasonable palette settings that do not hog the colormap include `5/5/4` and `6/6/5`. You can use fewer shades of blue because the human eye is less sensitive to blue.

After you create an image you can operate on it. Table 38–8 lists the image instance operations. In the table, `$p` is a photo image handle returned by the `image create photo` command.

Table 38–9 lists the options available when you copy data from one image to another. The regions involved in the copy are specified by the upper-left and lower-right corners. If the lower-right corner of the source is not specified, then it

Table 38–8 Photo image operations.

`$p blank`	Clears the image. It becomes transparent.
`$p cget option`	Returns the configuration attribute `option`.
`$p configure ...`	Reconfigures the photo image attributes.
`$p copy source options`	Copies another image. Table 38–9 lists the `copy` options.
`$p get x y`	Returns the pixel value at position $x\ y$.
`$p put data ?-to x1 y1 x2 y2?`	Inserts `data` into the image. `data` is a list of rows, where each row is a list of colors.
`$p read file options`	Loads an image from a file. Table 38–10 lists the read options.
`$p redither`	Reapplies the dithering algorithm to the image.
`$p write file options`	Saves the image to `file` according to `options`. Table 38–11 lists the `write` options.

defaults to the lower-right corner of the image. If the lower-right corner of the destination is not specified, then the size is determined by the area of the source. Otherwise, the source image may be cropped or replicated to fill the destination.

Table 38–9 Copy options for photo images.

`-from x1 y1 ?x2 y2?`	Specifies the location and area in the source image. If $x2$ and $y2$ are not given, they are set to the bottom-right corner.
`-to x1 y1 ?x2 y2?`	Specifies the location and area in the destination. If $x2$ and $y2$ are not given, the size is determined by the source. The source may be cropped or tiled to fill the destination.
`-shrink`	Shrinks the destination so that its bottom right corner matches the bottom right corner of the data copied in. This has no effect if the `width` and `height` have been set for the image.
`-zoom x ?y?`	Magnifies the source so each source pixel becomes a block of x by y pixels. y defaults to x if it is not specified.
`-subsample x ?y?`	Reduces the source by taking every xth pixel in the X direction and every yth pixel in the Y direction. y defaults to x.

Table 38–10 lists the `read` options, and Table 38–11 lists the `write` options. The `-format` option is more important for writing, because the first format found is used. With reading, the format is determined automatically. If there are multiple image types that can read the same data, you may specify a read format.

V. Tk Details

Table 38–10 Read options for photo images.

`-format` *format*	Specifies the format of the data. By default, the format is determined automatically.
`-from` *x1 y1 ?x2 y2?*	Specifies a subregion of the source data. If *x2* and *y2* are not given, the size is determined by the data.
`-to` *x1 y1*	Specifies the top-left corner of the new data.
`-shrink`	Shrinks the destination so that its bottom-right corner matches the bottom-right corner of the data read in. This has no effect if the width and height have been set for the image.

Table 38–11 Write options for photo images.

`-format` *format*	Specifies the format of the data.
`-from` *x1 y1 ?x2 y2?*	Specifies a subregion of the data to save. If *x2* and *y2* are not given, they are set to the lower-right corner.

The Text Insert Cursor

The text, entry, and canvas widgets have a second cursor to mark the text insertion point. The text insert cursor is described by a set of attributes. These attributes can make the insert cursor vary from a thin vertical line to a large rectangle with its own relief. Table 38–12 lists these attributes. The default insert cursor is a two-pixel-wide vertical line. You may not like the look of a wide insert cursor. The cursor is centered between two characters, so a wide one does not look the same as the block cursors found in many terminal emulators. Instead of occupying the space of a single character, it partially overlaps the two characters on either side:

Table 38–12 Cursor attribute resource names.

`cursor`	The mouse cursor. See text for sample formats. All widgets.
`insertBackground`	Color for the text insert cursor. Widgets: `canvas`, `entry`, and `text`.
`insertBorderWidth`	Width for three dimensional appearance. Widgets: `canvas`, `entry`, and `text`.
`insertOffTime`	Milliseconds the cursor blinks off. (Zero disables blinking.) Widgets: `canvas`, `entry`, and `text`.
`insertOnTime`	Milliseconds the cursor blinks on. Widgets: `canvas`, `entry`, and `text`.
`insertWidth`	Width of the text insert cursor, in screen units. Widgets: `canvas`, `entry`, and `text`.

The Mouse Cursor

The cursor attribute defines the mouse cursor. Example 38–6 shows the cursors that come built into Tk:

Example 38–6 The Tk cursors.

✖ X_cursor	⊡ dotbox	🔭 man	sizing
↗ arrow	↕ double_arrow	middlebutton	✳ spider
⊤ based_arrow_down	↗ draft_large	mouse	spraycan
⊥ based_arrow_up	↗ draft_small	✎ pencil	☆ star
⇀ boat	draped_box	☠ pirate	◈ target
bogosity	↻ exchange	+ plus	+ tcross
⌐ bottom_left_corner	✛ fleur	? question_arrow	↖ top_left_arrow
⌐ bottom_right_corner	gobbler	↗ right_ptr	top_left_corner
⊥ bottom_side	gumby	→| right_side	⊐ top_right_corner
⊥ bottom_tee	hand1	⊣ right_tee	⊤ top_side
box_spiral	hand2	rightbutton	⊤ top_tee
↑ center_ptr	♡ heart	rtl_logo	⚲ trek
O circle	icon	sailboat	⌐ ul_angle
clock	iron_cross	↓ sb_down_arrow	umbrella
coffee_mug	↖ left_ptr	↔ sb_h_double_arrow	⌐ ur_angle
╬ cross	|← left_side	⇐ sb_left_arrow	⌾ watch
✳ cross_reverse	⊢ left_tee	⇒ sb_right_arrow	I xterm
+ crosshair	leftbutton	↑ sb_up_arrow	
⊕ diamond_cross	⌐ ll_angle	↕ sb_v_double_arrow	
● dot	⌐ lr_angle	shuttle	

A foreground and background color for the cursor can be specified. Here are some example cursor specifications:

```
$w config -cursor watch              ;# stop-watch cursor
$w config -cursor {gumby blue}       ;# blue gumby
$w config -cursor {X_cursor red white}   ;# red X on white
```

V. Tk Details

The other form for the cursor attribute specifies a file that contains the definition of the cursor bitmap. If two file names are specified, then the second specifies the cursor mask that determines what bits of the background get covered up. Bitmap editing programs like *idraw* and *iconedit* can be used to generate these files. Here are some example cursor specification using files. You need to specify a foreground color, and if you specify a mask file, then you also need to specify a background color:

```
$w config -cursor "@timer.xbm black"
$w config -cursor "@timer.xbm timer.mask black red"
```

The cursors shown in Example 38–6 are available on all platforms. However, on Windows and Macintosh some of the cursors are mapped to native cursors and appear differently. On Windows the following cursors are mapped to native cursors: arrow, ibeam, icon, crosshair, fleur, sb_v_double_arrow, sb_h_double_arrow, center_ptr, watch, and xterm. These additional cursors are defined on Windows: starting, size, size_ne_sw, size_ns, size_nw_se, size_we, uparrow, and wait. On Windows, use the no cursor to eliminate the cursor. On Macintosh, the following cursors are mapped to native cursors: ibeam, xterm, cross, crosshair, plus, watch, arrow. These additional cursors are defined on Macintosh: text and cross-hair.

## CHAPTER 39

Fonts and Text Attributes

This chapter describes the naming conventions for fonts. Tk has a font object
that you can dynamically configure and associate with widgets. This
chapter also describes other text-related attributes such as justification,
anchoring, and geometry gridding.

Fonts describe how characters look on the
screen. Tk widgets like buttons, labels, and listboxes have a `font` attribute that
determines which font they use to display their text. The text widget has `font`
attributes on tags that are applied to different regions of text. Tk has a platform-
independent way to name fonts (e.g., `times 12 bold`), plus it gracefully handles
missing fonts. You can define named font objects and then associate those with
widgets and text tags. When the font objects are reconfigured, the widgets using
them update their display automatically. You can use the resource database to
define the fonts used in your interface.

X font names (e.g., `-*-times-bold-r-normal-*-12-*`) were used in versions of Tk before 8.0, and the widgets would raise errors if a font could not be
found. The X names have a pattern matching scheme that helps avoid some
missing font errors. You can still use X font names in current versions of Tk.
However, the Tk font system does not do font substitutions if you use X font
names; if you use them, you must be prepared for errors. In general, you should
use the platform-independent font names.

After describing fonts, the chapter explains a few of the widget attributes
that relate to fonts. This includes justification, anchors, and geometry gridding.

Naming a Font

There are two basic ways to name a font. You can use predefined font names (e.g., system), or you can specify a set of font attributes with a platform-independent name:

```
label .foo -text "Hello" -font {times 12 bold}
```

In this form, the font is specified with a three element list. The first element is the font family, the second is the size, in points, and the third is a list of style parameters. The family determines the basic look, such as courier or helvetica.

The complete set of style parameters are normal, bold, roman, italic, underline, and overstrike. For example, to specify both **bold** and *italic*:

```
label .foo -text "Hello" -font {times 12 {bold italic}}
```

The font size is points, which are 1/72 inch. Tk maintains a scale factor that maps from points to pixels. The default scale is derived from the screen resolution, and you can change it with the tk scaling command, which is described on page 580. You can specify pixel-based sizes with negative numbers. The advantage of points over pixels is that text appears about the same size regardless of the screen resolution. (This works better on Windows and Macintosh than on Unix.) However, sometimes you want to control font size relative to other widget geometry, in which case pixel-based sizes are better.

An alternate way to name font attributes uses name-value pairs. These are summarized in Table 39–1. The format is less compact, but it is useful for changing part of a font configuration because you do not need to specify everything. The same specification can be made like this:

```
label .foo -text "Hello" -font \
    {-family times -size 12 -weight bold -slant italic}
```

Table 39–1 Font attributes.

-family *name*	The *name* can be times, courier, helvetica, and others returned by the font families command.
-size *points*	The font size is given in points, which are 1/72 inch.
-weight *value*	The value is bold or normal.
-slant *value*	The value is roman or italic.
-underline *bool*	If *bool* is true, an underline is drawn.
-overstrike *bool*	If *bool* is true, an overstrike line is drawn.

Tk matches a font specification with the fonts available on your system. It will use the best possible font, but it may have to substitute some font parameters. Tk guarantees that the Times, Courier, and **Helvetica** families exist. It also understands the synonyms of Courier New for Courier, and Arial or Geneva for Helvetica. The font actual command returns the parameters chosen to match a font specification:

```
font actual {times 13 bold}
-family Times -size 13 -weight bold -slant roman
    -underline 0 -overstrike 0
```

The Macintosh and Windows platforms have a system-defined default size. You can get this size by specifying a size of 0 in your specification. The system font uses this:

```
font actual system
-family Chicago -size 0 -weight normal -slant roman
    -underline 0 -overstrike 0
```

Named Fonts

You can define your own names for fonts with the `font create` command. Creating a named font provides a level of indirection between the font parameters and the widgets that use the fonts. If you reconfigure a named font, the widgets using it will update their display automatically. This makes it easy to support a user preference for font size. For example, we can define a font name `default` on all platforms:

```
font create default -family times -size 12
```

The `default` font can be made larger at any time with `font configure`. Widgets using the fonts will update automatically:

```
font configure default -size 14
```

System Fonts

The Windows and Macintosh platforms have system-defined fonts that are used by most applications. When you query the configuration of the Tk widgets, you will see the system font names. The parameters for the system fonts can be tuned by the user via the system control panel. You can find out the attributes of the system font with `font actual`. These are the system fonts for each platform:

- The Windows platform supports `system`, `systemfixed`, `ansi`, `ansifixed`, `device`, `oemfixed`. The `fixed` suffix refers to a font where each character is the same size.
- The Macintosh platform has `system` and `application`.
- The UNIX platform has `fixed`. This is the only X font name that is guaranteed to exist. X font names are described in the next section.

Unicode Fonts

Tk does character-by-character font substitution when it displays Unicode characters. This supports mixed display of ASCII and Kanji characters, for example. The great thing about this is that you do not have to worry too much about choosing fonts in the simple case. The problem with font substitution is that it can be slow. In the worst case, Tk will query every font installed in your

V. Tk Details

system to find out whether it can display a particular character. If you know you will be displaying characters in a particular character set, you can optimize your interface by specifying a font that matches what you expect to display.

X Font Names

Fonts can be specified with X font names on all platforms, and you must use X font names in versions of Tk before Tk 8.0. The name `fixed` is an example of a short X font name. Other short names might include `6x12`, `9x15`, or `times12`. However, these aliases are site-dependent. In fact, all X font names are site dependent because different fonts may be installed on different systems. The only font guaranteed to exist on the UNIX platform is named `fixed`.

The more general form of an X font name has several components that describe the font parameters. Each component is separated by a dash, and the asterisk (`*`) is used for unspecified components. Short font names are system-defined aliases for these more complete specifications. Here is an example:

```
-*-times-medium-r-normal-*-18-*-*-*-*-*-iso8859-1
```

The components of X font names are listed in Table 39–2 in the order in which they occur in the font specification. The table gives the possible values for the components. If there is an ellipsis (...), then there are more possibilities, too.

Table 39–2 X Font specification components.

Component	Possible values
foundry	adobe xerox linotype misc ...
family	times helvetica lucida courier symbol ...
weight	bold medium demibold demi normal book light
slant	i r o
swidth	normal sans narrow semicondensed
adstyle	sans
pixels	8 10 12 14 18 24 36 48 72 144 ...
points	0 80 100 120 140 180 240 360 480 720 ...
resx	0 72 75 100
resy	0 72 75 100
space	p m c
avgWidth	73 94 124 ...
registry	iso8859 xerox dec adobe jisx0208.1983 ...
encoding	1 fontspecific dectech symbol dingbats

The most common attributes chosen for a font are its family, weight, slant, and size. The weight is usually **bold** or medium. The slant component is a bit cryptic, but i means *italic*, r means roman (i.e., normal), and o means *oblique*. A given font family might have an italic version, or an oblique version, but not both. Similarly, not all weights are offered by all font families. Size can be specified in pixels (i.e., screen pixels) or points. Points are meant to be independent of the screen resolution. On a 75dpi font, there are about 10 points per pixel. Note: These "points" are different than the printer points Tk uses in screen measurements. When you use X font names, the size of the font is *not* affected by the Tk scaling factor described on page 580.

It is generally a good idea to specify just a few key components and use * for the remaining components. The X server attempts to match the font specification with its set of installed fonts, but it fails if there is a specific component that it cannot match. If the first or last character of the font name is an asterisk, then that can match multiple components. The following selects a 12-pixel times font:

```
*times-medium-r-*-*-12*
```

Two useful UNIX programs that deal with X fonts are *xlsfonts* and *xfontsel*. These are part of the standard X11 distribution. *xlsfonts* simply lists the available fonts that match a given font name. It uses the same pattern matching that the server does. Because asterisk is special to most UNIX shells, you need to quote the font name argument if you run *xlsfonts* from your shell. *xfontsel* has a graphical user interface and displays the font that matches a given font name.

Font Failures before Tk 8.0

Unfortunately, if a font is missing, versions of Tk before 8.0 do not attempt to substitute another font, not even fixed. Current versions of Tk do substitutions only if you use platform-independent font names. Otherwise, the widget creation or reconfiguration command raises an error if the font does not exist. Example 39–1 shows one way to deal with missing fonts, which is to create a wrapper, the FontWidget procedure, around the Tk widget creation routines:

Example 39–1 The FontWidget procedure handles missing fonts.

```
proc FontWidget { args } {
    # args is a Tcl command
    if {[catch $args w]} {
        # Delete the font specified in args, if any
        set ix [lsearch $args -font]
        if {$ix >= 0} {
            set args [lreplace $args $ix [expr $ix+1]]
        }
        # This font overrides the resource database
        # The "fixed" font is UNIX-specific
        set w [eval $args {-font fixed}]
    }
    return $w
}
```

You call `FontWidget` like this:

```
FontWidget button .foo -text Foo -font garbage
```

The `FontWidget` procedure reverts to a default font if the widget creation command fails. It is careful to eliminate the font specified in `args`, if it exists. The explicit font overrides any setting from the resource database or the Tk defaults. Of course, widget creation might fail for some more legitimate reason, but that is allowed to happen in the backup case. Again, the missing font problem disappears when you use platform-independent font names, so you only need to resort to using `FontWidget` in early versions of Tk.

Font Metrics

The `font metrics` command returns measurement information for fonts. It returns general information about all the characters in the font:

```
font metrics {times 10}
-ascent 9 -descent 2 -linespace 11 -fixed 0
```

The `fixed` setting is true for fonts where each character fits into the same-sized bounding box. The `linespace` is the distance between the baselines of successive lines. The `ascent` and `descent` are illustrated in Example 39–2:

Example 39–2 Font metrics.

The `font measure` command returns the width of a string that will be displayed in a given font. The width does not account for heavily slanted letters that overhang their bounding box, nor does it do anything special with tabs or newlines in the string.

The `font` Command

Table 39–3 summarizes the `font` command. In the table, `font` is either a description of font parameters, a logical font name, a system font name, or an X font name. The `-displayof` option applies to X where you can have windows on different displays that can support different fonts. Note that when you delete a logical font name with `font delete`, the font is not really deleted if there are widgets that use that font.

Table 39–3 The `font` command.

`font actual` *font* `?-displayof` *window*`? ?`*option*`?`	Returns the actual parameters of *font*.
`font configure` *fontname* `?`*option*`? ?`*value option* *value*`?`	Sets or queries the parameters for *fontname*.
`font create ?`*fontname*`?` `?`*option value* `...?`	Defines *fontname* with the specified parameters.
`font delete` *fontname* `?`*name2* `...?`	Removes the definition for the named fonts.
`font families ?-displayof` *win*`?`	Returns the list of font families supported on the display of *win*.
`font measure` *font* `?-displayof` *win*`? `*text*	Returns the width of *text* displayed in *win* with *font*.
`font metrics` *font* `?-displayof` *win*`? ?`*option*`?`	The *option* can be `-ascent`, `-descent`, `-linespace`, or `-fixed`.
`font names`	Returns the names of defined fonts.

Text Attributes

Layout

Table 39–4 summarizes two simple text layout attributes: `justify` and `wrapLength`. The `text` widget has several more layout-related attributes, and Chapter 33 describes those in detail. The two attributes described in this section apply to the various button widgets, the label, entry, and message widgets. Those widgets are described in Chapters 27, 29, and 31. The `justify` attribute causes text to be centered, left-justified, or right-justified. The default justification is `center` for all the widgets in the table, except for the entry widget, which is left-justified by default.

The `wrapLength` attribute specifies how long a line of text is before it is wrapped onto another line. It is used to create multiline buttons and labels. This attribute is specified in screen units, however, not string length. It is probably easier to achieve the desired line breaks by inserting newlines into the text for the button or label and specifying a `wrapLength` of 0, which is the default.

Table 39–4 Layout attribute resource names

`justify`	Text line justification. Values: `left`, `center`, or `right`. Widgets: `button`, `checkbutton`, `entry`, `label`, `menubutton`, `message`, and `radiobutton`.
`wrapLength`	Maximum line length for text, in screen units. Widgets: `button`, `checkbutton`, `label`, `menubutton`, and `radiobutton`.

Selection Attributes

Table 39–5 lists the selection-related attributes. The exportSelection attribute controls if the selection is exported for cut and paste to other widgets. The colors for selected text are set with selectForeground and selectBackground. The selection is drawn in a raised relief, and the selectBorderWidth attribute affects the 3D appearance. Choose a border width of zero to get a flat relief.

Table 39–5 Selection attribute resource names.

exportSelection	Share selection. Widgets: entry, canvas, listbox, and text.
selectForeground	Foreground of selected text.
selectBackground	Background of selected text.
selectBorderWidth	Width of 3D raised border for selection highlight.

Gridding, Resizing, and Geometry

The text, listbox, and canvas widgets support geometry gridding. This is an alternate interpretation of the main window geometry that is in terms of grid units, typically characters, as opposed to pixels. The setGrid attribute is a boolean that indicates if gridding should be turned on. The listbox and text widgets define a grid size that matches their character size. Example 41–1 on page 570 sets up gridding for a canvas.

When a widget is gridded, its size is constrained to have a whole number of grid units displayed. The height will be constrained to show a whole number of text lines, and the width will be constrained to show a whole number of average width characters. This affects interactive resizing by users, as well as the various window manger commands (wm) that relate to geometry. When gridding is turned on, the geometry argument (e.g., 24x80) is interpreted as grid units; otherwise, it is interpreted as pixels. The window manager geometry commands are summarized in Table 41–1 on page 571.

The following example creates a listbox with gridded geometry enabled. Try resizing the window in the following example with and without the -setgrid flag, and with and without the wm minsize command, which sets the minimum size of the window. The Scrolled_Listbox procedure is defined in Example 30–3 on page 430.

Example 39–3 A gridded, resizable listbox.

```
wm minsize . 5 3
button .quit -text Quit -command exit
pack .quit -side top -anchor e
Scrolled_Listbox .f -width 10 -height 5 -setgrid true
pack .f -side top -fill both -expand true
```

A Font Selection Application

This chapter concludes with an example that lets you select fonts. It is written as a dialog that you can add to your application. The menus are tied to elements of the `font` array that are used in `font configure` commands. The actual settings of the font are shown above a sampler of what the font looks like. When the user clicks the OK button, the font configuration is returned:

Example 39–4 Font selection dialog.

```
proc Font_Select {{top .fontsel}} {
    global font

    # Create File, Font, Size, and Format menus

    toplevel $top -class Fontsel -bd 10
    set menubar [menu $top.menubar]
    $top config -menu $menubar
    foreach x {File Font Size Format} {
        set menu [menu $menubar.[string tolower $x]]
        $menubar add cascade -menu $menu -label $x
    }
    $menubar.file add command -label Reset -command FontReset
    $menubar.file add command -label OK \
        -command {set font(ok) ok}
    $menubar.file add command -label Cancel \
        -command {set font(ok) cancel}

    # The Fonts menu lists the available Font families.

    set allfonts [font families]
    set numfonts [llength $allfonts]
    set limit 20
    if {$numfonts < $limit} {

        # Display the fonts in a single menu

        foreach family $allfonts {
            $menubar.font add radio -label $family \
                -variable font(-family) \
                -value $family \
                -command FontUpdate
```

```
        }
    } else {

        # Too many fonts. Create a set of cascaded menus to
        # display all the font possibilities

        set c 0 ; set l 0
        foreach family $allfonts {
            if {$l == 0} {
                $menubar.font add cascade -label $family... \
                    -menu $menubar.font.$c
                set m [menu $menubar.font.$c]
                incr c
            }
            $m add radio -label $family \
                -variable font(-family) \
                -value $family \
                -command FontUpdate
            set l [expr ($l +1) % $limit]
        }
    }

    # Complete the other menus

    foreach size {7 8 10 12 14 18 24 36 72} {
        $menubar.size add radio -label $size \
            -variable font(-size) \
            -value $size \
            -command FontUpdate
    }
    $menubar.size add command -label Other... \
            -command [list FontSetSize $top]
    $menubar.format add check -label Bold \
            -variable font(-weight) \
            -onvalue bold -offvalue normal \
            -command FontUpdate
    $menubar.format add check -label Italic \
            -variable font(-slant) \
            -onvalue italic -offvalue roman \
            -command FontUpdate
    $menubar.format add check -label underline \
        -variable font(-underline) \
        -command FontUpdate
    $menubar.format add check -label overstrike \
        -variable font(-overstrike) \
        -command FontUpdate

    # FontReset initializes the font array, which causes
    # the radio menu entries to get highlighted.

    FontReset

    # This label displays the current font

    label $top.font -textvar font(name) -bd 5
```

```
    # This message displays a sampler of the font.

    message $top.msg -aspect 1000 \
                -borderwidth 10 -font fontsel \
                -text "
ABCDEFGHIJKLMNOPQRSTUVWXYZ
abcdefghijklmnopqrstuvwxyz
0123456789
!@#$%^&*()_+-=[]{};:\"''~,.<>/?\\|
"

    # Lay out the dialog

    pack $top.font $top.msg -side top
    set f [frame $top.buttons]
    button $f.ok -text Ok -command {set font(ok) 1}
    button $f.cancel -text Cancel -command {set font(ok) 0}
    pack $f.ok $f.cancel -padx 10 -side left
    pack $f -side top

    # Dialog_Wait is defined in Example 36-1 on page 519

    set font(ok) cancel
    Dialog_Wait $top font(ok)
    destroy $top
    if {$font(ok) == "ok"} {
        return [array get font -*]
    } else {
        return {}
    }
}

# FontReset recreates a default font

proc FontReset {} {
    catch {font delete fontsel}
    font create fontsel
    FontSet
}

# FontSet initializes the font array with the settings
# returned by the font actual command

proc FontSet {} {
    global font

    # The name is the font configuration information
    # with a line break so it looks nicer

    set font(name) [font actual fontsel]
    regsub -- "-slant" $font(name) "\n-slant" font(name)

    # Save the actual parameters after any font substitutions

    array set font [font actual fontsel]
```

```
}

# FontSetSize adds an entry widget to the dialog so you
# can enter a specific font size.

proc FontSetSize {top} {
    set f [frame $top.size -borderwidth 10]
    pack $f -side top -fill x
    label $f.msg -text "Size:"
    entry $f.entry -textvariable font(-size)
    bind $f.entry <Return> FontUpdate
    pack $f.msg -side left
    pack $f.entry -side top -fill x
}

# FontUpdate is called when any of the font settings
# are changed, either from the menu or FontSetSize

proc FontUpdate { } {
    global font

    # The elements of font that have a leading - are
    # used directly in the font configuration command.

    eval {font configure fontsel} [array get font -*]
    FontSet
}
```

Send

This chapter describes the `send` command that invokes Tcl commands in other applications. This chapter also presents an alternative to `send` that uses network sockets.

*T*he `send` command lets Tk applications on the same display send each other Tcl commands and cooperate in very flexible ways. A large application can be structured as a set of smaller tools that cooperate instead of one large monolith. This encourages reuse, and it exploits your workstation's multiprogramming capabilities.

The `send` facility provides a name space for Tk applications. The `winfo interps` command returns the names of all the Tk applications reachable with `send`. The `send` communication mechanism is limited to applications running on one display. Multiple screens on one workstation still count as the same display on X. In UNIX, `send` uses properties on the X display for communication and to record the application names. As of Tk 8.0, `send` is not yet implemented on Macintosh or Windows. There is an extension for Windows that uses DDE to emulate `send`.

This chapter also describes an alternative to `send` that uses network sockets. The facility is not limited to a single display, and can be used in conjunction with safe interpreters to limit the capabilities of remote operations. A number of Tcl extensions provide similar functionality, including *GroupKit* and *Tcl-DP*. You can find these extensions on the Tcl archive and the CD-ROM.

V. Tk Details

559

The send Command

The `send` command invokes a Tcl command in another application. The general form of the command is:

```
send options interp arg ?arg...?
```

The `send` command behaves like `eval`; if you give it extra arguments, it concatenates them to form a single command. If your argument structure is important, use `list` to build the command. Table 40–1 lists the options to `send`:

Table 40–1 Options to the `send` command.

`-async`	Does not wait for the remote command to complete.
`-displayof window`	Sends to the application on the same display as `window`
`--`	Delimits options from the `interp` argument. Useful if the `interp` begins with a dash.

The `interp` argument is the name of the other application. An application defines its own name when it creates its main window. The *wish* shell uses as its name the last component of the file name of the script. For example, when *wish* interprets `/usr/local/bin/exmh`, it sets its application name to `exmh`. However, if another instance of the `exmh` application is already running, *wish* chooses the name `exmh #2`, and so on. If *wish* is not executing from a file, its name is just `wish`. You may have noticed `wish #2` or `wish #3` in your window title bars, and this reflects the fact that multiple *wish* applications are running on your display. If you use Tk 3.6 or earlier and your application crashes, it can forget to unregister its name. The *tkinspect* program has a facility to clean up these old registrations.

A script can find out its own name, so you can pass names around or put them into files in order to set up communications. The `tk appname` command queries or changes the application name:

```
set myname [tk appname]
tk appname aNewName
```

In Tk 3.6 and earlier, you have to use the `winfo name` command to get the name of the application:

```
set myname [winfo name .]
```

Send and X Authority

The `send` command relies on the X authority mechanism for authorization. A command is rejected by the target interpreter if you do not have X authority set up. There are two ways around this problem. First, you can disable the access check by compiling the `tkSend.c` file with the `-DTK_NO_SECURITY` compile flag. If you must worry about malicious programs that send your programs commands, then you should not do this.

The second option is to start your X server with its -auth flag, which initializes the X authority mechanism. The details vary depending on your X server, and most modern X servers do this automatically. The general picture is that you generate a pseudo-random string and store it into a file, which is usually named ~/.Xauthority and must be readable only by your account. The -auth flag specifies the name of this file to the X server. Each X application reads this file and sends the contents to the X server when opening the connection to the server. If the contents match what the server read when it started, then the connection is allowed. The system is slightly more complicated than described here. The file actually contains a sequence of records to support multiple displays and client hosts. Consult your local X guru or the documentation for the details particular to your system.

Your xhost list must be clear.

Tk also requires that the *xhost* list be empty. The *xhost* mechanism is the old, not-so-secure authentication mechanism in X. With *xhost* you allow all programs on a list of hosts to connect to your display. The problem with this is that multiuser workstations allow remote login, so essentially anybody could log in to a workstation on the *xhost* list and gain access to your display. The Xauthority mechanism is much stronger because it restricts access to your account, or to accounts that you explicitly give a secret token to. The problem is that even if Xauthority is set up, the user or a program can turn on *xhosts* and open up access to your display.

If you run the *xhost* program with no argument, it reports the status and what hosts are on the list. The following output is generated when access control is restricted, but programs running on sage are allowed to connect to the display:

```
exec xhost
=> Access control enabled: all hosts being restricted
sage
```

This is not good enough for Tk send. It will fail because sage is on the list. I work in an environment where old scripts and programs are constantly adding things to my *xhost* list for reasons that are no longer valid. I developed a version of send that checks for errors and then does the following to clean out the *xhost* list. You have to enable access control and then explicitly remove any hosts on the list. These are reported after an initial line that says whether or not hosts are restricted:

```
xhost - ;# enable access control in general
foreach host [lrange [split [exec xhost] \n] 1 end] {
    exec xhost -$host ;# clear out exceptions
}
```

The Sender Script

The following example is a general-purpose script that reads input and then sends it to another application. You can put this at the end of a pipeline to get a loopback effect to the main application, although you can also use `fileevent` for similar effects. One advantage of `send` over `fileevent` is that the sender and receiver can be more independent. A logging application, for example, can come and go independently of the applications that log error messages:

Example 40–1 The sender application.

```
#!/usr/local/bin/wish
# sender takes up to four arguments:
# 1) the name of the application to send to.
# 2) a command prefix.
# 3) the name of another application to notify
#    after the end of the data.
# 4) the command to use in the notification.

# Hide the unneeded window
wm withdraw .
# Process command line arguments
if {$argc == 0} {
    puts stderr "Usage: send name ?cmd? ?uiName? ?uiCmd?"
    exit 1
} else {
    set app [lindex $argv 0]
}
if {$argc > 1} {
    set cmd [lindex $argv 1]
} else {
    set cmd Send_Insert
}
if {$argc > 2} {
    set ui [lindex $argv 2]
    set uiCmd Send_Done
}
if {$argc > 3} {
    set uiCmd [lindex $argv 3]
}
# Read input and send it to the logger
while {[gets stdin input] >= 0} {
    # Ignore errors with the logger
    catch {send $app [concat $cmd [list $input\n]]}
}
# Notify the controller, if any
if [info exists ui] {
    if [catch {send $ui $uiCmd} msg] {
        puts stderr "send.tcl could not notify $ui\n$msg"
    }
}
# This is necessary to force wish to exit.
exit
```

The *sender* application supports communication with two processes. It sends all its input to a primary "logging" application. When the input finishes, it can send a notification message to another "controller" application. The logger and the controller could be the same application.

Use list to quote arguments to send.

Consider the send command used in the example:

```
send $app [concat $cmd [list $input\n]]
```

The combination of concat and list is tricky. The list command quotes the value of the input line. This quoted value is then appended to the command, so it appears as a single extra argument. Without the quoting by list, the value of the input line will affect the way the remote interpreter parses the command. Consider these alternatives:

```
send $app [list $cmd $input]
```

This form is safe, except that it limits $cmd to a single word. If cmd contains a value like the ones given below, the remote interpreter will not parse it correctly. It will treat the whole multiword value as the name of a command:

```
.log insert end
.log see end ; .log insert end
```

This is the most common wrong answer:

```
send $app $cmd $input
```

The send command concatenates $cmd and $input together, and the result will be parsed again by the remote interpreter. The success or failure of the remote command depends on the value of the input data. If the input included Tcl syntax like $ or [ ], errors or other unexpected behavior would result.

Communicating Processes

Chapter 22 presented two examples: a browser for the examples in this book, and a simple shell in which to try out Tcl commands. In that chapter they are put into the same application. The two examples shown below hook these two applications together using the send command. Example 40–2 changes the Run and Reset procedures of the browser to send EvalEcho commands to the shell.

Example 40–2 Hooking the browser to an eval server.

```
# Replace the Run and Reset procedures of the browser in
# Example 22-3 on page 322 with these procedures

# Start up the evalsrv.tcl script.
proc StartEvalServer {} {
    global browse
    # Start the shell and pass it our name.
    exec evalsrv.tcl [tk appname] &
    # Wait for evalsrv.tcl to send us its name
    tkwait variable browse(evalInterp)
}
proc Run {} {
    global browse
    set apps [winfo interps]
```

```
    set ix [lsearch -glob $apps evalsrv.tcl*]
    if {$ix < 0} {
        # No evalsrv.tcl application running
        StartEvalServer
    }
    if {![info exists browse(evalInterp)]} {
        # Hook up to already running eval server
        set browse(evalInterp) [lindex $apps $ix]
    }
    if [catch {send $browse(evalInterp) {info vars}} err] {
        # It probably died - restart it.
        StartEvalServer
    }
    # Send the command asynchronously. The two
    # list commands foil the concat done by send and
    # the uplevel in EvalEcho
    send -async $browse(evalInterp) \
        [list EvalEcho [list source $browse(current)]]
}
# Reset the shell interpreter in the eval server
proc Reset {} {
    global browse
    send $browse(evalInterp) {EvalEcho reset}
}
```

The number of lists created before the send command may seem excessive, but they are all necessary. The send command concatenates its arguments, so instead of letting it do that, we pass it a single list. Similarly, EvalEcho expects a single argument that is a valid command, so list is used to construct that.

The StartEvalServer procedure starts up the shell. Command-line arguments are used to pass the application name of the browser to the shell. The shell completes the connection by sending its own application name back to the browser. The browser stores the name of the shell application in browser(evalInterp). The code that the shell uses is shown in Example 40–3:

Example 40–3 Making the shell into an eval server.

```
# Add this to the shell application shown
# in Example 22-4 on page 327
if {$argc > 0} {
    # Send our application name to the browser
    send [lindex $argv 0] \
        [list set browse(evalInterp) [tk appname]]
}
```

Remote eval through Sockets

Network sockets provide another communication mechanism you can use to evaluate Tcl commands in another application. The "name" of the application is just the host and port for the socket connection. There are a variety of schemes you can use to manage names. A crude, but effective way to manage host and ports for your servers is to record them in a file in your network file system. These examples ignore this problem. The server chooses a port and the client is expected to know what it is.

Example 40–4 implements `Eval_Server` that lets other applications connect and evaluate Tcl commands. The `interp` argument specifies the interpreter in which to evaluate the Tcl commands. If the caller of `Eval_Server` specifies `{}` for the interpreter, then the commands are evaluated in the current interpreter. The `openCmd` is called when the connection is made. It can do whatever setup or authentication is required. If it doesn't like the connection, it can close the socket:

Example 40–4 Remote `eval` using sockets.

```
proc Eval_Server {port {interp {}} {openCmd EvalOpenProc}} {
    socket -server [list EvalAccept $interp $openCmd] $port
}
proc EvalAccept {interp openCmd newsock addr port} {
    global eval
    set eval(cmdbuf,$newsock) {}
    fileevent $newsock readable [list EvalRead $newsock $interp]
    if [catch {
        interp eval $interp $openCmd $newsock $addr $port
    }] {
        close $newsock
    }
}
proc EvalOpenProc {sock addr port} {
    # do authentication here
    # close $sock to deny the connection
}
```

Example 40–5 shows `EvalRead` that reads commands and evaluates them in an interpreter. If the `interp` is `{}`, it causes the commands to execute in the current interpreter. In this case an `uplevel #0` is necessary to ensure the command is executed in the global scope. If you use `interp eval` to execute something in yourself, it executes in the current scope:

Example 40–5 Reading commands from a socket.

```
proc EvalRead {sock interp} {
    global eval errorInfo errorCode
    if [eof $sock] {
        close $sock
    } else {
        gets $sock line
        append eval(cmdbuf,$sock) $line\n
        if {[string length $eval(cmdbuf,$sock)] && \
                [info complete $eval(cmdbuf,$sock)]} {
            set code [catch {
```

V. Tk Details

```
                    if {[string length $interp] == 0} {
                        uplevel #0 $eval(cmdbuf,$sock)
                    } else {
                        interp eval $interp $eval(cmdbuf,$sock)
                    }
                } result]
                set reply [list $code $result $errorInfo \
                    $errorCode]\n
                # Use regsub to count newlines
                set lines [regsub -all \n $reply {} junk]
                # The reply is a line count followed
                # by a Tcl list that occupies that number of lines
                puts $sock $lines
                puts -nonewline $sock $reply
                flush $sock
                set eval(cmdbuf,$sock) {}
            }
        }
    }
```

Example 40–6 presents Eval_Open and Eval_Remote that implement the client side of the eval connection. Eval_Open connects to the server and returns a token, which is just the socket. The main task of Eval_Remote is to preserve the information generated when the remote command raises an error

The network protocol is line-oriented. The Eval_Remote command writes the command on the socket. The EvalRead procedure uses info complete to detect the end of the command. The reply is more arbitrary, so server sends a line count and that number of lines. The regsub command counts up all the newlines because it returns the number of matches it finds. The reply is a list of error codes, results, and trace information. These details of the return command are described on page 80.

Example 40–6 The client side of remote evaluation.

```
proc Eval_Open {server port} {
    global eval
    set sock [socket $server $port]
    # Save this info for error reporting
    set eval(server,$sock) $server:$port
    return $sock
}
proc Eval_Remote {sock args} {
    global eval
    # Preserve the concat semantics of eval
    if {[llength $args] > 1} {
        set cmd [concat $args]
    } else {
        set cmd [lindex $args 0]
    }
    puts $sock $cmd
    flush $sock
    # Read return line count and the result.
```

```
        gets $sock lines
        set result {}
        while {$lines > 0} {
            gets $sock x
            append result $x\n
            incr lines -1
        }
        set code [lindex $result 0]
        set x [lindex $result 1]
        # Cleanup the end of the stack
        regsub "\[^\n]+$" [lindex $result 2] \
            "*Remote Server $eval(server,$sock)*" stack
        set ec [lindex $result 3]
        return -code $code -errorinfo $stack -errorcode $ec $x
    }
    proc Eval_Close {sock} {
        close $sock
    }
```

If an error occurs in the remote command, then a stack trace is returned.
This includes the command used inside EvalRead to invoke the command, which
is either the uplevel or interp eval command. This is the very last line in the
stack that is returned, and regsub is used to replace this with an indication of
where control transferred to the remote server:

```
catch [Eval_Remote sock6 set xx]
=> 1
set errorInfo
=> can't read "xx": no such variable
    while executing
"set xx
"
    ("uplevel" body line 1)
    invoked from within
*Remote Server sage:4000*
    invoked from within
"catch [Eval_Remote sock6 set xx]"
```

V. Tk Details

Window Managers and Window Information

The window manager controls the size and location of other applications' windows. The window manager is built into Windows and Macintosh, while it is a separate application on UNIX. The wm command provides an interface to the window manager. The winfo command returns information about windows.

Management of top-level windows is done by the *window manager*. The Macintosh and Windows platforms have the window manager built in to the operating system, but in UNIX the window manager is just another application. The window manager controls the position of top-level windows, provides a way to resize windows, open and close them, and implements a border and decorative title for windows. The wm command interacts with the window manager so that the application can control its size, position, and iconified state.

If you need to fine-tune your display, you may need some detailed information about widgets. The winfo command returns all sorts of information about windows, including interior widgets, not just top-level windows.

The wm Command

The wm command has about 20 operations that interact with the window manager. The general form of the command is:

```
wm operation win ?args?
```

In all cases the *win* argument must be a toplevel. Otherwise, an error is raised. In many cases, the operation either sets or queries a value. If a new value is not specified, then the current settings are returned. For example, this command returns the current window geometry:

```
wm geometry .
```

=> 300x200+327+20

This command defines a new geometry:

```
wm geometry . 400x200+0+0
```

There are lots of wm operations, and this reflects the complex protocol with UNIX window managers. The summary below lists the subset of operations that I find useful. The operations can be grouped into four main categories:

- *Size, placement and decoration of windows.* Use the geometry and title operations to position windows and set the title bar.
- *Icons.* Use the iconify, deiconify, and withdraw operations to open and close windows. On UNIX, closed windows are represented by an icon.
- *Long-term session state.* Use the protocol operation to get a callback when users destroy windows.
- *Miscellaneous.* Use the transient and overrideredirect operation to get specialized windows. Future versions of Tk may support a style operation to select different kinds of top-level windows.

Size, Placement, and Decoration

Each window has a title that appears in the title bar that the window manager places above the window. In a *wish* script, the default title of the main window is the last component of the file name of the script. Use the wm title command to change the title of the window. The title can also appear in the icon for your window, unless you specify another name with wm iconname.

```
wm title . "My Application"
```

Use the wm geometry command to adjust the position or size of your main windows. A geometry specification has the general form *WxH+X+Y*, where *W* is the width, *H* is the height, and *X* and *Y* specify the location of the upper-left corner of the window. The location +0+0 is the upper-left corner of the display. You can specify a negative *X* or *Y* to position the bottom (right) side of the window relative to the bottom (right) side of the display. For example, +0-0 is the lower-left corner, and -100-100 is offset from the lower-right corner by 100 pixels in the X and Y direction. If you do not specify a geometry, then the current geometry is returned.

Example 41–1 Gridded geometry for a canvas.

```
canvas .c -width 300 -height 150
pack .c -fill both -expand true
wm geometry .
=> 300x200+678+477
wm grid . 30 15 10 10
wm geometry .
=> 30x20+678+477
```

Example 41–1 sets up *gridded geometry* for a canvas, which means that the geometry is in terms of some unit other than pixels. With the canvas, use the wm grid command to define the size of the grid. The text and listbox widgets set a grid based on the size of the characters they display. They have a setgrid attribute that turns on gridding, which is described on page 554.

The wm resizable command controls whether a user can resize a window. The following command allows a resize in the X direction, but not in the Y direction:

```
wm resizable . 1 0
```

You can constrain the minimum size, maximum size, and the aspect ratio of a toplevel. The aspect ratio is the width divided by the height. The constraint is applied when the user resizes the window interactively. The minsize, maxsize, and aspect operations apply these constraints.

Some window managers insist on having the user position windows. The sizefrom and positionfrom operations let you pretend that the user specified the size and position in order to work around this restriction.

Table 41–1 summarizes the wm commands that deal with size, decorations, placement:

Table 41–1 Size, placement and decoration window manager operations.

wm aspect *win ?a b c d?*	Constrains *win*'s ratio of width to height to be between (*a/b* and *c/d*).
wm geometry *win ?geometry?*	Queries or sets the geometry of *win*.
wm grid *win ?w h dx dy?*	Queries or sets the grid size. *w* and *h* are the base size, in grid units. *dx* and *dy* are the size, in pixels, of a grid unit.
wm maxsize *win ?width height?*	Constrains the maximum size of *win*.
wm minsize *win ?width height?*	Constrains the minimum size of *win*.
wm positionfrom *win ?who?*	Queries or sets *who* to be program or user.
wm resizable *win ?xok yok?*	Queries or sets ability to resize interactively.
wm sizefrom *win ?who?*	Queries or sets *who* to be program or user.
wm title *win ?string?*	Queries or sets the window title to *string*.

Icons

UNIX window managers let you close a window and replace it with an icon. The window still exists in your application, and users can open the window later. You can open and close a window yourself with the deiconify and iconify operations, respectively. Use the withdraw operation to unmap the window without replacing it with an icon. The state operation returns the current state, which is one of normal, iconified, or withdrawn. If you withdraw a window, you can restore it to the normal state with deiconify.

Windows and Macintosh do not implement icons for program windows.

V. Tk Details

Instead, icons represent files and applications in the desktop environment. Tk does not provide facilities to set up desktop icons. When you `iconify` under Windows, the window gets *minimized* and users can open it by clicking on the taskbar at the bottom of the screen. When you `iconify` under Macintosh, the window simply gets withdrawn from the screen.

Windows and Macintosh applications have an additional state, `maximized`, which is not yet supported by Tk. This is a full-screen display mode. Future versions of Tk may support this state.

You can set the attributes of UNIX icons with the `iconname`, `iconposition`, `iconbitmap`, and `iconmask` operations. The icon's mask is used to get irregularly shaped icons. Chapter 38 describes how masks and bitmaps are defined. In the case of an icon, it is most likely that you have the definition in a file, so your command will look like this:

```
wm iconbitmap . @myfilename
```

Table 41–2 summarizes the `wm` operations that have to do with icons:

Table 41–2 Window manager commands for icons.

`wm deiconify win`	Opens the window `win`.
`wm iconbitmap win ?bitmap?`	Queries or defines the bitmap for the icon. UNIX.
`wm iconify win`	Closes the window `win`.
`wm iconmask win ?mask?`	Queries or defines the mask for the icon. UNIX.
`wm iconname win ?name?`	Queries or sets the name on the icon. UNIX.
`wm iconposition win ?x y?`	Queries or sets the location of the icon. UNIX.
`wm iconwindow win ?window?`	Queries or specifies an alternate window to display when in the iconified state. UNIX.
`wm state win`	Returns `normal`, `iconic`, or `withdrawn`.
`wm withdraw win`	Unmaps the window. No icon is displayed.

Session State

The window manager lets users delete windows with a close operation. When the main Tk window gets deleted, *wish* normally quits. If you have any special processing that must take place when the user deletes a window, you need to intercept the close action. Use the `wm protocol` operation to register a command that handles the `WM_DELETE_WINDOW` message from the window manager. This works on all platforms even though "delete" is a UNIX term and "close" is the Windows and Macintosh term:

```
wm protocol . WM_DELETE_WINDOW Quit
```

If you intercept close on the main Tk window (i.e., dot), you must eventually call `exit` to actually stop your application. However, you can also take the time to prompt the user about unsaved changes, or even let the user change their mind about quitting.

Other window manager messages that you can intercept are WM_SAVE_YOURSELF and WM_TAKE_FOCUS. The first is called periodically by some UNIX session managers, which are described below. The latter is used in the active focus model. Tk (and this book) assumes a passive focus model where the window manager assigns focus to a top-level window.

Saving session state.

Some UNIX window managers support the notion of a *session* that lasts between runs of the window system. A session is implemented by saving state about the applications that are running, and using this information to restart the applications when the window system is restarted.

An easy way to participate in the session protocol is to save the command used to start your application. The wm command operation does this. The *wish* shell saves this information, so it is just a matter of registering it with the window manager. argv0 is the command, and argv is the command-line arguments:

```
wm command . "$argv0 $argv"
```

If your application is typically run on a different host than the one with the display (like in an Xterminal environment), then you also need to record what host to run the application on. Use the wm client operation for this. You might need to use *hostname* instead of *uname* on your system:

```
wm client . [exec uname -n]
```

Table 41–3 describes the session-related window manager operations.

Table 41–3 Session-related window manager operations.

wm client *win* ?*name*?	Records the hostname in the WM_CLIENT_MACHINE property. UNIX.
wm command *win* ?*command*?	Records the start-up command in the WM_COMMAND property. UNIX.
wm protocol *win* ?*name*? ?*command*?	Registers a *command* to handle the protocol request *name*, which can be WM_DELETE_WINDOW, WM_SAVE_YOURSELF, or WM_TAKE_FOCUS.

Miscellaneous

The UNIX window managers work by reparenting an application's window so that it is a child of the window that forms the border and decorative title bar. The wm frame operation returns the window ID of the new parent, or the ID of the window itself if it has not been reparented. The wm overrideredirect operation can set a bit that overrides the reparenting. This means that no title or border will be drawn around the window, and you cannot control the window through the window manager.

The wm group operation defines groups of windows so that the window manager can open and close them together. One window, typically the main window, is chosen as the leader. The other members of the group are iconified when it is iconified. This is not implemented on Windows and Macintosh, and not all UNIX window managers implement this, either.

The `wm transient` operation informs the window manager that this is a temporary window and there is no need to decorate it with the border and decorative title bar. This is used, for example, on pop-up menus. On Windows, a `transient` window is a toolbar window that does not appear in the task bar. On Macintosh, the `unsupported1` command, which is described on page 417, lets you create different styles of top-level windows.

Table 41–4 lists the remaining window manager operations:

Table 41–4 Miscellaneous window manager operations.

`wm colormapwindows win ?windowList?`	Sets or queries the `WM_COLORMAP_WINDOWS` property that orders windows with different colormaps.
`wm focusmodel win ?what?`	Sets or queries the focus model: `active` or `passive`. (Tk assumes the `passive` model.)
`wm frame win`	Returns the ID of the parent of `win` if it has been reparented; otherwise, returns the ID of `win`.
`wm group win ?leader?`	Queries or sets the group leader (a toplevel) for `win`. The window manager may unmap all the group at once.
`wm overrideredirect win ?boolean?`	Sets or queries the override redirect bit that suppresses reparenting by the window manager.
`wm transient win ?leader?`	Queries or marks a window as a transient window working for `leader`, another widget.

The `winfo` Command

The `winfo` command has just over 40 operations that return information about a widget or the display. The operations fall into the following categories:

- Sending commands between applications.
- Family relationships.
- Size.
- Location.
- Virtual root coordinates.
- Atoms and IDs.
- Colormaps and visuals.

Sending Commands between Applications

Each Tk application has a name that is used when sending commands between applications using the `send` command, which is described in Chapter 40. The list of Tk applications is returned by the `interps` operation. The `tk appname` command is used to get the name of the application, and that command can also be used to set the application name. In Tk 3.6 and earlier, you had to use `winfo name .` to get the name of the application.

Example 41–2 shows how your application might connect up with several existing applications. It contacts each registered Tk interpreter and sends a short command that contains the application's own name as a parameter. The other application can use that name to communicate back.

Example 41–2 Telling other applications what your name is.

```
foreach app [winfo interps] {
    catch {send $app [list Iam [tk appname]]}
}
```

Table 41–5 summarizes these commands:

Table 41–5 `send` command information.

`tk appname ?newname?`	Queries or sets the name used with `send`.
`winfo name .`	Also returns the name used for `send`, for backward compatibility with Tk 3.6 and earlier.
`winfo name pathname`	Returns the last component of `pathname`.
`winfo ?-displayof win? interps`	Returns the list of registered Tk applications on the same display as `win`.

Family Relationships

The Tk widgets are arranged in a hierarchy, and you can use the `winfo` command to find out about the structure of the hierarchy. The `winfo children` operation returns the children of a window, and the `winfo parent` operation returns the parent. The parent of the main window is null (i.e., an empty string).

A widget is also a member of a class, which is used for bindings and as a key into the resource database. The `winfo class` operation returns this information. You can test for the existence of a window with `winfo exists`, and whether or not a window is mapped onto the screen with `winfo viewable`. Note that `winfo ismapped` is true for a widget that is managed by a geometry manager, but if the widget's top-level window is not mapped, then the widget is not `viewable`.

The `winfo manager` operation tells you what geometry manager is controlling the placement of the window. This returns the name of the geometry manager command. Examples include `pack`, `place`, `grid`, `canvas`, and `text`. The last two indicate the widget is embedded into a canvas or text widget.

Table 41–6 summarizes these `winfo` operations:

Table 41–6 Window hierarchy information.

`winfo children` *win*	Returns the list of children widgets of *win*.
`winfo class` *win*	Returns the resource class of *win*.
`winfo exists` *win*	Returns 1 if *win* exists.
`winfo ismapped` *win*	Returns 1 if *win* is mapped onto the screen.
`winfo manager` *win*	Geometry manager: `pack`, `place`, `grid`, `canvas`, or `text`.
`winfo parent` *win*	Returns the parent widget of *win*.
`winfo viewable` *win*	Returns 1 if *win* and all its parent windows are mapped.

Size

The `winfo width` and `winfo height` operations return the width and height of a window, respectively. Alternatively, you can ask for the requested width and height of a window. Use `winfo reqwidth` and `winfo reqheight` for this information. The requested size may not be accurate, however, because the geometry manager may allocate more or less space, and the user may resize the window.

Size is not valid until a window is mapped.

A window's size is not set until a geometry manager maps a window onto the display. Initially, a window starts out with a width and height of 1. You can use `tkwait visibility` to wait for a window to be mapped before asking its width or height, or you can use `update` to give Tk a chance to update the display. There are some potential problems with `update` that are discussed on page 522. `Dialog_Wait` in Example 36–1 on page 519 uses `tkwait visibility`.

The `winfo geometry` operation returns the size and position of the window in the standard geometry format: *WxH+X+Y*. In this case the X and Y offsets are relative to the parent widget, or relative to the root window in the case of the main window.

You can find out how big the display is, too. The `winfo screenwidth` and `winfo screenheight` operations return this information in pixels. The `winfo screenmmwidth` and `winfo screenmmheight` return this information in millimeters.

You can convert between pixels and screen distances with the `winfo pixels` and `winfo fpixels` operations. Given a number of screen units such as `10m`, `3c`, or `72p`, these return the corresponding number of pixels. The first form rounds to a whole number, while the second form returns a floating point number. The correspondence between pixels and sizes may not be accurate because users can adjust the pixel size on their monitors, and Tk has no way of knowing about that. Chapter 37 explains screen units on page 526. For example:

```
set pixelsToInch [winfo pixels . 2.54c]
```

Table 41–7 summarizes these operations:

Table 41–7 Window size information.

winfo fpixels *win num*	Converts *num*, in screen units, to pixels. Returns a floating point number.
winfo geometry *win*	Returns the geometry of *win*, in pixels and relative to the parent in the form *WxH+X+Y*
winfo height *win*	Returns the height of *win*, in pixels.
winfo pixels *win num*	Converts *num* to a whole number of pixels.
winfo reqheight *win*	Returns the requested height of *win*, in pixels.
winfo reqwidth *win*	Returns the requested width of *win*, in pixels.
winfo screenheight *win*	Returns the height of the screen, in pixels.
winfo screenmmheight *win*	Returns the height of the screen, in millimeters.
winfo screenmmwidth *win*	Returns the width of the screen, in millimeters.
winfo screenwidth *win*	Returns the width of the screen, in pixels.
winfo width *win*	Returns the width of *win*, in pixels.

Location

Table 41–8 Window location information.

winfo containing ?-displayof *win*? *win x y*	Returns the pathname of the window at *x* and *y*.
winfo pointerx *win*	Returns the X screen coordinate of the mouse.
winfo pointery *win*	Returns the Y screen coordinate of the mouse.
winfo pointerxy *win*	Returns the X and Y coordinates of the mouse.
winfo rootx *win*	Returns the X screen position of *win*.
winfo rooty *win*	Returns the Y screen position of *win*.
winfo screen *win*	Returns the display identifier of *win*'s screen.
winfo server *win*	Returns the version string of the display server.
winfo toplevel *win*	Returns pathname of toplevel that contains *win*.
winfo x *win*	Returns the X position of *win* in its parent.
winfo y *win*	Returns the Y position of *win* in its parent.

The winfo x and winfo y operations return the position of the upper-left corner of a window relative to its parent widget. In the case of the main window, this is its location on the screen. The winfo rootx and winfo rooty return the screen location of the upper-left corner of a widget, even if it is not a toplevel.

The winfo containing operation returns the pathname of the window that contains a point on the screen. This is useful in implementing menus and drag-and-drop applications.

The `winfo toplevel` operation returns the pathname of the toplevel that contains a widget. If the window is itself a toplevel, then this operation returns its own pathname.

The `winfo screen` operation returns the display identifier for the screen of the window.

Virtual Root Window

Some window managers use a virtual root window to give the user a larger virtual screen. At any given time, only a portion of the virtual screen is visible, and the user can change the view on the virtual screen to bring different applications into view. In this case, the `winfo x` and `winfo y` operations return the coordinates of a main window in the virtual root window (i.e., not the screen).

The `winfo vrootheight` and `winfo vrootwidth` operations return the size of the virtual root window. If there is no virtual root window, then these just return the size of the screen.

Correcting virtual root window coordinates.

The `winfo vrootx` and `winfo vrooty` are used to map from the coordinates in the virtual root window to screen-relative coordinates. These operations return 0 if there is no virtual root window. Otherwise, they return a negative number. If you add this number to the value returned by `winfo x` or `winfo y`, it gives the screen-relative coordinate of the window:

```
set screenx [expr [winfo x $win] + [winfo vrootx $win]]
```

Table 41–9 summarizes these operations:

Table 41–9 Virtual root window information.

winfo vrootheight *win*	Returns the height of the virtual root window for *win*.
winfo vrootwidth *win*	Returns the width of the virtual root window for *win*.
winfo vrootx *win*	Returns the X position of *win* in the virtual root.
winfo vrooty *win*	Returns the Y position of *win* in the virtual root.

Atoms and IDs

An *atom* is an X technical term for an identifier that is registered with the X server. Applications map names into atoms, and the X server assigns each atom a 32-bit identifier that can be passed between applications. One of the few places this is used in Tk is when the selection mechanism is used to interface with different toolkits. In some cases the selection is returned as atoms, which appear as 32-bit integers. The `winfo atomname` operation converts that number into an atom (i.e., a string), and the `winfo atom` registers a string with the X server and returns the 32-bit identifier as a hexadecimal string

Each widget has an ID assigned by the window system. The winfo id command returns this identifier. The winfo pathname operation returns the Tk pathname of the widget that has a given ID, but only if the window is part of the same application.

Embedding applications.

The id operation is useful if you need to embed another application into your window hierarchy. Wish takes a -use id command-line argument that causes it to use an existing window for its main window. Other toolkits provide similar functionality. For example, to embed another Tk app in a frame:

```
frame .embed -container true
exec wish -use [winfo id .embed] otherscript.tcl
```

Table 41–10 summarizes these operations:

Table 41–10 Atom and window ID information.

winfo atom ?-dis- playof *win*? *name*	Returns the 32-bit identifier for the atom *name*.
winfo atomname ?-dis- playof *win*? *id*	Returns the atom that corresponds to the 32-bit ID.
winfo id *win*	Returns the window ID of *win*.
winfo pathname ?-dis- playof *win*? *id*	Returns the Tk pathname of the window with *id*, or null.

Colormaps and Visuals

The winfo depth returns the number of bits used to represent the color in each pixel. The winfo cells command returns the number of colormap entries used by the visual class of a window. These two values are generally related. A window with 8 bits per pixel usually has 256 colormap cells. The winfo screendepth and winfo screencells return this information for the default visual class.

The winfo visualsavailable command returns a list of the visual classes and screen depths that are available. For example, a display with 8 bits per pixel might report the following visual classes are available:

```
winfo visualsavailable .
=> {staticgray 8} {grayscale 8} {staticcolor 8} \
    {pseudocolor 8}
```

The winfo visual operation returns the visual class of a window, and the winfo screenvisual returns the default visual class of the screen.

The winfo rgb operation converts from a color name or value to the red, green, and blue components of that color. Three decimal values are returned. Example 38–2 on page 537 uses this command to compute a slightly darker version of the same color.

Table 41–11 summarizes operations that return information about color-maps and visual classes, which are described in Chapter 38:

Table 41–11 Colormap and visual class information.

`winfo cells` *win*	Returns the number of colormap cells in *win*'s visual.
`winfo colormapfull` *win*	Returns 1 if the last color allocation failed.
`winfo depth` *win*	Returns the number of bits per pixel for *win*.
`winfo rgb` *win color*	Returns the red, green, and blue values for *color*.
`winfo screencells` *win*	Returns the number of colormap cells in the default visual.
`winfo screendepth` *win*	Returns the number of bits per pixel in the screen's default visual.
`winfo screenvisual` *win*	Returns the default visual of the screen.
`winfo visual` *win*	Returns the visual class of *win*.
`winfo visualsavailable` *win*	Returns a list of pairs that specify the visual type and bits per pixel of the available visual classes.

The `tk` Command

The `tk` command provides a few miscellaneous entry points into the Tk library. The `appname` operation is used to set or query the application name used with the Tk `send` command. If you define a new name and it is already in use by another application, (perhaps another instance of yourself), then a number is appended to the name (e.g., `#2`, `#3`, and so on). This is the syntax of the command:

```
tk appname ?name?
```

Fonts, canvas items, and widget sizes use screen units that are pixels, points, centimeters, millimeters, or inches. There are 72 points per inch. The `tk` `scaling` command, which was added in Tk 8.0, is used to set or query the mapping between pixels and points. A scale of 1.0 results in 72 pixels per inch. A scale of 1.25 results in 90 pixels per inch. This gives accurate sizes on a 90 dpi screen or it makes everything 25% larger on a 72 dpi screen. Changing the scale only affects widgets created after the change. This is the syntax of the command:

```
tk scaling ?num?
```

## CHAPTER 42

Managing User Preferences

This chapter describes a user preferences package. The resource database
stores preference settings. Applications specify Tcl variables that are
initialized from the database entries. A user interface lets the user
browse and change their settings.

User customization is an important part
of any complex application. There are always design decisions that could go
either way. A typical approach is to choose a reasonable default, but then let
users change the default setting through a preferences user interface. This chapter describes a preference package that works by tying together a Tcl variable,
which the application uses, and a resource specification, which the user sets. In
addition, a user interface is provided so that the user need not edit the resource
database directly.

App-Defaults Files

We will assume that it is sufficient to have two sources of application defaults: a
per-application database and a per-user database. In addition, we will allow for
some resources to be specific to color and monochrome displays. The following
example initializes the preference package by reading in the per-application and
per-user resource specification files. There is also an initialization of the global
array `pref` that will be used to hold state information about the preferences
package. The `Pref_Init` procedure is called like this:

```
Pref_Init $library/foo-defaults ~/.foo-defaults
```

We assume `$library` is the directory holding support files for the `foo` application, and that per-user defaults will be kept in `~/.foo-defaults`. These are
UNIX-oriented file names. When you write cross-platform Tk applications, you

will find that some file names are inherently platform-specific. The platform-independent operations described in Chapter 9 are great, but they do not change the fact that user preferences may be stored in `c:/webtk/userpref.txt` on Windows, `Hard Disk:System:Preferences:WebTk Prefs` on Macintosh, and `~/.webtk` on UNIX. I find it useful to have a small amount of platform-specific startup code that defines these pathnames. The preference package uses resource files that work on all platforms:

Example 42–1 Preferences initialization.

```
proc Pref_Init { userDefaults appDefaults } {
    global pref

    set pref(uid) 0;# for a unique identifier for widgets
    set pref(userDefaults) $userDefaults
    set pref(appDefaults) $appDefaults
    PrefReadFile $appDefaults startup
    if [file exists $userDefaults] {
        PrefReadFile $userDefaults user
    }
}
proc PrefReadFile { basename level } {
    if [catch {option readfile $basename $level} err] {
        Status "Error in $basename: $err"
    }
    if {[string match *color* [winfo visual .]]} {
        if [file exists $basename-color] {
            if [catch {option readfile \
                    $basename-color $level} err] {
                Status "Error in $basename-color: $err"
            }
        }
    } else {
        if [file exists $basename-mono] {
            if [catch {option readfile $basename-mono \
                    $level} err] {
                Status "Error in $basename-mono: $err"
            }
        }
    }
}
```

The `PrefReadFile` procedure reads a resource file and then looks for another file with the suffix `-color` or `-mono` depending on the characteristics of the display. With this scheme, a UNIX user puts generic settings in `~/.foo-defaults`. They put color specifications in `~/.foo-defaults-color`. They put specifications for black and white displays in `~/.foo-defaults-mono`. You could extend `PrefReadFile` to allow for per-host files as well.

Throughout this chapter we assume that the `Status` procedure displays messages to the user. It could be as simple as:

```
proc Status { s } { puts stderr $s }
```

Defining Preferences

This section describes the `Pref_Add` procedure that an application uses to define preference items. A preference item defines a relationship between a Tcl variable and a resource name. If the Tcl variable is undefined at the time `Pref_Add` is called, then it is set from the value for the resource. If the resource is not defined, then the variable is set to the default value.

Hide simple data structures with Tcl procedures.

A default value, a label, and a more extensive help string are associated with each item, which is represented by a Tcl list of five elements. A few short routines hide the layout of the item lists and make the rest of the code read better:

Example 42–2 Adding preference items.

```
proc PrefVar { item } { lindex $item 0 }
proc PrefRes { item } { lindex $item 1 }
proc PrefDefault { item } { lindex $item 2 }
proc PrefComment { item } { lindex $item 3 }
proc PrefHelp { item } { lindex $item 4 }

proc Pref_Add { prefs } {
    global pref
    append pref(items) $prefs " "
    foreach item $prefs {
        set varName [PrefVar $item]
        set resName [PrefRes $item]
        set value [PrefValue $varName $resName]
        if {$value == {}} {
            # Set variables that are still not set
            set default [PrefDefault $item]
            switch -regexp -- $default {
                ^CHOICE {
                    PrefValueSet $varName [lindex $default 1]
                }
                ^OFF {
                    PrefValueSet $varName 0
                }
                ^ON {
                    PrefValueSet $varName 1
                }
                default {
                    # This is a string or numeric
                    PrefValueSet $varName $default
                }
            }
        }
    }
}
```

V. Tk Details

The procedures `PrefValue` and `PrefValueSet` are used to query and set the value of the named variable, which can be an array element or a simple variable. The `upvar #0` command sets the variable in the global scope.

Example 42–3 Setting preference variables.

```
# PrefValue returns the value of the variable if it exists,
# otherwise it returns the resource database value
proc PrefValue { varName res } {
    upvar #0 $varName var
    if [info exists var] {
        return $var
    }
    set var [option get . $res {}]
}
# PrefValueSet defines a variable in the global scope.
proc PrefValueSet { varName value } {
    upvar #0 $varName var
    set var $value
}
```

An important side effect of the `Pref_Add` call is that the variables in the preference item are defined at the global scope. It is also worth noting that `PrefValue` will honor any existing value for a variable, so if the variable is already set at the global scope, then neither the resource value nor the default value will be used. It is easy to change `PrefValue` to always set the variable if this is not the behavior you want. Here is a sample call to `Pref_Add`:

Example 42–4 Using the preferences package.

```
Pref_Add {
    {win(scrollside) scrollbarSide {CHOICE left right}
        "Scrollbar placement"
"Scrollbars can be positioned on either the left or
right side of the text and canvas widgets."}
    {win(typeinkills) typeinKills OFF
        "Type-in kills selection"
"This setting determines whether or not the selection
is deleted when new text is typed in."}
    {win(scrollspeed) scrollSpeed 15 "Scrolling speed"
"This parameter affects the scrolling rate when a selection
is dragged off the edge of the window. Smaller numbers
scroll faster, but can consume more CPU."}
}
```

Any number of preference items can be specified in a call to `Pref_Add`. The list-of-lists structure is created by proper placement of the curly braces, and it is preserved when the argument is appended to `pref(items)`, which is the master list of preferences. In this example, `Pref_Add` gets passed a single argument that is a Tcl list with three elements. The Tcl variables are array elements, presumably related to the Win module of the application. The resource names are associated with the main application as opposed to any particular widget. They are specified in the database like this:

```
*scrollbarSide: left
*typeinKills: 0
*scrollSpeed: 15
```

The Preferences User Interface

The figure shows the interface for the items added with the Pref_Add command given in the previous section. The pop-up window with the extended help text appears after you click on "Scrollbar placement." The user interface to the preference settings is table-driven. As a result of all the Pref_Add calls, a single list of all the preference items is built. The interface is constructed by looping through this list and creating a user interface item for each:

Example 42–5 A user interface to the preference items.

```
proc Pref_Dialog {} {
    global pref
    if [catch {toplevel .pref}] {
        raise .pref
    } else {
        wm title .pref "Preferences"
        set buttons [frame .pref.but -bd 5]
        pack .pref.but -side top -fill x
        button $buttons.quit -text Dismiss \
            -command {PrefDismiss}
        button $buttons.save -text Save \
            -command {PrefSave}
        button $buttons.reset -text Reset \
            -command {PrefReset ; PrefDismiss}
        label $buttons.label \
            -text "Click labels for info on each item"
        pack $buttons.label -side left -fill x
        pack $buttons.quit $buttons.save $buttons.reset \
            -side right -padx 4

        frame .pref.b -borderwidth 2 -relief raised
        pack .pref.b -fill both
        set body [frame .pref.b.b -bd 10]
```

V. Tk Details

```
pack .pref.b.b -fill both

set maxWidth 0
foreach item $pref(items) {
    set len [string length [PrefComment $item]]
    if {$len > $maxWidth} {
        set maxWidth $len
    }
}
set pref(uid) 0
foreach item $pref(items) {
    PrefDialogItem $body $item $maxWidth
}
    }
}
```

The interface supports three different types of preference items: boolean, choice, and general value. A boolean is implemented with a checkbutton that is tied to the Tcl variable, which will get a value of either 0 or 1. A boolean is identified by a default value that is either ON or OFF. A choice item is implemented as a set of radiobuttons, one for each choice. A choice item is identified by a default value that is a list with the first element equal to CHOICE. The remaining list items are the choices, with the first one being the default choice. A regexp is used to check for CHOICE instead of using list operations. This is because Tcl 8.0 will complain if the value is not a proper list, which could happen with arbitrary values. If neither of these cases, boolean or choice, are detected, then an entry widget is created to hold the general value of the preference item:

Example 42–6 Interface objects for different preference types.

```
proc PrefDialogItem { frame item width } {
    global pref
    incr pref(uid)
    set f [frame $frame.p$pref(uid) -borderwidth 2]
    pack $f -fill x
    label $f.label -text [PrefComment $item] -width $width
    bind $f.label <1> \
        [list PrefItemHelp %X %Y [PrefHelp $item]]
    pack $f.label -side left
    set default [PrefDefault $item]
    if {[regexp "^CHOICE " $default]} {
        foreach choice [lreplace $default 0 0] {
            incr pref(uid)
            radiobutton $f.c$pref(uid) -text $choice \
                -variable [PrefVar $item] -value $choice
            pack $f.c$pref(uid) -side left
        }
    } else {
        if {$default == "OFF" || $default == "ON"} {
            # This is a boolean
            set varName [PrefVar $item]
            checkbutton $f.check -variable $varName \
```

```
                -command [list PrefFixupBoolean $f.check $varName]
            PrefFixupBoolean $f.check $varName
            pack $f.check -side left
        } else {
            # This is a string or numeric
            entry $f.entry -width 10 -relief sunken
            pack $f.entry -side left -fill x -expand true
            set pref(entry,[PrefVar $item]) $f.entry
            set varName [PrefVar $item]
            $f.entry insert 0 [uplevel #0 [list set $varName]]
            bind $f.entry <Return> "PrefEntrySet %W $varName"
        }
    }
}
proc PrefFixupBoolean {check varname} {
    upvar #0 $varname var
    # Update the checkbutton text each time it changes
    if {$var} {
        $check config -text On
    } else {
        $check config -text Off
    }
}
proc PrefEntrySet { entry varName } {
    PrefValueSet $varName [$entry get]
}
```

In this interface, when the user clicks a radiobutton or a checkbutton, the Tcl variable is set immediately. To obtain a similar effect with the general preference item, the <Return> key is bound to a procedure that sets the associated Tcl variable to the value from the entry widget. PrefEntrySet is a one-line procedure that saves us from using the more awkward binding shown below. Grouping with double quotes allows substitution of $varName, but then we must quote the square brackets to postpone command substitution:

```
    bind $f.entry <Return> "PrefValueSet $varName \[%W get\]"
```

The binding on <Return> is done as opposed to using the -textvariable option because it interacts with traces on the variable a bit better. With trace you can arrange for a Tcl command to be executed when a variable is changed, as in Example 42–10 on page 590. For a general preference item it is better to wait until the complete value is entered before responding to its new value.

The other aspect of the user interface is the display of additional help information for each item. If there are lots of preference items, then there isn't enough room to display this information directly. Instead, clicking on the short description for each item brings up a toplevel with the help text for that item. The toplevel is marked transient so that the window manager does not decorate it:

V. Tk Details

Example 42–7 Displaying the help text for an item.

```
proc PrefItemHelp { x y text } {
    catch {destroy .prefitemhelp}
    if {$text == {}} {
        return
    }
    set self [toplevel .prefitemhelp -class Itemhelp]
    wm title $self "Item help"
    wm geometry $self +[expr $x+10]+[expr $y+10]
    wm transient $self .pref
    message $self.msg -text $text -aspect 1500
    pack $self.msg
    bind $self.msg <1> {PrefNukeItemHelp .prefitemhelp}
    .pref.but.label configure -text \
        "Click on pop-up or another label"
}
proc PrefNukeItemHelp { t } {
    .pref.but.label configure -text \
        "Click labels for info on each item"
    destroy $t
}
```

Managing the Preferences File

The preference settings are saved in the per-user file. The file is divided into two parts. The tail is automatically rewritten by the preferences package. Users can manually add resource specifications to the beginning of the file and they will be preserved:

Example 42–8 Saving preferences settings to a file.

```
# PrefSave writes the resource specifications to the
# end of the per-user resource file,
proc PrefSave {} {
    global pref
    if [catch {
        set old [open $pref(userDefaults) r]
        set oldValues [split [read $old] \n]
        close $old
    }] {
        set oldValues {}
    }
    if [catch {open $pref(userDefaults).new w} out] {
        .pref.but.label configure -text \
        "Cannot save in $pref(userDefaults).new: $out"
        return
    }
    foreach line $oldValues {
        if {$line == \
                "!!! Lines below here automatically added"} {
```

```
            break
        } else {
            puts $out $line
        }
    }
    puts $out "!!! Lines below here automatically added"
    puts $out "!!! [exec date]"
    puts $out "!!! Do not edit below here"
    foreach item $preferences {
        set varName [PrefVar $item]
        set resName [PrefRes $item]
        if [info exists pref(entry,$varName)] {
            PrefEntrySet $pref(entry,$varName) $varName
        }
        set value [PrefValue $varName $resName]
        puts $out [format "%s\t%s" *${resName}: $value]
    }
    close $out
    set new [glob $pref(userDefaults).new]
    set old [file root $new]
    if [catch {file rename -force $new $old} err] {
        Status "Cannot install $new: $err"
        return
    }
    PrefDismiss
}
```

There is one fine point in PrefSave. The value from the entry widget for general-purpose items is obtained explicitly in case the user has not already pressed <Return> to update the Tcl variable.

The interface is rounded out with the PrefReset and PrefDismiss procedures. A reset is achieved by clearing the option database and reloading it, and then temporarily clearing the preference items and their associated variables and then redefining them with Pref_Add.

Example 42–9 Read settings from the preferences file.

```
proc PrefReset {} {
    global pref
    # Re-read user defaults
    option clear
    PrefReadFile $pref(appDefaults) startup
    PrefReadFile $pref(userDefaults) user
    # Clear variables
    set items $pref(items)
    set pref(items) {}
    foreach item $items {
        uplevel #0 [list unset [PrefVar $item]]
    }
    # Restore values
    Pref_Add $items
}
```

V. Tk Detai

```
proc PrefDismiss {} {
    destroy .pref
    catch {destroy .prefitemhelp}
}
```

Tracing Changes to Preference Variables

Suppose, for example, we want to repack the scrollbars when the user changes their scrollside setting from left to right. This is done by setting a trace on the win(scrollside) variable. When the user changes that via the user interface, the trace routine is called. The trace command and its associated procedure are shown in the next example. The variable must be declared global before setting up the trace, which is not otherwise required if Pref_Add is the only command using the variable.

Example 42–10 Tracing a Tcl variable in a preference item.

```
Pref_Add {
    {win(scrollside) scrollbarSide {CHOICE left right}
        "Scrollbar placement"
"Scrollbars can be positioned on either the left or
right side of the text and canvas widgets."}
}
global win
set win(lastscrollside) $win(scrollside)
trace variable win(scrollside) w ScrollFixup
# Assume win(scrollbar) identifies the scrollbar widget
proc ScrollFixup { name1 name2 op } {
    global win
    if {$win(scrollside) != $win(lastscrollside)} {
        set parent [lindex [pack info $win(scrollbar)] 1]
        pack forget $win(scrollbar)
        set firstchild [lindex [pack slaves $parent] 0]
        pack $win(scrollbar) -in $parent -before $firstchild \
            -side $win(scrollside) -fill y
        set win(lastscrollside) $win(scrollside)
    }
}
```

Improving the Package

One small improvement can be made to Pref_Add. If a user specifies a boolean resource manually, he or she might use "true" instead of one and "false" instead of zero. Pref_Add should check for those cases and set the boolean variable to one or zero to avoid errors when the variables are used in expressions.

The interface lets you dismiss it without saving your preference settings. This is either a feature that lets users try out settings without committing to them, or it is a bug. Fixing this requires introducing a parallel set of variables to shadow the real variables until the user hits `Save`, which is tedious to implement. You can also use a *grab* as described in Chapter 36 to prevent the user from doing anything but setting preferences.

This preference package is a slightly simplified version of one I developed for *exmh*, which has so many preference items that a two-level scheme is necessary. The first level is a menu of preference sections, and each section is created with a single call to `Pref_Add`. This requires additional arguments to `Pref_Add` to provide a title for the section and some overall information about the preference section. The display code changes a small amount. The code for the *exmh* is on the CD-ROM.

A User Interface to Bindings

This chapter presents a user interface to view and edit bindings.

A good way to learn about how a widget works is to examine the bindings that are defined for it. This chapter presents a user interface that lets you browse and change bindings for a widget or a class of widgets.

The interface uses a pair of listboxes to display the events and their associated commands. An entry widget is used to enter the name of a widget or a class. There are a few command buttons that let the user add a new binding, edit an existing binding, save the bindings to a file, and dismiss the dialog. Here is what the display looks like:

Example 43–1 A user interface to widget bindings.

```
proc Bind_Interface { w } {
   # Our state
   global bind
   set bind(class) $w

   # Set a class used for resource specifications
   set frame [toplevel .bindui -class Bindui]
   # Default relief
   option add *Bindui*Entry.relief sunken startup
   option add *Bindui*Listbox.relief raised startup
   # Default Listbox sizes
   option add *Bindui*key.width 18 startup
   option add *Bindui*cmd.width 25 startup
   option add *Bindui*Listbox.height 5 startup

   # A labeled entry at the top to hold the current
   # widget name or class.
   set t [frame $frame.top -bd 2]
   label $t.l -text "Bindings for" -width 11
   entry $t.e -textvariable bind(class)
   pack $t.l -side left
   pack $t.e -side left -fill x -expand true
   pack $t -side top -fill x
   bind $t.e <Return> [list Bind_Display $frame]

   # Command buttons
   button $t.quit -text Dismiss \
       -command [list destroy $frame]
   button $t.save -text Save \
       -command [list Bind_Save $frame]
   button $t.edit -text Edit \
       -command [list Bind_Edit $frame]
   button $t.new -text New \
       -command [list Bind_New $frame]
   pack $t.quit $t.save $t.edit $t.new -side right

   # A pair of listboxes and a scrollbar
   scrollbar $frame.s -orient vertical \
       -command [list BindYview \
           [list $frame.key $frame.cmd]]
   listbox $frame.key \
       -yscrollcommand [list $frame.s set] \
       -exportselection false
   listbox $frame.cmd \
       -yscrollcommand [list $frame.s set]
   pack $frame.s -side left -fill y
   pack $frame.key $frame.cmd -side left \
       -fill both -expand true

   foreach l [list $frame.key $frame.cmd] {
      bind $l <B2-Motion>\
          [list BindDragto %x %y $frame.key $frame.cmd]
      bind $l <Button-2> \
```

```
            [list BindMark %x %y $frame.key $frame.cmd]
        bind $l <Button-1> \
            [list BindSelect %y $frame.key $frame.cmd]
        bind $l <B1-Motion> \
            [list BindSelect %y $frame.key $frame.cmd]
        bind $l <Shift-B1-Motion> {}
        bind $l <Shift-Button-1> {}
    }
    # Initialize the display
    Bind_Display $frame
}
```

The `Bind_Interface` command takes a widget name or class as a parameter. It creates a toplevel and gives it the `Bindui` class so that resources can be set to control widget attributes. The `option add` command is used to set up the default listbox sizes. The lowest priority, `startup`, is given to these resources so that clients of the package can override the size with their own resource specifications.

At the top of the interface is a labeled entry widget. The entry holds the name of the class or widget for which the bindings are displayed. The `textvariable` option of the entry widget is used so that the entry's contents are available in a variable, `bind(class)`. Pressing `<Return>` in the entry invokes `Bind_Display` that fills in the display.

Example 43–2 `Bind_Display` presents the bindings for a widget or class.

```
proc Bind_Display { frame } {
    global bind
    $frame.key delete 0 end
    $frame.cmd delete 0 end
    foreach seq [bind $bind(class)] {
        $frame.key insert end $seq
        $frame.cmd insert end [bind $bind(class) $seq]
    }
}
```

The `Bind_Display` procedure fills in the display with the binding information. The `bind` command returns the events that have bindings, and what the command associated with each event is. `Bind_Display` loops through this information and fills in the listboxes.

A Pair of Listboxes Working Together

The two listboxes in the interface, `$frame.key` and `$frame.cmd`, are set up to work as a unit. A selection in one causes a parallel selection in the other. Only one listbox exports its selection as the PRIMARY selection. Otherwise, the last listbox to assert the selection steals the selection rights from the other widget. The following example shows the `bind` commands from `Bind_Interface` and the

`BindSelect` routine that selects an item in both listboxes:

Example 43–3 Related listboxes are configured to select items together.

```
foreach l [list $frame.key $frame.cmd] {
    bind $1 <Button-1> \
        [list BindSelect %y $frame.key $frame.cmd]
    bind $1 <B1-Motion> \
        [list BindSelect %y $frame.key $frame.cmd]
}
proc BindSelect { y args } {
    foreach w $args {
        $w select clear 0 end
        $w select anchor [$w nearest $y]
        $w select set anchor [$w nearest $y]
    }
}
```

A scrollbar for two listboxes.

A single scrollbar scrolls both listboxes. The next example shows the `scrollbar` command from `Bind_Interface` and the `BindYview` procedure that scrolls the listboxes:

Example 43–4 Controlling a pair of listboxes with one scrollbar.

```
scrollbar $frame.s -orient vertical \
    -command [list BindYview [list $frame.key $frame.cmd]]

proc BindYview { lists args } {
    foreach l $lists {
        eval {$l yview} $args
    }
}
```

The `BindYview` command is used to change the display of the listboxes associated with the scrollbar. The first argument to `BindYview` is a list of widgets to scroll, and the remaining arguments are added by the scrollbar to specify how to position the display. The details are essentially private between the scrollbar and the listbox. See page 429 for the details. The `args` keyword is used to represent these extra arguments, and `eval` is used to pass them through `BindYview`. The reasoning for using `eval` like this is explained in Chapter 10 on page 128.

The `Listbox` class bindings for `<Button-2>` and `<B2-Motion>` cause the listbox to scroll as the user drags the widget with the middle mouse button. These bindings are adjusted so that both listboxes move together. The following example shows the `bind` commands from the `Bind_Interface` procedure and the `BindMark` and `BindDrag` procedures that scroll the listboxes:

Example 43–5 Drag-scrolling a pair of listboxes together.

```
bind $l <B2-Motion>\
    [list BindDragto %x %y $frame.key $frame.cmd]
bind $l <Button-2> \
    [list BindMark %x %y $frame.key $frame.cmd]

proc BindDragto { x y args } {
    foreach w $args {
        $w scan dragto $x $y
    }
}
proc BindMark { x y args } {
    foreach w $args {
        $w scan mark $x $y
    }
}
```

The `BindMark` procedure does a `scan mark` that defines an origin, and `Bind-Dragto` does a `scan dragto` that scrolls the widget based on the distance from that origin. All Tk widgets that scroll support `yview`, `scan mark`, and `scan dragto`. Thus the `BindYview`, `BindMark`, and `BindDragto` procedures are general enough to be used with any set of widgets that scroll together.

The Editing Interface

Editing and defining a new binding are done in a pair of entry widgets. These widgets are created and packed into the display dynamically when the user presses the `New` or `Edit` button:

Example 43–6 An interface to define bindings.

```
proc Bind_New { frame } {
    if [catch {frame $frame.edit} f] {
        # Frame already created
```

```
            set f $frame.edit
        } else {
            foreach x {key cmd} {
                set f2 [frame $f.$x]
                pack $f2 -fill x -padx 2
                label $f2.l -width 11 -anchor e
                pack $f2.l -side left
                entry $f2.e
                pack $f2.e -side left -fill x -expand true
                bind $f2.e <Return> [list BindDefine $f]
            }
            $f.key.l config -text Event:
            $f.cmd.l config -text Command:
        }
        pack $frame.edit -after $frame.top -fill x
    }
    proc Bind_Edit { frame } {
        Bind_New $frame
        set line [$frame.key curselection]
        if {$line == {}} {
            return
        }
        $frame.edit.key.e delete 0 end
        $frame.edit.key.e insert 0 [$frame.key get $line]
        $frame.edit.cmd.e delete 0 end
        $frame.edit.cmd.e insert 0 [$frame.cmd get $line]
    }
```

The -width 11 and -anchor e attributes for the label widgets are specified so that the Event: and Command: labels will line up with the Bindings for label at the top.

Saving and Loading Bindings

All that remains is the actual change or definition of a binding and some way to remember the bindings the next time the application is run. The BindDefine procedure attempts a bind command that uses the contents of the entries. If it succeeds, then the edit window is removed by unpacking it.

The bindings are saved by Bind_Save as a series of Tcl commands that define the bindings. It is crucial that the list command be used to construct the commands properly.

Bind_Read uses the source command to read the saved commands. The application must call Bind_Read as part of its initialization to get the customized bindings for the widget or class. It also must provide a way to invoke Bind_Interface, such as a button, menu entry, or key binding.

Example 43-7 Defining and saving bindings.

```
proc BindDefine { f } {
    if [catch {
        bind [$f.top.e get] [$f.edit.key.e get] \
            [$f.edit.cmd.e get]
    } err] {
        Status $err
    } else {
        # Remove the edit window
        pack forget $f.edit
    }
}
proc Bind_Save { dotfile args } {
    set out [open $dotfile.new w]
    foreach w $args {
        foreach seq [bind $w] {
            # Output a Tcl command
            puts $out [list bind $w $seq [bind $w $seq]]
        }
    }
    close $out
    file rename -force $dotfile.new $dotfile
}
proc Bind_Read { dotfile } {
    if [catch {
        if [file exists $dotfile] {
            # Read the saved Tcl commands
            source $dotfile
        }
    } err] {
        Status "Bind_Read $dotfile failed: $err"
    }
}
```

V. Tk Details

C Programming

Part VI describes C programming and Tcl. The goal of this section is to get you started in the right direction. For serious C programming, you will need to consult the on-line reference material for detailed descriptions of the C APIs.

Chapter 44 provides an introduction to using Tcl at the C programming level. It gets you started with integrating Tcl and Tk into an existing application. Chapter 47 provides a survey of the facilities in the Tcl and Tk C libraries. Chapter 46 presents a sample digital clock Tk widget implementation in C.

C Programming and Tcl

This chapter explains how to extend a Tcl application with new built-in commands. Tcl 8.0 replaces the original string-based command interface with a more efficient dual-ported object interface. This chapter describes both interfaces.

Tcl is implemented in a C library that is easy to integrate into an existing application. By adding the Tcl interpreter to your application, you can configure and control it with Tcl scripts, and with Tk you can provide a nice graphical interface to it. This was the original model for Tcl. Applications would be largely application-specific C code and include a small amount of Tcl for configuration and the graphical interface. However, the basic Tcl shells proved so useful by themselves that relatively few Tcl programmers need to worry about programming in C or C++.

Tcl is designed to be easily extensible by writing new command implementations in C. A command implemented in C is more efficient than an equivalent Tcl procedure. A more pressing reason to write C code is that it may not be possible to provide the same functionality purely in Tcl. Suppose you have a new device, perhaps a color scanner or a unique input device. The programming interface to that device is through a set of C procedures that initialize and manipulate the state of the device. Without some work on your part, that interface is not accessible to your Tcl scripts. You are in the same situation if you have a C or C++ library that implements some specialized function such as a database. Fortunately, it is rather straightforward to provide a Tcl interface that corresponds to the C or C++ interface.

Note: Where this chapter says "C", you can always think "C or C++". There is also a package called *TclBlend* that lets you extend Tcl by writing Java instead of C, and to evaluate Tcl scripts from Java. Find out more about *TclBlend* at:

```
http://www.scriptics.com/java/
```

VI. Tcl and C

Basic Concepts

This chapter assumes that you know some C or C++. You do not have to be an expert programmer to use the Tcl APIs. Indeed, one of Tcl's strengths is the ease with which you can extend it by writing C code. This chapter provides a few working examples that explain how to initialize your application and create Tcl commands. It describes how to organize your code into packages. It concludes with notes about compiling Tcl under UNIX, Windows, and Macintosh.

Getting Started

There are two ways to get started writing C code for Tcl applications. The easiest way is to write an *extension* that just adds some new commands to a standard Tcl shell like *tclsh* or *wish*. With this approach the Tcl shell creates a basic framework for you, and your C code just extends this framework with new commands. Tcl supports dynamic loading, so you can compile your extension as a shared library (i.e., DLL) and load it into a running Tcl shell. This is the easiest approach because the Tcl shell handles the details of startup and shutdown, and it provides an interactive console to enter Tcl commands. In the case of *wish*, it also provides the framework for a graphical user interface. Finally, a loadable extension can be shared easily with other Tcl users.

The second way to use the Tcl library is to add it to an existing application. If your application is very simple, it may make sense to turn it into an extension for a standard Tcl shell, which brings you back to the first, simpler approach. However, if your application already has a complex framework (e.g., it is a long-running server process), then you can just add Tcl to it and export the functionality of your application as one or more Tcl commands. Once you do this, you will find that you can extend your application with all the features provided by Tcl.

C Command Procedures and Data Objects

The C or C++ code that implements a Tcl command is called a *command procedure*. The interface to a command procedure is much like the interface to a main program. The inputs are an array of values that correspond exactly to the arguments in the Tcl script command. The result of the command procedure becomes the result of the Tcl command.

There are two kinds of command procedures: string-based and "object-based." I've quoted "object" here because we are really talking about the data representation of the arguments and results. We are not talking about methods and inheritance and other things associated with object oriented programming. However, the Tcl C APIs use a structure called a `Tcl_Obj`, which is called a *dual ported object* in the reference material. I prefer the term "`Tcl_Obj` value".

The string interface is quite simple. A command procedure gets an array of strings as arguments, and it computes a string as the result. Tcl 8.0 generalized strings into the `Tcl_Obj` type, which can have two representations: both a string and another native representation like an integer, floating point number, list, or bytecodes. An object-based command takes an array of `Tcl_Obj` pointers as arguments, and it computes a `Tcl_Obj` as its result. The goal of the `Tcl_Obj` type is to reduce the number of conversions between strings and native representations. Object-based commands will be more efficient than the equivalent string-based commands, but the APIs are a little more complex. For simple tasks, and for learning, you can use just the simpler string-based command interface.

SWIG

David Beasley created a nice tool called SWIG (Simple Wrapper Interface Generator) that generates the C code that implements command procedures that expose a C or C++ API as Tcl commands. This can be a great time saver if you need to export many calls to Tcl. The only drawback is that a C interface may not feel that comfortable to the script writer. Handcrafted Tcl interfaces can be much nicer, but automatically-generated interfaces are just fine for rapid prototyping and for software testing environments. You can learn more about SWIG at its web site:

        http://www.swig.org/

Tcl Initialization

Before you can use your command procedures from Tcl scripts, you need to register them with Tcl. In some cases, you may also need to create the Tcl interpreter, although this is done for you by the standard Tcl shells.

If you are writing an extension, then you must provide an initialization procedure. The job of this procedure is to register Tcl commands with `Tcl_CreateCommand` or `Tcl_CreateObjCommand`. This is shown in Example 44–1 on page 608. The name of this procedure must end with `_Init`, as in `Expect_Init`, `Blt_Init`, or `Foo_Init`, if you plan to create your extension as a shared library. This procedure is called automatically when the Tcl script loads your library with the `load` command, which is described on page 607.

If you need to create the Tcl interpreter yourself, then there are two levels of APIs. At the most basic level there is `Tcl_CreateInterp`. This creates an interpreter that includes the standard commands listed in Table 1–4 on page 22. You still have to initialize all your custom commands (e.g., by calling `Foo_Init`) and arrange to run a script using `Tcl_Eval` or `Tcl_EvalFile`. However, there are a lot of details to get right, and Tcl provides a higher level interface in `Tcl_Main` and `Tcl_AppInit`. `Tcl_Main` creates the interpreter for you, processes command line arguments to get an initial script to run, and even provides an interactive command loop. It calls out to `Tcl_AppInit`, which you provide, to complete the initialization of the interpreter. The use of `Tcl_Main` is shown in Example 44–13 on page 629. There are even more details to get right with a Tk application because of the window system and the event loop. These details are hidden behind `Tk_Main`, which makes a similar call out to `Tk_AppInit` that you provide to complete initialization.

VI. Tcl and C

Calling Out to Tcl Scripts

An application can call out to the script layer at any point, even inside command procedures. `Tcl_Eval` is the basic API for this, and there are several variations depending on how you pass arguments to the script. When you look up `Tcl_Eval` in the reference material, you will get a description of the whole family of `Tcl_Eval` procedures.

You can also set and query Tcl variables from C using the `Tcl_SetVar` and `Tcl_GetVar` procedures. Again, there are several variations on these procedures that account for different types, like strings or `Tcl_Obj` values, and scalar or array variables. The `Tcl_LinkVar` procedure causes a Tcl variable to mirror a C variable. Modifications to the Tcl variable are reflected in the C variable, and reading the Tcl variable always returns the C variable's value. `Tcl_LinkVar` is built on a more general variable tracing facility, which is exposed to Tcl as the `trace` command, and available as the `Tcl_TraceVar` C API.

I think a well-behaved extension should provide both a C and Tcl API, but most of the core Tcl and Tk commands do not provide an exported C API. This forces you to eval Tcl scripts to get at their functionality. Example 44–15 on page 635 shows the `Tcl_Invoke` procedure that can help you work around this limitation. `Tcl_Invoke` is used to invoke a Tcl command without the parsing and substitution overhead of `Tcl_Eval`.

Using the Tcl C Library

Over the years the Tcl C Library has grown from a simple language interpreter into a full featured library. An important property of the Tcl API is that it is cross platform: its works equally well on UNIX, Windows, and Macintosh. One can argue that it is easier to write cross-platform applications in Tcl than in Java! Some of the useful features that you might not expect from a language interpreter include:

- A general hash table package that automatically adjusts itself as the hash table grows. It allows various types of keys, including strings and integers.
- A dynamic string (i.e., `DString`) package that provides an efficient way to construct strings.
- An I/O channel package that replaces the old "standard I/O library" found on UNIX with something that is cross-platform, does buffering, allows non-blocking I/O, and does character set translations. You can create new I/O channel types.
- Network sockets for TCP/IP communication.
- Character set translations between Unicode, UTF-8, and other encodings.
- An event loop manager that interfaces with network connections and window system events. You can create new "event sources" that work with the event loop manager.
- Multithreading support in the form of mutexes, condition variables, and thread-local storage.

- A registration system for exit handlers that are called when Tcl is shutting down.

This Chapter focuses just on the Tcl C API related to the Tcl interpreter. Chapter 47 gives a high-level overview of all the procedures in the Tcl and Tk C library, but this book does not provide a complete reference. Refer to the on-line manual pages for the specific details about each procedure; they are an excellent source of information. The manual pages should be part of every Tcl distribution. They are on the book's CD, and they can be found web at:

```
http://www.scriptics.com/man/
```

The Tcl source code is worth reading.

Finally, it is worth emphasizing that the source code of the Tcl C library is a great source of information. The code is well written and well commented. If you want to see how something really works, reading the code is worthwhile.

Creating a Loadable Package

You can organize your C code into a loadable package that can be dynamically linked into *tclsh*, *wish*, or your own Tcl application. The details about compiling the code into the shared library that contains the package are presented in Chapter 45. This section describes a package that implements the `random` Tcl command that returns random numbers.

The `load` Command

The Tcl `load` command is used to dynamically link in a compiled package:

```
load library package ?interp?
```

The `library` is the file name of the shared library file (i.e., the DLL), and `package` is the name of the package implemented by the library. This name corresponds to the `package_Init` procedure called to initialize the package (e.g., `Random_Init`) The optional `interp` argument lets you load the library into a slave interpreter. If the library is in `/usr/local/lib/random.so`, then a Tcl script can `load` the package like this:

```
load /usr/local/lib/random.so Random
```

On most UNIX systems, you can set the `LD_LIBRARY_PATH` environment variable to a colon-separated list of directories that contain shared libraries. If you do that, then you can use relative names for the libraries:

```
load librandom.so Random
```

On Macintosh, the `load` command looks for libraries in the same folder as the Tcl/Tk application (i.e., *Wish*) and in the `System:Extensions:Tool Command Language` folder:

```
load random.shlib Random
```

On Windows, `load` looks in the same directory as the Tcl/Tk application, the current directory, the `C:\Windows\System` directory (or `C:\Windows\System32` on

Windows NT), the `C:\Windows` directory, and then the directories listed in the `PATH` environment variable.

```
load random.dll Random
```

Fortunately, you usually do not have to worry about these details because the Tcl `package` facility can manage your libraries for you. Instead of invoking `load` directly, your scripts can use `package require` instead. The package facility keeps track of where your libraries are and knows how to call `load` for your platform. It is described in Chapter 12.

The Package Initialization Procedure

When a package is loaded, Tcl calls a C procedure named *package*_Init, where *package* is the name of your package. Example 44–1 defines `Random_Init`. It registers a command procedure, `RandomCmd`, that implements a new Tcl command, `random`. When the Tcl script uses the `random` command, the `RandomCmd` procedure will be invoked by the Tcl interpreter. Two styles of command registrations are made for comparison: the original `Tcl_CreateCommand` and the `Tcl_CreateObjCommand` added in Tcl 8.0. The command procedures are described in the next section:

Example 44–1 The initialization procedure for a loadable package.

```
/*
 * random.c
 */
#include <tcl.h>
/*
 * Declarations for application-specific command procedures
 */

int RandomCmd(ClientData clientData,
            Tcl_Interp *interp,
            int argc, char *argv[]);
int RandomObjCmd(ClientData clientData,
            Tcl_Interp *interp,
            int objc, Tcl_Obj *CONST objv[]);

/*
 * Random_Init is called when the package is loaded.
 */

int Random_Init(Tcl_Interp *interp) {
    /*
     * Initialize the stub table interface, which is
     * described in Chapter 45.
     */

    if (Tcl_InitStubs(interp, "8.1", 0) == NULL) {
        return TCL_ERROR;
    }
```

```
    /*
     * Register two variations of random.
     * The orandom command uses the object interface.
     */

    Tcl_CreateCommand(interp, "random", RandomCmd,
            (ClientData)NULL, (Tcl_CmdDeleteProc *)NULL);
    Tcl_CreateObjCommand(interp, "orandom", RandomObjCmd,
            (ClientData)NULL, (Tcl_CmdDeleteProc *)NULL);

    /*
     * Declare that we implement the random package
     * so scripts that do "package require random"
     * can load the library automatically.
     */
    Tcl_PkgProvide(interp, "random", "1.1");
    return TCL_OK;
}
```

Using `Tcl_PkgProvide`

`Random_Init` uses `Tcl_PkgProvide` to declare what package is provided by the C code. This call helps the `pkg_mkIndex` procedure learn what libraries provide which packages. `pkg_mkIndex` saves this information in a package database, which is a file named `pkgIndex.tcl`. The `package require` command looks for the package database files along your `auto_path` and automatically loads your package. The general process is:

- Create your shared library and put it into a directory listed on your `auto_path` variable, or a subdirectory of one of the directories on your `auto_path`.
- Run the `pkg_mkIndex` procedure in that directory, giving it the names of all the script files and shared libraries it should index. Now your shared library is ready for use by other scripts.
- A script uses `package require` to request a package. The correct `load` command for your system will be used the first time a command from your package is used. The `package` command is the same on all platforms:

    ```
    package require random
    => 1.1
    ```

This process is explained in more detail on page 165.

A C Command Procedure

Tcl 8.0 introduced a new interface for Tcl commands that is designed to work efficiently with its internal on-the-fly byte code compiler. The original interface to commands was string oriented. This resulted in a lot of conversions between strings and internal formats such as integers, double-precision floating point numbers, and lists. The new interface is based on the `Tcl_Obj` type that can store different types of values. Conversions between strings and other types are done in a lazy fashion, and the saved conversions help your scripts run more efficiently.

This section shows how to build a random number command using both interfaces. The string-based interface is simpler, and we start with that to illustrate the basic concepts. You can use it for your first experiments with command procedures. Once you gain some experience, you can start using the interfaces that use `Tcl_Obj` values instead of simple strings. If you have old command procedures from before Tcl 8.0, you need to update them only if you want extra efficiency. The string and `Tcl_Obj` interfaces are very similar, so you should find updating your command procedures straightforward.

The String Command Interface

The string-based interface to a C command procedure is much like the interface to the `main` program. You register the command procedure like this:

```
Tcl_CreateCommand(interp, data, "cmd", CmdProc, DeleteProc);
```

When the script invokes `cmd`, Tcl calls `CmdProc` like this:

```
CmdProc(data, interp, argc, argv);
```

The `interp` is type `Tcl_Interp *`, and it is a general handle on the state of the interpreter. Most Tcl C APIs take this parameter. The `data` is type `Client-Data`, which is an opaque pointer. You can use this to associate state with your command. You register this state along with your command procedure, and then Tcl passes it back to you when the command is invoked. This is especially useful with Tk widgets, which are explained in more detail in Chapter 46. Our simple `RandomCmd` command procedure does not use this feature, so it passes `NULL` into `Tcl_CreateCommand`. The `DeleteProc` is called when the command is destroyed, which is typically when the whole Tcl interpreter is being deleted. If your state needs to be cleaned up, you can do it then. `RandomCmd` does not use this feature, either.

The arguments from the Tcl command are available as an array of strings defined by an `argv` parameter and counted by an `argc` parameter. This is the same interface that a main program has to its command line arguments. Example 44–2 shows the `RandomCmd` command procedure:

Example 44–2 The `RandomCmd` C command procedure.

```
/*
 * RandomCmd --
 * This implements the random Tcl command. With no arguments
 * the command returns a random integer.
 * With an integer valued argument "range",
 * it returns a random integer between 0 and range.
 */
int
RandomCmd(ClientData clientData, Tcl_Interp *interp,
        int argc, char *argv[])
```

```
{
    int rand, error;
    int range = 0;
    if (argc > 2) {
        interp->result = "Usage: random ?range?";
        return TCL_ERROR;
    }
    if (argc == 2) {
        if (Tcl_GetInt(interp, argv[1], &range) != TCL_OK) {
            return TCL_ERROR;
        }
    }
    rand = random();
    if (range != 0) {
        rand = rand % range;
    }
    sprintf(interp->result, "%d", rand);
    return TCL_OK;
}
```

The return value of a Tcl command is really two things: a result string and a status code. The result is a string that is either the return value of the command as seen by the Tcl script, or an error message that is reported upon error. For example, if extra arguments are passed to the command procedure, it raises a Tcl error by doing this:

```
interp->result = "Usage: random ?range?";
return TCL_ERROR;
```

The `random` implementation accepts an optional argument that is a range over which the random numbers should be returned. The `argc` parameter is tested to see if this argument has been given in the Tcl command. `argc` counts the command name as well as the arguments, so in our case `argc == 2` indicates that the command has been invoked something like:

```
random 25
```

The procedure `Tcl_GetInt` converts the string-valued argument to an integer. It does error checking and sets the interpreter's result field in the case of error, so we can just return if it fails to return `TCL_OK`.

```
if (Tcl_GetInt(interp, argv[1], &range) != TCL_OK) {
    return TCL_ERROR;
}
```

Finally, the real work of calling `random` is done, and the result is formatted directly into the result buffer using `sprintf`. A normal return looks like this:

```
sprintf(interp->result, "%d", rand);
return TCL_OK;
```

VI. Tcl and C

Result Codes from Command Procedures

The command procedure returns a status code that is either TCL_OK or TCL_ERROR to indicate success or failure. If the command procedure returns TCL_ERROR, then a Tcl error is raised, and the result value is used as the error message. The procedure can also return TCL_BREAK, TCL_CONTINUE, TCL_RETURN, which affects control structure commands like foreach and proc. You can even return an application-specific code (e.g., 5 or higher), which might be useful if you are implementing new kinds of control structures. The status code returned by the command procedure is the value returned by the Tcl catch command, which is discussed in more detail on page 77.

Managing the String Result

There is a simple protocol that manages the storage for a command procedure's result string. It involves interp->result, which holds the value, and interp->freeProc, which determines how the storage is cleaned up. When a command is called, the interpreter initializes interp->result to a static buffer of TCL_RESULT_SIZE, which is 200 bytes. The default cleanup action is to do nothing. These defaults support two simple ways to define the result of a command. One way is to use sprintf to format the result in place:

```
sprintf(interp->result, "%d", rand);
```

Using sprintf is suitable if you know your result string is short, which is often the case. The other way is to set interp->result to the address of a constant string. In this case, the original result buffer is not used, and there is no cleanup required because the string is compiled into the program:

```
interp->result = "Usage: random ?random?";
```

In more general cases, the following procedures should be used to manage the result and freeProc fields. These procedures automatically manage storage for the result:

```
Tcl_SetResult(interp, string, freeProc)
Tcl_AppendResult(interp, str1, str2, str3, (char *)NULL)
Tcl_AppendElement(interp, string)
```

Tcl_SetResult sets the return value to be *string*. The *freeProc* argument describes how the result should be disposed of: TCL_STATIC is used in the case where the result is a constant string allocated by the compiler, TCL_DYNAMIC is used if the result is allocated with Tcl_Alloc, which is a platform- and compiler-independent version of malloc, and TCL_VOLATILE is used if the result is in a stack variable. In the TCL_VOLATILE case, the Tcl interpreter makes a copy of the result before calling any other command procedures. Finally, if you have your own memory allocator, pass in the address of the procedure that should free the result.

Tcl_AppendResult copies its arguments into the result buffer, reallocating the buffer if necessary. The arguments are concatenated onto the end of the existing result, if any. Tcl_AppendResult can be called several times to build a result. The result buffer is overallocated, so several appends are efficient.

`Tcl_AppendElement` adds the string to the result as a proper Tcl list element. It might add braces or backslashes to get the proper structure.

If you have built up a result and for some reason want to throw it away (e.g., an error occurs), then you can use `Tcl_ResetResult` to restore the result to its initial state. `Tcl_ResetResult` is always called before a command procedure is invoked.

The `Tcl_Obj` Command Interface

The `Tcl_Obj` command interface replaces strings with *dual-ported values*. The arguments to a command are an array of pointers to `Tcl_Obj` structures, and the result of a command is also of type `Tcl_Obj`. The replacement of strings by `Tcl_Obj` values extends throughout Tcl. The value of a Tcl variable is kept in a `Tcl_Obj`, and Tcl scripts are stored in a `Tcl_Obj`, too. You can continue to use the old string-based API, which converts strings to `Tcl_Obj` values, but this conversion adds overhead.

The `Tcl_Obj` structure stores both a string representation and a native representation. The native representation depends on the type of the value. Tcl lists are stored as an array of pointers to strings. Integers are stored as 32-bit integers. Floating point values are stored in double-precision. Tcl scripts are stored as sequences of byte codes. Conversion between the native representation and a string are done upon demand. There are APIs for accessing `Tcl_Obj` values, so you do not have to worry about type conversions unless you implement a new type. Example 44–3 shows the random command procedure using the `Tcl_Obj` interfaces:

Example 44–3 The `RandomObjCmd` C command procedure.

```
/*
 * RandomObjCmd --
 * This implements the random Tcl command from
 * Example 44-2 using the object interface.
 */
int
RandomObjCmd(ClientData clientData, Tcl_Interp *interp,
        int objc, Tcl_Obj *CONST objv[])
{
    Tcl_Obj *resultPtr;
    int rand, error;
    int range = 0;
    if (objc > 2) {
        Tcl_WrongNumArgs(interp, 1, objv, "?range?");
        return TCL_ERROR;
    }
    if (objc == 2) {
        if (Tcl_GetIntFromObj(interp, objv[1], &range) !=
                TCL_OK) {
            return TCL_ERROR;
```

```
        }
    }
    rand = random();
    if (range != 0) {
        rand = rand % range;
    }
    resultPtr = Tcl_GetObjResult(interp);
    Tcl_SetIntObj(resultPtr, rand);
    return TCL_OK;
}
```

Compare Example 44–2 with Example 44–3. You can see that the two versions of the C command procedures are similar. The Tcl_GetInt call is replaced with Tcl_GetIntFromObj call. This receives an integer value from the command argument. This call can avoid conversion from string to integer if the Tcl_Obj value is already an integer.

The result is set by getting a handle on the result object and setting its value. This is done instead of accessing the interp->result field directly:

```
        resultPtr = Tcl_GetObjResult(interp);

        Tcl_SetIntObj(resultPtr, rand);
```

The Tcl_WrongNumArgs procedure is a convenience procedure that formats an error message. You pass in objv, the number of arguments to use from it, and additional string. The example creates this message:

```
        wrong # args: should be "random ?range?"
```

Example 44–3 does not do anything obvious about storage management. Tcl initializes the result object before calling your command procedure and takes care of cleaning it up later. It is sufficient to set a value and return TCL_OK or TCL_ERROR. In more complex cases, however, you have to worry about reference counts to Tcl_Obj values. This is described in more detail later.

If your command procedure returns a string, then you will use Tcl_SetStringObj. This command makes a copy of the string you pass it. The new Tcl interfaces that take strings also take length arguments so you can pass binary data in strings. If the length is minus 1, then the string is terminated by a NULL byte. A command that always returned "boring" would do this:

```
        resultPtr = Tcl_GetObjResult(interp);

        Tcl_SetStringObj(resultPtr, "boring", -1);
```

This is a bit too boring. In practice you may need to build up the result piecemeal. With the string-based API, you use Tcl_AppendResult. With the Tcl_Obj API you get a pointer to the result and use Tcl_AppendToObj or Tcl_AppendStringsToObj:

```
        resultPtr = Tcl_GetObjResult(interp);

        Tcl_AppendStringsToObj(resultPtr, "hello ", username, NULL);
```

Managing `Tcl_Obj` Reference Counts

The string-based interfaces copy strings when passing arguments and returning results, but the `Tcl_Obj` interfaces manipulate reference counts to avoid these copy operations. References come from Tcl variables, from the interpreter's result, and from sharing caused when a value is passed into a Tcl procedure. Constants are also shared. When a C command procedure is called, Tcl does not automatically increment the reference count on the arguments. However, each `Tcl_Obj` referenced by `objv` will have at least one reference, and it is quite common to have two or more references.

The C type definition for `Tcl_Obj` is shown below. There are APIs to access all aspects of an object, so you should refrain from manipulating a `Tcl_Obj` directly unless you are implementing a new type:

Example 44–4 The `Tcl_Obj` structure.

```
typedef struct Tcl_Obj {
    int refCount;          /* Counts number of shared references */
    char *bytes;           /* String representation */
    int length;            /* Number of bytes in the string */
    Tcl_ObjType *typePtr;/* Type implementation */
    union {
        long longValue;  /* Type data */
        double doubleValue;
        VOID *otherValuePtr;
        struct {
            VOID *ptr1;
            VOID *ptr2;
        } twoPtrValue;
    } internalRep;
} Tcl_Obj;
```

Each type implementation provides a few procedures like this:

```
Tcl_GetTypeFromObj(interp, objPtr, valuePtr);
Tcl_SetTypeObj(resultPtr, value);
objPtr = Tcl_NewTypeObj(value);
```

The initial reference count is zero.

The `Tcl_NewTypeObj` allocates storage for a `Tcl_Obj` and sets its reference count to zero. `Tcl_IncrRefCount` and `Tcl_DecrRefCount` increment and decrement the reference count on an object. `Tcl_DecrRefCount` frees the storage for `Tcl_Obj` when it goes to zero. The initial reference count of zero was chosen because functions like `Tcl_SetObjResult` automatically increment the reference count on an object.

The `Tcl_GetTypeFromObj` and `Tcl_SetTypeObj` procedures just get and set the value; the reference count does not change. Type conversions are automatic. You can set a `Tcl_Obj` value to an integer and get back a string or double precision number later. The type implementations automatically take care of the storage for the `Tcl_Obj` value as it changes. Of course, if a `Tcl_Obj` stays the same type, then no string conversions are necessary and accesses are more efficient.

Modifying Tcl_Obj Values

It is not safe to modify a shared `Tcl_Obj`. The sharing is only for efficiency: Logically, each reference is a copy, and you must honor this model when creating and modifying `Tcl_Obj` values. `Tcl_IsShared` returns 1 if there is more than one reference to an object. If a command procedure modifies a shared object, it must make a private copy with `Tcl_DuplicateObj`. The new copy starts with a reference count of zero. You either pass this to `Tcl_SetResultObj`, which adds a reference, or you have to explicitly add a reference to the copy with `Tcl_IncrRefCount`.

Example 44–5 implements a `plus1` command that adds one to its argument. If the argument is not shared, then `plus1` can be implemented efficiently by modifying the native representation of the integer. Otherwise, it has to make a copy of the object before modifying it:

Example 44–5 The `Plus1ObjCmd` procedure.

```
/*
 * Plus1ObjCmd --
 * This adds one to its input argument.
 */
int
Plus1ObjCmd(ClientData clientData, Tcl_Interp *interp,
        int objc, Tcl_Obj *CONST objv[])
{
    Tcl_Obj *objPtr;
    int i;
    if (objc != 2) {
        Tcl_WrongNumArgs(interp, 1, objv, "value");
        return TCL_ERROR;
    }
    objPtr = objv[1];
    if (Tcl_GetIntFromObj(interp, objPtr, &i) != TCL_OK) {
        return TCL_ERROR;
    }
    if (Tcl_IsShared(objPtr)) {
        objPtr = Tcl_DuplicateObj(objPtr);   /* refCount 0 */
        Tcl_IncrRefCount(objPtr);            /* refCount 1*/
    }
    /*
     * Assert objPtr has a refCount of one here.
     * OK to set the unshared value to something new.
     * Tcl_SetIntObj overwrites the old value.
     */
    Tcl_SetIntObj(objPtr, i+1);
    /*
     * Setting the result object adds a new reference,
     * so we decrement because we no longer care about
     * the integer object we modified.
     */
    Tcl_SetObjResult(interp, objPtr);        /* refCount 2*/
    Tcl_DecrRefCount(objPtr);                /* refCount 1*/
    /*
```

```
     * Now only the interpreter result has a reference to objPtr.
     */
    return TCL_OK;
}
```

Pitfalls of Shared `Tcl_Obj` Values

You have to be careful when using the values from a `Tcl_Obj` structure. The Tcl C library provides many procedures like `Tcl_GetStringFromObj`, `Tcl_GetIntFromObj`, `Tcl_GetListFromObj`, and so on. These all operate efficiently by returning a pointer to the native representation of the object. They will convert the object to the requested type, if necessary. The problem is that shared values can undergo type conversions that may invalidate your reference to a particular type of the value.

Value references are only safe until the next `Tcl_Get*FromObj` call.

Consider a command procedure that takes two arguments, an integer and a list. The command procedure has a sequence of code like this:

```
Tcl_GetListFromObj(interp, objv[1], &listPtr);
/* Manipulate listPtr */
Tcl_GetIntFromObj(interp, objv[2], &int);
/* listPtr may be invalid here */
```

If, by chance, both arguments have the same value, (e.g., 1 and 1), which is possible for a Tcl list and an integer, then Tcl will automatically arrange to share these values between both arguments. The pointers in `objv[1]` and `objv[2]` will be the same, and the reference count on the `Tcl_Obj` they reference will be at least 2. The first `Tcl_GetListFromObj` call ensures the value is of type list, and it returns a direct pointer to the native list representation. However, `Tcl_GetInFromObj` then helpfully converts the `Tcl_Obj` value to an integer. This deallocates the memory for the list representation, and now `listPtr` is a dangling pointer! This particular example can be made safe by reversing the calls because `Tcl_GetIntFromObj` copies the integer value:

```
Tcl_GetIntFromObj(interp, objv[2], &int);
Tcl_GetListFromObj(interp, objv[1], &listPtr);
/* int is still a good copy of the value */
```

By the way, you should always test your `Tcl_Get*` calls in case the format of the value is incompatible with the requested type. If the object is not a valid list, the following command returns an error:

```
if (Tcl_GetListFromObj(interp, obj[1], &listPtr) != TCL_OK) {
    return TCL_ERROR;
}
```

VI. Tcl and C

The `blob` Command Example

This section illustrates some standard coding practices with a bigger example. The example is still artificial in that it doesn't actually do very much. However, it illustrates a few more common idioms you should know about when creating Tcl commands.

The `blob` command creates and manipulates blobs. Each blob has a name and some associated properties. The `blob` command uses a hash table to keep track of blobs by their name. The hash table is an example of state associated with a command that needs to be cleaned up when the Tcl interpreter is destroyed. The Tcl hash table implementation is nice and general, too, so you may find it helpful in a variety of situations.

You can associate a Tcl script with a blob. When you poke the blob, it invokes the script. This shows how easy it is to associate behaviors with your C extensions. Example 44–6 shows the data structures used to implement blobs.

Example 44–6 The `Blob` and `BlobState` data structures.

```
/*
 * The Blob structure is created for each blob.
 */
typedef struct Blob {
    int N;                  /* Integer-valued property */
    Tcl_Obj *objPtr;        /* General property */
    Tcl_Obj *cmdPtr;        /* Callback script */
} Blob;
/*
 * The BlobState structure is created once for each interp.
 */
typedef struct BlobState {
    Tcl_HashTable hash;     /* List blobs by name */
    int uid;                /* Used to generate names */
} BlobState;
```

Creating and Destroying Hash Tables

Example 44–7 shows the `Blob_Init` and `BlobCleanup` procedures. `Blob_Init` creates the command and initializes the hash table. It registers a delete procedure, `BlobCleanup`, that will clean up the hash table.

The `Blob_Init` procedure allocates and initializes a hash table as part of the `BlobState` structure. This structure is passed into `Tcl_CreateObjCommand` as the `ClientData`, and gets passed back to `BlobCmd` later. You might be tempted to have a single static hash table structure instead of allocating one. However, it is quite possible that a process has many Tcl interpreters, and each needs its own hash table to record its own blobs.

When the hash table is initialized, you specify what the keys are. In this case, the name of the blob is a key, so `TCL_STRING_KEYS` is used. If you use an integer key, or the address of a data structure, use `TCL_ONE_WORD_KEYS`. You can also have an array of integers (i.e., a chunk of data) for the key. In this case, pass in an integer larger than 1 that represents the size of the integer array used as the key.

The `BlobCleanup` command cleans up the hash table. It iterates through all the elements of the hash table and gets the value associated with each key. This value is cast into a pointer to a `Blob` data structure. This iteration is a special case because each entry is deleted as we go by the `BlobDelete` procedure. If you do not modify the hash table, you continue the search with `Tcl_NextHashEntry` instead of calling `Tcl_FirstHashEntry` repeatedly.

Example 44–7 The `Blob_Init` and `BlobCleanup` procedures.

```
/*
 * Forward references.
 */

int BlobCmd(ClientData data, Tcl_Interp *interp,
        int objc, Tcl_Obj *CONST objv[]);
int BlobCreate(Tcl_Interp *interp, BlobState *statePtr);
void BlobCleanup(ClientData data);

/*
 * Blob_Init --
 *
 *      Initialize the blob module.
 *
 * Side Effects:
 *      This allocates the hash table used to keep track
 *      of blobs. It creates the blob command.
 */
int
Blob_Init(Tcl_Interp *interp)
{
    BlobState *statePtr;
    /*
     * Allocate and initialize the hash table. Associate the
     * BlobState with the command by using the ClientData.
     */
    statePtr = (BlobState *)Tcl_Alloc(sizeof(BlobState));
    Tcl_InitHashTable(&statePtr->hash, TCL_STRING_KEYS);
    statePtr->uid = 0;
    Tcl_CreateObjCommand(interp, "blob", BlobCmd,
            (ClientData)statePtr, BlobCleanup);
    return TCL_OK;
}
/*
 * BlobCleanup --
 *      This is called when the blob command is destroyed.
 *
 * Side Effects:
 *      This walks the hash table and deletes the blobs it
 *      contains. Then it deallocates the hash table.
 */
```

VI. Tcl and C

```
void
BlobCleanup(ClientData data)
{
    BlobState *statePtr = (BlobState *)data;
    Blob *blobPtr;
    Tcl_HashEntry *entryPtr;
    Tcl_HashSearch search;

    entryPtr = Tcl_FirstHashEntry(&statePtr->hash, &search);
    while (entryPtr != NULL) {
        blobPtr = Tcl_GetHashValue(entryPtr);
        BlobDelete(blobPtr, entryPtr);
        /*
         * Get the first entry again, not the "next" one,
         * because we just modified the hash table.
         */
        entryPtr = Tcl_FirstHashEntry(&statePtr->hash, &search);
    }
    Tcl_Free((char *)statePtr);
}
```

Tcl_Alloc and Tcl_Free

Instead of using malloc and free directly, you should use Tcl_Alloc and Tcl_Free in your code. Depending on compilation options, these procedures may map directly to the system's malloc and free, or use alternate memory allocators. The allocators on Windows and Macintosh are notoriously poor, and Tcl ships with a nice efficient memory allocator that is used instead. In general, it is not safe to allocate memory with Tcl_Alloc and free it with free, or allocate memory with malloc and free it with Tcl_Free.

When you look at the Tcl source code you will see calls to ckalloc and ckfree. These are macros that either call Tcl_Alloc and Tcl_Free or Tcl_DbgAlloc and Tcl_DbgFree depending on a compile-time option. The second set of functions is used to debug memory leaks and other errors. You cannot mix these two allocators either, so your best bet is to stick with Tcl_Alloc and Tcl_Free everywhere.

Parsing Arguments and Tcl_GetIndexFromObj

Example 44–8 shows the BlobCmd command procedure. This illustrates a basic framework for parsing command arguments. The Tcl_GetIndexFromObj procedure is used to map from the first argument (e.g., "names") to an index (e.g., NamesIx). This does error checking and formats an error message if the first argument doesn't match. All of the subcommands except "create" and "names" use the second argument as the name of a blob. This name is looked up in the hash table with Tcl_FindHashEntry, and the corresponding Blob structure is fetched using Tcl_GetHashValue. After the argument checking is complete, BlobCmd dispatches to the helper procedures to do the actual work:

Example 44–8 The `BlobCmd` command procedure.

```
/*
 * BlobCmd --
 *
 *      This implements the blob command, which has these
 *      subcommands:
 *          create
 *          command name ?script?
 *          data name ?value?
 *          N name ?value?
 *          names ?pattern?
 *          poke name
 *          delete name
 *
 * Results:
 *      A standard Tcl command result.
 */
int
BlobCmd(ClientData data, Tcl_Interp *interp,
    int objc, Tcl_Obj *CONST objv[])
{
    BlobState *statePtr = (BlobState *)data;
    Blob *blobPtr;
    Tcl_HashEntry *entryPtr;
    Tcl_Obj *valueObjPtr;

    /*
     * The subCmds array defines the allowed values for the
     * first argument. These are mapped to values in the
     * BlobIx enumeration by Tcl_GetIndexFromObj.
     */

    char *subCmds[] = {
        "create", "command", "data", "delete", "N", "names",
        "poke", NULL
    };
    enum BlobIx {
        CreateIx, CommandIx, DataIx, DeleteIx, NIx, NamesIx,
        PokeIx
    };
    int result, index;

    if (objc == 1 || objc > 4) {
        Tcl_WrongNumArgs(interp, 1, objv, "option ?arg ...?");
        return TCL_ERROR;
    }
    if (Tcl_GetIndexFromObj(interp, objv[1], subCmds,
            "option", 0, &index) != TCL_OK) {
        return TCL_ERROR;
    }
    if (((index == NamesIx || index == CreateIx) &&
            (objc > 2)) ||
        ((index == PokeIx || index == DeleteIx) &&
            (objc == 4))) {
```

```
            Tcl_WrongNumArgs(interp, 1, objv, "option ?arg ...?");
            return TCL_ERROR;
        }
        if (index == CreateIx) {
            return BlobCreate(interp, statePtr);
        }
        if (index == NamesIx) {
            return BlobNames(interp, statePtr);
        }
        if (objc < 3) {
            Tcl_WrongNumArgs(interp, 1, objv,
                "option blob ?arg ...?");
            return TCL_ERROR;
        } else if (objc == 3) {
            valueObjPtr = NULL;
        } else {
            valueObjPtr = objv[3];
        }
        /*
         * The rest of the commands take a blob name as the third
         * argument. Hash from the name to the Blob structure.
         */
        entryPtr = Tcl_FindHashEntry(&statePtr->hash,
                Tcl_GetString(objv[2]));
        if (entryPtr == NULL) {
            Tcl_AppendResult(interp, "Unknown blob: ",
                    Tcl_GetString(objv[2]), NULL);
            return TCL_ERROR;
        }
        blobPtr = (Blob *)Tcl_GetHashValue(entryPtr);
        switch (index) {
            case CommandIx: {
                return BlobCommand(interp, blobPtr, valueObjPtr);
            }
            case DataIx: {
                return BlobData(interp, blobPtr, valueObjPtr);
            }
            case NIx: {
                return BlobN(interp, blobPtr, valueObjPtr);
            }
            case PokeIx: {
                return BlobPoke(interp, blobPtr);
            }
            case DeleteIx: {
                return BlobDelete(blobPtr, entryPtr);
            }
        }
    }
```

Creating and Removing Elements from a Hash Table

The real work of `BlobCmd` is done by several helper procedures. These form the basis of a C API to operate on blobs as well. Example 44–9 shows the `BlobCreate` and `BlobDelete` procedures. These procedures manage the hash table entry, and they allocate and free storage associated with the blob.

Example 44–9 `BlobCreate` and `BlobDelete`.

```
int
BlobCreate(Tcl_Interp *interp, BlobState *statePtr)
{
    Tcl_HashEntry *entryPtr;
    Blob *blobPtr;
    int new;
    char name[20];
    /*
     * Generate a blob name and put it in the hash table
     */
    statePtr->uid++;
    sprintf(name, "blob%d", statePtr->uid);
    entryPtr = Tcl_CreateHashEntry(&statePtr->hash, name, &new);
    /*
     * Assert new == 1
     */
    blobPtr = (Blob *)Tcl_Alloc(sizeof(Blob));
    blobPtr->N = 0;
    blobPtr->objPtr = NULL;
    blobPtr->cmdPtr = NULL;
    Tcl_SetHashValue(entryPtr, (ClientData)blobPtr);
    /*
     * Copy the name into the interpreter result.
     */
    Tcl_SetStringObj(Tcl_GetObjResult(interp), name, -1);
    return TCL_OK;
}
int
BlobDelete(Blob *blobPtr, Tcl_HashEntry *entryPtr)
{
    Tcl_DeleteHashEntry(entryPtr);
    if (blobPtr->cmdPtr != NULL) {
        Tcl_DecrRefCount(blobPtr->cmdPtr);
    }
    if (blobPtr->objPtr != NULL) {
        Tcl_DecrRefCount(blobPtr->objPtr);
    }
    /*
     * Use Tcl_EventuallyFree because of the Tcl_Preserve
     * done in BlobPoke. See page 626.
     */
    Tcl_EventuallyFree((char *)blobPtr, Tcl_Free);
    return TCL_OK;
}
```

Building a List

The `BlobNames` procedure iterates through the elements of the hash table using `Tcl_FirstHashEntry` and `Tcl_NextHashEntry`. It builds up a list of the names as it goes along. Note that the object reference counts are managed for us. The `Tcl_NewStringObj` returns a `Tcl_Obj` with reference count of zero. When that object is added to the list, the `Tcl_ListObjAppendElement` procedure increments the reference count. Similarly, the `Tcl_NewListObj` returns a `Tcl_Obj` with reference count zero, and its reference count is incremented by `Tcl_SetObjResult`:

Example 44-10 The `BlobNames` procedure.

```
int
BlobNames(Tcl_Interp *interp, BlobState *statePtr)
{
    Tcl_HashEntry *entryPtr;
    Tcl_HashSearch search;
    Tcl_Obj *listPtr;
    Tcl_Obj *objPtr;
    char *name;
    /*
     * Walk the hash table and build a list of names.
     */
    listPtr = Tcl_NewListObj(0, NULL);
    entryPtr = Tcl_FirstHashEntry(&statePtr->hash, &search);
    while (entryPtr != NULL) {
        name = Tcl_GetHashKey(&statePtr->hash, entryPtr);
        if (Tcl_ListObjAppendElement(interp, listPtr,
                Tcl_NewStringObj(name, -1)) != TCL_OK) {
            return TCL_ERROR;
        }
        entryPtr = Tcl_NextHashEntry(&search);
    }
    Tcl_SetObjResult(interp, listPtr);
    return TCL_OK;
}
```

Keeping References to `Tcl_Obj` Values

A blob has two simple properties: an integer `N` and a general `Tcl_Obj` value. You can query and set these properties with the `BlobN` and `BlobData` procedures. The `BlobData` procedure keeps a pointer to its `Tcl_Obj` argument, so it must increment the reference count on it:

Example 44–11 The `BlobN` and `BlobData` procedures.

```c
int
BlobN(Tcl_Interp *interp, Blob *blobPtr, Tcl_Obj *objPtr)
{
    int N;
    if (objPtr != NULL) {
        if (Tcl_GetIntFromObj(interp, objPtr, &N) != TCL_OK) {
            return TCL_ERROR;
        }
        blobPtr->N = N;
    } else {
        N = blobPtr->N;
    }
    Tcl_SetObjResult(interp, Tcl_NewIntObj(N));
    return TCL_OK;
}
int
BlobData(Tcl_Interp *interp, Blob *blobPtr, Tcl_Obj *objPtr)
{
    if (objPtr != NULL) {
        if (blobPtr->objPtr != NULL) {
            Tcl_DecrRefCount(blobPtr->objPtr);
        }
        Tcl_IncrRefCount(objPtr);
        blobPtr->objPtr = objPtr;
    }
    if (blobPtr->objPtr != NULL) {
        Tcl_SetObjResult(interp, blobPtr->objPtr);
    }
    return TCL_OK;
}
```

Using `Tcl_Preserve` and `Tcl_Release` to Guard Data

The `BlobCommand` and `BlobPoke` operations let you register a Tcl command with a blob and invoke the command later. Whenever you evaluate a Tcl command like this, you must be prepared for the worst. It is quite possible for the command to turn around and delete the blob it is associated with! The `Tcl_Preserve`, `Tcl_Release`, and `Tcl_EventuallyFree` procedures are used to handle this situation. `BlobPoke` calls `Tcl_Preserve` on the blob before calling `Tcl_Eval`. `BlobDelete` calls `Tcl_EventuallyFree` instead of `Tcl_Free`. If the `Tcl_Release` call has not yet been made, then `Tcl_EventuallyFree` just marks the memory for deletion, but does not free it immediately. The memory is freed later by `Tcl_Release`. Otherwise, `Tcl_EventuallyFree` frees the memory directly and `Tcl_Release` does nothing. Example 44–12 shows `BlobCommand` and `BlobPoke`:

VI. Tcl and C

Example 44–12 The `BlobCommand` and `BlobPoke` procedures.

```
int
BlobCommand(Tcl_Interp *interp, Blob *blobPtr,
    Tcl_Obj *objPtr)
{
    if (objPtr != NULL) {
        if (blobPtr->cmdPtr != NULL) {
            Tcl_DecrRefCount(blobPtr->cmdPtr);
        }
        Tcl_IncrRefCount(objPtr);
        blobPtr->cmdPtr = objPtr;
    }
    if (blobPtr->cmdPtr != NULL) {
        Tcl_SetObjResult(interp, blobPtr->cmdPtr);
    }
    return TCL_OK;
}
int
BlobPoke(Tcl_Interp *interp, Blob *blobPtr)
{
    int result = TCL_OK;
    if (blobPtr->cmdPtr != NULL) {
        Tcl_Preserve(blobPtr);
        result = Tcl_EvalObj(interp, blobPtr->cmdPtr);
        /*
         * Safe to use blobPtr here
         */
        Tcl_Release(blobPtr);
        /*
         * blobPtr may not be valid here
         */
    }
    return result;
}
```

It turns out that `BlobCmd` does not actually use the `blobPtr` after calling `Tcl_EvalObj`, so it could get away without using `Tcl_Preserve` and `Tcl_Release`. These procedures do add some overhead: They put the pointer onto a list of preserved pointers and have to take it off again. If you are careful, you can omit these calls. However, it is worth noting the potential problems caused by evaluating arbitrary Tcl scripts!

Strings and Internationalization

There are two important topics related to string handling: creating strings dynamically and translating strings between character set encodings. These issues do not show up in the simple examples we have seen so far, but they will arise in more serious applications.

The `DString` Interface

It is often the case that you have to build up a string from pieces. The `Tcl_DString` data type and a related API are designed to make this efficient. The `DString` interface hides the memory management issues, and the `Tcl_DString` data type starts out with a small static buffer, so you can often avoid allocating memory if you put a `Tcl_String` type on the stack (i.e., as a local variable). The standard code sequence goes something like this:

```
Tcl_DString ds;
Tcl_DStringInit(&ds);
Tcl_DStringAppend(&ds, "some value", -1);
Tcl_DStringAppend(&ds, "something else", -1);
Tcl_DStringResult(interp, &ds);
```

The `Tcl_DStringInit` call initializes a string pointer inside the structure to point to a static buffer that is also inside the structure. The `Tcl_DStringAppend` call grows the string. If it would exceed the static buffer, then a new buffer is allocated dynamically and the string is copied into it. The last argument to `Tcl_DStringAppend` is a length, which can be minus 1 if you want to copy until the trailing NULL byte in your string. You can use the string value as the result of your Tcl command with `Tcl_DStringResult`. This passes ownership of the string to the interpreter and automatically cleans up the `Tcl_DString` structure.

If you do not use the string as the interpreter result, then you must call `Tcl_DStringFree` to ensure that any dynamically allocated memory is released:

```
Tcl_DStringFree(&ds);
```

You can get a direct pointer to the string you have created with `Tcl_DStringValue`:

```
name = Tcl_DStringValue(&ds);
```

There are a handful of additional procedures in the `DString` API that you can read about in the reference material. There are some that create lists, but this is better done with the `Tcl_Obj` interface (e.g., `Tcl_NewListObj` and friends).

To some degree, a `Tcl_Obj` can replace the use of a `Tcl_DString`. For example, the `Tcl_NewStringObj` and `Tcl_AppendToObj` allocate a `Tcl_Obj` and append strings to it. However, there are a number of Tcl API procedures that take `Tcl_DString` types as arguments instead of the `Tcl_Obj` type. Also, for small strings, the `DString` interface is still more efficient because it can do less dynamic memory allocation.

Character Set Conversions

As described in Chapter 15, Tcl uses UTF-8 strings internally. UTF-8 is a representation of Unicode that does not contain NULL bytes. It also represents 7-bit ASCII characters in one byte, so if you have old C code that only manipulates ASCII strings, it can coexist with Tcl without modification.

However, in more general cases, you may need to convert between UTF-8 strings you get from `Tcl_Obj` values to strings of a particular encoding. For

VI. Tcl and C

example, when you pass strings to the operating system, it expects them in its native encoding, which might be 16-bit Unicode, ISO-Latin-1 (i.e., iso-8859-1), or something else.

Tcl provides an encoding API that does translations for you. The simplest calls use a `Tcl_DString` to store the results because it is not possible to predict the size of the result in advance. For example, to convert from a UTF-8 `string` to a `Tcl_DString` in the system encoding, you use this call:

```
Tcl_UtfToExternalDString(NULL, string, -1, &ds);
```

You can then pass `Tcl_DStringValue(&ds)` to your system call that expects a native string. Afterwards you need to call `Tcl_DStringFree(&ds)` to free up any memory allocated by `Tcl_UtfToExternalDString`.

To translate strings the other way, use `Tcl_ExternalToUtfDString`:

```
Tcl_ExternalToUtfDString(NULL, string, -1, &ds);
```

The third argument to these procedures is the length of `string` in bytes (not characters), and minus 1 means that Tcl should calculate it by looking for a NULL byte. Tcl stores its UTF-8 strings with a NULL byte at the end so it can do this.

The first argument to these procedures is the encoding to translate to or from. NULL means the system encoding. If you have data in nonstandard encodings, or need to translate into something other than the system encoding, you need to get a handle on the encoding with `Tcl_GetEncoding`, and free that handle later with `Tcl_FreeEncoding`:

```
encoding = Tcl_GetEncoding(interp, name);
Tcl_FreeEncoding(encoding);
```

The names of the encodings are returned by the `encoding names` Tcl command, and you can query them with a C API, too.

Windows has a quirky string data type called TCHAR, which is an 8-bit byte on Windows 95/98, and a 16-bit Unicode character on Windows NT. If you use a C API that takes an array of TCHAR, then you have to know what kind of system you are running on to use it properly. Tcl provides two procedures that deal with this automatically. `Tcl_WinTCharToUf` works like `Tcl_ExternalToUtfDString`, and `Tcl_WinUtfToTChar` works like `Tcl_UtfToExternalDString`:

```
Tcl_WinUtfToTChar(string, -1, &ds);
Tcl_WinTCharToUtf(string, -1, &ds);
```

Finally, Tcl has several procedures to work with Unicode characters, which are type `Tcl_UniChar`, and UTF-8 encoded characters. Examples include `Tcl_UniCharToUtf`, `Tcl_NumUtfChars`, and `Tcl_UtfToUniCharDString`. Consult the reference materials for details about these procedures.

Tcl_Main and Tcl_AppInit

This section describes how to make a custom main program that includes Tcl. However, the need for custom main programs has been reduced by the use of loadable modules. If you create your commands as a loadable package, you can just load them into *tclsh* or *wish*. Even if you do not need a custom main, this section will explain how all the pieces fit together.

The Tcl library supports the basic application structure through the Tcl_Main procedure that is designed to be called from your main program. Tcl_Main does three things:

- It calls Tcl_CreateInterp to create an interpreter that includes all the standard Tcl commands like set and proc. It also defines a few Tcl variables like argc and argv. These have the command-line arguments that were passed to your application.
- It calls Tcl_AppInit, which is not part of the Tcl library. Instead, your application provides this procedure. In Tcl_AppInit you can register additional application-specific Tcl commands.
- It reads a script or goes into an interactive loop.

You call Tcl_Main from your main program and provide an implementation of the Tcl_AppInit procedure:

Example 44–13 A canonical Tcl main program and Tcl_AppInit.

```
/* main.c */
#include <tcl.h>
int Tcl_AppInit(Tcl_Interp *interp);
/*
 * Declarations for application-specific command procedures
 */
int Plus1ObjCmd(ClientData clientData,
            Tcl_Interp *interp,
            int objc, Tcl_Obj *CONST objv[]);

main(int argc, char *argv[]) {
    /*
     * Initialize your application here.
     *
     * Then initialize and run Tcl.
     */
    Tcl_Main(argc, argv, Tcl_AppInit);
    exit(0);
}
/*
 * Tcl_AppInit is called from Tcl_Main
 * after the Tcl interpreter has been created,
 * and before the script file
 * or interactive command loop is entered.
 */
int
Tcl_AppInit(Tcl_Interp *interp) {
    /*
     * Tcl_Init reads init.tcl from the Tcl script library.
     */
    if (Tcl_Init(interp) == TCL_ERROR) {
        return TCL_ERROR;
```

VI. Tcl and C

```
      }
      /*
       * Register application-specific commands.
       */
      Tcl_CreateObjCommand(interp, "plus1", Plus1ObjCmd,
              (ClientData)NULL, (Tcl_CmdDeleteProc *)NULL);
      Random_Init(interp);
      Blob_Init(interp);
      /*
       * Define the start-up filename. This file is read in
       * case the program is run interactively.
       */
      Tcl_SetVar(interp, "tcl_rcFileName", "~/.mytcl",
          TCL_GLOBAL_ONLY);
      /*
       * Test of Tcl_Invoke, which is defined on page 635.
       */
      Tcl_Invoke(interp, "set", "foo", "$xyz [foo] {", NULL);
      return TCL_OK;
  }
```

The `main` program calls `Tcl_Main` with the `argc` and `argv` parameters passed into the program. These are the strings passed to the program on the command line, and `Tcl_Main` will store these values into Tcl variables by the same name. `Tcl_Main` is also given the address of the initialization procedure, which is `Tcl_AppInit` in our example. `Tcl_AppInit` is called by `Tcl_Main` with one argument, a handle on a newly created interpreter. There are three parts to the `Tcl_AppInit` procedure:

*   The first part initializes the various packages the application uses. The example calls `Tcl_Init` to set up the script library facility described in Chapter 12. The core Tcl commands have already been defined by `Tcl_CreateInterp`, which is called by `Tcl_Main` before the call to `Tcl_AppInit`.
*   The second part of `Tcl_AppInit` does application-specific initialization. The example registers the command procedures defined earlier in this Chapter.
*   The third part defines a Tcl variable, `tcl_RcFileName`, which names an application startup script that executes if the program is used interactively.

You can use your custom program just like *tclsh*, except that it includes the additional commands you define in your `Tcl_AppInit` procedure. The sample makefile on the CD creates a program named *mytcl*. You can compile and run that program and test `random` and the other commands.

Tk_Main

The structure of Tk applications is similar. The `Tk_Main` procedure creates a Tcl interpreter and the main Tk window. It calls out to a procedure you provide to complete initialization. After your `Tk_AppInit` returns, `Tk_Main` goes into an event loop until all the windows in your application have been destroyed.

Example 44–14 shows a Tk_AppInit used with Tk_Main. The main program processes its own command-line arguments using Tk_ParseArgv, which requires a Tcl interpreter for error reporting. The Tk_AppInit procedure initializes the clock widget example that is the topic of Chapter 46:

Example 44–14 A canonical Tk main program and Tk_AppInit.

```
/* main.c */
#include <tk.h>

int Tk_AppInit(Tcl_Interp *interp);

/*
 * A table for command line arguments.
 */
char *myoption1 = NULL;
int myint2 = 0;

static Tk_ArgvInfo argTable[] = {
    {"-myoption1", TK_ARGV_STRING, (char *) NULL,
        (char *) &myoption1, "Explain myoption1"},
    {"-myint2", TK_ARGV_CONSTANT, (char *) 1, (char *) &myint2,
        "Explain myint2"},
    {"", TK_ARGV_END, },
};

main(int argc, char *argv[]) {
    Tcl_Interp *interp;

    /*
     * Create an interpreter for the error message from
     * Tk_ParseArgv. Another one is created by Tk_Main.
     * Parse our arguments and leave the rest to Tk_Main.
     */

    interp = Tcl_CreateInterp();
    if (Tk_ParseArgv(interp, (Tk_Window) NULL, &argc, argv,
            argTable, 0) != TCL_OK) {
        fprintf(stderr, "%s\n", interp->result);
        exit(1);
    }
    Tcl_DeleteInterp(interp);

    Tk_Main(argc, argv, Tk_AppInit);
    exit(0);
}
int ClockCmd(ClientData clientData,
            Tcl_Interp *interp,
            int argc, char *argv[]);
int ClockObjCmd(ClientData clientData,
            Tcl_Interp *interp,
            int objc, Tcl_Obj *CONST objv[]);
```

```
   void ClockObjDestroy(ClientData clientData);

int
Tk_AppInit(Tcl_Interp *interp) {
   /*
    * Initialize packages
    */
   if (Tcl_Init(interp) == TCL_ERROR) {
      return TCL_ERROR;
   }
   if (Tk_Init(interp) == TCL_ERROR) {
      return TCL_ERROR;
   }
   /*
    * Define application-specific commands here.
    */
   Tcl_CreateCommand(interp, "wclock", ClockCmd,
      (ClientData)Tk_MainWindow(interp),
      (Tcl_CmdDeleteProc *)NULL);
   Tcl_CreateObjCommand(interp, "oclock", ClockObjCmd,
      (ClientData)NULL, ClockObjDestroy);

   /*
    * Define start-up filename. This file is read in
    * case the program is run interactively.
    */
   Tcl_SetVar(interp, "tcl_rcFileName", "~/.mytcl",
      TCL_GLOBAL_ONLY);
   return TCL_OK;
}
```

The Event Loop

An event loop is used to process window system events and other events like timers and network sockets. The different event types are described later. All Tk
applications must have an event loop so that they function properly in the window system environment. Tk provides a standard event loop with the
Tk_MainLoop procedure, which is called at the end of Tk_Main. The *wish* shell
provides an event loop automatically. The *tclsh* shell does not, although you can
add an event loop using pure Tcl as shown in Example 16–2 on page 220.

Some applications already have their own event loop. You have two choices
if you want to add Tk to such an application. The first is to modify the existing
event loop to call Tcl_DoOneEvent to process any outstanding Tcl events. The
unix directory of the source distribution has a file called XtTest.c that adds Tcl
to an Xt (i.e., Motif) application. The other way to customize the event loop is to
make your existing events look like Tcl *event sources*, and register them with the
event loop. Then you can just use Tk_Main. There are four event classes, and they
are handled in the following order by Tcl_DoOneEvent:

- Window events. Use the `Tk_CreateEventHandler` procedure to register a handler for these events. Use the `TCL_WINDOW_EVENTS` flag to process these in `Tcl_DoOneEvent`.

- File events. Use these events to wait on slow devices and network connections. On UNIX you can register a handler for all files, sockets, and devices with `Tcl_CreateFileHandler`. On Windows and Macintosh, there are different APIs for registration because there are different system handles for files, sockets, and devices. On all platforms you use the `TCL_FILE_EVENTS` flag to process these handlers in `Tcl_DoOneEvent`.

- Timer events. You can set up events to occur after a specified time period. Use the `Tcl_CreateTimerHandler` procedure to register a handler for the event. Use the `TCL_TIMER_EVENTS` flag to process these in `Tcl_DoOneEvent`.

- Idle events. These events are processed when there is nothing else to do. Virtually all the Tk widgets use idle events to display themselves. Use the `Tcl_DoWhenIdle` procedure to register a procedure to call once at the next idle time. Use the `TCL_IDLE_EVENTS` flag to process these in `Tcl_DoOneEvent`.

Invoking Scripts from C

The main program is not the only place you can evaluate a Tcl script. You can use the `Tcl_Eval` procedure essentially at any time to evaluate a Tcl command:

```
Tcl_Eval(Tcl_Interp *interp, char *command);
```

The `command` is evaluated in the current Tcl procedure scope, which may be the global scope. This means that calls like `Tcl_GetVar` and `Tcl_SetVar` access variables in the current scope. If for some reason you want a new procedure scope, the easiest thing to do is to call your C code from a Tcl procedure used for this purpose. It is not easy to create a new procedure scope with the exported C API.

`Tcl_Eval` *modifies its argument.*

You should be aware that `Tcl_Eval` may modify the string that is passed into it as a side effect of the way substitutions are performed. If you pass a constant string to `Tcl_Eval`, make sure your compiler has not put the string constant into read-only memory. If you use the *gcc* compiler, you may need to use the `-fwritable-strings` option. Chapter 45 shows how to get the right compilation settings for your system.

Variations on Tcl_Eval

There are several variations on `Tcl_Eval`. The possibilities include strings or `Tcl_Obj` values, evaluation at the current or global scope, a single string (or `Tcl_Obj` value) or a variable number of arguments, and optional byte-code compilation. The most general string-based eval is `Tcl_EvalEx`, which takes a counted string and some flags:

```
Tcl_EvalEx(interp, string, count, flags);
```

The flags are `TCL_GLOBAL_EVAL` and `TCL_EVAL_DIRECT`, which bypasses the byte-code compiler. For code that is executed only one time, `TCL_EVAL_DIRECT` may be more efficient. `Tcl_GlobalEval` is equivalent to passing in the `TCL_GLOBAL_EVAL` flag. The `Tcl_VarEval` procedure takes a variable number of strings arguments and concatenates them before evaluation:

```
Tcl_VarEval(Tcl_Interp *interp, char *str, ..., NULL);
```

`Tcl_EvalObj` takes an object as an argument instead of a simple string. The string is compiled into byte codes the first time it is used. If you are going to execute the script many times, then the `Tcl_Obj` value caches the byte codes for you. The general `Tcl_Obj` value interface to `Tcl_Eval` is `Tcl_EvalObjEx`, which takes the same flags as `Tcl_EvalEx`:

```
Tcl_EvalObjEx(interp, objPtr, flags);
```

For variable numbers of arguments, use `Tcl_EvalObjv`, which takes an array of `Tcl_Obj` pointers. This routine concatenates the string values of the various `Tcl_Obj` values before parsing the resulting Tcl command:

```
Tcl_EvalObjv(interp, objc, objv);
```

Bypassing `Tcl_Eval`

In a performance-critical situation, you may want to avoid some of the overhead associated with `Tcl_Eval`. David Nichols showed me how to call the implementation of a C command procedure directly. The trick is facilitated by the `Tcl_GetCommandInfo` procedure that returns the address of the C command procedure for a Tcl command, plus its client data pointer. The `Tcl_Invoke` procedure is shown in Example 44–15. It is used much like `Tcl_VarEval`, except that each of its arguments becomes an argument to the Tcl command without any substitutions being performed.

For example, you might want to insert a large chunk of text into a text widget without worrying about the parsing done by `Tcl_Eval`. You could use `Tcl_Invoke` like this:

```
Tcl_Invoke(interp, ".t", "insert", "insert", buf, NULL);
```

Or:

```
Tcl_Invoke(interp, "set", "foo", "$xyz [blah] {", NULL);
```

No substitutions are performed on any of the arguments because `Tcl_Eval` is out of the picture. The variable `foo` gets the following literal value:

```
$xyz [blah] {
```

Example 44–15 shows `Tcl_Invoke`. The procedure is complicated for two reasons. First, it must handle a Tcl command that has either the object interface or the old string interface. Second, it has to build up an argument vector and may need to grow its storage in the middle of building it. It is a bit messy to deal with both at the same time, but it lets us compare the object and string interfaces. The string interfaces are simpler, but the object interfaces run more efficiently because they reduce copying and type conversions.

Example 44–15 Calling C command procedure directly with `Tcl_Invoke`.

```
#include <tcl.h>

#if defined(__STDC__) || defined(HAS_STDARG)
#    include <stdarg.h>
#else
#    include <varargs.h>
#endif

/*
 * Tcl_Invoke --
 *      Directly invoke a Tcl command or procedure
 *
 *      Call Tcl_Invoke somewhat like Tcl_VarEval
 *      Each arg becomes one argument to the command,
 *      with no further substitutions or parsing.
 */
    /* VARARGS2 */ /* ARGSUSED */

int
Tcl_Invoke TCL_VARARGS_DEF(Tcl_Interp *, arg1)
{
    va_list argList;
    Tcl_Interp *interp;
    char *cmd;            /* Command name */
    char *arg;            /* Command argument */
    char **argv;          /* String vector for arguments */
    int argc, i, max;     /* Number of arguments */
    Tcl_CmdInfo info;     /* Info about command procedures */
    int result;           /* TCL_OK or TCL_ERROR */

    interp = TCL_VARARGS_START(Tcl_Interp *, arg1, argList);
    Tcl_ResetResult(interp);

    /*
     * Map from the command name to a C procedure
     */
    cmd = va_arg(argList, char *);
    if (! Tcl_GetCommandInfo(interp, cmd, &info)) {
        Tcl_AppendResult(interp, "unknown command \"",
            cmd, "\"", NULL);
        va_end(argList);
        return TCL_ERROR;
    }

    max = 20;             /* Initial size of argument vector */

#if TCL_MAJOR_VERSION > 7
    /*
     * Check whether the object interface is preferred for
     * this command
     */

    if (info.isNativeObjectProc) {
```

```
        Tcl_Obj **objv;      /* Object vector for arguments */
        Tcl_Obj *resultPtr; /* The result object */
        int objc;

        objv = (Tcl_Obj **) Tcl_Alloc(max * sizeof(Tcl_Obj *));
        objv[0] = Tcl_NewStringObj(cmd, strlen(cmd));
        Tcl_IncrRefCount(objv[0]); /* ref count == 1*/
        objc = 1;

        /*
         * Build a vector out of the rest of the arguments
         */

        while (1) {
            arg = va_arg(argList, char *);
            if (arg == (char *)NULL) {
                objv[objc] = (Tcl_Obj *)NULL;
                break;
            }
            objv[objc] = Tcl_NewStringObj(arg, strlen(arg));
            Tcl_IncrRefCount(objv[objc]); /* ref count == 1*/
            objc++;
            if (objc >= max) {
                /* allocate a bigger vector and copy old one */
                Tcl_Obj **oldv = objv;
                max *= 2;
                objv = (Tcl_Obj **) Tcl_Alloc(max *
                        sizeof(Tcl_Obj *));
                for (i = 0 ; i < objc ; i++) {
                    objv[i] = oldv[i];
                }
                Tcl_Free((char *)oldv);
            }
        }
        va_end(argList);

        /*
         * Invoke the C procedure
         */
        result = (*info.objProc)(info.objClientData, interp,
                objc, objv);

        /*
         * Make sure the string value of the result is valid
         * and release our references to the arguments
         */
        (void) Tcl_GetStringResult(interp);
        for (i = 0 ; i < objc ; i++) {
            Tcl_DecrRefCount(objv[i]);
        }
        Tcl_Free((char *)objv);

        return result;
    }
#endif
```

```
argv = (char **) Tcl_Alloc(max * sizeof(char *));
argv[0] = cmd;
argc = 1;

/*
 * Build a vector out of the rest of the arguments
 */
while (1) {
    arg = va_arg(argList, char *);
    argv[argc] = arg;
    if (arg == (char *)NULL) {
        break;
    }
    argc++;
    if (argc >= max) {
        /* allocate a bigger vector and copy old one */
        char **oldv = argv;
        max *= 2;
        argv = (char **) Tcl_Alloc(max * sizeof(char *));
        for (i = 0 ; i < argc ; i++) {
            argv[i] = oldv[i];
        }
        Tcl_Free((char *) oldv);
    }
}
va_end(argList);

/*
 * Invoke the C procedure
 */
result = (*info.proc)(info.clientData, interp, argc, argv);

/*
 * Release the arguments
 */
Tcl_Free((char *) argv);
return result;

}
```

This version of `Tcl_Invoke` was contributed by Jean Brouwers. He uses `TCL_VARARGS_DEF` and `TCL_VARARGS_START` macros to define procedures that take a variable number of arguments. These standard Tcl macros hide the differences in the way you do this on different operating systems and different compilers. It turns out that there are numerous minor differences between compilers that can cause portability problems in a variety of situations. Happily, there is a nice scheme used to discover these differences and write code in a portable way. This is the topic of the next chapter.

VI. Tcl and C

Compiling Tcl and Extensions

This chapter explains how to build Tcl from the source distribution, and how to create C extensions that are built according to the standard Tcl Extension Architecture (TEA).

C ompiling Tcl from the source distribution is easy. One of the strengths of Tcl is that it is quite portable, so it has been built on all kinds of systems including Unix, Windows, Macintosh, AS/400, IBM mainframes, and embedded systems. However, it can be a challenge to create a Tcl extension that has the same portability. The Tcl Extension Architecture (TEA) provides guidelines and samples to help extension authors create portable Tcl extensions. The TEA is a result of collaboration within the Tcl user community, and it will continue to evolve.

This chapter starts with a walk through of how Tcl itself is built. This serves as a model for building extensions. There are also some by-products of the Tcl build process that are designed to make it easier to build your extensions. So if you are an extension author, you will almost always want to get started by compiling Tcl itself.

You can find the Tcl and Tk sources on the CD-ROM, and on the Web:

```
http://www.scriptics.com/products/tcltk/
```

Source distributions can be found at the Scriptics FTP site:

```
ftp://ftp.scriptics.com/pub/tcl/
```

The on-line CVS repository for Tcl software is explained here:

```
http://www.scriptics.com/products/tcltk/netcvs.html
```

If you have trouble with these URLs, please check this book's Web site for current information about the Tcl sources:

```
http://www.beedub.com/book/
```

VI. Tcl and C

Standard Directory Structure

The Source Distribution

Table 45–1 describes the directory structure of the Tcl source distribution. The Tk distribution is similar, and you should model your own source distribution after this. It is also standard to place the Tcl, Tk, and other source packages under a common source directory (e.g., `/usr/local/src` or `/home/welch/cvs`). In fact, this may be necessary if the packages depend on each other.

Table 45–1 The Tcl source directory structure.

`tcl8.2`	The root of the Tcl sources. This contains a README and `license_terms` file, and several subdirectories.
`tcl8.2/compat`	This contains `.c` files that implement procedures that are otherwise broken in the standard C library on some platforms. They are only used if necessary.
`tcl8.2/doc`	This contains the reference documentation. Currently this is in *nroff* format suitable for use with the UNIX *man* program. The goal is to convert this to XML.
`tcl8.2/generic`	This contains the generic `.c` and `.h` source files that are shared among Unix, Windows, and Macintosh.
`tcl8.2/mac`	This contains the `.c` and `.h` source files that are specific to Macintosh. It also contains *Code Warrior* project files.
`tcl8.2/library`	This contains init.tcl and other Tcl files in the standard Tcl script library.
`tcl8.2/library/encoding`	This contains the Unicode conversion tables.
`tcl8.2/library/`*package*	There are several subdirectories (e.g., `http2.0`) that contain Tcl script packages.
`tcl8.2/test`	This contains the Tcl test suite. These are Tcl scripts that exercise the Tcl implementation.
`tcl8.2/tools`	This is a collection of scripts used to help build the Tcl distribution.
`tcl8.2/unix`	This contains the `.c` and `.h` source files that are specific to UNIX. This also contains the *configure* script and the `Makefile.in` template.
`tcl8.2/unix/dltest`	This contains test files for dynamic loading.
`tcl8.2/unix/`*platform*	These can be used to build Tcl for several different platforms. You create the *package* directories yourself.
`tcl8.2/win`	This contains the `.c` and `.h` source files that are specific to Windows. This also contains the *configure* script and the `Makefile.in` template. This may contain a `makefile.vc` that is compatible with *nmake*.

The Installation Directory Structure

When you install Tcl, the files end up in a different arrangement than the one in the source distribution does. The standard installation directory is organized so that it can be shared by computers with different machine types (e.g., Windows, Linux, and Solaris). The Tcl scripts, include files, and documentation are all in shared directories. The applications and programming libraries (i.e., DLLs) are in platform-specific directories. You can choose where these two groups of files are installed with the `--prefix` and `--exec-prefix` options to *configure*, which is explained in detail in the next section. Table 45–2 shows the standard installation directory structure:

Table 45–2 The installation directory structure.

`arch`/bin	This contains platform-specific applications. On Windows, this also contains binary libraries (i.e., DLLs). Typical `arch` names are `solaris-sparc`, `linux-ix86`, and `win-ix86`.
`arch`/lib	This contains platform-specific binary libraries on UNIX systems (e.g., `libtcl8.2.so`)
bin	This contains platform-independent applications (e.g., Tcl script applications).
doc	This contains documentation.
include	This contains public `.h` files.
lib	This contains subdirectories for platform-independent script packages. Packages stored here are found automatically by the Tcl auto loading mechanism described in Chapter 12.
lib/tcl8.2	This contains the contents of the `tcl8.2/library` source directory, including subdirectories.
lib/*package*	This contains Tcl scripts for *package*. **Example** *package* directories include `tk8.2` and `itcl3.0.1`.
man	This contains reference documentation in UNIX *man* format.

If you are an expert in *configure*, you may be aware of other options that give you even finer control over where the different parts of the installation go. However, because of the way Tcl automatically searches for scripts and binary libraries, you should avoid deviating from the recommended structure.

Building Tcl from Source

Compiling Tcl from the source distribution is a two-step process: configuration, which uses a *configure* script; then compiling, which is controlled by the *make* program. The *configure* script examines the current system and makes various settings that are used during compilation. When you run *configure*, you make some basic choices about how you will compile Tcl, such as whether you will compile with debugging systems, or whether you will turn on threading support. You also define the Tcl installation directory with *configure*. You use *make* to compile the source code, install the compiled application, run the test suite, and clean up after yourself.

The *make* facility is familiar to any Unix programmer. By using the freely available Cygwin tools, you can use *configure* and *make* on Windows, too. Tcl still uses the Microsoft VC++ compiler; it does not use *gcc* on Windows.

Windows and Macintosh programmers may not have experience with *make*. The source distributions may also include project files for the Microsoft *Visual C++* compiler and the Macintosh *Code Warrior* compiler, and it may be easier for you to use these project files, especially on the Macintosh. Look in the `win` and `mac` subdirectories of the source distribution for these project files. However, the focus of this chapter is on using *configure* and *make* to build your Tcl applications and extensions.

Configure and Autoconf

If you are the developer of a Tcl extension, there is a preliminary setup step that comes before configuration. In this step, you create templates for the *configure* script and the `Makefile` that drives *make*. Then, you use the *autoconf* program to create the *configure* script. By using *autoconf*, a developer on Windows or Linux can generate a *configure* script that is usable by other developers on Solaris, HP-UX, FreeBSD, AIX, or any system that is vaguely UNIX-like.

The three steps: setup, configuration and make, are illustrated by the build process for Tcl and Tk:

- The developer of a source code package creates a `configure.in` template that expresses the system dependencies of the source code. They use the *autoconf* program to process this template into a `configure` script. The developer also creates a `Makefile.in` template. Creating these templates is described later. The Tcl and Tk source distributions already contain the `configure` script, which can be found in the `unix` and `win` subdirectories. However, if you get the Tcl sources from the network CVS repository, you must run *autoconf* yourself to generate the configure script.
- A user of a source code package runs `configure` on the computer system they will use to compile the sources. This step converts `Makefile.in` to a `Makefile` suitable for the platform and configuration settings. If you have only one platform, simply run *configure* in the `unix` (or `win`) directory:

  ```
  % cd /usr/local/src/tcl8.2/unix
  % ./configure flags
  ```

  The *configure* flags are described in Table 45–3. I use `./configure` because I do not have `.` on my `PATH`. Furthermore, I want to ensure that I run the configure script from the current directory! If you build for multiple platforms, create subdirectories of `unix` and run *configure* from there. For example, here we use `../configure`:

```
% cd /usr/local/src/tcl8.2/unix
% mkdir solaris
% cd solaris
% ../configure flags
```

- The *configure* script uses the `Makefile.in` template to generate the `Makefile`. Once *configure* is complete, you build your program with *make*:

```
% make
```

You can do other things with *make*. To run the test suite, do:

```
% make test
```

To install the compiled program or extension, do:

```
% make install
```

The Tcl Extension Architecture defines a standard set of actions, or make targets, for building Tcl sources. Table 45–4 on page 650 shows the standard *make* targets.

Make sure you have a working compiler.

As the configure script executes, it prints out messages about the properties of the current platform. You can tell if you are in trouble if the output contains either of these messages:

```
checking for cross compiler ... yes
```

or

```
checking if compiler works ... no
```

Either of these means that *configure* has failed to find a working compiler. In the first case, it assumes that you are configuring on the target system but will cross-compile from a different system. *Configure* proceeds bravely ahead, but the resulting Makefile is useless. While cross-compiling is common on embedded processors, it is rarely necessary on UNIX and Windows. I see this message only when my UNIX environment isn't set up right to find the compiler.

Many UNIX venders no longer bundle a working compiler. Fortunately, the freely available *gcc* compiler has been ported to nearly every UNIX system. You should be able to search the Internet and find a ready-to-use *gcc* package for your platform.

On Windows there is a more explicit compiler check, and *configure* exits if it cannot find the compiler. Tcl is built with the Microsoft *Visual C++* compiler. It ships with a batch file, `vcvars32.bat`, that sets up the environment so that you can run the compiler from the command line. You should read that file and configure your environment so that you do not have to remember to run the batch file all the time. At this time, other Windows compilers are not supported by the *autoconf* macros.

Standard Configure Flags

Table 45–3 shows the standard options for Tcl configure scripts. These are implemented by a configure library file (`aclocal.m4`) that you can use in your own configure scripts. The facilities provided by `aclocal.m4` are described in more detail later.

Table 45–3 Standard configure flags.

`--prefix=`*dir*	Defines the root of the installation directory hierarchy. The default is `/usr/local`.
`--exec-prefix=`*dir*	This defines the root of the installation area for platform-specific files. This defaults to the `--prefix` value. An example setting is `/usr/local/solaris-sparc`.
`--enable-gcc`	Uses the *gcc* compiler instead of the default system compiler.
`--disable-shared`	Disables generation of shared libraries and Tcl shells that dynamically link against them. Statically linked shells and static archives are built instead.
`--enable-symbols`	Compiles with debugging symbols.
`--enable-threads`	Compiles with thread support turned on.
`--with-tcl=`*dir*	Specifies the location of the build directory for Tcl.
`--with-tk=`*dir*	Specifies the location of the build directory for Tk.
`--with-tclinclude=`*dir*	Specifies the directory that contains `tcl.h`.
`--with-tcllib=dir`	Specifies the directory that contains the Tcl binary library (e.g., `libtclstubs.a`).
`--with-x11include=dir`	Specifies the directory that contains `X11.h`.
`--with-x11lib=dir`	Specifies the directory that contains the X11 binary library (e.g., `libX11.6.0.so`).

Any flag with `disable` or `enable` in its name can be inverted. Table 45–3 lists the nondefault setting, however, so you can just leave the flag out to turn it off. For example, when building Tcl on Solaris with the *gcc* compiler, shared libraries, debugging symbols, and threading support turned on, use this command:

```
configure --prefix=/home/welch/install \
    --exec-prefix=/home/welch/install/solaris \
    --enable-gcc --enable-threads --enable-symbols
```

Keep all your sources next to the Tcl sources.

Your builds will go the most smoothly if you organize all your sources under a common directory. In this case, you can specify the same configure flags for Tcl and all the other extensions you will compile. In particular, you must use the same `--prefix` and `--exec-prefix` so that everything gets installed together.

If your source tree is not adjacent to the Tcl source tree, then you must use `--with-tclinclude` or `--with-tcllib` so that the header files and runtime library can be found during compilation. Typically, this can happen if you build an extension under your home directory, but you are using a copy of Tcl that has been installed by your system administrator. The `--with-x11include` and `--with-x11lib` flags are similar options necessary when building Tk if your X11 installation is in a nonstandard location.

Installation

The `--prefix` flag specifies the main directory (e.g., `/home/welch/install`). The directories listed in Table 45–2 are created under this directory. If you do not specify `--exec-prefix`, then the platform-specific binary files are mixed into the main `bin` and `lib` directories. For example, the *tclsh8.2* program and `libtcl8.2.so` shared library will be installed in:

```
/home/welch/install/bin/tclsh8.2
/home/welch/install/lib/libtclsh8.2.so
```

The script libraries and manual pages will be installed in:

```
/home/welch/install/lib/tcl8.2
/home/welch/install/man
```

If you want to have installations for several different platforms, then specify an `--exec-prefix` that is different for each platform. For example, if you use `--exec-prefix=/home/welch/install/solaris`, then the *tclsh8.2* program and `libtcl8.2.so` shared library will be installed in:

```
/home/welch/install/solaris/bin/tclsh8.2
/home/welch/install/solaris/lib/libtclsh8.2.so
```

The script libraries and manual pages will remain where they are, so they are shared by all platforms. Note that Windows has a slightly different installation location for binary libraries. They go into the `arch/bin` directory along with the main executable programs.

Using Stub Libraries

One problem with extensions is that they get compiled for a particular version of Tcl. As new Tcl releases occur, you find yourself having to recompile extensions. This was necessary for two reasons. First, the Tcl C library tended to change its APIs from release to release. Changes in its symbol table tie a compiled extension to a specific version of the Tcl library. Another problem occurred if you compiled *tclsh* statically and then tried to dynamically load a library. Some systems do not support back linking in this situation, so *tclsh* would crash. Paul Duffin created a *stub library* mechanism for Tcl that helps solve these problems.

The main idea is that Tcl creates two binary libraries: the main library (e.g., `libtcl8.2.so`) and a stub library (e.g., `libtclstub.a`). All the code is in the main library. The stub library is just a big jump table that contains addresses of functions in the main library. An extension calls Tcl through the jump table. The level of indirection makes the extension immune to changes in the Tcl library. It also handles the back linking problem. If this sounds expensive, it turns out to be equivalent to what the operating system does when you use shared libraries (i.e., dynamic link libraries). Tcl has just implemented dynamic linking in a portable, robust way.

To make your extension use stubs, you have to compile with the correct flags, and you must add a new call to your extensions `Init` procedure (e.g.,

VI. Tcl and C

Examplea_Init). The TCL_USE_STUBS compile-time flag turns the Tcl C API calls into macros that use the stub table. The Tcl_InitStubs call ensures that the jump table is initialized, so you must call Tcl_InitStubs as the very first thing in your Init procedure. A typical call looks like this:

```
if (Tcl_InitStubs(interp, "8.1", 0) == NULL) {
    return TCL_ERROR;
}
```

Tcl_InitStubs is similar in spirit to Tcl_PkgRequire in that you request a minimum Tcl version number. Stubs have been supported since Tcl 8.1, and the API will evolve in a backward-compatible way. Unless your extension uses new C APIs introduced in later versions, you should specify the lowest version possible so that it is compatible with more Tcl applications.

Using autoconf

Autoconf uses the *m4* macro processor to translate the configure.in template into the *configure* script. The *configure* script is run by /bin/sh (i.e., the Bourne Shell). Creating the configure.in template is simplified by a standard *m4* macro library that is distributed with *autoconf*. In addition, a Tcl distribution contains a tcl.m4 file that has additional *autoconf* macros. Among other things, these macros support the standard *configure* flags described in Table 45–3.

Creating configure templates can be complex and confusing. Mostly this is because a macro processor is being used to create a shell script. The days I have spent trying to change the Tcl configuration files really made me appreciate the simplicity of Tcl! Fortunately, there is now a standard set of Tcl-specific *autoconf* macros and a sample Tcl extension that uses them. By editing the configure.in and Makefile.in sample templates, you can ignore the details of what is happening under the covers.

The tcl.m4 File

The Tcl source distribution includes tcl.m4 and aclocal.m4 files. The *autoconf* program looks for the aclocal.m4 file in the same directory as the configure.in template. In our case, the aclocal.m4 file just includes the tcl.m4 file. *Autoconf* also has a standard library of m4 macros as part of its distribution. To use tcl.m4 for your own extension, you have some options. The most common way is to copy tcl.m4 into aclocal.m4 in your source directory. Or you can copy both aclocal.m4 and tcl.m4 and have aclocal.m4 include tcl.m4. If necessary, you can add more custom macros to this aclocal.m4 file. Alternatively, you can copy the tcl.m4 file into the standard *autoconf* macro library.

The tcl.m4 file defines macros whose names begin with SC_ (for Scriptics). The standard *autoconf* macro names begin with AC_. This book does not provide an exhaustive explanation of all these *autoconf* macros. Instead, the important ones are explained in the context of the sample extension.

The `tcl.m4` file replaces the `tclConfig.sh` found in previous versions of Tcl. (Actually, `tclConfig.sh` is still produced by the Tcl 8.2 *configure* script, but its use is deprecated.) The idea of `tclConfig.sh` was to capture some important results of Tcl's *configure* so that they could be included in the *configure* scripts used by an extension. However, it is better to recompute these settings when configuring an extension because, for example, different compilers could be used to build Tcl and the extension. So, instead of including `tclConfig.sh` into an extension's *configure* script, the extension's `configure.in` should use the `SC_` macros defined in the *tcl.m4* file.

Makefile Templates

Autoconf implements yet another macro mechanism for the `Makefile.in` templates. The basic idea is that the *configure* script sets shell variables as it learns things about your system. Finally, it substitutes these variables into `Makefile.in` to create the working `Makefile`. The syntax for the substitutions in `Makefile.in` is:

```
@configure_variable_name@
```

Often, the *make* variable and the shell variable have the same name. For example, the following statement in `Makefile.in` passes the `TCL_LIBRARY` value determined by *configure* through to the `Makefile`:

```
TCL_LIBRARY = @TCL_LIBRARY@
```

The `AC_SUBST` macro specifies what shell variables should be substituted in the `Makefile.in` template. For example:

```
AC_SUBST(TCL_LIBRARY)
```

The Sample Extension

This section describes the sample extension that is distributed as part of the Tcl Extension Architecture (TEA) standard. The goal of TEA is to create a standard for Tcl extensions that makes it easier to build, install, and share Tcl extensions. The sample Tcl extension is on the CD, and it can be found on the Web at:

```
ftp://ftp.scriptics.com/pub/tcl/examples/tea/
```

There is also documentation on the Web at:

```
http://www.scriptics.com/products/tcltk/tea/
```

The extension described here is stored in the network CVS repository under the module name `samplextension`. If you want direct access to the latest versions of Tcl source code, you can learn about the CVS repository at this web page:

```
http://www.scriptics.com/products/tcltk/netcvs.html
```

The sample extension implements the Secure Hash Algorithm (SHA1). Steve Reid wrote the original SHA1 C code, and Dave Dykstra wrote the original Tcl interface to it. Michael Thomas created the standard configure and Makefile templates.

VI. Tcl and C

Instead of using the original name, sha1, the example uses a more generic name, exampleA, in its files, libraries, and package names. When editing the sample templates for your own extension, you can simply replace occurrences of "exampleA" with the appropriate name for your extension. The sample files are well commented, so it is easy to see where you need to make the changes.

configure.in

The configure.in file is the template for the *configure* script. This file is very well commented. The places you need to change are marked with __CHANGE__. The first macro to change is:

```
AC_INIT(exampleA.h)
```

The AC_INIT macro lists a file that is part of the distribution. The name is relative to the configure.in file. Other possibilities include ../generic/tcl.h or src/mylib.h, depending on where the configure.in file is relative to your sources. The AC_INIT macro necessary to support building the package in different directories (e.g., either tcl8.2/unix or tcl8.2/unix/solaris). The next thing in configure.in is a set of variable assignments that define the package's name and version number:

```
PACKAGE = exampleA
MAJOR_VERSION = 0
MINOR_VERSION = 2
PATCH_LEVEL =
```

The package name determines the file names used for the directory and the binary library file created by the Makefile. This name is also used in several configure and Makefile variables. You will need to change all references to "exampleA" to match the name you choose for your package.

The version and patch level support a three-level scheme, but you can leave the patch level empty for two-level versions like 0.2. If you do specify a patch-level, you need to include a leading "." or "p" in it. These values are combined to create the version number like this:

```
VERSION = ${MAJOR_VERSION}.${MINOR_VERSION}${PATCH_LEVEL}
```

Windows compilers create a special case for shared libraries (i.e., DLLs). When you compile the library itself, you need to declare its functions one way. When you compile code that uses the library, you need to declare its functions another way. This complicates the exampleA.h header file. Happily, the complexity is hidden inside some macros. In configure.in, you simply define a build_*Package* variable. The sample defines:

```
AC_DEFINE(BUILD_exampleA)
```

This variable is set only when you are building the library itself, and it is defined only when compiling on Windows. We will show later how this is used in exampleA.h to control the definition of the Examplea_Init procedure.

The configure.in file has a bunch of magic to determine the name of the shared library file (e.g., packageA02.dll, packageA.0.2.so, packageA.0.2.shlib, etc.). All you need to do is change one macro to match your package name.

```
AC_SUBST(exampleA_LIB_FILE)
```

These should be the only places you need to edit when adapting the sample `configure.in` to your extension. It is worth noting that the last macro determines which templates are processed by the configure script. The sample generates two files from templates, `Makefile` and `mkIndex.tcl`:

```
AC_OUTPUT([Makefile mkIndex.tcl])
```

The `mkIndex.tcl` script is a script that runs `pkg_mkIndex` to generate the `pkgIndex.tcl` file. The `pkg_mkIndex` command is described in Chapter 12. The `mkIndex.tcl` script is more complex than you might expect because UNIX systems and Windows have different default locations for binary libraries. The goal is to create a `pkgIndex.tcl` script that gets installed into the *arch*/lib/*package* directory but that can find either *arch*/bin/*package*.dll or *arch*/lib/lib*package*.so, depending on the system. You may need to edit the `mkIndex.tcl.in` template, especially if your extension is made of both Tcl scripts and a binary library.

Makefile.in

The `Makefile.in` template is converted by the *configure* script into the `Makefile`. The sample `Makefile.in` is well commented so that it is easy to see where to make changes. However, there is some first class trickery done with the Makefile variables that is not worth explaining in detail. (Not in a Tcl book, at least!) There are a few variables with `exampleA` in their name. In particular, `exampleA_LIB_FILE` corresponds to a variable name in the configure script. You need to change both files consistently. Some of the lines you need to change are shown below:

```
exampleA_LIB_FILE = @exampleA_LIB_FILE@
lib_BINARIES = $(exampleA_LIB_FILE)
$(exampleA_LIB_FILE)_OBJECTS = $(exampleA_OBJECTS)
```

The *@varname@* syntax is used to substitute the configure variable with its platform-specific name (e.g., `libexamplea.dll` or `libexample.so`). The `lib_BINARIES` variable names the set of libraries built by the "make binaries" target. The `_OBJECT` variable is a clever trick to allow a generic library make rule, which appears in the `Makefile.in` template as `@MAKE_LIB@`. Towards the end of `Makefile.in,` there is a rule that uses these variables, and you must change uses of `exampleA` to match your package name:

```
$(exampleA_LIB_FILE) : $(exampleA_OBJECTS)
    -rm -f $(exampleA_LIB_FILE)
    @MAKE_LIB@
    $(RANLIB) $(exampleA_LIB_FILE)
```

You must define the set of source files and the corresponding object files that are part of the library. In the sample, `exampleA.c` implements the core of the Secure Hash Algorithm, and the `tclexampleA.c` file implements the Tcl com-

VI. Tcl and C

mand interface:

```
exampleA_SOURCES = exampleA.c tclexampleA.c
SOURCES = $(exampleA_SOURCES)
```

The object file definitions use the OBJEXT variable that is .o for UNIX and
.obj for Windows:

```
exampleA_OBJECTS = exampleA.${OBJEXT} tclexampleA.${OBJEXT}
OBJECTS = $(exampleA_OBJECTS)
```

The header files that you want to have installed are assigned to the
GENERIC_HDRS variable. The srcdir Make variable is defined during *configure* to
be the name of the directory containing the file named in the AC_INIT macro:

```
GENERIC_HDRS = $(srcdir)/exampleA.h
```

Unfortunately, you must specify explicit rules for each C source file. The
VPATH mechanism is not reliable enough to find the correct source files reliably.
The *configure* script uses AC_INIT to locate source files, and you create rules that
use the resulting $(srcdir) value. The rules look like this:

```
exampleA.$(OBJEXT) : $(srcdir)/exampleA.c
    $(COMPILE) -c '@CYGPATH@ $(srcdir)/exampleA.c' -o $@
```

The sample Makefile includes several standard targets. Even if you decide
not to use the sample Makefile.in template, you should still define the targets
listed in Table 45–4 to ensure your extension is TEA compliant. Plans for automatic build environments depend on every extension implementing the standard
make targets. The targets can be empty, but you should define them so that *make*
will not complain if they are used.

Table 45–4 TEA standard Makefile targets.

all	Makes these targets in order: binaries, libraries, doc.
binaries	Makes executable programs and binary libraries (e.g., DLLs).
libraries	Makes platform-independent libraries.
doc	Generates documentation files.
install	Makes these targets in order: install-binaries, install-libraries, install-doc.
install-binaries	Installs programs and binary libraries.
install-libraries	Installs script libraries.
install-doc	Installs documentation files.
test	Runs the test suite for the package.
depend	Generates makefile dependency rules.
clean	Removes files built during the make process.
distclean	Removes files built during the configure process.

Standard Header Files

This section explains a technique you should use to get symbols defined properly in your binary library. The issue is raised by Windows compilers, which have a notion of explicitly importing and exporting symbols. When you build a library you export symbols. When you link against a library, you import symbols. The BUILD_exampleA variable is defined on Windows when you are building the library. This variable should be undefined on UNIX, which does not have this issue. Your header file uses this variable like this:

```
#ifdef BUILD_exampleA
#undef TCL_STORAGE_CLASS
#define TCL_STORAGE_CLASS DLLEXPORT
#endif
```

The TCL_STORAGE_CLASS variable is used in the definition of the EXTERN macro. You must use EXTERN before the prototype for any function you want to export from your library:

```
EXTERN int Examplea_Init _ANSI_ARGS_((Tcl_Interp *Interp));
```

The _ANSI_ARGS_ macro is used to guard against old C compilers that do not tolerate function prototypes.

Using the Sample Extension

You should be able to configure, compile, and install the sample extension without modification. On my Solaris machine, the binary library is named exampleA0.2.so, while on my Windows NT machine the library is named exampleA02.dll. The package name is Tclsha1, and it implements the sha1 Tcl command. Ordinarily these names would be more consistent with the file names and package names in the template files. However, the names in the sample are designed to be easy to edit in the template. Assuming that you use make install to copy the binary library into the standard location for your site, you can use the package from Tcl like this:

```
package require Tclsha1
sha1 -string "some string"
```

The sha1 command returns a 128 bit encoded hash function of the input string. There are a number of options to sha1 you can learn about by reading the manual page that is included with the extension.

Writing a Tk Widget in C

This chapter describes the implementation of a simple clock widget. Two implementations are shown: the original string-based command interface and the Tcl_Obj command interface.

A custom widget implemented in C has the advantage of being efficient and flexible. However, it requires more work, too. This chapter illustrates the effort by explaining the implementation of a clock widget. It is a digital clock that displays the current time according to a format string. This is something you could implement in several lines of Tcl using a label widget, the `clock` command, and `after` for periodic updates. However, the point of the example is to show the basic structure for a Tk widget implemented in C, not how much easier Tcl programming is :-). The implementation of a widget includes:

- A data structure to describe one instance of the widget.
- A class procedure to create a new instance of the widget.
- An instance procedure to operate on an instance of the widget.
- A set of configuration options for the widget.
- A configuration procedure used when creating and reconfiguring the widget.
- An event handling procedure.
- A display procedure.
- Other widget-specific procedures.

Two implementations are compared: string-based and `Tcl_Obj` based. The version that uses `Tcl_Obj` values can interpret command line options more efficiently. A new option parsing package hides most of the details. The string-based version of each procedure is shown first, and then the `Tcl_Obj` version is shown for comparison. The display portion of the code is the same in the two versions.

VI. Tcl and C

653

Initializing the Extension

The widget is packaged as an extension that you can dynamically load into *wish*. Example 46–1 shows the `Clock_Init` procedure. It registers two commands, clock and oclock, which use the string-based and `Tcl_Obj` interfaces, respectively. It also initializes the stub table, which is described in Chapter 45, and declares a package so that scripts can load the widget with `package require`.

Example 46–1 The `Clock_Init` procedure.

```
int ClockCmd(ClientData clientData,
         Tcl_Interp *interp,
         int argc, char *argv[]);
int ClockObjCmd(ClientData clientData,
         Tcl_Interp *interp,
         int objc, Tcl_Obj *CONST objv[]);
void ClockObjDelete(ClientData clientData);

/*
 * Clock_Init is called when the package is loaded.
 */

int Clock_Init(Tcl_Interp *interp) {
    if (Tcl_InitStubs(interp, "8.1", 0) == NULL) {
        return TCL_ERROR;
    }
    Tcl_CreateCommand(interp, "wclock", ClockCmd,
            (ClientData)NULL, (Tcl_CmdDeleteProc *)NULL);
    Tcl_CreateObjCommand(interp, "oclock", ClockObjCmd,
            (ClientData)NULL, ClockObjDelete);
    Tcl_PkgProvide(interp, "Tkclock", "1.0");
    return TCL_OK;
}
```

The Widget Data Structure

Each widget is associated with a data structure that describes it. Any widget structure will need a pointer to the Tcl interpreter, the Tk window, and the display. The interpreter is used in most of the Tcl and Tk library calls, and it provides a way to call out to the script or query and set Tcl variables. The Tk window is needed for various Tk operations, and the display is used when doing low-level graphic operations. The rest of the information in the data structure depends on the widget. The different types will be explained as they are used in the rest of the code. The structure for the clock widget follows:

Example 46–2 The Clock widget data structure.

```c
#include "tk.h"
#include <sys/time.h>

typedef struct {
    Tk_Window tkwin;            /* The window for the widget */
    Display *display;           /* Tk's handle on the display */
    Tcl_Interp *interp;         /* Interpreter of the widget */
    Tcl_Command widgetCmd;      /* clock instance command. */
    Tk_OptionTable optionTable; /* Used to parse options */
    /*
     * Clock-specific attributes.
     */
    int borderWidth;            /* Size of 3-D border */
    Tcl_Obj *borderWidthPtr;    /* Original string value */
    int relief;                 /* Style of 3-D border */
    Tk_3DBorder background;     /* Color for border & background */
    XColor *foreground;         /* Color for the text */
    XColor *highlight;          /* Color for active highlight */
    XColor *highlightBg;        /* Color for neutral highlight */
    int highlightWidth;         /* Thickness of highlight rim */
    Tcl_Obj *highlightWidthPtr; /* Original string value */
    Tk_Font tkfont;             /* Font info for the text */
    char *format;               /* Format for time string */
    /*
     * Graphic contexts and other support.
     */
    GC textGC;                  /* Text graphics context */
    Tk_TimerToken token;        /* Periodic callback handle*/
    char *clock;                /* Pointer to the clock string */
    int numChars;               /* length of the text */
    int textWidth;              /* in pixels */
    Tcl_Obj *widthPtr;          /* The original width string value*/
    int textHeight;             /* in pixels */
    Tcl_Obj *heightPtr;         /* The original height string value*/
    int padX;                   /* Horizontal padding */
    Tcl_Obj *padXPtr;           /* The original padX string value*/
    int padY;                   /* Vertical padding */
    Tcl_Obj *padYPtr;           /* The original padY string value */
    int flags;                  /* Flags defined below */
} Clock;
/*
 * Flag bit definitions.
 */
#define REDRAW_PENDING 0x1
#define GOT_FOCUS      0x2
#define TICKING        0x4
```

The Widget Class Command

The Tcl command that creates an instance of a widget is known as the *class command*. In our example, the clock command creates a clock widget. The command procedure for `clock` follows. The procedure allocates the `Clock` data structure. It registers an event handler that gets called when the widget is exposed, resized, or gets the focus. It creates a new Tcl command that operates on the widget. Finally, it calls `ClockConfigure` to set up the widget according to the attributes specified on the command line and the default configuration specifications.

Example 46–3 The `ClockCmd` command procedure.

```
int
ClockCmd(clientData, interp, argc, argv)
    ClientData clientData;/* Main window of the app */
    Tcl_Interp *interp; /* Current interpreter. */
    int argc;               /* Number of arguments. */
    char **argv;            /* Argument strings. */
{
    Tk_Window main = (Tk_Window) clientData;
    Clock *clockPtr;
    Tk_Window tkwin;

    if (argc < 2) {
        Tcl_AppendResult(interp, "wrong # args: should be \"",
            argv[0], " pathName ?options?\"", (char *) NULL);
        return TCL_ERROR;
    }
    tkwin = Tk_CreateWindowFromPath(interp, main,
            argv[1], (char *) NULL);
    if (tkwin == NULL) {
        return TCL_ERROR;
    }
    /*
     * Set resource class.
     */
    Tk_SetClass(tkwin, "Clock");
    /*
     * Allocate and initialize the widget record.
     */
    clockPtr = (Clock *) Tcl_Alloc(sizeof(Clock));
    clockPtr->tkwin = tkwin;
    clockPtr->display = Tk_Display(tkwin);
    clockPtr->interp = interp;
    clockPtr->borderWidth = 0;
    clockPtr->highlightWidth = 0;
    clockPtr->relief = TK_RELIEF_FLAT;
    clockPtr->background = NULL;
    clockPtr->foreground = NULL;
    clockPtr->highlight = NULL;
    clockPtr->highlightBg = NULL;
    clockPtr->tkfont = NULL;
    clockPtr->textGC = None;
    clockPtr->token = NULL;
    clockPtr->clock = NULL;
    clockPtr->format = NULL;
    clockPtr->numChars = 0;
```

```
    clockPtr->textWidth = 0;
    clockPtr->textHeight = 0;
    clockPtr->padX = 0;
    clockPtr->padY = 0;
    clockPtr->flags = 0;
    /*
     * Register a handler for when the window is
     * exposed or resized.
     */
    Tk_CreateEventHandler(clockPtr->tkwin,
        ExposureMask|StructureNotifyMask|FocusChangeMask,
        ClockEventProc, (ClientData) clockPtr);
    /*
     * Create a Tcl command that operates on the widget.
     */
    clockPtr->widgetCmd = Tcl_CreateCommand(interp,
        Tk_PathName(clockPtr->tkwin),
        ClockInstanceCmd,
        (ClientData) clockPtr, (void (*)()) NULL);
    /*
     * Parse the command line arguments.
     */
    if (ClockConfigure(interp, clockPtr,
            argc-2, argv+2, 0) != TCL_OK) {
        Tk_DestroyWindow(clockPtr->tkwin);
        return TCL_ERROR;
    }
    interp->result = Tk_PathName(clockPtr->tkwin);
    return TCL_OK;
}
```

The Tcl_Obj version, ClockObjCmd, does some additional work to set up an option table that is used to efficiently parse the command line options to the clock command. The option table is created the first time the clock command is used. The clientData for ClockObjCmd is initially NULL; it is used to store the option table once it is initialized. While ClockCmd uses the clientData to store a reference to the main Tk window, ClockObjCmd uses the Tk_MainWindow procedure to get a reference to the main Tk window.

Example 46–4 The ClockObjCmd command procedure.

```
int
ClockObjCmd(clientData, interp, objc, objv)
    ClientData clientData;/* Main window of the app */
    Tcl_Interp *interp; /* Current interpreter. */
    int objc;           /* Number of arguments. */
    Tcl_Obj **objv;     /* Argument values. */
{
    Tk_OptionTable optionTable;
    Clock *clockPtr;
    Tk_Window tkwin;
```

```
if (objc < 2) {
   Tcl_WrongNumArgs(interp, 1, objv, "pathName ?options?");
   return TCL_ERROR;
}
optionTable = (Tk_OptionTable) clientData;
if (optionTable == NULL) {
   Tcl_CmdInfo info;
   char *name;

   /*
    * Initialize the option table for this widget the
    * first time a clock widget is created. The option
    * table is saved as our client data.
    */

   optionTable = Tk_CreateOptionTable(interp, optionSpecs);
   name = Tcl_GetString(objv[0]);
   Tcl_GetCommandInfo(interp, name, &info);
   info.objClientData = (ClientData) optionTable;
   Tcl_SetCommandInfo(interp, name, &info);
}
tkwin = Tk_CreateWindowFromPath(interp,
      Tk_MainWindow(interp),
      Tcl_GetString(objv[1]), (char *) NULL);
if (tkwin == NULL) {
   return TCL_ERROR;
}
/*
 * Set resource class.
 */
Tk_SetClass(tkwin, "Clock");
/*
 * Allocate and initialize the widget record.
 */
clockPtr = (Clock *) Tcl_Alloc(sizeof(Clock));
clockPtr->tkwin = tkwin;
clockPtr->display = Tk_Display(tkwin);
clockPtr->interp = interp;
clockPtr->optionTable = optionTable;
clockPtr->borderWidth = 0;
clockPtr->borderWidthPtr = NULL;
clockPtr->highlightWidth = 0;
clockPtr->highlightWidthPtr = NULL;
clockPtr->relief = TK_RELIEF_FLAT;
clockPtr->background = NULL;
clockPtr->foreground = NULL;
clockPtr->highlight = NULL;
clockPtr->highlightBg = NULL;
clockPtr->tkfont = NULL;
clockPtr->textGC = None;
clockPtr->token = NULL;
clockPtr->clock = NULL;
clockPtr->format = NULL;
clockPtr->numChars = 0;
clockPtr->textWidth = 0;
```

```
        clockPtr->widthPtr = NULL;
        clockPtr->textHeight = 0;
        clockPtr->heightPtr = NULL;
        clockPtr->padX = 0;
        clockPtr->padXPtr = NULL;
        clockPtr->padY = 0;
        clockPtr->padYPtr = NULL;
        clockPtr->flags = 0;
        /*
         * Register a handler for when the window is
         * exposed or resized.
         */
        Tk_CreateEventHandler(clockPtr->tkwin,
            ExposureMask|StructureNotifyMask|FocusChangeMask,
            ClockEventProc, (ClientData) clockPtr);
        /*
         * Create a Tcl command that operates on the widget.
         */
        clockPtr->widgetCmd = Tcl_CreateObjCommand(interp,
            Tk_PathName(clockPtr->tkwin),
            ClockInstanceObjCmd,
            (ClientData) clockPtr, (void (*)()) NULL);
        /*
         * Parse the command line arguments.
         */
        if ((Tk_InitOptions(interp, (char *)clockPtr,
                optionTable, tkwin) != TCL_OK) ||
            (ClockObjConfigure(interp, clockPtr,
                objc-2, objv+2, 0) != TCL_OK)) {
            Tk_DestroyWindow(clockPtr->tkwin);
            return TCL_ERROR;
        }
        Tcl_SetStringObj(Tcl_GetObjResult(interp),
            Tk_PathName(clockPtr->tkwin), -1);
        return TCL_OK;
    }
```

The Widget Instance Command

For each instance of a widget, a new command is created that operates on that widget. This is called the *widget instance command*. Its name is the same as the Tk pathname of the widget. In the clock example, all that is done on instances is to query and change their attributes. Most of the work is done by Tk_ConfigureWidget and ClockConfigure, which are shown in the next section. The ClockInstanceCmd command procedure is shown in the next example:

Example 46–5 The ClockInstanceCmd command procedure.

```
static int
ClockInstanceCmd(clientData, interp, argc, argv)
    ClientData clientData;/* A pointer to a Clock struct */
```

VI. Tcl and C

```
    Tcl_Interp *interp; /* The interpreter */
    int argc;              /* The number of arguments */
    char *argv[];          /* The command line arguments */
{
    Clock *clockPtr = (Clock *)clientData;
    int result = TCL_OK;
    char c;
    int len;
    if (argc < 2) {
        Tcl_AppendResult(interp, "wrong # args: should be \"",
            argv[0], " option ?arg arg ...?\"", (char *) NULL);
        return TCL_ERROR;
    }
    c = argv[1][0];
    len = strlen(argv[1]);
    if ((c == 'c') && (strncmp(argv[1], "cget", len) == 0)
            && (len >= 2)) {
        if (argc != 3) {
            Tcl_AppendResult(interp,
                "wrong # args: should be \"",
                argv[0], " cget option\"",
                (char *) NULL);
            return TCL_ERROR;
        }
        result = Tk_ConfigureValue(interp, clockPtr->tkwin,
            configSpecs, (char *) clockPtr, argv[2], 0);
    } else if ((c == 'c') && (strncmp(argv[1], "configure", len)
            == 0) && (len >= 2)) {
        if (argc == 2) {
            /*
             * Return all configuration information.
             */
            result = Tk_ConfigureInfo(interp, clockPtr->tkwin,
                configSpecs, (char *) clockPtr,
                (char *) NULL,0);
        } else if (argc == 3) {
            /*
             * Return info about one attribute, like cget.
             */
            result = Tk_ConfigureInfo(interp, clockPtr->tkwin,
                configSpecs, (char *) clockPtr, argv[2], 0);
        } else {
            /*
             * Change one or more attributes.
             */
            result = ClockConfigure(interp, clockPtr, argc-2,
                argv+2,TK_CONFIG_ARGV_ONLY);
        }
    } else {
        Tcl_AppendResult(interp, "bad option \"", argv[1],
            "\": must be cget, configure, position, or size",
            (char *) NULL);
        return TCL_ERROR;
    }
    return result;
}
```

Example 46–6 shows the `ClockInstanceObjCmd` procedure. It uses the `Tk_GetIndexFromObj` routine to map the first argument to an index, which is then used in a switch statement. It uses the `Tk_GetOptionValue` and `Tk_GetOptionInfo` procedures to parse the widget configuration options.

Example 46–6 The `ClockInstanceObjCmd` command procedure.

```
static int
ClockInstanceObjCmd(clientData, interp, objc, objv)
    ClientData clientData;/* A pointer to a Clock struct */
    Tcl_Interp *interp; /* The interpreter */
    int objc;            /* The number of arguments */
    Tcl_Obj *objv[];     /* The command line arguments */
{
    Clock *clockPtr = (Clock *)clientData;
    char *commands[] = {"cget", "configure", NULL};
    enum command {CLOCK_CGET, CLOCK_CONFIGURE};
    int result;
    Tcl_Obj *objPtr;
    int index;

    if (objc < 2) {
        Tcl_WrongNumArgs(interp, 1, objv,
            "option ?arg arg ...?");
        return TCL_ERROR;
    }
    result = Tcl_GetIndexFromObj(interp, objv[1], commands,
            "option", 0, &index);
    if (result != TCL_OK) {
        return result;
    }
    switch (index) {
        case CLOCK_CGET: {
            if (objc != 3) {
                Tcl_WrongNumArgs(interp, 1, objv,
                    "cget option");
                return TCL_ERROR;
            }
            objPtr = Tk_GetOptionValue(interp,
                    (char *)clockPtr,
                    clockPtr->optionTable,
                    (objc == 3) ? objv[2] : NULL,
                    clockPtr->tkwin);
            if (objPtr == NULL) {
                return TCL_ERROR;
            } else {
                Tcl_SetObjResult(interp, objPtr);
            }
            break;
        }
        case CLOCK_CONFIGURE: {
            if (objc <= 3) {
                /*
                 * Return one item if the option is given,
```

```
             * or return all configuration information.
             */
            objPtr = Tk_GetOptionInfo(interp,
                    (char *) clockPtr,
                    clockPtr->optionTable,
                    (objc == 3) ? objv[2] : NULL,
                    clockPtr->tkwin);
            if (objPtr == NULL) {
                return TCL_ERROR;
            } else {
                Tcl_SetObjResult(interp, objPtr);
            }
        } else {
            /*
             * Change one or more attributes.
             */
            result = ClockObjConfigure(interp, clockPtr,
                objc-2, objv+2);
        }
    }
    }
    return TCL_OK;
}
```

Configuring and Reconfiguring Attributes

When the widget is created or reconfigured, then the implementation needs to allocate the resources implied by the attribute settings. Each clock widget uses some colors and a font. These are described by graphics contexts that parameterize operations. Instead of specifying every possible attribute in graphics calls, a graphics context is initialized with a subset of the parameters, and this is passed into the graphic commands. The context can specify the foreground and background colors, clip masks, line styles, and so on. The clock widget allocates a graphics context once and reuses it each time the widget is displayed.

There are two kinds of color resources used by the widget. The focus highlight and the text foreground are simple colors. The background is a Tk_3DBorder, which is a set of colors used to render 3D borders. The background color is specified in the attribute, and the other colors are computed based on that color. The code uses Tk_3DBorderColor to map back to the original color for use in the background of the widget.

After the resources are set up, a call to redisplay the widget is scheduled for the next idle period. This is a standard idiom for Tk widgets. It means that you can create and reconfigure a widget in the middle of a script, and all the changes result in only one redisplay. The REDRAW_PENDING flag is used to ensure that only one redisplay is queued up at any time. The ClockConfigure procedure is shown in the next example:

Example 46–7 `ClockConfigure` allocates resources for the widget.

```c
static int
ClockConfigure(interp, clockPtr, argc, argv, flags)
    Tcl_Interp *interp;/* For return values and errors */
    Clock *clockPtr; /* The per-instance data structure */
    int argc;          /* Number of valid entries in argv */
    char *argv[];      /* The command line arguments */
    int flags;         /* Tk_ConfigureWidget flags */
{
    XGCValues gcValues;
    GC newGC;

    /*
     * Tk_ConfigureWidget parses the command line arguments
     * and looks for defaults in the resource database.
     */
    if (Tk_ConfigureWidget(interp, clockPtr->tkwin,
            configSpecs, argc, argv, (char *) clockPtr, flags)
              != TCL_OK) {
      return TCL_ERROR;
    }
    /*
     * Give the widget a default background so it doesn't get
     * a random background between the time it is initially
     * displayed by the X server and we paint it
     */
    Tk_SetWindowBackground(clockPtr->tkwin,
        Tk_3DBorderColor(clockPtr->background)->pixel);
    /*
     * Set up the graphics contexts to display the widget.
     * The context is used to draw off-screen pixmaps,
     * so turn off exposure notifications.
     */
    gcValues.background =
        Tk_3DBorderColor(clockPtr->background)->pixel;
    gcValues.foreground = clockPtr->foreground->pixel;
    gcValues.font = Tk_FontId(clockPtr->tkfont);
    gcValues.graphics_exposures = False;
    newGC = Tk_GetGC(clockPtr->tkwin,
        GCBackground|GCForeground|GCFont|GCGraphicsExposures,
        &gcValues);
    if (clockPtr->textGC != None) {
        Tk_FreeGC(clockPtr->display, clockPtr->textGC);
    }
    clockPtr->textGC = newGC;
    /*
     * Determine how big the widget wants to be.
     */
    ComputeGeometry(clockPtr);
    /*
     * Set up a call to display ourself.
     */
    if ((clockPtr->tkwin != NULL) &&
            Tk_IsMapped(clockPtr->tkwin)
```

VI. Tcl and C

```
                && !(clockPtr->flags & REDRAW_PENDING)) {
            Tk_DoWhenIdle(ClockDisplay, (ClientData) clockPtr);
            clockPtr->flags |= REDRAW_PENDING;
        }
        return TCL_OK;
}
```

Example 46–8 shows the ClockObjConfigure procedure. The
Tk_SetOptions interface, which is used to set fields in the Clock data structure,
has one potential problem. It is possible that some configuration options are correct, while others cause errors. In this case, ClockObjConfigure backs out the
changes, so the whole configuration has no effect. This requires a two-pass
approach, with the second pass used to restore the original values.
Tk_SetOptions has a feature that lets you classify changes to the widget. The
GEOMETRY_MASK and GRAPHICS_MASK are bits defined by the clock widget to divide
its attributes into two classes. It changes its graphics context or recomputes its
geometry only if an attribute from the appropriate class is changed.

Example 46–8 ClockObjConfigure allocates resources for the widget.

```
static int
ClockObjConfigure(interp, clockPtr, objc, objv)
    Tcl_Interp *interp;/* For return values and errors */
    Clock *clockPtr; /* The per-instance data structure */
    int objc;        /* Number of valid entries in argv */
    Tcl_Obj *objv[]; /* The command line arguments */
{
    XGCValues gcValues;
    GC newGC;
    Tk_SavedOptions savedOptions;
    int mask, error, new;
    Tcl_Obj *errorResult;
    /*
     * The first time through this loop we set the
     * configuration from the command line inputs. The second
     * pass is used to restore the configuration in case of
     * errors
     */
    new = (clockPtr->clock == NULL);
    for (error = 0 ; error <= 1 ; error++) {
        if (!error) {
            /*
             * Tk_SetOptions parses the command arguments
             * and looks for defaults in the resource
             * database.
             */
            if (Tk_SetOptions(interp, (char *) clockPtr,
                    clockPtr->optionTable, objc, objv,
                    clockPtr->tkwin, &savedOptions,
                    &mask) != TCL_OK) {
                continue;
            }
```

```
        } else {
            /*
             * Restore options from saved values
             */
            errorResult = Tcl_GetObjResult(interp);
            Tcl_IncrRefCount(errorResult);
            Tk_RestoreSavedOptions(&savedOptions);
        }
        if (new || (mask & GRAPHICS_MASK)) {
            /*
             * Give the widget a default background so it doesn't
             * get a random background between the time it is
             * initially displayed by the system and we paint it
             */
            Tk_SetBackgroundFromBorder(clockPtr->tkwin,
                    clockPtr->background);
            /*
             * Set up the graphics contexts to display the widget.
             * The context is used to draw off-screen pixmaps,
             * so turn off exposure notifications.
             */
            gcValues.background =
                Tk_3DBorderColor(clockPtr->background)->pixel;
            gcValues.foreground = clockPtr->foreground->pixel;
            gcValues.font = Tk_FontId(clockPtr->tkfont);
            gcValues.graphics_exposures = False;
            newGC = Tk_GetGC(clockPtr->tkwin,
            GCBackground|GCForeground|GCFont|GCGraphicsExposures,
                &gcValues);
            if (clockPtr->textGC != None) {
                Tk_FreeGC(clockPtr->display, clockPtr->textGC);
            }
            clockPtr->textGC = newGC;
        }
        /*
         * Determine how big the widget wants to be.
         */
        if (new || (mask & GEOMETRY_MASK)) {
            ComputeGeometry(clockPtr);
        }
        /*
         * Set up a call to display ourself.
         */
        if ((clockPtr->tkwin != NULL) &&
                Tk_IsMapped(clockPtr->tkwin)
                && !(clockPtr->flags & REDRAW_PENDING)) {
            Tk_DoWhenIdle(ClockDisplay,
                (ClientData) clockPtr);
            clockPtr->flags |= REDRAW_PENDING;
        }
    }
    if (!error) {
        Tk_FreeSavedOptions(&savedOptions);
        return TCL_OK;
    } else {
```

```
            Tcl_SetObjResult(interp, errorResult);
            Tcl_DecrRefCount(errorResult);
            return TCL_ERROR;
        }
    }
```

Specifying Widget Attributes

Several of the fields in the `Clock` structure are attributes that can be set when
the widget is created or reconfigured with the `configure` operation. The
`Tk_ConfigureWidget` procedure is designed to help you manage the default values, their resource names, and their class names. It works by associating a widget option with an offset into the widget data structure. When you use a
command line argument to change an option, `Tk_ConfigureWidget` reaches into
your widget structure and changes the value for you. Several types are supported, such as colors and fonts, and `Tk_ConfigureWidget` handles all the memory allocation used to store the values. Example 46–9 shows the `Tk_ConfigSpec`
type used to represent information about each attribute:

Example 46–9 The `Tk_ConfigSpec` typedef.

```
typedef struct Tk_ConfigSpec {
    int type;
    char *name;
    char *dbName;
    char *dbClass;
    char *defValue;
    int offset;
    int specflags;
    Tk_CustomOption *customPtr;
} Tk_ConfigSpec;
```

The initial field is a type, such as `TK_CONFIG_BORDER`. Colors and borders
will be explained shortly. The next field is the command-line flag for the
attribute, (e.g., `-background`). Then comes the resource name and the class
name. The default value is next, (e.g., `light blue`). The offset of a structure
member is next, and the `Tk_Offset` macro is used to compute this offset. The
`specflags` field is a bitmask of flags. The two used in this example are
`TK_CONFIG_COLOR_ONLY` and `TK_CONFIG_MONO_ONLY`, which restrict the application of the configuration setting to color and monochrome displays, respectively.
You can define additional flags and pass them into `Tk_ConfigureWidget` if you
have a family of widgets that share most, but not all, of their attributes. The
`tkButton.c` file in the Tk sources has an example of this. The `customPtr` is used
if you have a `TK_CONFIG_CUSTOM` type, which is explained in detail in the manual
page for `Tk_ConfigureWidget`. Example 46–10 shows the `Tk_ConfigSpec` specification of widget attributes for the clock widget.

Example 46–10 Configuration specs for the clock widget.

```
static Tk_ConfigSpec configSpecs[] = {
    {TK_CONFIG_BORDER, "-background", "background",
        "Background", "light blue",
        Tk_Offset(Clock, background), TK_CONFIG_COLOR_ONLY},
    {TK_CONFIG_BORDER, "-background", "background",
        "Background", "white", Tk_Offset(Clock, background),
        TK_CONFIG_MONO_ONLY},
    {TK_CONFIG_SYNONYM, "-bg", "background", (char *) NULL,
        (char *) NULL, 0, 0},
    {TK_CONFIG_SYNONYM, "-bd", "borderWidth", (char *) NULL,
        (char *) NULL, 0, 0},
    {TK_CONFIG_PIXELS, "-borderwidth", "borderWidth",
        "BorderWidth","2", Tk_Offset(Clock, borderWidth), 0},
    {TK_CONFIG_RELIEF, "-relief", "relief", "Relief",
        "ridge", Tk_Offset(Clock, relief), 0},
    {TK_CONFIG_COLOR, "-foreground", "foreground",
        "Foreground", "black", Tk_Offset(Clock, foreground),
        0},
    {TK_CONFIG_SYNONYM, "-fg", "foreground", (char *) NULL,
        (char *) NULL, 0, 0},
    {TK_CONFIG_COLOR, "-highlightcolor", "highlightColor",
        "HighlightColor", "red", Tk_Offset(Clock, highlight),
        TK_CONFIG_COLOR_ONLY},
    {TK_CONFIG_COLOR, "-highlightcolor", "highlightColor",
        "HighlightColor", "black",
        Tk_Offset(Clock, highlight),TK_CONFIG_MONO_ONLY},
    {TK_CONFIG_COLOR, "-highlightbackground",
        "highlightBackground", "HighlightBackground",
        "light blue", Tk_Offset(Clock, highlightBg),
        TK_CONFIG_COLOR_ONLY},
    {TK_CONFIG_COLOR, "-highlightbackground",
        "highlightBackground", "HighlightBackground",
        "black", Tk_Offset(Clock, highlightBg),
        TK_CONFIG_MONO_ONLY},
    {TK_CONFIG_PIXELS, "-highlightthickness",
        "highlightThickness","HighlightThickness",
        "2", Tk_Offset(Clock, highlightWidth), 0},
    {TK_CONFIG_PIXELS, "-padx", "padX", "Pad",
        "2", Tk_Offset(Clock, padX), 0},
    {TK_CONFIG_PIXELS, "-pady", "padY", "Pad",
        "2", Tk_Offset(Clock, padY), 0},
    {TK_CONFIG_STRING, "-format", "format", "Format",
        "%H:%M:%S", Tk_Offset(Clock, format), 0},
    {TK_CONFIG_FONT, "-font", "font", "Font",
        "Courier 18",
        Tk_Offset(Clock, tkfont), 0},
    {TK_CONFIG_END, (char *) NULL, (char *) NULL,
        (char *) NULL, (char *) NULL, 0, 0}
};
```

There is an alternative to the Tk_ConfigureWidget interface that understands Tcl_Obj values in the widget data structure. It uses a a similar type,

Tk_OptionSpec, and Tk_ConfigureWidget is replaced by the Tk_SetOptions, Tk_GetOptionValue, and Tk_GetOptionInfo procedures. Example 46–11 shows the Tk_OptionSpec type.

Example 46–11 The Tk_OptionSpec typedef.

```
typedef struct Tk_OptionSpec {
    Tk_OptionType type;
    char *optionName;
    char *dbName;
    char *dbClass;
    char *defValue;
    int objOffset;
    int internalOffset;
    int flags;
    ClientData clientData;
    int typeMask;
} Tk_OptionSpec;
```

The Tk_OptionSpec has two offsets, one for normal values and one for Tcl_Obj values. You can use the second offset to set Tcl_Obj values directly from the command line configuration. The TK_CONFIG_PIXELS type uses both offsets. The pixel value is stored in an integer, and a Tcl_Obj is used to remember the exact string (e.g., 0.2cm) used to specify the screen distance. Most of the functionality of the specflags field of Tk_ConfigSpec (e.g., TK_CONFIG_MONO_ONLY) has been changed. The flags field accepts only TK_CONFIG_NULL_OK, and the rest of the features use the clientData field instead. For example, the color types uses clientData for their default on monochrome displays. The typeMask supports a general notion of grouping option values into sets. For example, the clock widget marks attributes that affect geometry and color into different sets. This lets the widget optimize its configuration procedure. Example 46–12 shows the Tk_OptionSpec specification of the clock widget attributes.

Example 46–12 The Tk_OptionSpec structure for the clock widget.

```
#define GEOMETRY_MASK 0X1
#define GRAPHICS_MASK 0X2

static Tk_OptionSpec optionSpecs[] = {
    {TK_OPTION_BORDER, "-background", "background",
        "Background", "light blue", -1,
        Tk_Offset(Clock, background), 0,
        (ClientData) "white", GRAPHICS_MASK},
    {TK_OPTION_SYNONYM, "-bg", "background", (char *) NULL,
        (char *) NULL, -1, 0,0, (ClientData)"-background", 0},
    {TK_OPTION_PIXELS, "-borderwidth", "borderWidth",
        "BorderWidth", "2", Tk_Offset(Clock, borderWidthPtr),
        Tk_Offset(Clock, borderWidth),
        0, 0, GEOMETRY_MASK},
    {TK_OPTION_SYNONYM, "-bd", "borderWidth", (char *) NULL,
```

```
            (char *) NULL, -1,0,0,(ClientData)"-borderwidth", 0},
    {TK_OPTION_RELIEF, "-relief", "relief", "Relief",
        "ridge", -1, Tk_Offset(Clock, relief), 0, 0, 0},
    {TK_OPTION_COLOR, "-foreground", "foreground",
        "Foreground", "black",-1, Tk_Offset(Clock, foreground),
        0, (ClientData) "black", GRAPHICS_MASK},
    {TK_OPTION_SYNONYM, "-fg", "foreground", (char *) NULL,
        (char *) NULL, -1, 0,0,(ClientData) "-foreground", 0},
    {TK_OPTION_COLOR, "-highlightcolor", "highlightColor",
        "HighlightColor", "red",-1, Tk_Offset(Clock, highlight),
        0, (ClientData) "black", GRAPHICS_MASK},
    {TK_OPTION_COLOR, "-highlightbackground",
        "highlightBackground", "HighlightBackground",
        "light blue",-1, Tk_Offset(Clock, highlightBg),
        0, (ClientData) "white", GRAPHICS_MASK},
    {TK_OPTION_PIXELS, "-highlightthickness",
        "highlightThickness","HighlightThickness",
        "2", Tk_Offset(Clock, highlightWidthPtr),
        Tk_Offset(Clock, highlightWidth), 0, 0,
        GEOMETRY_MASK},
    {TK_OPTION_PIXELS, "-padx", "padX", "Pad",
        "2", Tk_Offset(Clock, padXPtr),
        Tk_Offset(Clock, padX), 0, 0, GEOMETRY_MASK},
    {TK_OPTION_PIXELS, "-pady", "padY", "Pad",
        "2", Tk_Offset(Clock, padYPtr),
        Tk_Offset(Clock, padY), 0, 0, GEOMETRY_MASK},
    {TK_OPTION_STRING, "-format", "format", "Format",
        "%H:%M:%S",-1, Tk_Offset(Clock, format), 0, 0,
        GEOMETRY_MASK},
    {TK_OPTION_FONT, "-font", "font", "Font",
        "Courier 18",
        -1, Tk_Offset(Clock, tkfont), 0, 0,
        (GRAPHICS_MASK|GEOMETRY_MASK)},
    {TK_OPTION_END, (char *) NULL, (char *) NULL,
        (char *) NULL, (char *) NULL, -1, 0, 0, 0, 0}
};
```

Table 46–1 lists the correspondence between the configuration type of the option and the type of the associated field in the widget data structure. The same types are supported by the Tk_ConfigSpec and Tk_OptionSpec types, with a few exceptions. The TK_CONFIG_ACTIVE_CURSOR configuration type corresponds to the TK_OPTION_CURSOR; both of these set the widgets cursor. The TK_CONFIG_MM and TK_CONFIG_CURSOR types are simply not supported by Tk_OptionSpec because they were not very useful. The TK_OPTION_STRING_TABLE replaces TK_CONFIG_CAP_STYLE and TK_CONFIG_JOIN_STYLE with a more general type that works with Tcl_GetIndexFromObj. In this case, the clientData is an array of strings that are passed to Tcl_GetIndexFromObj. The index value corresponds to the integer value returned from procedures like Tk_GetCapStyle.

VI. Tcl and C

Table 46–1 Configuration flags and corresponding C types.

TK_CONFIG_ACTIVE_CURSOR TK_OPTION_CURSOR	Cursor
TK_CONFIG_ANCHOR TK_OPTION_ANCHOR	Tk_Anchor
TK_CONFIG_BITMAP TK_OPTION_BITMAP	Pixmap
TK_CONFIG_BOOLEAN TK_OPTION_BOOLEAN	int (0 or 1)
TK_CONFIG_BORDER TK_OPTION_BORDER	Tk_3DBorder *
TK_CONFIG_CAP_STYLE	int (see Tk_GetCapStyle)
TK_CONFIG_COLOR TK_OPTION_COLOR	XColor * clientData **is monochrome default.**
TK_CONFIG_CURSOR	Cursor
TK_CONFIG_CUSTOM	
TK_CONFIG_DOUBLE TK_OPTION_DOUBLE	double
TK_CONFIG_END TK_OPTION_END	(signals end of options)
TK_CONFIG_FONT TK_OPTION_FONT	Tk_Font
TK_CONFIG_INT TK_OPTION_INT	int
TK_CONFIG_JOIN_STYLE	int (see Tk_GetJoinStyle)
TK_CONFIG_JUSTIFY TK_OPTION_JUSTIFY	Tk_Justify
TK_CONFIG_MM	double
TK_CONFIG_PIXELS TK_OPTION_PIXELS	int objOffset **used for original value.**
TK_CONFIG_RELIEF TK_OPTION_RELIEF	int (see Tk_GetRelief)
TK_CONFIG_STRING TK_OPTION_STRING	char *
TK_OPTION_STRING_TABLE	The clientData **is an array of strings used** **with** Tcl_GetIndexFromObj
TK_CONFIG_SYNONYM TK_OPTION_SYNONYM	(alias for other option) clientData **is the name of another option.**
TK_CONFIG_UID	Tk_Uid
TK_CONFIG_WINDOW TK_OPTION_WINDOW	Tk_Window

Displaying the Clock

There are two parts to a widget's display. First, the size must be determined. This is done at configuration time, and then that space is requested from the geometry manager. When the widget is later displayed, it should use the Tk_Width and Tk_Height calls to find out how much space was actually allocated to it by the geometry manager. Example 46–13 shows ComputeGeometry. This procedure is identical in both versions of the widget.

Example 46–13 ComputeGeometry computes the widget's size.

```
static void
ComputeGeometry(Clock *clockPtr)
{
    int width, height;
    Tk_FontMetrics fm;      /* Font size information */
    struct tm *tmPtr;       /* Time info split into fields */
    struct timeval tv;      /* BSD-style time value */
    int bd;                 /* Padding from borders */
    char clock[1000];       /* Displayed time */

    /*
     * Get the time and format it to see how big it will be.
     */
    gettimeofday(&tv, NULL);
    tmPtr = localtime(&tv.tv_sec);
    strftime(clock, 1000, clockPtr->format, tmPtr);
    if (clockPtr->clock != NULL) {
        Tcl_Free(clockPtr->clock);
    }
    clockPtr->clock = Tcl_Alloc(1+strlen(clock));
    clockPtr->numChars = strlen(clock);

    bd = clockPtr->highlightWidth + clockPtr->borderWidth;
    Tk_GetFontMetrics(clockPtr->tkfont, &fm);
    height = fm.linespace + 2*(bd + clockPtr->padY);
    Tk_MeasureChars(clockPtr->tkfont, clock,
        clockPtr->numChars, 0, 0, &clockPtr->textWidth);
    width = clockPtr->textWidth + 2*(bd + clockPtr->padX);

    Tk_GeometryRequest(clockPtr->tkwin, width, height);
    Tk_SetInternalBorder(clockPtr->tkwin, bd);
}
```

Finally, we get to the actual display of the widget! The routine is careful to check that the widget still exists and is mapped. This is important because the redisplay is scheduled asynchronously. The current time is converted to a string. This uses the POSIX library procedures gettimeofday, localtime, and strftime. There might be different routines on your system. The string is painted into a pixmap, which is a drawable region of memory that is off-screen. After the whole display has been painted, the pixmap is copied into on-screen

VI. Tcl and C

memory to avoid flickering as the image is cleared and repainted. The text is
painted first, then the borders. This ensures that the borders overwrite the text
if the widget has not been allocated enough room by the geometry manager.

This example allocates and frees the off-screen pixmap for each redisplay.
This is the standard idiom for Tk widgets. They temporarily allocate the off-
screen pixmap each time they redisplay. In the case of a clock that updates every
second, it might be reasonable to permanently allocate the pixmap and store its
pointer in the Clock data structure. Make sure to reallocate the pixmap if the
size changes.

After the display is finished, another call to the display routine is scheduled
to happen in one second. If you were to embellish this widget, you might want to
make the uptime period a parameter. The TICKING flag is used to note that the
timer callback is scheduled. It is checked when the widget is destroyed so that
the callback can be canceled. Example 46–14 shows ClockDisplay. This procedure is identical in both versions of the widget.

Example 46–14 The ClockDisplay procedure.

```
static void
ClockDisplay(ClientData clientData)
{
    Clock *clockPtr = (Clock *)clientData;
    Tk_Window tkwin = clockPtr->tkwin;
    GC gc;                      /* Graphics Context for highlight
*/
    Tk_TextLayout layout;    /* Text measurement state */
    Pixmap pixmap;           /* Temporary drawing area */
    int offset, x, y;        /* Coordinates */
    int width, height;       /* Size */
    struct tm *tmPtr;        /* Time info split into fields */
    struct timeval tv;       /* BSD-style time value */

    /*
     * Make sure the clock still exists
     * and is mapped onto the display before painting.
     */
    clockPtr->flags &= ~(REDRAW_PENDING|TICKING);
    if ((clockPtr->tkwin == NULL) || !Tk_IsMapped(tkwin)) {
        return;
    }
    /*
     * Format the time into a string.
     * localtime chops up the time into fields.
     * strftime formats the fields into a string.
     */
    gettimeofday(&tv, NULL);
    tmPtr = localtime(&tv.tv_sec);
    strftime(clockPtr->clock, clockPtr->numChars+1,
        clockPtr->format, tmPtr);
    /*
     * To avoid flicker when the display is updated, the new
```

```
 * image is painted in an offscreen pixmap and then
 * copied onto the display in one operation. Allocate the
 * pixmap and paint its background.
 */
pixmap = Tk_GetPixmap(clockPtr->display,
    Tk_WindowId(tkwin), Tk_Width(tkwin),
    Tk_Height(tkwin), Tk_Depth(tkwin));
Tk_Fill3DRectangle(tkwin, pixmap,
    clockPtr->background, 0, 0, Tk_Width(tkwin),
    Tk_Height(tkwin), 0, TK_RELIEF_FLAT);

/*
 * Paint the text first.
 */
layout = Tk_ComputeTextLayout(clockPtr->tkfont,
    clockPtr->clock, clockPtr->numChars, 0,
    TK_JUSTIFY_CENTER, 0, &width, &height);
x = (Tk_Width(tkwin) - width)/2;
y = (Tk_Height(tkwin) - height)/2;
Tk_DrawTextLayout(clockPtr->display, pixmap,
    clockPtr->textGC, layout, x, y, 0, -1);

/*
 * Display the borders, so they overwrite any of the
 * text that extends to the edge of the display.
 */
if (clockPtr->relief != TK_RELIEF_FLAT) {
    Tk_Draw3DRectangle(tkwin, pixmap,
        clockPtr->background,
        clockPtr->highlightWidth,
        clockPtr->highlightWidth,
        Tk_Width(tkwin) - 2*clockPtr->highlightWidth,
        Tk_Height(tkwin) - 2*clockPtr->highlightWidth,
        clockPtr->borderWidth, clockPtr->relief);
}
if (clockPtr->highlightWidth != 0) {
    GC gc;

    /*
     * This GC is associated with the color, and Tk caches
     * the GC until the color is freed. Hence no freeGC.
     */

    if (clockPtr->flags & GOT_FOCUS) {
        gc = Tk_GCForColor(clockPtr->highlight, pixmap);
    } else {
        gc = Tk_GCForColor(clockPtr->highlightBg, pixmap);
    }
    Tk_DrawFocusHighlight(tkwin, gc,
        clockPtr->highlightWidth, pixmap);
}
/*
 * Copy the information from the off-screen pixmap onto
 * the screen, then delete the pixmap.
 */
```

VI. Tcl and C

```
    XCopyArea(clockPtr->display, pixmap, Tk_WindowId(tkwin),
        clockPtr->textGC, 0, 0, Tk_Width(tkwin),
        Tk_Height(tkwin), 0, 0);
    Tk_FreePixmap(clockPtr->display, pixmap);

    /*
     * Queue another call to ourselves. The rate at which
     * this is done could be optimized.
     */
    clockPtr->token = Tk_CreateTimerHandler(1000,
        ClockDisplay, (ClientData)clockPtr);
    clockPtr->flags |= TICKING;
}
```

The Window Event Procedure

Each widget registers an event handler for expose and resize events. If it implements a focus highlight, it also needs to be notified of focus events. If you have used other toolkits, you may expect to register callbacks for mouse and keystroke events too. You should not need to do that. Instead, use the regular Tk bind facility and define your bindings in Tcl. That way they can be customized by applications. This procedure is identical in both versions of the widget.

Example 46–15 The `ClockEventProc` handles window events.

```
static void
ClockEventProc(ClientData clientData, XEvent *eventPtr)
{
    Clock *clockPtr = (Clock *) clientData;
    if ((eventPtr->type == Expose) &&
        (eventPtr->xexpose.count == 0)) {
            goto redraw;
    } else if (eventPtr->type == DestroyNotify) {
        Tcl_DeleteCommandFromToken(clockPtr->interp,
                clockPtr->widgetCmd);
        /*
         * Zapping the tkwin lets the other procedures
         * know we are being destroyed.
         */
        clockPtr->tkwin = NULL;

        if (clockPtr->flags & REDRAW_PENDING) {
            Tk_CancelIdleCall(ClockDisplay,
                (ClientData) clockPtr);
            clockPtr->flags &= ~REDRAW_PENDING;
        }
        if (clockPtr->flags & TICKING) {
            Tk_DeleteTimerHandler(clockPtr->token);
            clockPtr->flags &= ~TICKING;
        }
```

```
            /*
             * This results in a call to ClockDestroy.
             */
            Tk_EventuallyFree((ClientData) clockPtr,
                ClockDestroy);
    } else if (eventPtr->type == FocusIn) {
        if (eventPtr->xfocus.detail != NotifyPointer) {
            clockPtr->flags |= GOT_FOCUS;
            if (clockPtr->highlightWidth > 0) {
                goto redraw;
            }
        }
    } else if (eventPtr->type == FocusOut) {
        if (eventPtr->xfocus.detail != NotifyPointer) {
            clockPtr->flags &= ~GOT_FOCUS;
            if (clockPtr->highlightWidth > 0) {
                goto redraw;
            }
        }
    }
    return;
redraw:
    if ((clockPtr->tkwin != NULL) &&
            !(clockPtr->flags & REDRAW_PENDING)) {
        Tk_DoWhenIdle(ClockDisplay, (ClientData) clockPtr);
        clockPtr->flags |= REDRAW_PENDING;
    }
}
```

Final Cleanup

When a widget is destroyed, you need to free up any resources it has allocated.
The resources associated with attributes are cleaned up by Tk_FreeOptions. The
others you must take care of yourself. The ClockDestroy procedure is called as a
result of the Tk_EventuallyFree call in the ClockEventProc. The
Tk_EventuallyFree procedure is part of a protocol that is needed for widgets
that might get deleted when in the middle of processing. Typically the
Tk_Preserve and Tk_Release procedures are called at the beginning and end of
the widget instance command to mark the widget as being in use.
Tk_EventuallyFree will wait until Tk_Release is called before calling the
cleanup procedure. The next example shows ClockDestroy:

Example 46–16 The ClockDestroy cleanup procedure.

```
static void
ClockDestroy(clientData)
    ClientData clientData;/* Info about entry widget. */
{
    register Clock *clockPtr = (Clock *) clientData;
```

```
      /*
       * Free up all the stuff that requires special handling,
       * then let Tk_FreeOptions handle resources associated
       * with the widget attributes.
       */
      if (clockPtr->textGC != None) {
          Tk_FreeGC(clockPtr->display, clockPtr->textGC);
      }
      if (clockPtr->clock != NULL) {
          Tcl_Free(clockPtr->clock);
      }
      if (clockPtr->flags & TICKING) {
          Tk_DeleteTimerHandler(clockPtr->token);
      }
      if (clockPtr->flags & REDRAW_PENDING) {
          Tk_CancelIdleCall(ClockDisplay,
              (ClientData) clockPtr);
      }
      /*
       * This frees up colors and fonts and any allocated
       * storage associated with the widget attributes.
       */
      Tk_FreeOptions(configSpecs, (char *) clockPtr,
          clockPtr->display, 0);
      Tcl_Free((char *) clockPtr);
  }
```

The version of `ClockDestroy` that uses the `Tcl_Obj` interfaces calls `Tk_FreeConfigOptions` instead of `Tk_FreeOptions`. The `ClockObjDelete` command is called when the `oclock` command is removed from the interpreter. This has to clean up the option table used to parse options, if it has been initialized. There is no corresponding delete procedure for the string-based version of the widget. Example 46–17 shows `ClockObjDelete`.

Example 46–17 The `ClockObjDelete` command.

```
void
ClockObjDelete(ClientData clientData)
{
    Tk_OptionTable optionTable = (Tk_OptionTable) clientData;
    if (optionTable != NULL) {
        Tk_DeleteOptionTable(optionTable);
    }
}
```

C Library Overview

This chapter provides a bird's eye view of the facilities in the Tcl and Tk C
libraries. For details of the APIs, you will need to consult the on-line
reference material.

C libraries provide comprehensive access
to the Tcl and Tk implementation. You have complete control over the Tcl script
environment, plus you can extend Tcl and Tk by writing new features in C. You
can implement new commands, I/O channels, event sources, widgets, canvas
items, image types, and geometry managers. The platform-independent I/O subsystem and the event loop are available for use from C. This chapter provides an
overview of the Tcl and Tk C libraries.

For serious C programming, you need to consult the on-line reference material. The manual pages describe groups of related C procedures. For example, on
UNIX, you can run *man* on individual procedures and see the documentation for
the whole group of related procedures:

```
man Tcl_CreateCommand
```

The Windows Help and HTML versions are indexed by procedure. You can
find the HTML on the CD-ROM and the Web:

```
http://www.scriptics.com/man/
```

The Tcl and Tk sources are also excellent reference material. The code is
well written with a consistent style that encourages lots of comments. Virtually
all the exported APIs are used by Tcl and Tk themselves, so you can read the
source code to see how the APIs are used. The Tcl and Tk sources are on the CD-
ROM in `tcl8.2` and `tk8.2` directories. Chapter 45 describes the source directory
structure and how to build Tcl from the source code.

VI. Tcl and C

An Overview of the Tcl C Library

Application Initialization

The `Tcl_Main` and `Tcl_AppInit` procedures are illustrated by Example 44–13 on page 629. They provide a standard framework for creating main programs that embed a Tcl interpreter.

The `Tcl_InitStubs` procedure must be called during initialization by an extension that has been linked against the Tcl stub library, which is described on page 645. `Tcl_InitStubs` is illustrated in Example 44–1 on page 608.

Creating and Deleting Interpreters

A Tcl interpreter is created and deleted with the `Tcl_CreateInterp` and `Tcl_DeleteInterp` procedures. You can find out whether an interpreter is in the process of being deleted with the `Tcl_InterpDeleted` call. You can register a callback to occur when the interpreter is deleted with `Tcl_CallWhenDeleted`. Unregister the callback with `Tcl_DontCallWhenDeleted`.

Slave interpreters are created and manipulated with `Tcl_CreateSlave`, `Tcl_GetSlave`, `Tcl_GetSlaves`, `Tcl_GetMaster`, `Tcl_CreateAlias`, `Tcl_CreateAliasObj`, `Tcl_GetAlias`, `Tcl_GetAliasObj`, `Tcl_GetAliases`, `Tcl_GetInterpPath`, `Tcl_IsSafe`, `Tcl_MakeSafe`, `Tcl_ExposeCommand`, and `Tcl_HideCommand`.

Creating and Deleting Commands

Register a new Tcl command with `Tcl_CreateCommand`, and delete a command with `Tcl_DeleteCommand`. The `Tcl_DeleteCommandFromToken` procedure is useful if you need to delete a command that gets renamed. The `Tcl_GetCommandInfo` and `Tcl_SetCommandInfo` procedures query and modify the procedure that implements a Tcl command and the `ClientData` that is associated with the command. The command that uses the `Tcl_Obj` interface is created with `Tcl_CreateObjCommand`. Command procedures are illustrated in Chapter 44.

Dynamic Loading and Packages

`Tcl_PkgRequire` checks a dependency on another package. `Tcl_PkgProvide` declares that a package is provided by a library. These procedures are equivalent to the `package require` and `package provide` Tcl commands. The `Tcl_PkgPresent` procedure returns the version number of the package, if it is loaded. `Tcl_PkgProvideExx`, `Tcl_PkgRequireEx`, and `Tcl_PkgPresentEx` let you set and query the clientData associated with the package. The `Tcl_StaticPackage` call is used by statically linked packages so that scripts can `load` them into slave interpreters. The `Tcl_FindExecuatable` searches the system to determine the absolute file name of the program being run. Once this has been determined, `Tcl_GetNameOfExecutable` can be used to get the cached value of the program name.

Managing the Result String

The result string is managed through the `Tcl_SetResult`, `Tcl_AppendResult`, `Tcl_AppendElement`, `Tcl_GetStringResult`, and `Tcl_ResetResult` procedures. The object interface is provided by `Tcl_SetObjResult` and `Tcl_GetObjResult`.

Error information is managed with the `Tcl_AddErrorInfo`, `Tcl_AddObjErrorInfo`, `Tcl_SetErrorCode`, and `Tcl_PosixError` procedures. The `Tcl_WrongNumArgs` generates a standard error message. The `Tcl_SetErrno` and `Tcl_GetErrno` provide platform-independent access to the `errno` global variable that stores POSIX error codes.

Memory Allocation

The `Tcl_Alloc`, `Tcl_Realloc`, and `Tcl_Free` procedures provide platform- and compiler-independent functions to allocation and free heap storage. Use these instead of `alloc`, `realloc`, and `free`. The `Tcl_Preserve` and `Tcl_Release` procedures work in concert with `Tcl_EventuallyFree` to guard data structures against premature deallocation. These are described on page 625.

Lists

You can chop a list up into its elements with `Tcl_SplitList`, which returns an array of strings. You can create a list out of an array of strings with `Tcl_Merge`. This behaves like the `list` command in that it will add syntax to the strings so that the list structure has one element for each of the strings. The `Tcl_ScanElement` and `Tcl_ConvertElement` procedures are used by `Tcl_Merge`. The object interface to lists is provided by `Tcl_NewListObj`, `Tcl_SetListObj`, `Tcl_ListObjIndex`, `Tcl_ListObjAppendList`, `Tcl_ListObjAppendElement`, `Tcl_ListObjGetElements`, `Tcl_ListObjLength`, and `Tcl_ListObjReplace`.

Command Parsing

If you are reading commands, you can test for a complete command with `Tcl_CommandComplete`. You can do backslash substitutions with `Tcl_Backslash`. A more formal Tcl parser is provided by these procedures: `Tcl_ParseCommand`, `Tcl_ParseExpr`, `Tcl_ParseBraces`, `Tcl_ParseQuotedString`, `Tcl_ParseVarName`, and `Tcl_FreeParse`. The result of the parse is a sequence of tokens, which you can evaluate with `Tcl_EvalTokens`.

VI. Tcl and C

Command Pipelines

The `Tcl_OpenCommandChannel` procedure does all the work of setting up a pipeline between processes. It handles file redirection and implements all the syntax supported by the `exec` and `open` commands.

If the command pipeline is run in the background, then a list of process identifiers is returned. You can detach these processes with `Tcl_DetachPids`, and you can clean up after them with `Tcl_ReapDetachedProcs`.

Tracing the Actions of the Tcl Interpreter

There are several procedures that let you trace the execution of the Tcl interpreter and provide control over its behavior. The `Tcl_CreateTrace` registers a procedure that is called before the execution of each Tcl command. Remove the registration with `Tcl_DeleteTrace`.

You can trace modifications and accesses to Tcl variables with `Tcl_TraceVar` and `Tcl_TraceVar2`. The second form is used with array elements. Remove the traces with `Tcl_UntraceVar` and `Tcl_UntraceVar2`. You can query the traces on variables with `Tcl_VarTraceInfo` and `Tcl_VarTraceInfo2`.

Evaluating Tcl Commands

There is a large family of procedures that evaluate Tcl commands. `Tcl_Eval` evaluates a string as a Tcl command. `Tcl_VarEval` takes a variable number of string arguments and concatenates them before evaluation. The `Tcl_EvalFile` command reads commands from a file. `Tcl_GlobalEval` evaluates a string at the global scope. The `Tcl_EvalEx` procedure takes flags. The `TCL_GLOBAL_EVAL` flag causes evaluation at the global scope. The `TCL_EVAL_DIRECT` flags does evaluation without first compiling the script to byte codes.

`Tcl_EvalObj` and `Tcl_GlobalEvalObj` provide an object interface. Their argument is a script object that gets compiled into byte codes and cached. Use these procedures if you plan to execute the same script several times. The `Tcl_EvalObjEx` procedure takes the evaluation flags described above. The `Tcl_EvalObjv` procedure takes an array of `Tcl_Obj` that represent the command and its arguments. Unlike the other procedures, `Tcl_EvalObjv` does not do substitutions on the arguments to the command.

If you are implementing an interactive command interpreter and want to use the history facility, then call `Tcl_RecordAndEval` or `Tcl_RecordAndEval`. This records the command on the history list and then behaves like `Tcl_GlobalEval`.

You can set the recursion limit of the interpreter with `Tcl_SetRecursionLimit`. If you are implementing a new control structure, you may need to use the `Tcl_AllowExceptions` procedure. This makes it acceptable for `Tcl_Eval` and friends to return something other than `TCL_OK` and `TCL_ERROR`.

If you want to evaluate a Tcl command without modifying the current interpreter result and error information, use `Tcl_SaveResult`, `Tcl_RestoreResult`, and `Tcl_DiscardResult`.

Reporting Script Errors

If your widget makes a callback into the script level, what do you do when the callback returns an error? Use the `Tcl_BackgroundError` procedure that invokes the standard `bgerror` procedure to report the error to the user.

Manipulating Tcl Variables

You can set a Tcl variable with `Tcl_SetVar` and `Tcl_SetVar2`. These two procedures assign a string value, and the second form is used for array elements. The `Tcl_SetVar2Ex` procedure assigns a `Tcl_Obj` value to the variable, and it can be used with array elements. You can retrieve the value of a Tcl variable with `Tcl_GetVar` and `Tcl_GetVar2`. The `Tcl_GetVar2Ex` procedure returns a `Tcl_Obj` value instead of a string. In the rare case that you have the name of the variable in a `Tcl_Obj` instead of a simple string, you must use `Tcl_ObjSetVar2` procedure and `Tcl_ObjGetVar2`. You can delete variables with `Tcl_UnsetVar` and `Tcl_UnsetVar2`.

You can link a Tcl variable and a C variable together with `Tcl_LinkVar` and break the relationship with `Tcl_UnlinkVar`. Setting the Tcl variable modifies the C variable, and reading the Tcl variable returns the value of the C variable. If you need to modify the Tcl variable directly, use `Tcl_UpdateLinkedVar`.

Use the `Tcl_UpVar` and `Tcl_UpVar2` procedures to link Tcl variables from different scopes together. You may need to do this if your command takes the name of a variable as an argument as opposed to a value. These procedures are used in the implementation of the `upvar` Tcl command.

Evaluating Expressions

The Tcl expression evaluator is available through the `Tcl_ExprLong`, `Tcl_ExprDouble`, `Tcl_ExprBoolean`, and `Tcl_ExprString` procedures. These all use the same evaluator, but they differ in how they return their result. The object interface to expressions is implemented with `Tcl_ExprLongObj`, `Tcl_ExprDoubleObj`, `Tcl_ExprBooleanObj`, and `Tcl_ExprObj`. You can register the implementation of new math functions by using the `Tcl_CreateMathFunc` procedure.

Converting Numbers

You can convert strings into numbers with the `Tcl_GetInt`, `Tcl_GetDouble`, and `Tcl_GetBoolean` procedures. The `Tcl_PrintDouble` procedure converts a floating point number to a string. Tcl uses it any time it must do this conversion.

Tcl Objects

Tcl 8.0 uses dual-ported objects instead of strings to improve execution efficiency. The basic interface to objects is provided by `Tcl_NewObj`,

Tl_DuplicateObj, Tcl_IncrRefCount, Tcl_DecrRefCount, and Tcl_IsShared. Example 44–5 on page 616 and Example 44–15 on page 635 illustrate some of these procedures. You can define new object types. The interface consists of Tcl_RegisterObjType, Tcl_GetObjType, Tcl_AppendAllObjTypes, and Tcl_ConvertToType.

Primitive Object Types

The basic Tcl object types are boolean, integer, double-precision real, and string. The types provide procedures for creating objects, setting values, and getting values: Tcl_NewBooleanObj, Tcl_SetBooleanObj, Tcl_GetBooleanFromObj, Tcl_NewDoubleObj, Tcl_SetDoubleObj, Tcl_GetDoubleFromObj, Tcl_NewIntObj, Tcl_GetIntFromObj, Tcl_SetIntObj, Tcl_NewLongObj, Tcl_GetLongFromObj, and Tcl_SetLongObj.

String Object Types

The Tcl_Obj values are used to store strings in different encodings. The natural string value in a Tcl_Obj is UTF-8 encoded. There can also be Unicode (i.e., 16-bit characters) or ByteArray (i.e., 8-bit characters) format strings stored in a Tcl_Obj. Conversions among these string types are done automatically. However, certain operations work best with a particular string encoding, and the Tcl_Obj value is useful for caching an efficient representation.

These procedures operate on string objects with the UTF-8 encoding: Tcl_NewStringObj, Tcl_SetStringObj, Tcl_GetString, Tcl_GetStringFromObj, Tcl_AppendToObj, and Tcl_AppendStringsToObj. These procedures operate on Unicode strings: Tcl_NewUnicodeObj, Tcl_SetUnicodeObj, Tcl_AppendUnicodeToObj, Tcl_GetUnicode, Tcl_GetRange, and Tcl_GetUniChar. The Tcl_AppendObjToObj preserves the existing representation (e.g., Unicode or UTF-8) of the string being appended to.

The Tcl_GetCharLength returns the length in characters of the string. Tcl_SetObjLength procedure sets the storage size of the string in bytes, which is generally different from the character length. This can be used to overallocate a string in preparation for creating a large one.

The Tcl_Concat and Tcl_ConcatObj procedures operate like the concat Tcl command. Its input is an array of strings (for Tcl_Concat) or Tcl_Obj values (for Tcl_ConcatObj). They trim leading and trailing white space from each one, and concatenate them together into one string with a single space character between each value.

ByteArrays for Binary Data

The ByteArray Tcl_Obj type is used to store arbitrary binary data. It is simply an array of 8-bit bytes. These are its procedures: Tcl_NewByteArrayObj, Tcl_SetByteArrayObj, Tcl_GetByteArrayFromObj, and Tcl_SetByteArray-Length.

Dynamic Strings

The Tcl dynamic string package is designed for strings that get built up incrementally. You will need to use dynamic strings if you use the `Tcl_TranslateFileName` procedure. The procedures in the package are `Tcl_DStringInit`, `Tcl_DStringAppend`, `Tcl_DStringAppendElement`, `Tcl_DStringStartSublist`, `Tcl_DStringEndSublist`, `Tcl_DStringLength`, `Tcl_DStringValue`, `Tcl_DStringSetLength`, `Tcl_DStringFree`, `Tcl_DString-Result`, and `Tcl_DStringGetResult`. Dynamic strings are explained in more detail on page 627.

Character Set Encodings

The procedures that convert strings between character set encodings use an abstract handle on a particular encoding. The `Tcl_GetEncoding` and `Tcl_FreeEncoding` procedures allocate and release these handles. `Tcl_SetSystemEncoding` is called by Tcl to set the encoding for the current system. `Tcl_CreateEncoding` creates a new encoding. The `Tcl_GetEncodingName` and `Tcl_GetEncodingNames` procedures query the available encodings. The encodings are stored in files in default location, which you query and set with `Tcl_GetDefaultEncodingDir` and `Tcl_SetDefaultEncodingDir`.

There are three sets of procedures that translate strings between encodings. The easiest to use are `Tcl_ExternalToUtfDString` and `Tcl_UtfToExternalDString`, which put the result into a `Tcl_DString`. These are built on top of `Tcl_ExternalToUtf` and `Tcl_UtfToExternal`, which are harder to use because they have to deal with partial conversions at the end of the buffer. The `Tcl_WinTCharToUtf` and `Tcl_WinUtfToTChar` procedures are for use with Windows `TChar` type, which is an 8-bit character on Windows 98 and a 16-bit Unicode character on Windows N/T.

There are many utility procedures for operating on Unicode and UTF-8 strings: `Tcl_UniChar`, `Tcl_UniCharToUtf`, `Tcl_UtfToUniChar`, `Tcl_UniCharToUtfDString`, `Tcl_UtfToUniCharDString`, `Tcl_UniCharLen`, `Tcl_UniCharNcmp`, `Tcl_UtfCharComplete`, `Tcl_NumUtfChars`, `Tcl_UtfFindFirst`, `Tcl_UtfFindLast`, `Tcl_UtfNext`, `Tcl_UtfPrev`, `Tcl_UniCharAtIndex`, `Tcl_UtfAtIndex`, and `Tcl_UtfBackslash`.

These procedures convert Unicode characters to different cases: `Tcl_UniCharToUpper`, `Tcl_UniCharToLower`, and `Tcl_UniCharToTitle`. These procedures convert strings: `Tcl_UtfToUpper`, `Tcl_UtfToLower`, `Tcl_UtfToTitle`.

AssocData for per Interpreter Data Structures

If your extension needs to store information that is not associated with any particular command, you can associate it with an interpreter with *AssocData*. The `Tcl_SetAssocData` registers a string-valued key for a data structure. The `Tcl_GetAssocData` gets the data for a key, and `Tcl_DeleteAssocData` removes the key and pointer. The registration also includes a callback that is made when the interpreter is deleted. This is a layer on top of the hash table package described next.

Hash Tables

Tcl has a nice hash table package that automatically grows the hash table data structures as more elements are added to the table. Because everything is a string, you may need to set up a hash table that maps from a string-valued key to an internal data structure. The procedures in the package are Tcl_InitHashTable, Tcl_DeleteHashTable, Tcl_CreateHashEntry, Tcl_Delete-HashEntry, Tcl_FindHashEntry, Tcl_GetHashValue, Tcl_SetHashValue, Tcl_GetHashKey, Tcl_FirstHashEntry, Tcl_NextHashEntry, and Tcl_HashStats. Hash tables are used in the blob command example presented in Chapter 44.

Option Processing

The Tcl_GetIndexFromObj provides a way to look up keywords in a table. It returns the index of the table entry that matches a keyword. It is designed to work with options on a Tcl command. It is illustrated in Example 44–8 on page 621.

Regular Expressions and String Matching

The regular expression library used by Tcl is exported through the Tcl_RegExpMatch, Tcl_RegExpCompile, Tcl_RegExpExec, and Tcl_RegExpRange procedures. The Tcl_Obj version of this interface uses the Tcl_RegExpMatchObj, Tcl_GetRegExpFromObj, Tcl_RegExpExecObj and Tcl_GetRegExpInfo proce-dures. The string match function is available through the Tcl_StringMatch and Tcl_StringCaseMatch procedures.

Event Loop Implementation

The event loop is implemented by the *notifier* that manages a set of *event sources* and a queue of pending events. The *tclsh* and *wish* applications already manage the event loop for you. The simplest interface is provided by Tcl_DoOneEvent. In some cases, you may need to implement new event sources. Use Tcl_CreateEventSource and Tcl_DeleteEventSource to create and destroy an event source. An event source manipulates the events queue with Tcl_QueueEvent, Tcl_DeleteEvents, and Tcl_SetMaxBlockTime.

Each thread runs a notifier. You can enqueue events for another thread's notifier with Tcl_ThreadQueueEvent. After you do this, you must signal the other thread with Tcl_ThreadAlert. The ID of the current thread is returned from Tcl_GetCurrentThread.

The notifier is implemented with a public API so that you can replace the API with a new implementation for custom situations. This API consists of Tcl_InitNotifier, Tcl_FinalizeNotifier, Tcl_WaitForEvent, Tcl_Alert-

`Notifier`, `Tcl_Sleep`, `Tcl_CreateFileHandler`, and `Tcl_DeleteFileHandler`.

If you want to integrate Tcl's event loop with an external one, such as the Xt event loop used by Motif, then you can use the following procedures: `Tcl_WaitForEvent`, `Tcl_SetTimer`, `Tcl_ServiceAll`, `Tcl_ServiceEvent`, `Tcl_GetServiceMode`, and `Tcl_SetServiceMode`. There is an example application of this in the `unix/xtTest.c` file.

File Handlers

Use `Tcl_CreateFileHandler` to register handlers for I/O streams. You set up the handlers to be called when the I/O stream is ready for reading or writing, or both. File handlers are called after window event handlers. Use `Tcl_DeleteFileHandler` to remove the handler.

`Tcl_CreateFileHandler` is UNIX-specific because UNIX has a unified handle for files, sockets, pipes, and devices. On Windows and the Macintosh, there are different system APIs to wait for events from these different classes of I/O objects. These differences are hidden by the channel drivers for sockets and pipes. For nonstandard devices, the best thing is to create a channel driver and event source for them.

Timer Events

Register a callback to occur at some time in the future with `Tcl_CreateTimerHandler`. The handler is called only once. If you need to delete the handler before it gets called, use `Tcl_DeleteTimerHandler`.

Idle Callbacks

If there are no outstanding events, the Tk makes idle callbacks before waiting for new events to arrive. In general, Tk widgets queue their display routines to be called at idle time. Use `Tcl_DoWhenIdle` to queue an idle callback, and use `Tcl_CancelIdleCall` to remove the callback from the queue. The `Tcl_Sleep` procedure delays execution for a specified number of milliseconds.

Input/Output

The Tcl I/O subsystem provides buffering and works with the event loop to provide event-driven I/O. The interface consists of `Tcl_OpenFileChannel`, `Tcl_OpenCommandChannel`, `Tcl_MakeFileChannel`, `Tcl_GetOpenFile`, `Tcl_RegisterChannel`, `Tcl_UnregisterChannel`, `Tcl_Close`, `Tcl_Read`, `Tcl_ReadChars`, `Tcl_Gets`, `Tcl_Write`, `Tcl_WriteObj`, `Tcl_WriteChars`, `Tcl_Flush`, `Tcl_Seek`, `Tcl_Tell`, `Tcl_Eof`, `Tcl_GetsObj`, `Tcl_InputBlocked`, `Tcl_InputBuffered`, `Tcl_GetChannelOption`, and `Tcl_SetChannelOption`.

I/O Channel Drivers

Tcl provides an extensible I/O subsystem. You can implement a new channel (i.e., for a UDP network socket) by providing a Tcl command to create the channel and registering a set of callbacks that are used by the standard Tcl I/O commands like `puts`, `gets`, and `close`. The interface to channels consists of these procedures: `Tcl_CreateChannel`, `Tcl_GetChannel`, `Tcl_GetChannelType`, `Tcl_GetChannelInstanceData`, `Tcl_GetChannelName`, `Tcl_GetChannelHandle`, `Tcl_GetChannelMode`, `Tcl_BadChannelOption`, `Tcl_GetChannelBufferSize`, `Tcl_SetDefaultTranslation`, `Tcl_SetChannelBufferSize`, and `Tcl_NotifyChannel`.

The `Tcl_CreateChannelHandler` and `Tcl_DeleteChannelHandler` are used in the interface to the main event loop. The `Tcl_CreateCloseHandler` and `Tcl_DeleteCloseHandler` set and delete a callback that occurs when a channel is closed. The `Tcl_GetStdChannel` and `Tcl_SetStdChannel` are used to manipulate the standard input and standard output channels of your application.

Network sockets are created with `Tcl_OpenTcpClient` and `Tcl_OpenTcpServer`. The `Tcl_MakeTcpClientChannel` provides a platform-independent way to create a Tcl channel structure for a socket connection.

The `Tcl_StackChannel`, `Tcl_UnstackChannel`, and `Tcl_GetStackedChannel` procedures support layering of I/O channels. This can be used to push compression- or encryption-processing modules onto I/O channels.

Manipulating File Names

The `Tcl_SplitPath`, `Tcl_JoinPath`, and `Tcl_GetPathType` procedures provide the implementation for the `file split`, `file join`, and `file pathtype` Tcl commands that are used to manipulate file names in a platform-independent manner. The `Tcl_TranslateFileName` procedure converts a file name to native syntax. It also expands tilde (~) in file names into user home directories.

Examining the File System

The `Tcl_Stat` and `Tcl_Access` functions are thin layers on top of the UNIX `stat` and `access` system calls. `Tcl_Stat` returns information about a file, and `Tcl_Access` checks access permissions. The `Tcl_Chdir` procedure changes the current working directory, and `Tcl_GetCwd` returns the current working directory. These procedures are cross-platform, plus they support hooks used by *TclPro Wrapper* to store files inside an executable.

Thread Support

The Tcl library is thread safe. It uses the following procedures to serialize access to its data structures: `Tcl_MutexLock`, `Tcl_MutexUnlock`, `Tcl_ConditionWait`, and `Tcl_ConditionNotify`. Thread local storage is provided by `Tcl_GetThreadData`. All of these procedures are self-initializing, so there are no explicit initialization calls.

The `Tcl_CreateThreadExitHandler` procedure registers a procedure that is called when a thread is terminated. In particular, it can clean up thread local storage. Use `Tcl_DeleteThreadExitHandler` to remove a registration.

`Tcl_FinalizeThread` is called when a thread is exiting to clean up state. Currently, the thread creation API is still private (`TclpCreateThread`), and script-level access to threads is provided by an extension.

Working with Signals

Tcl provides a simple package for safely dealing with signals and other asynchronous events. You register a handler for an event with `Tcl_AsyncCreate`. When the event occurs, you mark the handler as ready with `Tcl_AsyncMark`. When the Tcl interpreter is at a safe point, it uses `Tcl_AsyncReady` to determine which handlers are ready, and then it uses `Tcl_AsyncInvoke` to call them. Your application can call `Tcl_AsyncInvoke`, too. Use `Tcl_AsyncDelete` to unregister a handler.

Exit Handlers

The `Tcl_Exit` procedure terminates the application. The `Tcl_Finalize` procedure cleans up Tcl's memory usage and calls exit handlers, but it does not exit. This is necessary when unloading the Tcl DLL. The `Tcl_CreateExitHandler` and `Tcl_DeleteExitHandler` set up callbacks that occur when `Tcl_Exit` is called.

An Overview of the Tk C Library

Main Programs and Command-Line Arguments

The `Tk_Main` procedure does the standard setup for your application's main window and event loop. The `Tk_ParseArgv` procedure parses command-line arguments. This procedure is designed for use by main programs. It uses a table of `Tk_ArgvInfo` records to describe your program's arguments. These procedures are illustrated by Example 44–14 on page 631.

If your extension uses the Tk library, you should link against the Tk stub library. In this case, you must call `Tk_InitStubs` in your extension's initialization routine.

Creating Windows

The `Tk_Init` procedure creates the main window for your application. The `Tk_CreateWindow` and `Tk_CreateWindowFromPath` are used to create windows for widgets. The actual creation of the window is delayed until an idle point. You can force the window to be created with `Tk_MakeWindowExist` or destroy a window with `Tk_DestroyWindow`.

VI. Tcl and C

The `Tk_MainWindow` procedure returns the handle on the application's main window. The `Tk_MapWindow` and `Tk_UnmapWindow` are used to display and withdraw a window, respectively. The `Tk_MoveToplevelWindow` call is used to position a top-level window.

Translate between window names and the `Tk_Window` type with `Tk_Name`, `Tk_PathName`, and `Tk_NameToWindow`. You can convert from an operating system window ID to the corresponding `Tk_Window` with `Tk_IdToWindow` procedure.

Application Name for Send

The name of the application is defined or changed with `Tk_SetAppName`. This name is used when other applications send it Tcl commands using the `send` command.

Configuring Windows

The configuration of a window includes its width, height, cursor, and so on. Tk provides a set of routines that configure a window and also cache the results. This makes it efficient to query these settings because the system does not need to be contacted. The window configuration routines are `Tk_ConfigureWindow`, `Tk_ResizeWindow`, `Tk_MoveResizeWindow`, `Tk_SetWindowBorderWidth`, `Tk_DefineCursor`, `Tk_ChangeWindowAttributes`, `Tk_SetWindowBackground`, `Tk_SetWindowColormap`, `Tk_UndefineCursor`, `Tk_SetWindowBackgroundPixmap`, `Tk_SetWindowBorderPixmap`, `Tk_MoveWindow`, and `Tk_SetWindowBorder`.

The `Tk_SetOptions`, `Tk_GetOptionValue`, `Tk_GetOptionInfo`, `Tk_RestoreSavedOptions`, `Tk_FreeSavedOptions`, `Tk_InitOptions`, `Tk_FreeConfigOptions`, and `Tk_DeleteOptionTable` procedures are used to parse command line options with procedures that use `Tcl_Obj` values. Canvas item types are supported by `Tk_CanvasTagsOption`.

Window Coordinates

The coordinates of a widget relative to the root window (the main screen) are returned by `Tk_GetRootCoords`. The `Tk_GetVRootGeometry` procedure returns the size and position of a window relative to the virtual root window. The `Tk_CoordsToWindow` procedure locates the window under a given coordinate.

Window Stacking Order

Control the stacking order of windows in the window hierarchy with `Tk_RestackWindow`. Windows higher in the stacking order obscure lower windows.

Window Information

Tk keeps lots of information associated with each window, or widget. The following calls are fast macros that return the information without calling the X server: `Tk_WindowId`, `Tk_Parent`, `Tk_Display`, `Tk_DisplayName`, `Tk_ScreenNumber`, `Tk_Screen`, `Tk_X`, `Tk_Y`, `Tk_Width`, `Tk_Height`, `Tk_Changes`, `Tk_Attributes`, `Tk_IsMapped`, `Tk_IsTopLevel`, `Tk_ReqWidth`, `Tk_ReqHeight`, `Tk_InternalBorderWidth`, `Tk_Visual`, `Tk_Depth`, and `Tk_Colormap`.

Configuring Widget Attributes

The `Tk_ConfigureWidget` procedure parses command-line specification of attributes and allocates resources like colors and fonts. Related procedures include `Tk_Offset`, `Tk_ConfigureInfo`, `Tk_ConfigureValue`, and `Tk_FreeOptions`. The `Tk_GetScrollInfo` parses arguments to scrolling commands like the `xview` and `yview` widget operations.

The Selection and Clipboard

Retrieve the current selection with `Tk_GetSelection`. Clear the selection with `Tk_ClearSelection`. Register a handler for selection requests with `Tk_CreateSelHandler`. Unregister the handler with `Tk_DeleteSelHandler`. Claim ownership of the selection with `Tk_OwnSelection`. Manipulate the clipboard with `Tk_ClipboardClear` and `Tk_ClipboardAppend`.

Event Loop Interface

The standard event loop is implemented by `Tk_MainLoop`. If you write your own event loop, you need to call `Tcl_DoOneEvent` so that Tcl can handle its events. Call `Tcl_DoOneEvent` with `TCL_DONT_WAIT` until it returns 0 to indicate no more events need to be processed. If you read window events directly, (e.g., through `Tk_CreateGenericHandler`), you can dispatch to the correct handler for the event with `Tk_HandleEvent`. Note that most of the event loop is implemented in the Tcl library, except for `Tk_MainLoop` and the window event handler interface that are part of the Tk library. You can create handlers for file, timer, and idle events after this call. Restrict or delay events with the `Tk_RestrictEvent` procedure.

Handling Window Events

Use `Tk_CreateEventHandler` to set up a handler for specific window events. Widget implementations need a handler for expose and resize events, for example. Remove the registration with `Tk_DeleteEventHandler`. You can set up a handler for all window events with `Tk_CreateGenericHandler`. This is useful in some modal interactions where you have to poll for a certain event. If you get an event you do not want to handle yourself, you can push it onto the event queue with `Tk_QueueWindowEvent`. Delete the handler with `Tk_DeleteGenericHandler`.

Event Bindings

The routines that manage bindings are exported by the Tk library, so you can manage bindings yourself. For example, the canvas widget uses the API to implement bindings on canvas items. The procedures are `Tk_CreateBindingTable`, `Tk_DeleteBindingTable`, `Tk_CreateBinding`, `Tk_DeleteBinding`, `Tk_BindEvent`, `Tk_GetBinding`, `Tk_GetAllBindings`, and `Tk_DeleteAllBindings`.

Handling Graphic Protocol Errors

You can handle graphic protocol errors by registering a handler with `Tk_CreateErrorHandler`. Unregister it with `Tk_DeleteErrorHandler`. UNIX has an asynchronous interface, so the error will be reported sometime after the offending call was made. You can call the Xlib `XSynchronize` routine to turn off the asynchronous behavior in order to help you debug.

Using the Resource Database

The `Tk_GetOption` procedure looks up items in the resource database. The resource class of a window is set with `Tk_SetClass`, and the current class setting is retrieved with `Tk_Class`.

Managing Bitmaps

Tk maintains a registry of bitmaps by name, (e.g., `gray50` and `questhead`). You can define new bitmaps with `Tk_DefineBitmap`, and you can get a handle on the bitmap from its name with `Tk_GetBitmap`. Related procedures include `Tk_NameOfBitmap`, `Tk_SizeOfBitmap`, `Tk_GetBitmapFromData`, `Tk_FreeBitmap`, `Tk_AllocBitmapFromObj`, `Tk_GetBitmapFromObj`, and `Tk_FreeBitmapFromObj`.

Creating New Image Types

The `Tk_CreateImageType` procedure is used to register the implementation of a new image type. The registration includes several procedures that call back into the implementation to support creation, display, and deletion of images. When an image changes, the widgets that display it are notified by calling `Tk_ImageChanged`. The `Tk_NameOfImage` procedure returns the Tcl name of an image. The `Tk_GetImageMasterData` returns the client data associated with an image type.

Using an Image in a Widget

The following routines support widgets that display images. `Tk_GetImage` maps from the name to a `Tk_Image` data structure. `Tk_RedrawImage` causes the image to update its display. `Tk_SizeOfImage` tells you how big it is. When the image is no longer in use, call `Tk_FreeImage`. The `Tk_DeleteImage` deletes an image.

Photo Image Types

One of the image types is `photo`, which has its own C interface for defining new formats. The job of a format handler is to read and write different image formats such as `GIF` or `JPEG` so that the `photo` image can display them. The `Tk_CreatePhotoImageFormat` procedure sets up the interface. There are several support routines for photo format handlers. The `Tk_FindPhoto` procedure maps from a photo name to its associated `Tk_PhotoHandle` data structure. The image is updated with `Tk_PhotoBlank`, `Tk_PhotoPutBlock`, and `Tk_PhotoPutZoomedBlock`. The image values can be obtained with `Tk_PhotoGetImage`. The size of the image can be manipulated with `Tk_PhotoExpand`, `Tk_PhotoGetSize`, and `Tk_PhotoSetSize`

Canvas Object Support

The C interface for defining new canvas items is exported via the `Tk_CreateItemType` procedure. The description for a canvas item includes a set of procedures that the canvas widget uses to call the implementation of the canvas item type. The `Tk_GetItemTypes` returns information about all types of canvas objects. The support routines for the managers of new item types are `Tk_CanvasGetCoord`, `Tk_CanvasDrawableCoords`, `Tk_CanvasSetStippleOrigin`, `Tk_CanvasTkwin`, `Tk_CanvasWindowCoords`, and `Tk_CanvasEventuallyRedraw`. The following procedures help with the generation of postscript: `Tk_CanvasPsY`, `Tk_CanvasPsBitmap`, `Tk_CanvasPsColor`, `Tk_CanvasPsFont`, `Tk_CanvasPsPath`, and `Tk_CanvasPsStipple`. If you are manipulating text items directly, then you can use the `Tk_CanvasGetTextInfo` procedure to get a description of the selection state and other details about the text item.

Geometry Management

A widget requests a certain size with the `Tk_GeometryRequest` procedure. If it draws a border inside that area, it calls `Tk_SetInternalBorder`. The geometry manager responds to these requests, although the widget may get a different size. The `Tk_ManageGeometry` procedure sets up the relationship between the geometry manager and a widget. The `Tk_MaintainGeometry` procedure arranges for one window to stay at a fixed position relative to another widget. This is used by the place geometry manager. The relationship is broken with the `Tk_UnmaintainGeometry` call. The `Tk_SetGrid` call enables gridded geometry management. The grid is turned off with `Tk_UnsetGrid`.

VI. Tcl and C

String Identifiers (UIDS)

Tk maintains a database of string values such that a string appears in it only once. The `Tk_Uid` type refers to such a string. You can test for equality by using the value of `Tk_Uid`, which is the string's address, as an identifier. A `Tk_Uid` is used as a name in the various `GetByName` calls introduced below. The `Tk_GetUid` procedure installs a string into the registry.

Note: The table of `Tk_Uid` values is a memory leak. The leak is not serious under normal operation. However, if you continually register new strings as `Tk_Uid` values, then the hash table that records them continues to grow. This table is not cleaned up when Tk is finalized. The mapping from a string to a constant is better served by the `Tcl_GetIndexFromObj` call.

Colors, Colormaps, and Visuals

Use `Tk_GetColor`, `Tk_GetColorByValue`, `Tk_AllocColorFromObj`, and `Tk_GetColorFromObj` to allocate a color. You can retrieve the string name of a color with `Tk_NameOfColor`. When you are done using a color, you need to call `Tk_FreeColor` or `Tk_FreeColorFromObj`. You can get a graphics context for drawing a particular color with `Tk_GCForColor`. Colors are shared among widgets, so it is important to free them when you are done using them. Use `Tk_GetColormap` and `Tk_FreeColormap` to allocate and free a colormap. Colormaps are shared, if possible, so you should use these routines instead of the platform-specific routines to allocate colormaps. The window's visual type is set with `Tk_SetWindowVisual`. You can get a visual context with `Tk_GetVisual`.

3D Borders

The three-dimensional relief used for widget borders is supported by `Tk_Get3DBorder`, `Tk_3DBorderGC`, `Tk_Draw3DRectangle`, `Tk_Fill3DRectangle`, `Tk_Draw3DPolygon`, `Tk_Free3DBorder`, `Tk_Fill3DPolygon`, `Tk_3DVerticalBevel`, `Tk_3DHorizontalBevel`, `Tk_SetBackgroundFromBorder`, `Tk_NameOf3DBorder`, `Tk_3DBorderColor`, `Tk_Alloc3DBorderFromObj`, `Tk_Get3DBorderFromObj`, and `Tk_Free3DBorderFromObj`. Widgets use `Tk_DrawFocusHighlight` to draw their focus highlight.

Mouse Cursors

Allocate a cursor with `Tk_GetCursor`, `Tk_GetCursorFromData`, `Tk_GetCursorFromObj`, and `Tk_AllocCursorFromObj`. Map back to the name of the cursor with `Tk_NameOfCursor`. Release the cursor resource with `Tk_FreeCursor` or `Tk_FreeCursorFromObj`.

Fonts and Text Display

Allocate a font with `Tk_GetFont`, `Tk_GetFontFromObj`, or `Tk_AllocFontFromObj`. Get the name of a font with `Tk_NameOfFont`. Release the font with `Tk_FreeFont` or `Tk_FreeFontFromObj`. Once you have a font, you can get information about it with `Tk_FontId`, `Tk_FontMetrics`, and `Tk_PostscriptFontName`. `Tk_MeasureChars`, `Tk_TextWidth`, `Tk_DrawChars`, and `Tk_UnderlineChars` measure and display simple strings. `Tk_ComputeTextLayout`, `Tk_FreeTextLayout`, `Tk_DrawTextLayout`, `Tk_UnderlineTextLayout`, `Tk_CharBbox`, `Tk_DistanceToTextLayout`, `Tk_PointToChar`, `Tk_IntersectTextLayout`, and `Tk_TextLayoutToPostscript` measure and display multiline, justified text.

Graphics Contexts

A graphics context records information about colors, fonts, line drawing styles, and so on. Instead of specifying this information on every graphics operation, a graphics context is created first. Individual graphics operations specify a particular graphic context. Allocate a graphics context with `Tk_GetGC` and free it with `Tk_FreeGC`.

Allocate a Pixmap

A pixmap is a simple color image. Allocate and free pixmaps with `Tk_GetPixmap` and `Tk_FreePixmap`.

Screen Measurements

Translate between strings like `4c` or `72p` and screen distances with `Tk_GetPixels`, `Tk_GetPixelsFromObj`, `Tk_GetMMFromObj`, and `Tk_GetScreenMM`. The first call returns pixels (integers); the second returns millimeters as a floating point number.

Relief Style

Window frames are drawn with a particular 3D relief such as raised, sunken, or grooved. Translate between relief styles and names with `Tk_GetRelief`, `Tk_GetReliefFromObj`, and `Tk_NameOfRelief`.

Text Anchor Positions

Anchor positions specify the position of a window within its geometry parcel. Translate between strings and anchor positions with `Tk_GetAnchor`, `Tk_GetAnchorFromObj`, and `Tk_NameOfAnchor`.

VI. Tcl and C

Line Cap Styles

The line cap defines how the end point of a line is drawn. Translate between line cap styles and names with `Tk_GetCapStyle` and `Tk_NameOfCapStyle`.

Line Join Styles

The line join style defines how the junction between two line segments is drawn. Translate between line join styles and names with `Tk_GetJoinStyle` and `Tk_NameOfJoinStyle`.

Text Justification Styles

Translate between line justification styles and names with `Tk_GetJustify`, `Tk_GetJustifyFromObj`, and `Tk_NameOfJustify`.

Atoms

An atom is an integer that references a string that has been registered with the system. Tk maintains a cache of the atom registry to avoid contacting the system when atoms are used. Use `Tk_InternAtom` to install an atom in the registry, and `Tk_GetAtomName` to return the name given an atom.

X Resource ID Management

Each window system resource like a color or pixmap has a resource ID associated with it. The `Tk_FreeXId` call releases an ID so it can be reused. This is used, for example, by routines like `Tk_FreeColor` and `Tk_FreePixmap`.

PART VII

Changes

Part VII describes the changes between versions of Tcl and Tk.

Chapter 48 has notes about porting your scripts to Tcl 7.4 and Tk 4.0. Chapter 49 describes changes in Tcl 7.5 and Tk 4.1. Chapter 50 describes changes in Tcl 7.6 and Tk 4.2. The Tcl and Tk version numbers were unified in the next release, Tcl/Tk 8.0, which is described in Chapter 51. New features added Tcl/Tk 8.1 are described in Chapter 52, and changes in Tcl/Tk 8.2 are described in Chapter 53.

Tcl/Tk 8.3 is in the planning stages as this book goes to press. An early view of these plans are presented in Chapter 54.

Tcl 7.4/Tk 4.0

This chapter has notes about upgrading your application to Tcl 7.4 and Tk 4.0 from earlier versions of Tk such as Tk 3.6. This includes notable new features that you may want to take advantage of as well as things that need to be fixed because of incompatible changes.

*P*orting your scripts from any of the Tk version 3 releases is easy. Not that many things have changed. The sections in this chapter summarize what has changed in Tk 4.0 and what some of the new commands are.

wish

The *wish* shell no longer requires a `-file` (or `-f`) argument, so you can drop this from your script header lines. This flag is still valid but no longer necessary.

The class name of the application is set from the name of the script file instead of always being `Tk`. If the script is `/usr/local/bin/foobar`, then the class is set to `Foobar`, for example.

Obsolete Features

Several features that were replaced in previous versions are now completely unsupported.

The variable that contains the version number is `tk_version`. The ancient (version 1) `tkVersion` is no longer supported.

Button widgets no longer have `activate` and `deactivate` operations. Instead, configure their `state` attribute.

Menus no longer have `enable` and `disable` operations. Instead, configure their `state` attribute.

The `cget` Operation

All widgets support a `cget` operation that returns the current value of the specified configuration option. The following two commands are equivalent:

```
lindex [$w config option] 4
$w cget option
```

Nothing breaks with this change, but you should enjoy this feature.

Input Focus Highlight

Each widget can have an input focus highlight, which is a border that is drawn in color when the widget has the input focus. This border is outside the border used to draw the 3D relief for widgets. It has the pleasant visual effect of providing a little bit of space around widgets, even when they do not have the input focus. The addition of the input focus highlight does not break anything, but it changes the appearance of your interfaces a little. In particular, the highlight on a canvas obscures objects that are at its edge. See page 529 for a description of the generic widget attributes related to the input focus highlight.

Bindings

The hierarchy of bindings has been fixed so that it is actually useful to define bindings at each of the global (i.e., `all`), class, and instance levels. The new `bindtags` command defines the order among these sources of binding information. You can also introduce new binding classes (e.g., `InsertMode`), and bind things to that class. Use the `bindtags` command to insert this class into the binding hierarchy. The order of binding classes in the `bindtags` command determines the order in which bindings are triggered. Use `break` in a binding command to stop the progression, or use `continue` to go on to the next level.

```
bindtags $w [list all Text InsertMode $w]
```

The various `Request` events have disappeared: `CirculateRequest`, `ConfigureRequest`, `MapRequest`, and `ResizeRequest`. The `Keymap` event is gone, too.

Extra modifier keys are ignored when matching events. Although you can still use the `Any` wild card modifier, it is no longer necessary. The `Alt` and `Meta` modifiers are set up in a general way so that they are associated with the `Alt_L`, `Alt_R`, `Meta_L`, and `Meta_R` keysyms.

Chapter 26 describes bindings starting at page 367.

Scrollbar Interface

The interface between scrollbars and the scrollable widgets has changed. Happily, the change is transparent to most scripts. If you hook your scrollbars to widgets in the straightforward way, the new interface is compatible. If you use the `xview` and `yview` widget commands directly, however, you might need to modify your code. The old interface still works, but there are new features of these operations that give you even better control. You can also query the view state, so you do not need to watch the scroll `set` commands to keep track of what is going on. Finally, scrollable widgets are constrained so that the end of their data remains stuck at the bottom (right) of their display. In most cases, nothing is broken by this change. Chapter 30 describes the scrollbar protocol starting at page 429.

pack info

Version 3 of Tk introduced a new syntax for the `pack` command, but the old syntax was still supported. This continues to be true in nearly all cases except the `pack info` command. If you are still using the old packer format, you should probably take this opportunity to convert to the new packer syntax.

The problem with `pack info` is that its semantics changed. The new operation used to be known as `pack newinfo`. In the old packer, `pack info` returned a list of all the slaves of a window and their packing configuration. Now `pack info` returns the packing configuration for a particular slave. You must first use the `pack slaves` command to get the list of all the slaves and then use the (new) `pack info` to get their configuration information. Chapter 23 describes the pack geometry manager starting at page 334.

Focus

The focus mechanism has been cleaned up to support different focus windows on different screens. The `focus` command takes a `-displayof` argument. Tk remembers which widget inside each toplevel has the focus. When the focus is given to a toplevel by the window manager, Tk automatically assigns focus to the right widget. The `-lastfor` argument queries which widget in a toplevel will get the focus by this means. Chapter 36 describes focus starting at page 516.

The `focus default` and `focus none` commands are no longer supported. There is no real need for `focus default` anymore, and `focus none` can be achieved by passing an empty string to the regular `focus` command.

The `tk_focusFollowsMouse` procedure changes from the default explicit focus model where a widget must claim the focus to one in which moving the mouse into a widget automatically gives it the focus.

The `tk_focusNext` and `tk_focusPrev` procedures implement keyboard traversal of the focus among widgets. Most widgets have bindings for `<Tab>` and `<Shift-Tab>` that cycle the focus among widgets.

The send Command

The send command has been changed so that it does not time out after five seconds but instead waits indefinitely for a response. Specify the -async option if you do not want to wait for a result. You can also specify an alternate display with the -displayof option. Chapter 40 describes send starting on page 560.

The name of an application can be set and queried with the new tk appname command. Use this instead of winfo name ".".

Because of the changes in the send implementation, it is not possible to use send between Tk 4.0 applications and earlier versions.

Internal Button Padding

Buttons and labels have new defaults for the amount of padding around their text. There is more padding now, so your buttons get bigger if you use the default padX and padY attributes. The old defaults were one pixel for both attributes. The new defaults are 3m for padX and 1m for padY, which map into three pixels and ten pixels on my display.

There is a difference between buttons and the other button-like widgets. An extra two pixels of padding is added, in spite of all padX and padY settings in the case of simple buttons. If you want your checkbuttons, radiobuttons, menubuttons, and buttons with all the same dimensions, you'll need two extra pixels of padding for everything but simple buttons.

Radiobutton Value

The default value for a radiobutton is no longer the name of the widget. Instead, it is an empty string. Make sure that you specify a -value option when setting up your radiobuttons.

Entry Widget

The scrollCommand attribute changed to xScrollCommand to be consistent with other widgets that scroll horizontally. The view operation changed to the xview operation for the same reason. Chapter 31 describes the entry widget starting on page 435.

The delete operation has changed the meaning of the second index so that the second index refers to the character immediately following the affected text. The selection operations have changed in a similar fashion. The sel.last index refers to the character immediately following the end of the selection, so deleting from sel.first to sel.last still works. The default bindings have been updated, of course, but if you have custom bindings, you must fix them.

Menus

The menu associated with a menubutton must be a child widget of the menubutton. Similarly, the menu for a cascade menu entry must be a child of the menu.

The @y index for a menu always returns a valid index, even if the mouse cursor is outside any entry. In this case, it simply returns the index of the closest entry, instead of none.

The selector attribute is now selectColor.

The postcascade operation posts the menu of a cascade entry:

```
$menu postcascade index
```

The insert operation adds a menu entry before a specified entry:

```
$menu insert index type options...
```

Chapter 27 describes menus starting at page 394.

Listboxes

Listboxes changed quite a bit in Tk 4.0. See Chapter 32 for all the details. There are now four Motif-like selection styles, and two of these support disjoint selections. The tk_listboxSingleSelect procedure no longer exists. Instead, configure the selectMode attribute of the listbox. A listbox has an active element, which is drawn with an underline. It is referenced with the active index keyword.

The selection commands for listboxes have changed. Change:

```
$listbox select from index1
$listbox select to index2
```

to:

```
$listbox select anchor index1
$listbox select set anchor index2
```

The set operation takes two indices, and anchor is a valid index, which typically corresponds to the start of a selection.

You can selectively clear the selection and query whether there is a selection in the listbox. The command to clear the selection has changed. It requires one or two indices. Change:

```
$listbox select clear
```

to:

```
$listbox select clear 0 end
```

No geometry Attribute

The frame, toplevel, and listbox widgets no longer have a geometry attribute. Use the width and height attributes instead. The geometry attribute was confused with geometry specifications for top-level windows. The use of `width` and `height` is more consistent. Note that for listboxes the `width` and `height` are in terms of lines and characters, while for frames and toplevels, they are in screen units.

Text Widget

The tags and marks of the text widgets have been cleaned up a bit, justification and spacing are supported, variable tab stops can be defined, and you can embed widgets in the text display.

A mark now has a gravity — either left or right — that determines what happens when characters are inserted at the mark. With right gravity you get the old behavior: The mark gets pushed along by the inserted text by sticking to the right-hand character. With left gravity it remains stuck. The default is right gravity. The `mark gravity` operation changes it.

When text is inserted, it picks up only tags that are present on both sides of the insert point. Previously it would inherit the tags from the character to the left of the insert mark. You can also override this default behavior by supplying tags to the insert operation.

The widget scan operation supports horizontal scrolling. Instead of using marks like `@y`, you need a mark like `@x,y`.

For a description of the new features, see Chapter 33.

Color Attributes

Table 48–1 lists the names of the color attributes that changed. These attributes are described in more detail in Chapter 38 starting at page 534.

Table 48–1   Changes in color attribute names.

Tk 3.6	Tk4.0
selector	selectColor
Scrollbar.activeForeground	Scrollbar.activeBackground
Scrollbar.background	troughColor
Scrollbar.foreground	Scrollbar.background
Scale.activeForeground	Scale.activeBackground
Scale.background	troughColor
Scale.sliderForeground	Scale.background
(did not exist)	highlightBackground
(did not exist)	highlightColor

Color Allocation and `tk colormodel`

In Tk 3.6, color allocations could fail if the colormap was full. In this case, Tk would revert its colormodel to monochrome and use only black and white. The `tk colormodel` command was used to query or set the colormodel. In Tk 4.0, color allocations do not fail. Instead, the closest possible color is allocated. Because of this, the `tk colormodel` operation is no longer supported. Use the `winfo visual` command, which is described on page 538, to find out the characteristics of your display.

Canvas `scrollincrement`

The canvas widget changed the `scrollIncrement` attribute to a pair of attributes: `xScrollIncrement` and `yScrollIncrement`. The default for these is now one-tenth the width (height) of the canvas instead of one pixel. Scrolling by one page scrolls by nine-tenths of the canvas display.

The Selection

The selection support has been generalized in Tk 4.0 to allow use of other selections such as the `CLIPBOARD` and `SECONDARY` selections. The changes do not break anything, but you should check out the new `clipboard` command. Some other toolkits, notably OpenLook, can paste data only from the clipboard. Chapter 35 describes the selection starting at page 505.

The `bell` Command

The `bell` command rings the bell associated with the terminal. You need to use the *xset* program to modify the parameters of the bell such as volume and duration. This command is described on page 426.

Tcl 7.5/Tk 4.1

Tk 4.1 is notable for its cross-platform support. Your Tk scripts can run on
Windows, Macintosh, and UNIX. The associated Tcl release, 7.5, saw
significant changes in event-driven I/O, network sockets, and multiple
interpreters.

Cross-platform support, network sockets,
multiple Tcl interpreters, and an enhanced `foreach` command are the highlights
of Tcl 7.5 and Tk 4.1.

Cross-Platform Scripts

Cross-platform support lets a Tcl/Tk script run unchanged on UNIX, Windows,
and Macintosh. However, you can still have platform dependencies in your program. The most obvious dependency is if your script executes other programs or
uses C-level extensions. These need to be ported for your script to continue to
work.

File Name Manipulation

File naming conventions vary across platforms. New file operations were
added to help you manipulate file names in a platform-independent manner.
These are the `file join`, `file split`, and `file pathtype` operations, which are
described on page 103. Additional commands to copy, delete, and rename files
were added in Tcl 7.6

Newline Translations

Windows and Macintosh have different conventions for representing the end of line in files. These differences are handled automatically by the new I/O subsystem. However, you can use the new `fconfigure` command described on page 221 to control the translations.

The `tcl_platform` Variable

In practice you may need a small amount of platform-specific code. The `tcl_platform` array holds information about the computer and operating system that your script is running on. This array is described on page 182. You can use a script file with the name of the platform to isolate all your platform-specific code. The following command sources either `unix.tcl`, `windows.tcl`, or `macintosh.tcl` from your script library:

```
source [file join $lib $tcl_platform(platform).tcl]
```

The `console` Command

The Windows and Macintosh versions of *wish* have a built-in console. The commands you enter in the console are evaluated in the main Tcl interpreter, but the console is really implemented in another Tcl interpreter to avoid conflicts. You can show and hide the console with the `console` command, which is described on page 28.

The `clock` Command

The `clock` command eliminates the need to `exec date` to get the time of day in Tcl. The equivalent is:

```
clock format [clock seconds]
```

The `format` operation takes an optional format string that lets you control the date and time string. There is also `clock scan` to parse clock values, and `clock clicks` to get high resolution clock values. The `clock` command is described on page 173.

The `load` Command

The `load` command supports shared libraries (i.e., DLLs) that implement new Tcl commands in compiled code. With this feature, the preferred way to package extensions is as a shared library. This eliminates the need to compile custom versions of *wish* if you use extensions. The details about creating shared libraries are described on page 607. For example, you could load the `Tix` library with:

```
load libtix.so Tix
```

The `info` command added two related operations, `sharedlibextention` and `nameofexecutable`, which are described on page 182.

The package Command

The package command provides an alternate way to organize script libraries. It also supports extensions that are added with the load command. The package command supports a provide/require model where packages are provided by scripts in a library, and your application specifies what it needs with package require commands. The package facility supports multiple versions of a package, if necessary. Packages are described on page 163.

Multiple foreach loop variables

This is one of my favorite features. The foreach command supports multiple loop variables and multiple value lists. This means that you can assign values to multiple variables during each loop iteration. The values can come from the same list or from lists that are processed in parallel. Multiple foreach loop variables are described on page 75. For example, you can iterate through the contents of an array with:

```
foreach {name value} [array get arrName] {
    # arrName($name) is $value
}
```

Event Loop Moves from Tk to Tcl

To support network sockets, the event loop was moved from Tk to Tcl. This means that the after and update commands are now part of Tcl. The fileevent command was added to support nonblocking I/O. The vwait command was added to Tcl and is equivalent to the tkwait variable command. Event-driven I/O is described in Chapter 16 starting on page 217.

The tkerror command has been replaced by bgerror. This is the procedure that is called when an error occurs while processing an event. Backwards compatibility is provided if you already define tkerror. These procedures are described on page 190.

Network Sockets

The socket command provides access to TCP/IP sockets. There are C APIs to define new *channels*, and there are extensions that provide UDP and other protocols. Chapter 17 describes sockets starting on page 226. Example 40–4 on page 565 uses sockets as a replacement for the Tk send command.

VII. Changes

```
info hostname
```

The `info hostname` command was added to find out your host identifier.

The `fconfigure` Command

The best way to use sockets is with event-driven I/O. The `fileevent` command provides part of the solution. You also need to be able to control the blocking behavior and buffering modes of sockets. The `fconfigure` command lets you do this and more. You can also control the newline translation modes and query socket-specific settings. The `fconfigure` command is described on page 221.

Multiple Interpreters and Safe-Tcl

Chapter 19 describes the new `interp` command and the Safe-Tcl security mechanism. You can create multiple Tcl interpreters in your application and control them with the `interp` command. You create command aliases so that the interpreters can exchange Tcl commands. If an interpreter is created in a safe mode, then its set of Tcl commands is restricted so that its scripts cannot harm your computer or application. However, with aliases you can give the untrusted scripts limited access to resources.

The `grid` Geometry Manager

Chapter 24 describes the new `grid` geometry manager that provides a table-like metaphor for arranging widgets. Like `pack`, `grid` is constraint-based, so the grid automatically adjusts if widgets change size or if widgets are added and deleted. The `grid` command was influenced by the `blt_table` geometry manager, but it is a whole new implementation.

The Text Widget

Several new operations were added to the text widget. The `dump` operation provides a way to get all the information out of the widget, including information about tags, marks, and embedded windows. The `mark next` and `mark previous` operations let you search for marks. The `tag prevrange` is the complement of the existing `tag nextrange` operation.

The Entry Widget

The `bbox` operation was added to the entry widget. This is used to refine the bindings that do character selection and set the input cursor.

C H A P T E R **50**

Tcl 7.6/Tk 4.2

Tk 4.2 saw improvements in its cross-platform support., including virtual events, additions to the `file` command, improvements to the `exec` command on Windows, and the addition of common dialogs for choosing colors and selecting files. The `grid` geometry manager was rebuilt to improve its layout algorithm.

Grid saw a major rewrite for Tk 4.2 to improve its layout algorithm. Cross-platform scripts were enhanced by the addition of standard dialogs and virtual events. Tcl 7.6 saw improvements in `exec` and pipelines on Windows. The Macintosh version got a significant performance boost from a new memory allocator.

More `file` Operations

The `file` command was rounded out with `copy`, `rename`, `delete`, and `mkdir` operations. These operations are described on page 105.

Virtual Events

The new `event` command defines virtual events like `<<Cut>>` `<<Copy>>` and `<<Paste>>`. These virtual events map to different physical events on different platforms. For example, `<<Copy>>` is `<Control-c>` on Windows and `<Command-c>` on Macintosh. You can write your scripts in terms of virtual events, and you can define new virtual events for your application. You can also use the `event` command to generate events for testing purposes. Virtual events and the `event` command are described starting at page 378.

Standard Dialogs

Several standard dialogs were added to Tk. These let you display alerts, prompt the user, choose colors, and select files using dialogs that are implemented in native look for each platform. For example, to ask the user a yes/no question:

```
tk_messageBox -type yesno \
    -message "Ok to proceed?" \
    -icon question
=> yes
```

To open an existing file:

```
set file [tk_getOpenFile]
```

The standard dialogs are described in Chapter 36 starting at page 513.

New `grid` Geometry Manager

The `grid` geometry manager was overhauled to improve its layout algorithm, and there were several user-visible changes. The weights on rows and columns that affect resize behavior were changed from floating point values to integers. A `-pad` row and column attribute was added to provide padding for a whole row or column. The `columnconfigure` and `rowconfigure` operations now return the current settings if given no arguments. There are two new `grid` operations. The `update` operation forces an update of the grid layout. The `remove` operation removes a widget from the grid but remembers all its grid settings, so it is easy to put it back into the grid later.

Macintosh `unsupported1` Command

The `unsupported1` command provides access to different window styles on the Macintosh. If supported, it might be a `style` operation in the `wm` command, but it is Macintosh-specific, so it is not fully supported. However, you can use it to get several different styles of Macintosh windows. This command is described on page 417.

Tcl/Tk 8.0

Tcl 8.0 includes an on-the-fly byte code compiler that improves performance of scripts from two to 20 times depending on what commands they use. The Tk version number was set to match Tcl. Tk 8.0 uses native buttons, menus, menubars, and scrollbars. Font objects allow flexible font handling in a platform-independent way.

Tcl 8.0 added a byte-code compiler that improves performance dramatically. The compiler is transparent to Tcl scripts, so you do not have to do anything special to take advantage of it. The other main addition to Tcl is support of binary data. It is now safe to read binary data into Tcl variables, and new commands convert between strings and binary representations.

Tk 8.0 has native look and feel on UNIX, Windows, and Macintosh. This is due to native buttons, native menus, native scrollbars, and a new cross-platform menu bar facility. A new cross-platform font facility improves the font support. Tk also has support for application embedding, which is used in the Web browser plug-in described in Chapter 20.

The Tcl Compiler

The Tcl Compiler is an *on-the-fly* compiler that is virtually transparent to Tcl scripts. The compiler translates a script to byte codes the first time it evaluates it. If the script is evaluated again, such as in a loop or in a procedure body, then the byte codes are executed and the translation step is saved. If a procedure is redefined, then the compiler discards any translated byte codes for it.

The compiler uses a dual-ported object model instead of the simple string-based model used in earlier versions of Tcl. The dual-ported objects hold a string value and a native representation of that string such as an integer, double-precision floating point value, or compiler byte codes. This makes it possible to save translations between strings and the native representations. The object model is described in Chapter 44 starting at page 613.

The performance improvement for your application will depend on what features you use. Math expressions and list accesses are much faster. Overall you should expect a factor of 2 speedup, and I have heard reports of 10 and 20 times improvement in parts of some applications.

Compile-Time Errors

The compiler catches some sorts of errors earlier than the pure interpreted version. The first time a compiler runs a procedure, it translates the whole thing to byte codes first. If there are syntax errors at the end of the procedure, it prevents any code in the procedure from running.

A similar problem occurs with list data. If a string is not a perfect list, then the list commands will fail when parsing it, even if they do not use the damaged part of the list. For example, `lindex` used to process only enough of a list to find the requested element. In Tcl 8.0 the whole list is converted into a native representation. Errors at the end of a list will prevent you from getting elements at the beginning. This is mainly an issue when you use list operations on arbitrary input data.

Binary String Support

Tcl now supports binary data. This means that an embedded NULL byte no longer terminates a value. Instead, Tcl keeps a byte count for its string objects. This is facilitated by the switch from simple strings to dual-ported objects.

The `binary format` and `binary scan` commands support conversions between binary data and strings. These are described on page 54. The `unsupported0` command was improved and became the `fcopy` command, which is described on page 237.

Namespaces

Chapter 14 describes the Tcl namespace facility that partitions the global scope for variables and procedures. Namespaces are optional. Simple scripts can avoid them, but larger applications can use them for structuring. Library packages should also use namespaces to facility code sharing without conflict.

Safe-Tcl

Hidden commands were added to the Safe-Tcl security model. Instead of removing unsafe commands from an interpreter, the commands are hidden. The master can invoke hidden commands inside a slave. This is necessary so that the command sees the correct context. This adds new operations to the interp command: invokehidden, hide, expose, and hidden. Hidden commands are described on page 279.

Initialization of a safe interpreter with a *safe base* that supports auto loading and a standard exit alias has been abstracted into a Tcl interface. The safe::interpCreate and safe::interpInit procedures create or initialize a slave with the safe base. The safe::interpDelete procedure cleans up. The safe base is described on page 282.

To support the Trusted security policy, the interp marktrusted command was added. This promotes an unsafe interpreter back into a trusted one. Of course, only the master can do this.

New lsort

The lsort command was reimplemented. The new implementation is reentrant, which means that you can use lsort inside a sorting function called by lsort. New options have lessened the need for custom sorting procedures, too. The -dictionary option sorts cases together, and it handles numbers better. The -index option sorts lists on a key field. These are described on page 65.

tcl_precision Variable

The tcl_precision variable was removed in the 8.0p2 release and added back in the 8.0.3 release. Its default value was increased from 6 to 12, which should be enough for most applications.

Year 2000 Convention

The clock command now implements the following standard convention for two-digit year names:

70–99 map to 1970–1999.
00–69 map to 2000–2069.

Actually, the ability to parse a date value after 2037 and before 1903 may be limited on your system by the size of an integer (e.g., 32-bits) and the clock *epoch*, which is January 1, 1970 on Windows and most UNIX systems.

Http Package

A Tcl implementation of the HTTP/1.0 protocol was added to the Tcl script library. The http::geturl command is described on page 238.

Serial Line I/O

Support for serial line devices was added to `fconfigure`. The `-mode` argument specifies the baud rate, parity setting, and the number of data and stop bits. The `-mode` option to `fconfigure` is described on page 224.

Windows has some special device names that always connect you to the serial line devices when you use `open`. They are `com1` and `com2`. UNIX has names for serial devices in `/dev`. Interactive applications can open the current terminal with `/dev/tty`.

As of this writing, there is no way to open serial devices on the Macintosh. I expect a new `serial` command for this purpose, or possibly a flag to `open`.

Platform-Independent Fonts

A platform-independent font-naming system was added in Tk 8.0. Names like `times 10 bold` are interpreted on all platforms. The `font` command lets you create font objects that can be associated with widgets. The `font metrics` command returns detailed size information. The `font` command is described on page 552.

The `tk scaling` Command

The `tk scaling` command queries or sets the mapping from pixels to points. Points are used with fonts, and points and other screen measures are used in the canvas. The `tk scaling` command is described on page 580.

Application Embedding

Tk supports application embedding. Frames and toplevels have a `-container` attribute that indicates that they embed another application. This is necessary for geometry management and focus protocols. Frames and toplevels have a `-use` parameter that embeds them into an existing window. *Wish* also takes a `-use` command-line argument. Embedding is described on pages 417 and 294.

Native Menus and Menubars

Tk 8.0 has a native menubar mechanism. You define a menu and associate it with a toplevel. On the Macintosh, this menu appears along the top of the screen when the window is activated. On Windows and UNIX, the menubar appears along the top of the window. This facility is described on page 395.

Tear-off menus now track any changes to the menu they were created from. As part of this, the `-transient` attribute was replaced with a `-type` attribute.

You can create multicolumn menus with the `-columnbreak` attribute.

CDE Border Width

On UNIX, the default border width changed from two to one to match the CDE look and feel.

Native Buttons and Scrollbars

Buttons, menus, and scrollbars are native widgets on Windows and Macintosh. This goes a long way to providing your applications with a native look. The bindings on the text and entry widgets were also tuned to match platform standard bindings. See page 330 for an example of the same Tk program on all platforms.
    Buttons on all platforms support a `-default` attribute, which has three values: `active`, `normal`, and `disabled`. The `active` state displays like a default button. The `normal` state displays like a regular button, but leaves room for the highlight used in the `active` state. The `disabled` state, which is the default, may be smaller. You still need to program a key binding that invokes the button.

Images in Text Widgets

The text widget supports embedded images. They work much like the embedded windows but provide a more efficient way to embed images. These are described on page 464.

No Errors from `destroy`

The `destroy` command used to raise an error if the window did not exist. Now it does not.

`grid rowconfigure`

The `grid columnconfigure` and `rowconfigure` commands take an argument that specifies a row or column. This value can be a list:

```
grid columnconfigure {0 3} -weight 1
```

The Patch Releases

There was a hiatus in the development of the 8.0 release as John Ousterhout left Sun Microsystems to form Scriptics Corporation. The 8.0p2 release was made in the fall of 1997, about the same time the first alpha release of 8.1 was made. Almost a year later, there were a series of patch releases: 8.0.3, 8.0.4, and 8.0.5, which were made in conjunction with releases of the *TclPro* development tools. The main changes in these patch releases were in C APIs, which were added to support *TclPro Wrapper* and *TclPro Compiler*. These tools are introduced on page

189. There were only a few changes after 8.0p2 that were visible to Tcl script writers, and these are documented here.

fconfigure -error

The `fconfigure -error` option was added so that you can find out whether or not an asynchronous socket connection attempt has failed. It returns an empty string if the connection completed successfully. Otherwise, it returns the error message.

tcl_platform(debug)

A new element was added to the `tcl_platform` variable to indicate that Tcl was compiled with debugging symbols. The motivation for this is the fact that a Windows application compiled with debugging symbols cannot safely load a DLL that has been compiled without debugging symbols. Similarly, an application compiled without debugging symbols cannot safely load a DLL that does have debugging symbols. The problem is an artifact of the Microsoft C runtime library.

When you build Tcl DLLs with debugging symbols their name has a trailing "d", such as `tcl80d.dll` instead of `tcl80.dll`. By testing `tcl_platform(debug)`, a savvy application can attempt to load a matching DLL.

tcl_findLibrary

The `tcl_findLibrary` procedure was added to help extensions find their script library directory. This is used by Tk and other extensions. The big picture is that Tcl has a complex search path that it uses to find its own script library. It searches relative to the location of *tclsh* or *wish* and assumes a standard installation or a standard build environment. The search supports sites that have several Tcl installations and helps extensions find their correct script library. The usage of `tcl_findLibrary` is:

```
tcl_findLibrary base version patch script enVar varName
```

The *base* is the prefix of the script library directory name. The *version* is the main version number (e.g., "8.0"). The *patch* is the full patch level (e.g., "8.0.3"). The *script* is the initialization script to source from the directory. The *enVar* names an environment variable that can be used to override the default search path. The *varName* is an output parameter that is set to the name of the directory found by `tcl_findLibrary`. A side effect of `tcl_findLibrary` is to source the script from the directory. An example call is:

```
tcl_findLibrary tk 8.0 8.0.3 tk.tcl TK_LIBRARY tk_library
```

`tcl_findLibrary` is described on page 170.

`auto_mkindex_old`

The `auto_mkindex` procedure was reimplemented by Michael McLennan to support [incr Tcl] classes and methods. This changed the semantics somewhat so that all procedures are always indexed. Previously, only procedures defined with the word "proc" starting at the beginning of a line were indexed. The new implementation sources code into a safe interpreter and watches for `proc` commands however they are executed, not how they are typed into the source file. The old version of `auto_mkindex` was saved as `auto_mkindex_old` for those applications that used the trick of indenting procedure definitions to hide them from the indexing process.

Windows Keysyms for Start and Menu Keys

The Microsoft keyboards have special keys that bring up the Start menu and trigger menu traversal. New keysyms `App`, `Menu_L`, and `Menu_R` were added for these keys.

The `MouseWheel` Event

The `MouseWheel` event was added to support the scrolling wheel built into Microsoft mice. There is a `%d` event parameter that gets replaced with a positive or negative number to indicate relative scrolling motion.

Transparent Fill on Canvas Text

Canvas text items now honor the convention that an empty `fill` attribute turns them transparent. This convention was previously implemented for all other canvas item types. This feature makes it easy to hide items with:

```
$canvas itemconfigure item -fill ""
```

`safe::loadTk`

This procedure was extended to take a `-display` *displayname* argument so that you can control where the main window of the safe interpreter is created. Its `-use` argument was extended to take either window IDs or Tk window pathnames.

Tcl/Tk 8.1

Tcl/Tk 8.1 features Unicode support for internationalization, thread safety, and
a new regular expression package.

Tcl 8.1 should probably have been
called Tcl 9.0. The internal changes required to support Unicode caused a major
overhaul that touched nearly the entire implementation. At the same time, the
code base was cleaned up so that it could be used in multithreaded environments, and it added a platform-independent dynamic loading facility (i.e., stub
libraries). Finally, an all new regular expression package was added thanks to
Henry Spencer. This package brings Advanced Regular Expressions to Tcl, which
are already familiar to Perl programmers. However, in spite of all these changes,
scripts written for earlier versions of Tcl are very compatible with Tcl 8.1.

Unicode and Internationalization

The effect of Unicode on Tcl scripts is actually very limited. There is a new backslash sequence, \u*XXXX*, that specifies a 16-bit Unicode character. There are also
facilities to work with character set encodings and message catalogs.

fconfigure -encoding

The Tcl I/O system supports character set translations. It automatically
converts files to Unicode when it reads them in, and it converts them to the
native system encoding during output. The `fconfigure -encoding` option can be
used to specify alternate encodings for files. This option is described on page 209.

The encoding Command

The encoding command provides access to the basic encoding mechanism used in Tcl. The encoding convertfrom and convertto operations convert strings between different encodings. The encoding system operation queries and sets the encoding used by the operating system. The encoding command is described on page 212.

The msgcat Package

Message catalogs are implemented by the msgcat package, which is described on page 216. A message catalog stores translations of user messages into other languages. Tcl makes message catalogs easy to use.

UTF-8 and Unicode C API

The effects of Unicode on the Tcl C API is more fundamental. Tcl uses UTF-8 to represent Unicode internally. This encoding is compatible with ASCII, so Tcl extensions that pass only ASCII strings to Tcl continue to work normally. However, to take advantage of Unicode, Tcl extensions need to translate strings into UTF-8 or Unicode before calling the Tcl C library. There is a C API for this. An example of its use is shown on page 627.

Thread Safety

The Tcl C library is thread-safe. This means that you can use Tcl in an application that uses threads. The threading model for Tcl is a thread can have one or more Tcl interpreters, but a Tcl interpreter cannot be used by different threads. For communication between threads, Tcl provides the ability to send Tcl scripts to an interpreter in another thread. You can also create an extension that implements shared data and does its own locking.

The Tcl C library provides mutex variables, condition variables, and thread local storage. These primitives are used by Tcl internally, and they are meant to be used by Tcl extensions to serialize access to their own data structures. The Tcl library allows different implementations of the threading primitives. This is done to support Unix, Windows, and Macintosh. Tcl uses native threads on Windows, and Posix pthreads on Unix. MacOS does not have true threads, so it is easy to provide the required thread API.

The testthread Command

Tcl 8.2 does not export threads to the script level, except through the testthread testing command. Instead of adding this to the Tcl core, this command will become an extension that is distributed along with Tcl. You can try out testthread by compiling the *tcltest* program instead of the regular *tclsh* shell.

Table 52–1 describes the `testthread` operations, which are implemented in the `generic/tclThreadTest.c` file. These operations are likely to be similar to those of the API provided by the more general threading extension, but you should check the documentation associated with that extension for more details.

Table 52–1 The `testthread` command.

`testthread create` `?script?`	Creates a new thread and a Tcl interpreter. Runs `script` after creating the Tcl interpreter. If no `script` is specified, the new thread waits with `testthread wait`.
`testthread id`	Returns the thread ID of the current thread.
`testthread errorproc proc`	Registers `proc` as a handler for errors from other threads. If they terminate with a Tcl error, this procedure is called with the error message and `errorInfo` values as arguments. Otherwise, a message is printed to `stderr`.
`testthread exit`	Terminates the current thread.
`testthread names`	Returns a list of thread IDs.
`testthread send id` `?-async? script`	Sends a script to another thread for evaluation. If `-async` is specified, the command does not wait for the result.
`testthread wait`	Enters the event loop. This is used by worker threads to wait for scripts to arrive for evaluation. Threads can also use `vwait` for this purpose.

Advanced Regular Expressions

An all new regular expression implementation supports Unicode and *Advanced Regular Expressions*, which are described in detail in Chapter 11. The new regular expression syntax has been added in a way that is compatible with earlier versions of regular expressions. There are also new `regexp` and `regsub` command options to control the new regular expression engine.

New String Commands

The string command was enhanced with several new operations that include string classification operations (`string is`), character string mappings (`string map`), title case conversion (`string totitle`), an easier-to-use equality test (`string equal`), and new string manipulation commands (`string repeat` and `string replace`). The `-nocase` and `-length` options have been added to commands like `string compare` and `string tolower`. These additions are listed in Table 4–1 on page 46 and explained in more detail in Chapter 4. Note: These only appeared in the Tcl 8.1.1 patch release.

The DDE Extension

Dynamic Data Exchange (DDE) is a communication protocol used among Windows applications. The protocol exchanges data with a server identified by name. Each service implements a number of operations known as *topics*. The data exchange can be synchronous or asynchronous. The dde command is implemented as an extension that is distributed with Tcl. You must use package require dde to load the extension. Table 52–2 summarizes the dde command.

Table 52–2 The dde command options.

dde servername ?*topic*?	Registers the current process as a DDE service with name TclEval and the given *topic*. If *topic* is not specified, this command returns the currently registered topic.
dde ?-async? execute service topic data	Sends *data* to the *service* with the given *topic*.
dde ?-async? eval topic cmd ?arg ...?	Sends *cmd* and its arguments to the TclEval service with the given *topic*. This is an alternative to the Tk send command.
dde ?-async? poke service topic data	Similar to the execute operation, but some services export operations under poke instead of execute.
dde ?-async? request service topic item	Fetches the named *item* from the *service* with the given *topic*.
dde services *server topic*	Returns *server* and *topic* if that server currently exists; otherwise, it returns the empty string.
dde services *server* {}	Returns all the topics implemented by *server*.
dde services {} *topic*	Returns all servers that implement *topic*.
dde services {} {}	Returns all server, topic registrations.

Miscellaneous

Serial Line I/O

The Windows serial line drivers were converted to use threads, so you can wait for I/O with fileevent when using serial devices. There is no API change here, but this was a limitation on Windows that was annoying in previous Tcl releases.

tcl_platform(user)

The tcl_platform(user) array element records the currently logged in user. This masks differences in environment variables and system calls used to get this information on different platforms.

Tcl/Tk 8.2

Tcl 8.2 is primarily a bug fix and stabilization release. This release is recommended instead of Tcl 8.1.

Tcl 8.2 adds almost no new features at the Tcl script level. Instead, it adds a few new C APIs that enable some interesting extensions to be added without having to modify the core Tcl distribution. At the same time, Scriptics focused on the outstanding bug reports in order to make the 8.2 release as stable as possible.

The Trf Patch

Andreas Kupries contributed a mechanism that allows I/O channel processing modules to be stacked onto open I/O channels. This adds a new `Tcl_StackChannel` C API, but there are no changes visible at the Tcl script level. However, it enables several interesting extensions such as compression and encryption (e.g., SSL) to be added to Tcl. Andreas has an extension that exports the channel filter mechanism to the Tcl script level. This is used primarily for testing, but you can also use it for script-level data filters.

Faster String Operations

The UTF-8 encoding has the drawback that characters are not all the same size: They are either one, two, or three bytes in length. The variable-sized characters make operations like `string length`, `string index`, and `string range` quite slow in comparison to a system that uses fixed-sized characters. A new Unicode string type, which uses 16-bit characters, was added to support faster string operations. This change does not cause any changes that are visible to Tcl scripts, except for improved performance in comparison to Tcl 8.1.

Empty Array Names

Perhaps the only change in Tcl 8.2 visible to Tcl scripts is support for empty array names. This is a quirk you can get by using name spaces or `upvar`, but it was previously difficult to use directly. For example, the syntax `$::foo::(item)` references an array. That worked in any version of Tcl that supported namespaces. However, in Tcl 8.2 you can also use `$(item)` directly, which implies that the array name is the empty string. This trick is exploited by Jean-Luc Fontain's *STOOOP* object-oriented extension.

Browser Plugin Compatibility

The Web Browser plugin requires changes to the event loop mechanism because Tcl is embedded in an application with its own event loop. While the C APIs have supported alternate event loops since Tcl 8.0.3, it has been difficult to do this sort of embedding without recompiling Tcl. The `Tcl_SetNotifier` API was added to support embedding a "stock" Tcl interpreter.

## CHAPTER 54

Tcl/Tk 8.3

This chapter provides a look ahead at the next Tcl release.

Tcl 8.3 is already in the planning stages as this book goes to press. The overall theme of 8.3 is to continue the incorporation of contributed patches, especially for Tk. Jan Nijtmans's dash and image patches have many handy features such as dashed lines on the canvas, improved image support, and more. These additions will be added in a compatible way. In many cases, a patch only makes small changes to the Tcl or Tk core library that enables a more sophisticated extension to be loaded without changing the core. The long-term goal for Tcl/Tk is that interesting additions can be made as extensions that do not require changes to the Tcl core. Many extensions are available today: You can find them on the Web at:

```
http://www.scriptics.com/resource/
```

However, some changes require changes to Tcl/Tk itself. If you are interested in contributing to the continued improvement of Tcl/Tk, you can help. Contributions should be made via the Scriptics Web site at:

```
http://www.scriptics.com/support/bugForm.html
```

All bug reports and patch submissions are logged in a database. Source code patches that are made according to the Tcl Engineering Manual guidelines have the most chance of adoption. These guidelines describe code appearance (e.g., indentation), test suite requirements, and documentation requirements.

Note: the changes proposed in this chapter are not guaranteed to actually appear in Tcl/Tk 8.3! These features are on the short list proposed by Jeff Hobbs, but the final contents of 8.3 will be a trade-off between features, effort, and schedule.

Proposed Tcl Changes

Octal Numbers

Invalid octal numbers (e.g., 08) have long been cause for confusion. The error message will be improved to alert users that a leading zero implies an octal number, which cannot contain digits eight or nine.

We are considering a new way to specify decimal numbers, probably `\0dXXX`, that will force interpretation of *XXX* as decimal, even if it has leading zeros.

`file channels`

The `file channels` command will return a list of open I/O channels, which can be sockets, regular files, or channels created by extensions. It will take an optional pattern argument (e.g., `sock*`) to constrain the list.

Changing File Modify Times

Either a new command, `file touch`, or a change to `file attributes -mtime` option will be made to let you change the modification date on a file.

`regsub -subst or -command`

The combination of `regsub` and `subst` is so powerful, we want to make it perform even better. The `-subst` option to `regsub` will run `subst` over the result of `regsub`, but only over the parts that were generated by `regsub`. The input data that is not matched by `regsub` is untouched by the subsequent `subst`. This can eliminate the need to quote special Tcl characters in input, which takes extra regsub passes. The `-command` option passes the replacement string to a command before substitution into the result. You can achieve similar effects with both `-subst` and `-command`, so we may only implement one option.

A `-start` option will be added to `regsub` and `regexp`. This indicates a starting offset into the string being matched.

New `glob` options

The `-dir`, `-join`, `-path`, and `-types` options may be added to glob to make it easier to manipulate directories in a platform-independent manner.

Internationalization

There are still some improvements that can be made in internationalization support, especially with respect to input methods.

Proposed Tk Changes

The Img Patch

The `Img` patch adds an alpha channel, better transparency support, and improved GIF support, including the ability to save GIF images. This patch also supports other image types (e.g., JPEG) that can be loaded as extensions.

Canvas Improvements

The canvas implementation needs to be converted to use `Tcl_Obj` values, which will improve its performance. Advanced tag searching may be added. This adds the ability to search for canvas items based on boolean expressions of tag values. Dashed lines will be added, even though we can support only single-pixel wide dashed lines on Windows 95. Windows NT, UNIX, and Macintosh can support thick dashed lines. Canvas coordinates may be specified as a single list argument instead of individual arguments, which makes it easier to construct commands. The "Visitors Patch" may be adopted, so that extensions can add new canvas operations without patching Tk directly.

Pointer Warping

Tk applications will have the ability to move the mouse under program control. Use the `wm warp` command:

```
wm warp x y
```

Hidden Text

We may add a new tag property that suppresses text display. This feature is used by the popular *TkMan* manual page browser.

Entry Widget Validation

New options may be added to the entry widget for input validation. The options specify command callbacks that are made at various times, such as when the entry widget takes input focus, loses input focus, or has its value change. The commands are subject to `%` keyword substitution similar to the substitutions in event bindings. The keywords are used to get the name of the entry widget (e.g., `%W`), the character that is being added, and so forth.

About The CD-ROM

This chapter describes what is available on the CD-ROM.

The CD-ROM contains the Tcl/Tk software distributions, the examples from the book, and a collection of Tcl-related software found on the Internet. The CD is one volume in a hybrid format that is readable on UNIX (ISO 9660 format with Rock Ridge extensions), Windows (Juliet format with long file names), and Macintosh (HFS). Kudos to the ISO standard for supporting multiple formats simultaneously, and to the Linux *mkhybrid* application used to create the disk image.

The Tcl/Tk distributions are in the tcl_76, tcl_80, and tcl_82 folders. The .tar.gz files there are source distributions that can be unpacked on a UNIX system with a command like this:

```
gunzip < tcl8.2.0.tar.gz | tar xvf -
```

You can compile the source code like this (there are more detailed instructions in Chapter 45):

```
cd tcl8.2.0/unix
./configure --enable-gcc
make
```

There are also source distributions in .zip files that contain the same files as the .tar.gz packages. There are Windows installers in .exe files that install ready-to-run Tcl/Tk interpreters and script libraries.

The binhex folder contains various Macintosh distributions in BINHEX format. The macintosh folder contains some of these already converted to native installers.

The `plugin` folder contains the Web browser plugin. There is a source distribution and binary distributions for a variety of UNIX platforms, Windows, and Macintosh.

The `tclpro` folder contains demo copies of *TclPro*, which is described in more detail on page 189. *TclPro* provides another way to get a free version of Tcl/Tk compiled for your platform. TclPro also has a nice set of development tools. You can get a demo license for the tools at:

    http://www.scriptics.com/registration/welchbook.html

The `exsource` folder contains the examples from the book. These are automatically extracted from Framemaker files. One thing to watch out for is that single quotes get extracted as `\"`. I have left these as-is. The `browser.tcl` script lets you view and try out the examples.

The `tclhttpd` directory contains an unpacked version of the TclHttpd distribution. You should be able to start the server by loading the `bin/httpd.tcl` script into `wish` or `tclsh`. This script starts a Web server on part 8015.

The `tea_sample` directory contains a sample Tcl extension from the Tcl Extension Architecture. This example illustrates how to create Tcl extensions on Windows and UNIX.

The `download` folder contains software downloaded from the Internet. Some of these have associated .README files. Others are described by files in the `index` folder. These descriptions are derived from the Tcl Resource Center found at:

    http://www.scriptics.com/resource/

The `index/index.html` file provides a listing and description of the software in the `download` folder.

The `CD_UTILS` folder contains software you may find helpful, such as Winzip and a version of Tar for Macintosh. I have also included the *mkhybrid* software used to create the CD image, as well as other scripts used in the process.

The `welch` folder contains a picture of me and a copy of my PGP key. The key ID is `7EDF9C79` and its fingerprint is:

    94 D8 90 6A FD 9C AE 94   40 E3 C6 D6 B1 90 E0 03

Technical Support

Prentice Hall does not offer technical support for this software. If there is a problem with the media, however, you may obtain a replacement CD by emailing a description of the problem. Send your email to:

    disc_exchange@prenhall.com

Index

Symbols

\#, pad with spaces in format 53
\$ in regular expressions 145
\$, dollar sign 18
% in clock format 174
% in event bindings 379
( ) for arrays 89
( ) in regular expressions 145
(?!re) in regular expressions 145
(?:re) in regular expressions 145
(?=re) in regular expressions 145
(?abc) in regular expressions 145
* in regular expressions 145
*, matching character 49
*? in regular expressions 145
+ in regular expressions 145
+, format character 53
+? in regular expressions 145
-, left justify string in format 53
., (dot) in regular expressions 145
/bin/sh to run a Tcl script 27
/debug, Application Direct URL 264
/mail, Application Direct URL 266
/status, Application Direct URL 263
? in regular expressions 145
?, string match character 49
?? in regular expressions 145
@ in binary format 55
[ ] in regular expressions 145
[ ] in string match 49
[ ], command substitution 18
[. .] in regular expressions 146
[: :] in regular expressions 146
[= =] 146
[incr Tcl] object system 204
\\, backslash 20
\0 in regular expressions 147
\A in regular expressions 146
\a in regular expressions 146
\a, bell 20
\B in regular expressions 146
\b in regular expressions 146
\b, backspace 20
\c in regular expressions 146
\cX in regular expressions 146
\D in regular expressions 146
\d in regular expressions 146
\e in regular expressions 147
\f in regular expressions 147
\f, form feed 20

\M in regular expressions 147
\m in regular expressions 147
\n in regular expressions 147
\n, newline 20
\r in regular expressions 147
\r, carriage return 20
\S in regular expressions 147
\s in regular expressions 147
\t in regular expressions 147
\t, tab 20
\uXXXX in regular expressions 147
\v in regular expressions 147
\v, vertical tab 20
\W in regular expressions 147
\x in regular expressions 147
\xhh in regular expressions 147
\xy in regular expressions 147
\xyz in regular expressions 147
\Y in regular expressions 147
\y in regular expressions 147
\Z in regular expressions 147
^ in regular expressions 145
{ } for argument grouping 4
{m,n} in regular expressions 145
{m,n}? in regular expressions 145
| in regular expressions 145
~ in file names 116

Numerics

0, o, in binary format 53
3D Border 692
3D relief sampler 528
3dDarkShadow, system color 536
3dLight, system color 536

A

A, a, in binary format 55
abbreviation of commands 169
-about, regexp option 148
-above, event option 379
abs(x), absolute value 21
AC_INIT 648
AC_OUTPUT 649
AC_SUBST 649
accepting socket connections 227
access time, file 102
acos(x), arccosine 21
activate window event 374
activate, button operation 398

B

736

H

X

Y

Z

LICENSE AGREEMENT AND LIMITED WARRANTY

READ THE FOLLOWING TERMS AND CONDITIONS CAREFULLY BEFORE OPENING THIS SOFTWARE MEDIA PACKAGE. THIS LEGAL DOCUMENT IS AN AGREEMENT BETWEEN YOU AND PRENTICE-HALL, INC. (THE "COMPANY"). BY OPENING THIS SEALED SOFTWARE MEDIA PACKAGE, YOU ARE AGREEING TO BE BOUND BY THESE TERMS AND CONDITIONS. IF YOU DO NOT AGREE WITH THESE TERMS AND CONDITIONS, DO NOT OPEN THE SOFTWARE MEDIA PACKAGE. PROMPTLY RETURN THE UNOPENED SOFTWARE MEDIA PACKAGE AND ALL ACCOMPANYING ITEMS TO THE PLACE YOU OBTAINED THEM FOR A FULL REFUND OF ANY SUMS YOU HAVE PAID.

1.   **GRANT OF LICENSE:** In consideration of your payment of the license fee, which is part of the price you paid for this product, and your agreement to abide by the terms and conditions of this Agreement, the Company grants to you a nonexclusive right to use and display the copy of the enclosed software program (hereinafter the "SOFTWARE") on a single computer (i.e., with a single CPU) at a single location so long as you comply with the terms of this Agreement. The Company reserves all rights not expressly granted to you under this Agreement.

2.   **OWNERSHIP OF SOFTWARE:** You own only the magnetic or physical media (the enclosed software media) on which the SOFTWARE is recorded or fixed, but the Company retains all the rights, title, and ownership to the SOFTWARE recorded on the original software media copy(ies) and all subsequent copies of the SOFTWARE, regardless of the form or media on which the original or other copies may exist. This license is not a sale of the original SOFTWARE or any copy to you.

3.   **COPY RESTRICTIONS:** This SOFTWARE and the accompanying printed materials and user manual (the "Documentation") are the subject of copyright. You may not copy the Documentation or the SOFTWARE, except that you may make a single copy of the SOFTWARE for backup or archival purposes only. You may be held legally responsible for any copying or copyright infringement which is caused or encouraged by your failure to abide by the terms of this restriction.

4.   **USE RESTRICTIONS:** You may not network the SOFTWARE or otherwise use it on more than one computer or computer terminal at the same time. You may physically transfer the SOFTWARE from one computer to another provided that the SOFTWARE is used on only one computer at a time. You may not distribute copies of the SOFTWARE or Documentation to others. You may not reverse engineer, disassemble, decompile, modify, adapt, translate, or create derivative works based on the SOFTWARE or the Documentation without the prior written consent of the Company.

5.   **TRANSFER RESTRICTIONS:** The enclosed SOFTWARE is licensed only to you and may not be transferred to any one else without the prior written consent of the Company. Any unauthorized transfer of the SOFTWARE shall result in the immediate termination of this Agreement.

6.   **TERMINATION:** This license is effective until terminated. This license will terminate automatically without notice from the Company and become null and void if you fail to comply with any provisions or limitations of this license. Upon termination, you shall destroy the Documentation and all copies of the SOFTWARE. All provisions of this Agreement as to warranties, limitation of liability, remedies or damages, and our ownership rights shall survive termination.

7.   **MISCELLANEOUS:** This Agreement shall be construed in accordance with the laws of the United States of America and the State of New York and shall benefit the Company, its affiliates, and assignees.

8.   **LIMITED WARRANTY AND DISCLAIMER OF WARRANTY:** The Company warrants that the SOFTWARE, when properly used in accordance with the Documentation, will operate in substantial conformity with the description of the SOFTWARE set forth in the Documentation. The Company does not warrant that the SOFTWARE will meet your requirements or that the operation of the SOFTWARE will be uninterrupted or error-free. The Company warrants that the media on which the SOFTWARE is delivered shall be free from defects in materials and workmanship under normal use for a period of thirty (30) days from the date of your purchase. Your only remedy and the Company's only obligation under these limited warranties is, at the Company's option, return of the warranted item for a refund of any amounts paid by you or replacement of the item. Any replacement of SOFTWARE or media under the warranties shall not extend the original warranty period. The limited warranty set forth above shall not apply to any SOFTWARE which the Company determines in good faith has been subject to misuse, neglect, improper installation, repair, alteration, or dam-

age by you. EXCEPT FOR THE EXPRESSED WARRANTIES SET FORTH ABOVE, THE COMPANY DISCLAIMS ALL WARRANTIES, EXPRESS OR IMPLIED, INCLUDING WITHOUT LIMITATION, THE IMPLIED WARRANTIES OF MERCHANTABILITY AND FITNESS FOR A PARTICULAR PURPOSE. EXCEPT FOR THE EXPRESS WARRANTY SET FORTH ABOVE, THE COMPANY DOES NOT WARRANT, GUARANTEE, OR MAKE ANY REPRESENTATION REGARDING THE USE OR THE RESULTS OF THE USE OF THE SOFTWARE IN TERMS OF ITS CORRECTNESS, ACCURACY, RELIABILITY, CURRENTNESS, OR OTHERWISE.

IN NO EVENT, SHALL THE COMPANY OR ITS EMPLOYEES, AGENTS, SUPPLIERS, OR CONTRACTORS BE LIABLE FOR ANY INCIDENTAL, INDIRECT, SPECIAL, OR CONSEQUENTIAL DAMAGES ARISING OUT OF OR IN CONNECTION WITH THE LICENSE GRANTED UNDER THIS AGREEMENT, OR FOR LOSS OF USE, LOSS OF DATA, LOSS OF INCOME OR PROFIT, OR OTHER LOSSES, SUSTAINED AS A RESULT OF INJURY TO ANY PERSON, OR LOSS OF OR DAMAGE TO PROPERTY, OR CLAIMS OF THIRD PARTIES, EVEN IF THE COMPANY OR AN AUTHORIZED REPRESENTATIVE OF THE COMPANY HAS BEEN ADVISED OF THE POSSIBILITY OF SUCH DAMAGES. IN NO EVENT SHALL LIABILITY OF THE COMPANY FOR DAMAGES WITH RESPECT TO THE SOFTWARE EXCEED THE AMOUNTS ACTUALLY PAID BY YOU, IF ANY, FOR THE SOFTWARE.

SOME JURISDICTIONS DO NOT ALLOW THE LIMITATION OF IMPLIED WARRANTIES OR LIABILITY FOR INCIDENTAL, INDIRECT, SPECIAL, OR CONSEQUENTIAL DAMAGES, SO THE ABOVE LIMITATIONS MAY NOT ALWAYS APPLY. THE WARRANTIES IN THIS AGREEMENT GIVE YOU SPECIFIC LEGAL RIGHTS AND YOU MAY ALSO HAVE OTHER RIGHTS WHICH VARY IN ACCORDANCE WITH LOCAL LAW.

ACKNOWLEDGMENT

YOU ACKNOWLEDGE THAT YOU HAVE READ THIS AGREEMENT, UNDERSTAND IT, AND AGREE TO BE BOUND BY ITS TERMS AND CONDITIONS. YOU ALSO AGREE THAT THIS AGREEMENT IS THE COMPLETE AND EXCLUSIVE STATEMENT OF THE AGREEMENT BETWEEN YOU AND THE COMPANY AND SUPERSEDES ALL PROPOSALS OR PRIOR AGREEMENTS, ORAL, OR WRITTEN, AND ANY OTHER COMMUNICATIONS BETWEEN YOU AND THE COMPANY OR ANY REPRESENTATIVE OF THE COMPANY RELATING TO THE SUBJECT MATTER OF THIS AGREEMENT.

Should you have any questions concerning this Agreement or if you wish to contact the Company for any reason, please contact in writing at the address below.

Robin Short
Prentice Hall PTR
One Lake Street
Upper Saddle River, New Jersey 07458